S0-BRT-271

Contemporary
Analytic
Philosophy

MILTON K. MUNITZ

Contemporary Analytic Philosophy

MACMILLAN PUBLISHING CO., INC.
New York
COLLIER MACMILLAN PUBLISHERS
London

Copyright © 1981. Milton K. Munitz
Printed in the United States of America

All rights reserved. No part of this book may be reproduced or
transmitted in any form or by any means, electronic or mechanical,
including photocopying, recording, or any information storage and
retrieval system, without permission in writing from the Publisher.

Macmillan Publishing Co., Inc.
866 Third Avenue, New York, New York 10022

Collier Macmillan Canada, Ltd.

Library of Congress Cataloging in Publication Data

Munitz, Milton Karl, (date)
Contemporary analytic philosophy.

Bibliography: p.
Includes index.
1. Analysis (Philosophy) 2. Philosophy, Modern—
20th century. 3. Languages—Philosophy. I. Title.
B808.5.M86   190   80-17263
ISBN 0-02-384840-5

Printing: 1 2 3 4 5 6 7 8   Year: 1 2 3 4 5 6 7 8

PREFACE

In writing this book I have had in mind primarily the needs of those students or other readers who, having had some introductory work in philosophy, are ready to undertake a variety of steps toward deepening their knowledge of the subject. For example, they may set out to explore particular periods or individual figures in the history of philosophy, or one or another specialized area of philosophy, each with its own budget of problems. I try to meet one aspect of this type of need by examining some of the leading thinkers and problems of twentieth-century analytic philosophy. Because this book is an introductory survey of its material, it does not aim at encyclopedic coverage or exhaustive detail. Selection, of course, is inevitable. Moreover, the important and representative thinkers I have chosen to dwell on, for all their diversity, have devoted themselves for the most part to topics in logic, the philosophy of language, and ontology. Hence it is on these topics that I have concentrated.

A feature of this book is its inclusion of extended quotations from the writings of the philosophers examined. I have integrated these quotations within my narrative and explanatory account. By this means, it is hoped, the reader will obtain a fair sample of the content and style of each thinker's way of putting matters. And of course a major purpose in my use of this device is to encourage readers to turn to the complete works of the thinkers whose ideas are here only briefly glimpsed and surveyed.

M. K. M.

ACKNOWLEDGMENTS

I first discussed the project of this book with Mr. Kenneth J. Scott, Senior Editor at Macmillan, and I wish to thank him for his general counsel and support. Professor William J. Earle of Long Island University read the manuscript in its entirety and gave me the benefit of a number of valuable comments.

For permission to make use of quoted excerpts from copyright material I am much indebted to the following publishers and individuals:

Basil Blackwell, Publisher
George Allen & Unwin
Routledge & Kegan Paul Ltd
Columbia University Press
Humanities Press Inc.
Harvard University Press
Prentice-Hall Inc.
New York University Press
Open Court Publishing Company
Macmillan Publishing Company, Inc.
Professor W.V.O. Quine
Professor Saul Kripke

CONTENTS

I. *Introduction*   I

1. 'Contemporary Philosophy'   I

2. On Characterizing the Present Epoch in Philosophy   3

II. *Belief, Inquiry, and Meaning*   14

1. Charles S. Peirce   17

2. The Nature of Belief   27

3 Methods of Effecting a Settlement of Opinion   34

4 Investigation: Truth and Reality   42

5. Meaning   48

6. Concluding Remarks About 'Pragmatism'   61

III. *The New Logic*   67

Gottlob Frege   70

The Language of Logic   80

Concept and Object   82

Sense and Reference   104

IV. *Logical Atomism*   119

Bertrand Russell   119

General Features of Russell's Philosophy   129

Descriptions and Existence   140

Classes and Types   156

Concluding Remarks   165

V. *The Limits of Language*   169

Ludwig Wittgenstein   169

A Preliminary View of the *Tractatus*   177

'What Can Be Said'   182

'What Can't Be Said'   201

VI. *Verificationism*   221

Wittgenstein's Return to Philosophy: The Transitional Phase   221
'Verificationism' and 'Hypotheses' in Wittgenstein's Philosophy   228
The Vienna Circle   237
The Main Doctrines of Logical Positivism   239
Problems About 'Verifiability'   257

VII. *Language-Games*   269

Wittgenstein's Later Philosophy   269
From 'Essences' to 'Family Resemblances'   274
Meaning and Use   279
Language-Games   283
Grammar and Grammatical Rules   287
Ostensive Definitions   293
The Autonomy of Grammar   295
Criteria   299
'Meaning' ('Intending') and 'Understanding'   303
The Private Language Argument   307
On 'Philosophy'   315
Common Sense and Certainty: A Critique of G. E. Moore   321

VIII. *Ontological Commitments*   349

Willard V. O. Quine   349
'On What There Is'   350
The Critique of Empiricism   357
Objects, Quantification, and Ontology   363
The Indeterminacy Thesis and Ontological Relativity   375
Referential Opacity, Modality, and Essentialism; Saul Kripke   380

Reference Notes   400
Selected Bibliography   413
Index   429

Contemporary
Analytic
Philosophy

CHAPTER I

Introduction

1. 'CONTEMPORARY PHILOSOPHY'

The major periods in the history of philosophy are commonly labeled 'ancient', 'medieval', 'modern', and 'contemporary'. Of these terms, 'ancient', 'medieval', and 'modern' are normally used in a fairly straightforward way to demarcate easily recognized blocks of a stabilized past. Each of the periods so designated has a structure that has been traversed often enough so that one can readily identify its broad outlines, characteristic features, undisputed peaks, and major accomplishments. For example, there is little disagreement that a study of ancient philosophy would begin with the pre-Socratic philosophers (e.g., Parmenides, Heraclitus, Anaximander, the Pythagoreans, Democritus) and the major Sophists. This would be followed by an analysis of the towering achievements of Socrates, Plato, and Aristotle. It would conclude with an examination of the philosophies of neo-Platonism, Epicureanism, Scepticism, Stoicism, and the earliest formulations of Jewish and Christian thought. In a similar fashion, the material encompassed by the label 'medieval philosophy' would range over the views of such thinkers as St. Anselm, St. Thomas Aquinas, Duns Scotus, William of Ockham, Maimonides, and Avicenna. Again, the long period covered by the term 'modern philosophy' would normally include a study of Francis Bacon and Thomas Hobbes; the works of the seventeenth-century rationalists—Descartes, Spinoza, and Leibniz; the writings of the British empiricists—Locke, Berkeley, and Hume; the critical philosophy of Immanuel Kant; and the contributions of Hegel, Schopenhauer, and Nietzsche, among others, in the nineteenth century.

By contrast with these earlier periods, and for a number of obvious or plausible reasons, what falls under the heading of 'contemporary philosophy' is not fixed or standardized to the same degree. For one thing, the sphere of the 'contemporary' has continually shifting boundaries with the advance of time. Thus an account of contemporary philosophy written in the 1980s has a partially different subject matter from one written, say, in the 1930s. Furthermore, like its cognate expressions 'now' or 'present', the term 'contemporary' has narrower and wider uses. It can be used to refer to what is most recent and current as well as to the entire period of the 'present century'. Most importantly, one must employ some principles of selection in deciding what to include, what to stress, what to identify as of primary and possibly enduring value, and what is of lesser significance. Because there are no simple or universally agreed-upon answers to these questions, at least of the degree of relative uniformity holding for earlier periods of the history of philosophy, there are greater opportunities for flexibility of approach and choice. The greatest differences of opinion are likely to concern the very recent past and what is currently under active discussion. Nevertheless, as one gains the advantage of a broadening perspective into the ever-lengthening past, the outlines begin to be clearer, the uncertainties fewer, and the possible divergences of opinion less pronounced.

With respect to the temporal span to be covered, 'contemporary philosophy' in its narrowest sense would signify only what is actively under discussion at the present time. In a slightly more liberal use, it might be extended to include philosophical discussions of the quite recent past, say the last two or three decades. The advantage of restricting the scope of 'contemporary philosophy' to the immediate present or the very recent past is that it leads directly to the active frontiers of research. One is plunged into an examination of the problems, options, and controversies that make up the content of lively ongoing discussion. Exploring this material in its various dimensions and directions provides an effective and stimulating way of participating in the activity of philosophical inquiry. One need not minimize or disparage these advantages in pointing to the possible shortcomings of this way of restricting the scope of 'contemporary philosophy'. These very advantages are enhanced and made more secure by enlarging the field to be covered beyond the narrow temporal limits just described. To have a better grasp of matters under current active discussion it is helpful to see them against the wider historical background out of which they arose. A broadening and deepening of that background is essential to a more adequate understanding of these discussions. To take one simple illustration: Certain questions in philosophical logic of a semantical nature—those for example having to do with 'the problem of singular reference'—are being much debated in the literature at the present time (as in the work of Kripke, Dummett,

Strawson, Quine, and others). However, these questions cannot be fully understood without seeing them in the context and against the background of a sequence of philosophical investigations stemming from the work of Gottlob Frege, who lived at the end of the last century and into the early part of this century. One is in a better position to understand the present-day controversies and distinctions if one is aware of how they are related to the earlier views not only of Frege but of Russell, Wittgenstein, Carnap, and others. Examples could easily be multiplied that make a similar point outside the domain of philosophical logic or the field of analytic philosophy generally.

In addition to the foregoing there is a more conventional reason that argues for broadening the scope of the field to be covered under the heading 'contemporary philosophy'. If, as indeed is the case, the term 'modern philosophy' is conventionally used to extend roughly until the end of the nineteenth century, then the term 'contemporary philosophy' can be usefully reserved to encompass the whole span of twentieth-century philosophy. And this is how we shall understand the temporal scope of our interest in what follows.

2.   ON CHARACTERIZING THE PRESENT EPOCH IN PHILOSOPHY

Our first task, before looking at the details concerning particular themes and individual thinkers, is to get some preliminary bird's-eye view of the main contours of our subject. What, if anything, sets off our age against earlier epochs? Even if we grant that philosophy, wherever and whenever it is pursued, tends to circle around certain fundamental and recurrent themes, still the differences between one period and another—changes in voice, emphasis, orientation, or prevalent doctrine—are noticeable and important features. Can we point, then, to some relatively distinctive and innovative features of the philosophic activity of our own time?

Our philosophic period is sometimes described as 'an age of analysis'. This characterization, although an oversimplification, calls attention to the fact that an outstanding feature of contemporary philosophy is the emergence of analytic philosophy to a position of dominance.

The expression 'analytic philosophy', as is the case with many classificatory labels, cannot be given a single, universally agreed-upon, precise definition. It can be used in wider or narrower senses. In its wider use it encompasses an assortment of differently oriented schools or philosophies that nevertheless have a number of points of overlap, affinity, and connection with one another. The term 'analytic philosophy' may be used in contemporary philosophy to cover the kind of analysis practiced by

George E. Moore; the conception of logical analysis championed by
Bertrand Russell; the central teachings of the logical positivists (e.g.,
Moritz Schlick, Rudolf Carnap, Hans Reichenbach, Alfred J. Ayer); the
'Oxford School of ordinary language philosophy' as led, for example, by
John Austin; the principal types of conceptual analysis associated with
the work of Ludwig Wittgenstein; the examination of various semantical
questions about reference and truth belonging to the sphere of philosophical logic associated with recent developments in formal logic and linguistics (e.g., the work of Willard Van Orman Quine, Peter F. Strawson,
Jaakko Hintikka, Saul Kripke, Donald Davidson, Michael Dummett). On
the other hand, the term 'analytic philosophy' might be used, more re-
strictively, to apply to the views of some particular thinker or school of
thought from among the above mentioned list.

Let us, for the moment, use the term 'analytic philosophy' in its
wider sense and try to describe what in an overall way is distinctive of it.
For this purpose, let us pause to take a brief backward glance at the history of modern philosophy from Descartes down to the end of the nineteenth and early part of the twentieth centuries, in order to see in what
way contemporary analytic philosophy represents a fresh development.
The major difference between the earlier epoch and that of contemporary
analytic philosophy is that whereas modern philosophy is dominated by a
concern with *epistemological* issues, contemporary analytic philosophy
represents a shift to issues of a *logico-linguistic* sort.

Modern philosophy, beginning with Descartes, has as its central preoccupation a concern with the problems of epistemology (the theory of
knowledge). These problems can be summed up in such questions as:
What are the powers of the mind in its efforts to achieve knowledge of the
external world? To what extent are the mind's faculties able to penetrate
the structure of reality? How adequate are the mind's ideas in representing and disclosing the nature of the world? What are the limits of the
mind's abilities to achieve the truth?

The terms in which I have just couched the traditional interests of
epistemology—terms such as '*the nature and limits of the powers (or faculties) of the mind*', '*the external world*', '*the extent to which the mind's
ideas adequately represent the nature of the external world*'—recall some
of the characteristic ways in which the problems of epistemology were
posed and discussed throughout the modern period of philosophy. This is
the case whether we turn to the writings of rationalists such as Descartes
and Leibniz or empiricists such as Locke, Berkeley, and Hume, or to the
philosophy of Kant and the major successors of Kant up to the end of the
nineteenth century. Indeed, these problems, so phrased, continue to preoccupy some thinkers well into the twentieth century. To be sure, there
are important differences in the ways the continental rationalists, the Brit-

ish empiricists, Kant, later representational dualists of various sorts, phenomenalists, as well as numerous other epistemologists went about their business and offered their own distinctive solutions to 'the problem of knowledge'. Yet for all their differences they shared certain underlying presuppositions in dealing with the problem of knowledge. In following the implications and consequences of these presuppositions they faced various dialectical problems that they tried to solve, each in his distinctive way.

The commonly shared orientation that pervades modern epistemology is the contrast between *subject* and *object*, i.e., the distinction between *the knowing mind* and *the external world* that it confronts and seeks to know. Descartes' philosophy helped set the pattern for this way of formulating the problems of epistemology. A primary feature of his philosophy is the stress it places on the fact that the one thing we can be sure of, even in the face of thoroughgoing radical scepticism, is the existence of the mind itself. *Cogito, ergo sum.* (I think, therefore I am.) Much of his philosophy, as it undertakes to escape from its own self-imposed sceptical beginnings, is devoted to examining how to get 'outside' the mind, how to reestablish grounds for a responsible belief in the external world (the world of physical phenomena) and a belief in God. The route to be followed was to examine the various ideas and beliefs that form the *contents* of the mind, to examine which among these ideas and beliefs are to be taken as *adequate representations* of those entities that presumably lie outside and independently of the mind, and are possessed of their own properties and relations. Descartes' philosophic criterion for judging the adequacy of ideas and beliefs in this representational role was strongly influenced by his use of mathematical knowledge as a model or paradigm. As a rationalist Descartes appealed to the standards that reason imposes when it operates in its most rigorous form, as is the case in the deductive demonstrations of mathematics. He demands, as an ideal to be aimed at, that all our accepted ideas in any intellectual domain, even outside of mathematics, be 'clear and distinct'. He also demands that our beliefs start, as they do in a deductive system of mathematics, from certain intuitively certain, axiomatic premisses, and that they proceed, step by step, through necessary deductive inference to securely established, demonstrable conclusions.

The British empiricists, for all their rebellion against some of the rationalists' claims, started with the same 'subject-object' dualistic framework, the same mentalistic model and orientation to the epistemological problem. Instead of appealing, with Descartes, to rationally certified clear and distinct ideas or to demonstrative proofs, they emphasized the appeal to the *data of sense experience* as the basis for determining any legitimate claim to knowledge. The empiricists stressed the need for showing not only that the *genesis* of all our ideas is to be found in certain sense-given originals, but also that it is to sense experience that appeal must be made in the end as the *testing ground* for all our beliefs. This is not the occasion to rehearse the full story of how the British empiricists, especially as we move from Locke to Berkeley and finally to Hume, worked out the dialectical consequences of this way of thinking. It will suffice to recall that the outstanding and impressive outcome of the relentless following out of the implications of the starting point of that philosophy was the scepticism of Hume. Hume's devastating critique carried out what Locke (to some extent) and Berkeley (more thoroughly in certain directions) had already shown: that the mind in fact is incapable of achieving any secure knowledge of an independently existing material world. What Hume called into question was the reliance upon, and appeal to, the very fundamental philosophic notions of *material or mental substances* and *necessary causal connections* as holding among such substances. Hume undermined the commonly employed framework of much of traditional metaphysics in its use of these concepts, in particular the way in which the epistemological problem was formulated insofar as it made use of these same concepts.

The monumental efforts of Kant's critical philosophy, as stated in *The Critique of Pure Reason,* were devoted in part to 'answering Hume'. Kant undertook to show how one can incorporate the best insights of the rationalists and empiricists and yet not agree with either one completely. His own solution to the problem of knowledge—what the mind can know and what it cannot—rested on recognizing the all-important distinction between what is *given* to the mind in the form of unordered data of sensory experience, and what the mind *contributes* as a result of imposing on given sensuous materials the *a priori* forms of the mind's own constitution. Kant's 'Copernican revolution' in philosophy consisted in challenging the commonly shared realism of older philosophies according to which knowledge is a *disclosure* of a preexistent structure in an independently existing world. For Kant, knowledge is a *product,* a construction, not a disclosure. Knowledge has to do with a domain of phenomena, of appearances. However, what things-in-themselves are, what lies beyond all actual or possible experience, is something of which no knowledge can ever be had. The claims of traditional metaphysics to know about the world as a whole, God, freedom, or the immortality of the soul, are, for Kant, also forever incapable of realization. These matters lie in the domain of the transcendent, the unknowable, the noumenal.

Kant's solution to the epistemological problem marks a milestone in the history of modern philosophy. However, in one respect it gives clear, unmistakable evidence of being itself dominated by the same subject-object dualism, of being constrained and guided by the same mentalistic model, as are all other varieties of epistemology in modern philosophy.

While in one respect Kant showed a way of answering Hume's scepticism, his philosophy raised a number of difficulties of its own. His successors and critics were quick to point these out. Chief among them was the problem of rendering coherent, even within the framework of Kant's own philosophy, the use of the 'concept' of things-in-themselves. How is it possible to give meaning to the very notion of a reality that is totally unknowable, that exists independently of all actual as well as possible experience? Kant left a rich but mixed legacy; it drove home even more deeply the difficulties of working with a philosophy whose central question is how it is possible for men to have knowledge of the external world, when we insist on construing the problem of knowledge as one of establishing a satisfactory relation between ideas as the contents of the mind and a world that exists beyond those ideas. What was needed in order to understand the nature of knowledge was to discard altogether the very model that lay at the center of the problem so conceived. That model required us to think in terms of the mind as a container, a substance facing the world beyond. It was a mind said to have certain ideas 'within' itself, and so presenting us with the need of somehow finding a way of breaking out of those ideas to determine the properties of the world 'outside'.

A noticeable feature of much of contemporary philosophy, beginning with the pragmatists, continuing with the work of the analytic philosophers deriving in one way or another from the Fregean concern with logico-linguistic issues, and continuing even into the efforts of many metaphysicians concerned with building world views, is the concerted effort to break away from the epistemological problem and its various 'solutions' as conceived in modern philosophy. This is not to say that such efforts always succeed, or indeed that they do not themselves betray in their very formulations the presence and continued influence of the older ways of thinking that they seek to replace. Still, insofar as we may make any valid generalization about the matter, what has happened in much of contemporary philosophy is the dropping altogether of the subject-object orientation for coming to understand the nature of knowledge. Instead of an *epistemological problem* as traditionally conceived, we find a concern (as in the pragmatists and analytic philosophies of the post-Fregean tradition) with questions of the *logic of inquiry* (methodology) and with clarifying the *language* in which we talk about knowledge and belief. Instead of asking *how,* or indeed *whether* it is possible for the mind to know an external world, these philosophies would start by presupposing the fact that we do already possess knowledge in many ways, and in any case can come to know the world. If scepticism or a doctrine of the essential unknowability of the world is the outcome of the dialectical tracing out of the consequences of our starting point, it is necessary to abandon the very model, paradigm, or set of presuppositions that leads to such an outcome. Such scepticism shows there is something wrong with the way the problem was set up to begin with. There is no *problem* of the external world if this means either we cannot be sure there is such a world, or (as another view might hold) we can never come to know *what* its structure is, though we may claim to know *that* it exists.

To avoid scepticism, we begin by examining the fact that not only in everyday life and on a commonsense level do we have all sorts of perfectly reliable bits of information, satisfactory insights and explanations as to why things happen, but in the sciences, especially, the progressive achievement of reliable knowledge about various subject matters is a basic fact. The problem is not to understand *whether* it is possible to achieve knowledge. The problem is to show the ways in which this comes about: the conditions and procedures for achieving such knowledge. The task is one of correctly describing how we go from doubt, ignorance, and inadequately supported or crude beliefs to well-established ones, how we distinguish sound from unsound beliefs, how we are able to make progress on the level of the enlargement as well as in terms of the refinement of our beliefs about the world and its multitudinous parts.

In a broad use of the term 'logic', as derived from the Greek term *logos,* one can say that in conformity with the complex meanings of the latter term, logic deals with man's distinctive power of speech, inference, conceptual thought, and rational inquiry. If we take the term 'logic' in this broad sense (and so not restricted, as it sometimes is, to the study of formal deductive inference alone), we could say that contemporary analytic philosophy is dominated by attention to matters logical. It centers on questions having to do with the means for achieving clarity of linguistic meaning; with the characterization of methods of responsible inquiry for reaching the truth; with the conditions for realizing soundness and validity in argument. Analytic philosophy, in this many-faceted concern with logic, goes beyond the answers traditional logic gave to these questions. It seeks to show how a rejuvenated and more subtly developed discipline of logic can guide the employment of reason.

In general, then, we shall find three types of themes given special attention in contemporary analytic philosophy as well as in the work of some of the pragmatist philosophers.

1. A study of the role of *language* in communication and thought; and, in particular, the problem of how to identify, achieve, or insure the presence of *meaning* in the use of language.
2. An examination of the logic of inquiry or *methodology,* insofar as this has to do with evaluating the variety of techniques and conditions for achieving *true* beliefs and warranted claims to knowledge.

3. A philosophical examination of the resources of *formal logic* in its modern, revitalized forms, and the several ways in which these resources may be applied in helping to solve various philosophical problems.

These three themes are closely interrelated. However, the specific manner of their interconnection is manifold and receives differing kinds and amounts of attention or emphasis by various writers and special schools.

There is one common feature, one characteristic emphasis that belongs to all analytic philosophies and to some pragmatist philosophers. This consists in the careful attention paid to the use of *language* as the medium of communication of thought, and to the various conditions and resources that language makes available for such communication. In this connection, special concern is shown for the *problem of meaning*. What are the ways of achieving or insuring the presence of meaning in our use of language? Are there certain conditions for meaningfulness that have to be met? What ways are available for making explicit and clear the meanings and uses of various linguistic expressions? Given the frequent failure, difficulty, or inadequacy in achieving a clear use of language, what are the standards and techniques for achieving clarification? The attempt to answer questions such as these is a marked characteristic of contemporary philosophy, beginning with the earliest efforts of the pragmatists, and continuing in one form or another down to the present day in the work of various analytic philosophers. It is true, of course, that a concern with the clarification of meaning has always been characteristic of and essential to the philosophic enterprise, ever since the days of Socrates at least. What distinguish the focal interest of this question in contemporary philosophy are the different motivations and occasions that provoked a fresh and intensified concern with it. We shall examine some of the details later, but for the moment let me summarize some of these special motivations.

In some cases, for example in Moore's elaborate and painstaking exercises in analysis, we find a continuation of what we may call the Socratic (Platonic) tradition. It consists in the demand that we make explicit and *become* clear about some of our basic concepts, even about the ordinary terms and words we use in everyday speech. While we do communicate readily enough by their means, when pressed to give a careful *analysis* of their meaning (a statement of their basic components), we are often baffled and unable to do so. For example, to give an analysis of 'perception', 'description', 'morally right', 'truth', 'reality', is a matter of the greatest difficulty. To spend one's philosophic efforts in trying to give an analysis of the meaning of these and other basic concepts—this, for Moore, is the inescapable and difficult challenge a philosopher must meet.

For some philosophers, a concern with 'the problem of meaning' arises from other motives. One of these is related to the program of examining the methods by which we may claim to know the truth about the world in which we live. Meaning and meaningfulness, however, are prior conditions for reaching the truth. Unless we know what some statement means, for example, we cannot even begin to inquire into or try to establish whether it is true or false. This motivation is to be found in Peirce's account of 'how to make our ideas clear' as a necessary component and step in carrying out a process of scientific investigation. This orientation to the problem of meaning is also characteristic of logical positivism. The interest that the logical positivists have in questions of meaning, and in fashioning what for them is a criterion of meaningfulness, stems primarily from two motives. On the one hand they are interested, in a positive way, in championing the method of the sciences as the only reliable way of giving us the truth. On the other hand, and in a negative way, they are interested in pointing out that what often passes for a statement of factual truth turns out to lack all possibility of being empirically confirmed or disconfirmed. Positivists make the charge that a good deal of traditional and contemporary writing in metaphysics needs to be exposed as utterly meaningless, whatever the emotional, edifying, or expressive qualities the use of metaphysical language may have. The interest of the positivists in the problem of meaning, then, is linked with the broader methodological question of analyzing the logic of the sciences, as well as in seeking to eliminate what they regard as the spurious truth-claims to be found in metaphysical, speculative systems of thought.

Still another motivation for concern with the problem of meaning stems from the conviction that many typical philosophic puzzlements—an inability to see one's way clear to resolving some philosophic difficulty—is due not so much to a lack of evidence or an insufficiency of strong arguments in support of one view or another, but to the fact that there has been a failure to draw necessary distinctions among various uses of words. We are ensnared in our use of language and frustrated. We experience puzzlement because we have failed to clarify, painstakingly, the sometimes subtly related yet different uses of terms as they occur in the course of struggling with some problem. However, once we can carry out a linguistic analysis, once we achieve clarification of the multiple uses of language, many of these puzzlements disappear. Difficulties are *resolved* by being *dissolved*. This approach to the benefits of looking for and obtaining clarification of the multiple uses of language is typical of the emphasis one finds in Wittgenstein's later philosophy. It is also stressed and exhibited in the practice of the 'Oxford' or 'ordinary-language' school of philosophers, whose main interest is in performing various kinds of 'conceptual analysis' and in carrying out various exercises in the use of 'informal logic'. For these philosophers, there is no *single* problem of meaning, nor is there a question of finding a *single* criterion of meaningfulness. There are, rather, many different 'problems of meaning'. These arise on those numerous occasions in which, in order to achieve philosophic clarity or insight, or to dissolve philosophic puzzlement, we need to perform a careful analysis of the varied uses of linguistic expressions. Indeed, such conceptual analyses are frequently appropriate and called for not only with respect to some of the standard problems of philosophy but in other areas as well—for example in religious discourse, politics, law, and science.

Another interest, for some analytic philosophers, is the matter of formulating a *theory* of meaning. This interest has come to the fore in recent decades with the development of the science of linguistics. If one says that the acquisition and mastery of a given language requires not only the ability to understand expressions in that language, but also the ability to construct new sentences in that language, upon what factors does such mastery depend? In what does the understanding and fresh use of expressions consist? Various philosophers of language—Noam Chomsky, Michael Dummett, Donald Davidson, and others—have devoted considerable effort to answering this question; it is currently the subject of much lively discussion and debate.

A central question for philosophy, ever since the days of the Greeks, has been one of giving an analysis of the concept of truth. Is truth a property of propositions, of certain linguistic expressions, or does it have some independent ontological status apart from the use of language or by virtue of the outcome of some process of inquiry? How is the concept of truth related to the concept of reality? What are the criteria to which one can appeal in applying the adjectives 'true' and 'false'? Are there certain preferred techniques and methods for reaching the truth? If so, what are these?

A special form in which the discussion of this broad theme is carried forward in contemporary analytic philosophy has to do with the examination of the method of science. What is it that distinguishes the method of scientific inquiry from other methods of warranting beliefs? On what does the claim to its superiority rest? A number of leading philosophers have devoted much of their attention to answering this and related questions. Here one should mention the contributions of C. S. Peirce, Bertrand Russell, Rudolf Carnap, Hans Reichenbach, and Ernest Nagel, among others.

Ever since the time of Aristotle, 'formal logic' has been recognized as a central part of the discipline of philosophy. A systematic study of the principles and rules of logic, and a training in their repeated application for the purpose of evaluating the soundness of various kinds of arguments, has been a universally accepted component, a fundamental step in acquiring technical competency in philosophy.

The underlying concern of formal logic is the formulation of the laws, rules, criteria, and methods for determining the formal validity of arguments, regardless of the subject matter of such arguments. To realize this goal, logic studies the formal structure or patterns of various types of arguments in order to be able to separate those that are sound from those that are unsound. It studies, at its most fundamental level, such concepts as 'necessary consequence', 'entailment', 'consistency', and 'implication'. Formal logic studies the formal connections between the premises of an argument and its conclusion. Does the conclusion follow validly from the given premises? This is the central question of formal logic, the study of deductive reasoning.

Toward the realization of these goals, Aristotle made a contribution whose central approach, techniques, and formulated rules remained so overwhelmingly influential that it constituted the unchallenged authority and stable core of the discipline until the end of the nineteenth century—a period of more than two thousand years. While, to be sure, there were over the centuries many different codifications, partial reformulations, and slight extensions of Aristotelian logic, the latter remained in its basic principles a relatively closed, complete, and unchanging system. Kant, writing in the eighteenth century, typically thought that classical Aristotelian logic was a discipline whose main principles were already thoroughly and exhaustively known: there was nothing essentially new left to be discovered!

One of the remarkable and important facts of the history of philosophy in its contemporary phase is the rebirth of the study of logic, the opening up of its domain to the introduction of vitally new ways of approaching its central themes. Logicians have devised new techniques, formulated fresh rules, and, in general, discovered means for bursting the traditional bounds of the subject. They have pointed the way to the exploration of ever-new and continually expanding areas of investigation.

The history of contemporary philosophy numbers among its leading names those who made important contributions to this revitalized study of logic. Although in the late nineteenth century the name of George Boole needs to be listed among the early pioneers in the new growth of formal logic, it is not until we come to the work of Gottlob Frege and Charles S. Peirce that we meet with the two giants whose original contributions laid the foundations, gave the orientation, and provided the impetus toward the development of logic in its modern forms. The subsequent work of Bertrand Russell, Alfred North Whitehead, Ludwig Wittgenstein, Stanislaw Lésniewski, Kurt Gödel, and Willard Van Orman Quine, among others, mark other important stages in the development of the subject down to the present day. It is the work of these logicians that has transformed the study of logic from its classic Aristotelian outlines. That older logic concentrated on the simple subject-predicate proposition as the basic type of proposition, and the syllogism (composed of such propositions) as the basic type of argument whose valid forms were to be studied. By contrast, modern logic has extended its investigations into a range of topics not explicitly recognized or studied in the older logic. We shall not stop here to study in any detail these modern developments. Much of it is highly technical and requires extensive study in its own right. Let it suffice for the moment to refer to the work of modern logic in the logic of relations, the truth-functional sentential calculus, and predicate calculi involving the use of techniques of quantification and multiple generality. All these, as well as other topics, point in the direction in which modern logic has become a flourishing part of contemporary philosophy, interacting in manifold ways with other dimensions and areas of philosophic interest. We shall have occasion, later in this book, to study some of these interconnections.

CHAPTER II

Belief, Inquiry, and Meaning

2.0.

The word 'pragmatic' has become part of our everyday vocabulary. It is instructive to look at some of its uses, since these reflect on their own level both the elements of unity and the differences in the various technical formulations of the philosophy of pragmatism. According to ordinary uses of the term, to be pragmatic includes the following: to be 'practical' and 'realistic'; to try out various ideas as one goes along with some project or plan of action to see how these ideas work out in practice in realizing one's goals and purposes; to be open-minded and flexible and not be committed in advance, in some fanatic or dogmatic way, to certain fixed principles; to judge ideas or beliefs by the extent to which they make for success. Closely related to these meanings is the idea that to be pragmatic means, in general, to judge or evaluate any thought, belief, theory, policy, or plan of action in terms of its consequences and its implications. "By their fruits shall ye know them" is a rough and ready formula for conveying the kernel of the pragmatic attitude.

These everyday uses of the term, whatever their appropriateness in various circumstances, serve (once you begin to examine them more closely) to provoke certain obvious *philosophical* questions. For example, do all these varied meanings belong to a single, unified philosophy, or are they rather pointers to divergent, perhaps even conflicting, viewpoints? What, for example, are we to understand by the appeal to 'consequences', 'implications', 'practical results'? What kinds should we look for? In what direction? For example, if we stress the idea of usefulness or success, how is this to be understood? How is it to be specified, exemplified, and warranted? Is the pragmatic viewpoint one that applies primarily or even exclusively to guiding a 'man of action'? Does it have to do, then, especially with the domain of social (political, economic, business) affairs? Are 'practical' results and 'success' to be measured in terms of pleasure or an increase in the possession of power and wealth? Does 'being pragmatic' mean looking for and finding expedient ways of handling situations? Does pragmatism, then, mean readiness to abandon principles altogether? Does pragmatism have anything to do with intellectual matters? If so, how does it function, for example, in science, or in philosophy itself? How, if at all, does it help to settle questions about the *meaning* of concepts or the *truth* of various beliefs? To what kind of attitudes, to what kinds of philosophies, is pragmatism opposed? For what reasons and in what ways does a pragmatic philosophy seek to replace its rivals and alternatives? What makes it (or made it) a "new way of thinking"?

It is clear that these and many other questions cannot be dealt with satisfactorily by staying with the ordinary, everyday uses of the term 'pragmatic', or by hoping to find answers to them by consulting a dictionary. One has to turn to philosophic efforts at answering these questions. This means that we had best study the views of those who in the first place elaborated and defended a pragmatist philosophy. In doing so, we should find that while indeed there are certain elements of unity, or at any rate overlapping and partially shared doctrines among these philosophers, there are also many important differences.

What is commonly referred to as the philosophy of pragmatism is closely identified with the views of three major American thinkers: Charles S. Peirce (1839–1914), William James (1842–1909), and John Dewey (1859–1952). Of these, Peirce is not only the founder of the movement but probably its most profound and, from a long-range perspective, most important representative. James, a lifelong friend of Peirce, in a lecture in 1898 credited Peirce with its original formulation. However, it was James who helped popularize the term 'pragmatism' and introduced it to a wide international audience. This he did in many of his lectures and writings, among them "Philosophical Conceptions and Practical Results," *Pragmatism,* and *The Meaning of Truth.* Peirce was quite dissatisfied with the way James interpreted the essential ideas of pragmatism. As a result, he chose to disassociate himself from what by that time was being characterized as 'pragmatism' by many writers in Europe and America. He therefore proposed to drop the term 'pragmatism' as a label for his own doctrines and to use instead the term 'pragmaticism'. He thought the latter term was "ugly enough to be safe from kidnappers." It turned out that Peirce was right in one respect: nobody did kidnap this term! The fact of the matter is that Peirce's name will always be associated with 'pragmatism' in all standard accounts of the subject. Over the years Peirce continued to write about and sometimes significantly reformulate his own version of pragmatism.

James' popularization of pragmatism influenced the thought of certain European thinkers, who in turn developed their own account of this philosophy. In particular, one should mention here the views of British philosopher Ferdinand C. S. Schiller (1864–1937) and Giovanni Papini (1881–1956) an Italian thinker. The third major American philosopher identified with the classic development of pragmatism is John Dewey. As a graduate student at Johns Hopkins, Dewey studied briefly with Peirce but at the time did not really appreciate the significance of what Peirce had to teach. Many years later Dewey, in working out his own brand of pragmatism, acknowledged his great indebtedness to Peirce's ideas.[1] Two other prominent American thinkers who contributed significantly to the later development of pragmatism were George Herbert Mead (1863–1931) and Clarence I. Lewis (1883–1964).

It is important to see Peirce's orientation to pragmatism in contrast with that of James or Dewey. Peirce's primary interests were in clarifying certain aspects of scientific inquiry. His pragmatism was a central part of his theory of scientific methodology. With James, pragmatism functioned as a theory of the technique for settling metaphysical disputes and as a philosophic support for upholding a "right to believe in the religious hypothesis." Even though James was a major contributor to the science of psychology and was trained as a medical doctor, his pragmatism did not derive primarily from these aspects of his scientific background.

Dewey, who was in many ways more closely indebted to Peirce than to James for certain aspects of his own version of pragmatism (which he called 'instrumentalism'), had different kinds of fundamental interests from those of either Peirce or James. With Dewey the method of inquiry ('experimental intelligence') was broadened to include all those aspects of human experience or culture in which we might use intelligence to solve problems, satisfy human needs, and adjust to our environment. For Dewey, a scientific interest in the truth represented only one interest or dimension of human experience. Neither empirical science as a disinterested quest for truth, nor a religious orientation to the world, was the driving force in Dewey's philosophy. Rather, humanistic and social concerns were at the center of his attention. The transformation of all areas of experience in which problematic situations arise (in politics, economics, education, law, personal behavior, and art) was the primary focus of his interests. In the context of these themes he developed his version of pragmatism, obtained his paradigms, and sought to apply the method of experimental intelligence.

My purpose in this chapter is not to explore in detail the historical and philosophical development of pragmatism in each of the above-named writers or in others. Instead, I shall focus on the way Peirce formulated some of the central ideas of pragmatism, principally in two of his classic essays, "The Fixation of Belief" (1877) and "How to Make Our Ideas Clear" (1878). About 1903 Peirce combined these two essays into a single chapter entitled "My Plea for Pragmatism" that was to be included in a book he planned, which remained unpublished. He wrote the following introduction to this material:

> The two chapters composing this Essay were first published without any title for the whole in the Popular Scientific Monthly for November 1877 and January 1878. . . . They received as little attention as they laid claim to; but some years later the potent pen of Professor James brought their chief thesis to the attention of the philosophic world (pressing it, indeed, further than the tether of their author would reach . . .).[2]

And in 1905 Peirce wrote:

> Much as the writer has gained from the perusal of what other pragmatists have written, he still thinks there is a decisive advantage in his original conception of the doctrine. From this original form every truth that follows from any of the other forms can be deduced, while some errors can be avoided into which other pragmatists have fallen.[3]

The history of the development of the pragmatist philosophy has confirmed Peirce's own estimate of the importance of these early classic papers. The ways in which pragmatism was interpreted by James, Dewey, Mead, and others are best understood either as further enrichments and consistent amplifications of what Peirce had in mind, or as wholly new departures—even travesties—of the original doctrine although parading under the same name of 'pragmatism'. Surely much that falls under the common usage of the term 'pragmatic' is a considerable simplification of the Peircean thesis, or simply has little connection with what Peirce understood by the term. In any case, we need to turn to these early essays. They are genuinely seminal—sowing the seeds of a powerful and important movement of thought. While we shall concentrate on these two essays, we shall from time to time, in clarification or elaboration of what is to be found there, refer to some of Peirce's later writings.

2.1.   CHARLES S. PEIRCE

Charles S. Peirce was born in Cambridge, Massachusetts, in 1839, the second son of Benjamin Peirce, a professor of mathematics and astronomy at Harvard University and the leading American mathematician of his day. From an early age, Charles showed great precocity. He had a strong interest in puzzles of all sorts and while still a boy set up his own chemical laboratory. At thirteen he mastered Archbishop Whately's

Elements of Logic. It had a profound influence on him, as he tells us in an account he wrote when he was seventy-two.

> When I was thirteen years old, being one day in the room of my elder brother, I picked up from his table a copy of Whately's Logic, and asked him what "logic" was. Being answered, I stretched myself out on the carpet with the book, and in a few days had mastered all the Archbishop had to say. From that week until I had reached my three score years and ten the central passion of my being was to find out,—not by any means what passed in my organism and my consciousness when I thought, but something anterior to all such knowledge, namely, what are the fundamentally different ways of reasoning, what kind and degree of assurance each could supply, and under precisely what conditions, and by what methods to proceed in order to gain such knowledge as is possible for human beings. The more I studied this subject the more and more deeply I felt *the shocking levity and looseness of thought with which these basic questions had been treated.*[4]

In a way that is reminiscent of another famous father-son case (that of James and John Stuart Mill), Benjamin Peirce took a strong hand in the supervision of Charles's early education, especially in mathematics. The training was demanding and rigorous. The father would give the boy various problems, individual cases or tables, and would require Charles to find the underlying principles through his own efforts.*

Father and son would work together at various card games and puzzles, especially those requiring strong concentration. These games would sometimes last from evening till sunrise, with the father carefully criticizing every error. "He educated me," Charles later wrote, "and if I do anything it will be his work." Of the kind of training Peirce received from his father, as it had to with its impact on his own work in philosophy and logic, he writes:

> The writers of logic-books, with rare exceptions, are themselves but shambling reasoners. How wilt thou say to thy brother, Let me cast out the mote out of thine eye; and lo, the beam is in thine own eye? In fact we may say of philosophers at large, both small and great, that their reasoning is mostly so loose and fallacious that it would be derided in mathematics, in political-economy, and in physical science. I felicitate myself that I was made to see this at an early age; for even in my teens, when I was reading Kant, Spinoza, and Hegel, my father, who was the celebrated mathematician Benjamin Peirce, not a powerful analyst of thought, so that his demonstrations were sometimes faulty, but a mind who never once failed, as well as I can remember, to draw the correct conclusion from given premises,

---

* "He preferred that I should myself be led to draw up the rules for myself, and quite forbade that I should be informed of the reason of my rule. Thus he showed me, himself, how to use a table of logarithms, and showed that in a couple of cases the sum of the logarithms was the logarithm of the product, but refused to explain why this should be or to direct me to the explanation of the phenomenon. That, he said, I must find out for myself, as I ultimately did in a more general way than that in which it is usually stated."[5]

unless by a mere slip, my father, I say, would induce me to tell him about the proofs offered by the philosophers, and in a very few words would almost invariably rip them up and show them empty. He had even less mercy for such philosophers as Hobbes, Hume, and James Mill. In that way, the bad habits of thinking which would have been impressed upon me by those mighty powers were in great measure, though I confess not entirely, overcome. Would that every young student of philosophy could enjoy a similar companionship with a stalwart practical reasoner.[6]

Charles Peirce attended Harvard College, entering in 1855 and graduating in 1859 (near the bottom of his class!). He received an M.A. in 1862, and in 1863 the degree of B.Sc. in chemistry, *summa cum laude*. In 1861 Peirce joined the United States Coast and Geodetic Survey, an association that lasted for the next thirty years. During this period, among other things Peirce performed many pendulum experiments, inventing types of pendulums that are now on display at the Smithsonian Institution. He served as a computer for the *American Ephemeris and Nautical Almanac,* and attended various international scientific conferences. The only book published by Peirce during his lifetime, *Photometric Researches* (1878), contains the fruits of his astronomical observations made during the years 1869 to 1872 while he was an assistant at the Harvard College Observatory. He made investigations in the field of spectroscopy that suggested ways of using the wavelength of light as a standard unit of measure. He also devised new techniques of making map projections of the earth. These varied direct experiences as a laboratory scientist had a deep impact in forming Peirce's views as a philosopher, logician, and student of the logic of inquiry.

In a series of published papers, as well as in a large number of manuscripts that were not to be published until many years after his death, Peirce laid the groundwork for lines of investigation that have since come to be recognized as of the highest importance. These included original investigations in the field of formal logic, especially in the logic of relations and the theory of quantification. The importance of this was acknowledged during Peirce's lifetime by Ernest Schröder who based some of his work in the *Vorlesungen über die Algebra der Logik* (1890–1905) on the studies of Peirce. In addition, Peirce did seminal work in the theory of signs (semiotics), the theory of probability, the theory of induction and scientific methodology, and in the general field of the foundations of mathematics. Along with these contributions to various aspects of analytic (empirical, logical, mathematical) studies, Peirce wrote voluminously and creatively on various topics in metaphysics, phenomenology, and the theory of categories. He also wrote on a number of other topics, for example Egyptology, psychical research, econometrics, political economy, religion, criminology, and the history of science. Something of his voracious intellectual appetite and the range of his interests is captured in a delightful reminiscence by John Jay Chapman, who records in one of his letters the following scene to which he was witness.

> Went to the Century, where I happened to sit down next to Charles Peirce, and stayed talking to him ever since, or rather he talking. He is a most genial man—got down books and read aloud. He began by saying Lincoln had the Rabelais quality. It appears he worships Rabelais. He read passages from Carlyle in a voice that made the building reverberate. He also read from an Elizabethan Thomas Nash—a great genius whom he said Carlyle got his style from, but he is wrong. Nash is better . . . and Peirce read with oriflamme appreciation. He then talked about—plasms—force, heat, light—Boston, Emerson, Margaret Fuller, God, Mammon, America, Goethe, Homer, Silver, but principally science and philosophy—a wonderful evening. It was ask and have, and, but that he talked himself positively to sleep with exertion, he would be talking yet, and I have many more things I want to ask him, chiefly Helmholtz. He is a physical mathematician mechanician, that sort of a man of a failed life so far as professional recognition goes, but of acknowledged extraordinary ability, and is positively the most agreeable person in the city. He is a son of old Professor Peirce, is about 55 and is like Socrates in his willingness to discuss anything and his delight in posing things and expressing things. In fact I got to answering him in the style of Plato's dialogues. . . .
>
> When you remember that I do not know anything whatever about the scientific things he was talking of most earnestly and most patiently most of the evening, you will see he is a very remarkable person. He has a theory that the laws of mind and matter are the same and he don't believe in the conservation of energy. He explained this at length—and he frightened two or three gentlemen who came near while he was doing it so that they won't come to the Club for a month. They looked at him in wonder, crossed themselves, and went away.[7]

The germinal formulation of the philosophy of pragmatism, as set out by Peirce in his early published papers, arose from certain discussions held at regular intervals in Cambridge, Massachusetts, in the 1870s among members of 'The Metaphysical Club'. This "club" numbered, along with Peirce, such other important figures as William James, Oliver Wendell Holmes, Jr., and Chauncey Wright. In an account of the 'origin of pragmatism' written in 1906, Peirce tells of this early period and of the circumstances of the birth of the philosophy of pragmatism.

> It was in the earliest seventies that a knot of us young men in Old Cambridge, calling ourselves, half-ironically, half-defiantly, "The Metaphysical Club,"—for agnosticism was then riding its high horse, and was frowning superbly upon all metaphysics—used to meet, sometimes in my study, sometimes in that of William James. It may be that some of our old-time confederates would today not care to have such wild-oats-sowings made public, though there was nothing but boiled oats, milk, and sugar in the mess. Mr. Justice Holmes, however, will not, I believe, take it ill that we are proud to remember his membership; nor will Joseph Warner, Esq. Nicholas St. John Green was one of the most interested fellows, a skillful lawyer and a learned one, a disciple of Jeremy Bentham.

His extraordinary power of disrobing warm and breathing truth of the draperies of long worn formulas was what attracted attention to him everywhere. In particular, he often urged the importance of applying Bain's definition of belief, as "that upon which man is prepared to act." From this definition, pragmatism is scarce more than a corollary; so that I am disposed to think of him as the grandfather of pragmatism. Chauncey Wright, something of a philosophical celebrity in those days, was never absent from our meetings. I was about to call him our corypheus; but he will better be described as our boxing-master whom we—I particularly—used to face to be severely pummelled. He had abandoned a former attachment to Hamiltonianism to take up with the doctrines of Mill, to which and to its cognate agnosticism he was trying to weld the really incongruous ideas of Darwin. John Fiske and, more rarely, Francis Ellingwood Abbot, were sometimes present, lending their countenances to the spirit of our endeavours, while holding aloof from any assent to their success. Wright, James, and I were men of science, rather scrutinizing the doctrines of the metaphysicians on their scientific side than regarding them as very momentous spiritually. The type of our thought was decidedly British. I, alone of our number, had come upon the threshing-floor of philosophy through the doorway of Kant, and even my ideas were acquiring the English accent.

Our metaphysical proceedings had all been in winged words (and swift ones, at that, for the most part), until at length, lest the club should be dissolved, without leaving any material *souvenir* behind, I drew up a little paper expressing some of the opinions that I have been urging all along under the name of pragmatism. This paper was received with such unlooked-for kindness, that I was encouraged, some half dozen years later, on the invitation of the great publisher, Mr. W. H. Appleton, to insert it, somewhat expanded, in the *Popular Science Monthly* for November 1877 and January 1878.[8]

Despite his lifelong dedication to philosophy and a painstaking concern with formulating his ideas in numerous writings, Peirce had only the briefest of opportunities for communicating his thought to academic audiences. He was able to see only a fraction of his vast literary output published during his lifetime. Peirce lectured on logic at the Johns Hopkins University from 1879 to 1884. Among his students were the philosophers Josiah Royce and John Dewey, the economist Thorstein Veblen, and the logician Christine Ladd-Franklin. At scattered intervals and for brief periods he gave individual lectures or series of lectures at Harvard, though never as a regular member of the department. Peirce's total teaching opportunities for his entire life did not add up to more than eight years! There were various reasons for this, among them certain aspects of his personality, his unconventional ways, marital difficulties, and the estrangement or hostility of some of those who might ordinarily have been thought eager to take note of and help a man of such undoubted genius. As a result, Peirce was deprived of the normal opportunities for communication and criticism by colleagues and students that would undoubtedly have been of help to him. William James—lifelong friend and staunch supporter of Peirce—described him as "a queer being" and said his lectures on pragmatism were "flashes of brilliant light relieved against Cimmerian darkness."[9] James remarked in one of his letters:

As for Charles Peirce, it is the most curious instance of talents not making a career. He dished himself at Harvard by inspiring dislike in Eliot. . . . He is now so mature in character, with rather fixed half-bohemian habits, and no habit of teaching, that it would be risky to appoint him. I yield to no one in admiration of his genius, but he is paradoxical and unsociable of intellect, and hates to *make connection* with anyone he is with.[10]

After his divorce from his first wife in 1883, Peirce remarried. At forty-eight he retired with his second wife (Juliette Froissy of Nancy, France) to a house in Milford, Pennsylvania where he spent the rest of his days amid his considerable philosophical and scientific library. He wrote articles on a variety of subjects for the *Century Dictionary* (6 volumes, 1889–1891), most of the articles on logic for Baldwin's *Dictionary of Philosophy and Psychology* (1901–1905), and many reviews for the *Nation*. These brought him a pittance, and despite occasional private benefactions from friends Peirce lived for many years in debt and on the verge of poverty. He was repeatedly rebuffed in his efforts to secure a publisher for his projects, for the books and memoirs he had written or offered to write. Despite all this, Peirce maintained a dogged and unflagging persistence in writing and rewriting his thoughts.*

Although throughout his life Peirce kept working at developing the vast and far-flung system of his thought, it was a 'system' that in fact never received a final, finished form of expression at his hands.

But I must tell you that all that you can find in print of my work on logic are simply scattered outcroppings here and there of a rich vein which remains unpublished. Most of it I suppose has been written down; but no human being could ever put together the fragments. I could not myself do so. All I could do would be to make an entirely new presentation and this I could only do in five or six years of hard work devoted to that alone. Since I am now 63 years old and since all this is matter calculated to make a difference in man's future intellectual development, I can only say that if the *genus homo* is so foolish as not to set me at the task, I shall lean back in my chair and take my ease. I have done a great work wholly without any kind of aid, and now I am willing to undergo the last great effort which must finish me up in order to give men the benefit of what I have done. But if I am not in

---

* "I have no itch at all to go into print and never will do so until I have gone over the subject so many times and elaborated so clear an idea of it that it seems a great pity that it should not be recorded. It is always anywhere from five to twenty years from my first having written the matter out. Of course I don't speak of newspaper contributions, though I sometimes leave these standing in type for months before I will consent to their going to press. This is because I know of the castigation that is coming to me from myself. For no sooner is the paper out that I set to work to raise all the objections I possibly can both of the trifling kind and of the dynamitic kind. And the result has always been that I have found that there were other men who were far better satisfied with them than I myself have been."[11]

a situation to do so but have to earn my living, why that will be infinitely the more comfortable way of completing the number of my days; and if anybody supposes that I shall regret missing the fame that might attach to the name of C. S. Peirce— a name that won't be mine much longer—I shall only say that he can indulge that fancy without my taking the trouble to contradict him. I have reached the age when I think of my home as being on the other side rather than on this uninteresting planet.[12]

Peirce died of cancer, lonely, poor, with hardly anybody to take notice of his achievements.*

After his death, Peirce's widow sold the extensive collection of his manuscripts to the Harvard Philosophy Department. Years later, by one of the ironies of fate, that same department which had refused to appoint Peirce to its staff, arranged for the handsome edition and publication of his *Collected Papers*.

Peirce's claim to be one of America's most original and influential philosophers and its greatest logician is now well established and universally recognized. Numerous studies of his thought continue to appear— books, monographs, collections of his writings, papers, as well as volumes of studies sponsored by the Peirce Society. All these attest to the continuing vitality and interest of his thought. James's remark that Peirce "is a goldmine of ideas for thinkers of the coming generation" has turned out to be a profoundly true prophecy. Yet Peirce's is but another case (too frequent, alas!) from a roster of creative geniuses neglected in their own time whose work came to be appreciated only by later generations.

---

* Here is a description of his last hours, as reconstructed by Professor Lenzen who, many years later, visited the town where Peirce had lived and who spoke to some of the old-time residents and neighbors who had known Peirce:

> During the middle of April in 1914, Charles J. Gassmann, Jr., aged 22, had not seen the Peirces about their house for some time. He went to their door, knocked, and was admitted by Juliette. Young Gassmann saw Peirce, whom he called the Professor, with his white beard, lying on a small cot in a dark room with only a little fire in the fireplace. The room was cold, and Juliette said that they had no wood. The Professor was glad to see the young neighbor and called him Charlie. Young Gassmann then went out and cut some wood which he brought in and placed on the fire. This made Juliette very happy. He saw that there was no food in the house and brought some from home. He said that he would be back the following day.
>
> About ten o'clock the next morning, Charles Gassmann, Jr., went to the Peirce home again. Juliette said, "Papa isn't so good to-day" (Juliette called Peirce papa, since she was younger than he, while he spoke of her as "My little girl"). Peirce was very thin, shriveled up, weak and ill; lying upon the cot he looked just like a little boy. Peirce said that he was cold. Young Gassman then put wood on the fire. To warm him better, the young man lifted the Professor from the cot and held him in his arms. The Professor gasped two or three times, then stiffened out, and died. Juliette wept, and Mrs. Gassmann came over to comfort her and bring some food. Thus, on the morning of the 19th of April, 1914, while resting in the arms of Charles J. Gassmann, Jr., the last breath passed from the mortal body of Charles Sanders Peirce.[13]

In a memorable and characteristic self-analysis, Peirce sums up his life's work as follows:

The reader has a right to know how the author's opinions were formed. Not, of course, that he is expected to accept any conclusions which are not borne out by argument. But in discussions of extreme difficulty, like these, when good judgment is a factor, and pure ratiocination is not everything, it is prudent to take every element into consideration. From the moment when I could think at all, until now, about forty years, I have been diligently and incessantly occupied with the study of methods [of] inquiry, both those which have been and are pursued and those which ought to be pursued. For ten years before this study began, I had been in training in the chemical laboratory. I was thoroughly grounded not only in all that was then known of physics and chemistry, but also in the way in which those who were successfully advancing knowledge proceeded. I have paid the most attention to the methods of the most exact sciences, have intimately communed with some of the greatest minds of our times in physical science, and have myself made positive contributions—none of them of any very great importance, perhaps—in mathematics, gravitation, optics, chemistry, astronomy, etc. I am saturated, through and through, with the spirit of the physical sciences. I have been a great student of logic, having read everything of any importance on the subject, devoting a great deal of time to medieval thought, without neglecting the works of the Greeks, the English, the Germans, the French, etc., and have produced systems of my own both in deductive and in inductive logic. In metaphysics my training has been less systematic; yet I have read and deeply pondered upon all the main systems, never being satisfied until I was able to think about them as their own advocates thought.

The first strictly philosophical books that I read were of the classical German schools; and I became so deeply imbued with many of their ways of thinking that I have never been able to disabuse myself of them. Yet my attitude was always that of a dweller in a laboratory, eager only to learn what I did not yet know, and not that of philosophers bred in theological seminaries, whose ruling impulse is to teach what they hold to be infallibly true. I devoted two hours a day to the study of Kant's *Critic of the Pure Reason* for more than three years, until I almost knew the whole book by heart, and had critically examined every section of it. For about two years, I had long and almost daily discussions with Chauncey Wright, one of the most acute of the followers of J. S. Mill.

The effect of these studies was that I came to hold the classical German philosophy to be, upon its argumentative side, of little weight; although I esteem it, perhaps am too partial to it, as a rich mine of philosophical suggestions. The English philosophy, meagre and crude, as it is, in its conceptions, proceeds by surer methods and more accurate logic. The doctrine of the association of ideas is, to my thinking, the finest piece of philosophical work of the prescientific ages. Yet I can but pronounce English sensationalism to be entirely destitute of any solid bottom. From the evolutionary philosophers, I have learned little; although I admit that, however hurriedly their theories have been knocked together, and however antiquated and ignorant Spencer's *First Principles* and general doctrines, yet they are under the guidance of a great and true idea, and are developing it by methods that are in their main features sound and scientific.

The works of Duns Scotus have strongly influenced me. If his logic and metaphysics, not slavishly worshipped, but torn away from its medievalism, be adapted to modern culture, under continual wholesome reminders of nominalistic criticisms, I am convinced that it will go far toward supplying the philosophy which is best to harmonize with physical science. But other conceptions have to be drawn from the history of science and from mathematics.

Thus, in brief, my philosophy may be described as the attempt of a physicist to make such conjecture as to the constitution of the universe as the methods of science may permit, with the aid of all that has been done by previous philosophers. I shall support my propositions by such arguments as I can. Demonstrative proof is not to be thought of. The demonstrations of the metaphysicians are all moonshine. The best that can be done is to supply a hypothesis, not devoid of all likelihood, in the general line of growth and scientific ideas, and capable of being verified or refuted by future observers.

Religious infallibilism, caught in the current of the times, shows symptoms of declaring itself to be only practically speaking infallible; and when it has thus once confessed itself subject to gradations, there will remain over no relic of the good old tenth-century infallibilism, except that of the infallible scientists, under which head I include, not merely the kind of characters that manufacture scientific catechisms and homilies, churches and creeds, and who are indeed "born missionaries," but all those respectable and cultivated persons who, having acquired their notions of science from reading, and not from research, have the idea that "science" means knowledge, while the truth is, it is a misnomer applied to the pursuit of those who are devoured by a desire to find things out. . . .

Though infallibility in scientific matters seems to me irresistibly comical, I should be in a sad way if I could not retain a high respect for those who lay claim to it, for they comprise the greater part of the people who have any conversation at all. When I say they lay claim to it, I mean they assume the functions of it quite naturally and unconsciously. The full meaning of the adage *Humanum est errare,* they have never waked up to. In those sciences of measurement which are the least subject to error—metrology, geodesy, and metrical astronomy—no man of self-respect ever now states his result, without affixing to it its *probable error;* and if this practice is not followed in other sciences it is because in those the probable errors are too vast to be estimated.

I am a man of whom critics have never found anything good to say. When they could see no opportunity to injure me, they have held their peace. The little laudation I have had has come from such sources, that the only satisfaction I have derived from it, has been from such slices of bread and butter as it might waft my way. Only once, as far as I remember, in all my lifetime have I experienced the pleasure of praise—not for what it might bring but in itself. That pleasure was beatific; and the praise that conferred it was meant for blame. It was that a critic said of me that I did not seem to be *absolutely sure of my own conclusions.* Never, if I can help it, shall that critic's eye ever rest on what I am now writing; for I owe a great pleasure to him; and, such was his evident animus, that should he find that out, I fear the fires of hell would be fed with new fuel in his breast.

My book will have no instruction to impart to anybody. Like a mathematical treatise, it will suggest certain ideas and certain reasons for holding them true; but then, if you accept them, it must be because you like my reasons, and the responsibility lies with you. Man is essentially a social animal: but to be social is one thing, to be gregarious is another: I decline to serve as bellwether. My book is meant for people who *want to find out;* and people who want philosophy ladled out to them can go elsewhere. There are philosophical soup shops at every corner, thank God!

The development of my ideas has been the industry of thirty years. I did not know as I ever should get to publish them, their ripening seemed so slow. But the harvest time has come, at last, and to me that harvest seems a wild one, but of course it is not I who have to pass judgment. It is not quite you, either, individual reader; it is experience and history.

For years in the course of this ripening process, I used for myself to collect my ideas under the designation *fallibilism;* and indeed the first step toward *finding out* is to acknowledge you do not satisfactorily know already; so that no blight can so surely arrest all intellectual growth as the blight of cocksureness; and ninety-nine out of every hundred good heads are reduced to impotence by that malady—of whose inroads they are most strangely unaware!

Indeed, out of a contrite fallibilism, combined with a high faith in the reality of knowledge, and an intense desire to find things out, all my philosophy has always seemed to me to grow.[14]

Peirce's choice of the themes 'fixation of belief' and 'the clarification of ideas', in his early and classic formulations of a pragmatic philosophy, shows a profound sense of what is of central importance for any philosophy that would undertake to illuminate the role of knowledge in human experience. For what is comprised under Peirce's use of the terms 'belief' and 'ideas' (in their wide sense) has to do with that which lies at the core of human existence, insofar as that existence is differentiated from other modes. Only human beings, as far as we know, have beliefs and construct and use ideas. These permeate all our activities; they are found in one form or another in every domain of human experience, whether personal or collective, from the everyday and the most trivial to the most rarified, exalted, or sophisticated. Wherever we turn, human beings are involved with beliefs and ideas: acting in terms of them, arguing about them, accepting or rejecting them. Nothing is so distinctively human as having and using beliefs and ideas. It is of the greatest importance, therefore, that we be able to understand as thoroughly as possible what beliefs are and on what basis they are held. What methods do we use, or should we use, for arriving at or justifying them? How do we (or might we) go about settling or resolving differences and conflicts with respect to them? The term 'pragmatism', as employed in connection with Peirce's philosophy, collects his various distinctive answers to these questions and the way he develops these themes.

2.2. THE NATURE OF BELIEF

As a first step in disentangling the strands in the complex web of Peirce's views, we turn to an examination of the term 'belief'. One way we may sum up the kinds of things Peirce has to say about the nature of belief, as gathered from various writings, is the following:

A belief is the assertion of a proposition a person holds to be true; it is that upon which a person is consciously prepared to act in a certain definite way; it marks a habit of mind; it is the opposite of a state of doubt.

Let us examine the various items in this composite formula.

Proposition

First of all, every belief is belief in a *proposition*. And a proposition can be thought of as having basically two components: a subject (or subjects) and a predicate.

Every belief is belief in a proposition. Now every proposition has its predicate which expresses *what* is believed, and its subjects which express *of what* it is believed. The grammarians of today prefer to say that a sentence has but one subject, which is put in the nominative. But from a logical point of view the terminology of the older grammarians was better, who spoke of the subject nominative and the subject accusative. I do not know that they spoke of the subject dative; but in the proposition, "Anthony gave a ring to Cleopatra," Cleopatra is as much a subject of what is meant and expressed as is the ring or Anthony. A proposition, then, has one predicate and any number of subjects. The subjects are either names of objects well known to the utterer and to the interpreter of the proposition (otherwise he could not interpret it) or they are virtually almost directions how to proceed to gain acquaintance with what is referred to. Thus, in the sentence "Every man dies," "Every man" implies that the interpreter is at liberty to pick out a man and consider the proposition as applying to him. In the proposition "Anthony gave a ring to Cleopatra," if the interpreter asks, What ring? the answer is that the indefinite article shows that it is a ring which might have been pointed out to the interpreter if he had been on the spot; and that the proposition is only asserted of the suitably chosen ring. The predicate on the other hand is a word or phrase which will call up in the memory or imagination of the interpreter images of such things such as he has seen or imagined and may see again. Thus, "gave" is the predicate of the last proposition; and it conveys its meaning because the interpreter has had many experiences in which gifts were made; and a sort of composite photograph of them appears in his imagination. I am told that "Saccharin is 500 times as sweet as cane-sugar." But I never heard of saccharin. On inquiry, I find it is the sulphimide of orthosulphobenzoic acid; that is, it is phthalimide in which one CO group is replaced by SO_2. I can see on paper that there might be such a body. That it is "500 times sweeter than sugar" produces a rather confused idea of a very familiar general kind. *What* I am to expect is expressed by the predicate, while the subjects inform me on what occasion I am to expect it.[15]

Assertion

Consider next what it means to say that a person who has a belief is ready to *assert* a certain proposition. Assertion represents a specific propositional attitude: the way we respond to, the mental or behavioral stance we adopt with respect to, a particular proposition. In addition to assertion, there are other possible *propositional attitudes*. One may state a proposition, doubt it, question it, command it (for adoption by someone else), report it, examine its logical or grammatical structure, and so on. But in order to have a belief in it, it is necessary to be ready in appropriate circumstances to *assert it*. This is marked by specific features of a person's attitude toward it that are quite different from other types of propositional attitudes to the same proposition.

In the first place, it is necessary to distinguish between a proposition and the assertion of it. To confound those two things is like confounding the writing of one's name idly upon a scrap of paper, perhaps for practice in chirography, with the attachment of one's signature to a binding legal deed. A proposition may be stated without being asserted. I may state it to myself and worry as to whether I shall embrace it or reject it, being dissatisfied with the idea of doing either. In that case, I doubt the proposition. I may state the proposition to you and endeavor to stimulate you to advise me whether to accept or reject it: in which [case] I put it interrogatively. I may state it to myself; and be deliberately satisfied to base my action on it whenever occasion may arise: in which case I judge it. I may state it to you: and assume a responsibility for it: in which case I assert it. I may impose the responsibility of its agreeing with the truth upon you: in which case I command it. All of these are different moods in which that same proposition may be stated. The German word *Urtheil* confounds the proposition itself with the psychological act of assenting to it.[16]

To *assert* a proposition, then, is to commit oneself to it: to affirm, underwrite, or in effect to bet that it is true. It is equivalent to making oneself responsible for its truth.

Now it is a fairly easy problem to analyze the nature of *assertion*. To find an easily dissected example, we shall naturally take a case where the assertive element is magnified—a very formal assertion, such as an affidavit. Here a man goes before a notary or magistrate and takes such action that if what he says is not true, evil consequences will be visited upon him, and this he does with a view to thus causing other men to be affected just as they would be if the proposition sworn to had presented itself to them as a perceptual fact.

We thus see that the act of assertion is an act of a totally different nature from the act of apprehending the meaning of the proposition and we cannot expect that any analysis of what assertion is (or any analysis of what *judgment* or *belief* is, if that act is at all allied to assertion), should throw any light at all on the widely different question of what the apprehension of the meaning of a proposition is.

What is the difference between making an *assertion* and *laying a wager*? Both are acts whereby the agent deliberately subjects himself to evil consequences if a certain proposition is not true. Only when he offers to bet he hopes the other man will make himself responsible in the same way for the truth of the contrary proposition; while when he makes an *assertion* he always (or almost always) wishes the man to whom he makes it to be led to do what he does. Accordingly in our vernacular "I will bet" so and so, is the phrase expressive of a private opinion which one does not expect others to share, while "You bet" is a form of assertion intended to cause another to follow suit.[17]

This analysis of the nature of assertion can also be applied to the assertion of propositions having to do with the past. Of course, one cannot promise to do something now or in the future that is already in the past, or to commit oneself to have done something that is already over and done with. One can only commit oneself to something or other if it can be ascertained now or in the future that something is true. Such ascertainment of the truth of a proposition, having to do with some event in the past, can, in turn, be the basis for making a moral judgment that will affect a person's present or future conduct. Thus, one can be held responsible now, say, for something one should have done (or not have done) in the past. Peirce puts the matter as follows:

It follows, then, that to contract to pay money if something in the past has been done or not done *can only* mean that the money shall be paid if it is ascertained that the event has happened or has not happened. . . . Hence there can be no meaning in making oneself responsible for a past event independent of its future ascertainment. But to assert a proposition is to make oneself responsible for its truth. Consequently, the only meaning which an assertion of a past fact can have is that, if in the future the truth be ascertained, so it shall be ascertained to be. There seems to be no rational escape from this.[18]

Habit of mind
A third component in the nature of belief is that it marks a habit as a result of which a person would act in a certain way should an occasion present itself that calls forth that belief.

A belief as a habit is not a *momentary* state of consciousness, like having a twinge of pain or seeing a flash of lightning. It endures or persists over time. A particular belief may, of course, be challenged, dissolved, or replaced by some other belief, in which case the new belief will mark a new and different habit of mind. A belief as a habit is something general. It can be brought to bear upon more than one occasion. One who adopts a belief will repeatedly and deliberately use the same ways of dealing with the matter to which the belief applies. This holds for all types of belief, whether practical or theoretical. For example:

I have no belief that prussic acid is poisonous unless when the particular occasion comes up I am led to the further belief that that particular acid is poisonous; and unless I am further led to the belief that it is a thing to avoid drinking.

For all these things are necessary to my acting on my belief. A belief which will not be acted on ceases to be a belief.[19]

Peirce points out that a belief may be acquired not only as a result of a series of actually undergone experiences, but on the basis of an exercise of imagination. In this situation one comes to adopt a belief on the basis of considering possible cases to which the belief might apply.

A mere imagination of reacting in a particular way seems to be capable after numerous repetitions of causing the imagined kind of reaction really to take place upon subsequent occurrences of the stimulus. In the formation of habits of deliberate action, we may imagine the occurrence of the stimulus, and think out what the results of different actions will be. One of these will appear particularly satisfactory; and then an action of the soul takes place which is well described by saying that the mode of reaction "receives a deliberate stamp of approval."[20]

Peirce gives an example of the latter kind of situation:

I well remember when I was a boy, and my brother Herbert, now our minister at Christiania, was scarce more than a child, one day, as the whole family were at table, some spirit from a "blazer," or "chafing-dish," dropped on the muslin dress of one of the ladies and was kindled; and how instantaneously he jumped up, and did the right thing, and how skillfully each motion was adapted to the purpose. I asked him afterward about it; and he told me that since Mrs. Longfellow's death, it was that he had often run over in imagination all the details of what ought to be done in such an emergency. It was a striking example of a real habit produced by exercises in the imagination.[21]

Since belief is of the nature of a habit, the having of a *particular* belief is to be recognized by the kinds of actions to which it leads—the practical consequences one expects it to have. One has to look to these actions—to these behavioral, practical consequences—as the primary criterion for determining what a person actually believes. It is not the merely verbal or linguistic formulation of the belief that is the crucial factor. The fact that there may be differences in verbal formulation of belief need not be taken as indicating that there is a genuine difference in belief. The only test of whether there are genuine differences in belief is to see whether there are different courses of action—different habits of expectation, different habits or 'practical consequences' in the behavior which the individual manifests, who has the belief in question.

The essence of belief is the establishment of a habit; and different beliefs are distinguished by the different modes of action to which they give rise. If beliefs do not differ in this respect, if they appease the same doubt by producing the same rule of action, then no mere differences in the manner of consciousness of them can make them different beliefs, any more than playing a tune in different keys is playing different tunes. Imaginary distinctions are often drawn between beliefs which differ only in their mode of expression;—the wrangling which ensues is real enough, however. To believe that any objects are arranged among themselves as

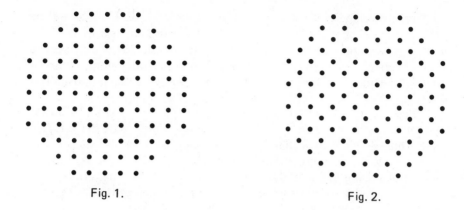

Fig. 1.   Fig. 2.

in Fig. 1, and to believe that they are arranged [as] in Fig. 2, are one and the same belief; yet it is conceivable that a man should assert one proposition and deny the other. Such false distinctions do as much harm as the confusion of beliefs really different, and are among the pitfalls of which we ought constantly to beware, especially when we are upon metaphysical ground. . . .

Another such deception is to mistake a mere difference in the grammatical construction of two words for a distinction between the ideas they express. In this pedantic age, when the general mob of writers attend so much more to words than to things, this error is common enough.[22]

Doubt and belief

Another important aspect of Peirce's analysis is the contrast he draws between belief and doubt. To begin with, they are contrasted propositional attitudes with respect to one and the same proposition. Belief marks the assertion or acceptance of the proposition, whereas doubt points to the presence of an active, genuine mental attitude of questioning with respect to it, the absence of any readiness to assert or accept it. Thus doubt has to be distinguished in this respect from ignorance, or a total lack of any awareness of the proposition in question.

There is something further removed from belief than doubt, that is to say not to conceive the proposition at all. Nor is doubt wholly without effect upon our conduct. It makes us waver. Conviction determines us to act in a particular way while pure unconscious ignorance alone which is the true contrary of belief has no effect at all.[23]

The contrast between doubt and belief is marked in additional ways. There is, first of all, the difference in immediate sensation or feeling that accompanies each. There is a difference in the state of mind involved. To be in a state of doubt is not simply to put a question mark after a proposition, to express it interrogatively. "We can throw any proposition into the interrogative mood at will; but we can no more call up doubt than we can call up the feeling of hunger at will."[24] What Peirce means by doubt is something genuinely felt, an active, living experience. It is a subjective state of genuine wavering or uncertainty that a person undergoes, an inability or hesitancy in some degree to commit oneself to the proposition in question.

Peirce contrasts genuine doubt and artificial doubt. What he means by doubt, as the opposite of belief, is genuine doubt, not the artificial kind. Thus Peirce claims that Descartes' 'method of doubt' is to be rejected as a faulty technique in philosophizing. It encourages the use of a method of raising artificial doubts. It asks us to doubt matters that we normally do not have the slightest reason or occasion for doubting.

Some philosophers have imagined that to start an inquiry it was only necessary to utter a question whether orally or by setting it down upon paper, and have even recommended us to begin our studies with questioning everything! But the mere putting of a proposition into the interrogative form does not stimulate the mind to any struggle after belief. There must be a real and living doubt, and without this all discussion is idle.[25]

Peirce maintains, contrary to Descartes, that all of us are equipped with many *indubitable* beliefs—beliefs that we are incapable of genuinely doubting at any given time, since we cannot and do not feel any genuine doubt about them.

We cannot begin with complete doubt. We must begin with all the prejudices which we actually have when we enter upon the study of philosophy. These prejudices are not to be dispelled by a maxim, for they are things which it does not occur to us *can* be questioned. Hence this initial skepticism will be a mere self-deception, and not real doubt; and no one who follows the Cartesian method will ever be satisfied until he has formally recovered all those beliefs which in form he has given up. It is, therefore, as useless a preliminary as going to the North Pole would be in order to get to Constantinople by coming down regularly upon a meridian. A person may, it is true, in the course of his studies, find reason to doubt what he began by believing; but in that case he doubts becasue he has a positive reason for it, and not on account of the Cartesian maxim. Let us not pretend to doubt in philosophy what we do not doubt in our hearts.[26]

It should be noted that Peirce's acceptance of various beliefs as 'indubitable' (as he understands this term) is in no way in conflict with his central adherence to the philosophy of fallibilism. For, according to Peirce, to say a proposition in which one believes is *indubitable* is not the same as saying that the belief (the proposition one asserts) is *incorrigible*. Any belief may be open to doubt and correction—when genuine doubt arises concerning it, and criticism and inquiry show it needs to be modified, corrected, or possibly discarded. Thus when Peirce uses the term 'indubitable', it means a belief one cannot *genuinely* doubt at a given time for there are no good reasons for actively doubting it. It remains indubitable, since it is actually undoubted. But the fact that a belief is in this sense indubitable is not equivalent to saying that it is forever incapable of being corrected, that it is *incorrigible*.[27]

A second crucial way in which belief and doubt are contrasted has to do with differences in behavior. There are differences to be noted in the way a person acts, not simply in the inner feelings or sensations the person experiences. To have a belief, as we have already seen, is to have a certain habit of mind that makes the believer expect certain consequences to hold. The individual acts in ways appropriate to the belief when relevant occasions present themselves. On the other hand, when a person is in doubt, that person's behavior does not show the regularity of response that characterizes one who has a belief. Doubt is characterized by hesitancy, wavering, indecision; there is no special pattern of behavior based on one's expecting certain definite matters to be enacted or observed. But even doubt has its *degrees,* as does belief itself, that are manifested in outward behavior.

Doubt has degrees and may approximate indefinitely to belief, but when I doubt, the effect of the mental judgment will not be seen in my conduct as invariably or to the full extent that it will when I believe. Thus, if I am perfectly confident that an insurance company will fulfill their engagements I will pay them a certain sum for a policy, but if I think there is a risk of their breaking, I shall not pay them so much.[28]

In any case, the main difference between doubt and belief is a *practical difference.*

Our beliefs guide our desires and shape our actions. The Assassins, or followers of the Old Man of the Mountain, used to rush into death at his least command, because they believed that obedience to him would insure everlasting felicity. Had they doubted this, they would not have acted as they did. So it is with every belief, according to its degree. The feeling of believing is a more or less sure indication of there being established in our nature some habit which will determine our actions. Doubt never has such an effect.[29]

Finally, the difference between doubt and belief is marked by the fact that to be in genuine doubt is to experience a tension, a state of irritation, unsettlement, and uneasiness, from which one seeks to escape, whereas the opposite is true of having a belief.

Doubt is an uneasy and dissatisfied state from which we struggle to free ourselves and pass into the state of belief; while the latter is a calm and satisfactory state which we do not wish to avoid, or to change to a belief in anything else. On the contrary, we cling tenaciously, not merely to believing, but to believing just what we do believe.[30]

METHODS OF EFFECTING A SETTLEMENT OF OPINION

Since to experience a state of genuine doubt is uncomfortable and irritating, a person in such a state craves and needs a belief that will overcome his or her hesitancy, wavering, and uncertainty. From a psychological point of view, having a belief is immensely preferable to being in a state of doubt. Accordingly, the need to escape from a state of doubt provides the occasion and the motivation for finding a way of overcoming the doubt and relieving the tension. "The irritation of doubt is the only immediate motive for the struggle to attain belief. . . . With the doubt, therefore, the struggle begins, and with the cessation of doubt it ends."[31]

Given this fundamental psychological fact, Peirce turns next to considering the possible means by which people seek to escape from a state of doubt and attain belief. He examines in detail the various methods for effecting a *settlement of opinion,* for achieving a *fixation of belief.* When he surveys the behavior of human beings, he finds there are basically four such methods. These are (1) *the method of tenacity,* or adhering obstinately to whatever happens to be one's existing opinions; (2) *the method of authority* (sometimes called "the method of persecution," since it consists in "spreading the opinions which happen to be approved by rulers"[32]); (3) the *a priori method* (sometimes called "the natural development of opinion," "the unimpeded action of natural preferences," or the method of "public opinion"[33]); and (4) *the method of science* (sometimes called simply "investigation," "inquiry," or "reasoning").

The phrase 'fixation of belief' (or its equivalent, 'settlement of opinion'), as Peirce uses it, has two distinguishable yet related aspects. The term 'fixation' (or 'settlement') can stand either for a way of *acquiring* a belief, or for a way of *justifying* the belief once acquired, or for both at once. By 'acquiring' a belief is meant the way one goes about finding or obtaining some belief to replace a state of doubt. By 'justifying' a belief is meant the way one responds—the kinds of things one does or says—in defense of the belief should that belief be challenged. Each of the methods of fixing belief is distinguished from the others by the way it functions. Let us now examine each of these methods to see in what each consists, and what can be said about it from a critical point of view.

The method of tenacity

Peirce describes the method of tenacity as follows:

If the settlement of opinion is the sole object of inquiry, and if belief is of the nature of a habit, why should we not attain the desired end, by taking as answer to a question any we may fancy, and constantly reiterating it to ourselves, dwelling on all which may conduce to that belief, and learning to turn with contempt and hatred from anything that might disturb it? This simple and direct method is really pursued by many men. I remember once being entreated not to read a certain newspaper lest it might change my opinion upon free-trade. "Lest I might be entrapped by its fallacies and misstatements," was the form of expression. "You are not," my friend said, "a special student of political economy. You might, therefore, easily be deceived by fallacious arguments upon the subject. You might, then, if you read this paper, be led to believe in protection. But you admit that free-trade is the true doctrine; and you do not wish to believe what is not true." I have often known this system to be deliberately adopted. Still oftener, the instinctive dislike of an undecided state of mind, exaggerated into a vague dread of doubt, makes men cling spasmodically to the views they already take. The man feels that, if he only holds to his belief without wavering, it will be entirely satisfactory. Nor can it be denied that a steady and immovable faith yields great peace of mind. It may, indeed, give rise to inconveniences, as if a man should resolutely continue to believe that fire would not burn him, or that he would be eternally damned if he received his *ingesta* otherwise than through a stomach-pump. But then the man who adopts this method will not allow that its inconveniences are greater than its advantages. He will say, "I hold steadfastly to the truth, and the truth is always wholesome." And in many cases it may very well be that the pleasure he derives from his calm faith overbalances any inconveniences resulting from its deceptive character. Thus, if it be true that death is annihilation, then the man who believes that he will certainly go straight to heaven when he dies, provided he have fulfilled certain simple observances in this life, has a cheap pleasure which will not be followed by the least disappointment. A similar consideration seems to have weight with many persons in religious topics, for we frequently hear it said, "Oh, I could not believe so-and-so, because I should be wretched if I did." When an ostrich buries its head in the sand as danger approaches, it very likely takes the happiest course. It hides the danger, and then calmly says there is no danger; and, if it feels perfectly sure there is none, why should it raise its head to see? A man may go through life, systematically keeping out of view all that might cause a change in his opinions, and if he only succeeds—basing his method, as he does, on two fundamental psychological laws—I do not see what can be said against his doing so. It would be an egotistical impertinence to object that his procedure is irrational, for that only amounts to saying that his method of settling belief is not ours. He does not propose to himself to be rational, and, indeed, will often talk with scorn of man's weak and illusive reason. So let him think as he pleases.[34]

The method of tenacity as a way of *acquiring* a belief consists in taking some belief, however arbitrarily chosen (whether at random, by imitation, or from any source whatever), that will serve to allay the doubt. By clinging to the belief obstinately, by repeating it and refusing to consider any alternative to it, a person satisfies the psychological need of resolving his or her state of doubt. The method of tenacity as a method of *justifying* a belief is marked by a refusal to budge, a refusal to examine openly and critically the relative merits of the belief, to examine or produce any evidence that might bear on its truth or soundness. The emotional security of having a belief, of not having it tampered with or opened to examination and so exposed to the danger of possible dislodgment, is preferred to everything else.

The method of tenacity as above characterized is approached by Peirce in primarily psychological terms. Peirce stresses the behavior and attitude of an individual whose emotional needs are dominant. However, even with strong psychological determinants there are two factors that are capable of breaking the stranglehold and discouraging continued reliance on the use of this method. One factor is some degree of sensitivity to logical considerations—what Peirce calls a sense of 'sanity'. A person may come to recognize, however dimly or intermittently, that other persons have beliefs incompatible with his. Indeed they may cling just as obstinately to theirs as he does to his. He may then come to realize that not all these beliefs can be true, since they are logically incompatible with one another. The seeds of doubt aroused by this logical consideration may be sufficiently disturbing to break his continued reliance on the method of tenacity. It may encourage the individual to seek some other method, some other way of acquiring and upholding his beliefs. The other factor (apart from a germinal sensitivity to logical considerations) that may cause a weakening of the hold of the method of tenacity is a countervailing psychological one, this time of a *social* dimension. We are, after all, not normally hermits. We crave and need the comfort of and the sense of being in agreement with our fellow men, of being part of a community of like-minded individuals. The method of tenacity

will be unable to hold its ground in practice. The social impulse is against it. The man who adopts it will find that other men think differently from him, and it will be apt to occur to him, in some saner moment, that their opinions are quite as good as his own, and this will shake his confidence in his belief. This conception, that another man's thought or sentiment may be equivalent to one's own, is a distinctively new step, and a highly important one. It arises from an impulse too strong in man to be suppressed, without danger of destroying the human species. Unless we make ourselves hermits, we shall necessarily influence each other's opinions; so that the problem becomes how to fix belief, not in the individual merely, but in the community.[35]

The method of authority

Where whole communities share in the adoption of a belief or set of beliefs, where such shared adoption of beliefs is the result of their having been imposed by some central source, and where the continued acceptance by the community of those beliefs is a matter of enforcement by the central authority, there is the use of what Peirce calls the method of authority. He describes it as follows:

Let the will of the state act, then, instead of that of the individual. Let an institution be created which shall have for its object to keep correct doctrines before the attention of the people, to reiterate them perpetually, and to teach them to the young; having at the same time power to prevent contrary doctrines from being taught, advocated, or expressed. Let all possible causes of a change of mind be removed from men's apprehensions. Let them be kept ignorant, lest they should learn of some reason to think otherwise than they do. Let their passions be enlisted, so that they may regard private and unusual opinions with hatred and horror. Then, let all men who reject the established belief be terrified into silence. Let the people turn out and tar-and-feather such men, or let inquisitions be made into the manner of thinking of suspected persons, and when they are found guilty of forbidden beliefs, let them be subjected to some signal punishment. When complete agreement could not otherwise be reached, a general massacre of all who have not thought in a certain way has proved a very effective means of settling opinion in a country. If the power to do this be wanting, let a list of opinions be drawn up, to which no man of the least independence of thought can assent, and let the faithful be required to accept all these propositions, in order to segregate them as radically as possible from the influence of the rest of the world.

This method has, from the earliest times, been one of the chief means of upholding correct theological and political doctrines, and of preserving their universal or catholic character. In Rome, especially, it has been practised from the days of Numa Pompilius to those of Pius Nonus. This is the most perfect example in history; but wherever there is a priesthood—and no religion has been without one—this method has been more or less made use of. Wherever there is an aristocracy, or a guild, or any association of a class of men whose interests depend, or are supposed to depend, on certain propositions, there will be inevitably found some traces of this natural product of social feeling. Cruelties always accompany this system; and when it is consistently carried out, they become atrocities of the most horrible kind in the eyes of any rational man. Nor should this occasion surprise, for the officer of a society does not feel justified in surrendering the interests of that society for the sake of mercy, as he might his own private interests. It is natural, therefore, that sympathy and fellowship should thus produce a most ruthless power.[36]

The method of authority differs from the method of tenacity both as a method of acquiring and of justifying beliefs. Insofar as an individual acquires his beliefs by this method, he does not do so by choosing some belief arbitrarily or at random. He does so rather by accepting his beliefs from some source regarded as authoritative. Indeed, what distinguishes this method from that of tenacity is that it normally rests on a commonly shared acceptance of a set of beliefs throughout an entire community. All members of this community, insofar as they use this method, acquire their commonly held beliefs from the same authoritative source. As Peirce suggests, this authoritative source is not ordinarily chosen as a result of some open and critically explored examination of possible alternatives. Rather, the authoritative source *imposes* the beliefs in question upon the community of believers. The techniques used for accomplishing this result and for achieving a uniformity of acceptance vary with respect to the kind of instruments or types of force used. Propaganda, brainwashing, the use of economic pressures, a control of the popular media (including the direction and manipulation of educational institutions) are familiar enough examples of the sort of thing Peirce has in mind. In justifying one's beliefs by this method, the believer will appeal to the authority from whom the belief is acquired. One who uses this method—out of fear, habit, conditioning, respect, confidence, or indoctrination—will appeal in an unquestioning way, if challenged, to the authority from whom the belief was derived as sanctioning the soundness of the belief in question. (The authority appealed to may, but need not, itself in turn appeal to and use the same method of authority in acquiring or justifying the beliefs it imposes on others.) It is the presence then, of these two factors that signalizes the use of the method of authority:

1. The imposition by the authority of certain beliefs on a community without tolerating any deviation, criticism, or modification of the beliefs, and without encouraging or permitting a rational examination of the merit of the beliefs in question;
2. The readiness of the recipient of such beliefs to justify the beliefs so acquired by referring unquestioningly to the authoritative source for their sanction.

Peirce recognizes the great success and widespread appeal of this method.

In judging this method of fixing belief, which may be called the method of authority, we must, in the first place, allow its immeasurable mental and moral superiority to the method of tenacity. Its success is proportionately greater; and, in fact, it has over and over again worked the most majestic results. The mere structures of stone which it has caused to be put together—in Siam, for example, in Egypt, and in Europe—have many of them a sublimity hardly more than rivalled by the greatest works of Nature. And, except the geological epochs, there are no periods of time so vast as those which are measured by some of these organized faiths. If we scrutinize the matter closely, we shall find that there has not been one of their creeds which has remained always the same; yet the change is so slow as to be imperceptible during one person's life, so that individual belief remains sensibly fixed. For the mass of mankind, then, there is perhaps no better method than this. If it is their highest impulse to be intellectual slaves, then slaves they ought to remain.[37]

It should be noted that Peirce's account of the method of authority is a description of what is more correctly described as the use of the *authoritarian* method. The authoritarian appeal to 'authority' needs to be carefully distinguished from the appeal to those authorities who, as *experts,* do not rest their expertise on force, whim, or the use of an authoritarian method. Their transmitted beliefs rest, rather, on an appeal to what is open to public inspection and confirmation—to what could be supported by a free, open, and critical examination of the evidence and arguments for the beliefs in question. Whenever we turn, for example, to a physician for a medical diagnosis or to a meteorologist for a weather forecast, we are not using the method of authority as Peirce describes it. In these cases, if we wish to question the expert we are free to do so. The expert rests his or her opinions on certain well-established generalizations, as well as on specific data or particular observations that constitute the relevant *evidence* for the judgment. Such evidence is open to public inspection. If we wished to do so—to take the time or effort and to undergo the requisite training—we too might examine the technical evidence for the belief in question. In short, the appeal to experts as 'authorities' is to those individuals who serve as intermediary, highly useful and reliable sources of opinion. They are not to be thought of as final, unquestionable, *authoritarian* sources.

The effectiveness of the use of the method of authority (in Peirce's sense) depends on two things: first, the possession of sufficient power by the authority to regulate and enforce the adoption of uniform beliefs; second, the readiness on the part of the community to accept whatever the authority dictates. Whenever either of these operative factors begins to weaken or disintegrate, the authority loses its grip.

This may happen where the authority is not able to regulate *all* opinions, yet where the need exists to find opinions on what is left undecided by the authority. In these circumstances, individuals will make up their own minds on the matters at issue. Having seized and exploited these opportunities, debates and a raising of questions or doubts (even about what has until then been decreed by higher authority) may tend to spread. This practice may result in the undermining of the attitude of unquestioning obedience hitherto granted to the authority. Furthermore, a uniformity of belief is normally achieved not only when sufficient force is exercised by the authority, but where the community is insulated from outside contacts. Once contact with other communities is established, once lines of communication are opened up, a community hitherto homogeneous will come to realize that there are other schemes of behavior and beliefs, that theirs is not the only one or necessarily the best. The seeds of doubt, perhaps of revolution, may thereby be planted. Finally, even in the most dictatorial, authoritarian, repressive, and isolated society, there will frequently be some few individuals who have enough imagination, initiative, courage, and creativity, to think otherwise than the herd. Their fresh ways of thinking, if somehow communicated to others, may be sufficient to disturb the otherwise uniform, static ways of thought of the society in which they live.

But no institution can undertake to regulate opinions upon every subject. Only the most important ones can be attended to, and on the rest men's minds must be left to the action of natural causes. This imperfection will be no source of weakness so long as men are in such a state of culture that one opinion does not influence another—that is, so long as they cannot put two and two together. But in the most priest-ridden states some individuals will be found who are raised above that condition. These men possess a wider sort of social feeling; they see that men in other countries and in other ages have held to very different doctrines from those which they themselves have been brought up to believe; and they cannot help seeing that it is the mere accident of their having been taught as they have, and of their having been surrounded with the manners and associations they have, that has caused them to believe as they do and not far differently. Nor can their candour resist the reflection that there is no reason to rate their own views at a higher value than those of other nations and other centuries; thus giving rise to doubts in their minds.

They will further perceive that such doubts as these must exist in their minds with reference to every belief which seems to be determined by the caprice either of themselves or of those who originated the popular opinions. The willful adherence to a belief, and the arbitrary forcing of it upon others, must, therefore, both be given up.[38]

The a priori *method*

The third method of fixing belief receives various designations by Peirce. Some expressions he uses for this purpose are 'the unimpeded action of natural preferences', 'the *a priori* method', 'the method of inclinations', 'the natural development of opinion', 'the appeal to what is agreeable to reason'. It will be convenient for our present purpose to fix on one label, and I shall use the expression 'the *a priori* method' since it is the one most commonly adopted. Here is the description of the method as given in the essay "The Fixation of Belief":

Let the action of natural preferences be unimpeded, then, and under their influence let men, conversing together and regarding matters in different lights, gradually develop beliefs in harmony with natural causes. This method resembles that by which conceptions of art have been brought to maturity. The most perfect example of it is to be found in the history of metaphysical philosophy. Systems of this sort have not usually rested upon any observed facts, at least not in any great degree. They have been chiefly adopted because their fundamental propositions seemed "agreeable to reason." This is an apt expression; it does not mean that which agrees with experience, but that which we find ourselves inclined to believe. Plato, for example, finds it agreeable to reason that the distances of the celestial spheres from one another should be proportional to the different lengths of strings which produce harmonious chords. Many philosophers have been led to their main conclusions by considerations like this; but this is the lowest and least developed form which the method takes, for it is clear that another man might find Kepler's theory, that the celestial spheres are proportional to the inscribed and circumscribed spheres of the different regular solids, more agreeable to *his* reason. But the shock of opinions will soon lead men to rest on preferences of a far more universal nature. Take, for example, the doctrine that man only acts selfishly—that is, from the consideration that acting in one way will afford him more pleasure than acting in another. This rests on no fact in the world, but it has had a wide acceptance as being the only reasonable theory.

    This method is far more intellectual and respectable from the point of view of reason than either of the others which we have noticed. Indeed, as long as no better method can be applied, it ought to be followed, since it is then the expression of instinct which must be the ultimate cause of belief in all cases. But its failure has been the most manifest. It makes of inquiry something similar to the development of taste; but taste, unfortunately, is always more or less a matter of fashion, and accordingly metaphysicians have never come to any fixed agreement, but the pendulum has swung backward and forward between a more material and a more spiritual philosophy, from the earliest times to the latest. And so from this, which has been called the *a priori* method, we are driven, in Lord Bacon's phrase, to a true induction. We have examined into this *a priori* method as something which promised to deliver our opinions from their accidental and capricious element. But development, while it is a process which eliminates the effect of some casual circumstances, only magnifies that of others. This method, therefore, does not differ in a very essential way from that of authority. The government may not have lifted its finger to influence my convictions; I may have been left outwardly quite free to choose, we will say, between monogamy and polygamy, and, appealing to my conscience only, I may have concluded that the latter practice is in itself licentious. But when I come to see that the chief obstacle to the spread of Christianity among people of as high culture as the Hindoos has been a conviction of the immorality of our way of treating women, I cannot help seeing that, though governments do not interfere, sentiments in their developments will be very greatly determined by accidental causes. Now, there are some people, among whom I must suppose that my reader is to be found, who, when they see that any belief of theirs is determined by any circumstance extraneous to the facts, will from that moment not merely admit in words that that belief is doubtful, but will experience a real doubt of it, so that it ceases in some degree at least to be a belief.[39]

    As may be gathered from the kinds of examples Peirce gives in the foregoing passage, the chief feature of the *a priori* method is that the choice of belief—both its acquisition and justification—is left to a matter of taste, of what seems self-evident, agreeable to reason, and so on. Unlike the method of tenacity, which relies on a blind, obstinate retention of a belief, or the method of authority, where beliefs are imposed by force, the *a priori* method yields beliefs which are neither arbitrarily capricious nor imposed from the outside. Its use allows for diversity and freedom of choice. It involves only the requirement that the belief be satisfying on the basis of some esthetic, intuitive, or intellectual sense of what is 'right', 'true', 'correct', or 'fitting'.

    Peirce identifies the use of these expressions as marks of the '*a priori*' method, because this method does not require that the beliefs be tested by publicly attainable observational experience. Yet, as Peirce remarks, for all its advance over the preceding two methods, it too suffers from serious deficiencies. For in intellectual matters, where we are concerned to get at the truth, the criterion of selection at work in this method is too subjective, too variable. What seems 'self-evident', 'obvious', 'a matter of intuitive certainty' to one individual, group, or culture, is notoriously not so for others. The beliefs sanctioned by this method are, as Peirce argues, too much subject to 'accidental causes'. The beliefs chosen by this method are deliverances of minds that have insufficiently exercised their capacity for a critical analysis of alternative options. They are too little guided by a concerted and prolonged investigation of the facts as these would come to be recognized by *all* human beings.

The method of science

The last of the methods to be examined for effecting a settlement of opinion is that of *science,* or *investigation.* For Peirce it is the most important and reliable. It is the one to whose clarification and advocacy the bulk of his thought and writing was devoted. Because it so outweighs the other three methods in Peirce's emphases, it will be treated separately in the section that follows.

2.4 INVESTIGATION: TRUTH AND REALITY

Peirce uses various terms to designate the method of investigation: "science," "inquiry," "reasoning." The study of this method in all its aspects belongs to *logic* in its widest and deepest sense. Peirce's pragmatism, critical common-sensism, fallibilism, theory of signs (semiotics), classification of the sciences, theory of modes of scientific reasoning (induction, abduction, deduction), his studies in formal logic, foundations of mathematics, theory of probability, and so on, are in one form or another different aspects of how—over a long career and with some changes in viewpoint—he conceived what this method amounts to. We shall on the present occasion consider only some of the basic themes and some of the emphases Peirce gives to this topic.

A brief introductory statement of these matters is contained in the following:

> Living doubt is the life of investigation. When doubt is set at rest inquiry must stop. . . .
>
> From this conception springs the desire to get a settlement of opinion [that] is some conclusion which shall be independent of all individual limitations, independent of caprice, of tyranny, of accidents of situation . . . —a conclusion to which every man would come who should pursue the same method and push it far enough. The effort to produce such a settlement of opinion is called *investigation.* Logic is the science which teaches whether such efforts are rightly directed or not.[40]

In considering the method of investigation it is important to see in what respects it differs in crucial respects from other methods of fixing belief.

There is an important difference between the settlement of opinion which results from investigation and every other such settlement. It is that investigation will not fix one answer to a question as well as another, but on the contrary it tends to unsettle opinions at first, to change them and to confirm a certain opinion which depends only on the nature of investigation itself. The method of producing fixity of belief by adhering obstinately to one's belief, tends only to fix such opinions as each man already holds. The method of persecution tends only to spread the opinions which happen to be approved by rulers; and except so far as rulers are likely to adopt views of a certain cast does not determine at all what opinions shall become settled. The method of public opinion tends to develop a particular body of doctrine in every community. Some more widely spread and deeply rooted conviction will gradually drive out the opposing opinions, becoming itself in the strife somewhat modified by these. But different communities, removed from mutual influence, will develop very different bodies of doctrine, and in the same community there will be a constant tendency to sporting which may at any time carry the whole public. . . .

Thus no one of these methods can as a matter of fact attain its end of settling opinions. Men's opinions will act upon one another and the method of obstinacy will infallibly be succeeded by the method of persecution and this will yield in time to the method of public opinion and this produces no stable result.

Investigation differs entirely from these methods in that the nature of the final conclusion to which it leads is in every case destined from the beginning, without reference to the initial state of belief. Let any two minds investigate any question independently and if they carry the process far enough they will come to an agreement which no further investigation will disturb.[41]

As already remarked, it is the task of logic as Peirce conceives it to explore the different aspects of the method of investigation. Logic as a normative science should undertake to formulate specific criteria by which to evaluate and guide investigation. Accordingly, Peirce offers us his distinctive views about what these criteria might be. We shall concentrate on two main aspects of Peirce's views. The first has to do with the way in which the use of the method of investigation is claimed to lead to a discovery of the nature of reality. The discussion of this theme constitutes Peirce's *theory of truth*. The second has to do with the way in which the method of investigation depends on the use of a procedure for clarifying ideas present in any beliefs. The discussion of this theme constitutes Peirce's *theory of meaning*.

Some commentators in discussing Peirce's 'pragmatism' think that his most distinctive contribution lay in the use of the 'pragmatic maxim' for making our ideas clear, that is, in his pragmatic theory of meaning. This puts the cart before the horse. For Peirce the main advantage and importance of the method of investigation is that when pursued it leads us to the truth, to the knowledge of reality. This, for him, is the primary matter. "Logic," he tells us, "is the doctrine of truth, its nature and the manner in which it is to be discovered."[42] The importance of the pragmatic theory of *meaning* is that it is a phase of the wider concern for ultimately elaborating a theory of how people might achieve the *truth*. Let us therefore begin by examining what Peirce has to say on this more fundamental theme.

Peirce treats the concepts of 'reality' and 'truth' on many different occasions. His remarks on these topics are scattered throughout his writings. If one were to try to extract the chief items he stresses, those items would come down to the following: Reality is that which is independent of any particular exercise of judgment, of any personal exercise of thought; true beliefs concerning reality can be established only by the persistent application of the method of investigation. Investigation requires the use of observation, reasoning, and the drawing of consequences from a belief, through a process of interpretation, itself to be tested and interpreted by still further interpretations, and so on without limits. The repeated application of the method of investigation will yield a growing agreement and uniformity of belief among the individuals making up the community of investigators. That which gradually comes to be increasingly agreed upon is forced or determined by the nature of things; it is independent of the judgment of any one person or group. The truth, thus gradually discovered and embodied in true beliefs, constitutes what Peirce understands by 'reality' in one of his uses of this term. Reality in this sense is that which awaits realization or actualization by our powers of thought. When it is actually known, the nature of reality is conveyed through some linguistic sign.

Even on the level of ordinary common sense (and apart from sophisticated philosophic theory) we distinguish what we say is real from what we say is only imagined (what is a figment, fiction, or a case of dreaming). We say that while what is a figment of the imagination (and so 'unreal') is not ordinarily taken as such by someone who is having a hallucination or dream, it is recognized to be such (i.e., unreal) by others. A figment (or what is unreal) is a product of a state of mind that is not shared by others.

Peirce takes over this commonsense distinction between that which is a subjective, variable exercise of imagination or private opinion and that which is a matter of objective, public recognition, and in this sense 'real'. "That is *real* which has such and such characters, whether anybody thinks it to have those characters or not. At any rate, that is the sense in which the pragmaticist uses the word".[43] When Peirce speaks of reality (or of a real object) as having such and such characters whether anybody thinks it to have those characters or not, he is saying that it is independent of what any *particular* person or *limited* group of persons thinks. Peirce's conception of reality as 'independent' is not to be thought of as some kind of thing-in-itself that has certain characters quite independently of *any* role of thought in determining those characters.

The objective final opinion is independent of the thoughts of any particular men, but is not independent of thought *in general*.[44]

The perversity or ignorance of mankind may make this thing or that to be held for true, for any number of generations, but it can not affect what would be the result of sufficient experience and reasoning. And this it is which is meant by the final settled opinion. This therefore is no particular opinion but is entirely independent of what you, I, or any number of men may think about it; and therefore it directly satisfies the definition of reality.[45]

Peirce's conception of 'reality' is best understood as equivalent in meaning to the concept of *'the truth'*. He is above all concerned to show that reality is determinable and expressible in thought.

It is unphilosophical to suppose that, with regard to any given question (which has any clear meaning), investigation would not bring forth a solution of it, if it were carried far enough. Who would have said, a few years ago, that we could ever know of what substances stars are made whose light may have been longer in reaching us than the human race has existed? Who can be sure of what we shall not know in a few hundred years? Who can guess what would be the result of continuing the pursuit of science for ten thousand years, with the activity of the last hundred? And if it were to go on for a million, or a billion, or any number of years you please, how is it possible to say that there is any question which might not ultimately be solved?[46]

The notion of a reality possessing certain characters forever incapable of being disclosed to investigation or conveyed through human beliefs is altogether alien to Peirce's philosophy. To say something is real is tantamount to saying it is *knowable*. The notion of independent reality means independence of what one person or limited group of persons might say or believe. It does not mean independence of what the entire community of investigators might discover.

Over against any cognition, there is an unknown but knowable reality; but over against all possible cognition, there is only the self-contradictory. In short, *cognizability* (in its widest sense) and *being* are not merely metaphysically the same, but are synonymous terms.[47]

To say *what* reality is requires that there be a 'saying', a belief that is arrived at as the result of investigation. It articulates or formulates in appropriate ways what the *knowable* properties of some real object (or of reality) are. But the knowability requires an active process of investigation by a community of investigators. It is not a property already possessed by some reality that is not or could never be disclosed to investigators. This would make no sense for Peirce.

In my exposition of Peirce's views on the nature of reality thus far, I have stressed those passages in which he seeks to link the notions of 'reality' and 'thought', and in a parallel fashion 'reality' and 'the truth'.

This approach has much in common with what is called the viewpoint of objective idealism, found in Josiah Royce and Francis H. Bradley, among other contemporaneous supporters. All such philosophies were united in their search for ways of overcoming the conception of an 'independent reality' that is said to be unknowable, a *ding-an-sich* (thing-in-itself). In this respect, such philosophies were preparing the ground for the 'realistic' philosophies that were to arise at the beginning of this century. (We shall later examine examples of realistic philosophies in the views of Bertrand Russell and G. E. Moore.)

The point to bear in mind for the moment is that Peirce's use of the term 'reality' reveals a certain tension and ambiguity resulting from his being caught up in the traditional model of reality as the 'object' facing the 'subject'; a conception of an external, independent reality *causing* certain ideas in the mind of the subject, and existing independently whether or not it is in causal interaction with a particular mind. This notion of a causally independent reality derives from a conception of reality different from that which Peirce wishes finally to adopt. The latter conception is found in his characterization of reality as that which is to be *identified* with the truth—with what is known as the outcome of a process of thorough investigation. This conception of reality does not lay stress on a *causal* independence or existence apart from thought, language, or the result of a process of inquiry. 'Independence' when assigned to reality means independence of the views of any one person or finite number of persons. At the same time, reality (in this latter usage) does depend for its existence on the fact that it is known and articulated in and through thought and language. These two uses of the term 'reality'—'the causal-independence' view, and the 'inquiry-linked' (language-linked) view are both found in Peirce's writings. He never freed himself from the first, the traditional *epistemological* approach. However, this epistemological approach does not cohere with the other approach he was also struggling to develop—the view that connects our conception of reality with the activity of language and inquiry. His adoption of the terminology of the objective idealists did not help to resolve this tension, since the 'solution' of objective idealism was itself derived from trying to work out a coherent view within the epistemological framework and through the retention of the subject-object dualism it inherited from the earlier Cartesian, British empiricist, and Kantian traditions.

Evidence of Peirce's ambivalent approach to the use of the term 'reality' is found in the following excerpt:

At first sight it seems no doubt a paradoxical statement that, "The object of final belief which exists only in consequence of the belief, should itself produce the belief"; . . . [However] there is nothing extraordinary . . . in saying that the existence of external realities depends upon the fact, that opinion will finally settle in the belief in them. And yet that these realities existed before the belief took rise, and were even the cause of that belief, just as the force of gravity is the cause of the falling of the inkstand—although the force of gravity consists merely in the fact that the inkstand and other objects will fall. . . .

But if it be asked us, whether some realities do not exist, which are entirely independent of thought; I would in turn ask, what is meant by such an expression and what can be meant by it. What idea can be attached to that of which there is no idea? For if there be an idea of such a reality, it is the object of that idea of which we are speaking, and which is not independent of thought. It is clear that it is quite beyond the power of the mind to have an idea of something entirely independent of thought—it would have to extract itself from itself for that purpose; and since there is no such idea there is no meaning in the expression. The experience of ignorance, or of error, which we have, and which we gain by means of correcting our errors, or enlarging our knowledge, does enable us to experience and conceive something which is independent of our own limited views; but as there can be no correction of the sum total of opinions, and no enlargement of the sum total of knowledge, we have no such means, and can have no such means of acquiring a conception of something independent of all opinion and thought.[48]

A characteristic way in which Peirce thinks of reality and to which I have given special attention and emphasis is that 'reality' stands for what is destined to disclose its character to a community of investigators. Reality as 'the truth' may not be adequately known at any given time. Even large groups may be duped and have false or inadequate beliefs as to what it is. Yet continued investigation will eventually correct those beliefs.

Changes of opinion are brought about by events beyond human control. All mankind were so firmly of opinion that heavy bodies must fall faster than light ones, that any other view was scouted as absurd, eccentric, and probably insincere. Yet as soon as some of the absurd and eccentric men could succeed in inducing some of the adherents of common sense to look at their experiments—no easy task—it became apparent that nature would not follow human opinion, however unanimous. So there was nothing for it but human opinion must move to nature's position. That was a lesson in humility. A few men, the small band of laboratory men, began to see that they had to abandon the pride of an opinion assumed absolutely final in any respect and to use all their endeavors to yield as unresistingly as possible to the overwhelming tide of experience, which must master them at last, and to listen to what nature seems to be telling us. The trial of this method of experience in natural science for these three centuries—though bitterly detested by the majority of men—encourages us to hope that we are approaching nearer and nearer to an opinion which is not destined to be broken down—though we cannot expect ever quite to reach that ideal goal.[49]

Peirce's linking of the concept of 'reality' with that of 'thought' is paralleled by his view that to talk about the Truth without linking it with beliefs held by human beings is equally futile.

If your terms "truth" and "falsity" are taken in such senses as to be definable in terms of doubt and belief and the course of experience (as for example they would be, if you were to define the "truth" as that to a belief in which belief would tend if it were to tend indefinitely toward absolute fixity), well and good: in that case, you are only talking about doubt and belief. But if by truth and falsity you mean something not definable in terms of doubt and belief in any way, then you are talking of entities of whose existence you can know nothing, and which Ockham's razor would clean shave off. Your problems would be greatly simplified, if, instead of saying that you want to know the "Truth," you were simply to say that you want to attain a state of belief unassailable by doubt.[50]

What we mean by *the* Truth, then, is connected with a property of those beliefs that would be arrived at as a result of a *process* of inquiry or investigation. It is not a property of beliefs independently of such a process. The concept of Truth needs to be understood in terms of an ongoing activity of search, testing, and submission to what experience sanctions.

The foregoing points about the meaning of 'reality' and 'truth' are summed up in the following passage from the essay, "How to Make Our Ideas Clear":

> Different minds may set out with the most antagonistic views, but the progress of investigation carries them by a force outside of themselves to one and the same conclusion. This activity of thought by which we are carried, not where we wish, but to a fore-ordained goal, is like the operation of destiny. No modification of the point of view taken, no selection of other facts for study, no natural bent of mind even, can enable a man to escape the predestinate opinion. This great hope is embodied in the conception of truth and reality. The opinion which is fated to be ultimately agreed to by all who investigate, is what we mean by the truth, and the object represented in this opinion is real. That is the way I would explain reality.

> But it may be said that this view is directly opposed to the abstract definition which we have given of reality, inasmuch as it makes the characters of the real depend on what is ultimately thought about them. But the answer to this is that, on the one hand, reality is independent, not necessarily of thought in general, but only of what you or I or any finite number of men may think about it; and that, on the other hand, though the object of the final opinion depends on what that opinion is, yet what that opinion is does not depend on what you or I or any man thinks. Our perversity and that of others may indefinitely postpone the settlement of opinion; it might even conceivably cause an arbitrary proposition to be universally accepted as long as the human race should last. Yet even that would not change the nature of the belief, which alone could be the result of investigation carried sufficiently far; and if, after the extinction of our race, another should arise with faculties and disposition for investigation, that true opinion must be the one which they would ultimately come to. "Truth crushed to earth shall rise again," and the opinion which would finally result from investigation does not depend on how anybody may actually think. But the reality of that which is real does depend on the real fact that investigation is destined to lead, at last, if continued long enough, to a belief in it.[51]

2.5. MEANING

The pragmatic theory of *meaning* is of crucial importance in working out a sound logic to guide investigation. For Peirce, attaining clarity of ideas is a basic condition that must be satisfied if one is primarily interested in the truth. One cannot achieve the truth, or know how to go about looking for it, if one has no sense what our ideas or beliefs mean. And so, for Peirce, the theory of meaning, by which we are to understand an account of what it takes to make our ideas clear, is an essential part of the logic of investigation.

The very first lesson that we have a right to demand that logic shall teach us is, how to make our ideas clear; and a most important one it is, depreciated only by minds who stand in need of it. To know what we think, to be masters of our own meaning, will make a solid foundation for great and weighty thought. It is most easily learned by those whose ideas are meagre and restricted; and far happier they than such as wallow helplessly in a rich mud of conceptions. A nation, it is true, may, in the course of generations, overcome the disadvantage of an excessive wealth of language and its natural concomitant, a vast, unfathomable deep of ideas. We may see it in history, slowly perfecting its literary forms, sloughing at length its metaphysics, and, by virtue of the untirable patience which is often a compensation, attaining great excellence in every branch of mental acquirement. The page of history is not yet unrolled that is to tell us whether such a people will or will not in the long run prevail over one whose ideas (like the words of their language) are few, but which possesses a wonderful mastery over those which it has. For an individual, however, there can be no question that a few clear ideas are worth more than many confused ones. A young man would hardly be persuaded to sacrifice the greater part of his thoughts to save the rest; and the muddled head is the least apt to see the necessity of such a sacrifice. Him we can usually only commiserate, as a person with a congenital defect. Time will help him, but intellectual maturity with regard to clearness is apt to come rather late. This seems an unfortunate arrangement of Nature, inasmuch as clearness is of less use to a man settled in life, whose errors have in great measure had their effect, than it would be to one whose path lay before him. It is terrible to see how a single unclear idea, a single formula without meaning, lurking in a young man's head, will sometimes act like an obstruction of inert matter in an artery, hindering the nutrition of the brain, and condemning its victim to pine away in the fullness of his intellectual vigour and in the midst of intellectual plenty. Many a man has cherished for years as his hobby some vague shadow of an idea, too meaningless to be positively false; he has, nevertheless, passionately loved it, has made it his companion by day and by night, and has given to it his strength and his life, leaving all other occupations for its sake, and in short has lived with it and for it, until it has become, as it were, flesh of his flesh and bone of his bone; and then he has waked up some bright morning to find it gone, clean vanished away like the beautiful Melusina of the fable, and the essence of his life gone with it. I have myself known such a man; and who can tell how many histories of circle-squarers, metaphysicians, astrologers, and what not, may not be told in the old German [French!] story?[52]

Peirce's proposed pragmatic method for showing what our ideas mean is a protest against a number of traditional views about the nature of meaning. He denies that the clarity of an idea consists simply in our being familiar with it, since the feeling of familiarity is subjective at best, and is no assurance that we have a genuine intellectual grasp of it. Nor is the clarification of ideas to be achieved by the use of a definition couched in abstract terms where the meaning of these abstract terms (in turn) depends on their seeming 'clear and distinct'. For these defining ideas may not in fact be so, nor need they give us anything more (once again) than a subjective feeling that they are so. What is at fault with these or other traditional criteria for specifying the meaning of an idea is that they are made to depend on a process of introspection—on an 'internal examination' of ideas as the contents of our minds and requiring nothing more than that these contents display certain marks. For an empiricist such as Berkeley this criterion amounted to the requirement that an idea (as the content of one's mind) be a distinct, particular, sensory image or combination of such images. For a rationalist such as Descartes the criterion of 'clearness and distinctness' was modeled on what one (presumably) finds in the definitions of geometry or some other branch of mathematics. Peirce protests against these traditional criteria. His pragmatic method for explicating the meaning of ideas would require that we turn not to some introspected, subjective contents of a mind but to the operations, actions, performances, uses, and observations that are *publicly* conducted and obtainable. These require overt behavior; they are exposed to (and are capable of) duplication by a community of investigators. "It is not 'my' experience," Peirce writes, "but 'our' experience that has to be thought of."[53]

Peirce's pragmatic criterion of meaning concerns what needs to be done when we seek to determine the meaning of some belief. This question arises in investigation when, for example, we need to see whether there is a genuine distinction of meaning among supposedly distinct and incompatible theories (beliefs), and to decide which among them, if any, is true.

It should be noted that, for Peirce, the determination of the meaning of ideas (concepts) is something performed in the context of examining the role of these concepts as parts of some belief. One cannot determine the meaning of an idea (concept) in isolation. It is rather as part of the statement of a belief that we are to examine the meaning of ideas. In one sense, then, when Peirce examines 'how to make our *ideas* clear' he is at the same time suggesting how we are to make clear what our *beliefs* mean.

The clarification of ideas, as a matter of determining their *meaning,* is *not* equivalent to determining the *truth or falsity* of the belief of which they are a part. It is a preliminary step. We have to know what a belief leads us to observe or do (its pragmatic meaning) before, and as a condition for, deciding—in the light of what we observe or do—whether the belief in question is true or false. The truth or falsity of a belief is a matter of evaluation *after* we have determined what the belief means. Even false beliefs have meaning. "It is certainly important to know how to make our ideas clear, but they may be ever so clear without being true."[54] However, we do not know whether or not they are false unless we first determine (on pragmatic grounds) what they mean.

Since, for Peirce, a belief is a habit of mind, something that leads us to perform certain types of action in relevant situations, the *meaning* of beliefs is primarily a matter of what specific actions a particular belief leads us to perform and what particular sensible effects will be found in experience as connected with the use of a concept or set of concepts. This crucial point is at the core of Peirce's pragmatic theory of meaning. He expresses the pragmatic maxim on various occasions and in slightly varying ways, but essentially they all come down to the same point. In the essay "How to Make Our Ideas Clear" he formulates the pragmatic maxim as follows:

Consider what effects, that might conceivably have practical bearings, we conceive the object of our conception to have. Then, our conception of these effects is the whole of our conception of the object.[55]

In the same essay he also puts the matter as follows:

The whole function of thought is to produce habits of action; . . . To develop its meaning, we have, therefore, simply to determine what habits it produces, for what a thing means is simply what habits it involves. Now, the identity of a habit depends on how it might lead us to act, not merely under such circumstances as are likely to arise, but under such as might possibly occur, no matter how improbable they may be. What the habit is depends on *when* and *how* it causes us to act. As for the *when*, every stimulus to action is derived from perception; as for the *how*, every purpose of action is to produce some sensible result. Thus, we come down to what is tangible and conceivably practical, as the root of every real distinction of thought, no matter how subtle it may be; and there is no distinction of meaning so fine as to consist in anything but a possible difference of practice.[56]

Let us consider, as Peirce does, some applications of the pragmatic maxim for attaining a clarification of ideas. Here are examples that Peirce himself gives in his essay "How to Make Our Ideas Clear":

Let us ask what we mean by calling a thing *hard*. Evidently that it will not be scratched by many other substances. The whole conception of this quality, as of every other, lies in its conceived effects. There is absolutely no difference between a hard thing and a soft thing so long as they are not brought to the test. Suppose, then, that a diamond could be crystallized in the midst of a cushion of soft cotton, and should remain there until it was finally burned up. Would it be false to say that that diamond was soft? This seems a foolish question, and would be so, in fact, except in the realm of logic. There such questions are often of the greatest utility as serving to bring logical principles into sharper relief than real discussions ever could. In studying logic we must not put them aside with hasty answers, but must consider them with attentive care, in order to make out the principles involved. We may, in the present case, modify our question, and ask what prevents us from saying that all hard bodies remain perfectly soft until they are touched, when their hardness increases with the pressure until they are scratched. Reflection will show that the reply is this: there would be no *falsity* in such modes of speech. They would involve a modification of our present usage of speech with regard to the words hard and soft, but not of their meanings. For they represent no fact to be different from what it is; only they involve arrangements of facts which would be exceedingly maladroit. This leads us to remark that the question of what would occur under circumstances which do not actually arise is not a question of fact, but only of the most perspicuous arrangement of them. . . .

Let us next seek a clear idea of Weight. This is another very easy case. To say that a body is heavy means simply that, in the absence of opposing force, it will fall. This (neglecting certain specifications of how it will fall, etc., which exist in the mind of the physicist who uses the word) is evidently the whole conception of weight. It is a fair question whether some particular facts may not *account* for gravity; but what we mean by the force itself is completely involved in its effects. . . .

Whether we ought to say that a force *is* an acceleration, or that it *causes* an acceleration, is a mere question of propriety of language, which has no more to do with our real meaning than the difference between the French idiom *"Il fait froid"* and its English equivalent *"It is cold."* Yet it is surprising to see how this simple affair has muddled men's minds. In how many profound treatises is not force spoken of as a "mysterious entity," which seems to be only a way of confessing that the author despairs of ever getting a clear notion of what the word means! In a recent admired work on *Analytic Mechanics* it is stated that we understand precisely the effect of force, but what force itself is we do not understand! This is simply a self-contradiction. The idea which the word force excites in our minds has no other function than to affect our actions, and these actions can have no reference to force otherwise than through its effects. Consequently, if we know what the effects of force are, we are acquainted with every fact which is implied in saying that a force exists, and there is nothing more to know.[57]

That Peirce's familiarity with the laboratory methods of the chemist served him with a fund of paradigms for the pragmatic criterion of meaning is made clear by the following:

If you look into a textbook of chemistry for a definition of *lithium,* you may be told that it is that element whose atomic weight is 7 very nearly. But if the author has a more logical mind he will tell you that if you search among minerals that are vitreous, translucent, grey or white, very hard, brittle, and insoluble, for one which imparts a crimson tinge to an unluminous flame, this mineral being triturated with lime or witherite rats-bane, and then fused, can be partly dissolved in muriatic acid; and if this solution be evaporated, and the residue be extracted with sulphuric acid, and duly purified, it can be converted by ordinary methods into a chloride, which being obtained in the solid state, fused, and electrolyzed with half a dozen powerful cells, will yield a globule of a pinkish silvery metal that will float on gasolene; and the material of *that* is a specimen of lithium. The peculiarity of this definition—or rather this precept that is more serviceable than a definition—is that it tells you what the word lithium denotes by prescribing what you are to *do* in order to gain a perceptual acquaintance with the object of the word.[58]

Let us now consider, in further detail, some of the main aspects of Peirce's pragmatic theory of meaning.

A crucial point to bear in mind is that the pragmatic theory of meaning has to do with the clarification of *intellectual concepts* as these occur in the statements of beliefs. An 'intellectual concept' is to be radically distinguished from pure sensations or feelings of any kind. A concept is *general*. It involves the exercise of a capacity for abstraction, and engages a distinctive human power of thought, understanding, and reason.

I understand pragmatism to be a method of ascertaining the meanings, not of all ideas, but only of what I call "intellectual concepts," that is to say, of those upon the structure of which, arguments concerning objective fact may hinge. Had the light which, as things are, excites in us the sensation of blue, always excited the sensation of red, and *vice versa,* however great a difference that might have made in our feelings, it could have made none in the force of any argument. In this respect, the qualities of hard and soft strikingly contrast with those of red and blue; because while red and blue name mere subjective feelings only, hard and soft express the factual behavior of the thing under the pressure of a knife-edge. (I use the word "hard" in its strict mineralogical sense, "would resist a knife-edge.") My pragmatism, having nothing to do with qualities of feelings, permits me to hold that the predication of such a quality is just what it seems, and has nothing to do with anything else. Hence, could two qualities of feeling everywhere be interchanged, nothing but feelings could be affected. Those qualities have no intrinsic significations beyond themselves. Intellectual concepts, however—the only sign-burdens that are properly denominated "concepts"—essentially carry some implication concerning the general behaviour either of some conscious being or of some inanimate object, and so convey more, not merely than any feeling, but more, too, than any existential fact, namely, the "would-acts," "would-dos" of habitual behaviour; and no agglomeration of actual happenings can ever completely fill up the meaning of a "would-be." But [Pragmatism asserts], that the *total* meaning of the predication of an intellectual concept is contained in an affirmation that, under all conceivable circumstances of a given kind (or under this or that more or less indefinite part of the cases of their fulfillment, should the predication be modal) the subject of the predication would behave in a certain general way—that is, it would be true under given experiential circumstances (or under a more or less definitely stated proportion of them, *taken as they would occur,* that is in the same order of succession, *in experience).*[59]

When Peirce speaks of clarifying *ideas* he means clarifying *concepts*. Concepts are necessarily employed in the statement of any belief. Suppose we are dealing with some individual object and make some statement about it. In making a statement about this individual object we shall be using some general concept. For example, in the statement 'This stone is hard', we are using two concepts: the concept 'stone' as part of the grammatical subject in referring to a particular object, and the concept 'hard' as the grammatical predicate in describing the individual object

Sometimes, as in the statement 'Lassie is a dog', we may use a proper name to refer to an individual object, whereas the grammatical predicate '(is) a dog' is a concept that describes the individual object selected. Peirce is concerned to explore what is involved in making clear the use of concepts in any statement (whether the statement deals with one object or some collection of objects). When Peirce uses the term 'object' in the pragmatic maxim quoted earlier, he means that *about which* we use some concept or concepts in statements we make about it. To 'conceive an object', then, means for Peirce to use a concept or concepts in the course of setting out our belief or beliefs about that object. The pragmatic theory of meaning concerns what is involved in making clear the use of such concepts.

There are a few additional points that need to be made about Peirce's approach, via the pragmatic maxim, to the clarification of concepts. These points have to do with the contrast between the use of expressions for concepts and other kinds of expressions in our language.

One such contrast consists in the fact that concepts are conveyed by the use of general words (common nouns, adjectives, verbs, and so on) and thus can be used to describe or apply to more than one individual or instance, whereas other types of expressions—such as proper names—are used to make reference only to a particular individual or instance. The pragmatic maxim is offered as a way of clarifying the meaning of general concepts and is not applicable to expressions for individual objects such as proper names.

[It] must be admitted that pragmaticism fails to furnish any translation or meaning of a proper name, or other designation of an individual object. . . . the pragmaticist grants that a proper name (although it is not customary to say that it has a *meaning*), has a certain denotative function peculiar, in each case, to that name and its equivalents; and that he grants that every assertion contains such a denotative or pointing-out function. In its peculiar individuality, the pragmaticist excludes this from the rational purport of the assertion, although *the like* of it, being common to all assertions, and so, being general and not individual, may enter into the pragmaticistic purport.[60]

A second broad distinction has to do with the fact that some expressions although general have a descriptive content, whereas others are purely formal and nondescriptive. Examples of the first would be terms such as 'dog', 'rain', and 'acceleration'; examples of the latter would be such purely logical (formal) expressions as 'not', 'if————then', 'or', and the like, that can be used in conjunction with descriptive expressions or to link entire propositions, but are not themselves descriptive in character. The latter types of formal or logical expressions are known as 'syncategorematic expressions'. The pragmatic maxim for clarifying concepts has to do with general descriptive concepts, not with purely formal, syncategorematic expressions.[61]

A concept is a *general* sign or expression (what Peirce, in his general classification of signs, calls a 'symbol'). To say it is 'general' signifies that its meaning can be stated as a rule or law, or, as Peirce also sometimes puts it, as a habit or regularity. The logical form for stating a rule, law, or habit, is by means of a conditional statement: "Whenever————then————" or "If————then————". (The part of the entire statement that follows the 'if' or 'whenever' is known as the *antecedent,* and the part that follows the 'then', is known as the *consequent.*)

According to the pragmatic criterion, "to predicate any . . . concept of a real or imaginary object is equivalent to declaring that a certain operation, corresponding to the concept, if performed upon that object would . . . be followed by a result of a definite general description."[62]

Let '*C*' stand for some general concept. Let '*R*' stand for some operation (or set of operations, tests, conditions of observation). Let '*E*' stand for 'sensible effects' ('practical results'). Then the pragmatic formula for explicating the meaning of *C* is:

$$C = (\text{if } R \text{ then } E)$$

Another way of making the same point is this: Let C_1 be the general concept (term, word) *to be* clarified. Let C_2 be the 'concept' that succeeds in clarifying C_1 according to the pragmatic maxim. Then C_2 is itself clarified by stating a general rule of procedure (a 'habit') of the general form: "If one performs such-and-such operations and fulfills such-and-such conditions of observations *('R'),* then certain sensible effects and practical results *('E')* may be expected to be observed." Let us express this rule as "If *R* then *E*." Let C_2 be a shorthand way of representing "If *R* then *E*." Then "$C_1 = C_2$" is a definition that sums up the pragmatic maxim.

The antecedent ('if *R*') of the definitional formula that gives the meaning of a general concept (e.g., 'hard'), states the various conditions of observation, the kinds of operations that need to be performed in order to put oneself in a position to note what would follow from, or accompany, these conditions of observation and these operations. The consequent ('then *E*') of the definitional formula states the various kinds of sensible, publicly observable effects expected to follow from those initial conditions of observation and operations. The property of being hard, as conveyed by the general word 'hard', means that if I apply, for example, certain scratch tests by means of a suitable type of knife edge (the operation *R*), I would observe that the object to which these tests had been applied would *not* show any scratches, incisions, depressions, as a result (sensible effects).

Take any general term whatever. I say of a stone that it is *hard.* That means that so long as the stone remains hard, every essay to scratch it by the moderate pressure of a knife will surely fail. To call the stone *hard* is to predict that no matter how often you try the experiment, it will fail every time. That innumerable series of conditional predictions is involved in the meaning of this lowly adjective.[63]

In the statement 'This stone is hard' the general concept 'hard' is used in asserting that this stone has this property. However, if *anything* is hard it will show certain sensible effects when certain operations are applied. To say this stone is hard is to assert by means of the predicate 'hard' that if one applies specific kinds of operations certain predictable sensible effects should be observed. This is what the statement *means*, as far as the use of this particular predicate is concerned.

There is an important and intimate connection between Peirce's theory of the truth of a belief and his pragmatic theory of the meaning of concepts. Since every belief involves the use of general concepts, the *meaning* of these concepts requires that one look to certain predicted, expected practical consequences or sensible effects. The method of investigation to settle the *truth* of a belief, however, involves an appeal to these same verifiable, experimental consequences of acting on that belief. Only if the expected practical consequences and sensible effects are found to hold in actual experience does one have a basis for continuing to accept the belief in question as *true*.

An understanding of the *meaning* of the general concepts employed in a belief is thus a necessary preliminary step in carrying out an investigation of testing the *truth* of a belief. Only if the expected results are found is there an evidential basis for saying that the concept used provides a *true* description of the case at hand, that it describes a property of the object to which the concept is applied.

Both the pragmatic theory of meaning and the theory of truth involve an appeal to consequences. But it is important to see that the appeal to consequences serves different purposes according to whether we are interested in setting out the meaning of a concept used *in* a belief, or whether we are interested in determining the truth of the belief *as a whole*. Where we are concerned with setting out in pragmatic terms the meaning of a concept used in stating the belief, the appeal to consequences has reference to selected *kinds of effects and bearings*. Where, however, we are concerned with the truth of the belief, the appeal to consequences has to do with finding out whether the types of predicted sensible effects are actually found in the particular case in hand. Here the appeal to consequences has to do with the verification of the belief as a whole, and with the question whether the concept in question is in fact warranted as an apt and correct description of the particular subject to which that concept is being applied.

It should be clear from our discussion thus far, and from the kinds of examples that Peirce gives of what a pragmatic clarification of ideas would come to, that his principal stress is upon those 'intellectual concepts' that occur in their most developed form in the empirical sciences. Peirce, as we have seen, is a 'laboratory' type of philosopher. His training as a chemist and geodesist provided him with the paradigms for what is involved in the use of concepts for purposes of description and explanation. He took the human interest in discovering the truth—the cognitive interest—as his primary context for analysis. His pragmatism was devoted to exploring what is involved in satisfying the interest in discovering the truth. It is within this context of the inquiry into discovering the truth that his pragmatism was worked out.

Yet even here we must take note of the broader as well as the narrower uses of the term 'science' and 'truth' Peirce himself employs. Thus in the narrower use of these terms science is restricted to the *empirical* sciences, and truth is that which is sought for as the outcome of investigation in these sciences. Peirce's examples of the concepts and methods to be used in this quest are, as we have seen, taken basically from one or another of these empirical sciences. Peirce writes:

The writer of this article has been led by much experience to believe that every physicist, and every chemist, and, in short, every master in any department of experimental science, has had his mind moulded by his life in the laboratory to a degree that is little suspected. The experimentalist himself can hardly be fully aware of it, for the reason that the men whose intellects he really knows about are much like himself in this respect. With intellects of widely different training from his own, whose education has largely been a thing learned out of books, he will never become inwardly intimate, be he on ever so familiar terms with them; for he and they are as oil and water, and though they be shaken up together, it is remarkable how quickly they will go their several mental ways, without having gained more than a faint flavor from the association. Were those other men only to take skillful soundings of the experimentalist's mind—which is just what they are unqualified to do, for the most part—they would soon discover that, excepting perhaps upon tactics where his mind is trammelled by personal feeling or by his bringing up, his disposition is to think of everything just as everything is thought of in the laboratory, that is, as a question of experimentation. Of course, no living man possesses in their fulness all the attributes characteristic of his type. But when you have found, or ideally constructed upon a basis of observation, the typical experimentalist, you will find that whatever assertion you may make to him, he will either understand as meaning that if a given prescription for an experiment ever can be and ever is carried out in act, an experience of a given description will result, or else he will see no sense at all in what you say.[64]

There is another side to Peirce's thought where the terms 'science' and 'the quest for truth' are used more widely. In these wider uses 'science' would encompass not only the empirical sciences, but mathematics and even a *reformed* philosophy as well. Correspondingly, truth would be sought not only in the empirical sciences but also in these other areas. Now, of course, it would be important, as it is for Peirce, to differentiate the special *kinds* of truth sought for in these various types of inquiry. Peirce writes:

> Confining ourselves to science, inference, in the broadest sense, is coextensive with the deliberate adoption, in any measure, of an assertion as true. For deliberation implies that the adoption is voluntary; and consequently, the observation of perceptual facts that are forced upon us in experience is excluded. General principles, on the other hand, if deliberately adopted, must have been subjected to criticism; and any criticism of them that can be called scientific and that results in their acceptance must involve an argument in favor of their truth. . . . As to the word "true," I may be asked what this means. Now the different sciences deal with different kinds of truth; mathematical truth is one thing, ethical truth is another, the actually existing state of the universe is a third; but all those different conceptions have in common something very marked and clear. We all hope that the different scientific inquiries in which we are severally engaged are going ultimately to lead to some definitely established conclusion, which conclusion we endeavor to anticipate in some measure. Agreement with that ultimate proposition that we look forward to,—agreement with that, whatever it may turn out to be, is the scientific truth.[65]

In this approach mathematics and philosophy, along with the empirical sciences, can be called 'sciences' provided they follow the method of scientific investigation. Some, for example many of the empirical sciences or mathematics, are already well developed. In other cases there is at least the possibility for developing them into disciplines that could merit the name 'science'. Thus Peirce himself is frequently highly critical of and negatively disposed to a good deal of what goes by the name of 'metaphysics' in the history of philosophy.

> Almost every proposition of ontological metaphysics is either meaningless gibberish—one word being defined by other words, and they by still others, without any real conception ever being reached—or else is downright absurd; so that all such rubbish being swept away, what will remain of philosophy will be a series of problems capable of investigation by the observational methods of the true sciences—the truth about which can be reached without those interminable misunderstandings and disputes which have made the highest of the positive sciences a mere amusement for idle intellects, a sort of chess—idle pleasure its purpose, and reading out of a book its method. In this regard, pragmaticism is a species of prope-positivism.[66]

Peirce envisaged that metaphysics, if properly investigated—as he conceived what this would amount to—could also become scientific. In order to be scientific it would first need to be a *cooperative* inquiry of many investigators (rather than an exercise of a private sort, the creation of systems of thought by 'intellectual nomads.') Second, it would need to base its discoveries on appeal to facts of observational experience, but of the kind that is the most elementary, common, and pervasive—what, so to speak, is before everyone's eyes. It need not appeal to special instruments, specialized technical observational data such as are obtained in the developed physical sciences. Peirce devoted a good deal of energy to sketching and working out, in some areas, what he took to be the character of such a *scientific metaphysics*. For example, he worked out various doctrines concerning the concepts of continuity ('synechism') and chance ('tychism'). He made contributions to the science of phenomenology ('phaneroscopy'). He worked and reworked a theory of basic metaphysical categories which he called Firstness, Secondness and Thirdness.* All of these topics and many others were concerned with setting up a discipline of scientific metaphysics, although he never reached a final comprehensive and systematic formulation of these matters. A study of these writings (which we shall not undertake here), for all the brilliance and ingenuity of their occasional insights, might raise in the mind of a critical reader the question whether, despite his claims for them, Peirce was being any more 'scientific' or less 'speculative' than others whom he condemns.

As we have seen, Peirce is prepared to encompass mathematics within a broad use of the term 'science'. However, as he is careful to

---

* My view is that there are three modes of being. I hold that we can directly observe them in elements of whatever is at any time before the mind in any way. They are the being of positive qualitative possibility, the being of actual fact, and the being of law that will govern facts in the future. . . .

Let us begin with considering actuality, and try to make out just what it consists in. If I ask you what the actuality of an event consists in, you will tell me that it consists in its happening *then* and *there*. The specifications *then* and *there* involve all its relations to other existents. The actuality of the event seems to lie in its relations to the universe of existents. A court may issue *injunctions* and *judgments* against me and I do not care a snap of my fingers for them. I may think them idle vapour. But when I feel the sheriff's hand on my shoulder, I shall begin to have a sense of actuality. Actuality is something *brute*. There is no reason in it. . . . On the whole, I think we have here a mode of being of one thing which consists in how a second object is. I call that Secondness.

Besides this, there are two modes of being that I call Firstness and Thirdness. Firstness is the mode of being which consists in its subject's being positively such as it is regardless of aught else. That can only be a possibility. For as long as things do not act upon one another there is no sense or meaning in saying that they have any being, unless it be that they are such in themselves that they may perhaps come into relation with others. The mode of being a *redness*, before anything in the universe was yet red, was nevertheless a positive qualitative possibility.

. . . .

Now for Thirdness. Five minutes of our waking life will hardly pass without our making some kind of prediction; and in the majority of cases these predictions are fulfilled in the event. Yet a prediction is essentially of a general nature, and cannot ever be completely fulfilled. To say that a prediction has a decided tendency to be fulfilled, is to say that the future events are in a measure really governed by law.

Some of the ideas of prominent Thirdness which, owing to their importance in philosophy and in science, require attentive study are generality, infinity, continuity, diffusion, growth, and intelligence.[67]

point out, what this comes to needs to be sharply distinguished from what we find in the empirical sciences. Peirce spoke from firsthand experience as a student of, and creative contributor to, the field of pure mathematics. In addition, he was much influenced by the work and conceptions of mathematics that his father, Benjamin Peirce, had worked out. For the father, as for the son, "mathematics is the science which draws necessary conclusions."[68] Mathematics, unlike the empirical sciences, is not concerned with existential truth, with the actual structure of the existing universe and all its parts. It is a purely hypothetical science, an exercise in rigidly controlled imagination. It sets up certain hypotheses or postulates and asks what necessarily follows from them as a matter of entailment or logical implication. In doing this sort of thing the mathematician draws diagrams and constructs simplified models. But his interest in them is not like that of an empirical scientist, who is ultimately guided by what he finds in the laboratory or in the field. The mathematician asks, "What *if* such and such were the case? What would follow necessarily from these starting points?" His interest is in *formal truth* rather than *factual truth,* in consistency of logical reasoning rather than in correspondence with observed fact.

The most abstract of all the sciences is mathematics. That this is so, has been made manifest in our day; because all mathematicians now see clearly that mathematics is only busied about *purely hypothetical questions.* As for what the truth of existence may be the mathematician does not (*qua* mathematician) care a straw.[69]

Now the services of the mathematician are called in when the physicist, the engineer, the insurance company, the lawgiver, etc. finds himself confronted with a complicated state of relations of fact and is in doubt whether or not it necessarily involves some other relation, or wishes to know precisely what relation it does involve of a certain kind. The mathematician is not responsible at all for the truth of the premises: that he is to assume. The first task before him usually is to substitute for the excessively complicated facts set before him, often confused in their statement, a comparatively simple system of relations, which while adhering as closely as possible to the given premises shall be within his powers as a mathematician to deal with. This he terms his *hypothesis.* Thereupon, he proceeds to show that the relations stated in that hypothesis involve as a part of them certain other relations, not explicitly taken account of.

Thus the mathematician is not concerned with real truth: he only studies the substance of hypotheses. This distinguishes mathematics from every other science. . . . Hence, the proper definition of mathematics is that it is the study of the substance of hypotheses, which it first frames and then traces to their consequences. . . .

There is *pure* mathematics and *applied* mathematics. Pure mathematicians would strenuously object to a definition which should limit their hypotheses to such as are subservient to the discovery of objective truth. A romancer who draws any necessary deductions from the situations he creates (as every romancer does) is beyond doubt doing mathematical work; and the charm of romance is in part due to the natural interest we have in tracing necessary consequences. But this is applied mathematics for the reason that the hypotheses are clothed with accidents which are not relevant to the forms of deduction. Mathematical hypotheses are such as are adapted to the tracing of necessary conclusions; and the hypotheses of *pure* mathematics are stripped of all accidents which do not affect the forms of deduction, that is, the relations of the conclusions to the premises.

We thus finally reach this definition. *Mathematics* is the study of the substance of hypotheses with a view to the drawing of necessary conclusions from them. It is *pure* when the hypotheses contain nothing not relevant to the forms of deduction.[70]

2.6. CONCLUDING REMARKS ABOUT 'PRAGMATISM'

Pragmatism, when looked at in wide perspective and against the background of earlier epochs of philosophic thought, is justified in thinking of itself as "a new way of thinking." In taking it as our first example of contemporary philosophic movements of an analytical cast, we see in it some of the intellectual forces that were already at work and were symptomatic of subsequent philosophic developments.

In the writings of Peirce, especially, we see the rich and powerful beginnings of a new logic, a concern with scientific methodology, a serious appreciation of the role of language (and signs, generally) in human experience, and a need for developing a general world view in the form of metaphysical theory of categories that would give us a schematic sense of the major features of reality and the principal distinctions among modes of being.

For Peirce, the method of pragmatism has to do primarily with the clarification of the meaning of concepts and with ways of establishing sound beliefs in the course of scientific inquiry. Peirce's pragmatism centers on man's *cognitive* interests, his interest in achieving reliable knowledge, in discovering the truth. A common misinterpretation of pragmatism, especially when this term is used to apply to Peirce's views, is to identify it as a philosophy that glorifies action for its own sake. Peirce was sensitive to this criticism and misunderstanding of his own philosophy. It led him to use the term 'pragmaticism' in order to distinguish his views from those more readily liable to this interpretation.

It must be admitted in the first place [he wrote in 1905] that if pragmaticism really made Doing to be the Be-all and the End-all of life, that would be its death. For to say that we live for the mere sake of action, as action, regardless of the thought it carries out, would be to say that there is no such thing as rational purport.[71]

No doubt, Pragmaticism makes thought ultimately *apply* to action exclusively—to *conceived* action. But between admitting that and either saying that it makes thought, in the sense of the purport of symbols, to consist in acts, or saying that the true ultimate purpose of thinking is action, there is much the same difference as there is between saying that the artist-painter's living art is applied to dabbing paint upon canvas, and saying that that art-life consists in dabbing paint, or that its ultimate aim is dabbing paint.[72]

Nor, of course, did Peirce's views of the pragmatic criterion for judging the truth of a belief appeal to the *utility* of holding a belief, if utility is understood in terms of increased power, material gain, or the satisfaction it brings to the individual. Peirce's appeal to 'practical bearings' in his formulation of the pragmatic maxim (as quoted in the previous section from his essay "How to Make our Ideas Clear") needs to be understood in the special way he intends it. That maxim asserts that we need to "consider what effects, that might conceivably have practical bearings, we conceive the object of our conception to have. Then, our conception of these effects is the whole of our conception of the object." Peirce is there concerned, as we have seen, with the clarification of concepts in the course of conducting an investigation into the truth of some belief. The use of the phrase 'practical bearings', as Peirce understood it, has to do with specifying the observable effects or results of performing certain operations in an experimental situation. Peirce's pragmatism was thus essentially a contribution to working out a logic of scientific inquiry. When seen in this context, Peirce's pragmatism is related by a certain 'family resemblance' to other empirically oriented, experimentalist, operationalist, and positivist philosophies of science. Whatever the obscurities and difficulties in Peirce's formulation of the pragmatic criterion, it opens up a new and important phase in the development of the theory of meaning and truth. If later philosophies were to probe more deeply, to provide more subtle or refined analysis, they do so only by carrying forward a line of thought for which Peirce's own philosophic investigations provided an epoch-making impetus and incentive.

William James's contribution to the development of pragmatism is marked by his breaking away from the dominantly cognitive, logical, scientifically oriented interests of Peirce, in order to give voice to the affective and practical sides of human nature. His pragmatism asks us to consider the broader aspects and contexts of life in which verbal, intellectual, and scientific theorizing are situated. Consider, he would urge, the bearing on the rest of life of adopting this or that theory whether it be in religion, science, metaphysics, or any intellectual sphere. What differences in our conduct, in our general attitudes toward the world, to the way we go about our daily business in the multifarious affairs of life, does the adoption of this or that belief have upon them? For James, the eventual total worth of any belief needs to be judged not by confining ourselves within a narrow and self-contained concern with examining the 'evidence' for the belief; it has to be judged rather by the way it *connects up,* for good or ill, with the rest of our experience. Only when we take into account these multiple interrelations of our beliefs and examine the total, variegated types of practical consequences of holding a belief on the rest of our experience, do we have a basis for judging the worth of that belief. Moreover, our estimate is not to be arrived at by using some criterion derived from *a priori* reason, fixed custom, or divine command. Rather, our judgments are *to be formed,* as we go along, in the light of our experience, in an open-ended future. The particularities of our ongoing experiences, the way our beliefs work themselves out for particular individuals and in particular circumstances—these are the directions and considerations that need to be looked at in order to arrive at our evaluations of the worth of our beliefs.

The pragmatic method is primarily a method of settling metaphysical disputes that otherwise might be interminable. Is the world one or many?—fated or free?—material or spiritual?—here are notions either of which may or may not hold good of the world; and disputes over such notions are unending. The pragmatic method in such cases is to try to interpret each notion by tracing its respective practical consequences. What difference would it practically make to any one if this notion rather than that notion were true? If no practical difference whatever can be traced, then the alternatives mean practically the same thing, and all dispute is idle. Whenever a dispute is serious, we ought to be able to show some practical difference that must follow from one side or the other's being right.[73]

It is astonishing to see how many philosophical disputes collapse into insignificance the moment you subject them to this simple test of tracing a concrete consequence. There can *be* no difference anywhere that doesn't *make* a difference elsewhere—no difference in abstract truth that doesn't express itself in a difference in concrete fact and in conduct consequent upon that fact, imposed on somebody, somehow, somewhere, and somewhen. The whole function of philosophy ought to be to find out what definite difference it will make to you and me, at definite instants of our life, if this world-formula or that world-formula be the true one.[74]

Pragmatism . . . asks its usual question. "Grant an idea or belief to be true," it says, "what concrete difference will its being true make in any one's actual life? How will the truth be realized? What experiences will be different from those which would obtain if the belief were false? What, in short, is the truth's cash-value in experiential terms?"[75]

The truth of an idea is not a stagnant property inherent in it. Truth *happens* to an idea. It *becomes* true, is *made* true by events. Its verity *is* in fact an event, a process; the process namely of its verifying itself, its veri-*fication.*[76]

'The true,' to put it very briefly, is only the expedient in the way of our thinking, just as 'the right' is only the expedient in the way of our behaving. Expedient in almost any fashion; and expedient in the long run and on the whole of course; for what meets expediently all the experience in sight won't necessarily meet all farther experiences equally satisfactorily. Experience, as we know, has ways of *boiling over,* and making us correct our present formulas.[77]

John Dewey, in his formulation of the philosophy of pragmatism, inherited and used some of the doctrines, emphases, and themes treated by Peirce and James. Like Peirce, Dewey stresses the role of the *logic of inquiry*. Much of his thought is devoted to working out the character of the *method of experimental intelligence* and how it can be applied in various situations. Peirce, as we have seen, was concerned to show how this method functions when used for primarily cognitive purposes—in the empirical sciences (and, by extension, in mathematics and even in metaphysics and philosophy—the latter if properly 'purified'!) Peirce, too, worked out in great technical detail, and in a fresh and original way, a theory of formal logic. Dewey's strengths and interests lay in altogether different quarters. Dewey was not a creative logician, nor was he especially trained in the physical sciences or mathematics. He had no deep interest in working out a metaphysics involving a broad concern with the cosmological dimensions of reality. Dewey's dominant interests (as Santayana once aptly summed it up) are in the *foreground of human experience*. His approach to human experience always keeps in view the biological conditions and social dimensions of that experience. Dewey was a naturalistic humanist. He made important contributions to the philosophy of education (its theory and practice), to political philosophy, to the philosophy of art and esthetic experience, and to ethical theory. For Dewey, experimental intelligence is to be used in *all* these areas. It is not to be confined to the scientific interest in coming to *know* (to describe, explain, predict) phenomena in the world about us. For Dewey, intelligence is an instrument for *transforming* the world. It is a means for bringing about changes in ourselves and in our environment that would serve human needs and solve various problems. For him the notion of *inquiry* is broadened beyond what Peirce envisaged. Dewey thought of inquiry as a method of solving problems of all sorts: cognitive, personal, political, economic, moral, technological, artistic, educational, and legal. The task of intelligence is to transform indeterminate (problematic) situations into determinate, solved ones. Its chief use and role is to find ways of resolving conflicts, relieving tensions, meeting needs of particular situations. Like James, Dewey stressed the importance of dealing with the fresh, multiple, *individual* (particular) circumstances and challenges that make up human life whether on a personal or a social level. Peirce called himself a 'realist' in the medieval sense: one who recognizes the reality of 'generals': habits, laws, universals *in rem*—what Peirce calls 'Thirdness'—as a basic feature of reality, whether human or nonhuman. He condemned nominalists of every stripe—those who rejected or denied the reality of such 'generals' and asserted instead the sole reality of individuals or particulars. For Peirce individuals or particulars belonged to the category of what he called 'Secondness' and so constituted one, but not the only, dimension of reality. Peirce recognized in James (as in others) nominalistic tendencies, and would no doubt have also recognized the same stress in Dewey. For Dewey too, in his methodology, emphasized the primary importance of confronting and dealing with the multiple, novel, *individual* cases in which problematic situations arise. General ideas (principles, plans of action, policies, laws, and the like) for Dewey play an instrumental and therefore subordinate role; their utility and worth are to be judged in terms of how well they help to resolve particular problems and deal with individual cases.

Pragmatism as a movement, when considered as a whole, is clearly a fresh development in philosophy. It was not, however, as we can see even from our summary account, a tightly unified movement. Its advocates did not always mean the same thing by "looking to the practical consequences." Nor did they share, as philosophers, the same interests and preoccupations. Nevertheless, pragmatism exhibited, in the work of Peirce and others, lines of thought that give a special cast to the philosophical concerns of the twentieth century.

Peirce's work remained largely unrecognized for many decades. It did not receive the attention and acclaim it deserves for the originality and fertility of its ideas until a long time after his death. Although some historians treat Peirce as a nineteenth-century figure, he is to be thought of more accurately as a twentieth-century philosopher since many of his insights were in advance of his time. It took the work of later logicians, building for the most part on the work of Frege (work that in some ways paralleled that of Peirce) to bring the sphere of formal and philosophical logic to its present state of development. Only today, with the benefit of hindsight, can we see that Peirce, like Frege, was a fountainhead of creative insights and fresh orientations in logico-linguistic studies. Frege's work, too, as we shall see, remained largely unnoticed for a long time. Only in recent years has it come to be recognized for its great importance. The lineage of Frege's influence—upon Russell, Wittgenstein, Carnap, Church, Geach, Dummett, and others—traces the main lines of succession in contemporary analytic philosophy. Peirce does not form part of this historical linkage in its earlier phases. Nevertheless he can now be reexamined from the vantage point of present-day perspectives as one whose work parallels or converges in certain respects upon the work of a number of writers in the 'main line' sequence. These reasons alone justify (quite independently of the seminal role he played in the development of pragmatic thought in American philosophy) assigning to him a place as one of the original founders of contemporary philosophy. The metaphysical scheme at which Peirce labored throughout his life has not had the impact that his work in logic has had. Nevertheless, in its own way, Peirce's venture into metaphysics showed the need for working out a world view and of serving the human quest for a comprehensive view of the nature of reality. The analytic movement, as derived in large part from

Frege's impetus, has often been either indifferent or hostile to satisfying this metaphysical interest. But even here there has been, very recently, a revival of interest in ontology that in part helps to satisfy this interest.

Pragmatism occupies a special and interesting place at the opening of twentieth-century philosophic thought. In the work of Peirce and others, it presents in germinal and symptomatic form much that is novel, arresting, and important in later thought.

CHAPTER III

The New Logic

3.0.

The development of analytic philosophy is a central and important aspect of twentieth-century thought. The term 'analytic philosophy', as we have remarked, does not designate a single, tightly organized, unified movement whose adherents subscribe to a well-defined body of commonly shared principles. There is much diversity—sometimes sharp antagonism of thought—among the various subgroups or individual thinkers collected under this heading. Yet despite this diversity, the utility of using the label 'analytic philosophy' derives from two principal considerations. First, there is enough (even if not total) unity to warrant the use of a common classificatory label for those philosophers whose broad orientation is 'analytic' in contradistinction to those falling outside this group. Second, and perhaps more to the point, the movement we are calling 'analytic philosophy' has special links to the germinal ideas of Frege. The multiple interconnections and influences among analytic philosophers are illuminated when seen as so many diverse offshoots of Frege's work. This is not to say that all analytic philosophers are 'Fregeans' in one form or another. This is emphatically not so. Many, to be sure, were directly influenced by Frege. They undertook to assimilate, interpret, and adapt what they found of value in Frege's work in their own thought. But even among these some found points on which they diverged from or criticized Frege. (Frege himself, for that matter, did not have a monolithic, unchanged set of doctrines to which he adhered.) Nevertheless, within the analytic movement there is by and large a direct line from Frege to other thinkers in which we can note a carrying out of an interpretation or amplification of Frege's themes, doctrinal emphases, and philosophic viewpoint. On the other hand, as we trace the unfolding of analytic philosophy, there are

other component movements or individual thinkers whose characteristic theses and claims are best seen as reactions to those who had a
more direct or sympathetic relation to Frege's views. Here the picture
gets more complicated as we seek to follow the multiple crisscrossing
interconnections. Suffice it to say for the moment that even the latter
post-Fregean analytic movements are better understood when seen in
terms of their place in relation to the Fregean matrix and starting point. I
shall not now attempt to work out the relevant details of this observation,
but will do so later at appropriate stages of our exposition. Yet it will be
helpful to illustrate, in a preliminary way, the sort of thing I have in
mind.

There are three major thinkers of an earlier period in the development of contemporary analytic philosophy whose acknowledgment of
direct indebtedness to Frege is a matter of record. They were in contact
with Frege while he was still alive, and their thought was strongly influenced by their knowledge of Frege's work. These three thinkers are
Bertrand Russell, Ludwig Wittgenstein, and Rudolf Carnap.

It is something of an exaggeration to say—although Russell himself
has encouraged and contributed to this widely shared belief—that Russell
'discovered' Frege and made his work known to the rest of the academic
world. Russell writes:

> In spite of the epoch-making nature of his discoveries, he [Frege] remained
> wholly without recognition until I drew attention to him in 1903.[1]

> In spite of the great value of this work [*Begriffsschrift*], I was, I believe, the
> first person who ever read it—more than twenty years after its publication.[2]

The fact remains that Frege's work exerted an enormous influence on
Russell's thought. In the great classic of modern symbolic logic, Russell
and Whitehead's *Principia Mathematica* (1910–1913), we have a major
and clear example of Frege's impact. In the Preface to Volume I of that
work the authors wrote:

> In all questions of logical analysis, our chief debt is to Frege.[3]

When Wittgenstein was a research student at Manchester University in England in 1910, working on certain problems in aeronautical engineering, he became interested in the philosophy of mathematics and
among other things studied Russell's *Principles of Mathematics* (1903).
Wittgenstein corresponded with Frege and visited him in Jena, Germany,
in 1911. Frege advised the young Wittgenstein to study with Russell,
which of course he did. Frege's influence on Wittgenstein's *Tractatus
Logico-Philosophicus* (written during World War I and first published in
1921) is of enormous importance in understanding that work. Wittgenstein, in the Preface of that work, says:

I do not wish to judge how far my efforts coincide with those of other philosophers. . . . I will only mention that I am indebted to Frege's great works and to the writings of my friend Mr. Bertrand Russell for much of the stimulation of my thoughts.[4]

Gertrude E. M. Anscombe, in her book *An Introduction to Wittgenstein's Tractatus* (1959), remarks:

In the *Tractatus* Wittgenstein assumes, and does not try to stimulate, an interest in the kind of questions that Frege wrote about; he also takes it for granted that his readers will have read Frege.[5]

Rudolf Carnap, one of the central figures in the movement of Logical Positivism, studied with Frege at the University of Jena, taking courses with him in the fall of 1910 and the summers of 1913 and 1914. In his ''Autobiography'' Carnap writes in considerable detail about his studies with Frege and the impact they had on him. At one point he says:

Although Frege gave quite a number of examples of interesting applications of his symbolism in mathematics, he usually did not discuss general philosophical problems. It is evident from his works that he saw the great philosophical importance of the new instrument which he had created, but he did not convey a clear impression of this to his students. Thus, although I was intensely interested in his system of logic, I was not aware at that time of its great philosophical significance. Only much later, after the first world war, when I read Frege's and Russell's books with greater attention, did I recognize the value of Frege's work not only for the foundations of mathematics, but for philosophy in general.[6]

Even when, as in the work of the later Wittgenstein or the Oxford school of ordinary-language analysis, reactions set in against the philosophy of positivism and against the appeal to the formal language of logic as the primary model and tool for dealing with philosophical problems, we cannot fully understand this phase of the development of analytic philosophy without seeing it in the context of, and in its interactions with, the work of previous Fregean interpreters (for example, Russell, the early Wittgenstein, and Carnap).

As we come closer to our own day we find an increasing attention paid to Frege as a result of the availability of translations of his works, anthologies of critical writings, and major book-length studies of his philosophy by various commentators. The influence of Frege's thought—whether direct or indirect—upon current writing in analytic philosophy is everywhere to be noticed. For example, the works of Strawson, Geach, Quine, Davidson, Kripke, and Dummett are best understood as offshoots, in one way or another, of Frege's work and as continuing to deal with themes to which he first gave special attention.

3./.   GOTTLOB FREGE

Gottlob Frege (1848–1925) was a professor of mathematics at the University of Jena. His work as a mathematician was virtually restricted to a single problem, that of providing firm logical foundations for that discipline. Frege believed that such foundations were lacking in all expositions of mathematics then available. His original studies in formal logic were intended to show how it is possible to re-express and derive the fundamental ideas of mathematics having to do with *number* from fundamental ideas of a purely logical sort. This effort represented the major drive of his work in the field of 'mathematical logic'. The thesis that the mathematical concepts of number and the mathematical theorems concerning numbers can be re-expressed in terms of concepts of a purely logical sort and derived from the principles of a purely logical character is known as the *logicist* thesis in studies of the foundations of mathematics. It was a thesis to which Russell and others at first subscribed, until later studies showed the program of logicism to be riddled with great difficulties. As a result, the logicist thesis, as Frege envisaged it, was eventually abandoned by Frege toward the end of his life as well as by others.

In the course of working out his views on the logical foundations of mathematics, Frege found it necessary and important to develop his views on a number of *philosophic* themes that might help clarify and support his work as a mathematician. Approximately half of his writings are thus taken up with these philosophic themes. In these writings Frege worked out some trail-blazing ideas of a logico-linguistic sort. The creative novelty and fertility of these philosophic ideas have served as a principal impetus to the work of others in the analytic tradition. Although Frege's work in philosophy proper was of a quite narrow compass as compared with the work of other great philosophers, what he had to say within his own restricted range of philosophic interest was of the highest importance.* Frege continued throughout his life to write on philosophic

---

* In a reminiscence by Wittgenstein of his visit with Frege, Wittgenstein reports:

> I was shown into Frege's study. Frege was a small neat man with a pointed beard, who bounced around the room as he talked. He absolutely wiped the floor with me, and I felt very depressed; but at the end he said "You must come again," so I cheered up.
>
> I had several discussions with him after that. Frege would never talk about anything but logic and mathematics; if I started on some other subject, he would say something polite and then plunge back into logic and mathematics. He once showed me an obituary on a colleague, who, it was said, never used a word without knowing what it meant; he expressed astonishment that a man should be *praised* for this!
>
> The last time I saw Frege, as we were waiting at the station for my train, I said to him "Don't you ever find *any* difficulty in your theory that numbers are objects?" He replied "Sometimes I *seem* to see a difficulty—but then again I *don't* see it"![7]

topics, and in addition to important sections devoted to these topics in his major works—*Conceptual Notation, the Foundations of Arithmetic,* and *The Basic Laws of Arithmetic*—he wrote an important series of papers, among them the classics *"Über Begriff und Gegenstand"* ("Concept and Object"), *"Funktion and Begriff"* ("Function and Concept"), and *"Über Sinn und Bedeutung"* ("Sense and Reference").*

There are relatively few known biographical details concerning Frege's life.† He was born in Wismar, Germany, on November 8, 1848. His father was the founder and principal of a girls' high school, and his mother was also a teacher and later a principal of a girls' school. Frege's father died when Gottlob was still a boy. He attended the University of Jena as a student during the years 1869–1871, and then enrolled at Göttingen for five years. During this period his work was concentrated in mathematics, physics, and chemistry, with some courses in philosophy. He earned his doctorate at Göttingen in 1873 and returned to the University of Jena, where he remained for the rest of his active teaching career, i.e., for a total of forty-four years.

He was a member of the mathematics department, in which he rose from the rank of Privat-dozent to that of Professor. He died on July 26, 1925, at the age of seventy-seven. His life was marked by a series of tragedies, including the death of his children while they were still young, and that of his wife. He received relatively little recognition during his lifetime, and his death passed virtually unnoticed. He is reported to have been a clear and effective teacher. However, he (correctly) believed his colleagues at Jena were incompetent to understand his work and said so publicly. He was a formidable polemicist and minced no words in condemning or belittling the views of those he considered weak or in error.

Concerning another side of Frege's mind, Michael Dummett, in his sympathetic, profound, and critical exposition of Frege's thought *(Frege: The Philosophy of Language)* makes the following highly interesting comment and startling disclosure.

There is some irony for me in the fact that the man about whose philosophical views I have devoted, over years, a great deal of time to thinking, was, at least at the end of his life, a virulent racist, specifically an anti-semite. This fact is revealed by a fragment of a diary which survives among Frege's Nachlass, but which was not published with the rest by Professor Hans Hermes in *Freges nachgelassene Schriften.* The diary shows Frege to have been a man of extreme right-

---

* These writings are collected in Geach and Black (editors), *Translations from the Philosophical Writings of Gottlob Frege* (Oxford, 1952).

† A biography of Frege by his adopted son, Alfred, was destroyed, along with other relevant materials, during World War II. No full-length biographical study of Frege is available at the present time, although some materials are to be found, for example, in Bynum's Introduction to his edition of Frege's *Conceptual Notation (Begriffsschrift),* and in Dummett's *Frege: The Philosophy of Language.*

wing political opinions, bitterly opposed to the parliamentary system, democrats, liberals, Catholics, the French and, above all, Jews, who he thought ought to be deprived of political rights and, preferably, expelled from Germany. When I first read that diary, many years ago, I was deeply shocked, because I had revered Frege as an absolutely rational man, if, perhaps, not a very likeable one. I regret that the editors of Frege's Nachlass chose to suppress that particular item. From it I learned something about human beings which I should be sorry not to know; perhaps something about Europe, also.[8]

There is a remarkable unity in Frege's work, from his earliest studies and published writings to the latest, although there are important developments and significant shifts of viewpoint. Before turning to a more detailed account of his views in philosophical logic, it will be useful, by way of preparation for this account, to summarize the main stages of development in Frege's thought.[9]

The earliest major work by Frege was his *Begriffsschrift (Conceptual Notation)*, published in 1879. In it many of the germinal ideas of his entire philosophy are to be found. It is also, from a wider perspective, one of the most important works in the entire history of logic. Although at the time none of Frege's contemporaries appreciated the significance of what he had accomplished, this work has slowly come to be recognized for the great achievement it is. Now, one hundred years later, it is universally acknowledged to be the first major classic in the development of modern logic.

Frege's purpose in this work is to provide a rigorous logical foundation for the proofs of arithmetic. He uses the term 'arithmetic' to include all those branches of mathematics that have to do with number—not simply ordinary 'arithmetic', but also, for example, algebra, the differential and integral calculus, and the theory of real and complex numbers. Although mathematics had traditionally been regarded as the very model and standard of a discipline that uses rigorous deductive reasoning to establish its conclusions, from Frege's point of view mathematics was still lacking in his own day the high degree of logical rigor of which it is capable. Frege sought to supply this needed rigor for the entire domain of arithmetic. He proposed to do this principally in two steps: (1) by making explicit all the assumptions and presuppositions as well as all the rules of inference that warrant the linking of statements within a proof to each other; (2) by providing a suitable, specially devised technical notation that would not retain any of the looseness and vagueness of ordinary natural language.

Frege sought to *prove* all the laws of arithmetic. In order to do this, he gave special attention to the notion of proof itself. He is not concerned with the *psychological processes* by which men may have come to discover proofs for some proposition or other. He is interested, rather, in the *logical* support (the logical relations a proposition has to others) such that we can say one proposition can be logically derived from these others. In the case of arithmetic, Frege wishes to find a way of establishing its conclusions by a chain of reasoning so tight and complete, so free of any appeals to 'intuition' and so 'free of gaps', that all necessary steps in the proof can be made explicit. Under these conditions, any one might check each formula and step and so come to verify the soundness of the reasoning.

To accomplish this broad purpose, Frege devised the system of Conceptual Notation—a system of Logic—that marks the beginning of this discipline in its modern form. We must state first how this accomplishment is to be understood in relation to Frege's purposes, and second what this amounted to when seen more generally from a broader historical perspective.

On the one hand, as already remarked, Frege was interested in providing a secure, rigorous formulation for the proofs of arithmetic. At the time this was his principal motive and purpose. In realizing this goal, Frege devised a new and improved system of logic. This system consisted of a special notation for expressing certain basic logical ideas. These included the notions of 'assertible content', 'negation', 'conditional proposition', 'the universal quantifier', and 'identity'. In addition, and very importantly, Frege pointed to a useful analogy between the mathematical notion of a *function* and the logical notion of a *concept*. He showed how this analogy could help clarify what in the older logic was called the *predicate* of a proposition. A predicate was traditionally understood as something that ascribes a certain property to a subject. However, what we mean by a 'subject' can be better understood (for purposes of logic) if we think of it on the analogy of what in mathematics is called the *argument* of a function. Thus, the entire combination of a 'function' and its 'arguments', when treated in this broadened logical sense, can now be thought of as having a *truth-value* (in analogy with the notion of a *numerical value* for the argument of a function in a strictly arithmetic context.) Frege showed how, in carrying out the analysis of the internal logical structure of a proposition, it is important to have at one's disposal the use of the notion of quantifiers and the variables they bind, in order to thereby express the concept of *generality*. (We shall consider all these ideas in greater detail later, together with some suitable examples.)

One of Frege's purposes, as mentioned, was to show how, with an arsenal of clear and precise ideas in logic, one can turn to the project of establishing rigorous proofs in arithmetic. On Frege's view, this meant specifically two things. It meant taking the basic ideas of a mathematical system (its primitive ideas and its rules of inference) and re-expressing them by means of the new conceptual notation. It also meant something stronger, however. It meant showing that the basic arithmetical ideas could be reduced to those of a purely logical sort. This is accomplished by redefining the arithmetical ideas in terms of logical ideas. One thereby shows that the mathematical ideas are at bottom nothing but ideas of logic. Similarly, the rules of arithmetic as used to draw inferences and to establish proofs could also be shown by a parallel process of redefinition and reduction to consist, at bottom, only of logical rules of inference. Insofar as one could carry through this project, one could show that arithmetic, as a fundamental branch of mathematics, is itself a branch of logic. This thesis was Frege's logicism, as it came to be known. It was a thesis to the establishment of whose truth all his major mathematical works were dedicated.

In the *Begriffsschrift* Frege took an important step in carrying out this program by showing how the central mathematical idea of 'following in a numerical sequence' (which lies at the base of the idea of mathematical induction—the procedure of adding one to an integer to get its successor) could be reduced to and redefined in terms of purely logical ideas. (These ideas have to do with what is known as a 'hereditary property' and the 'ancestral relation').[10] In his later major works, *Die Grundlagen der Arithmetik (The Foundations of Arithmetic)* (1884) and *Grundgesetze der Arithmetik (The Basic Laws of Arithmetic)* (vol. 1, 1893; vol. 2, 1903), Frege attempted to carry out this broad logistic project by showing how the notion of *number* could be defined in terms of the purely logical notion of *class*. All of the foregoing work then, as initiated in the *Begriffsschrift* and carried forward in the later works, represents one major side of Frege's highly motivated contributions to establishing a new logic. It was specifically devised to serve as a mathematical logic, that could provide both a precise logical notation for arithmetic and a means for reducing the basic ideas of arithmetic to purely logical ones, thereby absorbing arithmetic as a branch of logic.

Despite the eventual failure in the establishment of the logicist thesis, Frege's devotion to this thesis led him to develop the main ideas of logic in its modern form. What Frege accomplished here has endured as well as helped to spark other developments. Together, these are far from being failures. On the contrary, they are of the highest intellectual importance. When seen from this angle, Frege's creative contributions to logic have a utility and range of application that extend far beyond his original interests in upholding the logicist thesis. What Frege helped develop in his various logical writings could be used in areas other than mathematics, and for purposes quite different from those of furthering the logicist thesis. The logic he helped create provides a way of dealing with the formal structure of propositions—their logical interrelations among themselves, together with an analysis of their internal parts and components. It is a logic that can be employed regardless of the subject matter to which it is applied. The general rules and forms of logic can be used to express the structural features of discourse, whatever be the special subject matter. The rules of logic once formulated can be used to perform evaluations of the soundness of reasoning in any domain. When so used, moreover, the adoption of the tools of the new logic in no way commits one to the acceptance of either the logicist thesis or any analogue of it. It does not follow that if one uses the new logic and the vocabulary it makes available, one is thereby committed to the claim that this accomplishes a redefinition and reduction of some stretch of discourse into a branch of logic itself. The logical notation is only being used, rather, to extract the logical form of the discourse and to guide one in achieving precision of thought. There need be no claim made, in all this, that the language and discourse so codified and expressed concerning some subject matter has now become absorbed into and made a part of logic itself.

In clarifying the use of logical symbolism for expressing interrelations among propositions and the internal structural components of propositions, Frege found it necessary to work out his philosophy of what he was doing. This consisted in developing a theory of meaning, philosophy of language, and system of philosophical logic. The earliest stages of this side of his thought are to be found in his *Begriffsschrift,* where his comments are interspersed with his more formal, technical expositions.

Having laid the groundwork for many of his basic views in logic and in philosophical logic in his *Begriffsschrift,* Frege moved on to work out the details of his program in a series of books and articles. This he did despite the lack of comprehension or appreciation for what he had accomplished in the *Begriffsschrift* on the part of the few logicians or mathematicians who took the trouble to look at his work and who reviewed it unfavorably. His next major work was a masterpiece of clear exposition and a deepening of his ideas on the foundations of mathematics, *Die Grundlagen der Arithmetik (The Foundations of Arithmetic).* It too received very few reviews, all of them unfavorable, including one by the great mathematician George Cantor. Edmund Husserl also discussed and criticized it in his work on *The Philosophy of Arithmetic* (1891). Once again it took the passage of many years for the greatness of this work to come to be recognized; it is generally acknowledged today as containing the clearest and most felicitous statement of the core of Frege's thought.

In the Introduction to his work, Frege lays down three basic principles of philosophical logic. He writes:

> In the enquiry that follows, I have kept to three fundamental principles:
> always to separate sharply the psychological from the logical, the subjective from the objective;
> never to ask for the meaning of a word in isolation, but only in the context of a proposition;
> never to lose sight of the distinction between concept and object.[11]

The first principle expressed Frege's explicit rejection of any form of psychologism—the view that an understanding of the nature of meaning requires that one deal with certain subjective, 'inner' processes of the mind. On the contrary, Frege maintains, an understanding of the nature of meaning requires that we be able to examine certain objective features to be found in the use of *language*. These are public matters, open to inspection and examination. Thus, for him, concepts are not to be identified with ideas, images, or mental entities of any sort. Concepts, for Frege, are special types of objective entities. Concept-words are linguistic expressions that refer to these concepts. It is with these concept-words that the logician operates just as he does with other types of linguistic expressions. Frege was a realist in the technical sense of the term, who believed in the objective existence of concepts, relations, and objects. Thus objects are entities in the world designated by special types of linguistic expressions—what he calls 'proper names'—whereas 'concept-words' refer to concepts, relation-expressions to relations, and so on. The logician deals with linguistic expressions. He studies how various types of linguistic expressions might contribute to a logically perspicuous use of language in sentences and the logical connections of such sentences with one another. It is in this context of language-use, and not in the domain of psychological processes, that Frege would carry out his investigations into the nature of 'meaning'.

The second of the principles quoted above is similarly of fundamental importance in understanding the entire bent of Frege's philosophy. It tells us that the basic unit of language-use is the sentence. The fundamental move in the use of language is that in which one constructs and uses sentences—*to say something*. The understanding of individual words can only be successfully achieved when we see them as contributing to the formation and use of sentences. For Frege the major use of a sentence (at any rate the use he was principally interested in) was that in which we use it to make an assertion, to say something that is either *true* or *false*. Hence the understanding of the *meaning* of words is to be found in the link they have to our being able to specify ultimately the truth or falsity of a sentence of which they are constituents. The meaning of words is bound up with the way in which they contribute to and help to determine the *truth-conditions* of the sentences in which they figure. Another way of making this point is to say that Frege's approach to a philosophy of language was a *semantical* one. The question he was principally concerned with is, What distinctions of logical type need to be made among linguistic expressions in a logically purified language, where we wish to use that language to convey the truth and avoid falsity? In a broad sense, semantics is precisely that aspect of the study of language that concerns itself with matters of reference and truth. It studies the semantic roles of various types of expressions in the formation and use of sentences of varying degrees of logical complexity. It evaluates their contribution to the determination of the truth or falsity of the sentence of which these expressions are constituent parts.

The third principle Frege enunciates—the importance of recognizing the distinction between concepts and objects—is one to which he comes back over and over again in all his writings. The failure to make this distinction, he would say, lies at the base of many of the confusions and errors that pervade the history of philosophy. We shall turn later in this chapter to a detailed examination of what this distinction amounts to, and the kinds of uses to which it is put by Frege.

In the *Grundlagen* Frege argues for the main claims of his logicist thesis. He attacks the mathematicians of his day who failed to give a satisfactory analysis of the root idea of number, centering his fire primarily on those mathematicians and logicians who take a psychological approach to this concept. His own constructive treatment is carried out in a discursive manner, avoiding the novel, strange, and technical symbolism he had introduced in his *Begriffsschrift,* a symbolism that he was also to use later in his *Grundgesetze.* He argues in behalf of the broad thesis that the truths of arithmetic are *analytic a priori* (in opposition to the claim of Kant that they are *synthetic a priori*). In examining the central arithmetic concept of number, he proposes that this can be redefined and reduced to the logical notion of a *class,* where a class is treated as the extension of a concept. He defends, too, a form of Platonism with respect to mathematical truths, arguing that arithmetic, far from being simply a human *creation,* is a science engaged in making *discoveries* about the existence and properties of certain independently existing abstract objects—the numbers themselves. Arithmetic is not to be thought of, for example, as simply a 'game' in which we devise rules for manipulating various symbols (e.g., the *numerals*). Numbers are certain types of abstract objects to which numerals refer, but are not to be identified with numerals or any other kinds of linguistic symbols.

Following upon the publication of his *Grundlagen,* Frege devoted the next several years to two principal tasks. The first was to work out his views in philosophical logic, the philosophy of language, and the theory of meaning, in greater detail than he had up to that point. This he did principally in an important series of papers, among which the most celebrated are "Concept and Object" and "Sense and Reference." These writings, along with others in the same area, Frege hoped to transform eventually into a complete systematic book in philosophical logic. He never did succeed in writing this book. Meanwhile the papers as they stand are the most original and lasting contributions that Frege made in his role as a philosopher. Although these writings were intended to clarify and support his views about 'meaning' in connection with his work in the foundations of mathematics, they showed themselves to have a far wider significance and applicability than Frege envisaged for them. They have, in fact, served as the groundwork for much of the subsequent work in the theory of meaning in the later history of analytic philosophy.

At the same time that he was working out these ideas in the philosophy of language, Frege devoted himself to carrying out with full rigor and thoroughness, and with all the technical symbolic apparatus at his command, his general project of showing how the basic ideas and rules of arithmetic can be defined and formulated in purely logical terms—that arithmetic is a body of analytic truths, its axioms consisting entirely of truths of logic. This logicist thesis was now presented in this great work *Grundgesetze der Arithmetik,* two volumes of which appeared in 1893 and 1903. A third volume was planned but never appeared. In these works he carried out in technical detail the plans he already had presented in his *Begriffsschrift* and had informally sketched in the *Grundlagen.* In the *Grundgesetze* Frege not only makes full use of his newly developed ideas in philosophical logic (especially his views on the important distinctions between sense and reference, and between concept and object), but also makes fundamental use of the notion of *class* (set) as the extension of a concept in defining the nature of number.

When he had carried through this project to one stage of its completion in Volume 2 of the *Grundgesetze,* a shatteringly dramatic event took place. Frege received a letter from Bertrand Russell in which Russell pointed out a *contradiction* in Frege's use of the notion of class. The substance of Russell's argument has come to be known as the *Russell Paradox.* Frege tells us in his own words (in the Appendix to Volume 2 of the *Grundgesetze*) what this is.

Hardly anything more unwelcome can befall a scientific writer than that one of the foundations of his edifice be shaken after the work is finished.

I have been placed in this position by a letter of Mr. Bertrand Russell just as the printing of this [second] volume was nearing completion. It is a matter of my Basic Law (V). I have never concealed from myself its lack of the self-evidence which the others possess, and which must properly be demanded of a law of logic. . . . I should gladly have relinquished this foundation if I had known of any substitute for it. And even now I do not see how arithmetic can be scientifically founded, how numbers can be conceived as logical objects and brought under study, unless we are allowed—at least conditionally—the transition from a concept to its extension. Is it always permissible to speak of the extension of a concept, of a class? And if not, how do we recognize the exceptional cases? Can we always infer from the extension of one concept's coinciding with that of a second, that every object which falls under the first concept also falls under the second? These are the questions raised by Mr. Russell's communication.

Solatium miseris, socios habuisse malorum. I too have this solace, if solace it is; for everyone who in his proofs had made use of extensions of concepts, classes, sets, is in the same position. It is not just a matter of my particular method of laying the foundations, but of whether a logical foundation for arithmetic is possible at all.

But let us come to the point. Mr. Russell has discovered a contradiction, which may now be set out.

No one will want to assert of the class of men that it is a man. Here we have a class that does not belong to itself. That is, I say that something belongs to a class if it falls under the concept whose extension that class is. Now let us fix our attention upon the concept *class that does not belong to itself.* The extension of this concept (if we may speak of its extension) is accordingly the class of classes that do not belong to themselves. For short we shall call it the class *C*. Now let us ask whether this class *C* belongs to itself. First let us suppose that it does. If something belongs to a class, then it falls under the concept whose extension the class is; accordingly if our class *C* belongs to itself then it is a class that does not belong to itself. Thus our first supposition leads to a self-contradiction. Second, let us suppose that our class *C* does not belong to itself; then it falls under the concept whose extension it itself is, and thus does belong to itself: here again, a contradiction.[12]

The effect upon Frege in struggling with the Russell Paradox was, at first, to look for a way of overcoming its challenge. This he thought he succeeded in doing. It is known as 'Frege's Way Out', a solution he offers in the same Appendix. However, it was later proven by the Polish logician Leśniewski that Frege's "way out" didn't work, that the paradox reappears anyway. Frege eventually came to this realization and to admit that his lifelong efforts at grounding arithmetic in logic were a failure.

At the end of his life, Frege turned in another direction altogether in the project of grounding arithmetic. Although he had formerly believed that if his efforts had been successful he would have shown that the truths of arithmetic are analytic *a priori,* he now had to concede that this could not be shown by the procedures he had followed. Frege, from the very beginning, had not claimed that *all* the truths of mathematics could be established as analytic *a priori*. He had always exempted the truths of geometry from this claim, agreeing with Kant that they are synthetic *a priori.**

* For Frege the distinction between the use of the terms 'analytic' and 'synthetic' as well as the distinction between what is *'a priori'* and *'a posteriori'* have to do with the kinds of *justification* one can give in support of a proposition. He writes:

> Now these distinctions between a priori and a posteriori, synthetic and analytic, concern, as I see it, not the content of the judgement but the justification for making the judgement. . . . The problem becomes, in fact, that of finding the proof of the proposition, and of following it up right back to the primitive truths. If, in carrying out this process, we come only on general logical laws and on definitions, then the truth is an analytic one, bearing in mind that we must take account also of all propositions upon which the admissibility of any of the definitions depends. If, however, it is impossible to give the proof without making use of truths which are not of a general logical nature, but belong to the sphere of some special science, then the proposition is a synthetic one. For a truth to be a posteriori, it must be impossible to construct a proof of it without including an appeal to facts, i.e., to truths which cannot be proved and are not general, since they contain assertions about particular objects. But if, on the contrary, its proof can be derived exclusively from general laws, which themselves neither need nor admit of proof, then the truth is a priori.[13]

With the failure of the program to show that arithmetic consisted of analytic *a priori* truths, Frege thought he might be able to show that geometry, with its synthetic *a priori* truths, was the foundation upon which *all* the rest of mathematics could be erected. He never succeeded during the remaining years of his life in accomplishing this goal either. Since Frege's day other far-reaching, revolutionary developments in proof-theory, especially in the work of Gödel and others, have pointed to challenging questions and options that Frege had no way of anticipating. The current scene in the area devoted to working out a satisfactory philosophy in the foundations of mathematics no longer includes Frege's logicist thesis (as he formulated it) as a viable alternative.[14] The battle lines are drawn elsewhere, especially in the rival views of Intuitionists and Platonists. However, this is a topic—important and provocative as it is, though of a highly technical nature—that lies beyond the scope of the present survey, and we shall not enter into its ramifications in what follows.

THE LANGUAGE OF LOGIC

Let me now summarize and conclude these introductory remarks.

In his studies of the requirements for constructing a rigorous system of mathematics, as well as in his broader efforts at formulating the conditions for insuring clarity and exactness in our use of language in any domain of discourse, Frege worked out a system of logic. This logic embodies a specially devised notation (symbolism), with precisely assigned meanings and rules for its manipulation and use. It includes explicitly formulated rules for showing how various units of meaningfully employed discourse (for example, names and sentences) can be used to form more complex units of discourse. It states various rules of inference in accordance with which one may make logically warranted connections and establish linkages of implication among sentences of the language. In setting up such a logic—such a fund of specially devised symbols and rules for their manipulation—Frege believed we have at our disposal a crucial means for introducing the necessary clarity and rigor into any domain of inquiry in which we seek to determine what is true and to avoid or reject what is false. The logic makes available the tools for recasting any use of language that does not already embody or exhibit the necessary distinctions and forms of logic.

Frege belongs to that group of analytic philosophers who believe that a sound approach to the nature of language for purposes of philosophy requires that one draw a sharp distinction between the everyday uses of natural language and the ideal language of formal logic. From the point of view of such an ideal language, the natural languages and their everyday uses are infected with various deficiencies. These can only be recognized and removed if one can appeal to the standards set by, and exhibited in, the ideal language of formal logic. Philosophic clarity comes from using the tools of formal logic in criticism of and for purposes of overhauling the ordinary uses of natural language.

Much of our everyday use of natural language fails in possessing this logical rigor and clarity. Frequently, too, even specially constructed technical vocabularies (for example in the sciences), however clear and rigorous they may be in other respects, turn out to be deficient when it comes to abiding by the necessary forms and distinctions of logic. The advantage of having a carefully formulated system of logic is that with its aid one could set about removing the blemishes and weaknesses of prelogical or not-yet-reformed languages by imposing on them the standards of logic. The conceptual notation of the language of logic helps one to restate what is of essential value for truth-seeking, cognitive purposes.

In a logically reformed and purified language all expressions would have a precise and definite sense, and the ways in which all expressions might be used to construct more complex expressions out of less complex linguistic units (for example, entire phrases out of constituent words, or entire arguments out of individual sentences) would be governed by precise, explicitly formulated rules. Thus every name used in such a language to refer to an individual object would have a definite sense, and every sentence would be so formulated that one would know its truth-conditions (i.e., what conditions would need to be satisfied in order for it to be either true or false.) Any expression lacking either a clear and definite sense or used in such a way that it does not contribute in a precise way to the determination of the truth-value of a sentence in which it might figure, would be eliminated from a logically perspicuous language. Thus for the cognitive purposes of a logically reconstructed language, nothing is to be retained from ordinary language that involves, for example, expressing emotions, making puns, creating fictional works of literature, deliberately using language in an ambiguous, deceptive, or vague way (for instance, for social or diplomatic reasons), and so on. All variations—subtle or otherwise—in the use of terms with different 'colorings' or 'tones' would be eliminated. There would be only a single clear sense attached to every linguistic expression—its standard, explicit, uniform meaning. All variations or shadings of meaning would be excluded and prohibited. The deficiencies of ordinary language include vagueness and imprecision, and the multiple uses to which language can be put often stand in the way of or are confused with the use of language for strictly cognitive purposes. Consider, for example, the differences of tone or coloring in describing a person as a 'woman', 'female', 'lady', 'member of the opposite sex', 'member of the weaker sex', and so on. Or consider another example, this time from Frege. We sometimes intend different shades of meaning in using the word 'but' rather than 'and'. ''The speaker uses 'but' when he wishes to give a hint that what follows is different from what one might at first suppose."[15] However, from the point of view of logic, the truth-value of sentences in which they occur would be the same whether one used the word 'and' or the word 'but'. Thus the two sentences 'I was tired *and* met my appointment on time' and 'I was tired *but* met my appointment on time' have the same truth-value. Each sentence exhibits a form of proposition known as the 'conjunctive'. It is true, as a whole, only if each conjunct ('I was tired', and 'I met my appointment on time') is true. The use of the word 'but' in the second sentence has a different tone (coloring) from the tone-neutral use of the word 'and'. However, from the point of view of the logical analysis of these sentences, the differences in tone of 'but' and 'and' would be ignored.

Sometimes, too, the rules of ordinary grammar may be misleading in what they approve or disapprove as judged from the point of view of what a *logically* purified language would require. Frege gives the following example: In the sentences 'The emperor's carriage is drawn by four horses' and 'The emperor's carriage is drawn by black horses' the phrases 'four horses' and 'black horses' occupy the same grammatical position. They would therefore be treated, according to the ordinary rules of grammar, as performing the *same* grammatical role. However, according to *logic,* the phrases 'four horses' and 'black horses' play fundamentally *different* roles. The relation of the adjectives 'four' and 'black' to the term 'horse' is of a fundamentally *different logical* kind. (We shall later show why this is so.)

We proceed now to explore more fully some of Frege's basic contributions to philosophical logic, theory of meaning, and general philosophy of language. For this purpose we shall pay special attention to the distinctions between concept and object, and between sense and reference.

CONCEPT AND OBJECT

A central theme in Frege's philosophy of language, that already appears in his *Conceptual Notation* and that he develops in various ways in his later writings, is the importance for logic of taking the sentence as a whole as the basic item to be analyzed. In *The Foundations of Arithmetic,* as we have seen, he lays it down as a basic principle that "it is only in the context of a sentence that a word has meaning." It is the thought conveyed by a whole sentence of which, when asserted, we can ask whether it is true or false, and so as having possible cognitive significance. The task of logic, in starting with whole sentences, is to examine the type of components out of which a sentence is constructed. It is important to see the underlying logical role of these items and not to be misled by superficial grammatical similarities or dissimilarities. The disentangling of these logical components was accomplished by Frege in a pathbreaking way. What distinguishes much of modern logic (of the sort initiated by Frege) from traditional logic is the way sentences—in their internal components as well as in their interconnections in sequences of sentences to yield entire arguments—are analyzed.

As contrasted with a superficial grammatical distinction between subjects and predicates that underlay much of traditional logic, Frege distinguished between the linguistic expressions of *concept-words* and *proper names*. To accomplish this he showed the great importance of making a useful comparison between the idea of a mathematical function and its 'arguments' on the one hand, and the logical idea of a concept in application to an object on the other hand. In the light of this distinction he was able to point the way for using the important idea of *quantifiers* in expressing generality where this is found in certain types of sentences.

One underlying theme in Frege's analysis has to do with the notion of *assertion*. A sentence can be, but need not be, asserted. Consider, for example, the sentence 'Socrates is wise'. The sentence is grammatically well formed; it does not violate any standard, familiar rules of English grammar. Frege would say this entire sentence has a sense. We understand it. The sense of the sentence as a whole Frege calls a *thought* (what could also be called a *proposition*). We can understand the thought expressed by this sentence without asserting it. Insofar as the sentence is understood as expressing a thought, it has an *assertible content;* it would make sense to ask whether it is either true or false. To assert this sentence is to use it to make an actual truth-claim; one is prepared to claim that the sentence *is* true. And to assert this sentence is to use the sentence with an *assertoric force*. Instead of an assertoric force one might have given this same sentence an *interrogatory force*. Thus one might have asked a question by means of it: 'Socrates is wise?' or, by rearrangement of its words, 'Is Socrates wise?'

An interrogative sentence and an assertoric one contain the same thought; but the assertoric sentence contains something else as well, namely assertion. The interrogative sentence contains something more too, namely a request. Therefore two things must be distinguished in an assertoric sentence: the content, which it has in common with the corresponding propositional question; and assertion. The former is the thought or at least contains the thought. So it is possible to express a thought without laying it down as true. The two things are so closely joined in an assertoric sentence that it is easy to overlook their separability.[16]

In the formulation of sentences for cognitive purposes, everything that does not bear on their possible truth-value is to be eliminated. It is here, for example, that the discourse of science differs from that of poetry, or wherever the colorings and tones of our means of expression play an important role. All such distinctive colorings and tones are to be excluded in a sentence whose sole use is to express a *thought* capable of *logical analysis*.

An assertoric sentence often contains, over and above a thought and assertion, a third component not covered by the assertion. This is often meant to act on the feelings and mood of the hearer, or to arouse his imagination. Words like 'regrettably' and 'fortunately' belong here. Such constituents of sentences are more strongly prominent in poetry, but are seldom wholly absent from prose. They occur more rarely in mathematical, physical, or chemical expositions than in historical ones. What are called the humanities are closer to poetry, and are therefore less scientific, than the exact sciences, which are drier in proportion to being more exact; for exact science is directed toward truth and truth alone. Therefore all constituents of sentences not covered by the assertoric force do not belong to scientific exposition; but they are sometimes hard to avoid, even for one who sees the danger connected with them. Where the main thing is to approach by way of intimation what cannot be conceptually grasped, these constituents are fully justified. The more rigorously scientific an exposition is, the less the nationality of its authors will be discernible and the easier it will be to translate. On the other hand, the constituents of language to which I here want to call attention make the translation of poetry very difficult, for it is just in what largely makes the poetic value that languages most differ.

It makes no difference to the thought whether I use the word 'horse' or 'steed' or 'nag' or 'prad'. The assertoric force does not cover the ways in which these words differ. What is called mood, atmosphere, illumination in a poem, what is portrayed by intonation and rhythm, does not belong to the thought.[17]

To express the distinction between an assertible content and an assertion, Frege (in the *Begriffsschrift*) introduced the use of the symbols for the *content-stroke* and the *judgment-stroke* (the latter being the sign signalizing assertion). Thus, if we wished merely to *consider* the complete sentence 'Socrates is wise', we should put a content-stroke in front of it: '——— (Socrates is wise)'. Similarly, for any sentence or complete thought (let us represent it as '*F*') that can be treated as an assertible content, we could then write: '——— *(F)*'. Suppose now we wished to assert that Socrates is wise. For this, Frege introduces the assertion-sign or judgment-stroke: ' |———'. For the sentence 'Socrates is wise', as used with assertoric force, we should write:

|———(Socrates is wise).

In general, for some assertible sentence '*F*', as asserted, we should write:

$$\vdash\!\!\!\!\!———\ (F).$$

Of an asserted sentence it is appropriate to say it is either true or false. If there is some combination of words that could not be said to constitute a clear and complete sentence (to convey an assertible content), such a combination of words could not serve a cognitive role; it is one to which the rules of logic would not apply.

Frege makes a fundamental distinction, in the analysis of the internal logical structure of a sentence, between *concept-words* and *names*. Let us follow him as he works out this distinction: what leads him to make it, what clarifying help it accomplishes, what complications can be built on its foundation, and what kinds of applications can be made of it for the illumination of various philosophic topics.

In his important paper "Function and Concept" (1891), Frege makes clear how one can employ the *mathematical* idea of a *function* as a model by means of which to arrive, by analogy and generalization, at the important *logical* idea of a *concept*. Concepts play a crucial role in a great variety of well-formed sentences, regardless of the subject matter with which these sentences deal.

Let us consider a simple example that Frege gives from the domain of arithmetic in which the idea of 'function' makes its appearance. Take the following series of expressions, each of which stands for a number:

$$2 \cdot 1^3 + 1$$
$$2 \cdot 4^3 + 4$$
$$2 \cdot 5^3 + 5$$

The first expression designates the number 3, the second the number 132, the third the number 255. Frege points out that it is important to distinguish a numerical expression that stands for, signifies, or designates a number, from the number itself. In general we distinguish the sign for an object from the object itself, just as we distinguish the name 'Socrates' and the person Socrates. Similarly, Frege reminds us, we must distinguish a numeral or numerical expression from the number it represents. Thus the numeral '7' stands for the number 7. But the same number 7 could be represented by other symbols or expressions, for example, 'VII', '$2^2 + 3$', or '$4 + 3$'.

To return to our example above, each of the numerical expressions represents a different number—3, 132, 255. However, when we examine the three expressions '$2 \cdot 1^3 + 1$', '$2 \cdot 4^3 + 4$', and '$2 \cdot 5^3 + 5$', we recognize in them a *common pattern*. Although it is common practice among mathematicians to use a 'variable number' x to convey this common pattern by writing, for example '$2 \cdot x^3 + x$', Frege prefers to show what this common pattern is without making use of the notion of a 'variable number'. (He believes the expression 'variable number' is misleading; every number is determinate or definite; it cannot be 'variable'). Instead, he would show the pattern common to the series of numerical expressions in our example as

$$2 \cdot (\ )^3 + (\ )$$

The blank spaces enclosed in each of the two sets of parentheses can be filled by various numerals, provided (for the above pattern) the numeral that fills the first parenthesis also fills the second parenthesis. Thus we can substitute '1' in each of the above parentheses and obtain the first of the above expressions ('2 · 1^3 + 1'), and so on. The placement of a particular numeral in each of the above blank spaces is known as providing a symbol in an *argument place* to stand for an *argument*.* Thus in our example, '1', '4', and '5' are argument-expressions that appear in the above pattern; and, of course, there are other possible arguments as well, say 7, 38, and so on. What remains constant or invariant, even though the arguments may change from one example to the next, is the pattern '2 · $(\ )^3$ + $(\ )$'. This common pattern is known as the *function*. The same function reappears in each of the three sets of expressions ('2 · 1^3 + 1', '2 · 4^3 + 4', and '2 · 5^3 + 5') even though the arguments are different. Corresponding to a particular argument for the function under consideration, there is obtainable (in this case by simple arithmetical calculation) a particular *numerical value*. Thus for the argument 1, the above function has the numerical value 3; for the argument 4, it has the numerical value 132, and so on. The *numerical value* is the resultant of combining the *argument* and *function*. The function 'takes on' a particular *numerical value* for a particular *argument*. And, of course, we can have many different *types of function* in addition to the example we have considered.

Frege points out that in this way of analyzing what a function, argument, and (numerical) value are, we can say that the function is *unsaturated* (or *incomplete*). By itself, in other words, since a functional expression consists in part of blank spaces, it cannot designate any particular number. The argument, however, insofar as it is a particular number, is complete and determinate. Likewise, when one supplies a particular argument to a specific function, one obtains a complete or determinate numerical value (a particular number) that is also complete or saturated —a complete whole. Thus the notion of a function carries with it the important idea of a common pattern. It, however, is not a definite number. A function (in the mathematical sense) may be thought of as that which, though not itself a definite number, nevertheless connects up or

---

* The term 'argument' is here being used in its normal mathematical sense; it should not be confused, of course, with the use of the same word 'argument' in logic, where it means a logical sequence of statements, in which some of these statements serve as the premises from which another statement, the conclusion, is derived.

correlates two things that are definite numbers, namely arguments and values. For a particular number that is the argument in a given function, there is another particular number that is the numerical value for that argument—as established through the 'medium' of the particular function that connects them. As Frege puts it:

> In this respect functions differ fundamentally from numbers. Since such is the essence of the function, we can explain why, on the one hand, we recognize the same function in '2 · 1^3 + 1' and '2 · 2^3 + 2', even though these expressions stand for different numbers, whereas, on the other hand, we do not find one and the same function in '2 · 1^3 + 1' and '4 − 1' in spite of their equal numerical values.[18]

In the total mathematical expression such as '2 · 1^3 + 1', we can distinguish two components—the sign for the argument (in this case '1') and the expression for the function (in this case '2 · ( )^3 + ( )'), and these are dissimilar in their roles, "for the argument is a number, a whole complete in itself, as the function is not."[19]

With the foregoing background of how we are to think of the relations of 'function', 'argument', and 'value' in a mathematical context, Frege proceeds to exploit these distinctions for general logical or philosophical purposes. He shows how we can apply these distinctions to deal not only with expressions having to do with numbers, but how parallel distinctions among 'function', 'argument', and 'value' can be made in the logical analysis of language-uses in which are to be found descriptions or assertible sentences having to do with various types of subject matter. This will involve, among other things, showing the close connection between the mathematical notion of a *function* and the more general notion of a *concept*. It will also involve going beyond the idea of a *numerical value* to achieve the notion of a *truth-value* for a sentence as a whole. In summing up the main point of these moves, Frege asks us to consider "how closely that which is called a concept in logic is connected with what we call a function. Indeed, we may say at once: a concept is a function whose value is always a truth-value."[20]

Let us follow Frege as he makes these important moves, and as he extends in various directions the notions of 'function', 'argument', and 'value' from their normal mathematical uses.

One such extension is to think of objects of all sorts as the arguments of some function; they need not be restricted to numbers. For example, let us consider, in ordinary language, the way in which we refer to the capital of a country, state, or province. Consider the expression whose general form is 'The capital of _____', where the blank indicates we may substitute the name of some particular political unit—'The United States', 'France', 'The State of Maryland', 'The Province of Ontario', and so on. The incomplete expression 'The capital of _____' represents the common feature, the invariant form, in which we may put a name in the blank space. The expression 'The capital of _____' may thus be regarded as a *function;* in the present case the expression serves as a *descriptive function.* In the blank space of this descriptive function—its argument place—one may put the name for an individual political unit ('The United States', 'France'). By itself, the functional expression 'The capital of _____' does not represent a particular political entity (object). Once we substitute in the appropriate argument-place of this descriptive function the name of a political entity, we can then treat the resultant expression (the combination of the descriptive functional expression and the name in the argument-place) as an expression that designates a particular object or entity—this time (usually) a particular city. Thus when we put in the argument-place for the descriptive function 'The capital of _____' the name 'the United States', we have the complete expression 'The capital of the United States', and *this* linguistic expression has as its *value* the city Washington, D.C. Similarly, the value of the descriptive function 'The capital of _____' for the argument 'France' is Paris, and so on. The inter-related ideas of 'argument', 'function', and 'value' can now serve, by this mode of extension, beyond their purely mathematical uses, to represent types of objects other than numbers, types of functional connections other than numerical ones. Thus, in our example, the function is descriptive (specifically of a political area) and the objects that serve as arguments or as values for this function are political units, geographical regions, social units of one sort or another (countries, states, cities). Other examples of descriptive functions would be 'the child of_____', 'the wealthiest man in_____', and so on.

   Let us now follow Frege as he further extends the use of the model of 'function', 'argument', and 'value' to deal with other types of linguistic expressions beyond the purely mathematical cases. One such important extension has to do with the way we can examine *entire sentences* when used to make assertions. Consider the sentence 'Socrates is a philosopher'. Frege suggests that this sentence can be considered, for logical purposes, as made up of a functional part and an argument. One way of analyzing the sentence, in line with this suggestion, is to consider the expression '_____ is a philosopher', where we have put in place of the name 'Socrates' a blank (an 'argument-place') while retaining the rest of the sentence ('is a philosopher'). Having done this, we can treat the entire expression '_____ is a philosopher' as a function. Frege calls *this* kind of function a *concept.* The expression 'is a philosopher' stands for a concept. Instead of the name 'Socrates' we could, as Frege points out, use other names for individual objects—'Plato', 'Aristotle', '4', 'The Eiffel Tower', and so on. When we plug in the names of 'Socrates', 'Plato', and

'Aristotle' in the argument-place of this linguistic expression ('_____ is a philosopher') we obtain various complete sentences. For each of these resultant complete linguistic expressions (sentences) we can now ask whether it is *true* or *false*. Truth and Falsity are the possible *truth-values* for the sentence as a whole. For the sentence 'Socrates is a philosopher' we obtain the truth-value 'Truth' (and similarly for the complete sentences 'Plato is a philosopher', 'Aristotle is a philosopher'—where 'Plato' and 'Aristotle' are the expressions in the argument-places for the same concept (function), '_____ is a philosopher'.) For each of the aforementioned arguments (Socrates, Plato, Aristotle), with this function (concept) we obtain sentences whose truth-value is 'Truth'. However, when we put in the numeral '4' or the name 'The Eiffel Tower', we obtain sentences whose truth-value is 'The False' (or 'Falsity').

It is not only sentences in ordinary language that are either true or false. Frege points out that in mathematics we can regard equations as a whole as having truth-values. Thus algebraic equations make use of functional expressions and can receive arguments that make the entire equation true or false. Thus the equation '$x^2 = 4$' will be true for the arguments 2 and −2, and false for all other arguments.

The expression '_____ is a philosopher' is the incomplete or unsaturated part of a sentence which, when supplemented by the name or other designation for an object, yields a complete sentence whose truth-value can be determined. The unsaturated part ('_____ is a philosopher') Frege calls a *concept-word (Begriffswort)*. According to Frege, in order for the entire sentence to be capable of determination as true or false, the concept-word it contains must be given a clear and determinate meaning (sense), and the expressions used as argument-signs must designate some object, some individual entity. A concept-word is a linguistic expression; it stands for a concept; it serves as a predicate. However, a concept is, for Frege, something objective, not itself part of language. At the same time, a concept is not someone's idea, a mental occurrence or psychological event. In discussing concepts, one is not discussing a psychological phenomenon. That some object has a certain property—falls under a certain concept (as Frege would put it)—either is or is not the case, objectively. To say 'Socrates is a philosopher' is to say something about Socrates— that he has the property of being a philosopher, or falls under the concept 'philosopher'. It does not tell us anything about someone's—for example, the speaker's or hearer's—mental state. The *apprehension* of a concept is a psychological matter. However, the concept apprehended and the relations it bears to objects or other concepts is not a matter for psychological investigation.

What Frege calls a 'concept-word' *(Begriffswort)* takes the place of what, in the older logic or in a simple grammatical approach, would be called the *predicate* of the sentence. If we think of concept-words in Frege's sense as predicates, we must be careful to think of the term 'predicate' in the way he approaches the role of predicates in a perspicuous and logically correct restatement of the component parts of a sentence. A concept-word is a predicate, but many expressions that would have been considered predicates in the older logic are not so for Frege, and conversely what he assigns to a predicate role in his new logic would not have been recognized as such in the traditional logic or in simple 'surface' grammatical analyses.

To illustrate the foregoing points, let us consider some further examples of sentences taken from ordinary language, and see how Frege's new logic would handle the analysis of their internal structure. Take the sentence 'Brutus killed Caesar'. How shall we analyze it, in line with our broad reliance on the ideas of 'function', 'argument', and 'value'? To begin with, there are several equally legitimate ways of analyzing this sentence:

On one approach (and by way of analogy with our treatment of the sentence 'Socrates is a philosopher') we might say the functional part of this sentence is obtained if we put a blank space in place of the name 'Brutus'. In that case, we obtain the unsaturated expression

_____ killed Caesar.

If we adopt this approach, we would then say the expression 'killed Caesar' stands for the concept, and it may be completed by supplying a number of different argument-expressions. For some of these the entire sentence thus completed would be true, for others false. For the given sentence 'Brutus killed Caesar' the truth-value is Truth, whereas for the sentences 'Napoleon killed Caesar' or 'Antony killed Caesar' the truth-value is Falsity. Another characterization of this way of analyzing the original sentence would be to say that the concept-expression '_____ killed Caesar' is a *one-place predicate,* since there is only one blank space left in which to place an argument expression (name for an individual object). On the other hand, we might have approached the original sentence ('Brutus killed Caesar') in a slightly different way. We might have put a blank space where the name 'Caesar' occurs. We should then have 'Brutus killed _____'. And this too would be a functional expression, a way of expressing a concept, a one-place predicate. Except now, of course, the unsaturated concept expression is 'Brutus killed _____', whereas previously it was '_____ killed Caesar'. Once again, depending on what argument signs (names for objects, persons) we substitute in the blank space, we should get sentences that are either true or false. Notice that on this approach the expression 'Brutus killed _____' stands for a concept and so is a one-place *predicate,* even though for traditional grammar or classical logic the name 'Brutus' (by itself) would be treated as the *subject* of the sentence. What is the 'subject' and what the 'predicate', for Frege, cannot be determined by these ordinary grammatical criteria. Thus the first task would be to determine which expression, as unsaturated, can play the role of the predicate. Moreover, the two sentences 'Brutus killed Caesar' and 'Caesar was killed by Brutus', for logical purposes say the same thing (the difference between active and passive voices is irrelevant). Out of either of these sentences we could extract on one mode of analysis the concept expression '_____ killed Caesar' ('Caesar was killed by _____ '), *or* the completely different one-place predicate 'Brutus killed _____ ' ('_____ was killed by Brutus').

We might choose to analyze the predicate component (the unsaturated, functional part) of the sentence 'Brutus killed Caesar' in still another way. We could write the unsaturated part with *two* blank spaces, thus:

_____ killed _____ .

Here we would substitute argument names in each of the blanks. To make a complete sentence we have to fill in both blanks. We are at liberty to put in whatever names we choose—different ones, or even the same one in both blanks. Thus we could obtain:

Antony killed Napoleon.	(False)
Brutus killed Cassius.	(False)
Brutus killed Caesar.	(True)
Mark Antony killed Mark Antony.	(True)

The functional expression '_____ killed _____ ' is known as a two-place predicate.* (And obviously one could extend this terminology, as is done in modern logic, to identify many-place predicates.) On this approach, some relations such as 'killing', 'greater than', are two-place predicates; other relations such as '_____ gives _____ to _____ ' are three-place predicates, and so on.

In Frege's terminology the expression 'concept' is normally reserved for a one-place predicate, and he uses the expression 'relation' to

---

* The expression 'two-place predicate' in fact needs to be reserved, more strictly, for an expression that has argument places that receive *different* argument-signs; in our example, '*A* kills *B*', '*A*' and '*B*' would designate different persons. This would exclude a case such as our last example ('Mark Antony killed Mark Antony', i.e., cases of suicide) since for the statements of this form one substitutes the same argument-expression (the same proper name having the same reference) in the blanks. In this case, it is more accurate to regard such sentences as incorporating a *one-place* predicate, since one could always write such a sentence as 'Mark Antony killed himself', i.e., 'Mark Antony falls under the concept *commits suicide.*'

refer to a two-place predicate.* In a broader use of the term 'concept', we could say that a concept is the predicate part (whether one-place or many-place) of a sentence, and as such corresponds to the unsaturated part of the complete sentence.

When we have filled in the appropriate blank spaces in a one-place or many-place predicate, the resulting complete sentence is either true or false. Truth or falsity are the two possible truth-values of the thought expressed by a logically well-formed sentence. Another way of reading what truth or falsity amounts to is to say that for a sentence that is true as a whole, the predicate expression it contains is *true of* (or for false sentences, *false of*) the arguments of the sentence. For example, where we have the simple sentence 'Socrates is wise', we can say the predicate expression 'is wise' is *true of* (applies to) Socrates.

To summarize what has thus far been said about the use of concept-words: A concept-word is the predicative part of a sentence. As a predicate, a concept-word is to be understood in a logical rather than a psychological sense. It belongs to the use of language as analyzed and reconstructed to show its basic logical components. Frege does not use the term 'concept', as others do, to designate some part of the content of our mind, an image, or any other type of mental occurrence. Frege fre-

---

* If from a judgment-content which deals with an object a and an object b we subtract a and b, we obtain as remainder a relation-concept which is, accordingly, incomplete at two points. If from the proposition

'the Earth is more massive than the Moon'

we subtract 'the Earth', we obtain the concept 'more massive than the Moon'. If, alternatively, we subtract the object, 'the Moon', we get the concept 'less massive than the Earth'. But if we subtract them both at once, then we are left with a relation-concept, which taken by itself makes no [assertible] sense any more than a simple concept does: it has always to be completed in order to make up a judgment-content. There are, however, various different ways of completing it: instead of Earth and Moon I might, for example, put Sun and Earth; and it is just this fact that accounts for the possibility of the subtraction.

Each individual pair of correlated objects stands to the relation-concept much as an individual object stands to the concept under which it falls—we might call them the subject of the relation-concept. Only here the subject is a composite one. . . . The doctrine of relation-concepts is thus, like that of simple concepts, a part of pure logic. What is of interest to logic is not the special content of any particular relation, but only the logical form. And whatever can be asserted of this, is true analytically and known a priori. This is as true of relation-concepts as of other concepts.

Just as

'a falls under the concept F'

is the general form of a judgment-content which deals with an object a, so we can take

'a stands in relation ϕ to b'

as the general form of a judgment-content which deals with an object a and an object b.[21]

quently uses the term 'concept' in its narrower, special meaning, as synonymous with 'one-place predicate'. In this narrower use, 'concept' is differentiated from 'relation', since the latter expression is typically used by him to stand for a binary (two-place) predicate. In its broader use, we could extend the use of the term 'concept' to include all types of predicates, whether one-place (monadic, unary), or many-place (polyadic). A concept-word (or combination of concept-words) is incomplete or unsaturated. By itself it does not constitute an entire sentence. It can be joined, however, with the name (or names) of individual objects to yield a complete sentence. Such a complete sentence is either true or false; the predicate (concept) is either *true of* or *false of* (applies to or does not apply to) the objects of which it is predicated.

With these preliminary points in mind, let us proceed, with Frege, to amplify and refine the analysis of the distinction between concepts and objects so far presented.

As already remarked, a concept-word needs to be distinguished from those expressions, such as proper names, that designate individual objects. A concept-word (or predicative expression) is incomplete or unsaturated, whereas the expression designating an object is complete or saturated. It follows from this that the name for an object could never serve, as such and by itself, as the predicative part of a sentence.

Further, on Frege's analysis, the use of the word 'is' is not essential to marking the predicative part of a sentence. Although English contains the use of the word 'is', not all natural languages have equivalent words for 'is'.

Consider the sentences (Frege's example)

The morning star is Venus.

The morning star is a planet.

Although the word 'is' occurs in both sentences, it performs different roles in each. The first use of 'is' (in 'The morning star is Venus') marks the *identity* use of 'is'. The expressions 'the morning star' and 'Venus' that flank the word 'is' each designates the same object. Each expression serves as a *name* for an object. By itself, neither is predicative. In the sentence 'The morning star is a planet', the term 'is' is part of the predicate. The expression 'is a planet' stands for a *concept*. It is not a name for an object. The word 'is' (the copula) in this sentence is a sign of predication.

Go back to the sentence 'The morning star is Venus'. We said the word 'is' is here used in its *identity* rather than *predicative* sense. However, as Frege points out, it is possible to rewrite the sentence containing the identity use of 'is' so that it takes on a predicative form. For this purpose the sentence 'The morning star is Venus' would be written as

'The morning star *is no other than Venus*'. Now, however, the expression 'is no other than Venus' conveys a concept; it constitutes the predicate of the sentence. The name 'Venus' has been absorbed within the entire predicate ('is no other than Venus') and this predicate expression does *not* designate an individual object. Like all other predicates, it too is unsaturated. It represents a concept that could be used predicatively as a description (whether true or false) of any individual object. The word 'is' in the predicate 'is no other than Venus' is part of the entire predicative expression and so is a sign of predication. The predicative expression 'is no other than Venus' is still a *concept* even though only one object may fall under that concept.

In the identity use of 'is', the position of the two expressions 'The morning star' and 'Venus' is interchangeable or reversible. We have a meaningful and equally true (or equally false) statement by writing 'Venus is the morning star' or 'The morning star is Venus'. However, given the sentence

The morning star is a planet,

the expressions 'the morning star' and 'is a planet' are not interchangeable. (Let it be noted, by the way, that the sentence 'The morning star *is a planet*' is different from the sentence 'The morning star is *the planet Venus*'. The latter sentence employs the identity use of 'is', since the expression '*the* planet Venus' in Frege's usage is a *proper name* for a particular object.) The sentence 'The morning star is a planet' is not reversible since it makes use of the word 'is' in its predicative role.

The next point has to do with Frege's distinction between *falling under a concept* and *the marks of a concept*.

Consider once more the sentence

The morning star is a planet.

Following Frege, we say the expression 'the morning star' names an object, whereas the expression 'is a planet' is predicative and conveys a concept. Wherever we have a situation of this sort—where a sentence attaches a predicate expression to the name of an individual object—we can say *the object falls under the concept*. The notion of *falling under a concept* is Frege's way of expressing what is traditionally described by saying an individual (object) 'has a certain property', or (as some would interpret this) 'the universal (expressed by the predicate) is exemplified in the individual (subject)'. What is meant by the use of the phrase 'to fall under a concept' is that it holds for the relation between an individual object and a concept. It makes no sense, for example, on this stipulation of meaning to say that something or other falls under an object. It is only of *concepts* (as 'is wise', 'is a planet', 'is a square root') that one can say (truly or falsely) that some individual object falls under that concept.

Having made a sharp distinction between the use of names as standing for individual objects and concept-words (predicative expressions), Frege considers the possible objection to this distinction on the grounds that various concepts can serve as the subjects of a sentence, and not always, therefore, only in a predicative capacity. Take the sentence, for example,

All mammals have red blood.

Should we not say that in this sentence the *subject-concept* is 'all mammals', whereas the predicate is 'have red blood'? Frege points out that this would be a failure of sound logical analysis, whatever simple grammar or traditional logic says to the contrary. For the expression 'all mammals' is just as predicative in character in this sentence as is the expression 'have red blood'. He suggests that to show this we rewrite the foregoing sentence as

Whatever is a mammal has red blood

or

If anything is a mammal, then it has red blood.

In these restatements the genuine predicatve or conceptual nature of 'is a mammal' is brought out, and is seen to be on a par, logically, with 'has red blood'.

Let us consider next what is meant by speaking of 'the marks of a concept' as distinguished from the idea of 'falling under a concept'. Suppose an object a falls under the concept of P (i.e., as conventionally expressed, 'has the property P'). Let us assume that in addition to the property P, the same object has the properties $Q, R,$ and S (i.e., falls under the concepts $Q, R,$ and S. Then it is possible to combine the expressions 'Q' 'R' and 'S' and symbolize their conjunction by the concept-expression 'T'. We could then say that the object a has the property T, or, in Frege's terminology, 'falls under the concept T'. In this case, Q, R and S are not *properties* of T; rather, Q, R and S are *marks* of the complex concept T.

To take an example Frege gives:

Instead of saying:

'2 is a positive number' and
'2 is a whole number' and
'2 is less than 10'

we may also say

'2 is a positive whole number less than 10'.

Here

to be a positive number,
to be a whole number,
to be less than 10,

appear as properties of the object 2, and also as marks of the concept

positive whole number less than 10.

This is neither positive, nor a whole number, nor less than 10. It is indeed subordinate to the concept *whole number,* but does not fall under it.[22]

In other words, the *concept* 'positive whole number less than 10' does not have any of these component concepts (e.g., 'less than 10') as a *property* of the concept. Only the *marks* of the concept could be predicated, in our example, of the *individual object* 2.

Frege gives another example:

> If we say: 'a square is a rectangle in which the adjacent sides are equal', we define the concept *square* by specifying what properties a thing must have in order to fall under this concept. These properties I call 'characteristic marks' of the concept. But these characteristic marks of a concept, properly understood, are not the same as its properties. The concept *square* is not a rectangle; only such objects as may fall under this concept are rectangles, just as the concept *black cloth* is neither black nor a cloth.[23]

We may consider a further complication. We have thus far spoken of *objects,* of *objects falling under concepts,* of *the* (characteristic) *marks of concepts.* Recall, now, our original use of the mathematical model of function, argument, and value. This model was of help to form the logical distinctions among concept-words (in analogy with functions), names of objects (in analogy with arguments), and truth-values for entire sentences (in analogy with numerical values for functions supplied with arguments).

Frege now *extends* the logical idea of a concept by analogy with the way in which the mathematical idea of a function is used. There are in mathematics examples of functions whose arguments are numbers, and other functions whose arguments are *other functions.* Let us call those functions that take individual numbers as their arguments *first-order functions.* An example would be '$x^3 + 1$'—or better, '$(\ )^3 + 1$', where the gap-sign of the brackets stands for the function in which one can place various numerals, e.g., '2', '3', '7', and obtain a numerical value for each such substitution. Next, however, consider those types of mathematical function in which the arguments are *functions of the first order.* This is the case, for example, with the meaning of the *differential quotient* or the use of the *definite integral* in the calculus.* In the case of the definite integral, the first-order function is the *argument* for the operation of integration as a second-order function.

By analogy with the distinction between first-order and second-order functions in mathematics, Frege distinguishes different *levels* of con-

---

* The expression 'the limit, as n indefinitely increases, of $\phi(n)$' is an example of a second-order function. For the expression '$\phi(n)$, as n increases indefinitely' is a first-order function, whereas the expression 'the limit of $(\ )$' is a second-order function, which takes the first-order function, just mentioned, as one of its arguments.[24]

cepts. *First-level concepts* are those that take as their arguments individual objects—e.g., '_____ is wise'. We said individual objects—e.g., Socrates—fall under the concept 'wise'. Now form a *second-level concept* whose *arguments* are *first-level concepts,* but not individual objects. Take the sentence 'There are in fact people who are wise'. What this sentence asserts is that the *concept* 'is wise' is one that *has instances*. In this case the concept 'has instances' is a second-level concept that takes as its arguments first-level concepts. In the above example, the first-level concept that served as an argument for the second-level concept '_____ has instances' is the first-level concept 'is wise'. We should say this second-level predicative statement is true for this argument. However, if we had put in the place for a first-level concept the expression 'is a round square', then the sentence " 'Is a round square' *has instances*" would be false.* The second-level concept 'has instances' is false of (does not apply to) this first-level concept. A first-level concept can thus be related to a second-level concept insofar as the first-level concept *falls within* the second-level concept. So the relation of 'falling under' holds between an

---

* To the possible objection that the phrase 'round square' does not designate a proper first-level concept, since it expresses something self-contradictory, Frege would reply that this is not indeed a sound objection. He makes the following remark concerning concepts like 'round square', 'wooden iron', and 'not identical with itself':

> Now I believe that these old friends are not so black as they are painted. To be of any use is, I admit, the last thing we should expect of them; but at the same time, they cannot do any harm, if only we do not assume that there is anything which falls under them—and to that we are not committed by merely using them. That a concept contains a contradiction is not always obvious without investigation; but to investigate it we must first possess it and, in logic, treat it just like any other. All that can be demanded of a concept from the point of view of logic and with an eye to rigour of proof is only that its boundaries should be sharp, so that we can decide definitely about every object whether it falls under that concept or not. But this demand is completely satisfied by concepts which, like 'not identical with itself', contains a contradiction; for of every object we know that it does not fall under any such concept.[25]

Frege points out, at the same time, that while there are no logical objections to the use of a concept that is self-contradictory, it is an altogether different matter if one makes use of a self-contradictory concept as part of an expression that purports to describe a particular object. He writes:

> The definition of an object in terms of a concept under which it falls is a very different matter. For example, the expression 'the largest proper fraction' has no content, since the definite article claims to refer to a definite object. On the other hand, the concept 'fraction smaller than 1 and such that no fraction smaller than one exceeds it in magnitude' is quite unexceptionable: in order, indeed, to prove that there exists no such fraction, we must make use of just this concept, despite its containing a contradiction. If, however, we wished to use this concept for defining an object falling under it, it would, of course, be necessary first to show two distinct things:
> 1. that some object falls under this concept;
> 2. that only one object falls under it.

Now since the first of these propositions, not to mention the second, is false, it follows that the expression 'the largest proper fraction' is senseless.[26]

object and a first-level concept, and an analogous relation of 'falling within' holds between a first-level concept and a second-level concept.

It is important not to confuse the 'falling within' relation that holds between a first-level and a second-level concept and the species-genus relation. Thus the concept 'cows' is a species of the genus (concept) 'bovine'. For Frege, the relation between cows and bovine, as a species-genus relation, is a relation between concepts *both* of which are first-level. One could with equally logical correctness say 'Bossie is a cow' as well as 'Bossie is bovine'. However, where a concept is second-level, one could never use such a second-level concept expression to describe a property of an individual object (such as Bossie). One could use a second-level predicate only as applying to first-level concepts.

Similarly, the relation we previously considered, of the characteristic marks of a complex concept and the complex concept itself, has to do with concepts all of which are on the *same level,* not with concepts on one level and those on another level. Thus, as in our earlier example, the relation of the concept 'positive number', as a mark of the complex concept 'positive whole number less than 10' to that complex concept is a relation between concepts of the same level. It is not the case, in Frege's terminology, that the concept 'positive number' *falls within* the concept 'positive whole number less than 10'. It is not a *property* of the latter concept.

Instantiation is one example, among others, of this relation of 'falling within' between a first-level concept and a second-level concept. It should be noted that it would make no sense to say that an individual object falls under a second-level concept. For example, it makes no sense to say 'Socrates has instances'. The importance for Frege of this general distinction between first-level and second-level concepts is that the analysis of the concepts of *number* and *existence* is illuminated by this distinction, since on his approach what we mean by 'number' and 'existence' require the use of *second-level* concepts.

For Frege, the analysis of statements involving expressions for numbers, when these expressions are used adjectivally—e.g., 'four horses', 'zero moons'—requires the notion of 'falling within a concept'. He writes:

[A] statement of number contains an assertion about a concept. This is perhaps clearest with the number 0. If I say 'Venus has 0 moons', there simply does not exist any moon or agglomeration of moons for anything to be asserted of; but what happens is that a property is assigned to the *concept* 'moon of Venus', namely that of including nothing under it. If I say 'the King's carriage is drawn by four horses', then I assign the number four to the concept 'horse that draws the King's carriage'.[27]

(Here, incidentally, is the basis for the remark made at an earlier stage of our discussion that the logical status of the adjectival expressions 'black horses' and 'four horses' is different. For the use of the adjective 'four' involves the use of a *second-level* concept, whereas the use of the adjective 'black' is a *mark* of the *first-level* concept 'black horse'.)

Another example of the use of a second-level predicate is to be found in a sentence such as the following (which plays an important role in Frege's analysis of the concept of number):

There are just as many ϕ's as ψ's.

Here, let the letters 'ϕ' and 'ψ' stand for first-level predicates. The sentence makes use of the second-level relational expression 'just as many ____ as ____' where the argument-places take first-level concepts as their arguments.[28]

Existence, for Frege, requires the use of a second-level concept. The concept of existence, he would say, expresses essentially the idea that a first-level concept does have instances. To say that cows exist and mermaids do not exist is to say that there are instances to be found of the first-level concept 'cows', whereas no such instances can be found for the concept 'mermaids'. Accordingly it makes no sense to say that an *individual object exists,* for 'exists' is a second-level predicate that can only apply to a first-level concept. It cannot meaningfully be predicated of an individual object, to which only first-level predicates apply. This is Frege's way of supporting the traditional dictum that 'existence is not a predicate'—that existence cannot be a property of any object. Since existence is a second-level property of first-level *concepts,* it cannot be considered a property of any individual *object* that falls under a first-level concept. Frege thus agrees with some of the traditional criticisms of the ontological argument for the existence of God. For that type of argument presupposes that existence is a property that necessarily belongs to a special entity—the supreme being, God.

In this respect existence is analogous to number. Affirmation of existence is in fact nothing but denial of the number nought. Because existence is a property of concepts the ontological argument for the existence of God breaks down.[29]

Since for Frege 'existence' means 'instantiation' (or 'exists' means 'has instances'), when used in connection with first-level concepts, it would be an error to say that concepts exist if by that we intend to make an ontological remark that concepts are some special kind of *object.* Concepts, in Frege's view, are not like Platonic Forms—special types of 'objects'. We should not debate whether they have 'existence' or not—as in the traditional controversies between nominalists and realists. For concepts are not objects—not even abstract ones. And if existence has to do with a property of a *concept,* then the whole question as to whether there are such special types of *objects* as Forms or universals is misconceived. All that could be meant by saying that this or that specific first-level concept exists is that it has instances. And this is objectively true or not; the statement that a particular first-level concept is instantiated is itself either true or false. Such objectivity of instantiation is all that Frege means by 'existence', when the latter expression is used in connection with first-level concepts. Thus a second-level 'existence' statement (an instantiation claim) is objectively warranted if a certain first-level concept is found to be instantiated. It does not mean that this statement, if true, makes any reference to some special kind of object. Since there can be no such 'object' as the referent of a concept, it makes no sense to debate whether such an 'object' *exists*.[30]

The use of ordinary (natural) language, with its lack of any explicit recognition of the logical distinction among levels of predicates, frequently leads to confusions, puzzlements, or downright mistakes that could be avoided if we kept in mind the kind of distinction just examined. Consider, for example, the sentence

> Albert Einstein is out of the ordinary.

The expression 'out of the ordinary' looks as if it is a first-level predicate that describes Albert Einstein, just as would be the case with the use of the predicate 'a mathematician' in the sentence

> Albert Einstein is a mathematician.

From a simple, ordinary grammatical point of view, both expressions ('out of the ordinary' and 'a mathematician') would be regarded as offering descriptions of Albert Einstein. Yet this would be an error. For the expression 'out of the ordinary' is a second-level concept. When analyzed, it says something like the following:

> There are very few instances, in general, to be found among other human beings, of the combination of properties (first-level predicates) that are true of Albert Einstein.

The sentence says something *not* about Albert Einstein (as is the case with the sentence 'Albert Einstein is a mathematician') but about the first-level *predicates* used to describe Albert Einstein.

As a final example and application of the foregoing distinctions, we consider the important advance in logic that Frege accomplished (as did Peirce) by introducing the notion of *quantifiers*. By means of this type of expression, and the techniques for its use, it becomes possible for the first time to deal effectively with the notion of *generality*.

According to traditional logic, sentences such as

> All cows are herbivorous

> Some metals are good conductors

involve the use of two basic types of terms—a subject term and a predicate term. In the first sentence (classified as exhibiting a universal affirmative categorical proposition, an 'A' type) the subject term is 'cows' and the predicate term is 'herbivorous'. In the second sentence (classified as belonging to the particular affirmative, 'I' type of proposition), the subject term is 'metals' and the predicate term is 'good conductors'.

Frege pointed out that the expression 'cows', as used in the first sentence, plays a *predicative* role just as much as does the expression 'herbivorous'. For when rewritten, what the first sentence says is 'Whatever *is a cow is also herbivorous*'; 'is a cow' and 'is herbivorous' are both predicative. The term 'whatever' can be taken as standing for the *universal quantifier* and is to be distinguished from both predicative expressions ('is a cow' and 'is herbivorous'). In effect what the universal quantifier does is to perform the role of a *second-level concept*. It conveys the meaning, in this sentence, that any instance (object) that falls under the first-level concept 'cows' will also be found among the instances that fall under the concept 'herbivorous'.

In a similar fashion, the sentence

Some metals are good conductors

can be analyzed as involving the use of a *particular quantifier*. Again the term 'metals' plays a conceptual (predicative) role just as much as does the phrase 'good conductors'. The role of the particular quantifier is to convey the sense that *there are instances* of the concept formed by conjoining the properties 'metals' and 'good conductors'. The particular quantifier is thus a second-level concept that can be read as 'there are instances of _____', whose argument place is filled by expressions for a first-level concept. As second-level concepts, both the universal and particular quantifiers must therefore be distinguished from first-level predicates. Nor does either type of quantifier form part of a 'subject term', for there is no longer, on this analysis, any need for the use of the notion of a 'subject term' as this was understood in classical logic.*

* It is important to distinguish the sense in which Frege separates *first and second-level concepts* from the standard distinction, recognized in contemporary logic, between *first-order and second-order generalizations*. A first-order generalization is one in which the bound variables take, as substitutions (arguments) for the variables, names for individual objects, whereas in higher order generalizations the substitutions for the bound variables may be expressions other than those for individual objects. Thus consider a first-order generalization such as 'Some men are wise'. Let 'x' range over individuals; let 'M' stand for the predicate (first-level concept) 'men'; let 'W' stand for the predicate 'wise'; let '$\exists$' stand for the particular quantifier. Then 'Some men are wise' would be written as

$$(\exists x) : x \, M \cdot x \, W$$

This is a first-order generalization, since the possible substitutions for x can only be names for individuals. On the other hand, the predicate expressions 'M' and 'W', on Frege's analysis, are *first-level concepts,* since they can apply only to individuals. However, for Frege, the quantifier '$\exists$' is to be understood as standing for a *second-level concept*. It expresses the fact (if the entire statement is true) that *there are instances of M and W*.

Thus, combining the Fregean approach which makes the distinction between first- and second-level concepts, and the more recent, standard distinction between first-order and second-order generalizations, we could say that our sample sentence 'Some men are wise' states a first-order generalization in which are to be found a second-level concept (the particular quantifier), first-level concepts ('men' and 'wise'), and a variable ('x') serving as an argument-place in which one can put as substitutions the names for individual objects.

Sentences of the kind we have just been considering, since they do not involve the explicit use of names for individual objects, are known as *general* statements. In exhibiting their formal structure it is necessary to make use of *quantifiers* to bind variables. On the other hand, a sentence such as 'Socrates is wise' makes use explicitly of a proper name to designate an individual object (the person Socrates). One doesn't need the use of quantifiers (whether universal or particular) in formulating the logical structure of this type of sentence, since it is not a general statement.

The use of quantifiers is of great importance in all schemes of modern logic, as Frege first showed. They permit the analysis of complex general propositions that were beyond the power of such tools as traditional Aristotelian logic was able to employ. This is especially the case where a sentence involves multiple generality. Such sentences may involve complicated nested interrelations among several different variables, with different scopes, and would require, therefore, differently quantified variables and a notation that makes these interrelations clear. An example of such a sentence would be, 'Every president of the United States has some strong supporters among all those who are members of some religious sects'.

The following quotations from Frege will serve as a review and summary of a number of the points we have been considering in connection with the basic distinction between concepts and objects:

First of all, I must emphasize the radical difference between concepts and objects, which is of such a nature that a concept can never substitute for an object, or an object for a concept. . . . The nature of concepts can be characterized by the fact that they are said to have a predicative nature. An object can never be predicated of anything. When I say, 'The Evening Star is Venus', then I predicate not Venus, but *coinciding with Venus*. Linguistically, proper names correspond to objects, concept-words *(nomina appellativa)* to concepts. However, the sharpness of this distinction is somewhat blurred in ordinary language by the fact that what originally were proper names (e.g., 'Moon') can become concept-words, and what originally were concept-words (e.g. 'god') can become proper names. Concept-words occur with the indefinite article, with words like 'all', 'some', 'many', etc . . . Now between objects and (first-level) concepts there obtains a relation of subsumption: an object falls under a concept. For example, Jena is a university town. Concepts are generally composed of component-concepts—the characteristics. *Black silken cloth* has the characteristics *black, silken,* and *cloth.* An object falling under this concept has these characteristics as its properties. What is a characteristic with respect to a concept is a property of an object falling under that concept. Quite distinct from this relation of subsumption is that of the subordination of a first-level concept under a first-level concept, as in 'All squares are rectangles'. The *characteristics* of the superordinate concept (rectangle) are also *characteristics* of the subordinate one (square). When I say, 'There is at least one square root of 4', I am predicating something not of 2 or −2, but of the concept *square root of 4.* Neither am I giving a characteristic of this concept; rather, this concept must already be completely known. I am not singling out any components of this concept, but am stating a certain composition of the concept in virtue of which it differs for example from the concept *even prime number greater than 2*. I compare the individual characteristics of a concept to the stones constituting a house; I compare what is predicated in our proposition to a property of the house, e.g. its spaciousness. Here, too, something is predicated; not, however, a first-level concept, but a concept of the second level. *Square root of 4* relates to there-is-existence in a very similar way in which Jena relates to *university town*. Here we have a relation between concepts; not, however, a relation between first-level concepts, as in the case of subordination, but a relation of a first-level concept to a second-level concept, which is similar to the subsumption of an object under a first-level concept. The first-level concept here plays a role similar to that of an object in the case of subsumption. Here, too, one could speak of subsumption; but this relation, although indeed similar, nevertheless is not the same as that of the subsumption of an object under a first-level concept. I shall say that a first-level concept falls (not under, but) within a second-level concept. The distinction be-tween concepts of the first and second levels is just as sharp as that between objects and concepts of the first level; for objects can never substitute for con-cepts. Therefore an object can never fall under a second-level concept; such would be not false but nonsensical. If one tried something like this linguistically, one would get neither a true nor a false thought, but no thought at all. . . . A different feature of first-level concepts is expressed by the proposition that if an object falls under such a concept, another object distinct from the preceding one also falls under it. Here we have a second concept of the second level. From both, as second-level characteristics, we can form a third second-level concept within which fall all those first-level concepts under which fall at least two distinct ob-jects. The concepts *prime number, planet,* and *human being* would be such as fall within this second-level concept.[31]

Another useful summary statement of some central points concerning concepts and objects is the following excerpt from *The Foundations of Arithmetic:*

That a statement of number should express something factual independent of our way of regarding things can surprise only those who think a concept is something subjective like an idea. But this is a mistaken view. If, for example, we bring the concept of body under that of what has weight, or the concept of whale under that of mammal, we are asserting something objective; but if the concepts themselves were subjective, then the subordination of one to the other, being a relation between them, would be subjective too, just as a relation between ideas is. It is true that at first sight the proposition

'All whales are mammals'

seems to be not about concepts but about animals; but if we ask which animal then are we speaking of, we are unable to point to any one in particular. Even suppos-ing a whale is before us, our proposition still does not state anything about it. We cannot infer from it that the animal before us is a mammal without the additional premiss that it is a whale, as to which our proposition says nothing. As a general principle, it is impossible to speak of an object without in some way designating or naming it; but the word 'whale' is not a name for any individual creature. If it be replied that what we are speaking of is not, indeed, an individual definite object, but nevertheless an indefinite object, I suspect that 'indefinite object' is only another term for concept, and a poorer, more contradictory one at that. However true it may be that our proposition can only be verified by observing particular animals, that proves nothing as to its content; to decide what it is about, we do not need to know whether it is true or not, nor for what reasons we believe it to be true. If, then, a concept is something objective, an assertion about a concept can for its part contain something factual.

....

The business of a general term is precisely to signify a concept. Only when conjoined with the definite article or a demonstrative pronoun can it be counted as the proper name of a thing, but in that case it ceases to count as a general term. The name of a thing is a proper name. An object, again, is not found more than once, but rather, more than one object falls under the same concept. . . . A concept does not cease to be a concept simply because only one single thing falls under it, which thing, accordingly, is completely determined by it. It is to concepts of just this kind (for example, satellite of the Earth) that the number 1 belongs, which is a number in the same sense as 2 and 3. With a concept the question is always whether anything, and if so what, falls under it. With a proper name such questions make no sense. We should not be deceived by the fact that language makes use of proper names, for instance Moon, as general terms, and vice versa; this does not affect the distinction between the two. As soon as a word is used with the indefinite article or in the plural without any article, it is a general term.[32]

SENSE AND REFERENCE

In his work as a philosopher and logician, Frege constantly stresses the indissoluble link between thought and language. For him it is of crucial importance to examine the role that language plays in expressing and communicating thought, both in order to see what the actual resources of language are and how, under the guidance of critical logic, we may clarify and bring into the open an improved apparatus for using language to serve our cognitive interests. The use of language to give us *truth* about the world dominated and preoccupied Frege's approach to language. Logic, for him, is the tool by which we can best serve that interest.

We have thus far examined a number of topics that figure prominently in Frege's contributions to such logical studies. We have focused our attention on the basic distinction between concepts and objects—between concept-words and proper names. As contributing to the clarification and refinement of this basic distinction, we have followed Frege as he explores such subsidiary topics as the idea of 'falling under a concept', the analogy between function and concept, the distinction between first-level and second-level concepts, the role of quantifiers in expressing generality, the direction we might follow in exploring the use of terms such as 'existence' and 'number', and various other matters.

It is worth repeating that for Frege these or other distinctions that logic works out contribute to our underlying interest in *truth*. They provide us with various rules and criteria by which we can formulate, from the point of view of logic, our specifications of those conditions under which some sentences are true, others false. In furtherance of this overriding interest in truth, there is another aspect of Frege's work as a logician and philosopher of language that remains to be discussed. It has to do with what we may call, in a broad use of the term, his *theory of meaning*. It is not the case, of course, that in exploring up to now the basic distinction between concepts and objects we have ignored the question of meaning. On the contrary, in making clear the various distinctions among the different kinds of linguistic expression we have been examining, we could not avoid their different roles and 'kinds of meaning'. We studied the different ways in which they contribute to the construction of logically well-formed sentences and the way in which such sentences themselves are interrelated in various types of arguments. Still, another side of Frege's important work as a philosopher of language and philosophical logician, is the working out explicitly of the various meanings of 'meaning' itself. What he has to say here, especially as it relates to the basic distinction between *sense* and *reference,* is of the highest importance. This is the case from the point of view of understanding the internal structure of his own philosophy, as well as in terms of appreciating the influence his analysis has had on subsequent writings in the analytic, post-Fregean tradition. Since the basic distinction between sense and reference, as aspects of 'meaning', has a fundamental relevance to an overriding interest in the truth, it may be summed up by saying that the distinction has to do with making clear certain *truth-conditions* in our use of language. These truth-conditions need to be discriminated and satisfied in a logically controlled use of language.

The basic distinction between sense and reference was first worked out in Frege's classic paper *"Über Sinn und Bedeutung"* (1892) and subsequently employed by him in all his writings. Let us turn, then to an examination of the statement of this distinction as Frege presents it in that paper.

EQUALITY* gives rise to challenging questions which are not altogether easy to answer. Is it a relation? A relation between objects, or between names or signs of objects? In my *Begriffsschrift* I assumed the latter. The reasons which seem to favour this are the following: $a = a$ and $a = b$ are obviously statements of differing cognitive value; $a = a$ holds a priori and, according to Kant, is to be labelled analytic, while statements of the form $a = b$ often contain very valuable extensions of our knowledge and cannot always be established a priori. The

* I use this word strictly and understand '$a = b$' to have the sense of 'a is the same as b' or 'a and b coincide'.

discovery that the rising sun is not new every morning, but always the same, was one of the most fertile astronomical discoveries. Even to-day the identification of a small planet or a comet is not always a matter of course. Now if we were to regard equality as a relation between that which the names '*a*' and '*b*' designate, it would seem that $a = b$ could not differ from $a = a$ (i.e. provided $a = b$ is true). A relation would thereby be expressed of a thing to itself, and indeed one in which each thing stands to itself, but to no other thing. What is intended to be said by $a = b$ seems to be that the signs or names '*a*' and '*b*' designate the same thing, so that those signs themselves would be under discussion; a relation between them would be asserted. But this relation would hold between the names or signs only in so far as they named or designated something. It would be mediated by the connexion of each of the two signs with the same designated thing. But this is arbitrary. Nobody can be forbidden to use any arbitrarily producible event or object as sign for something. In that case the sentence $a = b$ would no longer refer to the subject matter, but only to its mode of designation; we would express no proper knowledge by its means. But in many cases this is just what we want to do. If the sign '*a*' is distinguished from the sign '*b*' only as object (here, by means of its shape), not as sign (i.e. not by the manner in which it designates something), the cognitive value of $a = a$ becomes essentially equal to that of $a = b$, provided $a = b$ is true. A difference can arise only if the difference between the signs corresponds to a difference in the mode of presentation of that which is designated. Let a, b, c be the lines connecting the vertices of a triangle with the midpoints of the opposite sides. The point of intersection of a and b is then the same as the point of intersection b and c. So we have different designations for the same point, and these names ('point of intersection of a and b', 'point of intersection of b and c') likewise indicate the mode of presentation; and hence the statement contains actual knowledge.

It is natural, now, to think of there being connected with a sign (name, combination of words, letter), besides that to which the sign refers which may be called the reference of the sign, also what I should like to call the *sense* of the sign, wherein the mode of presentation is contained. In our example, accordingly, the reference of the expressions 'the point of intersection of a and b' and 'the point of intersection of b and c' would be the same, but not their senses. The reference of 'evening star' would be the same as that of 'morning star', but not the sense.

It is clear from the context that by 'sign' and 'name' I have here understood any designation representing a proper name, which thus has as its reference a definite object (this word taken in the widest range), but not a concept or a relation, which shall be discussed further in another article. The designation of a single object can also consist of several words or other signs. For brevity, let every such designation be called a proper name.

The sense of a proper name is grasped by everybody who is sufficiently familiar with the language or totality of designations to which it belongs;† but this

---

† In the case of an actual proper name such as 'Aristotle' opinions as to the sense may differ. It might, for instance, be taken to be the following: the pupil of Plato and teacher of Alexander the Great. Anybody who does this will attach another sense to the sentence 'Aristotle was born in Stagira' than will a man who takes as the sense of the name: the teacher of Alexander the Great who was born in Stagira. So long as the reference remains the same, such variations of sense may be tolerated, although they are to be avoided in the theoretical structure of a demonstrative science and ought not to occur in a perfect language.

serves to illuminate only a single aspect of the reference, supposing it to have one. Comprehensive knowledge of the reference would require us to be able to say immediately whether any given sense belongs to it. To such knowledge we never attain.

The regular connexion between a sign, its sense, and its reference is of such a kind that to the sign there corresponds a definite sense and to that in turn a definite reference, while to a given reference (an object) there does not belong only a single sign. The same sense has different expressions in different languages or even in the same language. To be sure, exceptions to this regular behaviour occur. To every expression belonging to a complete totality of signs, there should certainly correspond a definite sense; but natural languages often do not satisfy this condition, and one must be content if the same word has the same sense in the same context. It may perhaps be granted that every grammatically well-formed expression representing a proper name always has a sense. But this is not to say that to the sense there also corresponds a reference. The words 'the celestial body most distant from the Earth' have a sense, but it is very doubtful if they also have a reference. The expression 'the least rapidly convergent series' has a sense; but it is known to have no reference, since for every given convergent series, another convergent, but less rapidly convergent, series can be found. In grasping a sense, one is not certainly assured of a reference.[33]

In the opening paragraph of the above passage, Frege makes it clear that his initial motive for introducing the distinction between sense and reference is that he might use that distinction in helping to solve the philosophic problem of how to correctly analyze certain types of identity statements. Frege will show that the reason for his earlier failure to deal successfully with these identity statements is that he failed to make the necessary distinction between sense and reference. Once made, the distinction has wider uses, for the distinction will clarify something of general importance in dealing with any form of linguistic expression employed for cognitive purposes. It will apply to types of sentences other than identity statements. It will apply not only to sentences taken as a whole, but to the constituents of sentences. While initially the distinction will be worked out in connection with his paradigm example—that of proper names—it will hold for concept-words as well. In short, not only names have their sense and reference; other constituent parts of well-formed sentences have their sense and reference too; and not only the constituent parts of sentences have sense and reference, but sentences as well, as wholes, have their sense and reference, and the sense of the constituent parts of sentences help determine the sense of the sentence as a whole. Frege will show that not only does the distinction between sense and reference have these multiple applications to different units of linguistic expression, it also serves to clarify the logical analysis to be given to the differences between direct and indirect speech.

In what follows we shall begin, as Frege does, by examining the question of what analysis to give to certain types of identity statements.

We shall then follow Frege in focusing our attention on the way in which the distinction between sense and reference appears in its clearest form in connection with proper names, and then turn briefly to the application of the distinction beyond these primary examples.

An identity statement (what Frege, in the first sentence of the passage quoted earlier, calls an 'equality') is of the general form '*a* = *b*'. It can be read as '*a* is the same as *b*' or '*a* and *b* coincide'. The problem is how to analyze such identity statements. What are their distinctive features? What logical roles are played by their several components?

The first question that may be asked has to do with how to understand the role of the identity (equality) sign, ' = ', translated as 'is the same as' (or 'coincides with'). It obviously expresses a *relation* of some sort—but between what? As it stands, the identity sign is an example of an incomplete or unsaturated expression. It needs to be completed by appropriate expressions which, together with the identity expression, will yield a complete sentence. The question Frege considers is this: If the identity sign ' = ' (or the words that translate it, 'is the same as') has to do with a special relation of some sort, then we must ask about what, between what, or as holding for what, does the identity relation have to do? This question is by no means a simple one. No quick, widely agreed-to answer is readily available. Frege tells us of his earlier attempts to answer this question and why he found these attempts to be unsatisfactory. He will then offer an answer that is superior to his earlier theories as well as to those of others. He identifies *two* such earlier (and now to be discarded) theories or attempted analyses of the nature of identity statements.

1. One possible answer to the question of what an identity statement asserts is this: Identity is a relation of *objects*. The general linguistic form of an identity statement makes use of an equality sign ' = ' flanked on either side by two other expressions. The expressions that flank the identity sign may be either the same or different. Thus '*a* = *a*' and '*a* = *b*' are both identity statements. If we take the identity relation as holding for *objects,* then one would interpret any identity statement, if true, as asserting that some object is the same as itself. If the object is designated by '*a*', then the statement '*a* = *a*' asserts that the *object* designated by '*a*' at the left of the identity sign is *the same object* as the object designated by the '*a*' at the right of the identity sign. And in the case of the identity statement '*a* = *b*', this interpretation of what an identity statement asserts would be: The *object* designated by '*a*' at the left of the identity sign is the *the very same object* designated by '*b*' at the right of the identity sign. In either case ('*a* = *a*' or '*a* = *b*'), what the identity relation has to do with is the relation of any object to itself, namely that it is *itself*—it is the very same object—and not some other. Let us call this interpretation of the 'identity relation' *the objectual self-identity interpretation*. (This label is

mine, not Frege's). Frege says this interpretation *fails* to give a satisfactory analysis of identity statements. For (as we may interpret his reasons) one might be in complete agreement with the claim, in a general ontological context, that every object is self-identical. It is true that every object has a relation to itself of *self-identity;* no other object has that same relation to it. However, this interpretation does not help us to deal with an obvious and important difference in the logical status of the two distinct examples of identity statements, '$a = a$' and '$a = b$'. While both are admittedly identity statements, the second type of statement can convey a kind of information that the first does not. They differ in *cognitive status.* The second kind of identity statement *('a = b')* may contain an important empirical *discovery*. That every object has a relation of self-identity to itself, while true, contains no special information; it contains no news. If every identity statement merely expressed the idea that every object has a relation of self-identity (and did not convey anything more than this fact), it would no doubt be a statement of an important ontological principle. But as such, this would not explain why it is that *some* identity statements give us more knowledge than this. They are genuinely informative and *add* to our knowledge over and above what we should accept on the basis of this broadly stated ontological principle about the self-identity of all objects. Frege's problem is how to explain what makes it possible for there to be such informative identity statements. And so, whatever our readiness to accept the general ontological thesis that an object is identical with itself (or has the relation of self-identity), this principle does not help explain the difference in cognitive status between '$a = a$' and '$a = b$'. The *objectual self-identity interpretation* of identity statements cannot suffice as a satisfactory analysis of identity statements. There is evidently something more to the analysis of an identity statement that we must take account of than a purely objectual or ontological analysis seems to provide.

2. Frege turns, next, therefore, to a second possible analysis of identity statements. And this time it is a theory he had defended in his earlier writings, specifically the *Begriffsschrift* (§8). This interpretation approaches the question of the identity relation not (as did the first interpretation) as having to do with the relation of an object to itself (self-identity), but rather as having to do with some special *relation between two names* insofar as they serve as signs for some object. The identity relation is a *sign relation,* not a purely *ontological* matter. As Frege points out, "What is intended to be said by $a = b$ seems to be that the signs or names 'a' and 'b' designate the same thing, so that those signs themselves would be under discussion, a relation between them would be asserted."

However, Frege finds fault with this theory as well, even though, in some respects, it is an advance over the first theory. It is an advance insofar as it stresses the need to bring in the connection (relation) between the signs, as essential to understanding the identity relation. One cannot get a satisfactory analysis of this relation by remaining exclusively on the ontological side, on the side of the object itself. If it is an identity *statement* one is interested in examining, one must examine something about the *linguistic* means used. This will involve studying the relation of the linguistic signs to each other, and the relation these signs have to the objects which in some way they signify. To realize even this much is an advance over the first approach. However, as we shall see, Frege will argue that it is not yet a complete answer because as a means of examining the identity relation insofar as this has to do with the relation between the sign and the thing signified, it fails to fasten on what is important in this part of the sign-relation as expressed by the identity statement. (What it fails to take into account, as we shall see, is the distinction between *sense* and *reference* in the way a sign functions.)

Consider the identity statement whose form is '$a = b$'. Let us assume that what is involved in the identity relation is that the sign 'a' and the sign 'b' are related by the identity relation to each other because each, independently, designates or refers to one and the same object. What we need, on the present interpretation, is that the following conditions be satisfied in order for the identity relation to hold: (1) there are signs that are readily distinguishable from one another in terms of their own physical properties—e.g., shape or sound—and serving, by virtue of these properties, as signs; (2) an object with which each sign is correlated; (3) the signs, though different from each other, refer to the same object. For the sake of having a label for this view, although Frege himself does not use it, let me call this the *pure reference* interpretation of the identity relation.

There is no requirement, on this pure reference approach, that the sign itself give us any information about the object. It is enough if both signs refer to the same object. It is enough if every sign have certain physical properties of its own by means of which it can be distinguished from another sign having the same reference. However, the properties of the sign need not be taken as giving us any information about the object to which it refers. One example of the identity statement '$a = b$' would be 'VII = 7'; another would be 'Tully = Cicero'. In the first case, though the numerical expressions 'VII' and '7' have different physical properties (e.g., shapes) they refer to the same object, i.e., the same number. Similarly, while the names 'Tully' and 'Cicero' differ as signs in terms of sound and lettering, they refer to the same person. Each sign, on this view, can thus be arbitrarily chosen in terms of its own physical properties. What the identity statement '$a = b$' tells us is the fact that two such arbitrarily chosen signs nevertheless refer to the same object. However the statement '*a* = *b*' need not give us any knowledge about the object co-referred to by '*a*' and '*b*'. Thus the statement '*a* = *b*' need not give us any more information or knowledge about the object than is contained in the statement '*a* = *a*.' The statement '*a* = *b*' would be known to be true, just as we know '*a* = *a*' is true. For if all that is involved in knowing that *a* = *b* is that the sign '*a*' refers to some object, and the sign '*b*' refers to some object, and the sign '=' means '*has the same referent as*', then the entire statement '*a* = *b*' is true *by virtue of this definition*.

Yet the fact remains, Frege argues, that the identity statement '*a* = *b*' is sometimes informative and is not known to be true merely in virtue of a definition. It gives us *knowledge about the object* referred to. And the information we get from an identity statement of the form '*a* = *b*' is not therefore simply exhausted by or reducible to the following items: (1) the material properties of the signs '*a*' and '*b*' are different; (2) there is an object, different from '*a*' and '*b*', of which '*a*' and '*b*' serve as signs; (3) one and the same object is being referred to by '*a*' and '*b*'. This kind or amount of knowledge is not enough to explain the fact that some identity statements themselves give us *additional knowledge (information) about the object* referred to by '*a*' and '*b*'. The identity statement ('*a* = *b*') that gives us such additional knowledge (knowledge which is now registered as a discovery) must evidently contain in its very statement some feature in the use of the signs '*a*' and '*b*' we have so far overlooked. It is this (so far) overlooked factor in the signs '*a*' and '*b*' that can yield knowledge about the object to which each refers. This missing element is what Frege's new theory will make explicit. It is what he calls the *sense* connected with the use of the sign in an identity statement. The pure-reference theory neglects to take into account this *sense* component in the use of a sign. It is the presence of the sense component, however, that explains the fact that some identity statements mark discoveries, and thereby register additions to our store of knowledge. The statement '*a* = *b*' can have cognitive value, he will argue, because the *senses* attached to the sign '*a*' and the sign '*b*' are *different*. Thus, if the senses of '*a*' and '*b*' were the same, '*a* = *b*' would not have any more cognitive value than '*a* = *a*'.

3. We turn, then, to the third theory of the identity-relation—one that Frege himself proposes in the paper *"Über Sinn und Bedeutung"*. This theory makes the crucial distinction between sense and reference in the use of a linguistic sign. It is necessary to take into account the presence of *both* factors in the use of a linguistic sign. In particular, by doing this, we shall understand, among other things, how certain identity statements can be informative and thus are not known to be true *a priori*.

What, then, does Frege mean by 'sense', and how is it different from reference in the use of a sign?

As a preparation for answering this question, let us pause to introduce, first, a clarification in our use of the term 'reference'. Let us distinguish between (1) *the relation of reference* and (2) *the referent*. Let us assume, by way of example, that we have a sign '*a*' that serves as a sign for some object *O*. We shall use the term 'reference' interchangeably with the terms 'designation', 'denotation', and 'standing for'. The sign '*a*' will be said to have a relation of reference to the object *O* when it designates, denotes, or stands for *O*. The sign is in the reference-relation to the object it designates. The object designated is the *referent* in the reference-relation. The sign (e.g., a proper name) is the linguistic sign in the reference-relation that refers to (designates, denotes, stands for) the object as referent.

Frege claims that in understanding the possibility of a reference-relation in which a sign refers to its referent, we should note *the sense* connected with the sign. The reference to the referent is not a wholly arbitrary or conventional matter. The reference-relation is established by virtue of the fact that there is a *sense* which belongs to the sign. Let us take some examples, first, of the sort of thing Frege means by 'sense'.

Consider the example Frege gives in the passage quoted.[34]

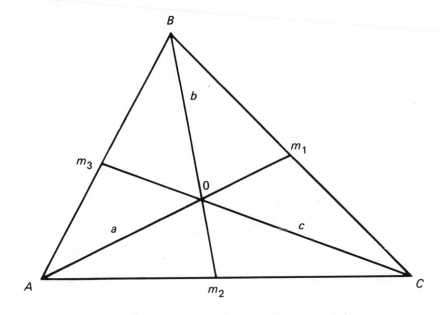

The line *a* joins the vertex *A* to the midpoint m_1; the line *b* joins the vertex *B* to the midpoint m_2; the line *c* joints the vertex *C* to the midpoint m_3. The phrase 'the point of intersection of lines *a* and *b*' can then be used as a linguistic means (a referring expression or proper name) to designate the point o. The point o is the referent of the referring expression 'the point of intersection of lines a and b.' Similarly, the expression 'the point of intersection of lines b and c' can be used as linguistic means (referring expression or proper name) to designate the point o. Point o is the referent of the referring expression 'the point of intersection of lines b and c'. The two referring expressions just introduced are different. One is: 'the point of intersection of lines a and b'; the other is: 'the point of intersection of lines b and c'. These two expressions are different because they have different *senses*. The *reference-relation* of the expression 'the point of intersection of lines a and b', has as its *referent* the point o. The sense of this first referring expression helps pick out (identify) as its referent the point o. Now consider the other referring expression, with its different sense ('the point of intersection of lines b and c'). It, too, helps us to pick out and identify as its referent the point o. We discover by these independent routes (by attending separately to the sense of each referring expression, first to one and then to other) that although the senses of both referring expressions are different from each other, they independently stand in the reference-relation to the *same referent*, the same o. This fact—this 'discovery'—can now be summed up in the statement: "The referring expression whose sense is 'the point of intersection of lines a and b' has the very same referent as the referring expression whose sense is 'the point of intersection of lines b and c'." This entire statement is an *identity statement*. It conveys an interesting and important discovery, an elementary truth, of the science of geometry.

Here is another famous example. The statement 'The Morning Star is the Evening Star' is an identity statement (the word 'is' expresses this identity relation). The expression 'The Morning Star' has a certain sense. By virtue of this sense, it tells us where and when to look for a certain heavenly body. The expression 'The Evening Star' has a *different* sense from that of the expression 'The Morning Star'. It tells us where and when to look for a certain heavenly body. Each, independently, and by virtue of its sense, serves as a referring device to pick out an object. The fact that the object thus picked out by each referring phrase, each having its own distinctive sense, nevertheless is the very same object—the planet Venus—was not always known. It represents an important astronomical discovery. It was not known *a priori*. Therefore the statement '$a = b$' (if taken to symbolize the sentence 'The Morning Star is the Evening Star') is not known *a priori* as would be the case with '$a = a$' (e.g., 'The Morning Star is the Morning Star').

One final example: 'The husband of Xanthippe is the teacher of Plato'. Here again, the same referent (the person Socrates) is referred to by two expressions, each of which has a different sense.

The sense of each referring expression offers a *mode of presentation* of its referent. The sense of an expression may serve as an item of information about, a description of, or a means of picking out the referent. It provides us, accordingly, with what may be called a *criterion of identification* for the object referred to by this means. Where we have different singular réferring expressions (proper names) each of which has its own sense, we have different criteria of identification for the same object. (Should the different senses be logically incompatible with each other, of course they could not then be used to describe properties of the same object. However, what may seem to be incompatible criteria of identification, may not in fact be logically incompatible. Thus the statement, 'The murderer of Mrs. Jones is the prisoner who is extremely devoted to helping injured birds' may be a true identity statement.)

The distinction between sense and reference clarifies the different ways in which we may approach the analysis of the term 'meaning' itself. For the preanalytic, rough use of the term 'meaning' can now be replaced by a number of distinctions in the use of the term. Thus we might mean by 'meaning' (1) the personal, subjective (and therefore variable) associations, images, or ideas an expression calls up in some mind; (2) the sense of the expression; (3) the referent of the expression. For Frege, only (2) and (3) are of relevance for logic and a scientific use of language. He rejects the relevance of subjective associations or ideas on the ground that they are inappropriate for the construction and use of a logically tight, scientific language.

The reference and sense of a sign are to be distinguished from the associated idea. If the reference of a sign is an object perceivable by the senses, my idea of it is an internal image, arising from memories of sense impressions which I have had and acts, both internal and external, which I have performed. Such an idea is often saturated with feeling; the clarity of its separate parts varies and oscillates. The same sense is not always connected, even in the same man, with the same idea. The idea is subjective: one man's idea is not that of another. There result, as a matter of course, a variety of differences in the ideas associated with the same sense. A painter, a horseman, and a zoologist will probably connect different ideas with the name 'Bucephalus'. This constitutes an essential distinction between the idea and the sign's sense, which may be the common property of many and therefore is not a part of a mode of the individual mind. For one can hardly deny that mankind has a common store of thoughts which is transmitted from one generation to another.

In the light of this, one need have no scruples in speaking simply of *the* sense, whereas in the case of an idea one must, strictly speaking, add to whom it belongs and at what time. It might perhaps be said: Just as one man connects this idea, and another that idea, with the same word, so also one man can associate this sense and another that sense. But there still remains a difference in the mode of connexion. They are not prevented from grasping the same sense; but they cannot have the same idea. . . . If two persons picture the same thing, each still has his own idea. It is indeed sometimes possible to establish differences in the ideas, or even in the sensations, of different men; but an exact comparison is not possible, because we cannot have both ideas together in the same consciousness.

The reference of a proper name is the object itself which we designate by its means; the idea, which we have in that case, is wholly subjective; in between lies the sense, which is indeed no longer subjective like the idea, but is yet not the object itself.[35]

While in accordance with the foregoing account we might use the term 'meaning' to encompass both the sense and the reference of a linguistic expression, there is a narrower use that restricts the term 'meaning' to the *sense* of an expression. According to this latter stipulation, to *understand* an expression—to know what it means—is to know what its *sense* is. This does not require, however, that the expression, though meaningful, i.e., with a determinate sense, must, therefore, have a referent. Consider the expression, 'the person who has a perfect command of all languages that have ever been used by human beings anywhere on earth and throughout the entire history of the human race'. While this expression has a sense, it does not follow that there is some actual person to which this description could be applied. Whether there is or is not such a referent remains to be established by whatever appropriate routes of inquiry or appeal to evidence is available. *Understanding* of meaning (sense) of a description, and factual *knowledge*—i.e., knowing there is an actual object to which a description applies—are thus two different matters. The latter, however, presupposes the former.

For Frege, all expressions in a well-constructed language have sense. Ideally, each expression would have a single, uniform sense, shared and understood by all competent users of the language. It is on the basis of the sense of an expression that one can specify the conditions for the truth or falsity of the sentence as a whole. For Frege, every constituent of a well-formed sentence has a clear and determinate sense. The sentence as a composite whole, too, must have a sense if we are going to be able to assess its truth or falsity. The sense of a sentence as a whole Frege calls *the thought*. This (let it be emphasized and repeated) is not some collection of subjective ideas. It is, for Frege, something objective, public, uniform. His use of the expression 'the thought' corresponds to what others intend by the word 'proposition'. The sense (thought) of a sentence—whatever the variable, conventional symbolic means for conveying that sense—is a definite proposition.

In his later writings Frege spoke of the referent of all true sentences as the True, and the referent of all false sentences as the False. In treating of the relation of reference of a sentence as a whole, he fell back on the model of a proper name. Just as a proper name, in a well-constructed language, has a sense and a referent, so too, Frege supposed, we can think of a sentence as a whole as expressing a sense (the thought) and as having a referent. Instead, however, of thinking of each true sentence as correlated with its own unique referent (as in the case of names, 'Socrates' refers to Socrates and 'Plato' refers to a different individual) Frege assimilated the referents of all true sentences to a single referent—'the True'.

We are therefore driven into accepting the *truth value* of a sentence as constituting its reference. By the truth value of a sentence I understand the circumstance that it is true or false. There are no further truth values. For brevity I call the one the True, the other the False. Every declarative sentence concerned with the reference of its words is therefore to be regarded as a proper name, and its reference, if it has one, is either the True or the False.[36]

The assimilation of the role of sentences, in this respect, to the role of names (whatever the conceptual economy achieved), is open to serious objections. It leads Frege to overlook the important differences between sentences and names, i.e., the need to distinguish the different ways in which we determine the 'referents' of each. Later philosophers, working broadly in the Fregean tradition, have criticized Frege on this score and have offered their own proposals for dealing with this question. Among others, as we shall see, Wittgenstein, in his *Tractatus Logico-Philosophicus,* introduces the notion of *facts* as the referential correlates of propositions. With each true atomic proposition is correlated its own referent, a unique fact in the world.

In addition to the foregoing ways of exploiting the distinction between sense and reference (for the analysis of identity statements, the treatment of proper names, and the way in which the distinction applies to entire sentences), Frege points out how this distinction can be helpful in dealing with various forms of *indirect speech.*

In the case of direct speech, the senses of the components of a sentence are among the relevant factors that determine the truth or falsity of the sentence as a whole. And where the sentence is a compound one, the references of the component sentences (their truth-values) determine the truth or falsity of the compound sentence as a whole. Thus in determining the truth of the simple sentence 'Earth is a planet', we need to understand the sense of the expression 'Earth' (a proper name) and the concept-word 'is a planet'. We identify the referent of the proper name 'Earth' and we establish the suitability of applying the concept 'is a planet' as a description of Earth. The truth of the entire sentence is thereby determined by taking into account the sense and references of the component expressions of the sentence. In determining the truth of a compound sentence, for example a conjunctive such as 'Plato is a philosopher and Darwin is a biologist', the truth or falsity of the entire sentence is determined by knowing the truth or falsity of the component conjuncts ('Plato is a philosopher' and 'Darwin is a biologist'). If either conjunct is false or both are false, the entire sentence is false. It is not only the senses of each constituent part of the entire sentence that affect the truth-value of the entire compound sentence; it is also the truth-value of each constituent conjunct, as determined, in turn, by *its* references, that affects the truth-value of the entire compound sentence.

Now, however, consider the sentence 'Dr. Velikovsky believes the planet Venus once collided with the planet Earth'. Here the entire sentence contains, as a subordinate part, the sentence 'The planet Venus once collided with the planet Earth'. This subordinate, constituent sentence *might* be evaluated separately as either true or false. But in the present case, it follows the words 'Dr. Velikovsky believes . . .'. Whether, in fact, the constituent sentence 'The planet Venus once collided with the planet Earth' is false rather than true, is *irrelevant* to establishing the truth of the entire sentence 'Dr. Velikovsky believes that the planet Venus once collided with the planet Earth'. To determine the truth of this entire sentence we need to know that there is an individual named 'Dr. Velikovsky', and that in fact he does believe the *quoted* constituent sentence. The quoted sentence 'The planet Venus once collided with the planet Earth' occurs here in *indirect speech*. The sentence 'The planet Venus once collided with the planet Earth' is *mentioned* in the sentence. However, someone (for example a newspaper reporter) uttering the entire sentence 'Dr. Velikovsky believes that the planet Venus once collided with the planet Earth' is not himself *directly asserting* the sentence 'The planet Venus once collided with the planet Earth'.

What Frege wishes to say about sentences of this and related types is that the determination of their truth-values calls upon other resources than the use of rules of simple truth-functional logic, of the kind operating in conjunctive or other types of compound sentences. Frege points out that even in sentences involving indirect (quoted) speech, there are references involved, but some of the *referents* may themselves be only *senses*. And this is indeed the case with the subordinate (quoted) sentence 'The planet Venus once collided with the planet Earth'. Here the *sense* of this entire quoted sentence is one of the *referents* of the primary sentence of which it is a part.

If words are used in the ordinary way, what one intends to speak of is their reference. It can also happen, however, that one wishes to talk about the words themselves or their sense. This happens, for instance, when the words of another are quoted. One's own words then first designate words of the other speaker, and only the latter have their usual reference. We then have signs of signs. In writing, the words are in this case enclosed in quotation marks. Accordingly, a word standing between quotation marks must not be taken as having its ordinary reference.

In order to speak of the sense of an expression 'A' one may simply use the phrase 'the sense of the expression "A"'. In reported speech one talks about the sense, e.g., of another person's remarks. It is quite clear that in this way of speaking words to not have their customary reference but designate what is usually their sense. In order to have a short expression, we will say: In reported speech, words are used *indirectly* or have their *indirect* reference. We distinguish accordingly the *customary* from the *indirect* reference of a word; and its *customary* sense from its *indirect* sense. The indirect reference of a word is accordingly its customary sense. Such exceptions must always be borne in mind if the mode of connexion between sign, sense, and reference in particular cases is to be correctly understood.[37]

In order to determine the truth or falsity of the entire sentence in indirect speech, one must be careful to include the indirectly quoted sentence with its given or equivalent sense. One cannot simply substitute for the quoted sentence some other sentence (having the same truth-value as the original) and assume that the truth-value of the original sentence is thereby preserved. For a person may believe p and not another sentence q, even though both p and q have the same truth-value. Thus Jones might believe that Katmandhu overlooks the Himalayas but not realize that Katmandhu is the capital of Nepal. Hence even though Jones believes that Katmandhu overlooks the Himalayas it does not necessarily follow that Jones believes that the capital of Nepal overlooks the Himalayas.

According to Frege, then, the difference between direct and indirect speech is the following: Although each in its own way involves making the distinction between the sense and reference of various aspects of these sentences, they differ in an important respect. In direct speech, the sense of an expression determines its ordinary direct *reference*. In the case of indirect speech, the sense of an expression determines its *indirect reference*, and this coincides with its ordinary *sense*.

In the foregoing pages I have sought to suggest, through my exposition of some of Frege's leading philosophic ideas, why he is a philosopher of great originality. Frege introduced distinctions and offered clarifications that prompted some of the leading analytic philosophers of our age to take hold of his suggestions, develop them, and adapt them to their own philosophic interest. There is much, of course, in Frege that has also been the occasion for controversial interpretation since what he means is not always crystal clear, and much of his writing is quite compressed. There are other features of his philosophy to which some philosophers have taken strong exception. As we proceed in our account of the development of some of the main figures and movements in post-Fregean analytic philosophy, we shall have occasion to study examples of the varied types of impact of Frege's thought—how his ideas were adopted, extended, and in some cases, rejected.

CHAPTER IV

Logical Atomism

BERTRAND RUSSELL

Bertrand Russell occupies a central and important place in the development of analytic philosophy in the twentieth century. As already noted, Russell was one of the few philosophers who recognized the importance of Frege's work at an early stage. However, Russell was not by any means restricted in his thought to following the lead of Frege. Russell's position in the development of analytic philosophy has to be seen in a much wider perspective than simply in terms of the 'Fregean-connecton', for Russell is a philosopher in the grand tradition. Although much of his work, like Frege's, deals with various problems in the philosophy of mathematics and undertakes a detailed elaboration of forms and techniques of logical analysis, unlike Frege's his very large body of writings ranges over almost the entire spectrum of human experience and traditional philosophical interests. His technical writings in philosophy beyond logic and the philosophy of mathematics deal with topics in epistemology, the philosophy of mind, ontology, ethics, political theory, the philosophy of science, and the history of philosophy. Russell also wrote on the theory and practice of education, the nature of religion, history, and international affairs. In addition, there are writings in fiction, several volumes of an autobiography, a vast trove of private correspondence, and various other incidental writings. Over a long and prolific career, Russell was the author of more than sixty books and a large number of published articles. What he had to say in all these is, to be sure, of uneven quality, ranging from the profound, highly technical, and original to the trivial and superficial. Still, the range of his mind, the combination of his intellectual vitality and his first-hand participation in practical affairs (including direct involvement in educational experiments, political movements, the efforts to influence the course of international affairs, as for example his pacifist activities and the campaign in behalf of nuclear disarmament) all testify to a life enormously rich and wide in its concerns. Virtually every facet of human experience was grist for the mill of his philosophic analysis, commentary, wit, and nimble pen.

The fascination of Russell's philosophy accordingly derives from many factors. Behind the writings stands one of the most colorful personalities of our age, whose life on the intellectual, public, and private sides provides endless occasions for exploring its manifold ramifications. On the purely philosophic side, Russell's mind and intellectual career — since he lived to the age of ninety-eight — spans a century of variegated and intense intellectual activity. His intellectual development offers the opportunity to see how certain major innovative ideas in twentieth century scientific and philosophic thought were filtered through his mind. At the same time, like other great philosophers, Russell was not simply a passive recipient, a weather vane for fashionable patterns of thought. He reacted upon and influenced their direction of development. In the course of responding to the challenges, puzzlements, and questions posed by a cultural life rife with intellectual and other types of revolution, Russell actively sought to come to terms with them. He advanced his own creative suggestions. In short, as a technical philosopher, as a popular writer, and as a public figure, Russell plays a unique role in bringing into focus the thought and tensions of our time.

Bertrand Russell was born on May 18, 1872. His parents died when he was very young and he was brought up in the household of his grandparents. His grandfather, Lord John Russell (later the first Earl Russell) was the author of the famous Reform Bill of 1832, and had twice been Prime Minister under Queen Victoria. Queen Victoria had given Lord Russell a large estate, Pembroke Lodge in Richmond Park, and here young Bertrand spent his boyhood and adolescence. He was not sent away to school, and his early education was supervised by governesses and private tutors. The grandfather died in 1878 within a few years after young Bertrand arrived. It was left to the grandmother to supervise the boy's upbringing. This she did in a spirit imbued with all the moral fervor and uncompromising religious conviction of her family's Scotch Presbyterian heritage. Upon the flyleaf of the Bible she had given to Bertrand when he was twelve years old, she inscribed the biblical quotation, "Thou shalt not follow a multitude to do evil." It is a maxim by which Russell claims to have been influenced throughout his life. In describing the household in which he was brought up, Russell writes:

The atmosphere in the house was one of puritan piety and austerity. There were family prayers at eight o'clock every morning. Although there were eight servants, food was always of Spartan simplicity, and even what there was, if it was at all nice, was considered too good for children. For instance, if there was an apple tart and rice pudding, I was only allowed the rice pudding. Cold baths all the year round were insisted upon, and I had to practise the piano from seven-thirty to eight every morning although the fires were not yet lit. My grandmother never allowed herself to sit in an armchair until the evening. Alcohol and tobacco were viewed with disfavour although stern convention compelled them to serve a little wine to guests. Only virtue was prized, virtue at the expense of intellect, health, happiness, and every mundane good.

I rebelled against this atmosphere first in the name of intellect. I was a solitary, shy, priggish youth. I had no experience of the social pleasures of boyhood and did not miss them. But I liked mathematics, and mathematics was suspect because it has not ethical content. I came also to disagree with the theological opinions of my family, and as I grew up I became increasingly interested in philosophy, of which they profoundly disapproved. Every time the subject came up they repeated with unfailing regularity, "What is mind? No matter. What is matter? Never mind." After some fifty or sixty repetitions, this remark ceased to amuse me.[1]

Russell went to Cambridge in October 1890, at age eighteen, having won a scholarship in mathematics at Trinity College. His examiner was a young man of twenty-nine named Alfred North Whitehead, with whom Russell was years later to write the three-volume classic of modern logic *Principia Mathematica*. The major part of his first three years at Cambridge was spent in the study of mathematics. During his fourth year he turned to an intensive study of philosophy. Among the many friends Russell made at Cambridge and who came to influence his views in philosophy were John M. E. McTaggart and G. E. Moore. From McTaggart, James Ward, and George F. Stout he acquired at first a strong attachment to German idealist philosophy, whether in its Kantian or Hegelian forms. Francis H. Bradley's *Appearance and Reality* was published at this time, and made a strong impact. However, of these influences McTaggart's proved for a while to be the strongest, and his 'Hegelianism' offered an attractive alternative to the empiricism of Henry Sidgwick and John Stuart Mill, to which Russell had earlier been sympathetic. Having during his adolescence lived through a period of questioning and a discarding of his earlier religious beliefs, Russell sought for some philosophically acceptable way of replacing these earlier certainties. He looked at first to mathematics and the framework of an idealist metaphysics.

My original interest in philosophy had two sources. On the one hand, I was anxious to discover whether philosophy would provide any defence for anything that could be called religious belief, however vague; on the other hand, I wished to persuade myself that something could be known, in pure mathematics if not elsewhere.[2]

Although he "thought about both these problems during adolescence, in solitude and with little help from books," it wasn't until he got to

Cambridge that he found a rich and sustaining atmosphere in which to pursue his intellectual interests.

At Cambridge I was introduced to the philosophy of Hegel who, in the course of nineteen abstruse volumes, professed to have proved something which would do quite well as an emended and sophisticated version of traditional beliefs. Hegel thought of the universe as a closely knit unity. His universe was like a jelly in the fact that, if you touched any one part of it, the whole quivered; but it was unlike a jelly in the fact that it could not really be cut up into parts. The appearance of consisting of parts, according to him, was a delusion. The only reality is the Absolute, which was his name for God. In this philosophy I found comfort for a time. As presented to me by its adherents, especially McTaggart, who was then an intimate friend of mine, Hegel's philosophy had seemed both charming and demonstrable. McTaggart was a philosopher some six years senior to me and throughout his life an ardent disciple of Hegel. He influenced his contemporaries very considerably, and I for a time fell under his sway. There was a curious pleasure in making oneself believe that time and space are unreal, that matter is an illusion, and that the world really consists of nothing but mind. In a rash moment, however, I turned from the disciples to the Master and found in Hegel himself a farrago of confusions and what seemed to me little better than puns. I therefore abandoned his philosophy.

For a time I found satisfaction in a doctrine derived, with modification, from Plato. According to Plato's doctrine, which I accepted only in a watered-down form, there is an unchanging timeless world of ideas of which the world presented to our senses is an imperfect copy. Mathematics, according to this doctrine, deals with the world of ideas and has in consequence an exactness and perfection which is absent from the everyday world. This kind of mathematical mysticism, which Plato derived from Pythagoras, appealed to me. But in the end I found myself obliged to abandon this doctrine also, and I have never since found religious satisfaction in any philosophical doctrine that I could accept.[3]

Russell's first philosophical book was *An Essay on the Foundations of Geometry* (1897), written as a Fellowship dissertation. In it he attempted to assess the development of non-Euclidean geometries from a modified Kantian point of view. Although even now it can be read with profit for its many valuable insights, Russell himself years later took a rather dim view of it.*

As Russell tells us, it was largely through the help and influence of Moore that he was able finally to break away from the philosophy of idealism. With Moore, Russell came to reestablish a healthy confidence in the

---

* "I took up Kant's question, 'how is geometry possible?' and decided that it was possible if, and only if, space was of one of the three recognized varieties, one of them Euclidean, the other two non-Euclidean but having the property of preserving a constant 'measure of curvature'. Einstein's revolution swept away everything at all resembling this point of view. The geometry in Einstein's General Theory of Relativity is such as I had declared to be impossible. The theory of tensors, upon which Einstein based himself, would have been useful to me, but I never heard of it until he used it. Apart from details, I do not think that there is anything valid in this early book."[4]

existence of an 'external world' of material things, and of space and time. At first this rebellion against idealism took the form of a defense of the naive realism of common sense, joined with a defense of realism in the Platonic sense.

> During 1898, various things caused me to abandon both Kant and Hegel. I read Hegel's *Greater Logic,* and thought, as I still do, that all he says about mathematics is muddle-headed nonsense. I came to disbelieve Bradley's arguments against relations, and to distrust the logical bases of monism. I disliked the subjectivity of the "Transcendental Aesthetic." But these motives would have operated more slowly than they did, but for the influence of G. E. Moore. He also had had a Hegelian period, but it was briefer than mine. He took the lead in rebellion, and I followed, with a sense of emancipation. Bradley argued that everything common sense believes in is mere appearance; we reverted to the opposite extreme, and thought that *everything* is real that common sense, uninfluenced by philosophy or theology, supposes real. With a sense of escaping from prison, we allowed ourselves to think that grass is green, that the sun and stars would exist if no one was aware of them, and also that there is a pluralistic timeless world of Platonic ideas. The world, which had been thin and logical, suddenly became rich and varied and solid.[5]

Looking back at this early exuberant defense of realism, Russell remarks, "I have not been able to retain this pleasing faith in its pristine vigour, but I have never again shut myself up in a subjective prison."[6]

Moore's rebellion against idealism was argued in his classic paper, "The Refutation of Idealism" (1903) (reprinted in his *Philosophical Studies*). That attack was directed mostly at the kind of philosophy espoused by Berkeley, the view that 'to be is to be perceived'—that reality is mind-dependent. Although a version of the mind-dependency thesis persists in the views of those who, following Hegel, believed that Reality is essentially spiritual (an Absolute Mind), the aspect of this philosophy that provoked Russell's attack (as contrasted with Moore's) was not so much the mind-dependency component as its *monism*. This consisted in the belief that Reality constitutes a single, all-inclusive rational Whole all of whose parts can only be ultimately understood when seen as 'appearances' of that absolute Whole. At the core of the monistic metaphysics of Absolute Idealism was the *doctrine of internal relations*. Russell, with an eye to what is fundamental, went for the jugular vein. His critical attack on Idealism focused on the doctrine of internal relations as that which supported its monistic metaphysics. In opposition, he argued for a *pluralistic* metaphysics, and what he called the *doctrine of external relations*.[7]

The doctrine of internal relations held that every relation between two terms expresses, primarily, intrinsic properties of the two terms and, in ultimate analysis, a property of the whole which the two compose. With some relations this view is plausible. Take, for example, love or hate. If A loves B, this relation exemplifies itself and may be said to consist in certain states of mind of A. Even an atheist must admit that a man can love God. It follows that love of God is a state of the man who feels it, and not properly a relational fact. But the relations that interested me were of a more abstract sort. Suppose that A and B are events, and A is earlier than B. I do not think that this implies anything in A in virtue of which, independently of B, it must have a character which we inaccurately express by mentioning B. Leibniz gives an extreme example. He says that, if a man living in Europe has a wife in India and the wife dies without his knowing it, the man undergoes an intrinsic change at the moment of her death. This is the kind of doctrine that I was combating. I found the doctrine of internal relations particularly inapplicable in the case of 'asymmetrical' relations—i.e., relations which, if they hold between A and B, do not hold between B and A. Let us take again the relation *earlier*. If A is earlier than B, then B is not earlier than A. If you try to express the relation of A to B by means of adjectives of A and B, you will have to make the attempt by means of dates. You may say that the date of A is a property of A and the date of B is a property of B, but that will not help you because you will have to go on to say that the date of A is earlier than the date of B, so that you will have found no escape from the relation. If you adopt the plan of regarding the relation as a property of the whole composed of A and B, you are in a still worse predicament, for in that whole A and B have no order and therefore you cannot distinguish between 'A is earlier than B' and 'B is earlier than A'. As asymmetrical relations are essential in most parts of mathematics, this doctrine was important.[8]

Russell's pluralistic metaphysics (later absorbed into, and renamed, 'logical atomism') and his championing of the method of analysis were formulated in embryo in this early period. It was, in its fundamental outlook, to remain with him in one form or another throughout the rest of his life. In 1959 (at age eighty-seven) he wrote:

Although I have changed my opinion on various matters since those early days, I have not changed on points which, then as now, seemed of most importance. I still hold to the doctrine of external relations and to pluralism, which is bound up with it. I still hold that an isolated truth may be quite true. I still hold that analysis is not falsification. I still hold that any proposition other than a tautology, if it is true, is true in virtue of a relation to *fact*, and that facts in general are independent of experience. I see nothing impossible in a universe devoid of experience. On the contrary, I think that experience is a very restricted and cosmically trivial aspect of a very tiny portion of the universe. On all these matters my views have not changed since I abandoned the teachings of Kant and Hegel.[9]

The years 1899–1900 mark a special turning point in Russell's career as a philosopher.

There is one major division in my philosophical work: in the years 1899–1900 I adopted the philosophy of logical atomism and the technique of Peano in mathematical logic. This was so great a revolution as to make my previous work, except such as was purely mathematical, irrelevant to everything that I did later. The change in these years was a revolution; subsequent changes have been of the nature of an evolution.[10]

Russell describes the circumstances that brought about this important re-orientation in his thought:

> The most important year in my intellectual life was the year 1900, and the most important event in this year was my visit to the International Congress of Philosophy in Paris. Ever since I had begun Euclid at the age of eleven, I had been troubled about the foundations of mathematics; when, later, I came to read philosophy, I found Kant and the empiricists equally unsatisfactory. I did not like the synthetic *a priori*, but yet arithmetic did not seem to consist of empirical generalizations. In Paris in 1900, I was impressed by the fact that, in all discussions, Peano and his pupils had a precision which was not possessed by others. I therefore asked him to give me his works, which he did. As soon as I had mastered his notation, I saw that it extended the region of mathematical precision backwards towards regions which had been given over to philosophical vagueness. Basing myself on him, I invented a notation for relations. Whitehead, fortunately, agreed as to the importance of the method, and in a very short time we worked out together such matters as the definitions of series, cardinals, and ordinals, and the reduction of arithmetic to logic. For nearly a year, we had a rapid series of quick successes. Much of the work had already been done by Frege, but at first we did not know this. The work that ultimately became my contribution to *Principia Mathematica* presented itself to me, at first, as a parenthesis in the refutation of Kant.[11]

Russell's philosophy of pluralism (logical atomism) has important connections with his work in logic. Of these connections, two original contributions by Russell are of special importance and were worked out by him in the early years of this century. One was his celebrated Theory of Types, in which he offered a solution to the 'Russell paradox' (the contradiction) he had found in Frege's philosophy of mathematics. An early version of this theory was suggested by Russell in an appendix to his *Principles of Mathematics*, published in 1903. It was developed in a more adequate form in *Principia Mathematica* (1910–1913). The other theory, for which Russell is perhaps best remembered and which we shall examine in detail in the next section in this chapter, is his Theory of Definite Descriptions. This was first broached in his paper "On Denoting" in 1905. It has been regarded by many as Russell's most important contribution to logic and has been characterized as "a paradigm of philosophy."

In line with Russell's own summary statement, one may look upon all of his technical work in philosophy as filling out the details of his philosophy of logical atomism. In connection with the inspiration toward the formulation of that philosophy in its earliest phases, there are (in addition to the work of Giuseppe Peano) two thinkers whose work Russell singles out for special attention, Gottlob Frege and Ludwig Wittgenstein.

Concerning Frege, Russell has the following to relate:

> With the beginning of the twentieth [century], I became aware of a man for whom I had and have the very highest respect although at that time he was practi-

cally unknown. This man is Frege. It is difficult to account for the fact that his work did not receive recognition. Dedekind had been justly acclaimed, but Frege on the very same topics was much more profound. My relations with him were curious. They ought to have begun when my teacher in philosophy, James Ward, gave me Frege's little book *Begriffsschrift* saying that he had not read the book and did not know whether it had any value. To my shame I have to confess that I did not read it either, until I had independently worked out a great deal of what it contained. The book was published in 1879 and I read it in 1901. I rather suspect that I was its first reader. What first attracted me to Frege was a review of a later book of his by Peano accusing him of unnecessary subtlety. As Peano was the most subtle logician I had at that time come across, I felt that Frege must be remarkable. I acquired the first volume of his book on arithmetic (the second volume was not yet published). I read the introduction with passionate admiration, but I was repelled by the crabbed symbolism which he had invented and it was only after I had done the same work for myself that I was able to understand what he had written in the main text. He was the first to expound the view which was and is mine, that mathematics is a prolongation of logic, and he was the first to give a definition of numbers in logical terms. He did this in 1884 but nobody noticed that he had done it.

Frege thought, as I thought for a few months at the turn of the century, that the reduction of mathematics to logic had been definitively completed. But in June 1901 I came across a contradiction which proved that something was amiss. I wrote to Frege about it and he behaved with a noble candour which cannot be too highly praised. The second volume of his arithmetic had been passed through the press but not yet published. He added an appendix saying that in view of the contradiction that I had brought to his notice "die Arithmetik ist ins Schwanken geraten." I understand that in later years, like the Pythagoreans when confronted with irrationals, he took refuge in geometrical treatment of arithmetic. In this I cannot follow him, but it is interesting to observe the repetition of ancient history in a new context. To my lasting regret, I never met Frege, but I am glad to have done all that lay in my power to win him the recognition which he deserved.[12]

In an Appendix to his *Principles of Mathematics* Russell offered the earliest account in English of Frege's work. By his frequent references to Frege's work in his own later, philosophical writings, he showed that he shared with Frege not only certain views about the foundations of mathematics, but about the overall importance of using the techniques of the new logic for conducting logical analyses and thereby exhibiting logic to be "the essence of philosophy."

Ludwig Wittgenstein, on Frege's advice, came to Cambridge in 1912 in order to study with Russell. Wittgenstein had studied Russell's *Principles of Mathematics* while he was a student of aeronautical engineering at Manchester University. He was in contact with Russell from 1912 until the outbreak of World War I in 1914. Russell's discussions with Wittgenstein during this period exerted a strong influence on his own thought, as Russell acknowledges. In the Preface to his book *Our Knowledge of the External World* (based on the Lowell lectures delivered at Harvard in

April 1914) Russell asserts: "In pure logic . . . I have had the benefit of vitally important discoveries, not yet published, by my friend Mr. Ludwig Wittgenstein." In his book *My Philosophical Development* Russell writes:

> Wittgenstein's doctrines influenced me profoundly. . . . Wittgenstein's impact upon me came in two waves: the first of these was before the First World War; the second was immediately after the War when he sent me the manuscript of his *Tractatus*. His later doctrines, as they appear in his *Philosophical Investigations,* have not influenced me at all.

> At the beginning of 1914, Wittgenstein gave me a short typescript consisting of notes on various logical points. This, together with a large number of conversations, affected my thinking during the war years while he was in the Austrian army and I was, therefore, cut off from all contact with him. What I knew of his doctrines at this time was derived entirely from unpublished sources. I do not feel sure that, either then or later, the views which I believed to have derived from him were in fact his views. He always vehemently repudiated expositions of his doctrines by others, even when those others were ardent disciples. The only exception that I know of was F.P. Ramsey. . . . At the beginning of 1918, I gave a course of lectures in London which were subsequently printed in *The Monist* (1918 and 1919). I prefaced these lectures by the following acknowledgement of my indebtedness to Wittgenstein: 'The following articles are the first two lectures of a course of eight lectures delivered in London in the first months of 1918, and are very largely concerned with explaining certain ideas which I learnt from my friend and former pupil Ludwig Wittgenstein. I have had no opportunity of knowing his views since August 1914, and I do not even know whether he is alive or dead. He has therefore no responsibility for what is said in these lectures beyond that of having originally supplied many of the theories contained in them...'.

> It was in these lectures that I first adopted the name 'Logical Atomism' to describe my philosophy.[13]

Russell's most concentrated and creative philosophical work occupied the period 1900–1914. However, works of various kinds continued to pour from his pen up to the time of his death in 1970. The following are some of his more technical books in philosophy, in addition to those we have had occasion to mention: *Mysticism and Logic* (1918), *The Analysis of Mind* (1921), *The Analysis of Matter* (1927), *An Inquiry into Meaning and Truth* (1940), *Human Knowledge, Its Scope and Limits* (1948). Two useful collections of his technical papers are *Logic and Knowledge* and *Essays in Analysis.*

In his autobiographical essay for the volume devoted to his philosophy in the series The Library of Living Philosophers, Russell sums up his career in philosophy as follows:

> My intellectual journeys have been, in some respects, disappointing. When I was young I hoped to find religious satisfaction in philosophy; even after I had abandoned Hegel, the eternal Platonic world gave me something non-human to

admire. I thought of mathematics with reverence, and suffered when Wittgenstein led me to regard it as nothing but tautologies. I have always ardently desired to find some justification for the emotions inspired by certain things that seemed to stand outside human life and to deserve feelings of awe. I am thinking in part of very obvious things, such as the starry heavens and a stormy sea on a rocky coast; in part of the vastness of the scientific universe, both in space and time, as compared to the life of mankind; in part of the edifice of impersonal truth, especially truth which, like that of mathematics, does not merely describe the world that happens to exist. Those who attempt to make a religion of humanism, which recognizes nothing greater than man, do not satisfy my emotions. And yet I am unable to believe that, in the world as known, there is anything that I can value outside human beings, and, to a much lesser extent, animals. Not the starry heavens, but their effects on human percipients, have excellence; to admire the universe for its size is slavish and absurd; impersonal non-human truth appears to be a delusion. And so my intellect goes with the humanists, though my emotions violently rebel. In this respect, the "consolations of philosophy" are not for me.

In more purely intellectual ways, on the contrary, I have found as much satisfaction in philosophy as any one could reasonably have expected. Many matters which, when I was young, baffled me by the vagueness of all that had been said about them, are now amenable to an exact technique, which makes possible the kind of progress that is customary in science. Where definite knowledge is unattainable, it is sometimes possible to prove that it is unattainable, and it is usually possible to formulate a variety of exact hypotheses, all compatible with the existing evidence. Those philosophers who have adopted the methods derived from logical analysis can argue with each other, not in the old aimless way, but cooperatively, so that both sides can concur as to the outcome. All this is new during my lifetime; the pioneer was Frege, but he remained solitary until his old age. This extension of the sphere of reason to new provinces is something that I value very highly. Philosophic rationality may be choked in the shocks of war and the welter of new persecuting superstitions, but one may hope that it will not be lost utterly or for more than a few centuries. In this respect, my philosophic life has been a happy one.[14]

At various times in his life Russell was associated with Trinity College, Cambridge. At one point (in 1916), he was dismissed from membership in Trinity College because of his active participation in antiwar activities. In May 1918 he wrote an article attacking the United States, and for this allegedly libelous attack on a wartime ally he was sentenced to a prison term of six months. During this period in prison (having been given access to books and writing materials) Russell wrote *An Introduction to Mathematical Philosophy*. Over the course of his long life he visited many countries and belonged on an intermittent basis to many universities and other educational institutions. Because of the opposition he aroused in various groups for his unconventional views on politics, sex, religion, and education, Russell was very often the target of bitter attacks by those strongly opposed to his views. One such occasion consisted of the notorious 'Bertrand Russell Case' (1940) in which the legal actions of his opponents succeeded in preventing him from taking up an appointment as Professor of Philosophy at the City College of New York.

Russell's life was far from a cloistered academic one. His work as a philosopher made up only one side of his checkered and complex life. Intermingled with and running parallel to his work as a technical philosopher were Russell's often turbulent, passionate involvements—his personal, emotional crises and private affairs (several marriages, as well as numerous romantic attachments), his travels to various countries, his friendships with eminent persons, his setting up of an experimental school for children, his activities as a pacifist and campaigner for nuclear disarmament, his work as a writer of popular books and articles, and much else. The many facets of his life provide material for a lively autobiography and are the subject of a number of biographical studies. The reader is referred to some of these in the Selected Bibliography for highly absorbing details. Our interest in what follows is with Russell's contribution to the development of analytic philosophy, and it is to a fuller statement of this that we turn next.

GENERAL FEATURES OF RUSSELL'S PHILOSOPHY

As we have seen, Russell chooses the expression 'logical atomism' as a label for his philosophy. While to do so would be useful and apt in certain respects, it would not prove profitable to try to give this expression a precise definition, for Russell's own accounts of what he intends by this phrase do not always agree with one another. In any case, one should not look for some tightly knit system of principles and doctrines, neatly interwoven to give an unchanging, fixed, and carefully worked-out system. There are too many loose connections, as well as modifications and changes of detail, to justify such an approach. Nevertheless, there is an overall unity in Russell's philosophy. This unity can be shown by making explicit the underlying themes to which he gave his primary attention as a philosopher, as well as by pointing out the techniques and principles that guided him in dealing with these themes. If the expression 'logical atomism' has any value it is to call attention to these characteristic themes, techniques, and principles.

In its most general light and as developed over a long career, Russell's philosophy may be looked at as devoted to two principal themes, *ontology* and *theory of knowledge*. By 'ontology' is meant a concern with establishing 'what there is'—some account of what are taken to be basic or fundamental types of reality. By 'theory of knowledge' is meant a critical examination of ways to justify our claims to know the truth about something or other—by what types of arguments and methods, using what types of premisses and rules of inference, we might

undertake to uphold our conclusions. For Russell these two themes—
'what there is' and 'the justification of what we believe to be true'—are
closely intertwined. Ontology requires a theory of knowledge, and the
theory of knowledge has as one of its ultimate purposes to sanction an
ontology.

One important link in Russell's writings between these two themes
is the *theory of meaning*. Russell's treatment of 'knowledge and truth' as
well as of 'what there is' is mediated by his concern (held in common with
other contemporary philosophers) with the 'problem of meaning'. For
Russell (as for Peirce and Frege) the analysis of the nature of meaning is
part of the wider concern with formulating a theory of truth (of what can
be known or said to be the case) and also, therefore, with what is real (or
exists). With Russell, the consideration of the nature of meaning focuses
on the role of language as the 'carrier' of meanings. This concern took
various forms. An important example of his contribution to this topic is
his Theory of Definite Descriptions. This theory had important repercus-
sions for ontology, and exhibited the advantages in using certain techniques of the new logic.

This last point reminds us of another way in which we may look at
Russell's overall work in philosophy, for his use of the language and techniques of modern logic provides another important link between his ontology and his theory of knowledge. Wherever possible, Russell brings to
bear the distinctions brought to light by the new logic (of Frege, Peano,
and his own and Whitehead's work) in dealing with the questions raised in
ontology and the theory of knowledge. For Russell, logic in one sense is
the 'essence' of philosophy. It offers some of the basic tools for conducting a responsible conceptual inquiry and for setting out in clear and precise language such results as one may reach. As with Peirce and Frege,
Russell looks to logic as giving us the criteria by which we can confront
and evaluate the everyday uses of language ('natural language') in the
light of what a purified, ideal logical language would require. The logic to
which Russell appeals is an 'atomistic' one; its formal syntax is set out in
Principia Mathematica.

The logic which I shall advocate is atomistic, as opposed to the monistic
logic of the people who more or less follow Hegel. When I say that my logic is
atomistic, I mean that I share the common-sense belief that there are many separate things; I do not regard the apparent multiplicity of the world as consisting
merely in phases and unreal division of a single indivisible reality.[15]

In a logically perfect language the words in a proposition would correspond
one by one with the components of the corresponding fact, with the exception of
such words as 'or', 'not', 'if', 'then', which have a different function. In a logically
perfect language, there will be one word and no more for every simple object, and
everything that is not simple will be expressed by a combination of words, by a

combination derived, of course, from the words for the simple things that enter in, one word for each simple component. A language of that sort will be completely analytic, and will show at a glance the logical structure of the facts asserted or denied. The language which is set forth in *Principia Mathematica* is intended to be a language of that sort. It is a language which has only syntax and no vocabulary whatsoever. Barring the omission of a vocabulary I maintain that it is quite a nice language. It aims at being that sort of a language that, if you add a vocabulary, would be a logically perfect language. Actual languages are not logically perfect in this sense, and they cannot possibly be, if they are to serve the purposes of daily life.[16]

Although Russell at various times shifted his acceptance of and allegiance to some particular item in his total philosophic enterprise, the goals of that enterprise remained remarkably constant. They were, as we stated, the goals of ontology and the theory of knowledge; their pursuit and implementation were conducted with the aid of distinctions and techniques worked out in the theory of meaning and in logic.

In carrying through his various philosophic projects in ontology, theory of knowledge, theory of meaning, and logic, Russell adheres to a major procedural principle that is a characteristic feature of his 'logical atomism'. He gives this principle a variety of formulations, and acknowledges its ancestry in 'Ockham's Razor'—the principle that "plurality is not to be posited without necessity." Russell sometimes expresses this principle as a search for "minimum vocabularies" and sometimes as a matter of preferring "constructions out of known entities for inferences to unknown entities."[17] Is it possible, for example, in one's ontological commitments, to dispense with affirming that certain entities are real by showing that these alleged entities are reducible to (or disguised forms of) other entities that *are* genuinely real? In general, Russell's project is always one of finding, in *any* type of inquiry, the minimum number of entities, factors, premisses, elements—'logical atoms'—that might suffice to give a consistent and complete account of the domain under investigation. In ontology or in any other inquiry, the finding of a minimum vocabulary is an exercise in intellectual economy. The vocabulary one looks for is such that the terms of that minimum vocabulary are independent of one another. This means that no term belonging to the minimum vocabulary can be defined in terms of other words in the minimum vocabulary. However, all the other terms of the language—other than the set of terms that make up the minimum vocabulary—can be defined by using the terms of the minimum vocabulary. Thus if one has a minimum vocabulary, "all definitions are theoretically superfluous, and therefore the whole of any science can be expressed by means of a minimum vocabulary for that science."[18]

Another version of Russell's adherence to Ockham's razor takes the form of preferring 'constructions' to 'inferences'. Russell sums up what this means, as follows:

The supreme maxim in scientific philosophising is this:

Wherever possible, logical constructions are to be substituted for inferred entities.

Some examples of the substitution of construction for inference in the realm of mathematical philosophy may serve to elucidate the uses of this maxim. Take first the case of irrationals. In old days, irrationals were inferred as the supposed limits of series of rationals which had no rational limit; but the objection to this procedure was that it left the existence of irrationals merely optative, and for this reason the stricter methods of the present day no longer tolerate such a definition. We now define an irrational number as a certain class of ratios, thus constructing it logically by means of ratios, instead of arriving at it by a doubtful inference from them. Take again the case of cardinal numbers. Two equally numerous collections appear to have something in common: this something is supposed to be their cardinal number. But so long as the cardinal number is inferred from the collections, not constructed in terms of them, its existence must remain in doubt, unless in virtue of a metaphysical postulate *ad hoc*. By defining the cardinal number of a given collection as the class of all equally numerous collections, we avoid the necessity of this metaphysical postulate, and thereby remove a needless element of doubt from the philosophy of arithmetic. A similar method, as I have shown elsewhere, can be applied to classes themselves, which need not be supposed to have any metaphysical reality, but can be regarded as symbolically constructed fictions.

The method by which the construction proceeds is closely analogous in these and all similar cases. Given a set of propositions nominally dealing with the supposed inferred entities, we observe the properties which are required of the supposed entities in order to make these propositions true. By dint of a little logical ingenuity, we then construct some logical function of less hypothetical entities which has the requisite properties. This constructed function we substitute for the supposed inferred entities, and thereby obtain a new and less doubtful interpretation of the body of propositions in question.[19]

The basic idea in Russell's adherence in one form or another to 'Ockham's Razor' is that in performing any logical analysis, i.e., in treating of the meaning of any complex symbol or idea, as well as in determining what is real and what is true, one should persist in trying to find what these are by identifying the minimum genuine constituents or components out of which they are composed. In carrying out an analysis in accordance with this guiding principle, the emphasis may fall on one or another aspect of what it means to carry out such an analysis. Sometimes it takes the form of reducing an initially given complex of elements or supposedly large multiplicity of independent entities to a smaller number of such entities or elements. Sometimes the emphasis falls on decomposing a complex whole into its simpler elements. Sometimes the emphasis falls on finding those truths or other given primitive starting points from which to derive or construct more remote consequences.

In a fully developed, philosophically satisfactory language, there will be two basic components. One of these will be purely formal or syntactical. It will be constructed to exemplify and abide by the forms and rules (the syntax) of formal logic, i.e., the logic of *Principia Mathematica*. The second major component will consist of a vocabulary (singular expressions and general terms) to be used in connection with the subject matter of the specific domain under investigation. These latter expressions in the vocabulary are 'nonlogical' or nonformal. Thus terms such as 'or', 'and', 'if . . . then' belong to the syntactical (formal) language of logic. On the other hand, terms such as 'red', 'Socrates', 'is older than' belong to some nonformal vocabulary.

In every proposition and in every inference there is, besides the particular subject-matter concerned, a certain *form,* a way in which the constituents of the proposition or inference are put together. If I say, "Socrates is mortal," "Jones is angry," "The Sun is hot," there is something in common in these three cases, something indicated by the word "is". What is in common is the *form* of the proposition, not an actual constituent. . . . We might understand all the separate words of a sentence without understanding the sentence: if a sentence is long and complicated, that is apt to happen. In such a case we have knowledge of the constituents, but not of the form. We may also have knowledge of the form without having knowledge of the constituents. If I say, "Rorarius drank the hemlock," those among you who have never heard of Rorarius (supposing there are any) will understand the form, without having knowledge of all the constituents. In order to understand a sentence, it is necessary to have knowledge both of the constituents and of the particular instance of the form. It is in this way that a sentence conveys information, since it tells us that certain known objects are related according to a certain known form.[20]

The philosophical questions having to do with the matter of 'meaning', to which Russell's philosophy of logical atomism addresses itself as one of the areas of its application, are directed principally to the 'vocabulary' component of a reconstructed language. It is assumed that the formal or syntactical questions, and the distinctions they embody, have been satisfactorily dealt with in the logical symbolism set forth in *Principia Mathematica.* The principal question for a theory of meaning is the question of specifying the kinds of criteria needed to establish the meaning of some term in the nonformal vocabulary of a sentence. Here Russell's chief emphasis is upon what is required to carry through an *analysis* of such a term.

For Russell, it is important to make a crucial distinction between complex, analyzable terms and those that are simple and so unanalyzable. Any expression in a logically satisfactory vocabulary, reconstructed in accordance with the guiding principles of the philosophy of logical atomism, must be either analyzable into a set of terms that are simple and so not further analyzable, or else be itself a simple, unanalyzable term. Moreover, while some complex terms designate existent things and others do not, it is a requirement on Russell's view that every simple expression to which analysis leads, if it is going to be meaningful, must designate some real entity. Its meaning will consist of the entity so designated.

Certain features of this philosophy of logical atomism, as set forth by Russell, reappear in Moore's use of the method of analysis, as well as in Wittgenstein's *Tractatus Logico-Philosophicus*. Moore, for example, applied the techniques and goals of analysis in the domain of ethics. In his book *Principia Ethica* (1903), Moore upheld the claim that in carrying out the analysis of various terms used in making moral judgments (of what is right or wrong, good or bad), we shall reach, eventually, a level at which no further analysis is possible. It is necessary at that point to appeal to certain basic intuitions; these will not be supported by arguments, but will embody nevertheless infallible judgments. These moral intuitions, according to Moore, are not subjective; on the contrary, they provide disclosures of objective and fixed moral values.* For a while Russell shared these views of Moore, for example as expressed in Russell's early essay "The Elements of Ethics" (reprinted in *Philosophical Essays* (1910)). Russell, however, later abandoned these intuitionistic views in ethics, largely as the result of the criticisms of George Santayana in the latter's book *Winds of Doctrine*.[21]

Russell's reliance on the method of analysis is used by him principally in the examination of *factual* discourse as well as in the discussion of mathematical foundations. Wittgenstein, too, in his *Tractatus*, appeals to the broad principles of the philosophy of logical atomism in dealing with factual discourse. There are, however, important differences in the way that Russell and Wittgenstein formulate their respective conceptions of what such analysis amounts to. Both Russell and Wittgenstein are in agreement that every complex can be analyzed into simples; that propositions, if molecular, can be analyzed into atomic propositions, and that the truth of a proposition is a matter of the correspondence of a proposition with an independently existing fact in the world. As we shall see in Chapter V Wittgenstein nowhere undertakes to specify the nature of the 'simples' out of which complex facts (states of affairs in the world) are constituted. Russell, on the other hand, does express certain definite views

---

* Moore writes: "My point is that 'good' is a simple notion, just as 'yellow' is a simple notion; that, just as you cannot, by any manner of means, explain to anyone who does not already know it, what yellow is, so you cannot explain what good is. Definitions of the kind that I was asking for, definitions, which describe the real nature of the object or notion denoted by a word, and which do not merely tell us what the word is used to mean, are only possible when the object or notion in question is something complex. You can give a definition of a horse, because a horse has many different properties and qualities, all of which you can enumerate. But when you have enumerated them all, when you have reduced a horse to his simplest terms, then you can no longer define those terms. . . . But yellow and good, we say, are not complex: they are notions of that simple kind, out of which definitions are composed and with which the power of further defining ceases." (*Principia Ethica*, sec. 7)

about the character of such 'simples', for Russell was influenced by the British empirical tradition (particularly Hume's version of it) far more than Wittgenstein ever was. Insofar as Russell undertakes to give an analysis of the use of singular expressions that refer to individual 'concrete' objects, he requires for their meaning certain basic sense-data (the analogues of Hume's 'impressions'). Furthermore, in addition to his empiricism (as providing the epistemological 'filling' for his logical atomism), Russell also adheres to an attenuated form of Platonism. He maintains that among the 'simples' of every atomic proposition, one must use expressions that have reference to some abstract entity, some universal. Thus whereas Wittgenstein shied away from specifying the nature of atomic simples, Russell did not hesitate to characterize what these must be, at least in a general way.

We must now consider more fully Russell's views concerning the methods and criteria for determining the meaning of nonlogical expressions in a language reconstructed in accordance with the guiding principles of logical atomism. For this purpose we shall examine Russell's important distinction between *knowledge by acquaintance* and *knowledge by description*.

Russell shares with Frege and most other philosophers the view that in exploring the logic of our language we must draw a broad distinction between those expressions such as proper names, demonstratives, and other devices that purport to refer to individual objects, and those expressions such as adjectives, common nouns, verbs, and other terms that are general. The philosophy of logical atomism, insofar as it is a theory of meaning, makes certain claims about and offers techniques for performing the analysis of both kinds of expressions. According to Russell, within each group we find some expressions that are complex and therefore analyzable, and others that are simple and so not further analyzable.

In the interest of determining the meaning of both kinds of expression, Russell introduces the distinction between knowledge by acquaintance and knowledge by description. Before proceeding to explore what this distinction is, let me pause to stress the fact that the distinction is relevant to a theory of *meaning*. Russell makes a distinction between kinds of knowledge (by acquaintance and by description), but *'knowledge'* of either kind, as he uses this term in this context, has to do with specifying the *meaning* of expressions. It does *not*, as such, have to do directly with making certain claims about the *truth* of some proposition as a whole, and therefore as contributing to our knowledge about some state of affairs. In order to appreciate this distinction, let us first follow Russell in drawing a distinction between having (or claiming to have) *knowledge* of certain *truths*, and being in a position to *understand the meaning* of some expression in a sentence quite apart from knowing (or being interested in knowing) whether the entire sentence is true or false.

In one use of the word 'know' we are said to have knowledge, as opposed to error. It is this sense of 'know' that is present when we know *that* something is the case. This kind of knowledge is conveyed by an entire proposition, sentence, or judgment. This is the sense of 'knowledge' in which we can be said to have knowledge of *truths*. If the proposition as a whole states the truth about something (e.g., 'This table is brown', 'It is raining outside now', 'Today is Tuesday', 'All cows are mammals') the proposition conveys an item of knowledge about some fact (some state of affairs).

Now, however, let the question be raised, not about whether the entire proposition is *true* or not, but about the *meaning* of some expression *in* the proposition. For example, given the proposition 'This table is brown', we may wish to specify, for purposes of philosophical and logical analysis, the ways for establishing the meaning of the expression 'this table' or the expression 'brown'. At this point and in this context Russell's distinction between knowledge by acquaintance and knowledge by description comes into play. To have knowledge by acquaintance or knowledge by description is to know the individual objects—whether concrete or abstract—and any other types of designata connected with an expression used *in* a proposition. Thus one may know of an individual object by acquaintance or by description. There are some objects that are known by acquaintance, whereas others may be known by description. And what some person may know by acquaintance, someone else may know only by description. This sense of 'know' is involved in the distinction between knowledge by acquaintance and knowledge by description. Thus given the statement 'The Empire State Building is in New York City', the question may be put to someone whether he knows the meaning of the expression 'the Empire State Building'. He may respond by saying, "Yes, I know the Empire State Building, I am quite well acquainted with it, having seen it many times, and having been inside it." On the other hand, given the same expression, 'the Empire State Building', another person may say, "Although I have never seen the Empire State Building with my own eyes, I nevertheless know what the name refers to, for I have read about it and have seen pictures of it, and I can describe it, since I have various bits of information about it." It is the use of the term 'know' as it figures in sentences of this sort that Russell is interested in making more precise by drawing the distinction between knowledge by acquaintance and knowledge by description.

First, then, let us consider what Russell means by 'knowledge by acquaintance':

We shall say that we have *acquaintance* with anything of which we are directly aware, without the intermediary of any process of inference or any knowledge of truths. Thus in the presence of my table I am acquainted with the sense-data that make up the appearance of my table—its colour, shape, hardness, smoothness, etc.; all these are things of which I am immediately conscious when I am seeing and touching my table. The particular shade of colour that I am seeing may have many things said about it—I may say that it is brown, that it is rather dark, and so on. But such statements, though they make me know truths *about* the colour, do not make me know the colour itself any better than I did before: so far as concerns knowledge of the colour itself, as opposed to knowledge of truths about it, I know the colour perfectly and completely when I see it, and no further knowledge of it itself is even theoretically possible. Thus the sense-data which make up the appearance of my table are things with which I have acquaintance, things immediately known to me just as they are.[22]

Russell claims that in addition to *sense-data* there are various other examples of things known by acquaintance. Among particulars known by acquaintance are those given through *memory* and *introspection*.

It is obvious that we often remember what we have seen or heard or had otherwise present to our senses, and that in such cases we are still immediately aware of what we remember, in spite of the fact that it appears as past and not present. This immediate knowledge by memory is the source of all our knowledge concerning the past: without it, there could be no knowledge of the past by inference, since we should never know that there was anything past to be inferred.

The next extension to be considered is acquaintance by *introspection*. We are not only aware of things, but we are often aware of being aware of them. When I see the sun, I am often aware of my seeing the sun; thus "my seeing the sun" is an object with which I have acquaintance. When I desire food, I may be aware of my desire for food; thus "my desiring food" is an object with which I am acquainted. Similarly we may be aware of our feeling pleasure or pain, and generally of the events which happen in our minds. This kind of acquaintance, which may be called self-consciousness, is the source of all our knowledge of mental things. It is obvious that it is only what goes on in our own minds that can be thus known immediately. What goes on in the minds of others is known to us through our perception of their bodies, that is, through the sense-data in us which are associated with their bodies. But for our acquaintance with the contents of our own minds, we should be unable to imagine the minds of others, and therefore we could never arrive at the knowledge that they have minds.[23]

According to Russell, we have knowledge by acquaintance not only of particulars of the sort we have just mentioned, but also of the special kinds of entities we call 'universals'. For example, we have acquaintance with the universals

whiteness, diversity, brotherhood, and so on. Every complete sentence must contain at least one word which stands for a universal, since all verbs have a meaning which is universal.

. . . .

Awareness of universals is called *conceiving*, and a universal of which we are aware is called a *concept*. Not only are we aware of particular yellows, but if we have seen a sufficient number of yellows and have sufficient intelligence, we are aware of the universal *yellow*; this universal is the subject in such judgments as "yellow differs from blue" or "yellow resembles blue less than green does." And the universal yellow is the predicate in such judgments as "this is yellow," where "this" is a particular sense-datum. And universal relations, too, are objects of awareness; up and down, before and after, resemblance, desire, awareness itself, and so on, would seem to be all of them objects of which we can be aware.[24]

While there are some entities, whether concrete (particular) or abstract (universal), of which we have knowledge by acquaintance, there are also various entities that we know by means of description.

Let us turn, then, to see what Russell intends by the use of the phrase 'knowledge by description'. A description, first of all, is a linguistic expression. Russell distinguishes two types of phrases that can serve a descriptive role: what he calls 'ambiguous' (or indefinite) descriptions, and 'definite' descriptions.

> By a "description" I mean any phrase of the form "a so-and-so" or "the so-and-so." A phrase of the form "a so-and-so" I shall call an "ambiguous" description; a phrase of the form "the so-and-so" (in the singular) I shall call a "definite" description. Thus "a man" is an ambiguous description, and "the man with the iron mask" is a definite description.[25]

Russell's principal interest is with definite descriptions, i.e. those of the general form '*the* so-and-so'. The use of the word 'the' implies that "there is one object, and no more, having a certain property; and it will generally be implied that we do not have knowledge of the same object by acquaintance."[26] Typical examples of objects of which we may be said to have knowledge by means of definite description are particular ('concrete') objects (persons or material objects), e.g., the first President of the United States, the author of the *Iliad*, the candidate who will get the most votes, and the outermost planet of the solar system. Other objects of which we may have knowledge by means of definite descriptions are abstract, e.g., numbers, as by using the (definite) description, 'the least prime number'.

Our knowledge of objects, depending on the circumstances of those having the knowledge as well as on the kind of objects of which knowledge is had, involves various modes of use of knowledge by acquaintance and knowledge by description.

> It will be seen that there are various stages in the removal from acquaintance with particulars: there is Bismarck to people who knew him, Bismarck to those who only know of him through history, the man with the iron mask, the longest-lived of men. These are progressively further removed from acquaintance with particulars; the first comes as near to acquaintance as is possible in regard to another person; in the second, we shall still be said to know "who Bismarck was"; in the third, we do not know who was the man with the iron mask, though we can know many propositions about him which are not logically deducible from the fact that he wore an iron mask; in the fourth, finally, we know nothing beyond what is logically deducible from the definition of the man. There is a similar hierar-

chy in the region of universals. Many universals, like many particulars, are only known to us by description.[27]

Suppose we have a definite description of some entity. If the description is going to be applicable to that entity, it is necessary at some point to come down from the level of description to the level of acquaintance. For Russell, we can only make direct contact with what is real through acquaintance. If we are going to establish that some offered definite description does in fact describe some actual entity, the only way we can assure ourselves of there being such an entity is by relying, at some point, on knowledge by acquaintance. Russell enunciates the following epistemological principle concerning propositions containing descriptions: *"Every proposition which we can understand must be composed wholly of constituents with which we are acquainted."*[28] And he offers the following illustration of the sort of thing he has in mind to back up this principle:

Suppose some statement made about Bismark. Assuming that there is such a thing as direct acquaintance with oneself, Bismarck himself might have used his name directly to designate the particular person with whom he was acquainted. In this case, if he made a judgment about himself, he himself might be a constituent of the judgment. Here the proper name has the direct use which it always wishes to have, as simply standing for a certain object, and not for a description of the object. But if a person who knew Bismarck made a judgment about him, the case is different. What this person was acquainted with were certain sense-data which he connected (rightly, we will suppose) with Bismarck's body. His body as a physical object, and still more his mind, were only known as the body and mind connected with these sense-data. That is, they were known by description. It is, of course, very much a matter of chance which characteristics of a man's appearance will come into a friend's mind when he thinks of him; thus the description actually in the friend's mind is accidental. The essential point is that he knows that the various descriptions all apply to the same entity, in spite of not being acquainted with the entity in question.

When we, who did not know Bismarck, make a judgment about him, the description in our minds will probably be some more or less vague mass of historical knowledge—far more, in most cases, than is required to identify him. But, for the sake of illustration, let us assume that we think of him as "the first Chancellor of the German Empire." Here all the words are abstract except "German." The word "German" will again have different meanings for different people. To some it will recall travels in Germany, to some the look of Germany on the map, and so on. But if we are to obtain a description which we know to be applicable, we shall be compelled, at some point, to bring in a reference to a particular with which we are acquainted. Such reference is involved in any mention of past, present, and future (as opposed to definite dates), or of here and there, or of what others have told us. Thus it would seem that, in some way or other, a description known to be applicable to a particular must involve some reference to a particular with which we are acquainted, if our knowledge about the thing described is not to be merely what follows logically from the description. For example, "the most long-lived of men" is a description which must apply to some, but we can make no judgments concerning this man which involve knowledge about him beyond what the description gives. If, however, we say, "the first Chancellor of the German Empire was an astute diplomatist," we can only be assured of the truth of our judgment in virtue of something with which we are acquainted—usually a testimony heard or read. Considered psychologically, apart from the information we convey to others, apart from the fact about the actual Bismarck, which gives importance to our judgment, the thought we really have contains the one or more particulars involved, and otherwise consists wholly of concepts.[29]

So much for a brief summary of some general features of Russell's philosophy. We turn next to a more detailed examination of two areas in which that philosophy achieved a classic and influential formulation, the Theory of Descriptions and the Theory of Types.

DESCRIPTIONS AND EXISTENCE

Russell published his celebrated paper "On Denoting" in 1905. In it, he presented the first full statement of what has come to be known as 'The Theory of Descriptions'. A more accure label would be 'The Theory of Definite Descriptions', since it has to do with analysis of what Russell characterized as definite descriptions, as distinguished from 'ambiguous' or indefinite ones. This analysis constituted the major emphasis of the paper, exhibited its originality, and has had the greatest impact on subsequent thought. Various amplifications and refinements of the theory were worked out by Russell in other writings, among them *Principia Mathematica*, "The Philosophy of Logical Atomism," and *An Introduction to Mathematical Philosophy*.

The importance of the Theory of Descriptions can be looked at in two ways. On the one hand, it may be seen as marking a major stage in the development of Russell's philosophy. Specifically, the theory contributed to and illustrated in an important way some of the main goals and principles of the general philosophy of logical atomism. Russell claimed that the theory pointed the way to solving certain philosophic problems in ontology and semantics. It carried out one of the goals expressed by Russell's adherence to Ockham's Principle: it *reduced* the number of one's ontological commitments. It showed in an explicit and relatively precise way how one may apply the distinctions and symbolism of the new logic in formulating the recommendations contained in the theory.

The theory, when seen in wider historical perspective, has a further major importance. Frank P. Ramsey, in a much-quoted remark, characterized the Theory of Descriptions as a "paradigm of philosophy."[30] It showed, he claimed, the great powers and merits of what can be accomplished by philosophy when it practices the techniques of 'analysis', and when it makes use, to its great advantage, of the precise language and symbolic tools of modern logic. It could therefore serve as a model of what analytic philosophy might accomplish in other areas, and toward the solution of other long-standing philosophic problems. Though some 'analytic' philosophers have, in turn, criticized Russell's theory, and have offered rival solutions to the problems with which he was concerned, there is a widely shared belief that the theory *is* a major and important step in the development of twentieth-century philosophy.

In his paper "On Denoting," Russell points to three puzzles he undertakes to solve. Two of the puzzles have to do with the question of how to understand an ostensible reference to 'nonexistent entities'. The third has to do with the analysis of definite descriptions as contrasted with proper names as these occur in identity statements.

One of the puzzles in the first group is presented by Russell as follows:

> Consider the proposition '*A* differs from *B*'. If this is true, there is a difference between *A* and *B*, which fact may be expressed in the form 'the difference between *A* and *B* subsists'. But if it is false that *A* differs from *B*, then there is no difference between *A* and *B*, which fact may be expressed in the form 'the difference between *A* and *B* does not subsist'. But how can a non-entity be the subject of a proposition? . . . Hence, it would appear, it must always be self-contradictory to deny the being of anything. . . . Thus if *A* and *B* do not differ, to suppose either that there is, or that there is not, such an object as 'the difference between *A* and *B*' seems equally impossible.[31]

The problem here is illustrated by the use of the denoting phrase (the definite description) 'the difference between A and B', which serves as the subject of the statement 'The difference between A and B subsists'. If this statement is false, this would require that there is nothing to which the phrase 'the difference between A and B' refers: it lacks a referent. On the other hand, if that expression is to be used meaningfully it must refer to *something*. How can these obviously contradictory requirements be reconciled? How can it be true both that there is *nothing* for the subject expression to be about, and at the same time that there is *something* to which it does refer? As Russell in the above passage puts the matter: "How can a non-entity be the subject of a proposition? . . . It would appear it must always be self-contradictory to deny the being of anything." This type of puzzle is known as the problem of *negative existential statements*. (It was already known to and dealt with by Plato in his dialogue *The Sophist*.) Other examples might be given, e.g., if the statement 'Zeus doesn't exist', is true, this means there is no such entity as Zeus. On the other hand, if the expression 'Zeus' is meaningful, this requires that there is some entity to which the name succeeds in referring.

This type of puzzle apparently had not worried Russell as recently as 1903 when he published his *Principles of Mathematics*. For in it he had defended an ontological view that allowed for the being of all sorts of entities, even nonexistent ones.

Being is that which belongs to every conceivable term, to every possible object of thought—in short to everything that can possibly occur in any proposition, true or false, and to all such propositions themselves. Being belongs to whatever can be counted. If A be any term that can be counted as one, it is plain that A is something, and therefore that A is. "A is not" must always be either false or meaningless. For if A were nothing, it could not be said to be; "A is not" implies that there is a term A whose being is denied, and hence that A is. Thus unless "A is not" be an empty sound, it must be false—whatever A may be, it certainly is. Numbers, the Homeric gods, relations, chimeras and four-dimensional spaces all have being, for if they were not entities of a kind, we could make no propositions about them. Thus being is a general attribute of everything, and to mention anything is to show that it is.[32]

Moore, in his lectures in 1910–1911 (subsequently published in his book *Some Main Problems of Philosophy* (1953)), defended a similar viewpoint. He writes:

To say that a centaur is not real, seems to be equivalent to saying that there is no such thing as a centaur. We should insist most strongly that there really is no such thing; that it is pure fiction. But there is another fact, which seems at first sight to be equally clear. I certainly can imagine a centaur; we can all imagine one. And to imagine a centaur is certainly not the same thing as imagining *nothing*. On the contrary to imagine a centaur is plainly quite a different thing from imagining a griffin; whereas, it might seem, if both were nothing—pure non-entities, there would be no difference between imagining the one and the other. A centaur then, it seems, is not nothing: it is something which I do imagine. And if it is *something*, isn't that the same thing as saying that there is such a thing—that it is or has being? I certainly do imagine *something* when I imagine one; and what *is* 'something' it would seem, must *be*—there *is* such a thing as what I imagine. But it would also seem, that 'centaur' is just a name for this something which I do imagine. And it would seem, therefore, that there certainly must *be* such a thing as a centaur, else I could not imagine it. How, therefore, can we maintain our proposition which seemed so certain, that there is *no* such thing as a centaur?[33]

A doctrine similar to that of Russell and Moore, as contained in the foregoing quotations, is attributed by Russell to the Austrian philosopher Alexius Meinong (1853–1920).[34] It was from this sort of ontological view—one that luxuriantly populated the realm of being with all sorts of queer entities, including golden mountains, round squares, chimeras, and the like—that Russell sought to free himself by means of the Theory of Descriptions. One of the motives he had in developing his theory was to reduce his ontological commitments—his toleration of this proliferation of entities. It was a reduction supported by adherence to Ockham's Principle and to what he characterized as a "robust sense of reality." Russell put the matter as follows:

It is argued, e.g. by Meinong, that we can speak about "the golden mountain," "the round square," and so on; we can make true propositions of which these are the subjects; hence they must have some kind of logical being, since otherwise the propositions in which they occur would be meaningless. In such theories, it seems to me, there is a failure of that feeling for reality which ought to be preserved even in the most abstract studies. Logic, I should maintain, must no more admit a unicorn than zoology can; for logic is concerned with the real world just as truly as zoology, though with its more abstract and general features. To say that unicorns have an existence in heraldry, or in literature, or in imagination, is a most pitiful and paltry evasion. What exists in heraldry is not an animal, made of flesh and blood, moving and breathing of its own initiative. What exists is a picture, or a description in words. Similarly, to maintain that Hamlet, for example, exists in his own world, namely, in the world of Shakespeare's imagination, just as truly as (say) Napoleon existed in the ordinary world, is to say something deliberately confusing, or else confused to a degree which is scarcely credible. There is only one world, the "real" world: Shakespeare's imagination is part of it, and the thoughts that he had in writing Hamlet are real. So are the thoughts that we have in reading the play. But it is of the very essence of fiction that only the thoughts, feelings, etc., in Shakespeare and his readers are real, and that there is not, in addition to them, an objective Hamlet. When you have taken account of all the feelings roused by Napoleon in writers and readers of history, you have not touched the actual man; but in the case of Hamlet you have come to the end of him. If no one thought about Hamlet, there would be nothing left of him; if no one had thought about Napoleon, he would have soon seen to it that some one did. The sense of reality is vital in logic, and whoever juggles with it by pretending that Hamlet has another kind of reality is doing a disservice to thought. A robust sense of reality is very necessary in framing a correct analysis of propositions about unicorns, golden mountains, round squares, and other such pseudo-objects.[35]

Let us return to Russell's paper "On Denoting" and its statement of the kinds of puzzles to which his theory proposed to offer a solution. We have already considered the puzzle about the apparent contradiction in referring to a 'nonexistent entity', for example 'the difference between A and B', where there is no such difference, i.e., where this expression lacks a referent. A closely related type of example is formulated by Russell as follows, and is the second of the puzzles he asks us to consider:

By the law of excluded middle, either '*A* is *B*' or '*A* is not *B*' must be true. Hence either 'the present King of France is bald' or 'the present King of France is not bald' must be true. Yet if we enumerated the things that are bald, and then the things that are not bald, we should not find the present King of France in either list. Hegelians, who love a synthesis, will probably conclude that he wears a wig.[36]

Here the question is what to make of the use of the definite descriptive phrase, 'the present King of France', when such a phrase is used at a time when there is no monarchy in France. The expression 'the present King of France' is presumably meaningful. Yet when used as a subject in a sentence in which one either affirms or denies a predicate ('is bald' or 'is not bald') of this subject, in either case one gets a false proposition, since there is in fact nothing to which the expression 'the present King of France' can be applied. Yet according to the Law of Excluded Middle, of two contradictory statements one must be true, both cannot be false. How then can we resolve the apparent conflict of this situation with an accepted law of logic?*

The third puzzle introduced by Russell in his paper "On Denoting" has to do with the question of how to interpret a definite description used in an identity statement, where that statement is itself embedded in indirect or oblique discourse.

> If *a* is identical with *b*, whatever is true of the one is true of the other, and either may be substituted for the other in any proposition without altering the truth or falsehood of that proposition. Now George IV wished to know whether Scott was the author of *Waverley;* and in fact Scott was the author of *Waverley.* Hence we may substitute *Scott* for *the author of 'Waverley',* and thereby prove that George IV wished to know whether Scott was Scott. Yet an interest in the law of identity can hardly be attributed to the first gentleman of Europe.[38]

The puzzle Russell here describes is of a type we encountered in our discussions of Frege's philosophy. Frege sought to give an analysis of identity statements and to provide a means to distinguish the two identity statements '*a* =*a*' and '*a* =*b*'. Frege, too, was interested in examining the semantic status of those propositions that belong to indirect discourse. In the above example Russell combines both problems.

The special character of Russell's Theory of Descriptions is best approached and understood when seen against the background of Frege's contributions to semantics and logic. In elaborating his theory Russell adopts *some* of the Fregean distinctions and uses them for his own purposes. In other respects his proposed solution is quite different from the kind of approach Frege would have taken to the problems Russell considers. Before proceeding, therefore, to examine the main lines of Russell's theory, let us pause briefly to recall the relevant distinctions in Frege's philosophy.

---

* It should be noted that in order for Russell to argue that this is a serious puzzle, it is necessary for him to maintain, as indeed he does, that both statements are *false*, because the definite description, as used, fails to designate some real entity. A number of later critics of Russell, among them Geach and Strawson, argue that Russell's account of the matter is incorrect. Instead of saying, with Russell, that the statements 'The present King of France is bald' and 'The present King of France is not bald' are each of them false, it is more appropriate to hold, these critics say, that neither statement can be meaningfully asserted. Neither statement can arise, and be judged either true or false, since to make such a statement and allow for an appraisal of its truth, it is necessary to presuppose that there is in fact a referent for the expression 'the present King of France'. If this presupposition is denied (as it would have to be in the given circumstances) the sentence cannot be used to make a genuine statement.[37]

Frege makes a fundamental distinction between proper names and predicate expressions (concept-words and relations). Frege's use of the expression 'proper name' is a broad one. It includes not only what we should ordinarily recognize as proper names (e.g., 'Abraham Lincoln', 'Socrates'), but also any linguistic device such as definite descriptions— e.g., 'the tallest mountain in Alaska' — that might be used to designate an individual object. In short, Frege's use of the label 'proper name' is equivalent to that of 'singular term', whether simple or complex.

In Frege's view, proper names (as he understands this expression) stand for something *complete*. A proper name, in order to serve as such, has a sense associated with it. Not all proper names, however, have a referent. In a well-designed scientific language, every proper name would have both a single clear sense and a referent. It is by means of the sense of a proper name that we could pick out the individual referred to by that name. In ordinary language, a proper name such as 'Abraham Lincoln' has one or more senses or definite descriptions associated with it. We could use one of these senses or definite descriptions as a replacement for the proper name. For example, in place of 'Abraham Lincoln' we could use the expression 'the President of the United States assassinated during the Civil War' to pick out the individual meant.

Frege distinguishes concept-words and relation-expressions from 'proper names' (singular terms). Concept-words and relation-expressions are the predicative components of complete sentences. As such, predicative expressions are 'incomplete' or 'unsaturated'. By themselves they do not designate any object, nor can one ask whether they say anything true or false. It is only of a complete sentence that one can ask whether it is true or false. A complete sentence is formed in one of two ways: by joining a singular term (or terms) to a predicate expression (e.g., 'Socrates is a philosopher'), or by using quantifiers in a general proposition to bind variables (e.g., 'For all values of x, if x is a man, then x is mortal').

Now let us turn to Russell's Theory of Descriptions and see how he adapts, for his own purposes, some of Frege's distinctions, whereas in other respects — e.g., in his approach to the analysis of such expressions as 'the present King of France' or 'the author of *Waverley*' — he employs a method wholly different from that with which Frege would have approached the matter.

It would seem a reasonable inference from various passages in Russell's writings that he accepted the broad distinction between proper names and predicate expressions — a distinction that Frege made explicit and on which he placed great emphasis.

The only kind of word that is theoretically capable of standing for a particular is a *proper name*, and the whole matter of proper names is rather curious.

Proper names = words for particulars. Df.

I have put that down although, as far as common language goes, it is obviously false. It is true that if you try to think how you are to talk about particulars, you will see that you cannot ever talk about a particular particular except by means of a proper name. You cannot use general words except by way of description. How are you to express in words an atomic proposition? An atomic proposition is one which does mention actual particulars, not merely describe them but actually name them, and you can only name them by means of names.

. . . .

Particulars have this peculiarity, among the sort of objects that you have to take account of in an inventory of the world, that each of them stands entirely alone and is completely self-subsistent. It has that sort of self-subsistence that used to belong to substance, except that it usually only persists through a very short time, so far as our experience goes. That is to say, each particular that there is in the world does not in any way logically depend upon any other particular. Each one might happen to be the whole universe; it is merely empirical fact that this is not the case. There is no reason why you should not have a universe consisting of one particular and nothing else. That is a peculiarity of particulars. In the same way, in order to understand a name for a particular, the only thing necessary is to be acquainted with that particular. When you are acquainted with that particular, you have a full, adequate, and complete understanding of the name, and no further information is required. No further information as to the facts that are true of that particular would enable you to have a fuller understanding of the meaning of the name.[39]

The distinction between proper names as denoting particular objects and general predicative expressions is a distinction that Russell leans on and uses in the several accounts he gives of the Theory of Descriptions. However, we should not be misled into thinking that Russell's acceptance and use of this broad distinction is precisely the same as that in which Frege understood it. Thus in Frege's case there is connected with the distinction the further distinction between sense and reference. However, Russell does not accept Frege's distinction between sense and reference in the treatment he (Russell) gives to the 'meaning' of singular terms. Instead, Russell uses the single (undifferentiated) concept of 'the meaning' of a name. Moreover, he equates what he calls 'the meaning' of a name with its *denotation* —the object or person to which the name applies. Russell writes, "A name is a simple symbol, directly designating an individual which is its meaning, and having this meaning in its own right, independently of the meaning of all other words."[40]

While he does not accept Frege's distinction between sense and reference, and instead claims that the meaning of a name is its denotation (the object itself), Russell nevertheless wishes to avoid subscribing to an ontology bloated by a proliferation of objects. Russell sought to reduce the number of objects or entities in his ontology and to eliminate certain expressions altogether from the category of singular terms. This is one of his main motivations in developing the Theory of Descriptions. In this theory he did not give up the controlling assumption that the meaning of a name consists in the object denoted by the name. If he had accepted Frege's distinction between sense and reference, Russell could have recognized the legitimate use of various singular expressions in ordinary language even though they lacked a referent provided they had a clear sense. He need not have required that there be a realm of objects to serve as the designata of *all* names. And he need not, therefore, have had the incentive to depopulate this realm by eliminating a certain number of those objects from that realm. Nor, finally, need he have ceased to think of certain singular terms as genuinely belonging to that semantic category. For not every singular term must, to be meaningful, denote an object. It is enough if it has a clear sense. And the fact that it has a sense does not require that there be an individual object this sense picks out. However, Russell did not travel this path. Holding on to his view that the meaning of a name is the denoted object, he worked out the Theory of Descriptions as a way of reducing the ontological excesses of a Meinongian as well as of his own earlier philosophy.

Russell, unlike Frege, considers it important to distinguish proper names from definite descriptions. According to Russell, whereas a proper name if it has meaning must denote an object, there are definite descriptions that have no denotation whatever—and in *that* sense have no 'meaning'. Instead of surrendering the claim that meaning is tantamount to having a denotation, Russell will undertake to show that definite descriptions do not function like names at all. Hence when analyzed they disappear as putatively denoting phrases. We need not look for their meaning in the form of denoted objects. Definite descriptions, unlike proper names, are not 'complete'. They have no meaning 'in isolation', i.e., they do not stand for some object apart from their role in a sentence. Definite descriptions are not to be treated like proper names; they are 'incomplete symbols'. Their meaning cannot be specified in isolation, but only in the context of a sentence. In order to do this one has to decompose the entire definite description into several component parts. These parts will be of diverse logical kinds, performing different logical or semantic roles in the sentence into which they have now been reassigned. When all this is accomplished it may be found that a definite description need not have a denotation at all. It need not designate some actual entity or object at all. In realizing all this, we shall be spared the excesses of a 'Meinongian' ontology.

Let us begin by examining four examples of sentences in which definite descriptions occur:

The present king of France is bald.
The golden mountain doesn't exist.
The author of *Waverley* exists.
Scott is the author of *Waverley*.

The definite description 'the present King of France' is used as a grammatical subject in the first sentence, the definite description 'the golden mountain' is used as grammatical subject in the second, and the definite description 'the author of *Waverley*' as subject in the third. The first sentence has as its grammatical predicate 'is bald', the second has as its grammatical predicate 'doesn't exist', and the third has as its grammatical predicate 'exists'. The fourth sentence expresses an identity, with the definite description 'the author of *Waverley*' flanking one side of the identity use of 'is', and the ordinary proper name 'Scott' the other side.

The main technique of the Theory of Descriptions consists in rewriting sentences such as the above, in each of which a definite description occurs, so that the definite description that appears in the original sentence as a seemingly complete singular referring expression disappears in the sentence as rewritten. This is done in order to bring out its true logical form. In the course of doing this, it is replaced by other expressions. The sentence as rewritten will take full advantage of the distinctions among quantifiers, quantified variables, arguments, and predicative functions as these are understood in modern logic.

Consider first, for example, the sentence 'The present King of France is bald'. As rewritten, the expression 'the present King of France' will now be displaced from its original position as logical subject of a subject-predicate proposition. According to Russell's recommendations, the sentence will now read:

> There is somebody or other of whom it is true that (1) he is a present King of France, (2) nobody other than this person is so, and (3) he is bald.

> Or equivalently: There is an individual object, say c, such that (1) an object is a present King of France, (2) one and only one object is identical with c, and (3) c is bald.

In this restatement, the original definite description ('the present King of France') no longer appears. In its place we now have the existential quantifier ('there is'), the *new predicate* expression 'a present King of France', the original predicate ('is bald'), the use of a constant ('c') to denote a particular individual, and the expression for identity. The original definite description no longer appears in the argument place of the original predicate ('is bald'). Instead, there is a new predicate expression ('is a present King of France') extracted from the original definite description. This new predicate is now joined as a predicate to the original predicate ('is bald'). Both of these predicate expressions ('is a present King of France' and 'is bald') are, in Russell's terminology, *incomplete symbols* (Frege called them 'unsaturated'). As incomplete symbols, they constitute what Russell calls 'propositional functions', i.e., expressions with *argument places*. Once supplied with arguments in appropriate argument places (either through the use of quantified variables or by means of individual constants), the propositional functions (predicates) are transformed into propositions, and as such are either true or false. The sentence of our initial example, rewritten with the aid of these logical ideas, conveys the claim that there is one and only one object to which the predicates 'is present King of France' and 'is bald' apply. Since there is, in fact, no individual having the property conveyed by the predicate 'is present King of France', *the entire sentence is false*. This is essentially the solution Russell proposes to one of the puzzles we mentioned earlier as stated in the paper "On Denoting".

> If I say 'The present King of France is bald', that implies that the present King of France exists. If I say, 'The present King of France has a fine head of hair', that also implies that the present King of France exists. Therefore unless you understand how a proposition containing a description is to be denied, you will come to the conclusion that it is not true either that the present King of France is bald or that he is not bald, because if you were to enumerate all the things that are bald you would not find him there, and if you were to enumerate all the things that are not bald, you would not find him there either. The only suggestion I have found for dealing with that on conventional lines is to suppose that he wears a wig. You can only avoid the hypothesis that he wears a wig by observing that the denial of the proposition 'The present King of France is bald' will not be 'The present King of France is not bald', if you mean by that 'There is such a person as the King of France and that person is not bald'. The reason of this is that when you state that the present King of France is bald you say 'There is a c such that c is now King of France and c is bald' and the denial is not 'There is a c such that c is now King of France and c is not bald'. It is more complicated. It is: 'Either there is not a c such that c is now King of France, or, if there is such a c, then c is not bald.' Therefore you see that, if you want to deny the proposition 'The present King of France is bald', you can do it by denying that he exists, instead of by denying that he is bald. In order to deny this statement that the present King of France is bald, which is a statement consisting of two parts, you can proceed by denying either part. You can deny the one part, which would lead you to suppose that the present King of France exists but is not bald, or the other part, which will lead you to the denial that the present King of France exists; and either of those two denials will lead you to the falsehood of the proposition 'The present King of France is bald'.[41]

Consider next the statement

> The golden mountain doesn't exist.

An essential condition for avoiding the puzzle into which one lands if this condition is not recognized is to treat this sentence as not having a subject-predicate form, despite surface grammatical appearances. The expression 'the golden mountain' is not to be taken as a denoting phrase i.e., as functioning in the way a name does, nor is 'doesn't exist' to be taken as a predicate.

(An) important distinction between names and descriptions is that a name cannot occur significantly in a proposition unless there is something that it names, whereas a description is not subject to this limitation. Meinong, for whose work I had had a great respect, had failed to note this difference. He pointed out that one can make statements in which the logical subject is 'the golden mountain' although no golden mountain exists. He argued, if you say that the golden mountain does not exist, it is obvious that there is something that you are saying does not exist—namely, the golden mountain; therefore the golden mountain must subsist in some shadowy Platonic world of being, for otherwise your statement that the golden mountain does not exist would have no meaning. I confess that, until I hit upon the theory of descriptions, this argument seemed to me convincing. The essential point of the theory was that, although 'the golden mountain' may be grammatically the subject of a significant proposition, such a proposition when rightly analyzed no longer has such a subject. The proposition 'the golden mountain does not exist' becomes 'the propositional function "x is golden and a mountain" is false for all values of x.'[42]

Once again, the definite description has been rewritten so that it no longer appears, as such, as the logical subject of the sentence. The existential quantifier (read as 'there is') replaces the original grammatical predicate ('doesn't exist'). The descriptive expressions 'made of gold' and 'a mountain' are extracted from the original definite description and treated as *predicates* in the rewritten sentence. And what the entire sentence now says, with the aid of bound variables and the sign for negation, is that there are *no* argument expressions (to represent individual objects) that could be used in the argument-places of the conjointly used predicates 'made of gold' and 'a mountain' to yield a true proposition. This true negative existential statement avoids the puzzle that results from taking the original statement as basically of a subject-predicate form.

In line with the foregoing mode of analysis, it is easy to see how one needs to rewrite the sentence 'The author of *Waverley* exists'.

'The author of *Waverley* exists': there are two things required for that. First of all, what is 'the author of *Waverley*'? It is the person who wrote *Waverley*, i.e., we are coming now to this, that you have a propositional function involved, viz., 'x writes *Waverley*', and the author of *Waverley* is the person who writes *Waverley*, and in order that the person who writes *Waverley* may exist, it is necessary that this propositional function should have two properties:

1. It must be true for *at least* one x.
2. It must be true for *at most* one x.

If nobody had ever written *Waverley* the author could not exist, and if two people had written it, *the* author could not exist. So that you want these two properties, the one that it is true for at least one x, and the other that it is true for at most one x, both of which are required for existence.

. . . .

That is what I mean when I say that the author of *Waverley* exists. When I say 'the author of *Waverley* exists', I mean that there is an entity *c* such that '*x* wrote *Waverley*' is true when *x* is *c,* and is false when *x* is not *c.* 'The author of *Waverley*' as a constituent has quite disappeared there, so that when I say 'The author of *Waverley* exists' I am not saying anything about the author of *Waverley.* You have instead this elaborate to-do with propositional functions, and 'the author of *Waverley*' has disappeared.[43]*

In the analysis of the foregoing sentences in which 'exists' and 'does not exist' appear as grammatical predicates, Russell adopts the view (already argued by Frege) that 'existence' is not a predicate that can be meaningfully affirmed or denied of an individual. Russell clearly opts for the use of the existential quantifier as conveying the notion of existence; the meaning of 'exists' is expressed by the words 'there is'. This reading of the existential quantifier is to be sharply differentiated from the meaning of a descriptive predicate.

There is a vast amount of philosophy that rests upon the notion that existence is, so to speak, a property that you can attribute to things, and that the things that exist have the property of existence and the things that do not exist do not. That is rubbish, whether you take kinds of things, or individual things described. When I say, e.g., 'Homer existed', I am meaning by 'Homer' some description, as 'the author of the Homeric poems', and I am asserting that those poems were written by one man, which is a very doubtful proposition; but if you could get hold of the actual person who did actually write those poems (supposing there was such a person), to say of him that he existed would be uttering nonsense, not a falsehood but nonsense, because it is only of persons described that it can be significantly said that they exist. . . . It is an entire mistake to argue: 'This is the author of the Homeric poems and the author of the Homeric poems exists, therefore this exists'. It is only where a propositional function comes in that existence may be significantly asserted. You can assert 'The so-and-so exists', meaning that there is just one *c* which has those properties, but when you get hold of a *c* that has them, you cannot say of this *c* that it exists, because that is nonsense: it is not false, but it has no meaning at all.

*The symbolism of *Principia Mathematica* may be used to convey the form of the analyses we have just examined.

Let the symbol $(\imath x)\,(\phi x)$ represent the form of a definite description, 'the so-and-so'; it is to be read as 'the unique *x* which has the property ϕ'.

Given a statement in ordinary language which has the form 'The so-and-so exists', we write this as

E! $(\imath x)\,(\phi x)$

The symbol 'E! $(\imath x)\,(\phi x)$' is defined in *Principia Mathematica* as follows:

$$(14.02)\ \text{E!}\,(\imath x)\,(\phi x)\ .\ =\ :\ (\exists b)\ :\ \phi x\ .\equiv_x x = b\ \text{Df.}$$

What this says is:

'The so-and-so exists' is to be understood as: 'For all values of *x* there is some *b* such that there is one and only one *x*, identical with *b,* that has the property ϕ'.

So the individuals that there are in the world do not exist, or rather it is nonsense to say that they exist and nonsense to say that they do not exist. It is not a thing you can say when you have named them, but only when you have described them. When you say 'Homer exists', you mean 'Homer' is a description which applies to something. A description when it is fully stated is always of the form 'the so-and-so'.[44]

Finally, consider the identity

Scott is the author of *Waverley.*

Once again, the expression 'the author of *Waverley*' is replaced by an expression in which one makes use of quantified variables, arguments, and genuine predicate expressions. Then the sentence 'Scott is the author of *Waverley*' can be rewritten as 'It is not always false that x wrote *Waverley,* that it is always true of y that if y wrote *Waverley,* y is identical with $x,$ and that Scott is identical with x'; or, in slightly less complicated form: 'One and only one entity wrote *Waverley,* and Scott was identical with that one'. [45] And if the entire identity sentence 'Scott is the author of *Waverley*' occurs in indirect discourse, as in the sentence 'George IV wished to know whether Scott is the author of *Waverley*', this can be rewritten to take advantage of the above elimination of the phrase 'the author of *Waverley*'; it is not a phrase to be treated in the way one does a proper name or as replaceable by the name 'Scott'.

The puzzle about George IV's curiosity is now seen to have a very simple solution. The proposition 'Scott was the author of *Waverley*' which was written out in its unabbreviated form in the preceding paragraph, does not contain any constituent 'the author of *Waverley*' for which we could substitute 'Scott'. [46]

For Russell, as we have seen, definite descriptions are treated in such a way that they are taken to be 'incomplete symbols'. Such meaning as they have is not to be found by considering them in isolation, i.e., as designating an object in the way a name does, but only by seeing how the various linguistic components into which they may be analyzed contribute in their several ways to the logical structure of the sentence as a whole. We can then proceed to evaluate whether the sentence as a whole is true or not.

It remains, however, to say something about Russell's views on proper names. Does what falls within this category wholly exclude definite descriptions? The answer to this question is somewhat complicated. If we were to cull the passages in which Russell discusses this matter, we should find that, if taken collectively and without regard to the periods at which they were written or the audiences for which they were intended, they would show some internal looseness, variation, even inconsistency.

There are passages in which Russell would wish to contrast *ordinary proper names* with definite descriptions. On these occasions, in order to bring out the contrast between them, he speaks of an ordinary proper name as 'complete' — as having a meaning consisting of its denotation (its object) — as contrasted with a definite description. This is the case, for example, in the following passage:

> You sometimes find people speaking as if descriptive phrases were names, and you will find it suggested, e.g., that such a proposition as 'Scott is the author of *Waverley*' really asserts that 'Scott' and the 'the author of *Waverley*' are two names for the same person. That is an entire delusion; first of all, because 'the author of *Waverley*' is not a name, and, secondly, because, as you can perfectly well see, if that were what is meant, the proposition would be one like 'Scott is Sir Walter', and would not depend upon any fact except that the person in question was so called, because a name is what a man is called.
>
> . . . .
>
> If you were to try to substitute for 'the author of *Waverley*' in that proposition any name whatever, say '*c*', so that the proposition becomes 'Scott is *c*', then if '*c*' is a name for anybody who is not Scott, that proposition would become false, while if on the other hand, '*c*' is a name for Scott, then the proposition will become simply a tautology. It is at once obvious that if '*c*' were 'Scott' itself, 'Scott is Scott' is just a tautology. But if you take any other name which is just a name for Scott, then if the name is being used *as* a name and not as a description, the proposition will still be a tautology. For the name itself is merely a means of pointing to the thing, and does not occur in what you are asserting, so that if one thing has two names, you make exactly the same assertion whichever of the two names you use, provided they are really names and not truncated descriptions.
>
> So there are only two alternatives. If '*c*' is a name, the proposition 'Scott is *c*' is either false or tautologous. But the proposition 'Scott is the author of *Waverley*' is neither, and therefore is not the same as any proposition of the form 'Scott is *c*', where '*c*' is a name. That is another way of illustrating the fact that a description is quite a different thing from a name.[47]

Russell's major purpose, in the foregoing passage, is to bring out the nature of definite descriptions. In order to do this, he uses ordinary proper names as a foil, as if they were different from definite descriptions. This pretension about ordinary proper names (e.g., 'Scott') being wholly different from definite descriptions (e.g., 'the author of *Waverley*') is to be understood, in the present context, as only serving a pedagogic purpose. It is not to be taken, however, as giving an analysis of the nature of proper names from a more thorough, technical point of view. For Russell would defend the view that even ordinary proper names are themselves only disguised or truncated definite descriptions. Thus, if we wished to set out the 'meaning' of such ordinary proper names, we should first need to translate them, explicitly, into the definite descriptions with which they may be equated. Indeed, only by so doing could we avoid, for example, what would otherwise be the paradox of using an ordinary proper name in a negative existential statement. Thus in the sentence 'Romulus did not exist' we must replace 'Romulus' by some definite description, and then we could show how it is possible for the statement 'Romulus did not exist' to be both meaningful and true.

What pass for names in language, like 'Socrates', 'Plato', and so forth, were originally intended to fulfil this function of standing for particulars, and we do accept, in ordinary daily life, as particulars all sorts of things that really are not so. The names that we commonly use, like 'Socrates', are really abbreviations for descriptions; not only that, but what they describe are not particulars but complicated systems of classes or series. A name, in the narrow logical sense of a word whose meaning is a particular, can only be applied to a particular with which the speaker is acquainted, because you cannot name anything you are not acquainted with. You remember, when Adam named the beasts, they came before him one by one, and he became acquainted with them and named them. We are not acquainted with Socrates, and therefore cannot name him. When we use the word 'Socrates', we are really using a description. Our thought may be rendered by some such phrase as, 'The Master of Plato', or 'The philosopher who drank the hemlock', or 'The person whom logicians assert to be mortal', but we certainly do not use the name as a name in the proper sense of the word. [48]

This proposition 'Romulus existed' or 'Romulus did not exist' does introduce a propositional function, because the name 'Romulus' is not really a name but a sort of truncated description. It stands for a person who did such-and-such things, who killed Remus, and founded Rome, and so on. It is short for 'the person who was called "Romulus".' If it were really a name, the question of existence could not arise, because a name has got to name something or it is not a name, and if there is no such person as Romulus there cannot be a name for that person who is not there, so that this single word 'Romulus' is really a sort of truncated or telescoped description, and if you think of it as a name you will get into logical errors. When you realize that it is a description, you realize therefore that any proposition about Romulus really introduces the propositional function embodying the description, as (say) 'x was called "Romulus".' That introduces you at once to a propositional function, and when you say 'Romulus did not exist', you mean that this propositional function is not true for one value of x. [49]

In general, Russell would say that *any ordinary* proper name could be — and for purposes of logical analysis *should* be — replaced by one or more definite descriptions. This would be the case not only for ordinary proper names for which there are no denotations (e.g., Santa Claus, Zeus), or for ordinary proper names where it is questionable or controversial that there is a denotation (e.g., Romulus, Homer), but for ordinary proper names where we are quite confident the name does have a denotation (e.g., Abraham Lincoln, Aristotle). In every case, including the last, we should need to replace an ordinary proper name by a definite description and proceed to handle the replacement as an incomplete symbol in the manner previously discussed. In short, every subject-predicate statement in which such an ordinary proper name appears as subject, e.g.,

'Socrates is wise', would be restated in the same way as we would reformulate a statement such as 'The present King of France is bald', i.e.,
with the aid of quantifiers, predicates (propositional functions), and the
sign for identity.

   If for Russell, then, ordinary proper names are only disguised or
truncated definite descriptions, are there any proper names that are not so
replaceable or reducible? Russell's view is that there are, and he calls
these genuine proper names *'logically proper names'*. They are not to be
confused with ordinary proper names. A logically proper name is what
emerges from performing a correct and thorough logical and epistemological analysis. A logically proper name designates something simple. What
it designates cannot be conveyed by means of a definite description. The
drive to find logically proper names is motivated by Russell's view that
ordinary proper names are not logically proper names. Yet, he believes,
there must be some expressions that could serve in this capacity. He is
supported in this conviction by his general epistemological view that all
descriptions, if meaningful, must rest upon data which are known directly, by acquaintance. A typical example, for Russell, of what a logically proper name denotes is provided by a sense datum. It is had by a
particular person at a particular moment of his experience. He can point
to this datum by means of a demonstrative such as 'this' or 'that'. It is this
pure demonstrative that is a logically proper name. It identifies a bare
particular, the object of this demonstrative. A logically proper name,
functioning as a pure demonstrative, has only a denotative role; it has no
connotation. It does not express or convey any properties. It has no latent
predicative components. A logically proper name *indicates* something. It
does not *describe* anything, either explicitly or implicitly.

   That makes it very difficult to get any instance of a name at all in the proper
strict logical sense of the word. The only words one does use as names in the
logical sense are words like 'this' or 'that'. One can use 'this' as a name to stand
for a particular with which one is acquainted at the moment. We say 'This is
white'. If you agree that 'This is white', meaning the 'this' that you see, you are
using 'this' as a proper name. But if you try to apprehend the proposition that I am
expressing when I say 'This is white', you cannot do it. If you mean this piece of
chalk as a physical object, then you are not using a proper name. It is only when
you use 'this' quite strictly, to stand for an actual object of sense, that it is really a
proper name. And in that it has a very odd property for a proper name, namely
that it seldom means the same thing two moments running and does not mean the
same thing to the speaker and to the hearer. It is an *ambiguous* proper name, but it
is really a proper name all the same, and it is almost the only thing I can think of
that is used properly and logically in the sense that I was talking of for a proper
name. The importance of proper names, in the sense of which I am talking, is in
the sense of logic, not of daily life. You can see why it is that in the logical language set forth in *Principia Mathematica* there are not any names, because there
we are not interested in particular particulars but only in general particulars, if I
may be allowed such a phrase. [50]

CLASSES AND TYPES

For Russell, as for Frege, much effort went into arguing for the merits of the logicist thesis in the foundations of mathematics. In carrying through this project, both writers give special attention to showing that the mathematical concept of number, so fundamental to many branches of mathematics, could be defined in terms of (and so 'reduced' to) the purely logical notions of 'class', 'membership in a class', and 'similarity'. In a manner that he explicitly acknowledges is strongly influenced by Frege's approach, Russell sums up the matter as follows:

Many philosophers, when attempting to define number, are really setting to work to define plurality, which is quite a different thing. *Number* is what is characteristic of numbers, as *man* is what is characteristic of men. A plurality is not an instance of number, but of some particular number. A trio of men, for example, is an instance of the number 3, and the number 3 is an instance of number; but the trio is not an instance of number.

. . . .

Number is a way of bringing together certain collections, namely, those that have a given number of terms. We can suppose all couples in one bundle, all trios in another, and so on. In this way we obtain various bundles of collections, each bundle consisting of all the collections that have a certain number of terms. Each bundle is a class whose members are collections, *i.e.* classes; thus each is a class of classes. The bundle consisting of all couples, for example, is a class of classes: each couple is a class with two members, and the whole bundle of couples is a class with an infinite number of members, each of which is a class of two members.

. . . .

Two classes are said to be "similar" when there is a one–one correlation which correlates the terms of the one class each with one term of the other class, in the same manner in which the relation of marriage correlates husbands with wives.

. . . .

We may thus use the notion of "similarity" to decide when two collections are to belong to the same bundle . . . . We want to make one bundle containing the class that has no members: this will be for the number 0. Then we want a bundle of all the classes that have one member: this will be for the number 1. Then, for the number 2, we want a bundle consisting of all couples; then one of all trios; and so on. Given any collection, we can define the bundle it is to belong to as being the class of all those collections that are "similar" to it. It is very easy to see that if (for example) a collection has three members, the class of all those collections that are similar to it will be the class of trios. And whatever number of terms a collection may have, those collections that are "similar" to it will have the same number of terms. We may take this as a *definition* of "having the same number of terms."

. . . .

We naturally think that the class of couples (for example) is something different from the number 2. But there is no doubt about the class of couples: it is indubitable and not difficult to define, whereas the number 2, in any other sense, is a metaphysical entity about which we can never feel sure that it exists or that we have tracked it down. It is therefore more prudent to content ourselves with the class of couples, which we are sure of, than to hunt for a problematical number 2 which must always remain elusive. Accordingly we set up the following definition:—

The number of a class is the class of all those classes that are similar to it.

Thus the number of a couple will be the class of all couples. In fact, the class of all couples will *be* the number 2, according to our definition. At the expense of a little oddity, this definition secures definiteness and indubitableness; and it is not difficult to prove that numbers so defined have all the properties that we expect numbers to have.[51]

Here, then, in this sketch of the fundamental orientation of the logicist program, we can see the operation of Ockham's Principle clearly at work in the drive to reduce one's ontological commitments. If it can be shown that numbers are at bottom classes of similar classes, then the ontological account of what there is need not affirm the independent reality (being) of numbers. If the reduction of numbers to classes can be effected, it is enough to posit, in one's ontology, the reality of classes. Such was Russell's underlying, initial motivation when he set out to uphold the logicist program.

But at an early stage in carrying through this project, as we previously noted, the young Russell had confronted Frege with a major snag, the famous paradox about the class of all classes that are not members of themselves. It was this 'Russell paradox' to which Russell called Frege's attention in 1902, when the latter's *Grundgesetze der Arithmetik* was nearing publication. The challenge was serious enough, as both Frege and Russell realized, to require an effective solution if the logicist program was to be carried through. In the course of searching for such an effective solution, Russell not only carefully reexamined the particular paradox he had uncovered, but the very 'logical' notions of class and membership in a class that lay at the center of the whole approach. The Russell paradox, as was soon clearly recognized, was only one of a whole group of similar paradoxes. The solution, if it was to be found, should if possible resolve them all, since they all showed certain common features. What these features are, what diagnosis one was to give of them, and how to resolve the difficulties — is precisely what Russell sought to achieve by his Theory of Types. In an appendix to his *Principles of Mathematics* (1903), Russell had suggested a simple, 'crude' version of this theory. In subsequent writings, for example in his important paper "Mathematical Logic as Based on a Theory of Types" (1908), as well as in numerous other writings, Russell refined and revised the main thrust of the theory. The problems raised in these various discussions, and the controversies they provoked, continue to be of active concern to philosophers, mathematicians, and logicians down to the present day. Much of this discussion is of a highly technical nature, and the details of this topic lie beyond the scope of our present interest. Nevertheless it will be both relevant and important to obtain at least a brief glimpse of the main lines of Russell's approach.

For purposes of setting out the basic features of the Theory of Types, we may borrow an analogy from medicine, and distinguish three stages: (1) identifying the 'disease', (2) diagnosing the reason or causes for its occurrence, and (3) proposing a method for its cure. In our present case, the 'disease' consists in certain breakdowns in our reasoning. These consist in a number of paradoxes or antinomies. In each case we arrive at a contradiction though reasoning in an apparently cogent way. How can we avoid such a result? The paradox calls for a resolution, a pointing out of the 'error' whatever it is, and not, of course, in surrendering the Law of Contradiction and accepting the inconsistency. The second step is to locate the 'error'. Here Russell's 'diagnosis' consists in calling attention to a common, recurrent feature in the classic paradoxes (including the one he himself discovered). Russell claims that the cause for the error in each case is the violation of The Vicious-Circle Principle. The violation involves making reference to *illegitimate totalities*. (We shall explain this terminology shortly.) The third step in Russell's Theory of Types is the recommendation of a positive 'cure' for the diagnosed ailment. This calls for distinguishing different *logical types*, and avoiding the improper mixture of types.

We shall select three well-known paradoxes as representative of the kinds of puzzlements from which the Theory of Types takes its point of departure. Russell summarizes each of these puzzles in "The Philosophy of Logical Atomism."

The first is associated with the name of Georg Cantor, the founder of set theory; it has to do with the question whether or not there is a greatest cardinal number.

Every class of things that you can choose to mention has some cardinal number. That follows very easily from the definition of cardinal numbers as classes of similar classes, and you would be inclined to suppose that the class of all things there are in the world would have about as many members as a class could be reasonably expected to have. The plain man would suppose you could not get a larger class than the class of all the things there are in the world. On the other hand, it is very easy to prove that if you take selections of some of the members of a class, making those selections in every conceivable way that you can, the number of different selections that you can make is greater than the original number of terms. That is easy to see with small numbers. Suppose you have a class with just three numbers, a, b, c. The first selection that you can make is the selection of no terms. The next of a alone, b alone, c alone. Then bc, ca, ab, *abc*, which makes in all 8 (i.e., 2^3) selections. Generally speaking, if you have *n* terms, you can make 2^n selections. It is very easy to prove that 2^n is always greater than *n*, whether *n* happens to be finite or not. So you find that the total number of things in the world is not so great as the number of classes that can be made up out of those things. I am asking you to take all these propositions for granted, because there is not time to go into the proofs, but they are all in Cantor's work. Therefore you will find that the total number of things in the world is by no means the greatest number. On the contrary, there is a hierarchy of numbers greater than that. That, on the face of it, seems to land you in a contradiction. You have, in fact, a perfectly precise arithmetical proof that there are *fewer* things in heaven or earth than are dreamt of in *our* philosophy.[52]

The second famous paradox is the one Russell discovered, and that we previously noted in our account of its impact on Frege. Here is Russell's summary:

I pass now to the contradiction about classes that are not members of themselves. You would say generally that you would not expect a class to be a member of itself. For instance, if you take the class of all the teaspoons in the world, that is not in itself a teaspoon. Or if you take all the human beings in the world, the whole class of them is not in turn a human being. Normally you would say you cannot expect a whole class of things to be itself a member of that class. But there are apparent exceptions. If you take, e.g., all the things in the world that are not teaspoons and make up a class of them, the class obviously (you would say) will not be a teaspoon. And so generally with negative classes. And not only with negative classes, either, for if you think for a moment that classes are things in the same sense in which things are things, you will then have to say that the class consisting of all the things in the world is itself a thing in the world, and that therefore this class is a member of itself. Certainly you would have thought that it was clear that the class consisting of all the classes in the world is itself a class. That I think most people would feel inclined to suppose, and therefore you would get there a case of a class which is a member of itself. If there is any sense in asking whether a class is a member of itself or not, then certainly in all the cases of the ordinary classes of everyday life you find that a class is not a member of itself. Accordingly, that being so, you could go on to make up the class of all those classes that are not members of themselves, and you can ask yourself, when you have done that, is that class a member of itself or is it not?

Let us first suppose that it is a member of itself. In that case it is one of those classes that are not members of themselves, i.e., it is not a member of itself. Let us then suppose that it is not a member of itself. In that case it is not one of those classes that are not members of themselves, i.e., it is one of those classes that are members of themselves, i.e., it is a member of itself. Hence either hypothesis, that it is or that it is not a member of itself, leads to its contradiction. If it is a member of itself, it is not, and if it is not, it is.[53]

Finally, there is the well-known paradox illustrated by the statement 'This sentence is false'. If it is true, it is false; if it is false, it is true. The prototype of this is the famous paradox of the liar—the saying of Epimenides the Cretan that 'All Cretans are liars'.

Epimenides was a man who slept for sixty years without stopping, and I believe that it was at the end of that nap that he made the remark that all Cretans were liars. It can be put more simply in the form: if a man makes the statement 'I am lying', is he lying or not? If he is, that is what he said he was doing, so he is speaking the truth and not lying. If, on the other hand, he is not lying, then plainly he is speaking the truth in saying that he is lying, and therefore he is lying, since he says truly that that is what he is doing. It is an ancient puzzle, and nobody treated that sort of thing as anything but a joke until it was found that it had to do with such important and practical problems as whether there is a greatest cardinal or ordinal number. Then at last these contradictions were treated seriously.[54]

According to Russell, what underlies these and other standard paradoxes is the error committed in making reference to certain *illegitimate totalities,* or, what amounts to the same thing, reasoning in a *viciously circular* way. A clear example of this is to be found in Russell's diagnosis of the third of the above-mentioned paradoxes — the one about 'All Cretans are liars'.

The man who says 'I am lying' is really asserting 'There is a proposition which I am asserting and which is false'. That is presumably what you mean by lying. In order to get out the contradiction you have to take that whole assertion of his as one of the propositions to which his assertion applies; i.e., when he says 'There is a proposition which I am asserting and which is false', the word 'proposition' has to be interpreted as to include among propositions his statement to the effect that he is asserting a false proposition. Therefore you have to suppose that you have a certain totality, viz., that of propositions, but that that totality contains members which can only be defined in terms of itself. Because when you say 'There is a proposition which I am asserting and which is false', that is a statement whose meaning can only be got by reference to the totality of propositions. You are not saying which among all the propositions there are in the world it is that you are asserting and that is false. Therefore it presupposes that the totality of propositions is spread out before you and that some one, though you do not say which, is being asserted falsely. It is quite clear that you get into a vicious circle if you first suppose that this totality of propositions is spread out before you, so that you can without picking any definite one say 'Some one out of this totality is being asserted falsely', and that yet, when you have gone on to say 'Some one out of this totality is being asserted falsely', that assertion is itself one of the totality you were to pick out from. That is exactly the situation you have in the paradox of the liar. You are supposed to be given first of all a set of propositions, and you assert that some one of these is being asserted falsely, then that assertion itself turns out to be one of the set, so that it is obviously fallacious to suppose the set already there in its entirety. If you are going to say anything about 'all propositions', you will have to define propositions, first of all, in some such way as to exclude those that refer to all the propositions of the sort already defined. It follows that the word 'proposition', in the sense in which we ordinarily try to use it, is a meaningless one, and that we have got to divide propositions up into sets and can make statements about all propositions in a given set, but those propositions will not themselves be members of the set. For instance, I may say 'All atomic propositions are either true or false', but that itself will not be an atomic proposition. If you try to say 'All propositions are either true or false', without qualification, you are uttering nonsense, because if it were not nonsense it would have to be itself a proposition and one of those included in its own scope, and therefore the law of excluded middle as enunciated just now is a meaningless noise. You have to cut propositions up into different types, and you can start with atomic propositions or, if you like, you can start with those propositions that do not refer to sets of propositions at all. Then you will take next those that refer to sets of propositions of that sort that you had first. Those that refer to sets of propositions of the first type, you may call the second type, and so on.

If you apply that to the person who says 'I am lying', you will find that the contradiction has disappeared, because he will have to say what type of liar he is. If he says 'I am asserting a false proposition of the first type', as a matter of fact that statement, since it refers to the totality of propositions of the first type, is of the second type. Hence it is not true that he is asserting a false proposition of the first type, and he remains a liar. Similarly, if he said he was asserting a false proposition of the 30,000th type, that would be a statement of the 30,001st type, so he would still be a liar. And the counter-argument to prove that he was also not a liar has collapsed.[55]

The analysis of the fallacy involved in the Epimenides paradox can be generalized to apply to other well-known paradoxes. It would be found that in every case the paradox results from reference to illegitimate totalities (to the use of viciously circular reasoning) and consequently to the failure to make appropriate distinctions of logical type.

An illegitimate totality results from treating a certain totality or class as presumably properly formed, when in fact it is not so. The Vicious-Circle Principle rules out such guilty or illegitimate totalities. In *Principia Mathematica* this Principle is given the following formulation:

"Whatever involves *all* of a collection must not be one of the collection": or, conversely: "If, provided a certain collection had a total, it would have members only definable in terms of that total, then the said collection has no total."

Another formulation is as follows:

Given any set of objects such that, if we suppose the set to have a total, it will contain members which presuppose this total, then such a set cannot have a total. By saying that a set has "no total," we mean, primarily, that no significant statement can be made about "all its members."[56]

The key idea in the Vicious-Circle Principle is that once the range of instances or members of some totality has been determined, such an 'original' determination of the totality cannot be modified. However, it is precisely such an 'illegitimate' modification in the form of an 'enlargement' of the totality that is involved in all of the paradoxes mentioned.

For each, in one form or another, would change the 'original' makeup of the totality to include a 'new' or different member of that totality. That change in the 'original' makeup of the totality would be brought about by treating as an instance or member of the original totality what is contained in the very statement about (or reference to) the 'original' totality.

To see this more clearly, let us put the matter in terms of sets (classes), and use the standard symbolism of logic.

Let the symbol 'ϵ' represent membership in a class. Let the variable 'x' range over individuals. Let 'A' represent a class whose members are selected in terms of their possessing some property ϕ, where 'possessing the property ϕ' is represented by 'ϕx'. The formula

$$(x)\,(x \in A \leftrightarrow \phi x)$$

states that for all values of x, x is a member of A, if and only if x has ϕ. Then what the Vicious-Circle Principle asserts is that the class A cannot be found within the range of the bound variable x.

The Vicious-Circle Principle constitutes the 'diagnosis' of the root error committed in the various paradoxes we have considered. The Principle may be looked upon as saying something 'negative'—as pointing to what we should *not* do, if illegitimate totalities are to be avoided. However, Russell also sought to give the whole matter a positive cast, to point to what would hold for 'healthy', 'nonpathological' cases. This positive account is what he undertook to provide in his Theory of Types. The formulation of this theory underwent various stages of refinement and amplification. As a result of these developments, it would be necessary in any full account of the theory to distinguish, among other things, (1) the simple and ramified theory of types, (2) the differences between the set-theoretical and semantic paradoxes, (3) the 'no classes' version of the theory as contrasted with other versions of the theory. The details of these and other distinctions are of a highly technical, complex nature and lie beyond the scope of the present discussion. I content myself instead with indicating the general line of approach Russell adopts on the level of the Simple Theory of Types. Russell offers a simple summary of the matter as follows:

> Given any propositional function, say fx, there is a certain range of values of x for which this function is 'significant'—i.e. either true or false. If a is in this range, then fa is a proposition which is either true or false. In addition to substituting a constant for the variable x, there are two other things that may be done with a propositional function: one is to assert that it is always true; and the other, that it is sometimes true. The propositional function, 'if x is human, x is mortal' is always true; the propositional function, 'x is human' is sometimes true. There are thus three things that can be done with a propositional function: the first is to substitute a constant for the variable; the second is to assert all values of the function; and the third is to assert some values or at least one value. The proposi-

tional function itself is only an expression. It does not assert or deny anything. A class, equally, is only an expression. It is only a convenient way of talking about the values of the variable for which the function is true . . . . When I assert all values of a function *fx*, the values that *x* can take must be definite if what I am asserting is to be definite. There must be, that is to say, some totality of possible values of *x*. If I now proceed to create new values defined in terms of that totality, the totality appears to be thereby enlarged and therefore the new values referring to it will refer to that enlarged totality. But, since they must be included in the totality, it can never catch up with them. The process is like trying to jump on to the shadow of your head. We can illustrate this most simply by the paradox of the liar. The liar says, 'everything that I assert is false'. This is, in fact, an assertion which he makes, but it refers to the totality of his assertions and it is only by including it in that totality that a paradox results. We shall have to distinguish between propositions that refer to some totality of propositions and propositions that do not. Those that refer to some totality of propositions can never be members of that totality. We may define first-order propositions as those referring to no totality of propositions; second-order propositions, as those referring to totalities of first-order propositions; and so on, *ad infinitum*. Thus our liar will now have to say, 'I am asserting a false proposition of the first order which is false'. But this is itself a proposition of the second order. He is thus not asserting any proposition of the first order. What he says is, thus, simply false, and the argument that it is also true collapses. Exactly the same argument applies to any proposition of higher order.

It will be found that in all the logical paradoxes there is a kind of reflexive self-reference which is to be condemned on the same ground: viz. that it includes, as a member of a totality, something referring to that totality which can only have a definite meaning if the totality is already fixed.[57]

The basic idea underlying the Theory of Types is that of a 'range of significance of a propositional function'. "A *type* is defined as the range of significance of a propositional function, i.e. as the collection of arguments for which the said function has values."[58] A propositional function is Russell's label for what in Frege's terminology is an unsaturated predicate expression, one that becomes a proposition when supplied with appropriate expressions (proper names or quantified variables) in its 'blank spaces'. A propositional function is an expression containing one or more variables such that when values are assigned to these variables, the expression becomes a proposition. An example of a propositional function is '*x* is human'. As long as *x* is undetermined, it is not either true or false. However, when an appropriate argument or range of arguments is assigned to *x*, the entire expression becomes a proposition and is either true or false. The 'range of significance' of a propositional function has to do with the possible substitution values in the blank space (or spaces) of a propositional function that can be used to convert a propositional function to a proposition. The notion of a propositional function can be used to determine a class. A class is all the objects satisfying some propositional function.

A proposition about a class is always to be reduced to a statement about a function which defines the class, *i.e.* about a function which is satisfied by members of the class and by no other arguments. Thus a class is an object derived from a function and presupposing the function, just as, for example, $(x) . \phi x$ presupposes the function $\phi \hat{x}$.[59]

Given the foregoing distinctions, Russell sums up the main thrust of the Theory of Types as follows:

You can lay it down that a totality of any sort cannot be a member of itself. That applies to what we are saying about classes. For instance, the totality of classes in the world cannot be a class in the same sense in which they are. So we shall have to distinguish a hierarchy of classes. We will start with the classes that are composed entirely of particulars: that will be the first type of classes. Then we will go on to classes whose members are classes of the first type: that will be the second type. Then we will go on to classes whose members are classes of the second type: that will be the third type, and so on. Never is it possible for a class of one type either to be or not to be identical with a class of another type. That applies to the question I was discussing a moment ago, as to how many things there are in the world. Supposing there are three particulars in the world. There are then, as I was explaining, 8 classes of particulars. There will be 2^8 (i.e., 256) classes of classes of particulars, and 2^{256} classes of classes of classes of particulars, and so on. You do not get any contradiction arising out of that, and when you ask yourself the question: 'Is there, or is there not a greatest cardinal number?' the answer depends entirely upon whether you are confining yourself within some one type, or whether you are not. Within any given type there is a greatest cardinal number, namely, the number of objects of that type, but you will always be able to get a larger number by going up to the next type. Therefore, there is no number so great but what you can get a greater number in a sufficiently high type. There you have the two sides of the argument: the one side when the type is given, the other side when the type is not given.[60]

When looked at in wide perspective, the Russellian Theory of Types is a major example of a concern we find running throughout the development of contemporary analytic philosophy: *a concern to distinguish sense and nonsense*. This distinction between sense and nonsense, it is commonly held, needs to be made with respect to the various *questions* human beings raise, as well as with respect to the various kinds of *statements* they make. We saw, earlier, an important example of this interest in Frege's insistence on drawing a distinction between proper names and predicates, as well as a distinction among different levels of concepts. He showed the kinds of nonsense that result from failing to abide by the forms, rules, and criteria that govern the use of these varied types of expressions. Russell's Theory of Types belongs to the same genre, and exemplifies the same kind of concern. We shall study, later, further important examples of this preoccupation with the sense-nonsense distinction in the work of Wittgenstein and in the Logical Positivists. If Russell's Theory of Types has not come to be universally accepted at the present time, this is not to belittle its importance as a contribution to this topic. On the contrary, the ideas behind the Vicious-Circle Principle and the distinctions among types in terms of 'ranges of significance' continue to be of great help as suggestive guidelines, if not as final dogmas or perfected doctrines, to those who continue to be devoted to the general project of demarcating sense from nonsense. In this perspective, Russell's Theory of Types marks a major and memorable step in the formulation of this problem as well as an important attempt to solve it.

CONCLUDING REMARKS

My purpose in the foregoing discussion has been not to explore or summarize all the many different facets of Russell's philosophy. I have not even touched on, much less given even a moderately full account of, his views in the philosophy of mind, the theory of perception, the theory of truth, the philosophy of science, or the philosophy of religion. I have sought, instead, through a few examples, to help the reader get a sense of the quality of his mind, to see the characteristic method of his approach, and the 'go' of his thought. For Russell's impact, great as it has been, has not been to bequeath a more or less finished *system*. He did not found a school of philosophy, nor did he gather about him a group of disciples to expound and propagate a special set of doctrines. Much of what he defended at one time or another in his career he abandoned at a later stage. Much, too, that he stressed has proved evanescent or has retained only a slight technical interest. Yet for all that, it is the style and method of his thinking that inspired others. Even when they came to strongly disagree with his conclusions, the kind of approach Russell adopted in dealing with philosophic problems caught the attention of many philosophers and led them to emulate his efforts. It was, thus, the *methodical* side of his thought, rather than its *doctrinal* side, that needs to be stressed in any estimate of Russell's role in twentieth-century thought.

Having made this point, I must add that it is important not to be misled into trying to sum up the value of Russell's thought by giving undue importance to terms such as 'analysis', 'logical atomism', 'logical constructions', and the like. In Russell's mind all these labels for various emphases, techniques, tools, and methods, were not ends in themselves. On the contrary, at the heart of his interest in philosophy was the traditional one of developing a world view, an ontology or metaphysics. To fail to see this side of his thought is to miss the crucial fact. With Russell the 'problems', 'puzzles', 'difficulties', and 'paradoxes' to be solved must be seen for what they are. They are phases or parts of a *method* to be used in philosophizing. It is typical of his method to begin from these questions and to construct 'theories' to solve the problems. However, it would be a mistake to think that the ultimate goal or value of philosophy, for Russell, consisted in the extent to which he achieved such successful 'theories', such solutions to problems. Both the problems and their solutions were, together, subordinate to a concern on Russell's part with the traditional interest of philosophy—one that he shares with other great philosophers—in working out a satisfactory world view, an ontology. If he rebelled and frequently said harsh things against 'metaphysics', it was usually directed against particular forms or versions of this type of inquiry—for example against Hegelianism or some bloated, excessive Platonism, not against the enterprise as such. For throughout his life Russell was interested in working out his own way of conceiving 'what there is'—the basic kinds of reality there are.

In his *Problems of Philosophy* (1912), there occurs the following passage:

> The world of universals, therefore, may also be described as the world of being. The world of being is unchangeable, rigid, exact, delightful to the mathematician, the logician, the builder of metaphysical systems, and all who love perfection more than life. The world of existence is fleeting, vague, without sharp boundaries, without any clear plan or arrangement, but it contains all thoughts and feelings, all the data of sense, and all physical objects, everything that can do either good or harm, everything that makes any difference to the value of life and the world. According to our temperaments, we shall prefer the contemplation of the one or of the other. The one we do not prefer will probably seem to us a pale shadow of the one we prefer, and hardly worthy to be regarded as in any sense real. But the truth is that both have the same claim on our impartial attention, both are real, and both are important to the metaphysician. Indeed no sooner have we distinguished the two worlds than it becomes necessary to consider their relations.[61]

The contrast Russell here paints between 'the world of universals' and 'the world of existence' has its clear ancestry in Plato. Like Plato, Russell sought a backing to accommodate his variegated interests through a suitable two-tiered metaphysics. The numerous and varied shifts in Russell's views over the course of his life are not to be looked upon as involving an abandonment of the basic schema provided by this type of philosophy. The changes, rather, were ones of detail. They concerned the specific makeup and order of priorities or dependencies *within* this overall picture of two basic realms of reality. His conception of the constitution of the two realms was not always the same. They shifted as he submitted his detailed studies to the pressures of solving various 'problems', to his reliance on Ockham's Principle, to the use of the techniques of logic, and the choice of ways of implementing and satisfying his general affinities with the tradition of British empiricism.

Even Russell's characteristic approach to the problems of the theory of knowledge—what we can know and with what degree of certainty—was linked to his underlying interest in ontology. Given a 'world of universals' and a 'world of existence', what, he asked himself, is the *minimum* number of constituent entities of each with which we can have acquaintance, and the knowledge of which has therefore the *maximum* certainty? What are the basic, 'simple', irreducible constituents of each domain? What are the interrelations within each domain of the identified simples to the complexes that are built up out of these simples? What are the relations between the elements (whether simple or complex) of one domain and those of another? These are the sorts of questions that were always at the center of Russell's thought and philosophic motivations. He never changed these questions or his allegiance to the goal of attempting to answer them, whatever the specific changes in the actual content of his answers.

What I myself have had to say, whether about mathematics or about physics or about perception or about the relation of language to fact, has proceeded always by a certain method. Taking it for granted that, broadly speaking, science and common sense are capable of being interpreted so as to be true in the main, the question arises: what are the minimum hypotheses from which this broad measure of truth will result? This is a technical question and it has no unique answer. A body of propositions, such as those of pure mathematics or theoretical physics, can be deduced from a certain apparatus of initial assumptions concerning initial undefined terms. Any reduction in the number of undefined terms and unproved premisses is an improvement since it diminishes the range of possible error and provides a smaller assemblage of hostages for the truth of the whole system. It was for this reason that I was glad to find mathematics reducible to logic. Kronecker said that God created the natural numbers and the mathematicians created the rest: viz. fractions, real numbers, imaginary numbers and complex numbers. But the natural numbers themselves, on this view, remained at an infinite set of mysterious entities. It was comforting to find that they could all be swept into limbo, leaving Divine Creation confined to such purely logical concepts as *or* and *not* and *all* and *some*. It is true that when this analysis had been effected, philosophical problems remained as regards the residue, but the problems were fewer and more manageable. It had formerly been necessary to give some kind of Platonic being to all the natural numbers. It was not now necessary to *deny* being to them, but only to abstain from *asserting* it, that is to say one could maintain the truth of pure mathematics with fewer assumptions than were formerly necessary.[62]

If anyone should wish to set up a contrast and opposition between 'analytic philosophers' on the one side, and those engaged in formulating a world view on the other, and claim that Russell belonged to the first group of philosophers but not to the second, he would simply be wrong. In Russell's case it is clear that the use of the techniques of logic and the role of 'analysis' are in the service of ontology. In this he is not alone, and we shall see the same underlying intellectual forces at work in several of the major 'analytic' philosophers of our time. An impressive, highly influential, and clear example of this is to be found in the early work of the philosopher by whom Russell was himself so much influenced, as he acknowledges—Ludwig Wittgenstein, the author of the *Tractatus Logico-Philosophicus*. We turn next to an examination of the thought contained in this major work of contemporary analytic philosophy.

CHAPTER V

The Limits of Language

LUDWIG WITTGENSTEIN

Ludwig Wittgenstein's *Tractatus Logico-Philosophicus* is an acknowledged classic of contemporary philosophy. Along with his later major work, *Philosophical Investigations,* this book assures him of an enduring place in the history of philosophy. In the present chapter we shall focus our attention on the *Tractatus.* The 'later' philosophy of Wittgenstein, as represented mainly by *Philosophical Investigations,* will be examined in Chapter VII.

In the Preface to his *Tractatus* Wittgenstein says, "I am indebted to Frege's great works and to the writings of my friend Mr. Bertrand Russell for much of the stimulation of my thoughts." The fact that Wittgenstein singles out Frege and Russell for acknowledgment is important. The linkage of his work with these two contemporaries must be borne in mind if we are to get a proper introduction to some of the kinds of problems with which he was concerned. From their writings Wittgenstein acquired not only the stimulation but also in large part the technical vocabulary and an awareness of the network of problems in logic that preoccupied the early stages of this thought. It is necessary to grasp this *background* in order not to go astray in understanding Wittgenstein.

At the same time we must not dwell exclusively on the connection between Wittgenstein's thought and that of Frege and Russell. It should be noted that Wittgenstein speaks of the *stimulation* given by Frege and Russell to his thought. He was led to think of certain problems by the way they introduced them. He took over much of their terminology and many of their conceptual distinctions, and he shared in some of the philosophic concerns they had. However he was far from being a disciple of either, for he developed his own thought and conclusions through the force of his intellectual genius. He enlarged the scope and altered the orientation of the problems these philosophers were concerned with, to fit them more clearly with his primary interests. The underlying context of his thought was provided by his own philosophic concerns and motivations, and the latter were not, on the whole, those of either Frege or Russell. So 'stimulation' should not be read as 'closely following in the footsteps.'

Indeed, when the *Tractatus* was finally finished Wittgenstein tells us it was not understood at all by Frege, and fundamentally misunderstood by Russell. In a letter written to Russell from the prison camp to which Wittgenstein was confined at the end of the World War I, there occurs the following passage:

Now I'm afraid you haven't really got hold of my main contention, to which the whole business of logical prop[osition]s is only a corollary. The main point is the theory of what can be expressed [*gesagt*] by prop[osition]s—i.e. by language—(and, which comes to the same, what can be *thought*) and what can not be expressed by prop[osition]s, but only shown [*gezeigt*]; which, I believe, is the cardinal problem of philosophy.—

I also sent my M.S. to Frege. He wrote me a week ago and I gather that he doesn't understand a word of it all. So my only hope is to see *you* soon and explain all to you, for it is VERY hard not to be understood by a single soul![1]

On the same point, Ludwig's sister Hermine Wittgenstein, in her Family Recollections, writes the following:

By the way, I have to mention that Ludwig, who had become such close friends with Professor Frege before the war that several times he spent a few days with him, sent him the first section of his book in typescript during the war. Surprisingly enough Frege did not understand the book at all and wrote this quite honestly to Ludwig. It seems that somehow Ludwig had developed away from him and the friendship was never reassumed [*sic*]. Things fared similarly with Russel [*sic*], who had even translated Ludwig's book into English during the war and had it published in a bilingual edition: as far as I know, Ludwig took some of his more popularized essays amiss, and the friendship did not endure.[2]

Wittgenstein was a complex and many-sided figure. His work in the philosophy of language and logic—his 'Fregean' heritage—was only one side of his total philosophic concern. To appreciate something of the other dimensions of his life and thought it is helpful, among other things, to study his Viennese background. He was part of an intellectual milieu that numbered many avant garde writers, creative artists, musicians, architects, and others whose work marked the *fin de siécle* of the Austro-Hungarian Hapsburg monarchy. Among the prominent names of this group are those of the influential journalist Karl Kraus, the architects Paul Engelmann and Adolf Loos, the writers Fritz Mauthner, Robert Mu-

sil, and Otto Weininger, the scientists Heinrich Hertz and Ludwig Boltzmann, the composer Arnold Schönberg, and many others.[3]

In addition, one must mention the following as having played their
varying roles in stimulating Wittgenstein's mind: the writings of Schopenhauer; and as mediated through the latter, the essential 'message' of
Kant's philosophy as well as that of Buddhism; the novels of Dostoyevsky; Tolstoy's writings and preachment in behalf of the Gospels; some
of the writings of Sören Kierkegaard, the Danish theologian and founder
of modern existentialism; and William James's *Varieties of Religious Experience*.

It should be recognized, too, that beyond these historical, intellectual, and cultural influences there is in the case of Wittgenstein something
that transcends them all. His was a mind and spirit able by virtue of its
deep sensitivities and genius to respond to the recurrent and abiding features of the world and human existence quite independently of the colora-
tions or influences that shape people's minds in the special character of an
age, language, or culture. There comes a point at which, simply because
people are people and live under the same sky, certain individuals will
raise the same basic questions and give voice to the same basic human
queries and feelings. Wittgenstein's mind was able to operate on that universal level in an important and original way. He didn't have to be steeped
in the history of philosophy (he wasn't) or to be a deeply learned scholar
in order to come upon these questions or to be provoked to meditate
about them. When he did, he was able to give expression to them in a
distinctively personal and arresting way.

Ludwig Wittgenstein was born in Vienna in 1891. He was the young-
est of a family of eight children (five brothers and three sisters) born to
Karl and Leopoldine Wittgenstein. The father was the head of the largest
iron and steel company of Austria. The heritage of the family was predominantly Jewish (three of Ludwig's grandparents were Jewish). His pa-
ternal grandfather had converted to Protestant Christianity, and two others
of his grandparents had been baptised as children.[4] Ludwig's mother was
Catholic, and he was baptized as a Catholic.

As a member of a wealthy and artistically gifted family, Ludwig
grew up in an environment in which the intellectual and artistic currents
of the cultural life of Vienna were dominant. Music was a part of the daily
life of the home. (Brahms was a friend of the family and a frequent visitor,
along with other prominent musicians of the day. Ludwig's brother Paul,
who had lost his right arm, was an internationally famous concert pianist
for whom Ravel had been commissioned to write his Concerto for Left
Hand.) Ludwig played the clarinet, had a great gift for whistling, and retained a passionate devotion to music throughout his life.

Up to the age of fourteen Ludwig was educated at home, and then
attended the Real Gymnasium at Linz, Austria, for three years. He later

became a student at the Technische Hochschule in Berlin-Charlottenburg, where he remained until the spring of 1908. From boyhood on Ludwig possessed a deep interest and unusual facility in all things technical and mechanical. (He even constructed, at the age of ten, a sewing machine out of little sticks and pieces of wire—one that actually worked!) In following out this type of interest and aptitude, Ludwig at first prepared himself for a career in engineering. By the summer of 1908 he was in England, and for a brief time was associated with the Kite Flying Upper Atmosphere Station of Derbyshire. By the autumn of 1908 he realized that the future development of aeronautics lay in the design of efficient engines. Accordingly he enrolled in and did research at the Engineering Laboratory of the University of Manchester, where he remained until the winter term of 1911. While there he worked on the design of jet-reaction engines and propellers; some of his work proved to have genuine practical value.*

Wittgenstein's work on the design of jet-reaction engines and propellers required the extensive use of applied mathematics. In the course of these researches he developed an interest in the discipline of pure mathematics, and this proved to be his major entry point into the formal study of philosophy. In exploring the whole area having to do with the 'foundations' of mathematics, Wittgenstein came upon Bertrand Russell's *Principles of Mathematics,* published in 1903. He read this with great interest. Through the study of this book he learned of Frege's 'new logic'. Wittgenstein became so absorbed in these studies that he decided to give up aeronautical engineering as a career. He went to Jena to seek advice from Frege, and on Frege's suggestion he went to Cambridge to study with Russell. This proved a major turning point in his life. He arrived in Cambridge in the autumn of 1911 and enrolled at first as an undergraduate, then later as an 'advanced student'. In this first period of his affiliation with Cambridge University, Wittgenstein remained for the three terms of 1912 and for the first two terms of 1913. There is a well-known and colorful reminiscence of Wittgenstein at this time, by Bertrand Russell, who writes:

I knew Wittgenstein first at Cambridge before the War. He was an Austrian, and his father was enormously rich. Wittgenstein had intended to become an engineer, and for that purpose had gone to Manchester. Through reading mathematics he became interested in the principles of mathematics, and asked at Manchester who there was who worked at this subject. Somebody mentioned my name, and he took up his residence at Trinity. He was perhaps the most perfect example I

---

*"Wittgenstein's idea of a combustion chamber together with a tangential reaction nozzle at the tip of a propeller blade did get a practical application at a much later date. It was brought into practical use for the rotor blade of a helicopter by the Austrian designer Doplhoff during the Second World War. It has been adopted by Fairey's for their Jet Gyrodyne, as well as by other aviation firms."[5]

have ever known of genius as traditionally conceived, passionate, profound, intense, and dominating. He had a kind of purity which I have never known equalled except by G. E. Moore. I remember taking him once to a meeting of the Aristotelian Society, at which there were various fools whom I treated politely. When we came away he raged and stormed against my moral degradation in not telling these men what fools they were. His life was turbulent and troubled, and his personal force was extraordinary. He lived on milk and vegetables, and I used to feel as Mrs. Patrick Campbell did about Shaw: 'God help us if he should ever eat a beefsteak.' He used to come to see me every evening at midnight, and pace up and down my room like a wild beast for three hours in agitated silence. Once I said to him: 'Are you thinking about logic or about your sins?' 'Both', he replied, and continued his pacing. I did not like to suggest that it was time for bed, as it seemed probable both to him and me that on leaving me he would commit suicide. At the end of his first term at Trinity, he came to me and said: 'Do you think I am an absolute idiot?' I said: 'Why do you want to know?' He replied: 'Because if I am I shall become an aeronaut, but if I am not I shall become a philosopher.' I said to him: 'My dear fellow, I don't know whether you are an absolute idiot or not, but if you will write me an essay during the vacation upon any philosophical topic that interests you, I will read it and tell you.' He did so, and brought it to me at the beginning of the next term. As soon as I read the first sentence, I became persuaded that he was a man of genius, and assured him that he should on no account become an aeronaut. At the beginning of 1914 he came to me in a state of great agitation and said, 'I am leaving Cambridge, I am leaving Cambridge at once.' 'Why?' I asked. 'Because my brother-in-law has come to live in London, and I can't bear to be so near him.' So he spent the rest of the winter in the far north of Norway. In early days I once asked G. E. Moore what he thought of Wittgenstein. 'I think very well of him', he said. I asked why, and he replied: 'Because at my lectures he looks puzzled, and nobody else ever looks puzzled.'[6]

In the autumn of 1913 Wittgenstein went to Norway with a young mathematician friend from Cambridge, David Pinsent. (Pinsent was later killed in World War I, and the *Tractatus* is dedicated to him.) While in Norway Wittgenstein built himself a hut near Skjolden, where he was able to carry on his writing and research in seclusion. He remained there until the outbreak of the war in 1914.

During the entire period from 1911 to the end of the war, Wittgenstein was engaged in original researches in the field of logic. These researches culminated in the publication of the *Tractatus*. Some of the earliest notes for, and drafts of, this work have been preserved and are of great value in helping to clarify the ideas behind the highly compressed final form in which the *Tractatus* appears.[7] Throughout his life it was Wittgenstein's habit to write down his thoughts in the form of 'remarks' in separate paragraphs, and to collect these in a series of notebooks. (In some cases he also dictated these 'remarks' to a colleague or students.) Wittgenstein volunteered for military service in the Austrian army and saw active service at the front, yet managed to find time during this period to do some writing. He carried the manuscript of his work in his rucksack, and it was with him when he was captured at the end of the war, was made a prisoner, and confined at Monte Cassino in 1918.

The story of his repeated frustrations in trying to get his manuscript published at the end of the war marks one among the many unhappy chapters in his life. Wittgenstein desperately and repeatedly sought a publisher for his book and was turned down by five publishers! It narrowly missed not being published at all. Only through the assistance that Russell gave by offering to write an Introduction did it finally appear in 1922 in English. (It had appeared in German under the title *Logisch-Philosophische Abhandlung* in the final issue of the *Annalen der Naturphilosophie* edited by Wilhelm Ostwald in 1921.)[8]

Of the various items of correspondence having to do with Wittgenstein's efforts at getting his manuscript published, there are two letters to Russell of special interest. In the first, written from his prison camp, Wittgenstein informs Russell about his book. In the second, written a year later, after he had exhausted all his efforts at getting it published, he indicates that he has given up the whole enterprise.

[Cassino, Provincia Caserta, Italy]
13.3.19

Dear Russell,

Thanks so much for your postcards dated 2[nd] and 3[rd] of March. I've had a *very* bad time, not knowing whether you were dead or alive! I can't write on Logic as I'm not allowed to write more than two p[ost] c[ard]s a week (15 lines each). This letter is an exception, it's posted by an Austrian medical student who goes home tomorrow. I've written a book called "Logisch-Philosophische Abhandlung" containing my work of the last six years. I believe I've solved our problems finally. This may sound arrogant but I can't help believing it. I finished the book in August 1918 and two months after was made Prigioniere. I've got the manuscript here with me. I wish I could copy it out for you; but its pretty long and I would have no safe way of sending it to you. In fact you would not understand it without a previous explanation as it's written in quite short remarks. (this of course means that *nobody* will understand it; although I believe, it's all as clear as crystal. But it upsets all our theory of truth, of classes, of numbers and all the rest.) I will publish it as soon as I get home. Now I'm afraid this *won't* be "before long". And consequently it will be a long time yet till we can meet. I can hardly imagine seeing you again! It will be too much! I suppose it would be impossible for you to come and see me here? or perhaps you think it's colossal cheek of me even to think of such a thing. But if you were on the other end of the world and I *could* come to you I would do it.

Please write to me how you are, remember me to Dr. Whitehead. Is old Johnson still alive? Think of me often!

Ever yours
Ludwig Wittgenstein [9]

, Wien III
Rasumofskygasse 24/II
bei Herrn Zimmermann
7.7.20

Dear Russell,

Very many thanks for your kind letter. Reclam has, naturally, not accepted my book and for the moment I won't take any further steps to have it published. But if you feel like getting it printed, it is entirely at your disposal and *you can do what you like with it.* (Only, if you change anything in the text, *indicate that the change was made by you.*)

Today I got my certificate, and I can now become a teacher. How things will go for me—how I'll endure life—God only knows. The best for me, perhaps, would be if I could lie down one evening and not wake up again. (But perhaps there is something better left for me.) We shall see.

Warmest regards from your devoted friend

Ludwig Wittgenstein [10]

Upon the death of his father, Karl Wittgenstein, in 1912, Ludwig inherited a large sum of money. The first thing he did upon his return from military service was to give away all this money. He insisted on living in great simplicity and frugality, as he did for the rest of his life. His 'unconventional' dress, his sparsely furnished rooms at Cambridge and elsewhere, his very few possessions, all testify (in a way somewhat reminiscent of Spinoza) to a life totally dedicated to matters of intellect and spirit, a life unencumbered by distractions of material goods, 'power', and status.

His personality, as all who knew him attest, was of an intense, sensitive sort. There are many anecdotes and reminiscences by former students and colleagues that make absorbing reading.[11] However, there is also a considerable mystique that has grown up around his name and person, with the danger that much of what is written or recalled may be exaggerated and wide of the mark. There is no full biography of him, and it is unlikely that enough has been retained or would be discovered to permit a full, detailed record and analysis of his life. Here are some brief recollections by some persons who knew him.

Rudolf Carnap writes:

In general, he was of a sympathetic temperament and very kind; but he was hypersensitive and easily irritated. Whatever he said was always interesting and stimulating, and the way in which he expressed it was often fascinating. His point of view and his attitude toward people and problems, even theoretical problems, were much more similar to those of a creative artist than to those of a scientist; one might almost say, similar to those of a religious prophet or a seer. When he started to formulate his view on some specific philosophical problem, we often felt the internal struggle that occurred in him at that very moment, a struggle by which he tried to penetrate from darkness to light under an intense and painful strain, which was even visible on his most expressive face. When finally, some-times after a prolonged arduous effort, his answer came forth, his statement stood before us like a newly created piece of art or a divine revelation. Not that he asserted his views dogmatically. Although some of the formulations of the *Tracta-tus* sound as if there could not be any possibility of a doubt, he often expressed the feeling that his statements were inadequate. But the impression he made on us was as if insight came to him as through a divine inspiration, so that we could not help feeling that any sober rational comment or analysis of it would be a profana-tion.[12]

The philosopher Karl Britton, who attended one of Wittgenstein's seminars at Cambridge in 1931, reports the following:

Wittgenstein spoke without notes but knew very well what he wanted to discuss and what he wanted to "put across," though sometimes he seemed to change his mind on some point while he was speaking. . . . On the whole, Wittgenstein was tremendously impatient in his discussion: not impatient of the raw newcomer to philosophy, but of the man who had developed philosophical views of his own. Wittgenstein talked often standing up and walking excitedly about—writing on the blackboard, pointing, hiding his face in his hands. But the most characteristic of all his attitudes was a very quiet, very intense stare—suddenly adopted and leading to a slow deliberate utterance of some new point. Very often he got thoroughly "stuck": appealed in vain to his hearers to help him out: he would walk about in despair murmuring: "I'm a fool, I'm a fool." And such was the difficulty of the topics he discussed, that all this struggle did not seem to us to be in the least excessive.[13]

Paul Engelmann, a close friend of Wittgenstein during the war years and after, writes:

The various military citations and reports concerning Wittgenstein and some reminiscences by fellow-soldiers show, as might be expected, that he stood out as a man of education and culture. Yet he is described as *'guter Kame-rad'*. . . . In this respect the harsh circumstances of the war seem to have imposed a naturalness and a freedom from artificiality which were congenial to him. On troops under his command he had a good effect, particularly in battle, calming them and getting the best out of them, principally by reason of his own ability to continue steadily with his tasks as artillery observer even under heavy fire. It is natural to suppose that the hardships and effort of those years were partly respon-sible for the withdrawal from the world and the search for peace of the years that followed, though Wittgenstein himself would have been more likely to ascribe them to inner reasons.[14]

M. O'C. Drury, a psychiatrist who had studied with Wittgenstein at Cambridge, and was a friend of many years standing, writes:

Anyone who knew Wittgenstein at all well will appreciate the hesitation I feel in speaking about him. He would have found a panegyric extremely distaste-ful. But since his death there have grown up so many false legends about him and his teaching that I think it necessary for some of us who knew him well to try to give them their quietus.

Some people seem to think that Wittgenstein was a rather cantankerous, arrogant, tormented genius; content to dwell aloof in the profundity of his own speculations. That was not the man at all. During the twenty years or so I knew him he was the most warm-hearted, generous, and loyal friend anyone could wish to have. Friendship meant a great deal to him. Two incidents come to my mind out of a host of similar memories. Wittgenstein looking for a birthday present for a friend and saying: "You don't need a lot of money to give a nice present but you do need a lot of time." Wittgenstein saying goodbye to me as I boarded a troop-ship for the Middle East, giving me a silver cup and saying: "Water tastes so much nicer out of silver; there is only one condition attached to it—you are not to worry if it gets lost."

He was a delightful companion. His conversation and interests extended over an immense range of topics. After I left Cambridge we seldom discussed specific philosophical problems. He preferred me to tell him about books I was reading or the medical problems I was at present engaged with. He had the ability to make one see a question in an entirely new light. For instance, I was telling him of some psychiatric symptoms that puzzled me greatly. Wittgenstein said: "You should never cease to be amazed at symptoms mental patients show. If I became mad the thing I would fear most would be your common-sense attitude. That you would take it all as a matter of course that I should be suffering from delusions."[15]

A PRELIMINARY VIEW OF THE *TRACTATUS*

At one point in his search for a publisher of the *Logisch-Philosophische Abhandlung,* Wittgenstein wrote to Ludwig von Ficker, editor of *Der Brenner* and head of a small publishing firm, who he thought might be willing to undertake its publication.[16] In an undated letter to von Ficker (probably September or October, 1919), Wittgenstein wrote as follows:

The book's point is an ethical one. I once meant to include in the preface a sentence which is not in fact there now but which I will write out for you here, because it will perhaps be a key to the work for you. What I meant to write, then, was this: My work consists of two parts: the one presented here plus all that I have *not* written. And it is precisely this second part that is the important one. My book draws limits to the sphere of the ethical from the inside as it were, and I am convinced that this is the ONLY *rigorous* way of drawing those limits. In short, I believe that where *many* others today are just *gassing,* I have managed in my book to put everything firmly in place by being silent about it. And for that reason, unless I am very much mistaken, the book will say a great deal that you yourself want to say. Only perhaps you won't see that it is said in the book. For now, I would recommend you to read the *preface* and the *conclusion,* because they contain the most direct expression of the point of the book.[17]

When, following Wittgenstein's suggestion to von Ficker, we turn to the Preface and Conclusion, we find the following relevant passages. In the Author's Preface to the *Tractatus,* he writes:

The book deals with the problems of philosophy, and shows, I believe, that the reason why these problems are posed is that the logic of our language is misunderstood. The whole sense of the book might be summed up in the following words: what can be said at all can be said clearly, and what we cannot talk about we must pass over in silence.

Thus the aim of the book is to set a limit to thought, or rather—not to thought, but to the expression of thoughts: for in order to be able to set a limit to thought, we should have to find both sides of the limit thinkable (i.e. we should have to be able to think what cannot be thought.)

It will therefore only be in language that the limit can be set, and what lies on the other side of the limit will simply be nonsense.[18]

And toward the very end of the *Tractatus* we find the following relevant passages:

6.52   We feel that even when *all possible* scientific questions have been answered, the problems of life remain completely untouched. Of course there are then no questions left, and this itself is the answer.

6.521   The solution of the problem of life is seen in the vanishing of the problem. (Is not this the reason why those who have found after a long period of doubt that the sense of life became clear to them have then been unable to say what constituted that sense?)

6.522   There are, indeed, things that cannot be put into words. They *make themselves manifest*. They are what is mystical.

6.54   My propositions serve as elucidations in the following way: anyone who understands me eventually recognizes them as nonsensical, when he has used them—as steps—to climb up beyond them. (He must, so to speak, throw away the ladder after he has climbed up it.)

He must transcend these propositions, and then he will see the world aright.

7   What we cannot speak about we must pass over in silence.[19]

I have begun our preliminary bird's-eye view of Wittgenstein's early philosophy by quoting the above passages, since it is essential to keep them fully in mind as stating what, according to Wittgenstein himself, is the purpose of his thought. It is necessary to stress this because if one examines the considerable secondary literature that has grown up around the *Tractatus,* it is by no means evident that many of those who undertake to expound or criticize his thought are sufficiently attentive to what Wittgenstein himself urges his readers to take seriously as constituting the mainsprings of his thought. This is especially the case because of the hostility or indifference to Wittgenstein's version of 'mysticism' and 'the transcendent' that one finds displayed both by Logical Positivists and some other 'analytic' or 'linguistic' philosophers who otherwise find much of value or interest in his writing. For these interpreters, the primary stress must be placed on Wittgenstein's contribution to logic and the analysis of language. Even if they should come to disagree with

Wittgenstein's views in these areas, they would still agree that it is here, if anywhere, that his historical and philosophical importance lies. As for Wittgenstein's 'mysticism'—well, this is a personal, private aberration of his, they would say. Consequently they tend either to disparage or to ignore it. Yet for Wittgenstein this 'mystical' side of his thought is *as important* as (probably *more* important than) what he has to say about logic and language.

After Russell had met with Wittgenstein in the Hague in 1919, at the end of World War I, he wrote to Lady Ottoline Morell an account of this meeting, in which he writes:

> I have much to tell you that is of interest. I leave here today, after a fortnight's stay, during a week of which Wittgenstein was here, and we discussed his book every day. I came to think even better of it than I had done; I feel sure it is a really great book, though I do not feel sure it is right. I told him I could not refute it, and that I was sure it was either all right or all wrong, which I considered the mark of a good book; but it would take me years to decide this. This of course didn't satisfy him, but I couldn't say more.
>
> I had felt in his book a flavour of mysticism, but was astonished when I found that he has become a complete mystic. He reads people like Kierkegaard and Angelus Silesius, and he seriously contemplates becoming a monk. It all started from William James's Varieties of Religious Experience, and grew (not unnaturally) during the winter he spent alone in Norway before the war, when he was nearly mad. Then during the war a curious thing happened. He went on duty to the town of Tarnov in Galicia, and happened to come upon a bookshop, which, however, seemed to contain nothing but picture postcards. However, he went inside and found that it contained just one book: Tolstoy on The Gospels. He bought it merely because there was no other. He read it and re-read it, and thenceforth had it always with him, under fire and at all times. But on the whole he likes Tolstoy less than Dostoewski (especially Karamazov). He has penetrated deep into mystical ways of thought and feeling, but I think (though he wouldn't agree) that what he likes best in mysticism is its power to make him stop thinking. I don't much think he will really become a monk—it is an idea, not an intention. His intention is to be a teacher. He gave all his money to his brothers and sisters, because he found earthly possessions a burden. I wish you had seen him.[20]

And so, as we ourselves set out to examine the main lines of Wittgenstein's thought, it is essential that we attempt to give a balanced account. We must not be deflected from this goal either by the brevity of his remarks about 'the mystical' (and the need to be silent), nor by the relatively small quantity of his remarks on this topic, as compared to the relatively large number of his remarks about 'what can be said' (the world, logic, language, and the relations among them). If we take Wittgenstein himself as our guide in his explicit declarations of intent, we shall give equal attention to these two sides of his philosophy—both to what can be said and to what must be passed over in silence.

In his memoir of Wittgenstein, Paul Engelmann underscores the point I have just been making; what he has to say is worth quoting.

If we are to understand this author and his book, the following point seems particularly important to me: Wittgenstein was stimulated to write the *Tractatus* by his study of the works of Frege and Russell who, together with the physicist Heinrich Hertz, can be regarded as his principal teachers. But Wittgenstein's system of thought, born of deep personal experience and conflicts and setting out by entirely original methods to present a comprehensive philosophical picture of the world, diverges in some points from the logical systems conceived by those teachers, the founders of modern logic. As a result of such divergencies special attention came to be focused on those particular elements in the rational exposition of that complex pattern of mystical experience which were at the same time corrections of errors made by those teachers, whom Wittgenstein held in such high esteem. (Russell, according to his own statements, has accepted these corrections, at least in part.) Yet we do not understand Wittgenstein unless we realize that it was philosophy that mattered to him and not logic, which merely happened to be the only suitable tool for elaborating his world picture. . . .

Bur irrespective of the process of growth of this system of thought, logic and mysticism have here sprung from one and the same root, and it could be said with greater justice that Wittgenstein drew certain logical conclusions from his fundamental mystical attitude to life and the world. That he should have chosen to devote five-sixths of his book to the logical conclusions is due to the fact that about them at least it is possible to speak.

A whole generation of disciples was able to take Wittgenstein for a positivist because he has something of enormous importance in common with the positivists: he draws the line between what we can speak about and what we must be silent about just as they do. The difference is only that they have nothing to be silent about. Positivism holds—and this is its essence—that what we can speak about is all that matters in life. *Whereas Wittgenstein passionately believes that all that really matters in human life is precisely what, in his view, we must be silent about.* When he nevertheless takes immense pains to delimit the unimportant, it is not the coastline of that island which he is bent on surveying with such meticulous accuracy, but the boundary of the ocean.[21]

Wittgenstein places much emphasis on the use of the expression 'limit'. It is used by him in such phrases as "the limit to thought," "the limit to language," "the limit of the world," "the world as a limited whole." However, the term 'limit' as used in these phrases is itself a metaphor, and is therefore subject to possible variations of interpretation. In its original, literal, philological derivation a 'limit' is a spatial or physical boundary such as a threshold or wall—a *physical* line of separation of some sort—between two regions, areas, domains—e.g., the fields, houses, or territories belonging to, or under the control of, different 'owners' or rulers. Its complement—'to transcend' a limit—also retains something of this original physical sense; thus to 'transcend' means, literally, to scale or climb over a barrier such as a wall.

When used metaphorically, however, the expressions 'limit' and 'transcend' obviously have their own *limitations;* they are *hedged* in by various dangers of misuse. Let us mention some examples of such possible misuse—at least in the context of Wittgenstein's thought.

It is clear that in interpreting Wittgenstein's use of this terminology (as he himself cautions us) we must avoid thinking of two 'worlds', two 'domains', and so on. The temptations would then be strong to give a *description* of *each,* to say what is on *both* sides of the limit, just as we are readily able to do in the primary case of physical regions separated by a physical boundary. This, according to Wittgenstein, would be a fundamental mistake. There is only *one* world and one domain of meaningful uses of a logic-governed language. The language we can use to describe this one world must be restricted to this one world. There is no other language because there is no other world. The logic of this language is the logic that sets out the basic thinkable possibilities of this world. The limits of language (and logic) are identical with the limits of the world. For this reason Wittgenstein insists we can only set out the limits of the world and language from 'this side'—from 'within' the world or 'within' a logically possible use of language. We cannot *say* anything about this world from the 'other side', as if we could jump over a fence and look back or describe both the region into which we have landed and the one we had left.

We must also guard ourselves against other dangers in the use of the expression 'limit'. It does not signify some *quantitative,* 'finite' domain. When Wittgenstein speaks of the world as a 'limited whole', this is not to be understood, for example, in the same way in which cosmologists might raise the question about whether the *physical universe* as a whole is finite or infinite in space, in time, or in space-time. Wittgenstein's use of the term 'world' is an ontologic one, not a cosmologic one.

Again, in Wittgenstein's use of the term 'limit' in connection with language, logic, and the world, it would make no sense to speak of *approaching* the limit. The notion of approaching a limit does have a sense in connection with a physical boundary. It has a sense, too, in mathematics where, for example, given a series of fractions of increasing magnitude lying between two integers—say 1 and 2—one may speak of these fractions 'approaching 2 as the limit'. Neither of these standard meanings, however, or any other involving questions of degree, proximity, approximation, and so on, has relevance to Wittgenstein's use of the concept of limit.

Further, the limit—whether of the world or of language—is not itself *part* of the world or of language, in the way in which a wall is part of the landscape that separates two regions, or even in the sense in which the number 2, being a number itself and a part of the domain of numbers, separates the rational numbers smaller than 2 from those larger than 2. The limit of language cannot be formulated *within* language; it is not a proposition *in* language. Nor is the limit of the world, or the world as a limited whole, a fact *in* the totality of facts that make up the world.

These are some cautionary remarks we must bear in mind as we use the term 'limit' in our effort at understanding the main lines of Wittgenstein's philosophy. We must try to do two things at once. We must retain the basic distinction between what can be said, and what (for all its importance) must be passed over in silence. At the same time, in our effort to do this we must not let ourselves be beguiled into saying things about the unsayable, as a result of unconsciously retaining some of the inappropriate literal meanings of the notion of a 'limit'.

'WHAT CAN BE SAID'

'What can be said', for Wittgenstein, has to do with language, logic, and the world. His views on all three are interconnected in a very special way. The questions he raises in connection with language follow, in the main, Frege's cognitive orientation. What are the essential or necessary conditions, in the use of factual language, that assure its having meaning, sense, and truth? The concern with logic centers on the question of what explains logical necessity. Can its source be found in the general form of a proposition, or in the nature of the world, or in both? The concern with ontology—with what can be said about the world—expresses itself in such questions as: What is the essential nature of the world? What is necessarily true of the world? What must be its basic constituents?

To answer each of these questions is thereby to give the limits of meaningful discourse, of logical necessity, of the basic constituents of the world. Indeed, an answer to any one of these sets of questions will turn out to be of the same underlying form and to involve at the same time the answers to the other two. The three (theory of language, theory of logic, theory of the world) are essentially interconnected. They are three different aspects or versions of one and the same philosophic enterprise. That enterprise (in part) is to give an account of what can be said, and, having given such an account, to 'disappear' as 'nonsense'. The theories of language, logic, and the world 'exhibit', 'make manifest', 'elucidate', 'clarify' what are the most fundamental, essential, necessary aspects of what can be said, of what can be known, of what exists. In setting out these fundamental, essential, and necessary aspects, one is thereby setting out the *limits* of what can be said in language that is meaningful and true, of what can be known with logical necessity, of what exists. But in doing all this, philosophy is *not* using language to give descriptions of some particular matters of fact (to give factual knowledge and information or to register any factual discoveries). It is not doing what everyday uses of language or the sciences do. It is only pointing out the 'limits', the 'domain', within which such particular meaningful use of language can take place, in which specific arguments having logical necessity can be offered, and in which detailed empirical knowledge can be communciated about what *happens* to be the case.

The philosophy of the *Tractatus* is an integrated, carefully worked out system, covering a large number of topics. It is exceedingly brief and compressed—only twenty thousand words long. It is written in an unconventional style—numbered statements, mostly short and aphoristic. These are arranged in such a way that there are altogether seven leading propositions, numbered 1 through 7. Each of the leading propositions (except number 7) is followed by others arranged in decimal fashion, e.g., 3.26, 3.261, 3.263. The last digit in any one of these numbered statements marks a comment on, or application or extension of, the idea contained in the preceding proposition.

Wittgenstein arranged the major divisions of propositions in an order he considered helpful and important in getting a sense of the logical interconnections of his system, and of how it unfolds and develops out of certain basic theses. It is possible surely to read with profit the statements arranged in this order. Indeed, once one has worked through the book in a variety of ways—after seeing it from various angles and in the multiple inner interrelationships among its several parts—Wittgenstein's order of exposition *is* a *prime* way of examining it. However, for purposes of 'getting into' his network of thoughts, there are several different possible entry points, each of which has its special advantage or insight to offer. It is by no means clear that Wittgenstein's arrangement offers the best sequence to follow on one's first approach to his thought. Accordingly, while there is no unique, absolutely preferable entry point among these several possibilities, I shall in what follows choose one such sequence—one line of unfoldment of his ideas—which, though admittedly not absolutely preferable to all others, has its special advantages.

I begin with two propositions that will allow us to explore, through the orientation they provide and through an expansion of their ideas, an important side of Wittgenstein's thought. They have the advantage of reminding us of how Wittgenstein adapted for his own purposes some key suggestions of Frege and Russell, thereby illustrating the kind of 'stimulation' he owed to their thought.

3.3   Only propositions have sense; only in the nexus of a proposition does a name have meaning.

3.318   Like Frege and Russell I construe a proposition as a function of the expressions contained in it.

The second half of the first of these statements recalls (it is virtually an exact restatement of) a dictum we encountered in Frege—one of the basic principles he enumerates in his *Foundations of Arithmetic*. Wittgenstein was evidently sufficiently impressed by the importance of this dictum to adopt it as his own, and indeed it does play a fundamental role in his system of thought. (It plays a different role at different stages in the development of his philosophy; thus it means something rather different in his later thought from what it means in the *Tractatus*. It is only with its use in the *Tractatus* that we are for the moment concerned.)[22]

Wittgenstein adopts Frege's distinction between sense *(Sinn)* and reference *(Bedeutung)*, but applies it differently from the way Frege did. The term *'Bedeutung'*, as used by Wittgenstein, is translated by Pears and McGuiness by the word 'meaning', and I shall adopt this usage in what follows. 'Meaning' *(Bedeutung)*, for Wittgenstein, corresponds to 'reference' *(Bedeutung)* as distinguished from 'sense'.

According to Frege, as we had seen, both names and sentences (propositions) have both sense and reference. The sense of a sentence is a function of the sense of its component parts. The sense of a name is the 'route' by which one makes reference to an object, where the object is the referent of the name. While all names have sense, some lack referents, although in a scientific or perfected language all names would have referents. According to Frege, the referent of a sentence is its truth or falsity. If it is a compound (molecular) sentence, whose constituents are other sentences, its truth or falsity as a whole is functionally dependent on the truth or falsity of its constituent sentences. Once again, every well-formed sentence must be either true or false. The senses of the constituent parts of a sentence (names, concept-words, relation-expressions) provide the *truth-conditions* (provide the basis for determining the truth or falsity) of the sentence as a whole.

In the *Tractatus* Wittgenstein accepts some features and elements of Frege's semantics, just briefly summarized, and rejects others.

Wittgenstein differs from Frege in that for him *only sentences* have *sense;* names do not. He agrees with Frege, however, in claiming that the sense of a sentence is the way in which it specifies the truth-conditions of that sentence. By understanding the sense of a sentence we have a way by which to distinguish—among all possible states of affairs—those in which it is true from those in which it is false.

4.063 . . . in order to be able to say, '"p" is true (or false)', I must have determined in what circumstances I call 'p' true, and in so doing I determine the sense of the proposition.

To *understand* a proposition is to understand its sense. However, this is not tantamount to *knowing* whether the proposition is true.

4.024 To understand a proposition means to know what is the case if it is true.
(One can understand it, therefore, without knowing whether it is true.)
It is understood by anyone who understands its constituents.

Names, whose semantic role is to stand for objects, have meaning, i.e., reference. They do not, however, have sense. Since a name is not a sentence it is not either true or false. A name does not refer to a state of affairs or to a fact. States of affairs and facts are particular combinations or configurations of objects. They are complex, just as sentences are particular combinations of names and are also, therefore, complex.

4.032 It is only in so far as a proposition is logically segmented that it is a picture of a situation.

(Even the proposition, *Ambulo,* is composite: for its stem with a different ending yields a different sense, and so does its ending with a different stem.)

In referring to an object, a name is not *saying* anything; it is therefore, as a name, not either true or false. It just 'points to' the object. A sentence can distinguish one state of affairs from another, one that holds or obtains, as contrasted with those that are not allowed by the sentence. This is what its sense accomplishes. But a name doesn't 'disallow' anything; it only singles out a particular object, in referring to it.

What does it mean to say that "only in the nexus of a proposition does a name have meaning"? Are there not situations—for example calling a roster of names, making a laundry list, using names as labels on bottles, and so on—where names are used meaningfully, though not in these circumstances in sentences? The point would be granted both by Frege and Wittgenstein. What they are interested in stressing is not incompatible with the use of names in nonsentential roles. Rather, they maintain, it is because we know how to use names (we know their semantic role) in sentences that we can also use them in nonsentential settings. For example, if a person's nickname is 'Red', we know how to differentiate the use of this name from the word 'red' in the sentence 'Red is red', or 'Red is a Red (a Communist)'.[23] When we call, address, or list the person named 'Red' we are not using the word 'red' as referring to a type of color, or to a type of political affiliation. Similarly, if a bottle is labeled 'Aspirin', and in this context we treat it as a mere label or name, this use also depends on our knowing how the name 'aspirin' can be joined to other words in a well-formed *sentence,* and how its role in such a sentence is different from, and can be linked with, other terms, for example, 'the', 'two', 'Bayer', 'after', and so on.

For Wittgenstein a sentence does not have as its referent truth or falsity, as Frege maintained. A sentence as a whole pictures a particular configuration of objects. A sentence, according to Wittgenstein, when fully analyzed, is made up of *names.* While each name refers to an object, the group of names that make up a sentence depicts the group of objects in some determinate interconnection with one another. These objects in their interconnections are in the world. A sentence, as a group of names, is also a group of objects. The special character of the names making up the sentence is that these serve as *signs for other* objects and their configurations.

As we had seen, Frege distinguished names, in the sense of 'singular terms', from concept-words and expressions for relations. And under the heading of 'names' he included what we should recognize as ordinary proper names (e.g., 'Socrates') and definite descriptions. On Wittgenstein's view, neither ordinary proper names nor definite descriptions are logically proper names. (We might borrow the expression 'logically proper names' from Russell, to serve as another way of referring to what Wittgenstein simply calls 'names'. However, 'names' in Wittgenstein's use are not to be equated with Russell's use of 'logically proper names'. Russell takes primarily an epistemological approach to them, and illustrates them by the use of the demonstratives 'this' or 'that' in connection with some sense-datum—e.g., 'this red now'. However, Wittgenstein's approach is primarily semantic and metaphysical. There is no reason to believe he would have accepted Russell's account, or the examples Russell gives, as explicating his own conception of names and the objects for which they stand.)

A name, for Wittgenstein, is something logically simple. It is a simple sign; it cannot be analyzed or decomposed into other expressions as constituents; it cannot be defined. What a particular name stands for (what it represents, the 'meaning' it has) is a particular object. An object, too, is something metaphysically simple, not further decomposable.

2.02   Objects are simple.

2.0201   Every statement about complexes can be resolved into a statement about their constituents and into the propositions that describe the complexes completely.

3.2   In a proposition a thought can be expressed in such a way that elements of the propositional sign correspond to the objects of the thought.

3.201   I call such elements 'simple signs', and such a proposition 'completely analyzed'.

3.202   The simple signs employed in propositions are called names.

3.203   A name means an object. The object is its meaning. ('*A*' is the same sign as '*A*'.)

3.21   The configuration of objects in a situation corresponds to the configuration of simple signs in the propositional sign.

3.22   In a proposition a name is the representative of an object.

3.221   Objects can only be *named*. Signs are their representatives. I can only speak *about* them; I cannot *put them into words*. Propositions can only say *how* things are, not *what* they are.

As already remarked, for Wittgenstein there is a parallel or correlation between the use of simple signs (names) on the one hand, and objects as the simple constituents of the world on the other. The semantic situation with respect to simple signs (names) is matched by the ontological status of objects in the world. Wittgenstein's logical atomism is thus correlated with his ontological atomism.

What justification is there, however, for believing that there are simple objects? Wittgenstein gives an argument (very compressed in its formulation) for this thesis, that we must now examine.

2.021   Objects make up the substance of the world. That is why they cannot be composite.

2.0211   If the world had no substance, then whether a proposition had sense would depend on whether another proposition was true.

2.0212   In that case we could not sketch out any picture of the world (true or false).

The argument as here presented seeks to establish that there are, in the world, simple objects that make up the substance of the world. The presupposition of the argument is that it must be possible to sketch out a picture of the world that is true or false. The argument undertakes to show that if this presupposition is denied, then indeed there is no logical necessity for believing that there are simple objects. But since it is absurd to deny this presupposition, the truth of this presupposition requires that there are simple objects. And this in turn would allow the possibility of giving a sketch of the substance of the world that is true or false.

Let the statement 'The world has no substance' be represented by '*p*'. Let the statement 'Whether a proposition had sense would depend on whether another proposition was true' be represented by '*q*'. Let the statement 'We could not sketch out any picture of the world which is true or false' be represented by '*r*'. Then the entire argument has the form:

> If *p* then *q*, and if *q* then *r*.
> But *r* is false.
> Hence *q* is false. (By denying the consequent of 'if *q* then *r*' we can deny the antecedent *q*.)
> And if *q* is false, then *p* is false. (By denying the consequent of 'if *p* then *q*', we can deny the antecedent *p*.)
> Hence *p* is false.

It is false, in other words, that the world has no substance; on the contrary, it *does* contain simple objects.

The key step in this argument is 2.0211 above: If the world had no substance (i.e., if there were no simple objects), then whether a proposition had sense would depend on whether another proposition was true. If all objects were complex (nonsimple), then given any complex object its analysis (its description and its decomposition into other objects) would not be terminal. For the complex object or objects reached at one stage of analysis would require further analysis—into further descriptions and still further complex objects. The process of analysis would lead to an infinite regress. Under these circumstances the sense of the original proposition could not be given *completely*. Its sense would not be completely determinate. And since the sense of a proposition is what specifies the conditions, the states of affairs that allow for the determination of the truth or falsity of the proposition, the original proposition, in being partly indeterminate in its sense, could not have its truth or falsity established. However, this result is incompatible with our initial presupposition that every proposition having sense is either true or false. We must therefore give up the belief that there are only complex, nonsimple objects in the world. The substance of the world must therefore consist of simple objects.

Once having established that the world consists of simple objects as its substance, various consequences and corollaries follow. Thus, a simple object, since it does not contain any parts, cannot undergo any change; it must be unalterable. For change or alterability imply different arrangements of or modifications in the makeup of something.

2.0271   Objects are what is unalterable and subsistent; their configuration is what is changing and unstable.

A man, for example, being a complex object, may have his hair change color or fall out altogether. However, if an object is truly simple, no change can take place in *it*. The only changes possible for a simple object are external ones, not internal ones. These external changes have to do with the various configurations or arrangements with other simple objects into which a particular simple object may enter. These configurations may change, not their constituents.

Since objects are simple and unalterable, they are also the 'building blocks', the units, out of which any possible world as well as the actual world is composed. They are common to all 'worlds'. The actual world is one of these possible worlds, the one that happens to obtain, though through no logical necessity. The actual world is one in which the objects it contains (its substance) are arranged in particular ways. They happen to have such and such configurations. These configurations are 'accidental', i.e., non-necessary. What defines the domain of necessary configurations is the totality of all possible configurations. The limits of this domain are what ontology and logic explore. Everyday experience and the various sciences, on the other hand, deal with the world as it is—the configuration of things (objects) that belong to the actual world.

The meaning of a logically proper name is the simple object it designates. Such a name occurs in a fully analyzed proposition. The *sense* of the entire proposition is thus dependent, in part, on the *references* (the 'meanings') of the names in a fully analyzed proposition. To understand what else the sense of a proposition depends on we must recognize that the objects in the world can belong to various configurations. The way in which particular objects are related to others in some particular configuration in the world constitutes the basis for determining whether or not the names for these objects are themselves connected with one another in a proposition to correspond with the configuration of the objects in the world.

Although simple objects constitute the substance of the world—its content—it is also necessary to take into account their possible combinations and interrelations with one another. The possibilities for combination of any one object with other objects is as necessary to its ontological status as the fact that it is simple, unalterable, and common to all possible worlds.

2.0123   If I know an object I also know all its possible occurrences in states of affairs.
(Every one of these possibilities must be part of the nature of the object.)
A new possibility cannot be discovered later.

2.0124   If all objects are given, then at the same time all *possible* states of affairs are also given.

2.013   Each thing is, as it were, in a space of possible states of affairs.

The possibilities of the combinations of an object with other objects is what Wittgenstein calls the *form* of the object.

2.014   Objects contain the possibility of all situations.

2.0141   The possibility of its occurring in states of affairs is the form of an object.

Each simple object has its distinctive form, its distinctive possibilities for interconnection and concatenation with other objects. Every object exists in its own 'space' of possibilities. Thus a color exists in a 'color space', a spatial object in a 'spatial space', a musical note or sound in a 'sound space', and so on.

2.013   Each thing is, as it were, in a space of possible states of affairs. This space I can imagine empty, but I cannot imagine the thing without the space.

2.0131   A spatial object must be situated in infinite space. (A spatial point is an argument-place.)
A speck in the visual field, though it need not be red, must have some colour: it is, so to speak, surrounded by colour-space. Notes must have *some* pitch, objects of touch *some* degree of hardness, and so on.

We can thus conceive that for each simple object there is a range of possibilities for linkage with other objects. The form of an object defines its *internal properties,* its distinctive range of *possible* configurations with other objects. The internal properties of an object are such that it is unthinkable that the object should be without them.

4.123   A property is internal if it is unthinkable that its object should not possess it.

(This shade of blue and that one stand, *eo ipso,* in the internal relation of lighter to darker. It is unthinkable that *these* two objects should not stand in this relation.)

What *particular, determinate* linkages an object has with other objects constitutes its *external* properties and relations. These belong to the particular configurations (from among all possible ones) into which an object happens to fall. The internal properties and relations of objects are, however, not explicitly stated in a proposition that contains names for such simple objects. The proposition can only explicitly *state* the relations holding among objects. It thereby *shows,* at the same time, the internal, formal properties and relations of the objects involved.

4.122   In a certain sense we can talk about formal properties of objects and states of affairs, or, in the case of facts, about structural properties: and in the same sense about formal relations and structural relations.

(Instead of 'structural property' I also say 'internal property'; instead of 'structural relation', 'internal relation'.

I introduce these expressions in order to indicate the source of the confusion between internal relations and relations proper (external relations), which is very widespread among philosophers.)

It is impossible, however, to assert by means of propositions that such internal properties and relations exist: rather, they make themselves manifest in the propositions that represent the relevant states of affairs and are concerned with the relevant objects.

The interconnections among particular objects, in Wittgenstein's ontology, constitutes their *structure*. It is in such structure, in the interconnections of objects, that *properties* are to be found.

2.0231   The substance of the world *can* only determine a form, and not any material properties. For it is only by means of propositions that material properties are represented—only by the configuration of objects that they are produced.

2.0232   In a manner of speaking, objects are colourless.

The *form* of the particular objects involved in a particular state of affairs determines the *structure* of the state of affairs. Given particular objects, each of which has its own form (its own range of possibilities for connections with other objects), the way in which those particular objects are connected with one another constitutes a state of affairs having a particular structure.

2.032   The determinate way in which objects are connected in a state of affairs is the structure of the state of affairs.

2.033   Form is the possibility of structure.

A *state of affairs (Sachverhalt)* is thus what results from a particular configuration of objects.

2.0272   The configuration of objects produces states of affairs.

2.03   In a state of affairs objects fit into one another like the links of a chain.

2.031   In a state of affairs objects stand in a determinate relation to one another.

Each state of affairs is simple; it is not composed of other states of affairs. It is composed of objects (themselves simple) in a particular configuration. The counterpart, in language, of a state of affairs is an elementary proposition, i.e., a proposition not containing other propositions as its components; an elementary proposition contains only names in a particular configuration with one another.

Among possible states of affairs we can distinguish existing states of affairs from nonexisting states of affairs. As a guide to this distinction let us consider the following pair of possibilities that concern objects in the ordinary, everyday use of the term 'object' (not in Wittgenstein's technical sense). We could say (1) George Washington was elected to be the first President of the United States, and (2) Thomas Jefferson was elected to be the first President of the United States. Both statements describe possible states of affairs. However, only the first statement is true. It describes an existing state of affairs. The second statement is false. It describes a possible state of affairs, but a nonexisting one. In a similar way, in Wittgenstein's ontology the simple objects can enter into various configurations with one another. An existing state of affairs is one containing particular objects in which a certain configuration holds or obtains.

An existing state of affairs is a *fact (Tatsache)*.

2.   What is the case—a fact—is the existence of states of affairs.

Since a state of affairs is simple, an existing state of affairs may be thought of as an *atomic fact*. A true atomic proposition is one that describes an atomic fact. Since, too, an existing state of affairs can be differentiated from nonexisting ones, it may also be considered a *positive* atomic fact.

Each state of affairs, being elementary, and whether existent or nonexistent, is *independent* of all other elementary states of affairs within the range of possibilities.

1.21   Each item can be the case or not the case while everything else remains the same.

2.061   States of affairs are independent of one another.

2.062   From the existence or non-existence of one state of affairs it is impossible to infer the existence or non-existence of another.

To understand what Wittgenstein means by the independence of states of affairs, let us use the following analogy.[24] Suppose we had a world consisting of parallelepipeds of various sorts, each having sides of some particular height, width, and length. For example, one parallelepiped may have a height of 5 feet, a width of 3 feet, a length of 6 feet; another parallelepiped has a height of 9 feet, a width of 6 feet, a length of 10 feet; and so on. The numerical value of any one of the three dimensions of any particular parallelepiped is numerically independent of the choice of the other two. And the particular combination of numerical values for any particular parallelepiped is numerically independent of the choices for values for any other parallelepiped. Of course, once the particular values of height, width, and length are settled for any particular parallelepiped, other matters pertaining to that figure (e.g., the volume, lengths of diagonals connecting end points) are dependent on and result from the initial independent choices for the three basic dimensions.

An elementary state of affairs may be compared to a parallelepiped. Each state of affairs, composed of its ontologically independent simple objects, has its properties determined by the structure into which the objects enter with one another. The objects and structural properties of one state of affairs are logically and ontologically independent of what holds for other states of affairs. Both existent and nonexistent states of affairs belong to the total range of possibilities. Existing states of affairs, however, are the only ones to be found in the world. Suppose in your home a certain collection of parallelepiped boxes is to be found. There are, in 'the world' of your home, the actual parallelepipeds ('the existing states of affairs') from among other possible ones. If one enlarged the scope of 'the world' to include a factory making boxes, or even all the boxes in the entire physical universe, these would still be the 'existing' boxes ('states of affairs') from among all possible ones.

The range of all possible states of affairs—existing and nonexisting—defines the domain of *logical space*. Logical space is the sum total of all possible states of affairs, existing and nonexisting. The world, as the totality of all facts or *existing* states of affairs, belongs to logical space.

1.13   The facts in logical space are the world.

Every existing state of affairs *(bestehende Sachverhalt)* constitutes an atomic fact. Such atomic facts may form parts of more complex—molecular—facts. The term 'fact' *(Tatsache)* can be used to comprehend anything that 'is the case', whether atomic or molecular, simple or complex. The world, therefore, can be characterized (as it is by Wittgenstein) as everything that is the case, the totality of facts.

1.   The world is all that is the case.

1.1   The world is the totality of facts, not of things.

1.11   The world is determined by the facts, and by their being *all* the facts.

1.12   For the totality of facts determines what is the case, and also whatever is not the case.

The term 'the world' *(Die Welt)* is used by Wittgenstein in its basic meaning to refer to the actual world, the sum total of existing states of affairs, of positive facts—whether atomic or molecular.

2.04   The totality of existing states of affairs is the world.

On the other hand, Wittgenstein sometimes uses the term 'the world' (as also the term 'reality' *(Wirklichkeit))* in a broader sense as well. In this use, 'the world' stands for the sum total of existing *and* nonexisting states of affairs, of positive and negative facts.

2.05   The totality of existing states of affairs also determines which states of affairs do not exist.

2.06   The existence and non-existence of states of affairs is reality.

(We also call the existence of states of affairs a positive fact, and their non-existence a negative fact.)

2.063   The sum-total of reality is the world.

In their broader uses, the terms 'the world' and 'reality' can also designate what Wittgenstein means by 'logical space', for the latter term stands for the sum total of all possible states of affairs. These broader uses of 'the world' and 'reality' are not incompatible with the use of the term 'the world' to mean the sum total of existing states of affairs, the sum total of facts, the sum total of what is the case. In standing for these parts of logical space, what is excluded is also thereby determined. In this way, the world as the sum total of positive facts 'includes', in the sense of determining, what is not the case, not in the sense of having 'negative facts' or nonexisting states of affairs as *parts* of the world. 'What is the case' and 'what is not the case' are inseparable. In being constituted by the first, the world at the same time also determines the second.[25]

For Wittgenstein there is a close interconnection between ontology (what can be said about the most general features of the world), logic, and language. It is futile to argue about whether, for him, the nature of the world is the 'prior' matter whose 'limits' determine the limits of language or of logic, or conversely whether it is the analysis of the basic features of language and logic that are 'prior' and determine what the world must be like. For Wittgenstein, there is no question of 'priority'. In exploring what can be said we are doing both—setting out both what can be said about *the world* and at the same time setting out what are the necessary features of any *'saying';* what must hold for *any* use of language as well as the necessary, unavoidable role of logic in any use of language.

Our expository comments thus far have been concerned mostly with Wittgenstein's ontology—with what can be said about the constituents of the world, its objects, states of affairs, and facts. Let us turn to consider, now, what for Wittgenstein is the other side of the coin—what is involved in the use of language and logic. It is to this 'critique of *language'* that the bulk of the *Tractatus* is devoted.

We begin, as Wittgenstein does, with some general comments about *pictures* and *thoughts* before coming to the heart of the matter—the use of *propositions*. Propositions are the basic units of language; they constitute special types of 'pictures' and express thoughts. The study of propositions forms the core of Wittgenstein's analysis of the nature of language and logic. In our review of what he has to say about propositions, we shall come upon such topics as his celebrated 'picture theory of language', the thesis that logical 'laws' are tautologies, the distinction between *a priori* and *empirical* uses of language, and other matters.

Wittgenstein tells us that he obtained an important clue to developing his theory of pictorial representation in general, and of propositions as pictures in particular, by reflecting on the practice in law courts of using small model toy automobiles and dolls to represent the pattern of a street accident. Von Wright, in his Biographical Sketch of Wittgenstein, reports the following:

> Wittgenstein told me how the idea of language as a *picture* of reality occurred to him. He was in a trench on the East front, reading a magazine in which there was a schematic picture depicting the possible sequence of events in an automobile accident. The picture there served as a proposition; that is, as a description of a possible state of affairs. It had this function owing to a correspondence between the parts of the picture and things in reality. It now occurred to Wittgenstein that one might reverse the analogy and say that a *proposition* serves as a *picture*, by virtue of a similar correspondence between *its* parts and the world. The way in which the parts of the proposition are combined—the *structure* of the proposition—depicts a possible combination of elements in reality, a possible state of affairs.[26]

Any type of picture (e.g., maps, photographs, representational paintings, diagrams, musical scores, and propositions) presents a certain structure of parts or elements. It is a fact. It articulates or presents a possible situation. It shows through what it presents, and through its own particular mode of representation, a specific arrangement of items.

2.14   What constitutes a picture is that its elements are related to one another in a determinate way.

It has a *sense* insofar as it presents a particular structural arrangement. It cannot be a picture without already doing this. Its presentation of a particular arrangement of elements, as a possibility, constitutes its *pictorial form*.

2.15   The fact that the elements of a picture are related to one another in a determinate way represents that things are related to one another in the same way.

Let us call this connexion of its elements the structure of the picture, and let us call the possibility of this structure the pictorial form of the picture.

2.151   Pictorial form is the possibility that things are related to one another in the same way as the elements of the picture.

Whether the structure of parts being presented by the pictorial form, as a possibility, actually exists or not in some situation or state of affairs in the world, cannot be read off from the picture alone. One has to go 'outside' the picture to determine that. However, even if the picture does not represent some existing structure in the world, the picture remains as it is with its determinate pictorial form. It depicts the same pictorial form whether there exists such a structural arrangement to correspond to it, or not.

2.22   What a picture represents it represents independently of its truth or falsity, by means of its pictorial form.

2.221   What a picture represents is its sense.

2.222   The agreement or disagreement of its sense with reality constitutes its truth or falsity.

4.06   A proposition can be true or false only in virtue of being a picture of reality.

Pictures vary in the materials used to convey what they signify. Some rely primarily on spatial arrangements, others on colors, still others on sounds, and so on. Also each type of picture will involve its distinctive mode of 'projection', its own representational form or conventions for relating the elements of the picture to what is being pictured. However, regardless of the special character of the material medium used and the conventions that govern the mode of representation, every picture also has at the same time a *logical form*.

2.18   What any picture, of whatever form, must have in common with reality, in order to be able to depict it—correctly or incorrectly—in any way at all, is logical form, i.e. the form of reality.

2.182   Every picture is *at the same time* a logical one. (On the other hand, not every picture is, for example, a spatial one.)

The logical form of any picture consists in its serving to distinguish the possible existence of a state of affairs from its nonexistence. This is the common underlying feature of any picture. Moreover, given any picture, whatever its special material medium of signs employed, it is also possible to *think* of what it would be like for some state of affairs to have the structure exhibited in the pictorial form. The *thinkable* aspects of any situation and of any pictorial form is its logical form.

2.202   A picture represents a possible situation in logical space.

3   A logical picture of facts is a thought.

3.001   'A state of affairs is thinkable': what this means is that we can picture it to ourselves.

In what does a thought consist? Is a thought necessarily conveyed by words, by linguistic signs? Russell, in studying the text of the *Tractatus*, asked Wittgenstein that very question. Russell wrote:

But a Gedanke [thought] is a Tatsache [fact]: what are its constituents and components, and what is their relation to those of the pictured Tatsache?[27]

And to this query, Wittgenstein replied:

> I don't know *what* the constituents of a thought are but I know *that* it must have such constituents which correspond to the words of Language. Again the kind of relation of the constituents of thought and of the pictured fact is irrelevant. It would be a matter of psychology to find it out. . . . Does a Gedanke consist of words? No! But of psychical constituents that have the same sort of relation to reality as words. What those constituents are I don't know.[28]

Insofar as a situation is thinkable, it *can* be conveyed by signs that are verbal, by linguistic signs. *Propositions* are the units of language, the structured ordering of linguistic signs by means of which one *says* something.

3.12   I call the sign with which we express a thought a propositional sign.—And a proposition is a propositional sign in its projective relation to the world.

A proposition depicts a possible state of affairs. It is thinkable. It can be said. We can understand it because it has sense. Its sense consists in depicting a position in logical space. This position in logical space is the structure of a possible situation.

4.031   In a proposition a situation is, as it were, constructed by way of experiment.

Instead of, 'This proposition has such and such a sense', we can simply say, 'This proposition represents such and such a situation'.

We can understand a proposition we never heard before because we can *think* about *possible* states of affairs.

4.027   It belongs to the essence of a proposition that it should be able to communicate a *new* sense to us.

4.03   A proposition must use old expressions to communicate a new sense.

Propositions are in this way different from names, for names are not pictures, in the way propositions are. The *meaning* of a name is established by convention, by correlating it with the object it refers to. This correlation needs to be explained or pointed out to us, otherwise we don't know what the name means. However, we *do* understand a proposition we never encountered before, for a proposition presents a concatenation of verbal signs, a structure. It has a *sense* we can understand. In having this sense, it need not have a reference in the way a name does.

4.022   A proposition *shows* its sense.

A proposition *shows* how things stand *if* it is true. And it *says that* they do so stand.

Another difference between a name and a proposition is this. A name to be meaningful must have an object for which it stands. If there is no object, the putative name is meaningless. However, a proposition, given its sense, could be false. There need not be any existing state of affairs (any fact) having the structure depicted in the proposition. Despite this, the proposition has sense. Even though the component names have meaning, the structure or arrangement depicted by the proposition need not exist among the objects themselves.

The sense of a proposition has a position in logical space. When we understand a proposition we understand what it says. What it says is its sense. Take the proposition, "Rome is on the same parallel of latitude as New York." Suppose we subsequently discover that what we have understood is in fact true. Or, conversely, suppose we subsequently discover that what we have understood is false. In either case we have understood the *same* proposition. It takes only *one* 'saying' to convey a proposition with sense. Yet, as conveyed, there are *two* possible truth-values for the same proposition: it is either true or false. However, there are not two different ways of saying what is true or false; there is only one way. And this one saying is the logical form of what is conveyed by or depicted in the kind of picture that a proposition is.

A proposition as a composite linguistic sign has a sense insofar as it *depicts* a possible state of affairs. It itself is a *picture*.

4.011 At first sight a proposition—one set out on the printed page, for example—does not seem to be a picture of the reality with which it is concerned. But no more does musical notation at first sight seem to be a picture of music, nor our phonetic notation (the alphabet) to be a picture of our speech.

And yet these sign-languages prove to be pictures, even in the ordinary sense, of what they represent.

4.012 It is obvious that a proposition of the form '*aRb*' strikes us as a picture. In this case the sign is obviously a likeness of what is signified.

What Wittgenstein means by saying that the propositional sign is a likeness of what is signified should not, of course, be interpreted as saying that the letters, words, or other linguistic signs that compose the proposition are themselves in any way material likenesses or spatial images of that which they represent. Rather, the signs as used are conventionally agreed-upon devices, and the way the conventional *signs* are linked to one another *as signs* can serve to mirror in their own way, in terms of their own 'syntax', the possible linkage of the reality they represent. This point is made by Wittgenstein as follows:

3.1432 Instead of, 'The complex sign "*aRb*" says that *a* stands to *b* in relation R', we ought to put, 'That "*a*" stands to "*b*" in a certain relation says *that aRb*.'

The fact that the *sign* "*a*" stands in a certain relation to the *sign* "*b*", and that this relation is represented in the proposition, enables the entire propositional sign to function as a logical picture of a possible situation. A proposition then has a logical form that is exhibited in the way the words that compose the proposition are related to one another. The form of the words—their interconnections—is exhibited by the propositional sign.

This form is not itself, however, another sign or element among the signs that compose the total propositional sign. It cannot be represented by a sign of some kind *in* the proposition. It can only be *shown* or displayed, *not said,* by that proposition. If one tries to *say* what that logical form is, one will necessarily have to use some *other* proposition, and this too, in turn, can only exhibit or show a certain form in saying what it does. It cannot *say* what its *own form* is.

A proposition as a logical picture says something. It has a determinate sense and therefore is either true or false. An ordinary descriptive or empirical proposition (whether elementary or compound) is true under certain conditions, for certain situations, and false for others. However, this is not the case with tautologies and contradictions. A tautology is always true; a contradiction is always false. Thus neither a tautology nor a contradiction is a picture of reality. A tautology cannot be false, and a contradiction cannot be true. A tautology—e.g., 'It is either raining or not raining', is always true, and for this reason does not give us any particular information about the weather. Similarly, a contradiction—e.g., 'This is black and not black', does not depict a particular state of affairs. It cannot be true, since it cancels itself.

4.461   Propositions show what they say: tautologies and contradictions show that they say nothing.

A tautology has no truth-conditions, since it is unconditionally true: and a contradiction is true on no condition.

Tautologies and contradictions lack sense.

(Like a point from which two arrows go out in opposite directions to one another.)

(For example, I know nothing about the weather when I know that it is either raining or not raining.)

4.4611   Tautologies and contradictions are not, however, nonsensical. They are part of the symbolism, just as '0' is part of the symbolism of arithmetic.

4.462   Tautologies and contradictions are not pictures of reality. They do not represent any possible situations. For the former admit *all* possible situations, and the latter *none*.

One of Wittgenstein's most important discoveries was that the so-called 'laws of logic' (the rules that guide inferences and determine their validity) are themselves *tautologies*. This can be shown by the technique that consists in drawing up a table of truth-values for the component propositional items in a law of logic, and showing that the truth-value of the entire composite proposition that formulates the law of logic has only *truth* as its truth-value, regardless of the combination of the truth-values of its component propositional elements.

6.1   The propositions of logic are tautologies.

6.11   Therefore the propositions of logic say nothing. (They are the analytic propositions.)

6.113   It is the peculiar mark of logical propositions that one can recognize that they are true from the symbol alone, and this fact contains in itself the whole philosophy of logic. And so too it is a very important fact that the truth or falsity of non-logical propositions *cannot* be recognized from the propositions alone.

6.12   The fact that the propositions of logic are tautologies *shows* the formal—logical—properties of language and the world.

Wittgenstein gives examples of the way in which it can be shown that the propositions of logic are tautologies:

6.1201   For example, the fact that the propositions 'p' and '$\sim p$' in the combination '$\sim(p \cdot \sim p)$' yield a tautology shows that they contradict one another. The fact that the propositions '$p \supset q$', 'p', and 'q', combined with one another in the form '$(p \supset q) \cdot (p) : \supset : (q)$', yield a tautology shows that q follows from p and $p \supset q$. The fact that '$(x) \cdot fx : \supset fa$' is a tautology shows that fa follows from $(x) \cdot fx$. Etc., etc.

Take the first proposition (the law of noncontradiction, $\sim (p \cdot \sim p)$; "It is not the case that both p and not p"). Let the truth-values of the component propositions (p, $\sim p$, and ($p \cdot \sim p$)) be represented as follows:

p	$\sim p$	$p \cdot \sim p$	$\sim (p \cdot \sim p)$
T	F	F	T
F	T	F	T

The last column shows that whatever the various combinations of the component propositions (p, $\sim p$, $p \cdot \sim p$), the truth-value of the law $\sim(p \cdot \sim p)$ is T (true). Similarly, for the law $(p \supset q) \cdot (p): \supset: (q)$ (the rule known as *modus ponens*, which says 'If (if p then q) and p, then q') we can show that this too is a tautology by the following truth-table diagram:

p	q	$p \supset q$	$(p \supset q) \cdot p$	$(p \supset q) \cdot (p) : \supset : q$
T	T	T	T	T
T	F	F	F	T
F	T	T	F	T
F	F	T	F	T

Once again, the last column contains only the truth-value T (true) for all possible combinations. A similar procedure would confirm Wittgenstein's general thesis that all propositions (laws) of logic are tautologies.

Wittgenstein draws the consequences of this analysis of the status of the laws of logic as tautological.

6.124   The propositions of logic describe the scaffolding of the world, or rather they represent it. They have no 'subject matter'. . . .

6.1251   Hence there can *never* be surprises in logic.

6.127   All the propositions of logic are of equal status: it is not the case that some of them are essentially primitive propositions and others essentially derived propositions.

Every tautology itself shows that it is a tautology.

Insofar as logical laws are tautologies, they exhaust all possibilities; they exhibit what is *necessary.* They can be known *a priori;* they are analytic. They do not give any substantial information about the world as a totality of *existing* states of affairs. Tautologies are true no matter what actually obtains in the world, hence logic itself is 'empty'; it says nothing. This is not to be understood, however, as claiming that logic is nonsensical. Rather they have to do with the *symbols* we use, not the *facts* in the world.

Elementary propositions consist of names for objects, arranged in a certain way. If true, they represent the existing states of affairs (the 'atomic facts') in the world. Propositions other than elementary ones consist of logical combinations of elementary ones. Such logical combinations make use of various logical constants, for example, 'not', 'and', 'if . . . then'. The truth or falsity of a composite (nonelementary) proposition depends on the particular type of logical constant used to link the elementary propositions that compose it and therefore on the particular combination of truth or falsity of the elementary propositions so linked. For example, the entire statement '*p and q*' is true only if both conjuncts are true; on the other hand, the entire statement '*p or q*' is true if at least one of the alternates is true or, otherwise put, 'not (not *p* and not *q*)'. Propositions other than elementary ones are thus *truth-functions* of elementary propositions. Logical constants, though used in the formulation of compound propositions, do not, however, represent either objects or configurations of objects in the world. There is nothing in the world to correspond to 'and', 'not', or to 'if———then'. The only objects in the world are those for which names can be provided in elementary propositions. These are objects that are configured in states of affairs. The logical constants (e.g., 'not', 'and', 'if———then') do not stand for or represent any kinds of special objects or structures of objects in the world in addition to the simple objects designated by names in elementary propositions and their configurations in states of affairs.

4.0311   One name stands for one thing, another for another thing, and they are combined with one another. In this way the whole group—like a *tableau vivant*—presents a state of affairs.

4.0312   The possibility of propositions is based on the principle that objects have signs as their representatives.

My fundamental idea is that the 'logical constants' are not representatives; that there can be no representatives of the *logic* of facts.

For the same reason, the signs '*T*' or '*F*' to mark the truth or falsity of propositions do not stand for any objects in the world.

4.441　It is clear that a complex of signs '*F*' and '*T*' has no object (or complex of objects) corresponding to it, just as there is none corresponding to the horizontal and vertical lines or to the brackets.—There are no 'logical objects'.

Let us summarize the main points thus far made about Wittgenstein's views about 'what can be said'. The domain of 'what can be said' concerns the use of language to describe the factual structure of the world. The basic unit of language in which something is said is a proposition. All genuine propositions have sense. The sense of a proposition consists in a picture of a possible state of affairs. When analyzed, ordinary language reveals its underlying logical form. Thus the constituents of an elementary proposition are seen to consist of names; these are configured in a determinate way, showing thereby the logical form of the proposition, and at the same time the logical form of a possible state of affairs. All propositions, when analyzed, are truth-functions of elementary propositions. True propositions are those that describe the structure of existing states of affairs. The totality of existing states of affairs constitutes facts. The world is the totality of facts. Whatever can be said can be said clearly, and would be said in one or more propositions. Logic provides, in an exhaustive and necessary way, the schematic forms for all possible propositions, and therefore 'the scaffolding', the 'grid of co-ordinates' of 'logical space' for use in the description of the actual structure of the world. Among all propositions that can be said clearly are some that are true, others false. The totality of true propositions belongs to natural science.

'WHAT CAN'T BE SAID'

We turn now to the second half, 'the other side', of Wittgenstein's philosophy as presented in the *Tractatus*. There are various locutions that can be used as labels to indicate what this comprises: 'what must be passed over in silence', 'what can only be shown, not said', 'the mystical', and so on. It will be our task to get some understanding of what Wittgenstein intends by such phrases and what lies behind them, however brief his remarks on this topic. This needs to be done despite the predominant tendency on the part of many commentators and 'followers' of Wittgenstein to either underplay or ignore this aspect of his philosophy altogether. For, as we have seen, it is for him a very important side of his total philosophy.

The first point to be made by way of introduction is that phrases such as those mentioned above, as well as the very title of this section, encompass a number of different though related matters. If used inter-changeably, they cloak various distinctions among what they cover. Thus, by way of example, the term 'mystical' is used by Wittgenstein sometimes in a broader and sometimes in a narrower sense. For instance, he says:

6.522   There are, indeed, things that cannot be put into words. They *make them-selves manifest*. They are what is mystical.

In this sentence Wittgenstein is using the term 'mystical' in a broad sense to include whatever 'cannot be put into words', for 'whatever makes itself manifest (but cannot be said)'. On the other hand he also says:

6.44   It is not *how* things are in the world that is mystical, but *that* it exists.

Here Wittgenstein is singling out one form of 'what can't be said' and identifying it, especially, as the mystical. The same point would hold gen-erally for the other phrases I have quoted. There are various types of things that 'can't be said': various types of matters that 'must be passed over in silence', 'can only be shown', or 'make themselves manifest'. It will be one of the purposes of our discussion to examine these cases and to show how each case, while having something in common with the others (and so justifying the use of the common label), is at the same time distinctive. So, if one refers to Wittgenstein as a 'mystic' or as upholding 'mysticism', this can be quite misleading unless clarified by examining the phrases he uses in particular contexts, and noting their special features in each case.

Wittgenstein's comments on 'what can't be said' may be collected and grouped under a number of specific headings. I shall distinguish, for our present purposes, the following four: (1) the status of *logical form;* (2) the nature of *philosophy;* (3) *ethics,* 'solipsism', and 'the problem of the meaning of life'; and (4) the special mystical feeling '*that* the world ex-ists.'

1.   In a letter to Russell, written shortly after he finished the *Tracta-tus,* Wittgenstein summed up the main thrust of his book as follows:

The main point is the theory of what can be expressed *(gesagt)* by proposi-tions—i.e., by language—(and, which comes to the same, what can be *thought)* and what can not be expressed by propositions, but only shown *(gezeigt);* which, I believe, is the cardinal problem of philosophy.[29]

The distinction between what can be expressed (said, represented) and what can be shown (displayed, exhibited) is one to which Wittgenstein comes back over and over again. A crucial section of the *Tractatus* in which this distinction is put to use, and also at the same time sums up a number of other passages in which the same general point is made, has to do with the notion of *logical form*. For, according to Wittgenstein, logical form can only be shown, not said.

4.12 Propositions can represent the whole of reality, but they cannot represent what they must have in common with reality in order to be able to represent it—logical form.

In order to be able to represent logical form, we should have to be able to station ourselves with propositions somewhere outside logic, that is to say outside the world.

4.121 Propositions cannot represent logical form: it is mirrored in them.

What finds its reflection in language, language cannot represent.

What expresses *itself* in language, *we* cannot express by means of language.

Propositions *show* the logical form of reality.

They display it.

4.1211 Thus one proposition '*fa*' shows that the object *a* occurs in its sense, two propositions '*fa*' and '*ga*' show that the same object is mentioned in both of them.

If two propositions contradict one another, then their structure shows it; the same is true if one of them follows from the other. And so on.

4.1212 What *can* be shown, *cannot* be said.

The first basic idea to be clear about in explicating the foregoing passage is the notion of *logical form*. By 'logical form', in its most general sense, is meant *possibilities of combination*. Objects in the world, and names in language, have various possibilities of combination with one another. By virtue of their individual forms, objects can combine to yield states of affairs. Among these possible determinate combinations or configurations are existing states of affairs. These are atomic facts. They, in turn, have various possibilities of combination to constitute more complex, molecular facts. Similarly, on the side of language, by virtue of their possibilities of combination with one another (their 'logical syntax'), names can combine to form elementary propositions. Each elementary proposition has its own determinate sense—its own picture of a possible determinate situation. If true, an elementary proposition, as a combination of names and through the sense of its pictorial form, represents the structure of an existing state of affairs. Various elementary propositions have all sorts of logical possibilities of combination with one another to constitute molecular propositions. The truth or falsity of these molecular propositions are truth-functions of the respective truth-possibilities of their component propositions.

The form of any item (name, object, state of affairs, proposition) thus consists of the particular determinate range of possibilities for combination with other elements that belong to it. The expression 'logical form', as used in its most general meaning, refers to the sum total of all these modes and types of possibilities for combination of elements, whether in the world or in language. (And, of course, language itself is one 'part' of the world; one type of facts, one kind of combinations of objects, 'sign-objects'.) In short, logical form has to do with the entire range of all possibilities of combination of items in the world and in language; it defines the domain of 'logical-space'.

The next point has to do with making clear Wittgenstein's claim that logical form cannot be represented or expressed in a proposition. Although propositions have logical form, and although reality, too, has logical form, and although propositions, in representing reality, have logical form in common with reality, propositions cannot represent the logical form which they have in common with reality. Logical form can only be *shown* or displayed in propositions, not represented or expressed in propositions. Logical form itself 'cannot be said' by any proposition. Why is this so?

A language, as analyzed, consists of particular names standing for particular objects, and of real propositions in which the names are so concatenated as to describe some particular determinate state of affairs. In the very use of such particular names and in the particular concatenation of these names in a real proposition, the language used thereby *exhibits* 'what it is to be a name' and 'what it is to be a concatenation of names'. Let us call such phrases as 'what it is to be a name', 'what it is to be a concatenation of names', as well as such expressions as 'object', 'fact', 'function', 'complex' and the like, *formal concepts* and *formal relations*. Another term that may be used for these expressions is *'pseudo-concepts'*, for they do not stand for or represent *particular* objects, concepts, complexes, functions, or relations. Nevertheless what they are is *shown* whenever we would use genuine names, concepts, functions, relations, and so on. These formal matters are shown in and displayed by real propositions, but are not the sort of matters that can be referred to or talked about by means of genuine or real propositions.

4.126   When something falls under a formal concept as one of its objects, this cannot be expressed by means of a proposition. Instead it is shown in the very sign for this object. (A name shows that it signifies an object, a sign for a number that it signifies a number, etc.)

Formal concepts cannot, in fact, be represented by means of a function, as concepts proper can.

For their characteristics, formal properties, are not expressed by means of functions.

The expression for a formal property is a feature of certain symbols.

So the sign for the characteristics of a formal concept is a distinctive feature of all symbols whose meanings fall under the concept.

So the expression for a formal concept is a propositional variable in which this distinctive feature alone is constant.

Suppose, further, we try to conceive of the use of a language in which there is only a *referring to,* a *talking about* something, but no *show-*

ing. Let us suppose, further, that the 'something' one undertakes to talk about, to refer to, is logical form itself—the possibilities of combination of elements. In this case, it would be necessary to use a language that does the talking about, the referring to, but (on the present hypothesis) does not itself *show* its own logical form. Moreover, if this hypothetically assumed 'language' is to have its own logical form in common with that to which it refers, or about which it offers a description, then it could not, by hypothesis, display or show its own logical form. This, however, is impossible. The hypothesis of such a 'language' is nonsensical. For it would in fact lack any articulation, any distinction of elements; it would lack any structure of parts, which is essential to providing a determinate sense, a particular description of some segment of reality. Thus any usable, genuine language must be a set of facts, a structured, articulated configuration of sign-objects. This means that any language already has and shows its own form. If we tried to get along without language in a genuine and usable form, we should have to go 'outside' the world, i.e., outside the domain of facts. This is impossible, not because it is 'difficult' but because such a prospect is wholly without meaning. It describes nothing at all! We cannot conceive, imagine, or picture what this 'going outside the world', or the having of a language not composed of facts (of sign-objects), would come to. Since every fact, whether in the world at large or in language in particular, already has a *form,* any language or a set of objects of any sort can't help *displaying* some form. The display of form is therefore inevitably present whenever we use language to say something, for to say something is to use sign-objects. The use of sign-objects (linguistic expressions) shows its own form in the very act of saying.

2. In the *Tractatus* Wittgenstein makes several remarks about the nature of philosophy. In none of these does he explicitly say that philosophy is one of those matters that 'can't be said'. Nevertheless, because of some of the things Wittgenstein does say about philosophy, we are justified in considering these remarks as providing another example of what, in a broad sense, 'can't be said'. The reasons for applying this label to philosophy will differ, in certain crucial respects, from its use in the other examples collected under this same heading.

The relevant passages in which Wittgenstein characterizes philosophy are the following:

4.11   The totality of true propositions is the whole of natural sciences (or the whole corpus of the natural sciences).

4.111   Philosophy is not one of the natural sciences.

(The word 'philosophy' must mean something whose place is above or below the natural sciences, not beside them.)

4.112   Philosophy aims at the logical clarification of thoughts.

Philosophy is not a body of doctrine but an activity.

A philosophical work consists essentially of elucidations.

Philosophy does not result in 'philosophical propositions', but rather in the clarification of propositions.

Without philosophy thoughts are, as it were, cloudy and indistinct: its task is to make them clear and to give them sharp boundaries.

6.53   The correct method in philosophy would really be the following: to say nothing except what can be said, i.e. propositions of natural science—i.e. something that has nothing to do with philosophy—and then, whenever someone else wanted to say something metaphysical, to demonstrate to him that he had failed to give a meaning to certain signs in his propositions. Although it would not be satisfying to the other person—he would not have the feeling that we were teaching him philosophy—*this* method would be the only strictly correct one.

6.54   My propositions serve as elucidations in the following way: anyone who understands me eventually recognizes them as nonsensical, when he has used them—as steps—to climb up beyond them. (He must, so to speak, throw away the ladder after he has climbed up it.)

He must transcend these propositions, and then he will see the world aright.

There are two salient points in the above remarks that justify our considering them as supporting the claim that philosophy is one of those matters that 'can't be said'. One of these points is essentially negative, the other positive.

The first, or negative point, is that philosophy cannot be conveyed through a series of philosophical propositions. Since, for Wittgenstein, propositions are the essential means by which something is said, and since there can be no genuine philosophical propositions, philosophy 'can't be said'.

Wittgenstein condemns much of what traditionally goes by the name 'philosophy' on the ground that philosophers have undertaken to give us true philosophical propositions. However, on Wittgenstein's view, these 'propositions' have been, for the most part, not false but senseless.

4.003   Most of the propositions and questions to be found in philosophical works are not false but nonsensical. Consequently we cannot give any answer to questions of this kind, but can only establish that they are nonsensical. Most of the propositions and questions of philosophers arise from our failure to understand the logic of our language.

(They belong to the same class as the question whether the good is more or less identical than the beautiful.)

And it is not surprising that the deepest problems are in fact *not* problems at all.

In order to understand Wittgenstein's claim that there are no philosophical propositions, and that philosophers who have undertaken to uphold certain philosophical theses or propositions as true have in fact produced nonsense instead, we must recall Wittgenstein's views about *sense,* as presented in the *Tractatus.* A proposition has sense when it offers a determinate picture or model of some possible state of affairs, of a possible fact. If the structure shown in the proposition is shared by an existing state of affairs, the proposition is true, otherwise false. All genuine propositions thus must be capable of describing factual situations. Such genuine factual propositions, having determinate sense, are to be found in everyday uses of language and in the sciences. Tautologies and contradictions do not offer any pictures of reality. They do not present any models of *particular* states of affairs. To this extent they do not have any *determinate* sense. On the other hand, they are not sense-less. They are, rather, limiting cases of ordinary propositions. Ordinary propositions, being contingent, can be either true or false. Tautologies and contradictions, however, are not contingent, since they offer no pictures of reality that *might be* true or *might be* false. On the contrary, a tautology is always and *necessarily* true; and similarly a contradiction is always and *necessarily* false. For this reason, they do not 'say' anything, since to say something is to offer a picture or model of a particular segment of reality, of a particular state of affairs. We may thus think of tautologies and contradictions as being degenerate, limiting cases of propositions. Each in its own way fills *all* of logical space. Together they provide the limits within which nontautological, noncontradictory sense-ful propositions can pick out, locate, describe, and inform us about some particular state of affairs.

As contrasted with genuine factual propositions—which say something and have sense—and as contrasted, too, with tautologies and contradictions—which do not say anything—the 'propositions' of philosophers are neither factual nor necessary. They have the surface grammatical appearance of being informative, of offering a certain kind of factual knowledge about the world. Yet when examined it turns out, Wittgenstein would say, that they fail in this purpose. They cannot be factual. They do not have any determinate sense. They are not descriptions or models of reality.

Typical propositions of philosophers that purport to give us factual knowledge include such expressions as 'reality', 'fact', 'object', 'class', 'form', 'concept', 'function', 'substance', 'number', 'relation', 'simple', 'complex', 'proposition', 'state of affairs', 'event', and so on. Of course, Wittgenstein's own book, the *Tractatus,* abounds with sentences containing such expressions. We find such statements as 'Objects are simple', 'The world is the totality of facts', and the like. And in the writings of other philosophers we find such statements as 'There are an infinite number of objects in the world', 'There is only one zero,' and the like. All such sentences look as if they are being used to make factual statements. Wittgenstein would say, however, that they are all logically malformed; they are nonsensical; they are pseudo-propositions.

At best such sentences have to do with what Wittgenstein calls 'formal concepts'. In all genuine propositions formal concepts make their appearance. If we had a set of completely analyzed genuine factual propositions, and a perspicuous notation by which to convey them, the formal concepts would not be explicitly mentioned and talked about; they would be *shown in the use of other expressions* that are not themselves formal concepts. Formal concepts cannot themselves be the factual subject matter about which sense-ful genuine propositions can be formulated, asserted, and confirmed as true.

Another way of making this same point is to equate formal concepts with variables of different types. Each variable (e.g., 'name', 'object', 'fact', 'function') is defined by its distinctive range of significance, by the values that can serve as arguments for the variable in question. The use of any expression for a value or argument implicitly shows the type of variable (formal concept) of which it is a value. The logical syntax of a value-expression as it appears in a genuine proposition is governed by a specific logical form or range of possible combinations with other expressions. However, it would be a misuse of the logic of language to treat a variable (a formal concept) as one of its *own* values (arguments). This is the essence of Wittgenstein's version of his Theory of Types—a more satisfactory view, he claims, than the one Russell had formulated. Yet this kind of logical mistake—of treating functions, variables and formal concepts as their own values—appears in all those pseudo-propositions of philosophers that fill the literature. In them, formal concepts are treated as if they were like particular objects, relations, properties, and so on, and about which, therefore, one could say something having sense, being informative, and conveying factual truth. There is thus a confusion in these pseudo-propositions between form and content. The formal concepts and properties exhibited in a perspicuous symbolism are treated as the content of that very symbolism. It can't be done. One can't 'say' these matters; one can only show them in a logically proper use of language. Once one has a perspicuous logical language and symbolism, and uses it, it would be impossible to form any philosophical propositions at all.

To the foregoing 'negative' remarks about philosophy, Wittgenstein adds that though philosophy does not consist in the statement of distinctive philosophical *propositions,* it nevertheless is a form of activity that has an important role and purpose. Wittgenstein describes this as one of 'elucidation', of 'serving as a critique of language', of 'setting a limit to thought'. In performing these functions philosophy of course uses language. After all, the *Tractatus* itself is a book, consisting of sentences. As Russell (in his introduction to the *Tractatus*) reminds us, "Mr. Wittgenstein manages to say a good deal about what cannot be said, thus suggesting to the sceptical reader that possibly there may be some loophole through a hierarchy of languages, or by some other exit." Wittgenstein would have rejected the suggestion that there is a hierarchy of languages in one part of which philosophy is to be found. However, he might acknowledge that there is some other exit. This other exit is to insist, as he does, that what he has himself been saying is *nonsense*. This expression needs to be understood in the special way he intends in the present context. Strictly speaking only full-fledged, genuine propositions have sense. Since there are no genuine philosophical propositions, and he himself has not provided any, what he has 'said' has no sense. Yet what he has 'said', though not to be taken as consisting of propositions, nevertheless has another kind of 'sense' in a looser, popular, and nontechnical use of this term. His use of language is part of the activity of elucidation. Insofar as language can be used to perform this function *in addition* to articulating propositions, his use of language in the *Tractatus* belongs to this other type of use. This other use is not one of fact-stating (as in science), or even one of setting out in an *a priori* way the propositions of logic. It is rather a use that clarifies these other, different uses of language, though not itself, in doing this, belonging to either the fact-stating uses or to formulating the laws of logic. At any rate, the distinctive character of the activity of philosophy as elucidatory is to give us an understanding of the logic of language—what can be said and what cannot be said. Once we have this understanding, we "can throw away the ladder." The philosophic activity ceases with this insight, though the insight gained cannot be stated in genuine propositions.

3. It will be recalled from a passage quoted earlier in this chapter that Wittgenstein, in a letter to Ludwig von Ficker describing the *Tractatus*, wrote, "The book's point is an ethical one." If the point of the book is 'ethical' we must ask, of course, what this term signifies for Wittgenstein. In our attempt to answer this question we are hampered to a large extent by the brevity, paucity, and unusual opacity and oracular quality of what Wittgenstein has to say on this topic. There are a few brief passages in the *Tractatus* and also some background passages of entries in 1916 in the *Notebooks* to which we can turn. Further, we know that Wittgenstein was much influenced by his reading of Schopenhauer, as well as by his intense admiration of Tolstoy's version of Christian ethics. In addition, we may conjecture that perhaps through his reading of Schopenhauer, Wittgenstein also acquired some insight into Buddhist ethics (a connection which makes some commentators find a similarity in certain ways between Wittgenstein and Zen). Beginning in 1929–1930, when Wittgenstein returned to research in philosophy after a lapse of several years since the end of World War I, he undertook a radical revision of his philosophy, especially in connection with his views on language (revisions that culminated in the *Philosophical Investigations*). There is a record of Wittgenstein's conversations with Moritz Schlick and Friedrich Waismann in 1929–1930, as well as a "Lecture on Ethics" prepared for delivery at Cambridge sometime between September, 1929, and December, 1930, in which further

ata on Wittgenstein's views on ethics are preserved.[30] It would appear from these sources that despite the radical changes his philosophy was beginning to undergo in other areas, his views on ethics are substantially unchanged from what we find in the *Tractatus* and the *Notebooks (1914–1916)*.

The relevant passages from the *Tractatus* are principally these:

6.41   The sense of the world must lie outside the world. In the world everything is as it is, and everything happens as it does happen: *in* it no value exists—and if it did exist, it would have no value.

If there is any value that does have value, it must lie outside the whole sphere of what happens and is the case. For all that happens and is the case is accidental.

What makes it non-accidental cannot lie *within* the world, since if it did it would itself be accidental.

It must lie outside the world.

6.42   And so it is impossible for there to be propositions of ethics.

Propositions can express nothing that is higher.

6.421   It is clear that ethics cannot be put into words.

Ethics is transcendental.

(Ethics and aesthetics are one and the same.)

6.422   When an ethical law of the form, 'Thou shalt . . .', is laid down, one's first thought is, 'And what if I do not do it?' It is clear, however, that ethics has nothing to do with punishment and reward in the usual sense of the terms. So our question about the *consequences* of an action must be unimportant.—At least those consequences should not be events. For there must be something right about the question we posed. There must indeed be some kind of ethical reward and ethical punishment, but they must reside in the action itself.

(And it is also clear that the reward must be something pleasant and the punishment something unpleasant.)

6.423   It is impossible to speak about the will in so far as it is the subject of ethical attributes.

And the will as a phenomenon is of interest only to psychology.

6.43   If the good or bad exercise of the will does alter the world, it can alter only the limits of the world, not the facts—not what can be expressed by means of language.

In short, the effect must be that it becomes an altogether different world. It must, so to speak, wax or wane as a whole.

The world of the happy man is a different one from that of the unhappy man.

6.52   We feel that even when *all possible* scientific questions have been answered, the problems of life remain completely untouched. Of course there are then no questions left, and this itself is the answer.

6.521   The solution of the problem of life is seen in the vanishing of the problem.

In analyzing these and other related remarks, let us begin by trying to make clear, in the first place, how Wittgenstein conceives the subject matter and interest of ethics. He gives us some help on this in his "Lecture on Ethics," where he says:

> Ethics is the enquiry into what is valuable, or into what is really important, or I could have said Ethics is the enquiry into the meaning of life, or into what makes life worth living, or into the right way of living.[31]

These phrases are not too far removed from the way in which others might also describe ethics. In fact, earlier in the same "Lecture on Ethics" Wittgenstein quotes with approval the definition given by Moore in the latter's *Principia Ethica,* which asserts, "Ethics is the general enquiry into what is good." Still, even though Wittgenstein uses certain familiar-sounding phrases to characterize ethics, we must be careful not to attribute to him a concern with certain themes that are frequently taken to be at the heart of ethics. Thus, for Wittgenstein, ethics is not concerned with proposing, analyzing, or justifying certain rules of conduct. He is not concerned with what we should or should not do—with our rights, duties, and obligations, with what we *ought* to do. For Wittgenstein what lies at the heart of ethics is a concern with 'the problem of life', the question about 'the meaning (or purpose) of life', with 'what makes life worth living'. Here again, however, it is important not to be misled by his use of these or similar phrases. For they might be taken to suggest—though mistakenly so—that what Wittgenstein is about to do is draw up a list of various 'goods', of things to aim at and prize, perhaps to even rank in some 'scale' or 'scheme' of values. Thus it might be thought that for him ethics undertakes to judge and guide us concerning such matters as health, power, wealth, material possessions, fame, pleasure, knowledge, adventure, esthetic enjoyment, security, peace, freedom, friendship, love, and so on. This is not what he either intends or does in his remarks on 'the meaning of life'. In a conversation held in 1929 with Schlick and Waismann, Wittgenstein remarked:

> I regard it as very important to put an end to all the chatter about ethics—whether there is knowledge in ethics, whether there are values, whether the Good can be defined, etc. In ethics, one constantly tries to say something that does not concern and can never concern the essence of the matter. It is a priori certain that, whatever definition one may give of the Good, it is always a misunderstanding to suppose that the formulation corresponds to what one really means. (Moore.) But the tendency, the thrust *points to something.*[32]

Ethics, in Wittgenstein's approach, is the search for the meaning of life. The term 'life' in the expression 'the meaning of life' does not refer to the biological, physiological, social (cultural), or psychological dimensions or types of phenomena (or any combination of these) that are normally meant in the use of this term. When Wittgenstein speaks of the 'meaning of life', he equates this with speaking of 'the meaning of the world'.

The World and Life are one.

Physiological life is of course not "Life". And neither is psychological life. Life is the world.

. . . .

Can there be any ethics if there is no living being but myself?

If ethics is supposed to be something fundamental, there can.

If I am right, then it is not sufficient for the ethical judgment that a world is given. Then the world in itself is neither good nor evil.

For it must be all one, as far as concerns the existence of ethics, whether there is living matter in the world or not. And it is clear that a world in which there is only dead matter is in itself neither good nor evil, so even the world of living things can in itself be neither good nor evil.[33]

In one sense—admittedly a paradoxical one—in order to deal with the problem of the meaning of life from an 'absolute' ethical point of view, one must ignore life altogether, one's own or that of any other living creature, human or otherwise.
     The 'life' whose 'meaning' Wittgenstein is concerned with is not something to be probed, described, understood, explained, analyzed, or classified scientifically. It is not that which is present in the body, not even in the mind or consciousness of some person—mine or someone else's. The 'life' Wittgenstein is talking about is what he calls 'the metaphysical subject', 'the philosophical I'. This 'I' is not an *object* of any kind *in* the world, situated in the world along with other objects.

The philosophical I is not the human being, not the human body or the human soul with the psychological properties, but the metaphysical subject, the boundary (not a part) of the world. The human body, however, my body in particular, is a part of the world among others, among animals, plants, stones, etc., etc.

Whoever realizes this will not want to procure a pre-eminent place for his own body or for the human body.

He will regard humans and animals quite naively as objects which are similar and which belong together.[34]

The 'I' or self Wittgenstein is alluding to is not then to be identified with a person's body, or with a 'thinking self' (an immaterial substance or soul, e.g., the *res cogitans* of Descartes), with any dualistic combination of these, or even with the organism as a whole. The 'philosophical I' (the 'metaphysical subject') is a subject, not an object.

Good and evil only enter through the *subject*. And the subject is not part of the world, but a boundary of the world.[35]

The 'philosophical I' may also be labeled a 'willing subject', that is, a subject that wills. But here, again, the 'will' is not to be located in or distributively identified with a variety of desires, needs, hopes, fears, goals, wishes, wants, impulses, and so on. Indeed, the essential—again paradoxical!—mark of the 'will' of the 'philosophical I' is that in solving the problem of the meaning of life, the philosophical I *loses* any sense of itself as an individual. It passes 'beyond good and evil'. It becomes wholly *egoless*. It becomes 'one with the world itself'. It says, "Thy will be done!" However, in 'saying' this (though not, of course, in proposi-tions), the subject that has 'solved' the problem of the meaning of life displays a certain attitude or stance toward the world (toward life) that distinguishes such a subject from others. The subject is a *happy* person. The 'happiness' however is not to be equated with pleasure, the gratifica-tion of desires, the achievement of goals and ambitions, and with the real-ization of 'success' *in* the world. *It cannot be described*.

What is the objective mark of the happy, harmonious life? Here it is again clear that there cannot be any such mark, that can be *described*.

This mark cannot be a physical one but only a metaphysical one, a transcendental one.[36]

It is marked by a kind of wordless serenity and contentment, evident in the way such a happy man conducts himself. Such a man feels *'absolutely safe'*; nothing that can or does happen in the world, as it would happen to himself *as object,* can affect or disturb *him*, because the 'him' is the philo-sophical I—and *it* can't be hurt since it has no desires and does not judge things in terms of 'good and evil'. Such wordless serenity or 'understand-ing' of the world is wholly absent in the life of an 'unhappy' person, one who has not solved the problem of life, because such a person is still living *altogether in* the world.

This is the essential point for understanding Wittgenstein's 'solip-sism'. In the *Tractatus,* he expresses this as follows:

5.62   . . . what the solipsist *means* is quite correct; only it cannot be *said*, but makes itself manifest.

The world is *my* world: this is manifest in the fact that the limits of *language* (of that language which alone I understand) mean the limits of *my* world.

5.621   The world and life are one.

5.63   I am my world. (The microcosm.)

To say that 'the world' is 'my world' is to be understood in such a way that the use of the word 'my' refers to the 'philosophical I', and not to myself as a particular body or mind—in short to a particular *object* in the world. If we take 'my world' to be that which holds for the 'philosophical I', then the individual ego (as one object among others) no longer operates as it does in solipsism as ordinarily understood (i.e., in the belief that everything that exists is part of my mind and that my mind and its con-tents is the *only* thing that exists—a form of madness, really). Instead, '*my* world', as involving the 'philosophical I', becomes identical with *the* world. Solipsism passes into and becomes identical with realism. And this indeed is how Wittgenstein conceives 'solipsism'. It is what emerges from an egoless attitude toward the world.

Here we can see that solipsism coincides with pure realism, if it is strictly thought out.

The I of solipsism shrinks to an extensionless point and what remains is the reality co-ordinate with it.[37]

And insofar as God and the world may be thought of as one and the same, one can say (from an egoless point of view), "*Thy* will be done!"

The use of the expression 'meaning' *(Sinn)* in the phrase 'the meaning of life' is not in any way to be identified or confused with the use of this word in the context of the analysis of language. The search for the 'meaning' of life has nothing to do with semantic matters; it does not depend on recalling the kinds of distinctions (for example between sense and reference) in the Fregean heritage and its application to the analysis of 'meaning' in *language*. On the other hand, if one should ask Wittgenstein (or anyone who 'understands' what he is driving at), "Well, in what sense of 'meaning' *are* you using the term when you speak of looking for the meaning of life?" he should have to respond by saying he cannot answer your question! He cannot say what this meaning is; he cannot use any propositions to describe it or its absence. It is thus, admittedly, 'nonsense', 'transcendental', 'supernatural'. And yet, for all that, Wittgenstein would say it is of supreme importance: it has absolute ethical value.

No description that I can think of would do to describe what I mean by absolute value. . . . That is to say: I see now that these nonsensical expressions were not nonsensical because I had not yet found the correct expressions, but that their nonsensicality was their very essence. For all I wanted to do with them was *to go beyond* the world and that is to say beyond significant language. My whole tendency and I believe the tendency of all men who ever tried to write or talk Ethics or Religion was to run against the boundaries of language. This running against the walls of our cage is perfectly, absolutely hopeless. Ethics so far as it springs from the desire to say something about the ultimate meaning of life, the absolute good, the absolutely valuable, can be no science. What it says does not add to our knowledge in any sense. But it is a document to a tendency in the human mind which I personally cannot help respecting deeply and I would not for my life ridicule it.[38]

One aspect of the solution to the problem of the meaning of life is to be found in living in the *present*. Such living in the present is not to be understood as a restriction in the *temporal* sense to that which is present as contrasted with that which is past or future. The 'present' in this non-temporal sense is tantamount to living in 'eternity'—to seeing things *sub specie aeternitatis*, 'under the aspect of eternity'. In living without hope, fear, or regrets, one focuses entirely on whatever *presents* itself. *Any-*

<u>*thing* can constitute 'the world' of egoless absorption</u>. The 'anything' can be the most 'trivial' or the most 'exalted'.

As a thing among things, each thing is equally insignificant; as a world each one equally significant.

If I have been contemplating the stove, and then am told: but now all you know is the stove, my result does indeed seem trivial. For this represents the matter as if I had studied the stove as one among the many things in the world. But if I was contemplating the stove *it* was my world, and everything colorless by contrast with it.

(Something good about the whole, but bad in details.)

For it is equally possible to take the bare present image as the worthless momentary picture in the whole temporal world, and as the true world among shadows.[39]

<u>Everything *in* the world, from the point of view of an egoless philosophical I (metaphysical subject) is of equal value, because in one sense nothing *in* the world has *any* value—good *or* evil. 'Values' for the philosophical I are beyond good and evil.</u> The philosophical I as a 'will-less' subject becomes one with God, the 'spirit' that 'belongs' to all things.

<u>Death, to such a philosophical I, to one who has 'solved the problem of the meaning of life', is nothing to be feared. It is not an event *in* life, i.e., in the 'life' of the philosophical I. Insofar as the 'I' is the philosophical I, then there is no death in *my* world.</u>

To believe in a God means to understand the question about the meaning of life.

To believe in a God means to see that the facts of the world are not the end of the matter.

To believe in God means to see that life has a meaning.

The world is *given* me, i.e., my will enters into the world completely from outside as into something that is already there.

(As for what my will is, I don't know yet.)

That is why we have the feeling of being dependent on an alien will.

However this may be, at any rate we *are* in a certain sense dependent, and what we are dependent on we can call God.

In this sense God would simply be fate, or, what is the same thing: The world— which is independent of our will.

I can make myself independent of fate.

There are two godheads: the world and my independent I.

I am either happy or unhappy, that is all. It can be said: good or evil do not exist.

A man who is happy must have no fear. Not even in the face of death.

Only a man who lives not in time but in the present is happy.

For life in the present there is no death.

Death is not an event in life. It is not a fact of the world.

If by eternity is understood not infinite temporal duration but non-temporality, then it can be said that a man lives eternally if he lives in the present.

In order to live happily I must be in agreement with the world. And that is what 'being happy' *means*.

I am then, so to speak, in agreement with that alien will on which I appear dependent. That is to say: 'I am doing the will of God'.

Fear in face of death is the best sign of a false, i.e., a bad, life.[40]

4.   At one point, in his discussion of the nature of logic in the *Tractatus*, Wittgenstein makes the following remark:

5.552 The 'experience' that we need in order to understand logic is not that something or other is the state of things, but that something *is:* that, however, is *not* experience.
     Logic is *prior* to every experience—that something *is so*.
     It is prior to the question 'How?', not prior to the question 'What?'

And in a celebrated remark at the end of the *Tractatus* he says:

6.44 It is not *how* things are in the world that is mystical, but *that* it exists.

The several distinctions with respect to the world here being signalized in a compressed way by the use of the expressions 'What', 'How', and 'That', are of great interest and importance in understanding Wittgenstein's philosophy.

To have an *experience (Erfahrung),* for Wittgenstein in the present context signifies having some determinate, selective, particular mode of identifying or describing a particular state of affairs, a particular structured situation of some sort. It is that which, when verbalized and articulated, is conveyed by a proposition of everyday language or science. To assert a proposition is to say *how* the world—or rather, some segment of the world—is. The 'how' is the specific way or ways—actually to be found in experience or even as conceived hypothetically and through imagination—some particular structure of objects, selected from among all possible structures, may be depicted.

The role of logic is to explore the entire domain of possible structures. It explores in an exhaustive way, through its tautologies and by means of a symbolic notation for its formal concepts, *what* the world is. 'What' here signifies the totality of structured possibilities of 'logical space'. We cannot have an *experience* of this, because experience is always of something determinate, specific, selective. Nevertheless, what logic explores provides the background (the 'logical space') for all particular experiences and determinate propositions of everyday language and science. The 'propositions' of logic are not nonsense. Yet they are not sense-ful in the way ordinary propositons are. The 'what' that logic's tautologies explore fill all of logical space. Hence the 'propositions' of logic are limiting, degenerate cases of propositions. They do not give us knowledge or information of *how* things are. Instead they give us an exhaustive, neutral account of all possible states of affairs without making any selection from among all the possibilities. Thus logic deals with the *what* of the world's (reality's) possibilities; everyday experience and science deal with the particular *hows* of the world.

What Wittgenstein calls 'the mystical' *(das Mystische)* is not an *experience* at all (in his use of this term). Neither is it something that can be thought, conceived, or articulated in a proposition, whether normal and determinate or tautological and degenerate. The mystical cannot be conveyed by propositions of any sort. Wittgenstein suggests at one point that we might use the expression 'mystical feeling' for referring to what he has in mind. Although Wittgenstein does not use the term 'awareness', I think it might also serve in the present context, provided we understand it is to be distinguished from both an experience and a propositionally conveyed thought. We should then be alluding to a mystical feeling or awareness *that* the world exists. This mystical feeling or awareness *that* the world exists is 'prior' even to the *thought* of *what* all possible states of affairs might be. It is also 'prior' to the *experience* of *how* some specific, determinate state of affairs might be described. The 'how' presupposes the 'what' and the 'what' presupposes the 'that'. But the awareness of the 'that' (the mystical feeling that the world exists) is not a type of *knowledge*. It belongs neither to logic nor to everyday experience and science.

In further clarifying what it signifies to have the mystical feeling or awareness *that* the world exists (as distinguished from its *what* or its *how*), Wittgenstein makes the following remark in the *Tractatus*, shortly after the passage I quoted earlier. He says:

6.5 When the answer cannot be put into words, neither can the question be put into words.
> *The riddle* does not exist.
> If a question can be framed at all, it is also *possible* to answer it.

The mystical feeling *that* the world exists must not be confused either with a *question* or a possible *answer,* since either could be conveyed by means of a proposition. The mystical feeling that the world exists cannot be *said:* it cannot be put into words that compose or articulate a proposition. Thus in having this feeling or awareness we are not, for example, asking such questions as, "Why does the world exist?" or "When did the world come into existence?" or "Did the world have a beginning in time?" or "How large (spatially) is the world?" or "Does the world embody some overall purpose or design?" and so on. All of these questions convey what may be thought of as 'riddles' about the existence of the world. Since many persons suppose it is meaningful to ask these questions, they also suppose there ought to be possible answers to them. Indeed there are, as we know, many proposed answers to these and similar questions that men have argued about and accepted. For Wittgenstein, however, neither the questions (the 'riddle') nor the 'answers' are legitimate expressions of what *he* intends by the mystical feeling or awareness *that* the world exists. He would insist most strongly, however, that one should not condemn, ignore, or belittle the quality and importance of having this feeling. For Wittgenstein, on the contrary, this mystical feeling was of the *highest importance*.

Can the mystical feeling aroused by being aware *that* the world exists be conveyed by a proposition in which one states one's *wonder* that the world exists? In his "Lecture on Ethics" Wittgenstein considers this very question. He indicates that although for him the mystical feeling alluded to is an example of something that has *absolute value,* and so is of the highest ethical importance, nevertheless the attempt to *describe* this in a proposition by using the term 'wonder' in its ordinary meaning would be a total misuse of language and therefore wholly nonsensical. His reasons are as follows:

> It has a perfectly good and clear sense to say that I wonder at something being the case, we all understand what it means to say that I wonder at the size of a dog which is bigger than anyone I have ever seen before or at any thing which, in the common sense of the word, is extra-ordinary. In every such case I wonder at something being the case which I *could* conceive *not* to be the case. I wonder at the size of this dog because I could conceive of a dog of another, namely the ordinary size, at which I should not wonder. To say 'I wonder at such and such being the case' has only sense if I can imagine it not to be the case. In this sense one can wonder at the existence of, say, a house when one sees it and has not visited it for a long time and has imagined that it had been pulled down in the meantime. But it is nonsense to say that I wonder at the existence of the world, because I cannot imagine it not existing. I could of course wonder at the world round me being as it is. If for instance I had this experience while looking into the blue sky, I could wonder at the sky being blue as opposed to the case when it's clouded. But that's not what I mean. I am wondering at the sky being *whatever it is.* One might be tempted to say that what I am wondering at is a tautology, namely at the sky being blue or not blue. But then it's just nonsense to say that one is wondering at a tautology.[41]

Wittgenstein thinks that the correct use of the expression 'to wonder at—' applies to a situation in which it could be said that one can conceive or imagine that it might *not* have been present, or might *not* be the case. In some cases there is a sense of surprise, marveling, or astonishment. One is apt to exclaim in the presence of that which evokes the sense of wonder, "How extraordinary!" although, of course, there need not be any explicit oral exclamation of this at all. The emotion felt is frequently (though not invariably) associated with our coming upon something that we did not *expect*. Thus, one could not speak of wonder in connection with a tautology. Since a tautology, by its very nature, exhaustively enumerates all the relevant, conceivable possibilities, there is no room left for some additional possibility that one could conceive or imagine. Thus one could legitimately wonder at some particular color of the sky, since it makes sense to say that it might have had some other color than the one it happens to have. But it would make no sense to say that if one enumerated all possible colors of the sky, one should wonder at this exhaustive enumeration.

For these reasons Wittgenstein alleges *it makes no sense to say that one wonders at something which, in general, might not be otherwise than it is*.

This last reason is the one he gives for saying that it makes no sense to say that one wonders at the existence of the world. For, Wittgenstein claims, one "cannot imagine it not existing." It is not, as I understand his point, that we can form a tautology in which we could exhaustively enumerate the possibilities, one of which happens to be true, but where the remaining possibility is conceivable. We could not say, "The world exists, and this is what arouses my wonder. But it is conceivable that the world *might not have existed*." This latter alternative Wittgenstein would say is not a meaningful alternative; the possibility of the world's not existing makes no sense. If this alternative drops out as even a meaningful possibility, then even the putative tautology as a whole, 'Either the world exists or does not exist' or 'It is conceivable that the world should exist or not exist', is nonsensical, for one of the disjuncts (that the world might not have existed) is itself inconceivable. If one were to say, therefore, that one wonders at the existence of the world, this would violate the essential condition of what it means to wonder at something, namely that it should make sense, in principle, for something that does exist not to have existed. This situation is not satisfied by the matter of the existence of the world. There could be no conceivable or possible alternative for which we might use the expression 'the nonexistence of the world'. That the world has this or that discernible and genuine feature, for example that it has human beings in it, is a legitimate ground for wonder, because we can imagine or conceive it not to have had this particular feature. But the *existence* of the world is not a *feature* of the world in the sense in which the fact that there are human beings in the world is a feature of the world. There is no conceivable alternative to the existence of the world; hence the existence of the world is not a feature of the world. Thus when Wittgenstein says that one cannot wonder at the sky *whatever* its color is, he here uses the tautologous statement of the possible colors of the sky as a symbol for the existence of the world as a whole. If we were to wonder at the sky *whatever* its color, what we are really expressing symbolically is that one wonders at the existence of the world as a whole. Such wonderment would be illegitimate in either case. For we cannot wonder at what cannot be otherwise than it is. No more than we can wonder at a tautologic enumeration of the sky's possible colors can we wonder at the existence of the world. Neither can be otherwise than it is.

With respect to the matter of astonishment or surprise as involved in what it means to wonder at something, there is this additional point. If we rule out wonder as an appropriate response to a situation of which possible alternatives are not imaginable or conceivable, as is the case with the matter of the existence of the world, then *a fortiori* the response of astonishment or surprise is likewise eliminated in connection with the existence of the world. We cannot meaningfully say, for example, "I am astonished at the existence of the world" or "How extraordinary that the world exists—I didn't *expect* the world to exist at all!"

CHAPTER VI

Verificationism

WITTGENSTEIN'S RETURN TO PHILOSOPHY: THE TRANSITIONAL PHASE

The bilingual German-English edition of Wittgenstein's *Tractatus* appeared in 1922. The translation into English was done by C. K. Ogden "with the assistance of Mr. F. P. Ramsey, of Trinity College, Cambridge."

During the period 1920 to 1926 Wittgenstein served as a schoolteacher in Trattenbach, Otterthal, and Puchberg, three villages in Lower Austria. In 1923 Ramsey came to visit Wittgenstein at Puchberg and spent a few weeks with him. In a letter dated September 20, 1923, written to his mother, Ramsey describes this visit:

Wittgenstein is a teacher in the Village school. He is very poor, at least he lives very economically. He has one *tiny* room whitewashed, containing a bed, washstand, small table and one hard chair and that is all there is room for. His evening meal which I shared last night is rather unpleasant coarse bread butter and cocoa. His school hours are 8 to 12 or 1 and he seems to be free all the afternoon.

He looks younger than he can possibly be; but he says he has bad eyes and a cold. But his general appearance is athletic. In explaining his philosophy he is excited and makes vigorous gestures but relieves the tension by a charming laugh. He has blue eyes.

He is prepared to give 4 or 5 hours a day to explaining his book. I have had two days and got through 7(+ incidental forward references) out of 80 pages. And when the book is done I shall try to pump him for ideas for its further development which I shall attempt. He says he himself will do nothing more, not because he is bored, but because his mind is no longer flexible. He says no one can do more than 5 or 10 years work at philosophy. (His book took 7). And he is sure Russell will do nothing more important. His idea of his book is not that anyone by reading it will understand his ideas, but that some day someone will think them out again for himself, and will derive great pleasure from finding in this book their exact expressions. I think he exaggerates his own verbal inspiration, it is much more careful than I supposed but I think it reflects the way the ideas came to him which might not be the same with another man.

He has already answered my chief difficulty which I have puzzled over for a year and given up in despair myself and decided he had not seen. (It is not in the 1st 7 pages but arose by the way.) He is great. I used to think Moore a great man but beside W!

He says I shall forget everything he explains in a few days; Moore in Norway said he understood W completely and when he got back to England was no wiser than when he started.

It's terrible when he says "Is that clear" and I say "no" and he says "Damn it's *horrid* to go through that again". Sometimes he says I can't see that now we must leave it. He often forgot the meaning of what he wrote within 5 min[ute]s, and then remembered it later. Some of his sentences are intentionally ambiguous having an ordinary meaning and a more difficult meaning which he also believes.

He is, I can see, a little annoyed that Russell is doing a new edit[ion] of Principia because he thought he had shown R that it was so wrong that a new edition would be futile. It must be done altogether afresh. He had a week with Russell 4 y[ea]rs ago.[1]

During the years 1923–1924 Ramsey made a number of efforts to induce Wittgenstein to return to Cambridge. In these efforts he had the encouragement and assistance of John Maynard Keynes. Nothing came of them. It wasn't until 1929 that Wittgenstein finally came to Cambridge and thus renewed an association with the university that, with some interruptions, was maintained until 1947. One of the persons with whom Wittgenstein was in close contact during the early period of his return to Cambridge was Ramsey. In the Preface to his *Philosophical Investigations* (written in 1945) Wittgenstein says:

Four years ago I had occasion to re-read my first book (the *Tractatus Logico-Philosophicus*) and to explain its ideas to someone. It suddenly seemed to me that I should publish those old thoughts and the new ones together: that the latter could be seen in the right light only by contrast with and against the background of my old way of thinking.

For since beginning to occupy myself with philosophy again, sixteen years ago, I have been forced to recognize grave mistakes in what I wrote in that first book. I was helped to realize these mistakes—to a degree which I myself am hardly able to estimate—by the criticism which my ideas encountered from Frank Ramsey, with whom I discussed them in innumerable conversations during the last two years of his life.[2]

(Ramsey, who had been made a fellow of King's College and a lecturer in mathematics, died in 1930, at the age of twenty-six. His premature death, as the editor of Ramsey's philosophical papers *The Foundations of Mathematics* remarks, "deprives Cambridge of one of its intellectual glories and contemporary philosophy of one of its profoundest thinkers.")

Wittgenstein's years of service as a schoolteacher during the period 1920–1926 were, on the whole, filled with considerable mental anquish and dissatisfaction. Apparently his life in the small villages in which he served did not fall in readily and happily with the adult members of those communities. However, his relations as a teacher with his pupils, involving the use of various innovative teaching techniques and a genuine dedication on Wittgenstein's part, were more rewarding since these were appreciated at least by the children themselves.[3] Although during this period Wittgenstein was not actively engaged in the writing of philosophy, it is quite likely that his lifelong preoccupation with the problems of language and meaning was not totally in abeyance. On the contrary, one may suppose that his day-to-day activities as a teacher, his composition of a word-book for children to help them to learn the grammar of their language, and the need to work with 'ordinary language' (as distinct from the highly technical artificial language of logic in which he had been absorbed during his earlier work in the Frege-Russell tradition)—all had significance for him. They left their deposit and had their eventual influence on the characteristic and novel doctrines concerning language, meaning, and communication that he came to formulate once he returned to active research in philosophy toward the end of the 1920s.

After discontinuing his work as a schoolteacher in 1926, Wittgenstein for a short time became a gardener's assistant in a monastery near Vienna. From 1926 to 1928 he remained in Vienna, where (together with his architect-friend Paul Engelmann) he designed a mansion for one of his sisters, Margaret Stonborough, and with great care and detail supervised its actual construction.[4]

During this period, upon his return to Vienna Wittgenstein first had occasion to meet with Moritz Schlick, the central figure in and founder of the Vienna Circle. Schlick had come to the University of Vienna as Professor of the Philosophy of the Inductive Sciences in 1922. He there gathered around him a number of philosophers, mathematicians, and scientists. They met regularly as a club and eventually came to be designated as the 'Vienna Circle'. The Vienna Circle was the group that gave birth to the philosophic movement known as 'logical positivism' (also sometimes referred to as 'logical empiricism').

Schlick had read Wittgenstein's *Tractatus* when it first appeared in Ostwald's *Annalen der Philosophie* in 1921. This work quickly became a matter of interest to others in the Vienna Circle. The mathematician Hans Hahn, one of its leading members, used it as a basis for a seminar given by him in 1922. It was given careful readings by all members of the Circle in

1924–1925, and again in 1925–1926. Schlick wrote to Wittgenstein in 1924 as follows:

> As an admirer of your *Tractatus Logico-Philosophicus* I have long intended to get in touch with you. My professorial and other duties are responsible for the fact that I have again and again put off carrying out my intention, though nearly five semesters have passed since I was called to Vienna. Every winter semester I have regular meetings with colleagues and gifted students who are interested in the foundations of logic and mathematics and your name has often been mentioned in this group, particularly since my mathematical colleague Professor Reidemeister reported on your work in a lecture which made a great impression on us all. So there are a number of people here—I am one of them myself—who are convinced of the importance and correctness of your fundamental ideas and who feel a strong desire to play some part in making your views more widely known.[5]

It wasn't until 1927 that Schlick succeeded in meeting with Wittgenstein. This was accomplished through the intermediary efforts of Margaret Stonborough. Schlick was to remain in contact with him for several years. Wittgenstein did not take part in the meetings of the Vienna Circle, preferring to meet privately with Schlick and Friedrich Waismann, and occasionally with one or two others. A published record of these conversations was kept by Waismann.[6] The influence on Schlick of Wittgenstein's ideas, both new and old, was very great. These ideas were indirectly transmitted to other members of the Vienna Circle, on some of whom they also had a great impact. Many of the characteristic theses identified with logical positivism owe their origin to the way in which the members of the Circle interpreted Wittgenstein's thought.

Another leading member of the Vienna Circle, Rudolf Carnap (1891–1970), was perhaps the most distinguished representative of the philosophy of logical positivism. In his intellectual autobiography, Carnap singled out Frege, Russell, and Wittgenstein as having exerted the greatest influence on the formation of his own thinking in its early stages. He writes:

> I was influenced by Frege first through his lectures and later, perhaps even to a greater extent, through his works, most of which I read only after the war. His main work, *Die Grundgesetze der Arithmetik* (2 vols., 1893 and 1903), I studied in 1920. From Frege I learned carefulness and clarity in the analysis of concepts and linguistic expressions, the distinction between expressions and what they stand for, and concerning the latter between what he called "*Bedeutung*" (denotation or *nominatum*) and what he called "*Sinn*" (sense or *significatum*). From his analysis I gained the conviction that knowledge in mathematics is analytic in the general sense that it has essentially the same nature as knowledge in logic. . . . From Frege I learned the requirement to formulate the rules of inference of logic without any reference to meaning, but also the great significance of meaning analysis. I believe that here are the roots of my philosophical interest—on the one hand in

logical syntax, and on the other hand in that part of semantics which may be regarded as a theory of meaning.

Whereas Frege had the strongest influence on me in the fields of logic and semantics, in my philosophical thinking in general I learned most from Bertrand Russell. In the winter of 1921 I read his book, *Our Knowledge of the External World, as a Field For Scientific Method in Philosophy.* Some passages made an especially vivid impression on me because they formulated clearly and explicitly a view of the aim and method of philosophy which I had implicitly held for some time. In the Preface he speaks about "the logical-analytic method of philosophy" and refers to Frege's work as the first complete example of this method. And on the very last pages of the book he gives a summarizing characterization of this philosophical method. . . . I felt as if this appeal had been directed to me personally. To work in this spirit would be my task from now on! And indeed henceforth the application of the new logical instrument for the purposes of analyzing scientific concepts and of clarifying philosophical problems has been the essential aim of my philosophical activity.

I now began an intensive study of Russell's books on the theory of knowledge and the methodology of science. I owe very much to his work, not only with respect to philosophical method, but also in the solution of special problems.[7]

Concerning Wittgenstein, Carnap has the following to say:

In the Vienna Circle, a large part of Ludwig Wittgenstein's book *Tractatus Logico-Philosophicus* was read aloud and discussed sentence by sentence. . . . Wittgenstein's book exerted a strong influence upon our Circle. But it is not correct to say that the philosophy of the Vienna Circle was just Wittgenstein's philosophy. We learned much by our discussions of the book, and accepted many views as far as we could assimilate them to our basic conceptions. The degree of influence varied, of course, for the different members.

For me personally, Wittgenstein was perhaps the philosopher who, besides Russell and Frege, had the greatest influence on my thinking. The most important insight I gained from his work was the conception that the truth of logical statements is based only on their logical structure and on the meaning of the terms.[8]

Upon his return to Cambridge in 1929, Wittgenstein applied for the Ph.D. degree, submitting the *Tractatus* (published eight years earlier) as his dissertation. The oral examining committee consisted of Moore and Russell. Russell's biographer reports what transpired:

Moore and Russell first chatted informally to Wittgenstein as old friends rather than as examiners and examinee. Then Russell turned to Moore. "Go on," he said, "you've got to ask him some questions—*you're* the Professor." There was a short discussion. Russell made a brief attempt to argue that Wittgenstein was inconsistent in stating that little could be said about philosophy and that it was possible to reach unassailable truth. Then the Viva ended unexpectedly with Wittgenstein clapping each of his examiners on the shoulder and exclaiming, "Don't worry, I know you'll *never* understand it."[9]

Wittgenstein received both the Ph.D. degree and, during the same month of June 1929, also a grant from Trinity College to carry on his research. By May 1930, when the Council of Trinity College was called upon to renew the grant, Wittgenstein had written "a bulky manuscript"—the *Philosophische Bemerkungen (Philosophical Remarks)*. He submitted this as evidence of his work. Russell, who had been asked by Moore to write a report evaluating this work, at first wrote to Moore:

> I do not see how I can refuse to read Wittgenstein's work and make a report on it. At the same time, since it involves arguing with him, you are right that it will require a great deal of work. I do not know anything more fatiguing than disagreeing with him in an argument.
>
> Obviously the best plan for me would be to read the manuscript carefully first, and see him afterwards.[10]

Philosophische Bemerkungen (Philosophical Remarks) deals with many of the themes that continued to preoccupy Wittgenstein in his later philosophy—the nature of propositions, the uses of language, what is involved in 'understanding', 'intending', and so on, and the foundations of mathematics. It was the first of a series of works that included *Philosophical Grammar, The Blue and Brown Books, Remarks on the Foundations of Mathematics,* and *Philosophical Investigations.* (None of these was published until after his death.) These works represent different stages in, and reworking of, the themes that belong to Wittgenstein's 'later' philosophy. There was no absolutely sharp break between the 'early' philosophy of the *Tractatus* and what emerged as the 'later' philosophy; instead there were various intermediate or transitional stages. The fresh orientation of Wittgenstein's thought as it became clearly evident in the *Philosophical Remarks,* was one with which Russell had no sympathy. Nevertheless in his report to the Council Russell wrote:

> The theories contained in this new work of Wittgenstein's are novel, very original, and indubitably important. Whether they are true, I do not know. As a logician who likes simplicity, I should wish to think that they are not, but from what I have read of them I am quite sure that he ought to have an opportunity to work them out, since when completed they may easily prove to constitute a whole new philosophy.[11]

By December 1930 Wittgenstein was appointed a Fellow of Trinity College. From that time forward, with some interruptions, he lectured at Cambridge until his retirement.

The record kept by Waismann of Wittgenstein's conversations held in Vienna with Schlick and himself cover the period from December 1929 to July 1932. The works subsequently published under the titles *Philosophical Remarks* and *Philosophical Grammar* belong to this transitional period. Although the members of the Vienna Circle had access to the *Tractatus,* their knowlege of Wittgenstein's newer ideas depended either on learning of them directly through conversations —as was the case with

Schlick, Waismann, and occasionally one or two others—or else indirectly and by report. Their understanding of Wittgenstein's philosophy was thus an amalgam of the interpretation given to what they took to be the message of the *Tractatus* and the influence of these newer ideas. This amalgam had considerable impact in the fashioning of the doctrines with which the movement of logical positivism became identified. At the center of the positivist philosophy was the appeal to the *Principle of Verification*. It was a 'principle' that Wittgenstein espoused in the period roughly between 1929 and 1932.

Contrary to what many people once believed, there is nothing that could be recognized and called a 'Principle of Verification' in the *Tractatus*. The whole philosophy of that work—its picture theory of meaning and truth-functional approach to propositions—is quite different in its orientation from the main thrusts of the later works. The suggestion for a verificationist approach makes its appearance in Wittgenstein's thought only with his return to philosophy in the late 1920s. If one studies the record of the conversations with Schlick and Waismann, as well as certain crucial passages in *Philosophical Remarks* and *Philosophical Grammar,* it is possible to collect various comments and doctrines and label them Wittgenstein's version of the 'Principle of Verification'. While this principle, so identified, did undoubtedly play its role at this stage of Wittgenstein's philosophy, it turned out, in the later course of the development of his philosophy, to have far less importance for him than what goes by the same name in the positivist philosophy.

During the heyday of the 'Verification Principle' and as popularized by the positivists, Wittgenstein is reported to have remarked at a meeting of the Moral Sciences Club at Cambridge University:

"I used at one time to say that, in order to get clear how a certain sentence is used, it was a good idea to ask oneself the question: 'How would one try to verify such an assertion?' But that's just one way among others of getting clear about the use of a word or sentence. For example, another question which it is often very useful to ask oneself is: 'How is this word learned?' 'How would one set about teaching a child to use this word?' But some people have turned this suggestion about asking for the verification into a dogma—as if I'd been advancing a *theory* about meaning."[12]

Despite Wittgenstein's attempt in the foregoing reported remark to downgrade the importance of the verification principle as of *sole* relevance in determining the meaning of a sentence, the fact remains that in his *Philosophical Remarks* he wrote:

The verification is not *one* token of the truth, it is *the* sense of the proposition.[13]

There is then *some* kinship between the two versions of the Verification Principle—that of Wittgenstein and of the logical positivists—and to the extent that there is one may ascribe a partial adherence or minimal sympathy on his part, at this stage, for a 'positivist' philosophy. However, his espousal of a 'Verification Principle' and the appeal to an emphasis on 'hypotheses' with which this was associated, underwent significant changes in the course of further development of his philosophy. So if we do ascribe a doctrine of 'verificationism' to Wittgenstein, it is important to see how he formulated it, how it was interpreted by the positivists and given a central status in their philosophy, and finally how the verificationism of the positivist philosophy had, as a result, a rather different cast and use from what it had in Wittgenstein's thought. In order to see these points more fully, in this chapter we shall first of all study the original stimulus to the formulation of a verificationist outlook as found in certain doctrines of Wittgenstein's writings and conversations during the early thirties. We shall then examine the main doctrines of the philosophy of logical positivism as developed by members of the Vienna Circle. In connection with the latter, we shall follow the fortunes of the attempts by the positivists to sponsor the doctrine of Verificationism as well as some of the problems that beset their efforts to give it a clear and defensible formulation.

'VERIFICATIONISM' AND 'HYPOTHESES' IN WITTGENSTEIN'S PHILOSOPHY

Some of the relevant passages in which Wittgenstein briefly sketches a verificationist approach to meaning are the following:
In *Philosophical Remarks* he writes:

The meaning of a question is the method of answering it: then what is the meaning of 'Do two men really mean the same by the word "white"?'

Tell me *how* you are searching, and I will tell you *what* you are searching for.[14]

To understand the sense of a proposition means to know how the issue of its truth or falsity is to be decided.[15]

Each proposition is a signpost for a verification.[16]

How a proposition is verified is what it says. Compare the generality of genuine propositions with generality in arithmetic. It is differently verified and so is of a different kind.[17]

In conversations with Schlick and Waismann he remarked:

The sense of a proposition is the method of its verification.[18]

This statement later became a slogan used by the positivists to sum up their own theory of meaning. In a passage foreshadowing an issue much discussed by the positivists—that having to do with the distinction between 'strong' and 'weak' verification—Wittgenstein comments:

> If I say, for example, 'Up there on the cupboard there is a book', how do I set about verifying it? Is it sufficient if I glance at it, or if I look at it from different sides, or if I take it into my hands, touch it, open it, turn over its leaves, and so forth? There are two conceptions here. One of them says that however I set about it, I shall never be able to verify the proposition completely. A proposition always keeps a back-door open, as it were. Whatever we do, we are never sure that we were not mistaken.
>
> The other conception, the one I want to hold, says, 'No, if I can never verify the sense of a proposition completely, then I cannot have meant anything by the proposition either. Then the proposition signifies nothing whatsoever.'
>
> In order to determine the sense of a proposition, I should have to know a very specific procedure for when to count the proposition as verified. In this respect everyday language oscillates very much, much more so than scientific language. There is a certain latitude here, and this means simply that the symbols of our everyday language are not unambiguously defined.[19]

In order to understand more fully Wittgenstein's conception of the role of verification, we need to examine the relation it has to *hypotheses* and *propositions*.

The matter of verification has a different role to perform in the case of a sentence describing some part of reality, as contrasted with the 'verification' of a sentence in a mathematical proof. In the former, the recognition of truth of the sentence is accomplished by confronting the sentence with reality. In the case of mathematical sentences Wittgenstein would say there is no requirement to consult reality, for mathematical sentences are, at bottom, 'grammatical rules' constructed by people and adopted by them as a matter of convention.

Sentences that would describe reality include what Wittgenstein in his *Philosophical Remarks* and *Philosophical Grammar* calls 'hypotheses' and 'propositions'. In the *wide sense* of the term, a 'proposition' is equivalent to a 'sentence'. In this wide sense, hypotheses are propositions (sentences). In the present context, however, we shall follow Wittgenstein in using the expression 'proposition' in the *narrower* sense, in order to *contrast it* with 'hypothesis'. The differences between 'hypotheses' and 'propositions' as here used is one of 'degrees of freedom'. This has to do with the kind of logical relation a sentence has to reality, the extent to which (or the manner in which) it is constrained by reality. If a sentence is not constrained at all by reality (as is the case with a tautology, a contradiction, or an arbitrary rule or convention) it has no degree of freedom, and has no sense as a reality-describing sentence.

A proposition, an hypothesis, is coupled with reality—with varying degrees of freedom. In the limit case there's no longer any connection, reality can do anything it likes without coming into conflict with the proposition: in which case the proposition (hypothesis) is senseless!

. . . .

A proposition construed in such a way that it can be uncheckably true or false is completely detached from reality and no longer functions as a proposition.[20]

The 'reality' to which reality-describing sentences must conform is not some *'ding-an-sich'*, some hidden and inaccessible thing-in-itself. It is, rather, what is given in sensory, observational experience.

All that matters is that the signs, in no matter how complicated a way, still in the end refer to immediate experience and not to an intermediary (a thing in itself).

All that's required for our propositions (about reality) to have a sense, is that our experience *in some sense or other* either tends to agree with them or tends not to agree with them. That is, immediate experience need confirm only something about them, *some* facet of them. And in fact this image is taken straight from reality, since we say 'There's a chair here', when we only see *one* side of it.

. . . .

A phenomenon isn't a symptom of something else: it is the reality.

A phenomenon isn't a symptom of something else which alone makes the proposition true or false: it itself is what verifies the proposition.[21]

The difference between a 'hypothesis' and a 'proposition' is that a hypothesis has a greater degree of freedom as compared to a proposition in conforming to reality. A hypothesis is a (proposed) 'law' that would connect various observations, many different immediate experiences. By contrast, a proposition describes a particular observation. By 'hypothesis' Wittgenstein means a "law for forming propositions. . . . A proposition is, so to speak, a particular cross-section of an hypothesis."[22] Consider the following situation: Let us draw a line to connect various points plotted on a graph that uses some particular coordinate system (method of representation). Let each *point* represent the results of some observation. The *line*—say a straight line, circle, parabola, or some other that connects these points —constitutes a 'hypothesis'. It represents an effort to interpret and discern the 'law' that connects not only the observed instances but also others that might be obtained in the future.

My experience speaks in favor of the idea that *this* hypothesis will be able to represent it and future experience *simply*. If it turns out that another hypothesis represents the material of experience more simply, then I choose the simpler method. . . . This is how someone might try to represent the course of an experience which presents itself as the development of a curve by means of various curves, each of which is based on how much of the actual course is known to us.

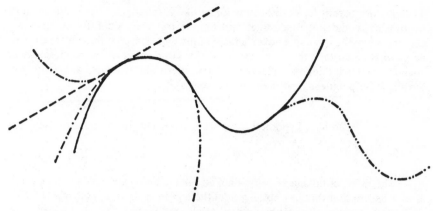

The curve ————— is the actual course, so far as it is to be observed at all. The curves ------, –··–··–, –·—·— , show different attempts to represent it that are based on a greater or lesser part of the whole material of observation.

We only give up an hypothesis for an even higher gain.[23]

The various expectations of future observations that would be found, if the hypothesis (the line or 'law' connecting the points) is correct, constitute *predictions*. Insofar as these predictions are borne out, they serve as verifications of the truth of the hypothesis. Each record of a particular observation is a 'proposition'. The various 'propositions' (observational reports) are so many 'verifications' of the hypothesis.

It is always single faces of hypotheses that are verified.

. . . .

The hypothesis, if *that* face of it is laid against reality, becomes a proposition.[24]

. . . .

If our experiences yield points lying on a straight line, the proposition that these experiences are various views of a straight line is a hypothesis.

The hypothesis is a way of representing this reality, for a new experience may tally with it or not, or possibly make it necessary to modify the hypothesis.

If for instance we use a system of coordinates and the equation for a sphere to express the proposition that a sphere is located at a certain distance from our eyes, this description has a greater multiplicity than that of a verification by eye. The first multiplicity corresponds not to *one* verification but to a *law* obeyed by verifications.[25]

All propositions that report what is directly observed are known with certainty. Their truth is established conclusively by describing what is immediately present to the observer.

It may be doubtful whether the body I see is a sphere, but it can't be doubtful that from here it looks to be something like a sphere. — The mechanism of hypothesis would not function if appearance too were doubtful so that one couldn't verify beyond doubt even a facet of the hypothesis. If there were a doubt here, what could take the doubt away? If this connection too were loose, there would be no such thing as confirming an hypothesis and it would hang entirely in the air, quite pointless (and therefore senseless).[26]

. . . .

There is nothing hypothetical in what connects the proposition with the given fact.[27]

. . . .

The point of talking of sense-data and immediate experience is that we're after a description that has nothing hypothetical in it. If an hypothesis can't be definitively verified, it can't be verified at all, and there's no truth or falsity for it.[28]

The relation a hypothesis has to reality is of a looser kind than that of a verified proposition. It cannot be established with certainty. The appeal to individual 'verifications'—i.e., to individual reports of observations (the 'cross sections' of the hypothesis) only tend to confirm or disconfirm the hypothesis with some *degree of probability*. 'Probability', accordingly, marks a logical relation of a hypothesis to reality. It is to be distinguished from the immediate truth of a 'verification', i.e., the *known* truth of an observation-sentence. Thus 'verifications' are known with certainty, conclusively; they mark the immediately recognized truths of 'propositions', whereas hypotheses are confirmed only with some degree of probability by appeal to these 'verifying' propositions. Hypotheses depend on the weight of evidence (the degree of confirmation) that the verifying propositions provide. It is the number and quality of these immediately known 'verifications' that lend support to an hypothesis. The logical status of the 'truth' of an hypothesis thus has to be distinguished from the truth of a verifying proposition. Furthermore, 'probability' in the sense of 'degree of confirmation', as applied to an hypothesis, is to be distinguished from the sense of 'probability' that has to do with the relative frequency of an event in a series of events to which it belongs.

The probability of an hypothesis has its measure in how much evidence is needed to make it profitable to throw it out.

It's only in this sense that we can say that repeated uniform experience in the past renders the continuation of this uniformity in the future probable.

If, in this sense, I now say: I assume the sun will rise again tomorrow, because the opposite is so unlikely, I here mean by "likely" and "unlikely" something completely different from what I mean by these words in the proposition "It's equally likely that I'll throw heads or tails". The two meanings of the word "likely" are, to be sure, connected in certain ways, but they aren't identical.[29]

Finally, if one uses the term 'verifiability' in connection both with 'hypotheses' *and* 'propositions', it is necessary to draw a distinction between the sense in which a hypothesis is verifiable and the sense in which a proposition is verifiable. The hypothesis is verifiable only with some degree of probability (degree of confirmation), never with certainty. On the other hand, the separate propositions that serve as 'confirmations' or 'verifications' of a hypothesis are *themselves not 'verifiable'* in the same sense in which hypotheses are. They are, rather, *verified* directly, conclusively, and with certainty. Such verifications (of propositions) are not a matter of probability.

What is essential to an hypothesis is, I believe, that it arouses an expectation by admitting of future confirmation. That is, it is of the essence of an hypothesis that its confirmation is never completed.

When I say an hypothesis isn't definitively verifiable, that doesn't mean that there is a verification of it which we may approach ever more nearly, without ever reaching it. That is nonsense—of a kind into which we frequently lapse. No, an hypothesis simply has a different formal relation to reality from that of verification. (Hence, of course, the words 'true' and 'false' are also inapplicable here, or else have a different meaning.)[30]

Let us pause to sum up and take stock of Wittgenstein's version of verificationism. His support of this philosophy was of relatively brief duration. It was formulated by him in the early stages of his return to philosophy in the late twenties and early thirties. In certain crucial respects Wittgenstein's verificationism showed deviations from the philosophy of the *Tractatus* period. However, it too was to mark only a transitional phase toward the full elaboration of his 'later' philosophy as this is conveyed in the *Philosophical Investigations*. This later philosophy superseded and displaced not only the philosophy of the *Tractatus* but the verificationism of this transitional phase as well. A quick, sloganized way of summing up these three periods, insofar as they are seen in terms of Wittgenstein's continuing concern with the 'critique of language' (the 'problem of meaning'), would be to say that in the *Tractatus* period the meaning of a proposition is to be identified with its serving as *a picture of a state of affairs*; in the 'middle' (transitional) period the meaning of a proposition is the mode of its *verification*; and in the later philosophy the meaning of any linguistic expression is to be found by examining its *use in some language-game*.

In the *Tractatus*, as we have seen, despite his various departures from Frege's detailed theses, Wittgenstein continued to work within the general Fregean orientation. Insofar as he dealt with the role of language as the medium for 'what can be said', he agreed with Frege in taking a primarily *cognitive* approach to the uses of language, and in stressing that a formal, truth-functional logic provides the necessary logical tools for probing the 'depth-grammar' of language. For this purpose, ordinary language needs to be recast into a language that consists entirely of certain basic expressions, viz., names and elementary propositions. To what extent can language, when thus carefully, clearly, and consistently articulated, give us the truth about the world? This is the guiding question. As a way of answering this question, Wittgenstein (as did Frege) attends first to the question of *meaning*. The meaning of a proposition is linked to its *truth-conditions*. Truth-conditions specify what would need to be the case for the entire proposition to be true, and what, in the absence or failure of satisfaction of this, would therefore make the entire proposition false. In the case of an elementary proposition what is required for the proposition to be true is that the pictorial form of the proposition be identical with the form of the state of affairs it represents. The concatenation of the names of the elementary proposition (its structural arrangement) must mirror, depict, serve as a model for, the structural arrangement of the objects in the state of affairs it purports to describe. If the pictorial structure of the proposition mirrors (coincides with) the actual structure of the state of affairs, the proposition is true, otherwise false. (Even if false, the proposition has meaning (sense) because it represents a *possible* state of affairs.) In order to have sense, to be meaningful, an elementary proposition must exhibit in its own pictorial, linguistic, and logical structure as a concatenation of names, a structure of some possible state of affairs. The matter of *truth*, on this approach, is bound up with *identity of structure* between proposition and fact. What is essential for truth is that there *be* an identity of form between proposition and fact, not that the truth be known or come to be recognized as a result of inquiry. The conception of truth here is a realistic one.

The situation for molecular (compound) propositions follows directly from that holding for elementary propositions. For the truth or falsity of a molecular proposition is dependent on the truth or falsity of the elementary propositions that compose it. The truth or falsity of a molecular proposition is thus determined in a truth-functional way. Its *meaning* is specified by its truth-conditions, as these are governed by the particular combinations of truth of falsity for the elementary propositions allowed by the rules for 'and', 'either————or', and 'if————then'. The truth-conditions of a molecular proposition consist of those conditions under which it is true and those conditions under which it is false. Whether a molecular proposition is in fact true is determined by the actual truth or falsity of the elementary propositions that compose it; it depends on the resultant combination of actual truth-values (truth or falsity) of the elementary propositions within the particular type of molecular proposition concerned.

So much for a brief reminder of the approach taken to 'meaning' and 'truth' by Wittgenstein in the *Tractatus*. When we turn, however, to

Wittgenstein's views on 'meaning' and 'truth' in his verificationist period, there are already very significant changes, although also some important elements of continuity with these earlier views. What remains unchanged is a continuing orientation to language in terms of its serving as an instrument for conveying knowledge—a cognitive interest. The preoccupation with language still has as its focus a setting out of those conditions for the use of language to state the truth about the world. Under what conditions can we say language so used is meaningful? The sharp difference between the kind of answer Wittgenstein would now give to this question and that which he had given earlier is that he no longer relies on a picture theory of meaning. For him, now, language is to be explored as we find it, not as it is 'sublimed' or submitted to a process of logical 'analysis' in accordance with the requirements of a truth-functional logic. In order to examine language as it is actually employed, rather than as transformed by logic, one should study it in its uses in everyday contexts, especially in the sciences. In examining the role of language for cognitive purposes from this perspective, Wittgenstein's views on 'meaning' and 'truth' show important changes from his earlier treatment. First, as we have seen, Wittgenstein finds it helpful to make a distinction between 'propositions' and 'hypotheses'. His new use of 'proposition' (and also, of course, of 'hypothesis') has an altogether different meaning. It no longer stands for an elementary or molecular proposition, as these were understood in the *Tractatus*. A proposition, as now understood, records a direct, immediate observation, a sense experience. It need not be composed entirely of names, nor need it refer by means of such names to simple objects. An hypothesis is a proposed 'law' for linking various observational data, as these are recorded in separate propositions. It also serves to enable predictions to be made beyond observations obtained. What, then, on this approach, becomes of 'meaning' and 'truth', both with respect to propositions and hypotheses? The materials for answering these questions have to be gathered from scattered passages in *Philosophical Remarks, Philosophical Grammar*, and the conversations with Schlick and Waismann (*Ludwig Wittgenstein and the Vienna Circle*). These do not add up to a fully developed theory. However, the suggestions for a verificationist approach are there, and they influenced the logical positivists who took them up and sought to give them a more polished and systematic elaboration. As for Wittgenstein's views, we may sum the matter up as follows.

What does it mean to say that the meaning of a proposition consists in its verification? Can one distinguish between the meaning of a proposition and its truth? It would appear from Wittgenstein's brief comments on this matter that as far as a proposition—in the special sense he gives to this—is concerned, its meaning *coincides* with its truth. A proposition, so understood, i.e., as recording a present, direct, immediate experience of an observer, is known with certainty, conclusively. It has no 'degree of freedom' and cannot be falsified. It is only when one introduces 'hypotheses' that one reintroduces the distinction between meaning and truth. The meaning of a hypothesis is the possibility of its being verified, its verifiability. Unless it allows predictions of what might be observed, it has no sense at all as a hypothesis. Moreover, its verifiability consists in its confirmability. It can receive a degree of confirmation, depending on the number and quality of the verifying propositions that can be adduced in its favor. The actual truth of a hypothesis is thus never established with certainty, in the way a proposition can be so established. Its truth is only a matter of probability, where this is equated with its degree of confirmation.

Since the truth of a proposition coincides with its meaning, i.e., its recording of the observations actually had by an individual observer, the fact of having such observational experience is essential.This view points in a different direction from the realism and the 'truth-conditions' analysis of the meaning of a proposition in the *Tractatus*. The latter system of semantics was set out independently of any appeal to the obtaining of observational data by individual persons, and concerned itself simply with a relation of identity of structure between proposition and fact. Now, however, in his verificationist semantics, Wittgenstein insists on the presence of an observer and on the fact that a proposition must record an actual observational experience. This *empirical* condition for the meaningfulness of a proposition is in sharp contrast to his earlier approach. Now the meaning (sense) of a proposition cannot be separated from the way in which its truth is actually established by a person using the language to record his observations. Similarly, the meaning of an hypothesis is bound up with the specification of the kinds of empirical observations that need to be obtained if the hypothesis is to be confirmed (established with some degree of probability). The meaning of a hypothesis is its verifiability—its openness to confirmation or disconfirmation, its being rendered probably true or probably false by data obtained through experience.

Wittgenstein gave up his 'verificationist' approach in the full flowering of his later philosophy. As we shall see, he abandoned the predominantly cognitivist orientation to language. He stressed, instead, the great variety and multiplicity of language uses. Furthermore, there are various semantic conditions, depending on the uses to which linguistic expressions are put, that sanction their use and so specify their meaning. The meaning of language-uses is given neither by means of truth-conditions nor by pointing to a mode of verification. Rather, the conditions for meaningful use of language are given by *various types of 'grammatical rules'*, i.e., by various *use-conditions*, among which *criteria* of meaning play an important role.

There were other important reasons why Wittgenstein abandoned verificationism. If, as we have seen, the meaning of a proposition collapses into its truth, a crucial distinction—between meaning and truth—is wiped out. This comes in conflict with a central thesis to which Wittgenstein had always subscribed, namely that a proposition of *any* kind must be either true *or* false. Furthermore, the whole idea of a proposition being meaningful or true for a single observer, and known only by him with certainty because of a direct, *private* experience, was seen to be wholly unacceptable. It conflicted with another central thesis of his later philosophy, namely that language cannot be private. (We shall explore all these ideas in greater detail, in the following chapter.)

THE VIENNA CIRCLE

As contrasted with individually produced schemes of thought of the kind, for example, we previously encountered in Peirce, Frege, Russell, and Wittgenstein, the philosophy of logical positivism was the fruit of a cooperative enterprise in which a number of like-minded scientists and philosophers participated. Apart from certain internal differences on particular matters, the philosophy of logical positivism is a unified set of doctrines, a commonly shared platform of principles, to which its adherents subscribed. At an early stage those who formed the nucleus of this movement published their own manifesto of principles, later held various international congresses, eventually published their own 'house organ', and succeeded in acquiring a number of affiliated groups and individual followers in various countries throughout the world to join in the advancement and support of their program. This is not to deny or to overlook that there are also important individual differences among logical positivists, and that some of the most creative members of this group—for example, Carnap and Reichenbach—produced highly individual results or engaged in special lines of research that reflected their personal interests.

The major activity and influence of the movement of logical positivism took place in the period 1926–1936. There were, to be sure, foreshadowings of the movement at earlier times. Nor is it the case that the movement suffered an immediate and total decline after 1936. Nevertheless, the most vigorous and cooperative period of its growth occurred during this time, and was dominated by the activities of the Vienna Circle.

The founder and moving spirit of the Vienna Circle was Moritz Schlick (1882–1936). He was appointed Professor of Philosophy at the University of Vienna in 1922. Schlick had done his doctoral thesis in physics under Max Planck (on the reflection of light in nonhomogeneous media) and had also published his *Space and Time in Contemporary Physics* in 1917, one of the earliest studies of Einstein's theory of relativity. Like the majority of those eventually belonging to the Vienna Circle,

Schlick combined a thorough, firsthand grounding in one or more of the sciences with a deep interest in the philosophical questions growing out of the sciences. One of Schlick's major works, written before the Vienna Circle came into being, was his *General Theory of Knowledge* (*Allgemeine Erkenntnislehre*) (first edition 1918, second edition 1925). In it he gave detailed expression to the importance of understanding the methods and goals of the sciences.

> We can carry on our work quite well in the sciences without providing them with epistemological foundations, but unless we do so, we shall never *understand* them in all their depth. An understanding of this kind is a peculiarly philosophical need, and the theory of knowledge is philosophy.[31]

By 1926 Schlick, through the force of his personality and intellectual gifts, had succeeded in gathering around him a select group of mathematicians, scientists, and philosophers. It was this group that came to be known as *Der Wiener Kreis* (The Vienna Circle). It included Friedrich Waismann, Hans Hahn, Herbert Feigl, Otto Neurath, Rudolf Carnap, Edgar Zilsel, Bela von Juhos, Kurt Gödel, Victor Kraft, Karl Menger, and others. The regular meetings of the group, and the cooperative character of their work, resulted in the clarification and adoption of certain fundamental views that served as the core of their platform of principles. An early statement of these principles was jointly published in 1929 by Hahn, Carnap, and Neurath (in the absence of Schlick, who was at that time in the United States lecturing at Stanford, California). This manifesto of principles was entitled *Wissenschaftlische Weltauffassung, Der Wiener Kreis* ("The Vienna Circle, Its Scientific Outlook").[32] It listed among its historical antecedents and precursors a great number of writers. Perhaps the most appropriate of these, and closest in spirit to what they stood for themselves, were David Hume and Ernst Mach—both sharing in a strong antimetaphysical and empiricist outlook.

In the same year, 1929, a meeting of mathematicians and scientists was held in Prague. Members of the Vienna Circle took the opportunity to participate in this international conference, and in so doing made important links with the Berlin group (the Society for Empirical Philosophy) led by Hans Reichenbach.

The periodical *Annalen der Philosophie* was taken over in 1930, renamed *Erkenntnis* (and still later renamed *Journal of Unified Science*), and served until its demise in 1940 as a major medium for publishing the views of members of the Vienna Circle and of others sympathetic to their viewpoint. Various monograph series were published over the next several years. During the same period, beginning in 1935 and continuing up to the outbreak of World War II in 1939, a yearly series of international congresses was held at which participants in the movement (by now spread to various countries throughout the world) met to discuss their common problems. Thus there were positivistically oriented thinkers in the United States (Charles W. Morris, Ernest Nagel, W.V.O. Quine); in England (A.J. Ayer, Susan Stebbing); in Germany (Hans Reichenbach, Carl Hempel, Kurt Grelling); in Scandinavia (Eino Kaila, Joergen Joergensen); as well as others in Poland, France, Czechoslavakia, and elsewhere.

With the rise of Nazism and the growing war clouds over Europe, the Circle began to lose much of its original physical cohesiveness and intimately cooperative character. Schlick was fatally wounded in 1936 by a mentally deranged former student. Hahn died in 1934. Carnap, Reichenbach, Hempel, Gödel, Neurath, Waismann, Zilsel, and other members of the original circle dispersed to other parts of the world. Many of them (e.g., Carnap, Reichenbach, and Hempel) settled in the United States where they found a congenial philosophic atmosphere in the traditions of pragmatism. However, wherever they managed to establish themselves positivists encountered strong reactions of hostility because of their opposition to entrenched dogmatic or speculative ways of thinking. There were many heated philosophic discussions and controversies in the 1930s and 1940s, aroused by positivist onslaughts on established ways of thinking.

Eventually, however, this 'positivist' period in the history of contemporary analytic philosophy came to an end. The movement lost its position of influence and cohesiveness. This was due partly to the exposure and critical examination of inherent weaknesses at the very heart of the positivist philosophy, especially with respect to the interpretation and status of the criterion of meaningfulness (the Principle of Verifiability), on which it relied so heavily. Meanwhile, too, the emergence and influence of the later philosophy of Wittgenstein, the flourishing of other types of 'ordinary language' philosophy at Oxford and elsewhere, along with developments in formal logic and linguistics, displaced logical positivism from its central position as the main example of 'analytic philosophy'. After World War II the preoccupations of analytic philosophers shifted from what they had been between the wars, and for all practical purposes logical positivism ceased to be an effective continuing philosophic movement.

THE MAIN DOCTRINES OF LOGICAL POSITIVISM

The basic problem to which positivist philosophers addressed themselves is that of giving a reasoned and detailed answer to the question, What justifies the philosophic belief that it is the method and results of the various sciences to which one must turn in order to obtain reliable claims to knowledge, i.e., as providing a true account of some subject matter?

Thus broadly stated, this problem defines the general domain within which positivist philosophers undertook to work out their detailed inquiries and analyses of various topics. These include the following: the differences between the formal and empirical sciences, as marked by the differences between the 'formal truth' reached in the disciplines of logic and mathematics, and the 'factual truth' achieved in the empirical sciences, e.g., physics, biology, psychology; the Principle of Verification as the criterion for determining the meaningfulness of any statement purporting to give the truth about some subject matter, and as the means for accomplishing the demarcation between genuine and pseudostatements; the elimination of metaphysics; and the interpretation of the use of language in ethics. In addition, there were a number of subsidiary topics related to the above that received extended attention, for example, the meaning of 'probability', the status of laws and theoretical entities in science, and the role of convention and definition in the formulation of scientific statements.

In a celebrated passage in his *Enquiry Concerning Human Understanding* (1748) Hume wrote:

The only objects of the abstract science or of demonstration are quantity and number, and . . . all attempts to extend this more perfect species of knowledge beyond these bounds are mere sophistry and illusion. . . . All other enquiries of men regard only matter of fact and existence; and these are evidently incapable of demonstration. What *is* may *not be*. No negation of a fact can involve a contradiction.

. . . .

When we run over libraries, persuaded of these principles, what havoc must we make? If we take in our hand any volume; of divinity or school metaphysics, for instance; let us ask, *Does it contain any abstract reasoning concerning quantity or number?* No. *Does it contain any experimental reasoning concerning matter of fact and existence?* No. Commit it then to the flames: for it can contain nothing but sophistry and illusion.[33]

The foregoing passage is a classic text that sums up in its way some of the distinctive claims of contemporary logical positivism. Like Hume, positivists make a fundamental distinction within the domain of scientific knowledge, broadly conceived, between the formal sciences of logic and mathematics on the one side, and the empirical sciences on the other. The statements of the former are *analytic a priori*, those of the latter *synthetic a posteriori*. Any claims to having knowledge *synthetic a priori* (such as one finds in Kant, and others) must be rejected. Likewise it is necessary to reject not simply as false but as meaningless (because empirically unverifiable) all claims of a metaphysical sort that purport to give knowledge about a reality or entities that transcend experience altogether. The adoption of the Principle of Verifiability accomplishes this demarcation and underlies these various claims. For this reason this principle occupies the central role in the philosophy of logical positivism.

(Meaningful) statements are divided into the following kinds. First there are statements which are true solely by virtue of their form ("tautologies" according to Wittgenstein; they correspond approximately to Kant's "analytic judgments"). They say nothing about reality. The formulae of logic and mathematics are of this kind. They are not themselves factual statements, but serve for the transformation of such statements. Secondly there are the negations of such statements ("*contradictions*"). They are self-contradictory, hence false by virtue of their form. With respect to all other statements the decision about truth or falsehood lies in the [elementary] protocol sentences. They are therefore (true or false) *empirical statements* and belong to the domain of empirical science. Any statement one desires to construct which does not fall within these categories becomes automatically meaningless. Since metaphysics does not want to assert analytic propositions, nor to fall within the domain of empirical science, it is compelled to employ words for which no criteria of application are specified and which are therefore devoid of sense or else to combine meaningful words in such a way that neither an analytic (or contradictory) statement nor an empirical statement is produced. In either case pseudo-statements are the inevitable product.[34]

Positivist philosophers wished to rid philosophy of fruitless inquiries and disagreements. In this aim they claimed their approach to be different from others who, throughout the history of philosophy, sought to criticize the views held by many philosophers. Unlike most critics who align themselves with one or another of the opposing views within a philosophic controversy, the positivists took a more radical view of such controversies in general. They maintained that such controversies were futile because *all* sides to the dispute were seeking to find answers to pseudoquestions, hence the 'answers' proposed, whatever they were, were also pseudoanswers. This is to say that there were no genuine statements involved in the disagreements, only pseudostatements. A genuine statement says something that is either true or false. If a combination of words can be shown to be not possibly true or false, then it has no cognitive value. This would be the case if the language used consisted of pseudostatements. There is no point in criticizing a position couched in pseudostatements on the ground that what it says is false, since it cannot be possibly true or false. Likewise, there is no point in upholding as true (or as 'closer' to the truth) some other position couched in pseudostatements, since it too could not be possibly true or false. What this entails is that the entire inquiry into finding the true view, and disagreements about which view can be said to embody it, are vacuous. No pseudostatement or combination of pseudostatements (however superficially they may appear to be genuine statements) can be either true or false. This is to say that such pseudostatements, not being either possibly true or possibly false, are strictly speaking *meaningless*. The logical positivists were convinced that many traditional philosophic controversies are of this character.

Nor would it be acceptable to suspend judgment about whether a statement is in fact true or in fact false, and adopt a position of agnosticism, of saying that because of the limitations of human capacities we should never know the truth, one way or the other. This agnostic position is rejected by positivists because it presumes that the question about which one is suspending judgment is meaningful. It is this very assumption that is denied by the positivists. In order for a factual statement to be meaningful it must be capable on empirical grounds of yielding a decision whether it is true or false. The agnostic rejects this type of appeal to empirical evidence because he believes certain questions transcend or lie beyond even the possibility of empirical decision; that the truth or falsity of certain statements cannot ever be decided by human beings because of inherent limitations in human capacity. Such agnosticism (as a third alternative to claiming 'dogmatically' that some view is true or that it is false) is denied by positivism as equally metaphysical, hence meaningless, as would be any positive dogmatic position.

With reference to the so-called *limitation of human knowledge* an attempt is sometimes made to save metaphysics by raising the following objection: metaphysical statements are not, indeed, verifiable by man nor by any other finite being; nevertheless they might be construed as conjectures about the answers which a being with higher or even perfect powers of knowledge would make to our questions, and as such conjectures they would, after all, be meaningful. To counter this objection, let us consider the following. If the meaning of a word cannot be specified, or if the sequence of words does not accord with the rules of syntax, then one has not even asked a question. (Just think of the pseudo-questions: "Is this table teavy?", "is the number 7 holy?", "which numbers are darker, the even or the odd ones?"). Where there is no question, not even an omniscient being can give an answer. Now the objector may say: just as one who can see may communicate new knowledge to the blind, so a higher being might perhaps communicate to us metaphysical knowledge, e.g. whether the visible world is the manifestation of a spirit. Here we must reflect on the meaning of "new knowledge." It is, indeed, conceivable that we might encounter animals who tell us about a new sense. If these beings were to prove to us Fermat's theorem or were to invent a new physical instrument or were to establish a hitherto unknown law of nature, then our knowledge would be increased with their help. For this sort of thing we can test, just the way even a blind man can understand and test the whole of physics (and therewith any statement made by those who can see). But if those hypothetical beings tell us something which we cannot verify, then we cannot understand it either; in that case no information has been communicated to us, but mere verbal sounds devoid of meaning though possibly associated with images. It follows that our knowledge can only be quantitatively enlarged by other beings, no matter whether they know more or less or everything, but no knowledge of an essentially different kind can be added. What we do not know for certain, we may come to know with greater certainty through the assistance of other beings; but what is unintelligible, meaningless for us, cannot become meaningful through someone else's assistance, however vast his knowledge might be. Therefore no god and no devil can give us metaphysical knowledge.[35]

The criterion of meaningfulness

This radical claim about the meaninglessness of many traditional philosophic disputes rests on the positivists' appeal to the *criterion* for determining the *meaningfulness* of any candidate for the cognitive use of language, that is, its capacity to be either true or false. The criterion of meaningfulness is the Principle of Verification (or Verifiability). The positivists used this criterion as a way of determining not whether a particular use of language *is* true, or whether on the contrary it *is* false. The criterion was not to be used as a method for determining the actual truth or falsity of a statement. It was to be used for determining the necessary condition for inquiring into truth, namely that it have *meaning*. A use of language must have meaning of appropriate type before it can be said to be true. The Principle of Verification was intended to serve as such a criterion of meaningfulness. Positivists did not undertake to determine which among several conflicting views (if any) is true, in some factual inquiry. They sought rather to settle the prior question—a philosophical or logical question—of whether the inquiry and the language in which it is couched is meaningful. If one adopts the positivists' answer by using the Principle of Verification as a criterion of meaningfulness, there will result far more radical criticisms of many traditional philosophic disputes than have been made by others, for these disputes will have been condemned as meaningless and so as entirely futile.

What, then, is this powerful weapon for judging the cognitive meaningfulness of a knowledge-promising, factual inquiry? What is this Principle of Verification that will serve in the role of passing judgment on this vital matter? Here is Schlick's answer to this question:

It is the peculiar business of philosophy to ascertain and make clear the *meaning* of statements and questions. The chaotic state in which philosophy has found itself during the greater part of its history is due to the unfortunate fact that, in the *first* place, it took certain formulations to be real questions before carefully ascertaining whether they really made any sense, and, in the *second* place, it believed that the answers to the questions could be found by the aid of special philosophical methods, different from those of the special sciences. . . .

When, in general, are we sure that the meaning of a question is clear to us? Evidently when and only when we are able to state exactly the conditions under which it is to be answered in the affirmative, or, as the case may be, the conditions under which it is to be answered in the negative. By stating these conditions, and by this alone, is the meaning of a question defined.

It is the first step of any philosophizing, and the foundation of all reflection, to see that it is simply impossible to give the meaning of any statement except by describing the fact which must exist if the statement is to be true. If it does not exist then the statement is false. The meaning of a proposition consists, obviously, in this alone, that it expresses a definite state of affairs. And this state of affairs must be pointed out in order to give the meaning of the proposition. One can, of course, say that the proposition itself already gives this state of affairs. This is true, but the proposition indicates the state of affairs only to the person who understands it. But when do I understand a proposition? When I understand the meanings of the words which occur in it? These can be explained by definitions. But in the definitions new words appear whose meanings cannot again be described in propositions, they must be indicated directly: the meaning of a word must in the end be *shown,* it must be *given.* This is done by an act of indication, of pointing; and what is pointed at must be given, otherwise I cannot be referred to it.

Accordingly, in order to find the meaning of a proposition, we must transform it by successive definitions until finally only such words occur in it as can no longer be defined, but whose meanings can only be directly pointed out. The criterion of the truth or falsity of the proposition then lies in the fact that under definite conditions (given in the definition) certain data are present, or not present. If this is determined then everything asserted by the proposition is determined, and I know its meaning. If I am *unable,* in principle, to verify a proposition, that is, if I am absolutely ignorant of how to proceed, of what I must do in order to ascertain its truth or falsity, then obviously I do not know what the proposition actually states, and I should then be unable to interpret the proposition by passing from the words, with the aid of the definitions, to possible experiences. For in so far as I am able to do this I am also able in the same way to state at least in principle the method of verification (even though, often, because of practical difficulties I am unable to carry it out). The statement of the conditions under which a proposition is true is *the same* as the statement of its meaning, and not something different.

And these *"conditions"* . . . must finally be discoverable in the given. Different conditions mean differences in the given. The *meaning* of every proposition is finally to be determined by the given, and by nothing else.[36]

One way of summing up Schlick's main point in the above is to use the formula (or slogan) that "the meaning of a statement is the method of its verification." Unless one can specify, in advance of actually setting out to perform acts of verification, what conditions would have to be met in observational, sensory experience in order for the statement to be judged true, and correspondingly those conditions in experience whose absence would be a basis for judging the statement to be false, the 'statement' is a pseudostatement; it is unverifiable and so meaningless.

Furthermore, what the Principle of Verification requires is *verifiability in principle;* it requires that one be able to say what specifically *would be* observed, even though at a given time the technical resources may be lacking to carry out the actual verifications. In the following quotation from a paper written in 1932, long before the development of technology to land on the moon and to take photographs of the other side of it, Schlick uses an example that is outdated but nevertheless clarifies his general point.

It is obvious that verifiability is used here in the sense of "verifiable in principle," for the meaning of a proposition is, of course, independent of whether the conditions under which we find ourselves at a specified time allow or prevent the actual verification. There is not the least doubt that the proposition "there is a mountain of height of 3000 meters on the other side of the moon" makes good sense, even though we lack the technical means of verifying it. And it would remain just as meaningful if one knew with certainty, on scientific grounds, that no man would ever reach the other side of the moon. The verification remains *conceivable;* we are always able to state what data we should have to experience in order to decide the truth or falsity of the proposition; the verification is *logically* possible, whatever be the case regarding its practical feasibility, and this alone concerns us.

But if someone should say: within every electron there is a nucleus which, though always present, never has in any way any external effects, so that its existence never manifests itself in nature—this would be a meaningless assertion. For we should have to ask the maker of the hypothesis: what do you really *mean* by the presence of that "nucleus"?; and he could answer only: I mean that something exists there in the electron. We should inquire further: what does that mean? What would be the case if it didn't exist? And he would have to answer: everything would remain exactly the same as before. For according to his assertion, the "somewhat" in the electron has no effects, and there would simply be no observable change: the realm of the given would not be affected in any way. We should judge that he had not succeeded in communicating the meaning of his hypothesis, and that therefore it made no sense. In this case the impossibility of verification is not factual, but *logical,* for by reason of the utter ineffectiveness of that nucleus a decision regarding it based on differences in the given is *in principle* excluded.

. . . .

For science, then, our standpoint does not represent something foreign and out of the ordinary, but it has in a certain sense always been more or less taken for granted. It could not be otherwise, because only from this standpoint is a proposition verifiable at all; and since all the activities of science consist in examining the truth of propositions, it continuously acknowledges the correctness of our insight by its practice.[37]

By way of further clarification of what the Principle of Verification stresses, it is helpful to point out, as Carnap does in the following passage, that while some statements are directly verifiable in immediate, present experience, others are indirectly verifiable by making predictions to future experience. Further, verifiable statements may be either singular, insofar as they have to do with some particular or individual situation or object, or universal or general, insofar as they formulate a uniformity or regularity among natural events.

What, then, is the method of verification of a statement? Here we have to distinguish between two kinds of verification: direct and indirect. If the question is about a statement which asserts something about a present perception, e.g. "Now I see a red square on a blue ground," then the statement can be tested directly by my present perception. If at present I do see a red square on a blue ground, the statement is directly verified by this seeing; if I do not see that, it is disproved. To be sure, there are still some serious problems in connection with direct verification. We will however not touch on them here, but give our attention to the question of indirect verification, which is more important for our purposes. A statement P which is not directly verifiable can only be verified by direct verification of statements deduced from P together with other already verified statements.

Let us take the statement P_1: "This key is made of iron." There are many ways of verifying this statement: e.g.: I place the key near a magnet; then I perceive that the key is attracted. Here the deduction is made in this way:

Premises:

P_1: "This key is made of iron"; the statement to be examined.

P_2: "If an iron thing is placed near a magnet, it is attracted"; this is a physical law, already verified.

P_3: "This object—a bar—is a magnet"; statement already verified.

P_4: "The key is placed near the bar"; this is now directly verified by our observation.

From these four premises we can deduce the conclusion:

P_5: "The key will now be attracted by the bar."

This statement is a prediction which can be examined by observation. If we look, we either observe the attraction or we do not. In the first case we have found a positive instance, an instance of verification of the statement P_1 under consideration; in the second case we have a negative instance, an instance of disproof of P_1.

In the first case the examination of the statement P_1 is not finished. We may repeat the examination by means of a magnet, i.e. we may deduce other statements similar to P_5 by the help of the same or similar premises as before. After that, or instead of that, we may make an examination by electrical tests, or by mechanical, chemical, or optical tests, etc. If in these further investigations all instances turn out to be positive, the certainty of the statement P_1 gradually grows. We may soon come to a degree of certainty sufficient for all practical purposes, but *absolute* certainty we can never attain. The number of instances deducible from P_1 by the help of other statements already verified or directly verifiable is infinite. Therefore there is always a possibility of finding in the future a negative instance, however small its probability may be. Thus the statement P_1 *can never be completely verified.* For this reason it is called an hypothesis.

So far we have considered a similar statement concerning one single thing. If we take a universal statement concerning all things or events at whatever time and place, a so-called natural *law*, it is still clearer that the number of examinable instances is infinite and so the statement is an hypothesis.

Every assertion P in the wide field of science has this character, that it either asserts something about present perceptions or other experiences, and therefore is verifiable by them, or that statements about future perceptions are deducible from P together with some other statements already verified. If a scientist should venture to make an assertion from which no perceptual statements could be deduced, what should we say to that? Suppose, e.g., he asserts that there is not only a gravitational field having an effect on bodies according to the known laws of gravitation, but also a levitational field, and on being asked what sort of effect this levitational field has, according to his theory, he answers that there is no observable effect; in other words, he confesses his inability to give rules according to which we could deduce perceptual statements from his assertion. In that case our reply is: your assertion is no assertion at all; it does not speak about any thing; it is nothing but a series of empty words; it is simply without sense.

It is true that he may have images and even feelings connected with his words. This fact may be of psychological importance; logically, it is irrelevant. What gives theoretical meaning to a statement is not the attendant images and thoughts, but the possibility of deducing from it perceptual statements, in other words, the possibility of verification. To give sense to a statement the presence of images is not sufficient; it is not even necessary. We have no actual image of the electromagnetic field, nor even, I should say, of the gravitational field. Nevertheless the statements which physicists assert about these fields have a perfect sense, because perceptual statements are deducible from them. I by no means object to the statement just mentioned about a levitational field that we do not know how to imagine or conceive such a field. My only objection to that statement is that we are not told how to verify it.[38]

Antimetaphysics

The intended result of formulating the Principle of Verification is that it could accomplish a demarcation between meaningful and meaningless uses of language. When used in this way, the Principle of Verification was specifically applied by the positivists to achieve the elimination of metaphysics on the ground that when construed as an inquiry into what transcends experience, the results of such an inquiry are meaningless because devoid, even in principle, of the possibility of verification or falsification. In this sense metaphysics is a vacuous discipline, its problems spurious, its proposed solutions of no possible truth or falsity, hence cognitively worthless. Let us consider two examples of this attack on metaphysics. The first is Schlick's analysis of the spuriousness of metaphysical (and epistemological) disputes about the 'reality of the external world'. The second is drawn from Carnap's attack on Heidegger's appeal to the use of the term 'Nothing' in the latter's treatment of ontology as a theory of Being.

In the ordinary language of common sense, we use the phrase 'external world' to designate the public world of things and events as distinguished from the 'inner, private world'. As used in this way, Schlick maintains the concept of the external world is not metaphysical. Rather, its meaning is in perfect agreement with the requirements of the Principle of Verification.

In opposition to the "inner world," which includes memories, thoughts, dreams, desires, feelings, the external world is simply the world of mountains and trees, of animals and men. Every child knows what is meant when we assert the existence of definite objects of this world; and we must insist that it really means absolutely nothing *more* than what the child knows. We all know how to verify the statement, say, that "there is a castle in the park outside the city." We act in certain ways and then if certain clearly describable facts are experienced we say: "Yes, there really is a castle there," otherwise we say the statement was wrong, or a lie. And if someone asks us: "Was the castle also there at night, when no one saw it?" We answer: "Undoubtedly! For it would have been impossible to build it since this morning; furthermore the condition of the building shows that not only was it there yesterday, but for hundreds of years, hence before we were born." Thus we possess quite definite empirical criteria with which to determine whether houses and trees existed when we did not see them, and whether they already existed before our birth, and whether they will exist after our death. This means that the statement that those things "exist independently of us" has a clear verifiable meaning, and is obviously to be affirmed. We can very well distinguish empirically things of this sort from those that are only "subjective" and "dependent upon us." If, for instance, because of some visual defect I see a dark spot when I look at the adjacent wall I say that the spot is there only when I look at it, but I say that the wall is there even when I do not look at it. The verification of this distinction is indeed quite easy, and both these statements say just what is contained in the verifications, and nothing else.

Hence if the phrase external world is taken with the signification it has in everyday life then the question regarding its existence is simply the question: are there in addition to memories, desires and ideas also stars, clouds, plants, animals, and my own body? We have just seen that it would be simply absurd to answer this question in the negative. There are, quite evidently, houses, clouds, and animals existing independently of us, and I said above that any thinker who denied the existence of the external world in this sense would have no claim on our respect. Instead of telling us what we mean when we speak of mountains and plants he would convince us that there aren't any such things at all![39]

According to Schlick, the same nonmetaphysical use of the concept of 'the external world' is to be found in science, where instead of dealing with ordinary objects, as in common sense, the scientist deals with entities of a more technical, rarefied sort. Yet for science, as for common sense, the objectivity of its entities, their belonging to the external world of Nature, is not anything requiring the notion of a transcendent reality.

But science! Does it, in opposition to common sense, mean something other than things like houses and trees when it speaks of the external world? It seems to me that nothing of the sort is the case. For atoms and electric fields, or whatever the physicist may speak of, are just what constitute houses and trees according to their theory; and therefore the one must be real in the same sense as the other. The objectivity of mountains and clouds is exactly the same as that of protons and energies—these latter stand in no greater opposition to "subjectivity," say to feelings and hallucinations, than do the former. In fact we are at last convinced that the existence of even the most subtle "invisible things," assumed by the scientist, is, in principle, verified exactly as is the reality of a tree or a star.[40]

Now, however, in contrast with these legitimate (because meaningful) uses in common sense and science of the concept of the external world, we must see how this same phrase is used by various metaphysicians and metaphysical epistemologists.

How is the transcendent or metaphysical external world distinguished from the empirical world? In philosophical systems it is thought of as somehow standing behind the empirical world, where the word "behind" indicates that it cannot be *known* in the same sense as can the empirical world, that it lies beyond a boundary which separates the accessible from the inaccessible.

This distinction has its original source in the view, formerly held by most philosophers, that in order to know an object it is necessary to perceive it directly; knowledge is a sort of intuition, and is perfect only when the object is directly present to the knower as a sensation or feeling. Hence according to this view what cannot be immediately experienced or perceived remains unknowable, incomprehensible, transcendent; it belongs to the realm of things in themselves.[41]

In opposition to this conception of a transcendent and unknowable external world, the positivist maintains that the very conception of such a 'world' is meaningless because unverifiable.

We must say: you designate here by existence or reality something which simply cannot in any way be given or explained. Yet despite this you believe that those words make sense. We shall not quarrel with you over this point. But this much is certain: according to the admission just made this sense can in no way become evident, it cannot be expressed in any written or spoken communication, nor by any gesture or conduct. For if this were possible we should have before us a verifiable empirical fact, and the world would be *different* if the proposition "there is an external world" were true, from what it would be if it were false. This difference would then constitute the meaning of the phrase "real external world," hence it would be an empirical meaning; that is, this real external world would again be only the empirical world, which, like all human beings, we also acknowledge. Even to speak of any other world is logically impossible. There can be no discussion concerning it, for a non-verifiable existence cannot enter meaningfully into any possible proposition. Whoever still believes—or believes himself to believe—in it must do so only silently. Arguments can relate only to what can be said.

. . . .

The denial of the existence of a transcendent external world would be just as much a metaphysical statement as its affirmation. Hence the consistent empiricist does not deny the transcendent world, but shows that both its denial and affirmation are meaningless.

This last distinction is of the greatest importance. I am convinced that the chief opposition to our view derives from the fact that the distinction between the falsity and the meaninglessness of a proposition is not observed. The proposition "Discourse concerning a metaphysical external world is meaningless" does *not* say: "There is no external world," but something altogether different. The empiricist does not say to the metaphysician "what you say is false," but, "what you say asserts nothing at all!" He does not contradict him, but says "I don't understand you."[42]

Among the various examples Carnap offers of the metaphysician's use of cognitively meaningless language, his selection of Heidegger's comments on the concept of Nothing is of interest because it is typical of the way a positivist, performing 'logical analysis', claims to show the cognitive emptiness of the metaphysician's 'statements'. In this case, Carnap argues Heidegger's comments on 'Nothing' display a flagrant violation of the most elementary rules of logical syntax. Here is the passage from Heidegger's essay "What is Metaphysics?" which Carnap quotes:

"What is to be investigated is being only and—*nothing* else; being alone and further—nothing; solely being, and beyond being—*nothing. What about this Nothing? . . . Does the Nothing exist only because the Not, i.e. the Negation, exists?* Or is it the other way around? . . . We assert: *the Nothing is prior to the Not and the Negation. . . .* Where do we seek the Nothing? How do we find the Nothing. . . . We know the Nothing. . . . *Anxiety reveals the Nothing. . . .* That for which and because of which we were anxious, was 'really'—nothing. Indeed: the Nothing itself—as such—was present. . . . *What about this Nothing?—The Nothing itself nothings.*"[43]

Carnap claims that these sentences of Heidegger are pseudostatements, devoid of meaning:

In order to show that the possibility of forming pseudo-statements is based on a logical defect of language, we set up the schema below. The sentences under I are grammatically as well as logically impeccable, hence meaningful. The sentences under II (excepting B3) are in grammatical respects perfectly analogous to those under I. Sentence form IIA (as question and answer) does not, indeed, satisfy the requirements to be imposed on a logically correct language. But it is nevertheless meaningful, because it is translatable into correct language. This is shown by sentence IIIA, which has the same meaning as IIA. Sentence form IIA then proves to be undesirable because we can be led from it, by means of grammatically faultless operations, to the meaningless sentence forms IIB, which are taken from the above quotation. These forms cannot even be constructed in the correct language of Column III. Nonetheless, their nonsensicality is not obvious at first glance, because one is easily deceived by the analogy with the meaningful sentences IB. The fault of our language identified here lies, therefore, in the circumstance that, in contrast to a logically correct language, it admits of the same grammatical form for meaningful and meaningless word sequences. To each sentence in words we have added a corresponding formula in the notation of symbolic logic; these formulae facilitate recognition of the undesirable analogy between IA and IIA and therewith of the origin of the meaningless constructions IIB.

I.	II.	III.
	Transition from	
Meaningful	*Sense to*	
Sentences of	*Nonsense in*	*Logically*
Ordinary	*Ordinary*	*Correct*
Language	*Language*	*Language*
A. What is Outside? Ou(?) Rain is outside Ou(r)	A. What is outside? Ou(?) Nothing is outside Ou(no)	A. There is nothing (does not exist anything) which is outside. $\sim (\exists x) \cdot Ou(x)$
B. What about this rain? (i.e. what does the rain do? or: what else can be said about this rain? ?(r)	B. "What about this Nothing?" ?(no)	B. None of these forms can even be constructed.
1. We know the rain K(r)	1. "We seek the Nothing" "We find the Nothing" "We know the Nothing" K(no)	
2. The rain rains R(r)	2. "The Nothing nothings" No(no)	
	3. "The Nothing exists only because . . . " Ex(no)	

On closer inspection of the pseudo-statements under IIB, we also find some differences. The construction of sentence (1) is simply based on the mistake of employing the word "nothing" as a noun, because it is customary in ordinary language to use it in this form in order to construct a negative existential statement (see IIA). In a correct language, on the other hand, it is not a particular *name*, but a certain *logical form* of the sentence that serves this purpose (see IIIA). Sentence IIB2 adds something new, viz, the fabrication of the meaningless word "to nothing." This sentence, therefore, is senseless for a twofold reason. We pointed out before that the meaningless words of metaphysics usually owe their origin to the fact that a meaningful word is deprived of its meaning through its metaphorical use in metaphysics. But here we confront one of those rare cases where a new word is introduced which never had a meaning to begin with. Likewise sentence IIB3 must be rejected for two reasons. In respect of the error of using the word "nothing" as a noun, it is like the previous sentences. But in addition it involves a contradiction. For even if it were admissible to introduce "nothing" as a name or description of an entity, still the existence of this entity would be denied in its very definition, whereas sentence (3) goes on to affirm its existence. This sentence, therefore, would be contradictory, hence absurd, even if it were not already meaningless.

In view of the gross logical errors which we find in sentences IIB, we might be led to conjecture that perhaps the word "nothing" has in Heidegger's treatise a meaning entirely different from the customary one. And this presumption is further strengthened as we go on to read there that anxiety reveals the Nothing, that the Nothing itself is present as such in anxiety. For here the word "nothing" seems to refer to a certain emotional constitution, possibly of a religious sort, or something or other that underlies such emotions. If such were the case, then the mentioned logical errors in sentences IIB would not be committed. But the first sentence of the quotation at the beginning of this section proves that this interpretation is not possible. The combination of "only" and "nothing else" shows unmistakenly that the word "nothing" here has the usual meaning of a logical particle that serves for the formulation of a negative existential statement. This introduction of the word "nothing" is then immediately followed by the leading question of the treatise: "What about this Nothing?"

But our doubts as to a possible misinterpretation get completely dissolved as we note the author of the treatise is clearly aware of the conflict between his questions and statements, and logic. *"Question and answer* in regard to the Nothing are equally *absurd* in themselves. . . . The fundamental rule of thinking commonly appealed to, the law of prohibited contradiction, general *'logic',* destroys this question." All the worse for logic! We must abolish its sovereignty: "If thus the power of the *understanding* in the field of questions concerning Nothing and Being is broken, then the fate of the sovereignty of 'logic' within philosophy is thereby decided as well. The very idea of 'logic' dissolves in the whirl of a more basic questioning." But will sober science condone the whirl of counter-logical questioning? To this question too there is a ready answer: "The alleged sobriety and superiority of science becomes ridiculous if it does not take the Nothing seriously." Thus we find here a good confirmation of our thesis; a metaphysician himself here states that his questions and answers are irreconcilable with logic and the scientific way of thinking.[44]

The status of ethics

The principal concern of positivist philosophers, as we have seen all along, is in determining the conditions for the meaningful use of language that need to be satisfied as part of the use of such language in serving the quest for knowledge. According to many traditionally oriented philosophers, philosophy itself, and not just science, is devoted to this quest for knowledge. In the case of philosophy, the knowledge sought for, they would say, is to be found in its three principal divisions—logic, metaphysics, and ethics. Positivists recognize basically only two types of cognitively meaningful statements: those which, as in formal logic and mathematics, are analytic and therefore at bottom tautologous; and those which, as in empirical science, are factual and open to verification or falsification by sense experience. With these criteria in mind, positivists recognize the contribution formal logic (especially in its modern post-Fregean developments) has made to the knowledge of 'formal truth'. On the other hand, they reject metaphysical claims to knowledge as spurious and vacuous.

Ethics, as a branch of philosophy, seeks for a special kind of knowledge of how men ought to act and what goals in life they ought to prize and pursue. Such knowledge, when had, would guide them in personal and social actions and justify their approval and disapproval of what they or others do. From its very beginnings ethics has been conceived as a quest for the knowledge of certain *norms*. These norms, variously interpreted as rules, standards, principles, moral laws, or values, would guide people in their private conduct and social behavior. There are, of course, many different ethical philosophies. They are distinguished one from the other by their divergent answers not only with respect to what the norms are but also by the way they would specify the method of *knowing* what the norms should be. Some appeal to intuition (moral sense), others to reason, still others to divine authority, and so on. Norms, when and however known, justify particular choices and sanction approval or disapproval of particular acts of a personal or social character. According to some ethical philosophies, norms may be structured in a systematic way, so that justification for certain norms may be given by showing them to be particular applications of more general or more fundamental norms. In any case, the knowledge of these norms, at one level or another, defines the sphere of normative ethics as a sphere of philosophic knowledge.

If positivists on the whole 'accept' logic and 'eliminate' metaphysics, how do they regard this general cognitive orientation of ethics as traditionally conceived? Can the norms of ethics, conveyed in ethical statements, be accommodated as *meaningful* by positivists? Are they, that is, analytic or are they empirically verifiable? And if neither, are they not therefore literally or cognitively meaningless?

In expounding the positivist response, our account has to be a qualified one, for there is no uniform, minimally standard answer. For some, ethics is interpreted as a 'factual' discipline, and so cognitively meaningful; for others, it is at best a domain in which one finds only an 'emotive' use of language, and so cognitively meaningless. Among the major representatives of the movement in its 'classic' phases, Schlick is the foremost exponent of the first of these views, Carnap of the second.

According to Schlick, ethical statements can be accommodated within the broad schema of meaningful statements. They are not analytic (or tautologous) as are the rules of logic. But they are not to be rejected as spuriously factual as are the statements of metaphysics, for, as Schlick interprets them, the statements of ethics are factual. One should not look for some 'absolute' *justification* of the norms of ethics. Instead, ethics can be regarded as an empirical science. What it has to say can be verified, for its norms are to be *explained*, not justified. The phenomena of ethical choice can be explained. This is done in the science of psychology, where one can give causal explanations of the ethical choices human beings make and the norms they adopt for making explicit the basis for their choices. Ethics thus becomes a branch of the empirical science of psychology.

In modern philosophy since Kant, the idea repeatedly appears that ethics as a normative science is something completely different from the "factual sciences." It does not ask, "When is a person judged to be good?" or, "Why is he judged to be good?" These questions concern mere facts and their explanation. But it does ask, "With *what right* is that person judged to be good?" It does not trouble itself with what is actually valued, but asks: "What is valuable? What should be valued?" And here obviously the question is quite different.

But *this* manner of opposing normative and factual sciences is fundamentally false. For if ethics furnishes a justification it does so only . . . in a relative-hypothetical way, not absolutely. It "justifies" a certain judgment only to the extent that it shows that the judgment corresponds to a certain norm; that this norm itself is "right," or justified, it can neither show nor, by itself, determine. Ethics must simply recognize this as a fact of human nature. Even as a normative science, a science can do no more than *explain*; it can never set up or establish a norm (which alone would be equivalent to an absolute justification). It is never able to do more than to discover the rules of the judgment, to read them from the facts before it; the origin of norms always lies outside and before science and knowledge. This means that their origin can only be apprehended by the science, and does not lie within it. In other words: if, or in so far as, the philosopher answers the question "What is good?" by an exhibition of norms, this means only that he tells us what "good" *actually* means; he can never tell us what good *must* or *should* mean. The question regarding the validity of a valuation amounts to asking for a higher acknowledged norm under which the value falls, and this is a question of *fact*. The question of the justification of the highest norms or the ultimate values is senseless, because there is nothing higher to which these could be referred. Since modern ethics, as we remarked, often speaks of this absolute justification as *the* fundamental problem of ethics, it must be said, unfortunately, that the formulation of the quesion from which it proceeds is simply meaningless.

. . . .

That man actually approves of certain actions, declares certain dispositions to be "good," appears not at all self-explanatory to the philosopher, but often very astonishing, and he therefore asks his "Why?" Now, in all of the natural sciences every explanation can be conceived as a *causal* explanation, a truth which we need not prove here; therefore the "why" has the sense of a question concerning the *cause* of that psychical process in which man makes a valuation, establishes a moral claim. (We must make clear that when we speak of the discovery of the "cause," we mean by the term "cause" only a popular abbreviation for the statement of the complete laws governing the event to be known.)

In other words, the *determination* of the contents of the concepts of good and evil is made by the use of moral principles and a system of norms, and affords a relative justification of the lower moral rules by the higher; scientific *knowledge* of the good, on the other hand, does not concern norms, but refers to the cause, concerns not the justification but the explanation of moral judgments. The theory of norms asks, "*What* does actually serve as the standard of conduct?" Explanatory ethics, however, asks "*Why* does it serve as a standard of conduct?"

. . . .

The problem which we must put at the center of ethics is a purely psychological one. For, without doubt, the discovery of the motives or laws of any kind of behavior, and therefore of moral behavior, is a purely psychological affair. Only the empirical science of the laws which describe the life of the soul can solve this problem. One might wish to derive from this a supposedly profound and destructive objection to our formulation of the problem. For, one might say, "In such case there would be no ethics at all; what is called ethics would be nothing but a part of psychology!" I answer, "Why shouldn't ethics be a part of psychology?" Perhaps in order that the philosopher have his science for himself and govern autonomously in this sphere? He would, indeed, thereby be freed of many burdensome protests of psychology. If he laid down a command, "*Thus* shall man act," he would not have to pay attention to the psychologist who said to him, "But man *cannot* act so, because it contradicts psychological laws!" I fear greatly that here and there this motive, though hidden, is at work. However, if one says candidly that "there is no ethics," because it is not necessary to label a part of psychology by a special name, then the question is merely terminological.

It is a poor recommendation of the philosophical spirit of our age that we so often attempt to draw strict lines of division between the sciences, to separate ever new disciplines, and to prove their autonomy. The true philosopher goes in the opposite direction; he does not wish to make the single sciences self-sufficient and independent, but, on the contrary, to unify and bring them together; he wishes to show that what is common to them is what is most essential, and that what is different is accidental and to be viewed as belonging to practical methodology. *Sub specie aeternitatis* there is for him only *one* reality and *one* science.

Therefore, if we decide that the fundamental question of ethics, "Why does man act morally?" can be answered only by psychology, we see in this no degradation of, nor injury to, science, but a happy simplification of the world-picture. In ethics we do not seek independence, but only the truth.[45]

A diametrically opposite view to that of Schlick, on the subject of ethics, is taken by Carnap. For him, there is no attempt to 'salvage' ethics as a cognitively meaningful inquiry by assimilating it to psychology as part of an empirical, factual discipline. Carnap insists on maintaining the traditional distinction between the use of language to say what one *ought* to do (i.e., by means of *prescription*) and what *is* the case (i.e., by means of *description*). For Carnap, since ethical statements are not either analytic or descriptive (hence factually not either true or false), they are cognitively meaningless. Ethical statements exhibit and contain an *emotive* use of language; they *express* certain attitudes of approval or disapproval. In addition to expressing feelings of approval or disapproval on the part of one who accepts or utters such statements, ethical judgments can also be interpreted as the use of language to *influence* the attitudes and behavior of other individuals. Those who use such ethical statements invite, command, or prescribe compliance and acceptance by others. In either case, as emotive or prescriptive, language is not being used to *describe* some factual state of affairs. Such statements cannot, therefore, be taken as verifiable. They are not capable, even in principle, of being either true or false. Hence they are cognitively meaningless.

"Ethics" is used in two different senses. Sometimes a certain empirical investigation is called "Ethics," viz. psychological and sociological investigations about the actions of human beings, especially regarding the origin of these actions from feelings and volitions and their effects upon other people. Ethics in this sense is an empirical, scientific investigation; it belongs to empirical science rather than to philosophy. Fundamentally different from this is ethics in the second sense, as the philosophy of moral values or moral norms, which one can designate normative ethics. This is not an investigation of facts, but a pretended investigation of what is good and what is evil, what it is right to do and what it is wrong to do. Thus the purpose of this philosophical, or normative, ethics is to state norms for human action or judgments about moral values.

It is easy to see that it is merely a difference of formulation, whether we state a norm or a value judgment. A norm or rule has an imperative form, for instance: "Do not kill!" The corresponding value judgment would be: "Killing is evil." This difference of formulation has become practically very important, especially for the development of philosophical thinking. The rule, "Do not kill," has grammatically the imperative form and will therefore not be regarded as an assertion. But the value statement, "Killing is evil," although, like the rule it is merely an expression of a certain wish, has the grammatical form of a declarative sentence. Most philosophers have been deceived by this form into thinking that a value statement is really an assertive statement, and must be either true or false. Therefore they give reasons for their own value statements and try to disprove those of their opponents. But actually a value statement is nothing but a command in a misleading grammatical form. It may have effects upon the actions of men, and these effects may either be in accordance with our wishes or not; but it is neither true nor false. It does not assert anything and can neither be proved nor disproved.

This is revealed as soon as we apply to such statements our method of logical analysis. From the statement "Killing is evil" we cannot deduce any statement about future experiences. Thus this statement is not verifiable and has no theoretical sense, and the same thing is true of all other value statements.

Perhaps somebody will contend in opposition that the following statement is deducible: "If a person kills anybody he will have feelings of remorse." But this statement is in no way deducible from the statement "Killing is evil." It is deducible only from psychological statements about the character and the emotional reactions of the person. These statements are indeed verifiable and not without sense. They belong to psychology, not to philosophy; to psychological ethics (if one wishes to use this word), not to philosophical or normative ethics. The statements of normative ethics, whether they have the form of rules or the form of value statements, have no theoretical sense, are not scientific statements (taking the word scientific to mean any assertive statement).

To avoid misunderstanding it must be said that we do not at all deny the possibility of importance of a scientific investigation of value statements as well as of acts of valuation. Both of these are acts of individuals and are, like all other kinds of acts, possible objects of empirical investigation. Historians, psychologists, and sociologists may give analyses and causal explanations of them, and such historical and psychological statements about acts of valuation and about value statements are indeed meaningful scientific statements which belong to ethics in the first sense of this word. But the value statements themselves are here only objects of investigation; they are not statements in these theories, and have, here as elsewhere, no theoretical sense. Therefore we assign them to the realm of metaphysics.[46]

PROBLEMS ABOUT 'VERIFIABILITY'

The Principle of Verification was intended by logical positivists to serve as a device of demarcation. It would serve, negatively, as the basis for rejecting meaningless uses of language and spurious claims to knowledge; it would also serve, positively, as a way of characterizing, in a fundamental way, the legitimate claims of science to provide examples of the meaningful uses of language for cognitive purposes. However, if the Principle of Verification was to do the jobs it was intended to do, it had to be itself both clear and adequate. Much depends on its own soundness and defensibility. Does it have these requisite features that allow it to carry the burden it does? Does it justify the confidence placed in it as a tool for achieving both the elimination of unwanted schemes of thought, and the illumination it would give to our understanding of the method of science? Positivists, in confronting these questions, came to realize that though they did not wish to surrender the goals for which the Principle of Verification had been fashioned, it was a matter of no small difficulty to give satisfactory answers to these questions. A good deal of the later history of positivism consisted in the efforts spent on refining and sharpening—and sometimes fundamentally changing—the formulation of the Principle of Verification. These efforts, and the modifications they brought about, were not simply or primarily occasioned by the criticisms of those hostile to the entire program of positivism, but, more importantly, by the self-questioning doubts and difficulties raised by persons internal to the movement itself.

If we start by saying in a general way that a putative meaningful statement must be capable of verification by appeal to what is found in sensory experience, such a 'criterion' hardly begins to do justice to the way in which we should need to understand, in some precise way, the actual relations between sensory, observational data and the statements of some advanced empirical science, for example physics. What are these relations? What are the logical connections between reports of observations and the highly abstract, mathematical formulae of the theories of physics? How does the appeal to sensory data serve to verify or falsify these theoretical statements? Quite apart from any negative use in eliminating metaphysics, it is essential to look into this question in order to be able to appeal with confidence and clarity to science itself as resting, allegedly, on the Principle of Verifiability. Care is needed in responding to this question, for it may turn out that an inadequate formulation of the Principle of Verification would not only eliminate metaphysics—it might even eliminate a good deal of science itself! This is one question, then, among several, with which many positivists concerned themselves.

Among other problems connected with giving an acceptable formulation to the Principle of Verification, the following were particularly troublesome and controversial:

1. An essential feature of the reliance on the Principle of Verification is the appeal to observational or sensory experience as providing the verifications for a meaningful statement and the basis on which the truth or falsity of the statement as a whole rests. Such empirical data are the logical foundations for a single statement or whole network or superstructure of statements. Let us call these empirical bases, these appeals to experience, the *'verifiers'* of a meaningful statement; and let us call the statements that report such experiences *'basic statements'*. (Some positivists preferred to speak of 'protocol statements', others of 'observation statements'.) One whole set of problems has to do with giving a satisfactory account of these verifiers themselves. Are they private or of a public sort? Are they established with certainty or are they themselves corrigible?

2. A basic claim of positivism is that all meaningful statements can

be divided into two groups: those that are analytic (tautologous) and those that are empirically verifiable. Consider now the statement of the Principle of Verification itself. How shall we characterize its logical status? Is it analytic and so tautologous? Or, if empirical, is its truth or falsity therefore a contingent matter? Either alternative seems unwelcome. In that case, isn't the Principle of Verification to be condemned, on positivist principles, as meaningless? This too seems absurd. How then interpret the logical status of the Principle of Verification?

Strong and weak Verifications

In the *Tractatus*, it will be recalled, Wittgenstein had argued for the need to recognize certain elementary propositions that, if true, would picture elementary states of affairs (atomic facts). Wittgenstein thought of these elementary propositions as made up of names, where each name designates an object, and where the logical concatenation of names in an elementary proposition would describe a logically possible state of affairs, a possible configuration of objects. Wittgenstein did not give any examples of such elementary propositions; neither did he give any examples of the names that constitute them nor of the objects they designate. He conceived his task as a logician and ontologist to be simply that of giving reasons for construing a cognitively adequate language as having its truth-functional base in such elementary propositions, and adequate ontology as requiring basic facts each of which is constituted of a configuration of simple objects.

When the positivists studied the *Tractatus* in the early and mid-twenties (i.e., before some of Wittgenstein's later thought on the nature of hypotheses, as developed in the early thirties, was being transmitted to the Vienna Circle), they found in it, and readily accepted its use of, a Fregean-inspired logic. In addition to their acceptance of a truth-functional logic as found in the *Tractatus*, the positivists brought to their initial interpretation of this work their own special empiricist orientation. To Frege they joined their admiration for the Humean tradition of British empiricism and certain aspects of empiricism as represented in the work of Ernst Mach and other positivists. This empiricist orientation and emphasis was largely absent from Wittgenstein's thought as expressed in the *Tractatus*. When some of the logical positivists, in relying exclusively on the *Tractatus*, gave an empiricist interpretation to Wittgenstein's logical atomism, they imported something that was not originally there. In this sense it was a fundamental error on their part to read the *Tractatus* as a positivist tract. Nevertheless some of them at first did so read it, and used it too to bolster their own hostility to metaphysics—a hostility they believed Wittgenstein shared. (And of course, in all this they rejected and ignored the 'mystical' side of the *Tractatus*, on which Wittgenstein placed such great store but which the positivists assimilated to 'metaphysics' as meaningless.)

However, the indebtedness of the members of the Vienna Circle to Wittgenstein's thought was not confined to their reading of the *Tractatus*. Beginning with Wittgenstein's return to Vienna in 1926, and starting with Schlick's first meeting with him in 1927, some of his newer philosophy was beginning to filter through to the Circle. This came about through Wittgenstein's conversations beginning in late 1929 and lasting up to 1932 with Schlick, Waismann, and a few others. (Carnap at first attended some of these conversations.)* Through these conversations the members of the Circle had access to Wittgenstein's new thoughts about the distinction between 'hypotheses' and 'propositions', and about the way he formulated his own adherence to a form of 'verificationism'. Included in these new ideas were Wittgenstein's view that propositions are directly verified with certainty, as contrasted with hypotheses that can only be established or confirmed with some degree of likelihood. It was these very fresh ideas of Wittgenstein that were taken up by some positivists, notably Schlick and Waismann, who incorporated them as part of their version of a logical positivist (scientific empiricist) point of view. The Principle of Verification, so understood, thus became interpreted in terms of these later ideas of Wittgenstein and did not have to rest on an empiricist reading of the *Tractatus*. In Wittgenstein's newer thought, positivists found a more convincing and directly available support for their empiricist outlook and for the antimetaphysical program they were committed to. All of this is reasonably clear when we turn, for example, to the writings of Schlick and Waismann, who were in direct contact with Wittgenstein.

When these ideas were presented to the Circle they did not meet with unanimous acceptance. Outstanding among the dissenters were Carnap and Neurath. Schlick, following Wittgenstein, argued for verifications that were themselves direct, final, and certain. These corresponded to what Wittgenstein had called 'propositions', although all hypotheses were only confirmable with some degree of probability, and never established with certainty. This was the doctrine of so-called 'strong' verification, as favored by the 'right wing' of the positivist group. Opposed to them were those like Carnap and Neurath who argued for the position of 'weak' verification and who saw no essential difference between the logical status of basic ('protocol') statements that are reports of observations, and those called 'hypotheses'; *all* empirical statements, according to

---

* Waismann collaborated with Wittgenstein in what was to have been a systematic exposition of Wittgenstein's thought in a book to be entitled *Logik, Sprache, und Philosophie*. Wittgenstein eventually broke off participating in this project. It was published eventually— much transformed from its early version—under Waismann's name alone, as *The Principles of Linguistic Philosophy*.

them, are at bottom 'hypothetical'. Let us see how these conflicting views are supported by their respective proponents.

In the following passage, Schlick echoes Wittgenstein's conception of a *hypothesis* that is verifiable (confirmable) with some degree of probability.

It is perfectly true that every statement about a physical object or an event *means* more than is verified, say, by the occurrence of a single experience. It is rather presupposed that the experience occurred under very definite conditions, whose realization of course can only be verified by something given, and it is presupposed further that ever more verifications are possible (confirmations etc.), which in their turn, naturally, reduce to certain given events. In this manner one can and must give an account of illusions of sense, and of error, and it is easy to see how those cases are to be included in which we should say the observer was merely dreaming, that the pointer indicated a definite line, or that he did not carefully observe, etc. . . . . Strictly speaking, the meaning of a proposition about physical objects would be exhausted only by an indefinitely large number of possible verifications, and we gather from this that such a proposition can in the last analysis never be shown to be absolutely true. It is indeed generally recognized that even the most certain propositions of science are always to be taken as hypotheses, which remain open to further refinement and improvement. This has certain consequences for the logical nature of such propositions, but these do not interest us here.

Once again: the meaning of a physical statement is never determined by a single isolated verification but it must be thought of in the form: If conditions x are given, the data y occur, where we can substitute an indefinitely large number of conditions for x, the proposition remaining true for each case. (This holds even when the statement refers to a single happening—a historical event, for such an event has innumerable consequences whose occurrences are verifiable). Thus the meaning of every physical statement is lodged finally in an endless concatenation of data; the isolated datum therefore is here uninteresting. Hence if any positivist ever said that the only objects of science are the given experiences themselves he was certainly quite mistaken; what alone the scientists seek are the rules which govern the connections among experiences, and by means of which they can be predicted. No one will deny that the sole verification of natural laws lies in the fact that they yield such true predictions. The common objection that the immediately given, which at most can be but the object of psychology, is thus falsely made into the object of physics is in this way refuted.[47]

At the same time, Schlick maintains that any single verifying experience of a hypothesis is *itself* known with finality and certainty.

Science makes prophecies that are tested by "experience." Its essential function consists in making predictions. It says, for example: "If at such and such a time you look through a telescope adjusted in such and such a manner you will see a point of light (a star) in coincidence with a black mark (cross wires)." Let us assume that in following out these instructions the predicted experience actually occurs. This means that we make an anticipated confirmation, we pronounce an expected judgment of observation, we obtain thereby a feeling of *fulfilment,* a quite characteristic satisfaction: we are *satisfied.* One is fully justified in saying the confirmation or observation statements have fulfilled their true mission as soon as we obtain this peculiar satisfaction.

And it is obtained in the very moment in which the confirmation takes place, in which the observation statement is made. This is of the utmost importance. For thus the function of the statements about the immediately experienced itself lies in the immediate present. Indeed we saw that they have so to speak no duration, that the moment they are gone one has at one's disposal in their place inscriptions, or memory traces, that can play only the role of hypotheses and thereby lack ultimate certainty. One cannot build any logically tenable structure upon the confirmations, for they are gone the moment one begins to construct. If they stand at the beginning of the process of cognition they are logically of no use. Quite otherwise however if they stand at the end; they bring verification (or also falsification) to completion, and in the moment of their occurrence they have already fulfilled their duty. Logically nothing more depends on them, no conclusions are drawn from them. They constitute an absolute end.

. . . .

The question hidden behind the problem of the absolutely certain basis of knowledge is, as it were, that of the legitimacy of this satisfaction with which verification fills us. Have our predictions actually come true? In every single case of verification or falsification a "confirmation" answers unambiguously with a yes or a no, with joy of fulfilment or disappointment. The confirmations are final.

. . . .

In other words: I can understand the meaning of a "confirmation" only by, and when, comparing it with the facts, thus carrying out that process which is necessary for the verification of all synthetic statements. While in the case of all other synthetic statements determining the meaning is separate from, distinguishable from, determining the truth, in the case of observation statements they coincide, just as in the case of analytic statements. However different therefore "confirmations" are from analytic statements, they have in common that the occasion of understanding them is at the same time that of verifying them: I grasp their meaning at the same time as I grasp their truth. In the case of a confirmation it makes as little sense to ask whether I might be deceived regarding its truth as in the case of a tautology. Both are absolutely valid. However, while the analytic, tautological, statement is empty of content, the observation statement supplies us with the satisfaction of genuine knowledge of reality.

It has become clear, we may hope, that here everything depends on the characteristic of immediacy which is peculiar to observation statements and to which they owe their value and disvalue; the value of absolute validity, and the disvalue of uselessness as an abiding foundation. . . .

If I make the confirmation "Here now blue," this is *not* the same as the protocol statement "M.S. perceived blue on the nth of April 1934 at such and such a time and such and such a place." The latter statement is a hypothesis and as such always characterized by uncertainty. The latter statement is equivalent to

"M.S. made . . . (here time and place are to be given) the confirmation 'here now blue.'" And that this assertion is not identical with the confirmation occurring in it is clear. In protocol statements there is *always* mention of perceptions (or they are to be added in thought—the identity of the perceiving observer is important for a scientific protocol), while they are never mentioned in confirmations. A genuine confirmation cannot be written down, for as soon as I inscribe the demonstratives "here," "now," they lose their meaning. Neither can they be replaced by an indication of time and place, for as soon as one attempts to do this, the result, as we saw, is that one unavoidably substitutes for the observation statement a protocol statement which as such has a wholly different nature.

· · · · · · · ·

If attention is directed upon the relation of science to reality the system of its statements is seen to be that which it really is, namely, a means of finding one's way among the facts; of arriving at the joy of confirmation, the feeling of finality. The problem of the "basis" changes then automatically into that of the unshakeable point of contact between knowledge and reality. We have come to know these absolutely fixed points of contact, the confirmations, in their individuality: they are the only synthetic statements that are not *hypotheses*.[48]

The views of Schlick as expressed in the foregoing are in sharp opposition to those of other positivists, e.g., Neurath and Carnap, who defended the notion of 'weak verifiability', and for whom the 'verifiers' are of the nature of 'protocol statements' or 'observation statements'. Such statements are, like all other statements in a scientific system of knowledge, of the nature of 'hypotheses' and so corrigible.

Neurath writes:

There is no way of taking conclusively established pure protocol sentences as the starting point of the sciences. No *tabula rasa* exists. We are like sailors who must rebuild their ship on the open sea, never able to dismantle it in dry-dock and to reconstruct it there out of the best materials.

· · · · · · · ·

Apart from tautologies, unified science consists of factual sentences. These may be divided into (a) protocol sentences (b) non-protocol sentences. Protocol sentences are factual sentences of the same form as the others except that, in them, a personal noun always occurs several times in a specific association with other terms. A complete protocol sentence might, for instance, read: "Otto's protocol at 3:17 o'clock: [At 3:16 o'clock Otto said to himself: (at 3:15 there was a table in the room perceived by Otto)]." This factual sentence is so constructed that, within each set of brackets, further factual sentences may be found, *viz.:* "At 3:16 o'clock Otto said to himself: (At 3:15 o'clock there was a table in the room perceived by Otto)" and "At 3:15 o'clock there was a table in the room perceived by Otto." These sentences are, however, not protocol sentences.

· · · · · · · ·

For a protocol sentence to be complete it is essential that the name of some person occur in it. "Now joy," or "Now red circle," or "A red die is lying on the table" are not complete protocol sentences. They are not even candidates for a position within the innermost set of brackets. For this they would, on our analysis, at least have to read "Otto now joy," or "Otto now sees a red circle," or "Otto now sees a red die lying on the table."

. . . .

We also allow for the possibility of discarding protocol sentences. A defining condition of a sentence is that it be subject to verification, that is to say, that it may be discarded.

. . . .

All of which means that *there are neither primitive protocol sentences nor sentences which are not subject to verification.*

. . . .

One cannot start with conclusively established, pure protocol sentences. Protocol sentences are factual sentences like the others, containing names of persons or names of groups of people linked in specific ways with other terms.[49]

The liberalization in the conception of empiricism represented by a shift from the emphasis on certainty and complete verification to the realization of the hypothetical status of *all* factual statements, and that as such these statements are capable only of some degree of probability or confirmability, was shared by Carnap in the later stages of his thought.

According to the original conception, the system of knowledge, although growing constantly more comprehensive, was regarded as a closed system in the following sense. We assumed that there was a certain rock bottom of knowledge, the knowledge of the immediately given, which was indubitable. Every other kind of knowledge was supposed to be firmly supported by this basis and therefore likewise decidable with certainty. This was the picture which I had given in the *Logischer Aufbau*; it was supported by the influence of Mach's doctrine of sensations as the elements of all knowledge, by Russell's logical atomism, and finally by Wittgenstein's thesis that all propositions are truth-functions of the elementary propositions. This conception led to Wittgenstein's principle of verifiability, which says that it is in principle possible to obtain either a definite verification or a definite refutation for any meaningful sentence.

Looking back at this view from our present position, I must admit that it was difficult to reconcile with certain other conceptions which we had at that time, especially in the methodology of science. Therefore the development and clarification of our methodological views led inevitably to an abandonment of the rigid frame in our theory of knowledge. The important feature in our methodological position was the emphasis on the hypothetical character of the laws of nature, in particular, of physical theories. This view was influenced by men like Poincaré and Duhem, and by our study of the axiomatic method and its application in the empirical sciences with the help of co-ordinative definitions or rules. It was clear that the laws of physics could not possibly be completely verified.[50]

The Logical Status of the Principle of Verifiability

The status of the Principle of Verifiability itself, whatever its preferred formulation, is a matter to which positivists were obliged to give their attention. Was the Principle of Verifiability a meaningful statement according to its own criterion of meaningfulness? Carnap writes:

> The following objection, which on first appearance seems indeed destructive, has been repeatedly raised:—"If every proposition which does not belong either to mathematics or to the empirical investigation of facts, is meaningless, how does it fare then with your own propositions? You positivists and antimetaphysicians yourselves cut off the branch on which you sit." This objection indeed touches upon a decisive point.[51]

In the *Tractatus* Wittgenstein had, of course, recognized this type of objection. When he came to comment on his own work he argued that philosophy is only an 'activity', that there are no distinctively philosophical propositions to be judged as factually true or false, and that his own use of language for philosophic purposes was, in this respect, 'nonsense'. Once one has climbed up and over the ladder, one 'throws the ladder away'. Carnap rejects this Wittgensteinian type of answer. He cannot admit that his own work and that of other logical positivists is nonsense, or that the Principle of Verifiability is an example of such nonsense. How, then, meet the challenge? How can one show the Principle of Verifiability to be a bona fide meaningful statement?

Carnap, at one stage of his philosophic development, stressed that the answer is to be found in recognizing that the distinctive role and status of philosophy is to be the logic of science.

> Philosophy deals with science only from the *logical* viewpoint. *Philosophy is the logic of science,* i.e., the logical analysis of the concepts, propositions, proofs, theories of science, as well as of those we select in available science as common to the possible methods of constructing concepts, proofs, hypotheses, theories.[52]

The Principle of Verifiability, along with other philosophic clarifications, belongs to the results of the logic of science.

According to Carnap's view of what such logic of science is, as expressed in his book *The Logical Syntax of Language* (1937) and other writings of this period, it is the theory of the formal structure of the language of science, i.e., the logical syntax of the language of science. The questions of logical syntax have to do with the various *rules of formation* (i.e., how the propositions of a scientific language can be built up out of its primitive symbols) and *rules of transformation* (i.e., rules that govern how new propositions can be derived from certain given ones). The study of the logical syntax of a language examines special problems in the purely mathematical sciences as well as in the empirical sciences. It is in connection with the empirical sciences that the matter of observational verification arises. According to Carnap, the matter of 'verification' is still to be approached in a syntactical way; that is, as a matter of the formal, syntactical coherence or consistency within the language of an empirical discipline, among the various propositions that compose it. Since any empirical science will need to include in its language the proto-col sentences that report the findings of empirical observations, it becomes a question of adjusting and rendering consistent with these obser-vation reports various other sentences, especially those of *theory*. "The problem of the verification of physical laws is the question concerning the syntactic deductive coherence between the physical laws (i.e., general propositions of a certain form) and the protocol propositions (singular propositions of a certain form)."[53]

But this solution, as given by Carnap, was open to numerous diffi-culties and objections. For one thing, by stressing as it did the matter of formal or syntactic rules as essential to the logical analysis of the language of a science, it tended to ignore important semantic questions having to do with questions of empirical reference and truth. (Carnap in his later work increasingly came to recognize this deficiency and devoted much of his attention to working out a suitable theory of semantics.) In any case, to leave the matter of the choice of a scientific language to questions of 'co-herence' would seem to make the use of the Principle of Verifiability a matter of conventional choice, one that is open for a critic to refuse to accept. It thereby weakens the initial claims of the positivists to have a secure basis for accomplishing the sharp demarcation between the mean-ingful use of language in science and 'metaphysical' uses. The Principle of Verification, in being reduced to a convention, loses much of its initially invested strength and absolute destructive power. Ayer, in commenting on this theme, begins by agreeing with Carnap in rejecting the Wittgen-steinian conception of philosophy as nonsense.

If the verification principle really is nonsensical, it states nothing; and if one holds that it states nothing, then one cannot also maintain that what it states is true.

The Vienna Circle tended to ignore this difficulty: but it seems to me fairly clear that what they were in fact doing was to adopt the verification principle as a convention. They were propounding a definition of meaning which accorded with common usage in the sense that it set out the conditions that are in fact satisfied by statements which are regarded as empirically informative. Their treatment of *a priori* statements was also intended to provide an account of the way in which such statements actually function. To this extent their work was descriptive; it became prescriptive with the suggestion that only statements of these two kinds should be regarded as either true or false, and that only statements which were capable of being either true or false should be regarded as literally meaningful.

But why should this prescription be accepted? The most that has been proved is that metaphysical statements do not fall into the same category as the laws of logic, or as scientific hypotheses, or as historical narratives, or judgments of perception, or any other common sense descriptions of the "natural" world. Surely it does not follow that they are neither true nor false, still less that they are nonsensical? No, it does not follow.[54]

If, then, as Ayer concedes, the Principle of Verification has the status of being a definition and not an empirical hypothesis, this means that as with other definitions it has no compelling power for its adoption. It is of the nature of a recommendation. Therefore one need not accept or abide by the recommendation! The Principle serves at best to offer a definition of how meaningfulness is to be understood in ordinary common sense and in scientific language. But it need not be binding upon, say, a metaphysician who chooses to adopt another or broader definition of meaningfulness. In the introduction to the second edition of his *Language, Truth and Logic,* Ayer writes:

Thus, while I wish the principle of verification itself to be regarded, not as an empirical hypothesis, but as a definition, it is not supposed to be entirely arbitrary. It is indeed open to anyone to adopt a different criterion of meaning and so to produce an alternative definition which may very well correspond to one of the ways in which the word "meaning" is commonly used. And if a statement satisfied such a criterion, there is, no doubt, some proper use of the word "understanding" in which it would be capable of being understood. Nevertheless, I think that, unless it satisfied the principle of verification, it would not be capable of being understood in the sense in which either scientific hypotheses or common-sense statements are habitually understood. I confess, however, that it now seems to me unlikely that any metaphysician would yield to a claim of this kind; and although I should still defend the use of a criterion of verifiability as a methodological principle, I realize that for the effective elimination of metaphysics it needs to be supported by detailed analyses of particular metaphysical arguments.[55]

The brief glimpse we have just had of the problems faced within the positivist movement of finding a precise formulation for the Principle of Verification that would be acceptable to all positivists (as well as the realization that the Principle was nothing more than a 'recommendation', and so not able to bring a total elimination of metaphysics) concentrated on the internal philosophic difficulties that led eventually to the dissolution of the movement of logical positivism as an effective philosophic force. To be sure, thinkers formerly close to the work of the Vienna Circle continued to carry on with their own individual researches, and made valuable contributions to various topics within the philosophy of science. But these were not in every case distinctively 'positivist' or even 'empiricist' in character. Moreover, the emergence of the impact on analytic philosophy of the later writings of Wittgenstein, along with the increasing attention paid to semantics and to various questions of an ontological character, led to a gradual loosening of the hold of positivist philosophy. We shall study some of the forms of these shifts in the winds of doctrine as we come closer to our own day. One early and important example of these shifts was the growing influence of the 'later' philosophy of Wittgenstein, and the stress it gave to the study of the use of expressions in 'natural' and 'ordinary' language. It is to this development in analytic philosophy that we turn next.

CHAPTER VII

Language-Games

WITTGENSTEIN'S LATER PHILOSOPHY

In 1939 Wittgenstein was appointed to the chair in philosophy at Cambridge University previously occupied by Moore. Because of the outbreak of the war in 1939 he did not take up his new duties, but instead volunteered for war service and served at first as a hospital porter and later as a laboratory assistant. (He had become a British subject some time previously.) After the war he resumed his post at the university and lectured there until his resignation from the professorship in 1947. He continued to work at his manuscripts. For a while he lived in seclusion in Ireland. He also spent three months on a visit to the United States, after which he returned to England. In 1949 it was discovered that he suffered from cancer. For the last few months of his life he lived in Cambridge at the home of his doctor. He continued to write on technical philosophical topics until two days before his death. He died on April 29, 1951.

The *Philosophical Investigations* was one of the many manuscripts left at his death. It was published posthumously and quickly achieved the status of a major classic. It represents the culmination and distillation of his fresh thought about the nature of language after his 'return' to philosophy in the late 1920s. In its Preface he suggests that it "could be seen in the right light only by contrast with and against the background of my old way of thinking." There can be no doubt that the later philosophy, as conveyed in the *Philosophical Investigations,* represents for him a radically new approach to language in contrast with that of the *Tractatus.* This is the basis for the remark, by now commonplace, that Wittgenstein is unique as a philosopher insofar as he was the creator of two completely different, original, highly influential philosophies, where the second philosophy was the outcome of the criticisms directed by the author himself against his own earlier scheme of thought. This summary statement needs immediate qualification. By stressing the element of sharp contrast between the two philosophies, such a summary tends to cloak the fact that the changeover was not abrupt but was mediated by various transitional phases. Furthermore, despite the major shifts that did occur, there were certain underlying elements of continuity that persisted to the end and that can be found both in the earliest pre-World War I writings and in those composed at the very end of his life.

In his *Notebooks 1914–1916* Wittgenstein wrote, "My *whole* task consists in explaining the nature of the proposition."[1] He might very well have made the same point throughout his life to describe his continuing philosophic preoccupation, since the same problem continues to lie at the center of all his writings up to the very end. What makes it possible to say something? How can words in combination signify something and be communicated to others? To be able to answer this broad question about the nature of language—how language functions and accomplishes its role in human life—provides the underlying motif and unchanging element of continuity in Wittgenstein's philosophy, early, middle, and late. What distinguishes the different periods in his philosophic development is the way he takes apart the question, understands its various possible guises, and having marked these, gives detailed answers to the problems thereby raised.

One way of summing up the major difference in the way he answered the question in his later philosophy as compared with the earlier is the following. In the earlier philosophy a proposition (*Satz*) says something because it is a picture or model of reality; it has a possible isomorphic relation to reality; its sense is determined by its truth-conditions. On the later account, a proposition—or better, a sentence—represents a 'move in a language-game'; it is a 'tool' used to accomplish a particular purpose, though not necessarily or exclusively one of describing reality; its sense is governed by various grammatical rules or conventions.

On the earlier approach, a proposition when thoroughly analyzed is always at bottom simply a concatenation of names, where every name stands for an object. Ordinary language has a concealed complexity that logical analysis brings to the surface and makes explicit. The basic role of language is to depict reality. The logical structure of language is to be viewed in terms of truth-functional relations of compound (molecular) propositions to elementary ones. The sense of an elementary proposition, in turn, consists in its relation of truth or falsity with respect to the reality of which it is a model. An elementary proposition depicts a possible state of affairs in the world.

In Wittgenstein's later philosophy, the logic of linguistic expressions is construed in altogether different terms. Language is not to be examined by means of a depth-grammar that points to truth-functions of elementary propositions as the essence of language. Nor are propositions in their 'basic' constituents made up of names. Language is ordinary language. It is not to be derived from something more fundamental in the form of elementary propositions. Language is languages. It is to be explored in all its great variety and complexity. It is to be described and understood *as it is found,* not reduced to some more basic structure. It has multiple uses, not simply one of describing reality and picturing facts.

It is wrong to say that in philosophy we consider an ideal language as opposed to our ordinary one. For this makes it appear as though we thought we could improve on ordinary language. But ordinary language is all right.[2]

In saying that ordinary language is "all right," Wittgenstein does not mean that for certain purposes we cannot find fault with some available linguistic tools and choose to replace them with others especially contrived and more suited to accomplish our purposes. This surely is the case whenever specialist vocabularies are constructed, as for example in scientific languages devised to deal with fresh and complex ranges of experience. Rather, what Wittgenstein stresses is the need for philosophy to recognize the ways in which language is employed in relation to an ever changing complex of activities. Ordinary language is "all right" when it is used successfully to accomplish the great variety of purposes in the forms of life in which particular language activities are embedded. To say that ordinary language is "all right" does not mean that its resources are always employed in ways that are free of failure and misuse. On the contrary, a special class of cases of such misuse arises, Wittgenstein would say, wherever pseudophilosophical problems arise due to the misapplication of the rules of ordinary language. In such cases it is appropriate for a critic to call attention to these misuses through a patient diagnosis of the resulting errors.

We want to establish an order in our knowledge of the use of language: an order with a particular end in view; one out of many possible orders; not *the* order. To this end we shall constantly be giving prominence to distinctions which our ordinary forms of language easily make us overlook. This may make it look as if we saw it as our task to reform language.

Such a reform for particular practical purposes, an improvement in our terminology designed to prevent misunderstandings in practice, is perfectly possible. But these are not the cases we have to do with. The confusions which occupy us arise when language is like an engine idling, not when it is doing work.[3]

In 1928, not long after his return to Vienna, Wittgenstein had an experience that is sometimes credited with inspiring him to take up once more an active interest in philosophy. On March 10, 1928, in the company of Herbert Feigl and Friedrich Waismann, he attended a lecture entitled

"Mathematics, Science, and Language" by the well-known Dutch mathematician Luitzen E. J. Brouwer, the leading figure of the Intuitionist school of mathematicians.[4] According to Feigl, he and Waismann spent a few hours with Wittgenstein in a cafe after the lecture and "it was fascinating to behold the change that had come over W[ittgenstein] that evening . . . . He became extremely voluble and began sketching ideas that were the beginnings of his later writings . . . . That evening marked the return of W[ittgenstein] to strong philosophical interests and activities."[5]

Brouwer's broad philosophic orientation, as expressed in the aforementioned lecture and elsewhere, has deep affinities with the Kantian tradition. That tradition defends in general the central role of the creative or constructive function of the human mind in providing the structures for organizing the data of sense experience. In particular, mathematics (along with science and language, generally) exemplifies such constructive activities of the mind. Mathematics constitutes a domain of intellectual inventions rather than one devoted to disclosures of antecedent or independent 'eternal' truths. Wittgenstein had already absorbed a good deal of this way of thought through his earlier attraction to Schopenhauer's philosophy. However, the main thrust of the *Tractatus* remained essentially realistic rather than conventionalistic or constructivistic. It affirmed that logic discloses the necessary structures inherent in all possible states of affairs. Mathematics, as a set of tautologies, is a disclosure of the necessities in the structure of reality, by virtue of stating exhaustively all possibilities. Furthermore, the sense of all propositions in a fully articulated and well-formulated language must be completely determinate in order to be correlated with objects in the world. This central doctrine of the *Tractatus* was evidence of Wittgenstein's adherence to and adoption of the realism he shared with Frege and Russell. (There was another strain, too, in the *Tractatus,* more closely linked to the Kantian tradition. It was one that showed the influence of Heinrich Hertz, and stressed the role of the free creations of the mind in natural science. But on the whole this strain was subordinated to and incorporated within the wider and more fundamental outlook of a realist philosophy.)

To adopt a broadly Kantian, conventionalistic, and constructivist view about man's intellectual activities, is to do a 180-degree turn. It does not look to the world to determine form, sense, and truth. It looks, rather, to the conceptual devices originating in the human mind and brought to experience for its interpretation. These devices (languages, conceptual schemes) are to be judged by their effectiveness in accomplishing our human purposes. The standards used in making judgments of effectiveness are on the whole pragmatic ones. How successful or convenient are the language-systems and conceptual tools man devises? Instead of looking for a matching or for a correspondence with some antecedent and independent structure to be captured and articulated by some uniquely preferred conceptual or linguistic scheme, one makes comparative judgments of relative adequacy among competing methods, languages, and conceptual schemes. Instead of a logic of 'truth-conditions' one relies on a logic of 'use-conditions'. The latter, when considered specifically with respect to the cognitive uses of language, have to do with the grounds or evidence to which one can appeal to *justify* the acceptance of a particular proposition. It was this broadly 'Kantian' orientation that Wittgenstein recognized in Brouwer's lecture. It aroused and strengthened a sympathetic chord in his own thought. The following out of this fresh impetus led to a new way of thinking and, over the period of the next decades, to the development of his 'later' philosophy.

The meaning (sense) of linguistic expressions is not to be determined by correlation with some antecedently and independently existing structure of reality. Instead of adopting a realistic view of meaning, Wittgenstein shifts to the adoption of a broadly conventionalistic one. The meaning of linguistic expressions is determined by rules of use that people devise and adopt. Grammar is autonomous; thought (and the language that conveys it) has its internal structures as articulated by the grammatical rules that belong to it. The choice of these rules, the grammar of thought, is not to be determined by establishing some isomorphic relation to reality. Reality does not have some language-independent structure to which our language, *considered as a system of rules,* conforms and to which it must stand in a relation of formal identity. Rather, thought (language) is structured by human conventions; it *brings to* reality its own structure. In order to describe reality, one must use these preestablished 'forms of thought' (rules of grammar). It is through the use and application of these rules that one can deal with reality in a 'thoughtful' (linguistic) way.

The task of 'logical analysis' — of philosophy — is to help us become aware of the rules, the 'grammars', as well as the contexts of daily living, in which the expressions and constructions of language find their use. The role of philosophy is to make us aware of how this is accomplished. By taking numerous examples and examining them in great detail, we come to see how language works. We study these uses by attending to the different kinds of 'language-games' we 'play'. We examine the nuances, the similarities and differences among the roles and uses to which the different 'pieces' (the expressions) of language are put in playing our language-games. The study of such 'grammar' is one of the important functions of philosophy. The failure to engage in this study accounts for the puzzlements, entanglements in pseudoproblems, and confusions that pervade much of traditional philosophy. The task of genuine philosophy is to free us from these snares. What goes by the name of 'philosophy', as traditionally practiced, is the disease of which philosophy as the examination of the logic of our language is the cure. In bringing the logic (the grammar) of our language to the surface, we do not change language or reduce it to something more basic. We leave everything as it is. But in becoming clear about the grammar of our language we achieve philosophic enlightenment. Our solutions to problems are dissolutions of pseudoproblems.

FROM 'ESSENCES' TO 'FAMILY RESEMBLANCES'

One of the major targets of attack in Wittgenstein's later philosophy is the pervasive 'craving for generality' — the belief in and search for common, uniform, essential properties — as a required condition for having an understanding of anything. The assumption that it is necessary to have a grasp of what is essential, uniform, general, and common in any multiplicity of instances is classically illustrated as a central feature of Plato's philosophy. It persists in one form or another throughout the entire subsequent history of Western philosophy. For example, it lies at the center of Frege's and Russell's philosophy. And it animated Wittgenstein's earlier philosophy in the *Tractatus*. It is this all-pervasive conception of the overriding importance of finding what is common, general, and essential, along with a correlated 'contempt for the particular case' and a parallel lack of concern for the *differences* among instances, to which Wittgenstein set himself in sharp opposition in his later philosophy. The consequences of this attack, the result of making this radical shift in orientation, is a key way of getting to understand the later philosophy.

First let us pause to recall the form that the craving for generality and the search for common essences took in the philosophy of the *Tractatus*. A major goal of the philosophy of the *Tractatus* is to determine *the* limits of language. It is assumed that one can lay down the boundary and universal conditions for separating in a sharp way sense from nonsense, what can be said from what cannot be said. The task of logic is said to be the making of these distinctions in a universal, necessary, and *a priori* way. The distinctions, once made, underlie and show the constraints on all meaningful uses of language that purport to convey knowledge of the world. It is claimed that there is a common, essential, underlying structure that links logic, language, and the world.

One of the philosophic goals in whose grip Wittgenstein was held and by which he was led in the *Tractatus* was to be able to characterize the general propositional form.

5.47   Wherever ther is compositeness, argument and function are present, and where these are present, we already have all the logical constants.

One could say that the sole logical constant was what *all* propositions, by their very nature, had in common with one another.

But that is the general propositional form.

5.471   The general propositional form is the essence of a proposition.

5.4711   To give the essence of a proposition means to give the essence of all description, and thus the essence of the world.

4.5   The general form of a proposition is: This is how things stand.

For Wittgenstein, following this line of thought, all propositions are truth-functions of elementary propositions; the latter are at bottom concatenations of names, where each name designates a simple object in the world, and where the configuration of the names in the proposition depicts a possible state of affairs. Here we have the an wer to the question how to state in a general way the essence of all language and the essence of the relation between language and the world. However, against the posing of the question itself and the assumptions underlying it, as well as the answer given to the question, Wittgenstein rebelled in his later philosophy.

If we look behind the search in the *Tractatus* for 'the essence of language', 'the general form of the proposition', and 'the limit of language', we find that one of the root causes of the illusory character of this search, as Wittgenstein later diagnosed the matter, is the craving for generality. He describes the sources of this prevalent craving as follows:

This craving for generality is the resultant of a number of tendencies connected with particular philosophical confusions. There is —

(a) The tendency to look for something in common to all the entities which we commonly subsume under a general term.— We are inclined to think that there must be something in common to all games, say, and that this common property is the justification for applying the general term "game" to the various games; whereas games form a *family* the members of which have family likenesses. Some of them have the same nose, others the same eyebrows and others again the same way of walking; and these likenesses overlap. The idea of a general concept being a common property of its particular instances connects up with other primitive, too simple, ideas of the structure of language. It is comparable to the idea that *properties* are *ingredients* of the things which have the properties; e.g., that beauty is an ingredient of all beautiful things as alcohol is of beer and wine, and that we therefore could have pure beauty, unadulterated by anything that is beautiful.

(b) There is a tendency rooted in our usual forms of expression, to think that the man who has learnt to understand a general term, say, the term "leaf", has thereby come to possess a kind of general picture of a leaf, as opposed to pictures of particular leaves. He was shown different leaves when he learnt the meaning of the word "leaf"; and showing him the particular leaves was only a means to the end of producing 'in him' an idea which we imagine to be some kind of general image. We say that he sees what is in common to all these leaves; and this is true if we mean that he can on being asked tell us certain features or properties which they have in common. But we are inclined to think that the general idea of a leaf is something like a visual image, but one which only contains what is common to all leaves. (Galtonian composite photograph.) This again is connected with the idea that the meaning of a word is an image, or a thing correlated to the word. (This roughly means, we are looking at words as though they all were proper names, and we then confuse the bearer of a name with the meaning of the name.)

(c) Again, the idea we have of what happens when we get hold of the general idea 'leaf', 'plant', etc. etc., is connected with the confusion between a mental state, meaning a state of a hypothetical mental mechanism, and a mental state meaning a state of consciousness (toothache, etc.).

(d) Our craving for generality has another main source: our preoccupation with the method of science. I mean the method of reducing the explanation of natural phenomena to the smallest possible number of primitive natural laws; and, in mathematics, of unifying the treatment of different topics by using a generalization. Philosophers constantly see the method of science before their eyes, and are irresistibly tempted to ask and answer questions in the way science does. This tendency is the real source of metaphysics, and leads the philosopher into complete darkness. I want to say here that it can never be our job to reduce anything to anything, or to explain anything. Philosophy really *is* 'purely descriptive'. (Think of such questions as "Are there sense data?" And ask: What method is there of determining this? Introspection?)

Instead of "craving for generality" I could also have said "the contemptuous attitude towards the particular case". If, e.g., someone tries to explain the concept of number and tells us that such and such a definition will not do or is clumsy because it only applies to, say, finite cardinals I should answer that the mere fact that he could have given such a limited definition makes this definition extremely important to us. (Elegance is *not* what we are trying for.) For why should what finite and transfinite numbers have in common be more interesting to us than what distinguishes them? Or rather, I should not have said "why should it be more interesting to us?"— it *isn't;* and this characterizes our way of thinking.

The attitude towards the more general and the more special in logic is connected with the usage of the word "kind" which is liable to cause confusion. We talk of kinds of numbers, kinds of propositions, kinds of proofs; and, also, of kinds of apples, kinds of paper, etc. In one sense what defines the kind are properties, like sweetness, hardness, etc. In the other the different kinds are different grammatical structures. A treatise on pomology may be called incomplete if there exist kinds of apples which it doesn't mention. Here we have a standard of completeness in nature. Supposing on the other hand there was a game resembling that of chess but simpler, no pawns being used in it. Should we call this game incomplete? Or should we call a game more complete than chess if it in some way contained chess but added new elements? The contempt for what seems the less general case in logic springs from the idea that it is incomplete. It is in fact confusing to talk of cardinal arithmetic as something special as opposed to something more general. Cardinal arithmetic bears no mark of incompleteness; nor does an arithmetic which is cardinal and finite. (There are no subtle distinctions between logical forms as there are between the tastes of different kinds of apples.)

If we study the grammar, say, of the words "wishing", "thinking", "understanding", "meaning", we shall not be dissatisfied when we have described various cases of wishing, thinking, etc. If someone said, "surely this is not all that one calls 'wishing'", we should answer, "certainly not, but you can build up more complicated cases if you like." And after all, there is not one definite class of features which characterize all cases of wishing (at least not as the word is commonly used). If on the other hand you wish to give a definition of wishing, i.e., to draw a sharp boundary, then you are free to draw it as you like; and this boundary will never entirely coincide with the actual usage, as this usage has no sharp boundary.

The idea that in order to get clear about the meaning of a general term one had to find the common element in all its applications, has shackled philosophical investigation; for it has not only led to no result, but also made the philosopher dismiss as irrelevant the concrete cases, which alone could have helped him to understand the usage of the general term. When Socrates asks the question, "what is knowledge?" he does not even regard it as a *preliminary* answer to enumerate cases of knowledge. (*Theaetetus*, 146 D-7c). If I wished to find out what sort of thing arithmetic is, I should be very content indeed to have investigated the case of a finite cardinal arithmetic. For

(a) this would lead me on to all the more complicated cases,

(b) a finite cardinal arithmetic is not incomplete, it has no gaps which are then filled in by the rest of arithmetic.[6]

In order to overcome the craving for generality and the contempt for the particular case, one must employ the remedy of making a careful study of numerous individual examples. Instead of assuming, because we subsume them under a *general* term or assign them to a *kind,* that they *must* have something in common (their 'essential' properties), Wittgenstein argues that we should look to the cases themselves. In studying them it is important to take note of their similarities and differences. It will not always be the case that there is, or must be, something common! There *may* be only overlapping similarities among particular cases, without there being a number of common properties shared by all. These overlapping similarities may suffice for our using the general term to describe all these particular cases, in the same way that members of a human family are recognized to resemble one another even though every one of the members need not have a set of characteristics shared by all other members. There may be only certain *family resemblances,* for example "build, features, color of eyes, gait, temperament, etc. etc." that overlap and crisscross in various ways.[7]

Wittgenstein uses the expression 'game' as an example of a term that covers a multitude of cases among which are to be found only 'family resemblances'.

Consider for example the proceedings that we call "games". I mean board-games, card-games, ball-games, Olympic games and so on. What is common to them all? Don't say: "There *must* be something common, or they would not be called 'games'"—but *look and see* whether there is anything common to all. — For if you look at them you will not see something that is common to *all*, but similarities, relationships, and a whole series of them at that. To repeat: don't think, but look! —Look for example at board-games, with their multifarious relationships. Now pass to card-games; here you find many correspondences with the first group, but many common features drop out, and others appear. When we pass next to ball-games, much that is common is retained, but much is lost. — Are they all 'amusing'? Compare chess with noughts and crosses. Or is there always winning and losing, or competition between players? Think of patience. In ball games there is winning and losing; but when a child throws his ball at the wall and catches it again, this feature has disappeared. Look at the parts played by skill and luck; and at the difference between skill in chess and skill in tennis. Think now of games like ring-a-ring-a roses; here is the element of amusement, but how many other characteristic features have disappeared! And we can go through the many, many other groups of games in the same way; can see how similarities crop up and disappear.

And the result of this examination is: we see a complicated network of similarities overlapping and criss-crossing: sometimes overall similarities, sometimes similarities of detail.[8]

The point illustrated here with respect to games can be shown to hold when we consider a large group of other general terms in ordinary use. Take, as another example, the term 'number'.

And for instance the kinds of number form a family in the same way. Why do we call something a "number"? Well, perhaps because it has a — direct — relationship with several things that have hitherto been called number; and this can be said to give it an indirect relationship to other things we call the same name. And we extend our concept of number as in spinning a thread we twist fibre on fibre. And the strength of the thread does not reside in the fact that some one fibre runs through its whole length, but in the overlapping of many fibres.[9]

However, one must not, from these or other examples, jump to the conclusion that *all* general terms can *only* be characterized by means of family resemblances. This would be to fall into the very trap from which the strictures against the craving for generality were intended to save us. Not all general terms have the 'essential' trait of being describable only by means of family resemblances. Some do and some do not. Look and see! Thus in science, the law, or in ordinary language it is quite possible to define certain general terms, i.e., to draw sharp boundaries for their meaning by *stipulating* that certain separately necessary and jointly sufficient conditions be present wherever that general term is to be applied. However, whether a general term has such a stipulated, fixed, and precise list of defining characteristics cannot be determined without inquiry. There are no antecedent ontological facts (as for example Plato assumed there are) that already exist in some timeless, objective (nonhuman) realm, and that embody the essential traits belonging to the meaning of each and every general term.

Philosophers very often talk about investigating, analysing, the meaning of words. But let's not forget that a word hasn't got a meaning given to it, as it were, by a power independent of us, so that there could be a kind of scientific investigation into what the word *really* means. A word has the meaning someone has given to it.[10]

The meanings of linguistic expressions are determined by human beings who create and use language. Thus the tightness or looseness, the unity or diversity, the changing or relatively fixed character of the sense of a general term can only be established by examining how it is actually used over a period of time in a linguistic community.

MEANING AND USE

Wittgenstein's warnings against the pitfalls that beset the craving for generality, and his recommendations of an antidote in the form of examining multiple individual cases in all their diversity and complex interrelationships, are illustrated in the later writings in his many detailed examinations of a variety of concepts. Among these, a fundamental example—one that sets the stage for many others, and so has a controlling, preliminary general interest—is the analysis of the term 'language' he gives at the very beginning of *Philosophical Investigations*. From everything we have seen thus far it follows that for Wittgenstein it would be a basic misdirection of effort to search for a common set of characteristics, some essence for the use of the general term 'language'. As a classic example of such misdirection of effort, and as a highly influential view of what the 'essence' of language supposedly is, he refers in the opening paragraphs of *Philosophical Investigations* to St. Augustine's theory as stated in the latter's *Confessions* (I,8):

"When they (my elders) named some object, and accordingly moved towards something, I saw this and I grasped that the thing was called by the sound they uttered when they meant to point it out. Their intention was shown by their bodily movements, as it were the natural language of all peoples: the expression of the face, the play of the eyes, the movement of other parts of the body, and the tone of voice which expresses our state of mind in seeking, having, rejecting, or avoiding something. Thus, as I heard words repeatedly used in their proper places in various sentences, I gradually learnt to understand what objects they signified; and after I had trained my mouth to form these signs, I used them to express my own desires.''

These words, it seems to me, give us a particular picture of the essence of human language. It is this: the individual words in language name objects — sentences are combinations of such names. — In this picture of language we find the roots of the following idea: Every word has a meaning. This meaning is correlated with the word. It is the object for which the word stands.

Augustine does not speak of there being any difference between kinds of words. If you describe the learning of language in this way you are, I believe, thinking primarily of nouns like "table", "chair", "bread", and of people's names, and only secondarily of the names of certain actions and properties; and of the remaining kinds of word as something that will take care of itself.[11]

Wittgenstein does not find fault with Augustine's theory of language on the ground that it takes language to be essentially a matter of using names to refer to entities or objects, and that he, Wittgenstein, would point to some other essential marks or constituents. On the contrary, it is the whole enterprise of finding a supposed common, fixed essence to language that is at fault. The term 'language' does not stand for some single unitary phenomenon with respect to which one should seek to disclose some fixed essence.

Language is not defined for us as an arrangement fulfilling a definite purpose. Rather "language" is for me a name for a collection and I understand it as including German, English, and so on, and further various systems of signs which have more or less affinity with these languages.

Language is of interest to me as a phenomenon and not as a means to a particular end.[12]

Not only is 'language' at best a term that collects a great diversity and multiplicity of languages — a host of natural languages along with a great number of artificial or technical languages — but in considering all of these, it is important to recognize the enormously rich and complex variety of *uses* (roles, functions, employments) these have within human life. For there is no single fundamental use of language.

Instead of producing something common to all that we call language, I am saying that these phenomena have no one thing in common which makes us use the same word for all, — but that they are *related* to one another in many different ways. And it is because of this relationship or these relationships, that we call them all "language".[13]

Even to say that in language every word or other expression *signifies* something is of no use.

When we say: "Every word in language signifies something" we have so far said *nothing whatever;* unless we have explained exactly *what* distinction we wish to make . . . .

Imagine someone's saying: "*All* tools serve to modify something. Thus the hammer modifies the position of the nail, the saw the shape of the board, and so on."—And what is modified by the rule, the glue-pot, the nails? — "Our knowledge of a thing's length, the temperature of the glue, and the solidity of the box." —Would anything be gained by this assimilation of expressions?[14]

The great variety of expressions and the great variety of uses to which expressions are put (whether these expressions are single words, phrases, entire sentences, or other combinations) are so diverse that it is frequently of little help to rely on groupings that involve only superficial similarities.

In order to illustrate the variety of uses of expressions in language, Wittgenstein employs a number of analogies.

Linguistic expressions may be compared to the tools in a toolbox:

Think of the tools in a tool-box; there is a hammer, pliers, a saw, a screwdriver, a rule, a glue-pot, glue, nails and screws. — The functions of words are as diverse as the functions of these objects. (And in both cases there are similarities.)

Of course, what confuses us is the uniform appearance of words when we hear them spoken or meet them in script and print. For their *application* is not presented to us so clearly. Especially not, when we are doing philosophy![15]

One may also compare language to the inside of a cabin of a locomotive.

It is like looking into the cabin of a locomotive. We see handles all looking more or less alike. (Naturally, since they are all supposed to be handled.) But one is the handle of a crank which can be moved continuously (it regulates the opening of a valve); another is the handle of a switch, which has only two effective positions, it is either off or on; a third is the handle of a brake-lever, the harder one pulls on it, the harder it brakes; a fourth, the handle of a pump: it has an effect only so long as it is moved to and fro.[16]

Or again, one may compare the variety of uses of words or the parts of a sentence with the lines on a map.

Compare the different parts of speech in a sentence with lines on a map with different functions (frontiers, roads, meridians, contours.) An uninstructed person sees a mass of lines and does not know the variety of their meanings.

Think of a line on a map crossing a sign out to show that it is void.[17]

Finally, one may compare the different roles of words and various parts of speech to the pieces in a game such as chess. All the pieces may be made of wood, but their different shapes are connected with the different rules that govern the way in which they can move, and these in turn are connected with the various strategies directed to the overall purpose of winning a game.

The difference between parts of speech is comparable to the differences between chessmen, but also to the even greater difference between a chessman and the chess board.[18]

Wittgenstein criticizes the prevalent view that all words are to be treated as if they were names for objects, and where the meaning of a word is identified with the object named. The error would be comparable to thinking that the only role of money is to buy an object. "Here the word, there the meaning. The money, and the cow you buy with it. (But contrast: money and its use.)"[19] The economic institution of money in any developed form (beyond perhaps the very elementary stage of barter in which money is one kind of object exchanged for another object) involves multiple and diverse uses. One can buy not only objects but also services, for example, not only a pair of shoes but a shoeshine, not only an automobile but a taxi ride. In addition, money has various other uses. It confers 'status', establishes credit, constitutes power, and so on. "Money, and what one buys with it. Sometimes a material object, sometimes the right to a seat in the theatre, or a title, or fast travel, or life, etc."[20] In turning to the institution of language, we need similarly to take note of the great variety of uses to which linguistic expressions can be put. To attempt to reduce them all to the role of names would be to commit a fundamental fallacy. This is illustrated in the failure of such a procrustean view of language to deal with the use of *exclamations*. Consider the following dialogue in which Wittgenstein first states the thesis of a proponent of the name-relation as adequate to explain all the variety of parts of speech, and then replies to this proposal.

"We name things and then we can talk about them: can refer to them in talk." — As if what we did next were given with the mere act of naming. As if there were only one thing called "talking about a thing." Whereas in fact we do the most various things with our sentences. Think of exclamations alone, with their completely different functions.

Water!
Away!
Ow!
Help!
Fine!
No!

Are you inclined still to call these words "names of objects"?[21]

Previous analyses of language, including Wittgenstein's in the *Tractatus*, were misled into thinking that all words function in the way names do. Just as an ordinary proper name for a person, or the name given to some physical object, is introduced in conjunction with some confronted individual or object, so, it is thought, all words must name some object or other. Many of the traditional disputes in philosophy—for example about the nature of 'universals' or other types of 'abstract objects', or about what is designated by such terms as 'mind', 'proposition', 'time', and the like, are guided by the model of proper names for individual objects or persons. For Wittgenstein, these disputes arise from the futile attempt to assimilate the varied uses of linguistic expressions to those of proper names.

> The questions "What is length?", "What is meaning?", "What is the number one?" etc., produce in us a mental cramp. We feel that we can't point to anything in reply to them and yet we ought to point to something. (We are up against one of the great sources of philosophical bewilderment: we try to find a substance for a substantive.)[22]

Instead of asking 'What is meaning?', we should ask 'What is an explanation of meaning?'. Instead of asking 'What is length?' we should ask 'How do we measure length?' Instead of asking 'What is number?' we should ask 'How are numerical expressions used?' In each case we would deflect the tendency to treat the substantive-sounding words as substantive-hungry expressions, and by fastening our attention on how to perform some activity within a relevant language-game avoid the mythology of looking for some 'object' as a correlate for some pseudoname.

LANGUAGE-GAMES

A major analytical device to which Wittgenstein appeals in examining the complex phenomena of language is that of a *language-game*. Language is not only languages. Languages themselves consist of and can be conceived as exhibiting many different types or combinations of language-games. Even Augustine's account of language might have a limited value if instead of claiming that it gives us the essence of all languages we should take it as a description of one type of language-game. In it human beings would communicate exclusively by means of names, and each name would be used to refer to some object. Wittgenstein gives an example in which this simple type of language-game might be 'played'.

> Let us imagine a language for which the description given by Augustine is right. The language is meant to serve for communication between a builder A and an assistant B. A is building with building-stones: there are blocks, pillars, slabs and beams. B has to pass the stones, and that in the order in which A needs them. For this purpose they use a language consisting of the words "block", "pillar", "slab", "beam". A calls them out;—B brings the stone which he has learnt to bring at such-and-such a call.—Conceive this as a complete primitive language.

Augustine, we might say, does describe a system of communication; only not everything that we call language is this system. And one has to say this in many cases where the question arises "Is this an appropriate description or not?" The answer is: "Yes, it is appropriate, but only for this narrowly circumscribed region, not for the whole of what you were claiming to describe."

It is as if someone were to say: "A game consists in moving objects about on a surface according to certain rules . . ."—and we replied: You seem to be thinking of board games, but there are others. You can make your definition correct by expressly restricting it to those games.[23]

For Wittgenstein the notion of a language-game serves a number of functions. Sometimes he thinks of a language-game as a simplified model of a language, a tool to be used in the analysis of complex, many-sided ordinary language. Such, for example, is the use of the simple language-game by the builder and his assistant, previously described, in which the only expressions used are names for objects and in which the primary purpose of the communication is that of *giving an order* to fetch a particular kind of object. A somewhat more complicated example of a related type of language-game, by which to illustrate the use of language to give orders to someone, might be that in which, in addition to using names for objects, one were also to employ color words or numerals as in sending someone shopping and giving him a slip marked 'five red apples'.[24]

Of course there are countless examples of both simplified and more complex language-games in which the basic function to which language is put is different from those illustrated in the foregoing.

There are as many language-games as there are uses of language or ways of using sentences.

But how many kinds of sentences are there? Say assertion, question, and command?—There are *countless* kinds: countless different kinds of use of what we call "symbols", "words", "sentences". And this multiplicity is not something fixed, given once for all; but new types of language, new language-games, as we may say, come into existence, and others become obsolete and get forgotten. (We can get a *rough picture* of this from the changes in mathematics.)

Here the term "language-*game*" is meant to bring into prominence the fact that the *speaking* of language is part of an activity, or a form of life.

Review the multiplicity of language-games in the following examples, and in others:

Giving orders, and obeying them—
Describing the appearance of an object, or giving its measurements—
Constructing an object from a description (a drawing)—
Reporting an event—
Speculating about an event—
Forming and testing a hypothesis—
Presenting the results of an experiment in tables and diagrams—
Making up a story; and reading it—
Play-acting—

Singing catches—
Guessing riddles—
Making a joke; telling it—
Solving a problem in practical arithmetic—
Translating from one language into another—
Asking, thanking, cursing, greeting, praying.

—It is interesting to compare the multiplicity of the tools in language and of the ways they are used, the multiplicity of kinds of word and sentence, with what logicians have said about the structure of language. (Including the author of the *Tractatus Logico-Philosophicus*.)[25]

A language-game in one of its uses, then, is a simplified model embedded in a form of life, a clear instance of some characteristic use of language in a typical life situation.

I shall in the future again and again draw your attention to what I shall call language games. These are ways of using signs simpler than those in which we use the signs of our highly complicated everyday language. Language games are the forms of language with which a child begins to make use of words. The study of language games is the study of primitive forms of language or primitive languages. If we want to study the problems of truth and falsehood, of the agreement and disagreement of propositions with reality, of the nature of assertion, assumption, and question, we shall with great advantage look at primitive forms of language in which these forms of thinking appear without the confusing background of highly complicated processes of thought. When we look at such simple forms of language, the mental mist which seems to enshroud our ordinary use of language disappears. We see activities, reactions, which are clear-cut and transparent. On the other hand we recognize in these simple processes forms of language not separated by a break from our more complicated ones. We see that we can build up the complicated forms from the primitive ones by gradually adding new forms.[26]

Further, a relatively simple language-game may not only be an analytical tool for understanding a more complex and rich language, it may, in some cases, constitute the entire rudimentary or primitive language actually used by some individuals. "It is easy to imagine a language consisting only of orders and reports in battle.—Or a language consisting only of questions and expressions for answering yes and no. And innumerable others."[27] Language-games are themselves languages.

The appeal to the notion of language-games is closely intertwined with the appeal to the notion of *use* as a major key to the analysis of the concept of meaning. To explain the meaning of a linguistic expression is to point to the use it has; and this in turn can be clarified by studying that use in some appropriate language-game.

I want to say the place of a word in grammar is its meaning.

But I might also say: the meaning of a word is what the explanation of its meaning explains. . . .

The explanation of the meaning explains the use of the word.

The use of a word in the language is its meaning.

Grammar describes the use of words in the language. So it has somewhat the same relation to the language as the description of a game, the rules of a game, have to the game.[28]

One of the fruits of this reorientation is that it not only overcomes the narrow constrictions of relying on the naming-relation as allegedly the key to all uses of language, but also shows up the inadequacy of thinking of the meaning of a name as consisting in the object correlated with the name. Let us dwell for a moment on this latter point.

When one asks for the meaning of a name, the traditional answer is that the name is correlated with its object and that the object so correlated *is the meaning* of the name. Thus in the case of a person's name, the meaning is the person referred to; the meaning of the name is identified with the *bearer* of the name. However, there is a fundamental difficulty with this conception of meaning. For suppose that the bearer of a name dies. It would follow, on the above view, that the name no longer has a meaning; one can no longer meaningfully say, on the present theory, for example, "Mr. N. N. is dead." Since the name, "Mr. N. N." no longer has a meaning, the entire sentence lacks sense. But this is absurd. Surely the correct view is that "when Mr. N. N. dies one says that the bearer of the name dies, not that the meaning dies."[29] The meaning of a name and the bearer of it are altogether different.

To overcome these kinds of difficulties and objections, while yet preserving the basic presupposition that the meaning of a name does consist of the object correlated with the name, various philosophic theories have been devised. One example is the theory of logical atomism of the kind Wittgenstein had defended in the *Tractatus*. According to that philosophy, there are *genuine* names and these are correlated with the indestructible simple objects that belong to the permanent nature of the world. Thus, according to this theory, while the sword Excalibur as a composite 'object' may be destroyed, the ultimate simples of which it is composed cannot be. How then, on this view, do we account for the fact that a sentence such as "Excalibur has a sharp blade" has sense, even if the object to which 'Excalibur' refers is broken into pieces? In order to get around this difficulty, the theory of logical atomism denies that the expression 'Excalibur' is a real name. "The word 'Excalibur' must disappear when the sense is analyzed and its place be taken by words which name simples. It will be reasonable to call these words real names."[30] The theory of meaning of logical atomism, the later Wittgenstein would say, is a desperate and misguided maneuver to preserve the claim that the meaning of a name is the object with which it is correlated. It results from a failure to examine the use of names (as of other types of linguistic expressions) in ordinary language.

The term 'language-game' is meant to bring into prominence the fact that the uses and applications of language are normally part of some wider activity or 'form of life'. Consider an ordinary sentence such as 'This is red'. One cannot read off straightaway, from this sentence, what its actual use might be, for what it means is as various as the contexts in which it might be used. For example, this same sentence could be employed in different language-games, depending on the surrounding activities in which it is used. Thus 'This is red' can be used to *describe* the color of some object or surface; to *define* ostensively, by means of a sample, the meaning of the word 'red'; *as a line in a play* uttered by an actor; *as an item of instruction* in teaching someone the English language; *as a coded message* or password in a secret undertaking; *as a translation* of a sentence from a foreign language; and so on. The sentence 'This is red' has no independent, self-contained, 'real' meaning apart from all these settings in which it might be used. Its particular sentence-meaning is a function of, and depends for its clarification on, the distinctive features of the particular context in which the sentence is used to accomplish some particular purpose.

GRAMMAR AND GRAMMATICAL RULES

The terms 'grammar', 'grammatical considerations', 'grammatical analysis', and the like, play a central role in Wittgenstein's treatment of language. Grammar is of fundamental importance in understanding the workings of language and therefore of human thought. To perform a grammatical analysis is to make explicit the rules that determine the meaning of a linguistic expression. The task of becoming clear through grammatical analysis of the use of some expression is not ordinarily simple. The relevant distinctions, the comparisons and contrasts, rarely lie on the surface. Very often what are, upon analysis, shown to be grammatical sentences, i.e., sentences that express some conventional rule for the use of some expression, do not appear as such. Metaphysical statements, for example, may often be defended as fact-stating and as true when in fact they are only grammatical and therefore neither fact-stating nor either true or false. Mathematical statements, too, will frequently not be recognized to be fundamentally grammatical sentences, and instead will be taken as disclosing some 'eternal' truth. In addition, each of the following is a grammatical sentence, although it appears in another guise: "The colors green and blue can't be in the same place simultaneously"; "3 x 18 inches won't go into 3 feet"; "Every rod has a length"; "This body has extension."[31]

The sense in which Wittgenstein uses the term 'grammar' has relatively little to do with ordinary syntactical distinctions or the classification of parts of speech. Indeed, in some cases a grammatical analysis in the present sense might even come into conflict with the ordinary use of the term 'grammar'. According to ordinary grammar the sentences, 'I have a toothache' and 'He has a toothache' are such that the use of the verb 'to have' has the *same* grammatical role in both sentences. According to Wittgenstein, however, the 'depth-grammar' of 'have' is *different* in each case. His reason is that there is no such thing, strictly speaking, as *verification* of the proposition 'I have a toothache', since the question 'How do you know that you have a toothache?' is nonsensical. Thus the statement 'I don't know whether I have a toothache' is absurd, whereas it makes perfectly good sense to say of another person 'I don't know whether he has a toothache'. Because of these differences, one cannot regard 'He has a toothache' and 'I have a toothache' as examples of the same underlying general form '*x has* a toothache'. The grammar of 'have' operates according to a rule for first person singular present tense use in connection with a pain that is different from the use of 'have' in connection with *other* persons.

A grammatical analysis in Wittgenstein's sense can serve to clear up a philosophic muddle that arises from not recognizing that in our use of a certain term we are tacitly appealing to some rule of use that does not belong to that term. Consider, as another example of this, St. Augustine's puzzlement over the question 'What is time?' In asking this question Augustine revealed that he was unclear about the grammar of the word 'time' and related expressions. Thus Augustine is puzzled by the alleged fact that we cannot measure time "for the past can't be measured, as it is gone by; and the future can't be measured because it has not yet come. And the present can't be measured for it has no extension." At the bottom of this puzzlement is Augustine's failure to be clear about the use of the word 'measurement', and to realize that far from having the same meaning when we speak of the measurement of lengths of spatial objects and the measurement of time, the term 'measurement' has different meanings in both cases. Augustine applies the word as if it had the same meaning; he applies the expressions 'length' and 'measurement of length' to time as if they meant what they do in connection with spatial objects.

Augustine, we might say, thinks of the process of measuring a *length:* say, the distance between two marks on a travelling band which passes us, and of which we can only see a tiny bit (the present) in front of us. Solving the puzzle will consist of comparing what we mean by "measurement" (the grammar of the word "measurement") when applied to a distance on a travelling band with the grammar of the word when applied to time. The problem may seem simple, but its extreme difficulty is due to the fascination which the analogy between the two similar structures can exert on us. (It is helpful here to remember that it is sometimes impossible for a child to believe that one word can have two meanings.)[32]

Let us take as a further example of the sort of grammatical analysis Wittgenstein is concerned with, the typical but frequent confusion on the part of philosophers of grammatical statements with factual or empirical statements.

The distinction between a grammatical rule (which is not either true or false), and an empirical assertion (and so either true or false), is a distinction not always easy to carry out in practice. Whether a sentence is to be assigned to one classification or the other can only be determined after analysis. Consider, for example, the controversies about whether machines can think. It may turn out, Wittgenstein suggests, that far from there being purely empirical questions at issue here, it is at bottom a matter to be settled by clarifying and reaching agreement about the grammar (the grammatical rules) for the terms 'machine' and 'think'.

Or take, as another example, the question whether every rod has a length. The statement 'Every rod has a length' is at first glance a statement that makes a generalization about all rods, and hence can be considered as either true or false. But Wittgenstein maintains this sentence is best regarded as a grammatical proposition. It tells us something about how we are to understand the use of the phrase 'the length of a rod'. While we can properly use the phrase 'the length of a rod' we do not use the expression 'length of a sphere' because there is no rule for determining the use of this phrase; it is a phrase without a meaning; it is not part of a language-game. With respect to the phrase 'the length of a rod', it makes no sense to imagine its opposite. The 'opposite' of a grammatical rule is simply a different grammatical rule. On the other hand, 'This table has the same length as the one over there' is either true or false; it puts to work the phrase ('length of an object'). With respect to this application one can say either the statement is true, or its opposite holds ('these two tables do not have the same length').[33]

Suppose that on measurement we found different values for the ratio of radius to circumference—should we then say that we had enclosed the number π in different intervals? [Should we assume that we had measured π in the same sense in which a physical constant is measured?] Obviously not. For if all those intervals happened to be too large, we should not suppose that the value of π was greater, but should say that we had made a mistake. But then the real significance of the number π is clear. No measurement can tell us the value of π or between what values it is to be found, the number π is rather the *standard* by which we judge the quality of a measurement. (We cannot measure the number π, for it is the number π by which we measure the precision of our observations.) The standard is given to us before we start measuring; this is why I cannot alter the measurement. Thus when we say, π has such and such a value, e.g., $\pi = 3.14159265$ . . . , this cannot mean that we want to say anything about the actual measurements, but only that we are stipulating when a measurement procedure is to be counted as correct and when not. Thus the axioms of geometry have the character of stipulations concerning the language in which we want to describe spatial objects. They are rules of syntax. The rules of syntax are not about anything; they are laid down by us.

We can stipulate only something that we ourselves do.

We can postulate only rules according to which we propose to speak. We cannot postulate states of affairs.

At first blush it seems as though the axioms of geometry did tell us something. Take, for example, the proposition that the sum of the angles of a triangle is 180°; does it not tell us something? Can it not be true or false? How can mere syntax teach us anything of this kind? Suppose a measurement had yielded 190°. What should we say? 'We have made a mistake.' Thus the only value attaching to the proposition that the sum of the angles of a triangle is 180° is this, that it distinguishes erroneous from non-erroneous methods of measuring angles. It can never tell us anything about a state of affairs. And this shows yet again that in geometry we are never dealing with reality but only with spatial possibilities.

Discoveries about space are discoveries about what there is in space.

In mathematics it is just as impossible to discover anything as it is in grammar.

Geometry plus physics is syntax for the totality.[34]

There is an important difference between saying 'This rod is three feet long' as a result of measuring some object, and saying 'The angle sum of a Euclidean triangle is 180 degrees'. For the first is not part of the grammar of ordinary arithmetic, nor of the grammar of using the word 'length'. It is a statement whose truth or falsity has to be established by examining the object through accepted measuring procedures. That this object is three feet long is not to assert something about the use of the terms 'length', 'object', 'three feet' or 'measurement'. The grammar of these terms, taken separately, is already established by certain grammatical rules. What results we are going to get, how we are going to apply these rules in the particular circumstances when we conduct the measurement of the length of a particular object, cannot be established simply by consulting the grammar of these terms. It must be determined by appealing to the observational results of measuring this object. Thus it is perfectly compatible with the grammar of the expressions 'length', 'measurement', and 'physical object' for the length of this physical object to be 3 feet, 6 feet, or some other length. The rules of grammar for these expressions have nothing to say about that. Any one of these results would fall within range of possible applications of these terms and be compatible with the grammar of these terms. Which one of these applications we are going to select as a correct description of the length of this object will have to be established by an appeal to observation, not by consulting the grammatical rules that set out the uses of the terms in question.

On the other hand, to say that the sum of the angles of a Euclidean triangle is 180 degrees is to make a grammatical assertion; it is to say something about the way in which the term 'triangle' is being used in a system of rules specified by the postulates and theorems of Euclidean geometry. These constitute the language of Euclidean geometry and serve to define how the term 'triangle' is being used in this language-game. Thus if we find by measuring the angle sum of a triangular object that its angle sum is not 180 degrees, we shall be obliged to say not that we have found a falsification of the statement 'The angle sum of a triangle is 180 degrees' but rather that we cannot describe that object as triangular. The statement 'The angle sum of a triangle is 180 degrees' goes along with the meaning of 'triangle' (in the Euclidean language-game). If we find any other result than 180 degrees we shall simply have to forefeit our right to use the term 'triangle' in the Euclidean sense to describe the object. In short, if we insist on using the term 'Euclidean triangle' to describe the object before us, then if the outcome of our measurements is such that the sum of the angles is other than 180 degrees, we shall have to say that *we have made a mistake in our measurements*. For we cannot say 'this is a triangle' in the Euclidean sense and have anything else than an angle sum of 180 degrees. It would be a violation of the rule of use of the term 'triangle' in the Euclidean sense to allow for any other angle sum, and therefore no possible experience or measurement of a physical object or configuration can possibly alter the language of Euclidean geometry or disturb its rules and how they specify the meanings of its terms.

When Wittgenstein claims that the explanation of the meaning of various expressions in a language-game involves making explicit the grammatical rules that govern their use, he does not intend by this that all rules are of the kind we find in a carefully formulated, rigorous calculus. Some languages are of this character, for example mathematics and some scientific languages. The rules there are carefully formulated and codified. On the other hand, there are many languages in which the mastery of rules, the acquisition of competence in their use, is not necessarily accompanied by any capacity on the part of one who has this competence to state the rules. Nor need it be the case that in every such language the rules, even if made explicit, are sharp, rigorous, and exact. Some rules are rough, others exact; some implicit, others explicit. Yet, whatever kind they may be these rules determine the meaning, i.e., the correct use of expressions.

I said that the meaning of a word is its role in the calculus of language. (I compared it to a piece in chess). Now let us think how we calculate with a word, for instance with the word "red". We are told where the color is situated; we are told the shape and size of the colored patch of the colored object; we are told whether the color is pure or mixed, light or dark, whether it remains constant or changes, etc. etc. Conclusions are drawn from the propositions, they are translated into diagrams and into behavior, there is drawing, measurement, and calculation. But think of the meaning of the word "oh!" If we were asked about it, we would say "'oh'! is a sigh; we say, for instance, things like 'Oh, it is raining already'". And that would describe the use of the word. But what corresponds now to the calculus, the complicated game that we play with other words? In the use of the words "oh!", or "hurrah", or "hm", there is nothing comparable.[35]

Frege's conception of sense, and Wittgenstein's views as stated in the *Tractatus,* require that a logically sound language employ only those expressions that have exact and determinate sense. The crystalline model of a logically perspicuous language, if the latter is going to picture the ultimate structure of reality, cannot tolerate fuzziness, inexactness, or indeterminacy. The rules of such a language must be the rules of a rigorously formulated calculus. In his *Philosophical Investigations* Wittgenstein describes the 'illusion' that infects this kind of philosophy, the very one that he had developed in the *Tractatus:*

> Thought, language, now appear to us as the unique correlate, picture, of the world. These concepts: proposition, language, thought, world, stand in line one behind the other, each equivalent to each. . . .
> Thought is surrounded by a halo.—Its essence, logic, presents an order, in fact the a priori order of the world: that is, the order of *possibilities,* which must be common to both world and thought. But this order, it seems, must be *utterly simple.* It is *prior* to all experience, must run through all experience; no empirical cloudiness or uncertainty can be allowed to affect it—it must rather be of the purest crystal. But this crystal does not appear as an abstraction; but as something concrete, indeed, as the most concrete, as it were the *hardest* thing there is (*Tractatus Logico-Philosophicus* No. 5.5563).
> We are under the illusion that what is peculiar, profound, essential, in our investigation, resides in its trying to grasp the incomparable essence of language. That is, the order existing between the concepts of proposition, word, proof, truth, experience, and so on. This order is a *super*-order between—so to speak—*super*-concepts. Whereas, of course, if the words "language", "experience", "world", have a use, it must be as humble a one as that of the words "table", "lamp", "door".[36]

It is against this conception of the nature of meaning and language that Wittgenstein's later philosophy rebelled. Neither language nor logic is something sublime. Grammar, as the newer version of what 'logic' is, must take language as we find it in actual life in all its diversity and richness; it is not something crystalline and 'pure'. Language is enmeshed in life. As a result we must attend, in our grammar, to whatever degrees of exactness or inexactness, clarity or fuzziness, the various uses of language as a living activity display.

> For remember that in general we don't use language according to strict rules—it hasn't been taught us by means of strict rules, either. *We,* in our discussions on the other hand, constantly compare language with a calculus proceeding according to exact rules.
> This is a very one-sided way of looking at language. In practice we very rarely use language as such a calculus. For not only do we not think of the rules of usage—of definitions, etc.—while using language, but when we are asked to give such rules, in most cases we aren't able to do so. We are unable clearly to circumscribe the concepts we use; not because we don't know their real definition, but because there is no real 'definition' to them. To suppose that there *must* be would

be like supposing that whenever children play with a ball they play a game according to strict rules.

When we talk of language as a symbolism used in an exact calculus, that which is in our mind can be found in the sciences and in mathematics. Our ordinary use of language conforms to this standard of exactness only in rare cases. Why then do we in philosophizing constantly compare our use of words with one following exact rules? The answer is that the puzzles which we try to remove always spring from just this attitude towards language.[37]

OSTENSIVE DEFINITIONS

There are various techniques for explaining the meaning of a linguistic expression. One technique, helpful in explaining the meaning of those general terms whose meaning is fixed with precision by means of a verbal stipulative definition, consists in specifying the necessary and sufficient conditions—the common, essential properties—of the concept represented by the term. Where no such fixed, essential properties are specified, one may explain the meaning of a general term by giving many examples (of which there are normally an indefinitely large number) that fall under the concept represented by the term, even though these various examples may be related only by certain family resemblances.

Still another technique for explaining the meaning of a term is the use of *ostensive definitions*. Wittgenstein discusses at length this last type of explanation of meaning in *Philosophical Grammar* and in *Philosophical Investigations*. It is worth pausing to explore what he has to say in connection with this topic, since it brings to the fore an important aspect of what it is to be a grammatical rule—what we shall later examine under the heading of 'the autonomy of grammar'.

To give an ostensive definition of some expression—for example of the name of a color, some material, a numeral, a chess piece—is to point to some *sample*. That sample becomes a constituent of the grammatical rule itself—the definition that explains the expression being defined in this way. The sample serves as a *paradigm*. Insofar as the sample serves in this way, we are dealing with a matter of grammar, not with an *application* of the grammatical rule thus established.

The interpretation of written and spoken signs by ostensive definitions is not an *application* of language, but part of the grammar. The interpretation remains at the level of generality preparatory to any application.

. . . .

That one empirical proposition is true and another false is no part of grammar. What belongs to grammar are all the conditions (the method) necessary for comparing the proposition with reality. That is, all the conditions necessary for the understanding (of the sense).[38]

An ostensive definition, being a grammatical rule, is a *preparation* for 'making a move in a language-game'; it is not itself such a 'move'. It is part of learning how to play a game, not yet to actually play a particular game. The playing of an actual game—the use of the rule, along with other rules—belongs to the domain of *application*.

Consider the case of the use of the term 'meter'. We define the use of this term by saying that anything will have the length of one meter if it can be made to coincide at its end points with a particular bar kept in Paris. But what of that bar kept in Paris? Does it have a length of one meter? Wittgenstein points out that it makes no sense to say that it does. The reason is that the bar plays the very special role in the language-game which defines what it is to be a meter. Insofar as this bar plays that role in this language-game, it cannot itself be an object to which we *apply* the term 'one meter long'.[39] A similar situation would hold if we were to define what a particular color is, say, sepia, by keeping a sample of it. "Let us imagine samples of colour being preserved in Paris like the standard meter. We define: sepia means the color of the standard sepia which is there kept hermetically sealed. Then it will make no sense to say of this sample either that it is of this color or that it is not."[40] The reason we cannot say that the samples are, respectively, of a length of one meter or colored sepia is that each, respectively, constitutes the paradigm by which meter lengths or being colored sepia can be ascribed or applied to *other* objects. Paradigms are rules in a language-game that establish a means of representation, a way of speaking; but the object used as paradigm, in being part of the rule that sets out the meaning of a term, is not itself something to which the term is applied. "This sample is an instrument of the language used in ascriptions of color. In this language-game it is not something that is represented, but is a means of representation."[41]

If by an 'ostensive definition' one intends a direct correlation between a name and an object, without involving or presupposing a whole network of signs in interconnection with one another, then this is a view of ostensive definition (as it is found in the *Tractatus*) that Wittgenstein now rejects.

It may seem to us as if the other grammatical rules for a word had to follow from its ostensive definition; since after all an ostensive definition, e.g. "that is called 'red' " determines the meaning of the word "red".

But this definition is only those words plus pointing to a red object, e.g. a red piece of paper. And is this definition really unambiguous? Couldn't I have used the very same one to give the word "red" the meaning of the word "paper", or "square", or "shiny", or "light", or "thin" etc. etc.?

However, suppose that instead of saying "that is called 'red'" I had phrased my definition "that color is called 'red'". That certainly is unambiguous, but only because the expression 'color' settles the grammar of the word "red" up to this last point. (But here questions could arise like "do you call just *this* shade of color red, or also other similar shades?'') Definitions might be given like this: the color of this patch is called "red", its shape "ellipse".

I might say: one must already understand a great deal of a language in order to understand that definition. Someone who understands that definition must already know where the words ("red", "ellipse") are being put, where they belong in language.[42]

In order then for an ostensive definition to work, it is necessary that it be considered as part of a wider system or 'calculus' of rules and concepts. It cannot stand by itself or work in a vacuum. If for example one is going to explain by means of an ostensive definition what the color sepia is by offering a sample of this color, it is necessary for the person to whom this definition is being offered to understand, among other things, the concept of being colored. Without this preparatory background of a network of other concepts and rules, the ostensive definition will not perform successfully.

So one might say: the ostensive definition explains the use—the meaning— of the word when the overall role of the word in language is clear. Thus if I know that someone means to explain a color-word to me the ostensive definition "That is called 'sepia'" will help me to understand the word. . . . One has already to know (or be able to do) something in order to be capable of asking a thing's name. But what does one have to know?

When one shows someone the king in chess and says: "This is the king", this does not tell him the use of this piece—unless he already knows the rules of the game up to this last point: the shape of the king. You could imagine his having learnt the rules of the game without ever having been shown an actual piece. The shape of the chessman corresponds here to the sound or shape of a word.

. . . .

Consider this further case: I am explaining chess to someone; and I begin by pointing to a chessman and saying: "This is the king; it can move like this, . . . and so on."—In this case we shall say: the words "This is the king" (or "This is called the 'king'") are a definition only if the learner already 'knows what a piece in a game is'. That is, if he has already played other games, or has watched other people playing 'and understood'—*and similar things*. Further, only under these conditions will he be able to ask relevantly in the course of learning the game: "What do you call this?"—that is, this piece in a game.[43]

THE AUTONOMY OF GRAMMAR

Can an ostensive definition come into collision with the other rules for the use of a word?—It might appear so; but rules can't collide, unless they contradict each other. That aside, it is they that determine a meaning; there isn't a meaning that they are answerable to and could contradict.[44]

There is a sense in which we say that the result of using or applying a grammatical rule, for example an ostensive definition, in some particular circumstances, is not arbitrary; that what one says is supported by observations, or can be supported in some way by reasons of an acceptable sort. Thus with an already accepted rule for measuring (i.e., for representing, defining) lengths in terms of inches, and given the procedures for carrying out a measurement, I can report that the length of this object is nine inches. This treatment is not arbitrary. It can be adequately supported by observations. On the other hand, the adoption of the rules for *defining* what it is to be an inch are not to be characterized as *not* arbitrary in the foregoing sense. One cannot give reasons for saying the adoption of the rules is not arbitrary in the same way, in which the *application* of the rules can be said to give a result that is not arbitrary.

The rules of grammar are arbitrary in the same sense as the choice of a unit of measurement. But that means no more than that the choice is independent of the length of the objects to be measured and that the choice of one unit is not 'true' and of another 'false' in the way that a statement of length is true or false. Of course that is only a remark on the grammar of the word "unit of length".[45]

It would make no sense to say, for example, that the metric system, as contrasted with the British Imperial system, is the one according to which Nature 'really' works. *Any* system one adopts is a matter of convention. One cannot appeal to some description of reality by which to justify, i.e., to give reasons for, the adoption of some grammatical rule or system of grammatical rules (language system, conceptual scheme).

The connection between "language and reality" is made by definitions of words, and these belong to grammar, so that language remains self-contained and autonomous.[46]

One cannot give a description of reality that does not already use some grammatical rule in the giving of such a description.

If I explain the meaning of a word 'A' to someone by pointing to someone and saying 'This is A', then this expression may be meant in two different ways. Either it is itself a proposition already, in which case it can only be understood once the meaning of 'A' is known, i.e. I must now leave it to chance whether he takes it as I meant it or not. Or the sentence is a definition. Suppose I have said to someone 'A is ill', but he doesn't know who I mean by 'A', and I now point at a man, saying 'This is A'. Here the expression is a definition, but this can only be understood if he has already gathered what kind of object it is through his understanding of the grammar of the proposition 'A is ill'. But this means that any kind of explanation of a language presupposes a language already. . . . I cannot use language to get outside language.[47]

The rules of grammar are *conventions*. They are neither true nor false. On the other hand, one may assert various *propositions* that purport to describe some segment of reality. Such propositions are either true or false. However, the formulation of these propositions rests upon and makes use of various grammatical conventions. Their *sense* (if not their actual truth or falsity) is based on the use of some grammatical rule (or rules). The justification of the grammatical rules does not rest on the propositions; it is the other way around—the sense of the proposition rests on the grammatical system it employs, and its truth or falsity upon what we find to be the case.

I do not call a rule of representation a convention if it can be justified in propositions: propositions describing what is represented and showing that the representation is adequate. Grammatical conventions cannot be justified by describing what is represented. Any such description already presupposes the grammatical rules. That is to say, if anything is to count as nonsense in the grammar which is to be justified, then it cannot at the same time pass for sense in the grammar of the propositions that justify it (etc.). . . .

The possibility of explaining these things always depends on someone else using language in the same way as I do. If he states that a certain string of words makes sense to him, and it makes none to me, I can only suppose that in this context he is using words with a different meaning from the one I give them, or else is speaking without thinking.[48]

Since there are any number of possible ways of describing reality—by using one or another grammatical rule in giving such descriptions, there is no absolute, language-independent, preferential status that attaches to one rule rather than another; there are no reasons in the nature of things, i.e., in reality, to justify the adoption of one rule rather than another. We are obliged to use some method of representation, and this already commits us to the use of some language scheme. The adoption of one rather than another language system for accomplishing a description cannot be supported by appealing to reality, for this would involve giving a *description* of reality and this makes use of some system of conceptual (grammatical) representation. It is in this sense that the adoption of any language system is arbitrary.

Grammar is not accountable to any reality. It is grammatical rules that determine meaning (constitute it) and so they themselves are not answerable to any meaning and to that extent are arbitrary.[49]

. . . .

The rules of grammar cannot be justified by showing that their application makes a representation agree with reality. For this justification would itself have to describe what is represented. And if something can be said in the justification and is permitted by its grammar—why shouldn't it also be permitted by the grammar that I am trying to justify? Why shouldn't both forms of expressions have the same freedom? And how could what the one says restrict what the other can say?[50]

Since the adoption of a language system (a set of grammatical rules) is a matter of convention, and so arbitrary, one cannot say that any one system of rules as such is either in agreement or in conflict with reality. It would not of course be correct to justify the adoption of some particular language system for the description of reality by the fact that this is the way in which certain terms are in fact used. Facts of usage are, to be sure, matters that can be established by empirical investigation. However, such descriptions of usage *mention* rather than *use* the words in question. What is in question now in the matter of establishing whether or not grammatical rules are arbitrary is the way in which we *use* various terms of language, not our mentioning them. With respect to the rules that govern the use of terms, there is no way of giving reasons for the adoption of one language system rather than another. One cannot give a reason for the adoption of one language system in the same sense in which one can give reasons for the result of applying a particular grammatical rule in some particular circumstance. One cannot give a reason for example for calling something a 'foot' "in the same sense of the word 'reason' as that in which a well-conducted measurement may give a 'reason' for the statement that a particular rod is less than four feet long."[51] It is the irrelevance of reasons in this sense to the adoption of language rules that is described by saying that their adoption is *arbitrary*.

While it is possible to derive logically some rules from other rules and thus give 'reasons' for the former, the adoption of the rules from which the first set is derived cannot appeal to reasons in the same sense. *They* must rest on convention and not either reason or reality. "A *reason* can only be given *within* a game. The links of the chain of reasons come to an end, at the boundary of the game."[52] Thus the adoption of an entire conceptual scheme or network of language (whatever the possibilities and options for logical ordering *within* the network) rests on convention and in this sense is arbitrary.

To say that *any* language-game is arbitrary is but another way of calling attention to the fact that it constitutes the result of an explicit or tacit adoption of certain conventions or rules for using the language in question. Languages vary in the precise ways in which they come to be adopted and the way their conventional rules are established. The growth of a natural language as spoken by countless individuals over the centuries is one thing, and the deliberate construction of a mathematical calculus by some individual creative mathematician or the invention of a theory in physics is another. Both are constructions. But whatever their internal differences, the important fact for our present consideration is that no language, whether ordinary or technical or rigidly formulated in terms of carefully stated rules, can claim for itself to be derived from something 'outside' in reality, and to whose logical structure it conforms. Rather, the construction of languages, of all sorts and varieties, is an exercise in human ingenuity; it is a product of man's activity, and cannot be understood in its status and function without taking into account that it is a human product.

CRITERIA

There are various types of grammatical rules. For example, some are ostensive definitions, others are verbal definitions that state 'necessary and sufficient conditions' as constituting the meaning of a general term. Still another variety of grammatical rule is that which formulates *criteria* for the meaning of a term. This last type is one to which Wittgenstein devoted much attention in his later philosophy, and plays an important role in his treatment of semantic questions. It has had a considerable influence on other philosophers, although it has also been the subject of much controversy and diverse interpretations.[53]

What is a criterion? As a first step in answering this question, let us say that in supplying a criterion or a group of criteria one is providing a justification for using a certain linguistic expression in a particular situation. On what basis, with what warrant, is one applying and using the expression under examination? The expression in question may, for example, be a proper name for a person (or object), or an adjective or verb used in a sentence to describe one or more individuals. In appealing to a criterion or set of criteria, one makes explicit a type of grammatical rule that governs the use of the expression in question. The rule calls attention to various kinds of items, the recognition of which may be used in order for the expression to be appropriately used.

Consider, by way of example, the use of the proper name 'Moses' in the Bible. An important way of making clear *who* is referred to in using that name in some sentence, is to provide criteria for that use. The criteria, so supplied, consist of a series or cluster of descriptions that help identify to whom one is referring, to whom one is applying the name 'Moses'.

We may say, following Russell: the name "Moses" can be defined by means of various descriptions. For example, as "the man who led the Israelites through the wilderness", "the man who lived at that time and place and was then called 'Moses'", "the man who as a child was taken out of the Nile by Pharaoh's daughter" and so on. . . .

But when I make a statement about Moses,—am I always ready to substitute some *one* of these descriptions for "Moses"? I shall perhaps say: By "Moses" I understand the man who did what the Bible relates of Moses, or at any rate a good deal of it. But how much? Have I decided how much must be proved false for me to give up my proposition as false? Has the name Moses got a fixed and unequivocal use for me in all possible cases?—Is it not the case that I have, so to speak, a whole series of props in readiness, and am ready to lean on one if another should be taken from under me and vice versa?[54]

To take another example, suppose someone were to assert that another person, John, is in pain. We might ask for evidence supporting the assertion. Among the grounds given by way of reply would be an appeal to criteria for ascribing the property pain to John. The use of the predicate 'pain' to describe John's state rests on certain criteria for the use of this predicate. These criteria call attention to various forms of behavior associated with pain, e.g., moaning, writhing, wincing, making grimaces.

John says he is in pain,
John is moaning,
John is writhing on the floor,
John is making various facial grimaces,
John is holding the part of his body where he locates his pain,
.
· (etc.),
.
Therefore, John is in pain.

What is *meant* by 'is in pain' is made clear by appealing to various behavioral *criteria* of pain.

The use of criterial evidence, as a way of explaining the meaning of a term and justifying its application, is normally done by appealing to multiple criteria, not to a single, isolated criterion. Thus, in accounting for our having the notion of personal identity, i.e., in using the phrase 'the same person' as applying to a particular individual,

many characteristics which we use as the criteria for identity coincide in the vast majority of cases. I am as a rule recognized by the appearance of my body. My body changes its appearance only gradually and comparatively little, and likewise my voice, characteristic habits, etc. only change slowly and within a narrow range. We are inclined to use personal names in the way we do, only as a consequence of these facts.[55]

The use of multiple criteria as a way of explaining the meaning of a term can be seen to hold both for singular terms (e.g., proper names) as well as for general terms (i.e., those conveying concepts).

Although the use of criterial evidence normally involves using several different criteria in combination, it is not the case that there is some *complete* list of such criteria either already available or to be sought for as an ideal. The notion of completeness is inapplicable to the concept of a criterial rule.

How should we have to imagine a complete list of rules for the employment of a word?—What do we mean by a complete list of rules for the employment of a piece in chess? Couldn't we always construct doubtful cases, in which the normal list of rules does not decide? Think e.g. of such a question as: how to determine who moved last, if a doubt is raised about the reliability of the players' memories?

The regulation of traffic in the streets permits and forbids certain actions on the part of drivers and pedestrians; but it does not attempt to guide the totality of their movements by prescription. And it would be senseless to talk of an 'ideal' ordering of traffic which should do that; in the first place we should have no idea what to imagine as this ideal. If someone wants to make traffic regulations stricter on some point or other, that does not mean that he wants to approximate to such an ideal.[56]

The use of criteria is not one of logical necessity or of mutual entailment. Thus the statement 'I see my hand move' may be taken as providing a criterion for asserting 'My hand moves'; or the statement 'I feel my finger touch my eye' may be taken as a criterion for 'My finger touches my eye'. Yet it is possible for the first statement in each pair to be true and the second false.

To say that my finger in tactile and kinaesthetic space moves from my tooth to my eye . . . means that I have those tactile and kinaesthetic experiences which we normally have when we say "my finger moves from my tooth to my eye". But what we regard as evidence for this latter proposition is, as we all know, by no means only tactile and kinaesthetic. In fact if I had the tactile and kinaesthetic sensations referred to, I might still deny the proposition "my finger moves etc. . . ." because of what I saw. The proposition is a proposition about physical objects. . . . The grammar of propositions which we call propositions about physical objects admits of a variety of evidences for every such proposition. It characterizes the grammar of the proposition "my finger moves, etc." that I regard the propositions "I see it move", "I feel it move", "He sees it move", "He tells me that it moves", etc. as evidences for it. Now if I say "I see my hand move", this at first sight seems to presuppose that I agree with the proposition "my hand moves". But if I regard the proposition "I see my hand move" as one of the evidences for the proposition "my hand moves", the truth of the latter is, of course, not presupposed in the truth of the former.[57]

To take another example, we normally regard our having certain sensations of wet and cold, certain visual experiences, and the presence of a falling barometer as criteria for our asserting that it is raining. However, it is possible that the statements reporting the former items (the criterial evidence) may be true, and the latter statement ('It is raining') to be false.[58]

Unlike, therefore, the Fregean requirement that in an ideal language the sense of an expression must be wholly determinate and exact, Wittgenstein, in turning to the workings of actual language, stresses that the sense of an expression can be partially indeterminate and inexact and yet be none the worse for this. The concepts we use and the sense we give them by criterial rules, can be exact enough for many purposes and therefore usable. While we can always make our concepts more precise to

serve some special purpose—while we can *add* criteria to already available ones to make the term so defined *more* determinate—there is no absolutely ideal language, no perfectly determinate sense to attach to every
expression in a language. The fact that a term may have some element of
indeterminateness of sense does not mean that it is therefore altogether
lacking in sense, that it is nonsensical, and that it can be of no use in a
language-game. The meanings of linguistic expressions need to be relativ-
ized to the languages in which they appear, to the purposes they serve,
and judged in terms of their effectiveness within conventionally established limits. We must always bear in mind that the limits are ones *we*
draw, and so we can always redraw them. There is no absolutely ideal and
uniquely correct way of doing this.

Wittgenstein frequently speaks of criteria as being types of *evidence*. It is important not to be misled by the use of this expression. For
we normally use the term 'evidence' to refer to those factual statements
(observational reports of individual occurrences or generalizations based
on observational data) that sanction the claim to the truth (or probable
truth) of some other statement that serves as the conclusion based on this
evidence. The term 'evidence' as Wittgenstein uses it to take into account
criterial evidence is wider than this ordinary use. 'Evidence', in his use,
includes ordinary factual evidence as well as 'criterial evidence'. In this
broad sense, a piece of 'evidence' serves as a justification or warrant for
using some expression or for making an assertion. In the case of criterial
evidence the reason, warrant, or justification consists in appealing to
some grammatical rule in support of one's use (application) of a linguistic
expression in a particular situation. The grammatical rule appealed to is
not to be regarded as a piece of factual (empirical) evidence. (However,
the adoption of the criterial rule may have been originally suggested by
such experience.) Once something functions as a criterion it is part of a
grammatical rule, and so is a matter of conventional decision, not of factual truth or falsity.

Thus Wittgenstein wishes to distinguish *criteria,* as grammatical and
so as having to do with explanations of the *meaning* of some expression,
from *symptoms,* which are factual, empirical, a matter of what is *found* to
hold in experience. Criteria are adopted as a matter of convention; their
adoption calls for a decision. Symptoms are found in experience, and are
not a matter of choice or decision. To distinguish these two types of 'evidence', we might say that criteria provide *noninductive* evidence,
whereas symptoms or other reports of observed phenomena constitute
inductive evidence.

Let us introduce two antithetical terms in order to avoid certain elementary
confusions: To the question "How do you know that so-and-so is the case?", we
sometimes answer by giving *'criteria'* and sometimes by giving *'symptoms'*. If
medical science calls angina an inflammation caused by a particular bacillus, and

we ask in a particular case "why do you say this man has got angina?" then the answer "I have found the bacillus so-and-so in his blood" gives us the criterion, or what we may call the defining criterion of angina. If on the other hand the answer was, "His throat is inflamed", this might give us a symptom of angina. I call "symptom" a phenomenon of which experience has taught us that it coincided, in some way or other, with the phenomenon which is our defining criterion. Then to say "A man has angina if this bacillus is found in him" is a tautology or it is a loose way of stating the definition of "angina". But to say, "A man has angina whenever he has an inflamed throat" is to make a hypothesis.[59]

Although there is an important distinction between criteria and symptoms, one cannot tell by simple inspection of a particular sentence whether it appeals to a criterion or describes a symptom. In certain situations—for example at a particular stage in the development of a science—what up to that point had been regarded as an empirically established 'symptom', may henceforth be treated as a criterion. A sentence can readily pass from being one that describes a symptom to one treated as a criterion. However, if a sentence is treated as a criterion—as a grammatical rule explanatory of the meaning of an expression—it cannot at the same time also be treated as a factual hypothesis, an empirical correlation whose truth rests upon observationally obtained data.

In practice, if you were asked which phenomenon is the defining criterion and which is a symptom, you would in most cases be unable to answer this question except by making an arbitrary decision *ad hoc*. It may be practical to define a word by taking one phenomenon as the defining criterion, but we shall easily be persuaded to define the word by means of what, according to our first use, was a symptom. Doctors will use names of diseases without ever deciding which phenomena are to be taken as criteria and which as symptoms; and this need not be a deplorable lack of clarity. For remember that in general we don't use language according to strict rules—it hasn't been taught us by means of strict rules, either.[60]

. . . .

Nothing is commoner than for the meaning of an expression to oscillate, for a phenomenon to be regarded sometimes as a symptom, sometimes as a criterion, of a state of affairs. And mostly in such a case the shift of meaning is not noted. In science it is usual to make phenomena that allow of exact measurement into defining criteria for an expression; and then one is inclined to think that now the proper meaning has been *found*. Innumerable confusions have arisen in this way.[61]

'MEANING' ('INTENDING') AND 'UNDERSTANDING'

When a speaker or writer uses a word we say he *intends* or *means* something by it, and when someone else hears or reads what has been said, he may *understand* what has been said. According to Wittgenstein, these two concepts—of meaning (intending) and understanding—are frequently identified with special types of consciousness or mental processes that 'accompany' the use of linguistic signs and make the latter 'come to life'. Meaning (intending) and understanding are taken to be certain types of 'inner' mental states, events, processes, or 'mechanisms' that are hidden from public view. They are said to take place 'in the mind' and to have a special mode of existence different from what can be observed in the form of 'outward behavior' in the 'material world'. Wittgenstein is radically opposed to this Cartesian, dualistic type of philosophy. According to him, meaning (intending) and understanding, along with other modes of 'thought', are identical with various activities in the use of language. Thinking, meaning, and understanding are not processes going on parallel to the use of language. They *are* the use of language, not separate from it.

Taken superficially, the two phrases 'to say (utter) something' and 'to mean something' seem comparable in that each may be taken to designate a special type of process. Moreover it would seem to make sense to say that the process designated by the latter phrase accompanies or 'lies behind' the process designated by the first phrase. But to believe this is to be caught in a philosophical mistake induced by the surface grammar of these expressions. There are not two *processes* here; for understanding and meaning (intending) are not processes at all. Hence it cannot be the case that one should 'accompany' or 'lie behind' the other. An explanation of what I mean (intend) by a word "is a definition; not a description of what goes on in me when I utter the word."[62] "Meaning it is not a process which accompanies a word."[63]

To understand an expression is to know how it can be used. To know how it can be used is to have acquired a competency, a mastery of the technique of using the expression in some language-game in accordance with the rules that govern its use. The evidence of having such understanding is not to be found by looking to see whether some mental process is taking place in the individual, but by seeing whether the individual can use the linguistic expression correctly in actual situations.

What does "to understand a word" mean?

We say to a child "No, no more sugar" and take it away from him. Thus he learns the meaning of the word "no". If, while saying the same words, we had given him a piece of sugar he would have learnt to understand the word differently. (In this way he has learnt to use the word, but also to associate a particular feeling with it, to experience it in a particular way.)

What constitutes the meaning of a word like "perhaps"? How does a child learn the use of the word "perhaps"? It may repeat a sentence it has heard from an adult like "*perhaps* she will come"; it may do so in the same tone of voice as the adult. (That is a kind of a game.) In such a case the question is sometimes asked: Does it already understand the word "perhaps" or is it only repeating it?—What shows that it really understands the word?—Well, that it uses it in particular circumstances in a particular manner—in certain contexts and with a particular intonation.

What does it mean "to understand the word 'perhaps'"?—Do *I* understand the word "perhaps"?—And how do I judge whether I do? Well, something like this: I know how it's used, I can explain its use to somebody, say by describing it in made-up cases. I can describe the occasions of its use, its position in sentences, the intonation it has in speech.—Of course this only means that "I understand the word 'perhaps'" comes to the same as: "I know how it is used etc."; not that I try to call to mind its entire application in order to answer the question whether I understand the word. More likely I would react to this question immediately with the answer "yes", perhaps after having said the word to myself once again, and as it were convinced myself that it's familiar, or else I might think of a single application and pronounce the word with the correct intonation and a gesture of uncertainty. And so on.[64]

To take another example, suppose, in a class in elementary arithmetic, the teacher has explained how to perform the operation of division of one number by another, and a pupil says "Now I understand." How does the teacher determine whether the pupil does understand? Is it a question of establishing whether there is some internal state, image, private experience, or process going on in the pupil's mind? Isn't it rather a matter of giving the pupil fresh test examples, and seeing whether the pupil can correctly *perform* the calculation, i.e., use the rules of division? Doesn't the pupil have an understanding of the expression 'division' by showing, through repeated application to various new examples that the pupil knows how to correctly apply the rules? Thus, since the rules constitute the sense of the expression 'division', can we not now say whether the pupil understands the concept 'division'?

Furthermore, consider the fact that a process of any kind takes place over a stretch of time, long or short. Heating a pot of water until it comes to a boil occupies a certain interval of time, just as does counting from one to a hundred, whether silently or out loud. Consider, however, a sentence such as "Today is Tuesday." Does the *intending* of this sentence (*not* the act of uttering it) or the *understanding* of it, take time, i.e., occupy a temporal interval? Wittgenstein suggests it would be misleading to describe intending and understanding as processes, for they do not occupy a time interval.

The understanding of language, as of a game, seems like a background against which a particular sentence acquires meaning.—But this understanding, the knowledge of the language, isn't a conscious state that accompanies the sentences of the language. Not even if one of its consequences is such a state. It's much more like the understanding or mastery of a calculus, something like the *ability* to multiply.

. . . .

In order to get clearer about the grammar of the word "understand", let's ask: *when* do we understand a sentence?—When we've uttered the whole of it? Or while uttering it?—Is understanding, like the uttering of a sentence, an articulated process and does its articulation correspond exactly to that of the sentence? Or is it non-articulate, something accompanying the sentence in the way a pedal note accompanies a melody?

How long does it take to understand a sentence?

And if we understand a sentence for a whole hour, are we always starting afresh?[65]

Moreover, let us ask ourselves how we decide whether someone intends something by a verbal sign, or understands it. What criteria do we use? Is it enough, indeed, to identify, even if we could, some physiologic (e.g., neural) process as going on? Would the criteria for such processes be identical with the criteria for establishing that there is something we should call 'intending' or 'understanding'? Shouldn't these be distinguished, so that, for example, we might be able to identify some process as taking place, and yet legitimately question whether there is some intention or understanding?

If I try to describe the process of intention, I feel first and foremost that it can do what it is supposed to only by containing an extremely faithful picture of what it intends. But further, that that too does not go far enough, because a picture, whatever it may be, can be variously interpreted; hence this picture too in its turn stands isolated. When one has the picture in view by itself it is suddenly dead, and it is as if something had been taken away from it, which had given it life before. It is not a thought, not an intention; whatever accompaniments we imagine for it, articulate or inarticulate processes, or any feeling whatsoever, it remains isolated, it does not point outside itself to a reality beyond.[66]

What all this adds up to is the rejection of any philosophy that would seek to assign the meaning of such terms as 'intending' and 'understanding' to private mental mechanisms or processes that are distinct from the multiple publicly observable occasions in which language is used. To understand 'understanding', 'intending' ('meaning'), and similar 'acts of thought', one should examine what is involved in acquiring competence in the use of language through overtly discoverable reliance on various teaching and learning situations. They have to do with the mastery of techniques for the application of various grammatical rules that govern the use of different linguistic expressions. The acquisition and mastery of techniques in the use of language are public matters. That a person has acquired and can use these techniques does not involve any appeal to hidden, private, mental mechanisms or processes. They can be tested for in a public way.

An 'inner process' stands in need of outward criteria.

. . . .

If I give anyone an order I feel it to be *quite enough* to give him signs. And I should never say: this is only words, and I have got to get behind the words. Equally, when I have asked someone something and he gives me an answer (i.e., a sign) I am content—that was what I expected—and I don't raise the objection: but that's a mere answer.

But if you say: "How am I to know what he means, when I see nothing but the signs he gives?" then I say: "How is *he* to know what he means, when he has nothing but the signs either?"[67]

THE PRIVATE LANGUAGE ARGUMENT

As previously noted, an important aspect of Wittgenstein's conception of language is that it is embedded in a 'form of life'—a set of activities in which the rules of a language-game serve as a basis for communication. Language exists in a linguistic community; it involves the use and application of grammatical rules. The rules include ostensive definitions, criteria, and 'strict' definitions that stipulate necessary and sufficient conditions. If one recognizes the foregoing crucial features of language, Wittgenstein would say, it should lead to the rejection of even the possibility of a private language. The very notion of a 'private language' would dispense with the requirement that language be embedded in the activities and practices of a linguistic community; it would also dispense with the requirement that the language be guided by the availability of grammatical rules for public adoption and use.

The conception of a private language appears in the writings of a number of modern and contemporary philosophers who have been influenced by the Cartesian theory of body-mind dualism. An important reason why Wittgenstein devoted an extended discussion in the *Philosophical Investigations* (Secs. 243–315) to arguing against the possibility of a private language is that, along with his analysis of psychological verbs (e.g., 'understanding', 'intending', 'expecting', 'wishing', 'willing', 'remembering', 'thinking'), it enabled him to mount a vigorous attack on the Cartesian tradition in the philosophy of mind. His 'private language argument' (i.e., his argument *against* the possibility of a private language) is one side of his general criticism of Cartesian dualism.

The theory of mind-body dualism envisages the mind as a substance different from yet linked to the body. The mind is an immaterial 'spiritual' or 'thinking' substance. To it belong various mental events, states, processes, and powers; it has its own internal 'mechanisms'. Mental phenomena are totally different from bodily (material) phenomena. The body as a distinct material substance has its distinctive physical (biological, physiologic, chemical, electrical, and so on) events, states, processes, causal connections, and powers. According to this philosophy, whereas bodily (physical) phenomena are accessible *externally,* i.e., to observation, description, and exploration, the mind's activities, states, and processes are accessible only to 'internal' observation, to introspection. Mental experiences are *private*. They cannot be known by others in the same direct and immediate way as they are known by the person whose experiences they are. What goes on in someone else's mind is known only at best by inference and by analogy. Certain philosophic sceptics would urge that they are never known at all. This Cartesian tradition is summed up in Gilbert Ryle's colorful phrase as the acceptance of the model of "the ghost in the machine."[68] Although it received a classic formulation and defense by Descartes, this theory was taken over with various modifications by other philosophers. It was adopted in one form or another by modern rationalists as well as by the classic British empiricists. It has persisted under many transformations in discussions of the philosophy of mind and epistemology well into our own day. This traditional conception of mind was a major target of Wittgenstein's later philosophy.

A good example of how this conception of mind affected the treatment of language is to be found in John Locke's *An Essay Concerning Human Understanding* (1690). Wittgenstein, in his assault on the notion of a private language, does not explicitly attack Locke's views. Nevertheless, it will be useful to quote the following passage as giving a clear and explicit statement of the kind of approach that Wittgenstein found objectionable. Locke writes:

> Words, in their primary or immediate signification, stand for nothing but *the ideas in the mind of him that uses them,* how imperfectly soever or carelessly those ideas are collected from the things which they are supposed to represent. When a man speaks to another, it is that he may be understood: and the end of speech is, that those sounds, as marks, may make known his ideas to the hearer. That then which words are the marks of are the ideas of the speaker: nor can any one apply them as marks, immediately, to anything else but the ideas that he himself hath: for this would be to make them signs of his own conceptions, and yet apply them to other ideas; which would be to make them signs and not signs of his ideas at the same time; and so in effect to have no signification at all. . . . A man cannot make his words the signs either of qualities in things, or of conceptions in the mind of another, whereof he has none in his own. Till he has some ideas of his own, he cannot suppose them to correspond with the conceptions of another man; nor can he use any signs for them: for thus they would be the signs of he knows not what, which is in truth to be the signs of nothing. But when he represents to himself other men's ideas by some of his own, if he consent to give them the same names that other men do, it is still to his own ideas; to ideas that he has, and not to ideas that he has not.[69]

Wittgenstein gives his formulation of what the conception of a private language would be.

> But could we also imagine a language in which a person could write down or give vocal expression to his inner experiences—his feelings, moods, and the

rest—for his private use?—Well, can't we do so in our ordinary language?—But that is not what I mean. The individual words of this language are to refer to what can only be known to the person speaking; to his immediate private sensations. So another person cannot understand the language.[70]

It is important, in understanding the sense in which Wittgenstein is using the phrase 'private language', not to confuse it with other uses of this expression. Thus it might be used to describe some specially devised code that a person could construct for his or her private use. In the latter case, if we use the term 'private language' to characterize such a code, we must recognize that it *could be* decoded; its rules *might be* deciphered and communicated to others. In that case not only would one understand what its originator meant by various expressions, but also in being made public it might be adopted by others. It is not this kind of 'private language' with which Wittgenstein is concerned. For such a language is a genuine language. It might, in fact, come to serve an entire linguistic community; its grammatical rules could be made explicit and employed by those who gain a competency in its use.

There is another common use of the term 'private' in connection with our ordinary experience that Wittgenstein does not wish to call into question and is not to be equated with the use of a 'private language' in the present sense. As Peter Geach reports:

> Of course Wittgenstein did not want to deny the obvious truth that people have a 'private' mental life, in the sense that they have for example thoughts they do not utter and pains they do not show; nor did he try to analyse away this truth in a neo-behaviouristic fashion. In one of his lectures he mentioned Lytton Strachey's imaginative description of Queen Victoria's dying thoughts. He expressly repudiated the view that such a description is meaningless because 'unverifiable'; it has meaning, he said, but only through its connexion with a wider, public, 'language-game' of describing people's thoughts; he used the simile that a chess-move worked out in a sketch of a few squares on a scrap of paper has significance through its connexion with the whole practice of playing chess.[71]

In the same vein, when Wittgenstein wishes to single out 'private language' for criticism he does not wish to deny the possibility of the use of a public language by some solitary, isolated individual (e.g., a Robinson Crusoe) or a soliloquizing monologuist. The use of language under these circumstances rests on and presupposes the presence of a public language, and so is not 'private' in the sense of the present discussion. Anyone coming upon such a private soliloquizing speaker might translate or interpret what the speaker is saying 'to himself'.

> A human being can encourage himself, give himself orders, obey, blame and punish himself; he can ask himself a question and answer it. So we could imagine human beings who spoke only in monologue; who accompanied their activities by talking to themselves.—An explorer who watched them and listened to their talk might succeed in translating their language into ours. (This would enable him to

predict these peoples's actions correctly, for he also hears them making resolutions and decisions.)[72]

By contrast with the foregoing uses of the term 'private language', the kind of 'private language' Wittgenstein is singling out for attack is not, he would say, a genuine language at all. It *cannot* in principle ever be made public. Its 'rules' are not only not communicable to others but, as he will argue, not genuine grammatical rules—not even for the person who would presumably 'use' such a 'language'. Wittgenstein's examination of this characterization of a putative 'private language' will show that the very notion of such a language is incoherent; it cannot therefore have any possible existence. Insofar as Cartesianism leads to the claim that the language to be used in describing mental experiences is a private language, it fails not only as a philosophy of mind but also as a philosophy of language.

With these preliminaries in mind, let us turn to an examination of Wittgenstein's strictures against the possibility of a private language. First, let us consider more carefully the characteristics of and claims made in behalf of private language by those who appeal to this idea.

The main characteristics of a private language are those that Wittgenstein states briefly in the passage quoted from *Philosophical Investigations*. They are three: (1) "The individual words of this language are to refer to what can only be known to the person speaking"; (2) The individual words of this language are to refer "to his immediate private sensations"; (3) "Another person cannot understand the language."

The first item has to do with the matter of *knowledge* of that to which the words in the private language refer. Only the person using the language can have this knowledge, since only the person speaking the language knows what the objects are to which the words in the language refer. The language is private because the knowledge is private, and the knowledge is private because the objects referred to by the words in the language are known only to the speaker of the language. To the sensations, known with certainty by the person who has them, names are assigned to refer to them as 'objects' of private experience. "It is as if when I uttered the word I cast a sidelong glance at the private sensation, as it were in order to say to myself: I know all right what I mean by it."[73] For the adherent of the concept of private language, the knowledge a person has of his or her own mental experiences (sensations such as colors seen, sounds heard, pains felt) are known *directly*, "from the inside," whereas any attempt to *know* what goes on in the mind of someone else can never be achieved. At best it is only possible to make an inference by analogy, to have a belief; for we must rely on a method that is "indirect" and "from the outside." All that we have access to is the "outward behavior" of the other person, never his private mental experiences. Any inference about what goes on in someone else's mind may be wrong. The advocate of private language could thus claim:

"So-and-so has excellent health, he never had to go to the dentist, never complained about toothache; but as toothache is a private experience, we can't know whether he hasn't had terrible toothache all his life."[74]

"I can only *believe* that someone else is in pain, but I *know* it if I am."[75]

"Well, only I can know whether I am really in pain: another person can only surmise it."[76]

The second characteristic of private language has to do with another sense of 'privacy', that of ownership. The words of the language are to refer to those mental experiences had by only one person—the speaker of the language. These sensations had by the speaker cannot be had by someone else; they cannot be shared by another person. "Another person can't have my pains."[77]

The third item draws the consequence of these two aspects of privacy (private knowledge, private ownership). The language is private in the sense that it cannot be *understood* by anyone but the speaker; it is *incommunicable* as a language.

Wittgenstein's criticism of the notion of a private language is conducted on several fronts. One criticism focuses on the supposed use of names to refer to private sensations. Such names, it is assumed, may be assigned by a process of private ostension. The speaker has a particular sensation (say the pain of a toothache, or the visual experience of seeing red), and to this sensation S, he assigns by private ostension in his own vocabulary the name 'S'. He may, it is claimed, be thought of as building up a table of such names by associating certain symbols with certain sensory experiences. He is henceforth able to use these names for other sensations insofar as the later sensations resemble the initial paradigm (exemplar) that served to assign the name in the original ostensive definition.

However, this putative process of assigning names to private experiences by means of private ostensive definitions fails to make available a set of usable names. The private ostensive definitions are not effective grammatical rules. One cannot appeal to such 'rules' to clarify or confirm the meaning of the symbols so introduced. One cannot justify using a name in new situations if it is, in principle, impossible to recapture in any reliable way the situation of the original introduction of the ostensive definition. Yet such impossibility would always be the case with private ostensive definitions. The ostensive definition could now only be appealed to in memory (or in imagination), and there is no way of checking a present memory image against the original sensory experience that provided the occasion for the introduction of the name in an ostensive definition. The 'rule' therefore is not an effectively usable rule. There are no reliable procedures for distinguishing correct from incorrect applications of a name in a private language.

Let us imagine the following case. I want to keep a diary about the recurrence of a certain sensation. To this end I associate it with the sign "E" and write this sign in a calendar for every day on which I have the sensation.—I will remark first of all that a definition of the sign cannot be formulated.—But still I can give myself a kind of ostensive definition.—How? Can I point to this sensation? Not in the ordinary sense. But I speak, or write the sign down, and at the same time I concentrate my attention on the sensation—and so, as it were, point to it inwardly.—But what is this ceremony for? For that is all it seems to be! A definition surely serves to establish the meaning of a sign.—Well, that is done precisely by the concentrating of my attention; for in this way I impress on myself the connexion between the sign and the sensation.—But "I impress it on myself" can only mean: this process brings it about that I remember the connexion *right* in the future. But in the present case I have no criterion of correctness. One would like to say: whatever is going to seem right to me is right. And that only means that here we can't talk about 'right'.

. . . .

Let us imagine a table (something like a dictionary) that exists only in our imagination. A dictionary can be used to justify the translation of a word X by a word Y. But are we also to call it a justification if such a table is to be looked up only in the imagination?—"Well, yes; then it is a subjective justification."—But justification consists in appealing to something independent.—"But surely I can appeal from one memory to another. For example, I don't know if I have remembered the time of departure of a train right and to check it I call to mind how a page of the time-table looked. Isn't it the same here?"—No; for this process has got to produce a memory which is actually *correct*. If the mental image of the time-table could not itself be *tested* for correctness, how could it confirm the correctness of the first memory? (As if someone were to buy several copies of the morning paper to assure himself that what it said was true.)

Looking up a table in the imagination is no more looking up a table than the image of the result of an imagined experiment is the result of an experiment.[78]

. . . .

Making sure that you know what 'seeing red' means, is good only if you can make use of this knowledge in a further case. Now what if I see a color again, can I say I made sure I knew what 'red' was so now I shall know that I recognize it correctly? In what sense is having said the words 'this is red' before a guarantee that I now see the same color when I say again I see red?[79]

Another consideration that shows the incoherence of the notion of a private language is its incapacity to serve as a language not only for the originator of the language, but as a possible medium of communication for others. The 'rules' of the private language cannot be adopted and used by anyone else, since the 'objects' (the sensations or private experiences that are the designata of the names of the privately established ostensive definitions) are inaccessible to anyone else. Such 'rules' cannot be learned by anyone. And if there are a number of such private languages, none of these can serve as a basis for intersubjective communication. There could be no linguistic community. If no sharing of a language is even possible, why use the term 'language' at all to describe what is so 'constructed'? Wittgenstein uses the following analogy between the possession of private 'beetle-boxes' and private languages to bring out this critical difficulty.

If I say of myself that it is only from my own case that I know what the word "pain" means—must I not say the same of other people too? And how can I generalize the *one* case so irresponsibly?

Now someone tells me that *he* knows what pain is only from his own case!—Suppose everyone had a box with something in it: we call it a "beetle". No one can look into anyone else's box, and everyone says he knows what a beetle is only by looking at *his* beetle.—Here it would be quite possible for everyone to have something different in his box. One might even imagine such a thing constantly changing.—But suppose the word "beetle" had a use in these people's language?—If so it would not be used as the name of a thing. The thing in the box has no place in the language-game at all; not even as a *something:* for the box might even be empty.—No, one can 'divide through' by the thing in the box; it cancels out, whatever it is.

That is to say: if we construe the grammar of the expression of sensation on the model of 'object and name' the object drops out of consideration as irrelevant.[80]

. . . .

The essential thing about private experience is really not that each person possesses his own exemplar, but that nobody knows whether other people also have *this* or something else. The assumption would thus be possible—though unverifiable—that one section of mankind had one sensation of red and another section another.[81]

Another criticism of the conception of a private language has to do with the claim made that the speaker of such a language is in a privileged position in having knowledge, i.e., complete certainty, with respect to the existence and character of that speaker's inner sensations. Only I can know, it is said, that I am in pain; others, who can only observe my outward behavior, can only surmise or infer it, and their belief may be wrong. This thesis, Wittgenstein responds, is either false or nonsense.

In what sense are my sensations *private?*—Well, only I can know whether I am really in pain; another person can only surmise it.—In one way this is false, and in another nonsense. If we are using the word "to know" as it is normally used (and how else are we to use it?), then other people very often know when I am in pain.—Yes, but all the same not with the certainty with which I know it myself!—It can't be said of me at all (except perhaps as a joke) that I *know* I am in pain. What is it supposed to mean—except perhaps that I *am* in pain?

Other people cannot be said to learn of my sensations *only* from my behaviour,—for *I* cannot be said to learn of them. I *have* them.

The truth is: it makes sense to say about other people that they doubt whether I am in pain; but not to say it about myself.[82]

In denying that only I can know whether I am in pain, Wittgenstein points out that in the way we ordinarily use the term 'know', we say that there are many cases in which others can know (be correct in their assertions) that someone is in pain. As justification for their ascribing (predicating) pain to someone, they use various criteria for pain, and also rely on various symptoms and publicly obtainable observational evidence. Of course, we may sometimes be wrong in our ascriptions of pain to someone else on the basis of such criteria and observational data. For example, a person who shows all 'outward' signs of pain behavior may be only pretending, e.g., may be a very skillful actor. However, not all judgments ascribing pain are wrong. Pretense of pain cannot be universal, if the term 'pain' is to have any meaning and usable criteria. Some ascriptions of pain to others are correct, and we can therefore be said to know that someone else is in pain. Hence it is false to say that we never know that someone else is in pain, and that only the sufferer knows he is in pain.

Moreover, Wittgenstein argues, it is nonsense to say that the one who suffers pain *knows* he is in pain. It is not nonsense to say that others can know this. The person who has the pain *expresses* that pain in various ways, for example by exhibiting various types of pain behavior and also by uttering the sentence "I have pain." But the uttering of this sentence is not to claim *knowledge about* the pain being suffered. It is rather an *avowal* of pain, a way of expressing the pain, like holding one's cheek when one has a toothache. The utterance of the sentence "I have a toothache" is neither true nor false. It makes no sense for the one uttering this sentence either to verify it or falsify it. Others may verify or falsify the sentence (in third-person ascription) "He has a toothache." But the person who utters the sentence (in present tense first person singular) "I have a toothache" is not uttering a sentence that is a claim to privileged knowledge. To say "I *know* I am in pain" means no more than "I *am* in pain." Since the notion of doubt does not have any applicability or foothold in connection with the latter sentence, neither does any claim to certainty (absence of doubt). Since neither certainty nor doubt has any bearing on the sentence "I am in pain," that sentence cannot be equated with the sentence "I know I am in pain." And so the claim by the pain sufferer to be in a uniquely privileged position to have such *knowledge* is without any sense. Furthermore, since self-ascriptions of pain are expressions rather than statements, they are not made on the basis of criteria in the way the term 'pain' is used in third-person ascriptions. Hence the use of terms in a putative private language cannot be based on any effective grammatical rules (whether ostensive definitions or criterial rules) in the way such rules are present and operative in ordinary languages used by a linguistic community.

ON 'PHILOSOPHY'

In his discussions of various topics in *Philosophical Investigations* (as well as in his other later writings), Wittgenstein often pauses to make comments about the nature of philosophy. In the *Tractatus,* too, as we have noted, he devotes some attention to what philosophy is, and contrasts his views with certain standard conceptions. It will be of interest to examine Wittgenstein's later remarks about philosophy to see wherein they are similar to, and wherein they mark a shift from, his earlier views. We shall find that he continues to hold to the view that philosophy should be pursued as an activity of clarification rather than as a discipline that asserts various substantive propositions or factual claims about the world. The primary role of philosophy for him continues to be to serve as a 'critique of language'. However, given the radical shift in his approach to the nature of language in his later writings, the way in which philosophy performs this role shifts accordingly. Briefly the difference is this. In the earlier writings, the drive is to probe beneath the surface use of ordinary language in order to uncover a logical grammar that articulates and circumscribes the limits of thought. The role of philosophy is to point to the areas in which sense is present in a healthy use of language. Having done this, philosophy itself 'disappears' and leaves behind no substantive claims, no detailed or specific factual propositions about the world. In the later writings, Wittgenstein abandons this type of search for a depth logic. He stresses the need for an acceptance of the great multiplicity of language-games as they exist, and therefore as 'all right'. Philosophy continues to be an activity of clarification. However, it no longer seeks to draw a single encompassing limit to the meaningful use of language. It would help to disentangle various knots and mental cramps that result from a failure to understand and use available languages in a perspicuous way. It helps, furthermore, to make us aware that the desire to reform ordinary language often parades as a factual discovery when it is merely a proposal for a change in the grammar of our thought.

It was Wittgenstein's belief that the way he went about discussing the themes of his later philosophy exemplifies *a new method* of practicing philosophy. He wishes to contrast this new method with older, more traditional conceptions, even though some might suppose they could all be collected under the common label of 'philosophy'.

If, e.g., we call our investigations "philosophy", this title, on the one hand, seems appropriate, on the other hand it certainly has misled people. (One might say that the subject we are dealing with is one of the heirs of the subject which used to be called "philosophy".)[83]

Moore, in his account of Wittgenstein's lectures in 1930–1933, makes the following comment:

> I was a good deal surprised by some of the things he said about the difference between 'philosophy' in the sense in which what he was doing might be called 'philosophy' (he called this 'modern philosophy'), and what has traditionally been called 'philosophy'. He said that what he was doing was a 'new subject', and not merely a stage in a 'continuous development'; that there was now, in philosophy, a 'kink' in the 'development of human thought', comparable to that which occurred when Galileo and his contemporaries invented dynamics; that a 'new method' had been discovered, as had happened when 'chemistry was developed out of alchemy'; and that it was now possible for the first time that there should be 'skillful' philosophers, though of course there had in the past been 'great' philosophers.[84]

What, then, is the 'new method' that, according to Wittgenstein, sets apart his approach to philosophy from what was so designated in earlier epochs? Let us follow him as he gives an account, sometimes in positive terms and more often in negative ones, of what the aim of philosophy should be. Both the positive and negative elements are hinted at in the following statement:

> A main source of our failure to understand is that we do not *command a clear view* of the use of our words.—Our grammar is lacking in this sort of perspicuity. A perspicuous representation produces just that understanding which consists in 'seeing connexions'. Hence the importance of finding and inventing *intermediate cases.*
> The concept of a perspicuous representation is of fundamental significance for us. It earmarks the form of the account we give, the way we look at things. (Is this a 'Weltanschauung'?)[85]

From a positive point of view, the goal of philosophy is to achieve a perspicuous representation, to command a clear view of the use of our words, to produce understanding through coming to see connections. The initial or primary subject matter to which philosophy addresses itself is the varied and complex use of language by human beings. Through language human thought is conveyed. Thought and language, in this broad sense, constitute the 'way we look at things'; they make up our modes of representation. But what the structure is—the interconnections among the various parts, the rules, and the complex linkages—of our human modes of representation, this is not easily discernible. We know bits and pieces, but we do not readily have a grasp of very large or complex segments of it. Nor need we assume that there is anything like a complete, finished system to be taken in. Nevertheless, to be able to *survey* larger and larger segments, to discern the patterns and interconnections among the component parts, all of this is essential if we are to achieve under-standing and not 'get lost'. The analogy with surveying, map-making, and finding one's way about in a spatial domain readily comes to mind and is exploited by Wittgenstein. Just as in order to 'know' the layout of a por-tion of the earth's surface, and to be able to get about successfully on it, one should have a reliable map, a surveyable picture of the terrain (the contours, locations, distances, and so on, of items of relevance and inter-est), so with the 'terrain' that interests the philosopher. The philosopher too needs to make a survey, to have a 'perspicuous representation'. But of what? The answer is, of language, of thought, of the basic features to be found in our various 'modes of representation', of the 'conceptual sys-tems' and 'language-games' of all sorts that people devise and use to 'get around' in the world. The subject matter for surveyability by philosophy consists of human modes of representation that people use. What is needed is a perspicuous representation of our modes of representation (languages, methods of measurement, grammatical rules, and so on). To achieve such a 'survey', to have such an overview, is the goal of philoso-phy. It would give us a 'geography' of our conceptual resources. If we had such a 'map', we would take these all in and find our way clearly and with confidence among them because we would then 'understand' them; we would see them in their interconnections with one another; we would be able to take in the lay of the 'conceptual land' at a glance, and would get about without getting lost or entangled.

The absence of such a reliable map, the reliance instead on partial or misleading ones, is what accounts for the manifold pathologies of human thinking, for the existence of numerous philosophic 'problems'. Wittgen-stein's account of philosophy, although it recognizes the positive goal of achieving 'understanding', tends nevertheless on the whole to stress the negative weaknesses of 'philosophy' as ordinarily practiced. He is much more concerned to illustrate, diagnose, and treat the failures of misguided philosophic thinking than to exhibit its positive accomplishments.

> The philosopher is the man who has to cure himself of many sicknesses of the understanding before he can arrive at the notions of the sound human under-standing.
>
> If in the midst of life we are in death, so in sanity we are surrounded by madness.[86]

When put thus in negative terms, the 'madness' or 'illness' that philoso-phy must seek to cure is manifested in the existence and persistence of various philosophic 'problems'. "The philosopher's treatment of a ques-tion is like the treatment of an illness."[87] A symptom of the existence of such a problem or 'illness' is its persistence; one has a sense of continuing failure to see the kinds of conceptual distinctions and connections that, if seen, would enable one to be at (intellectual) peace because one would then know how to get about effectively in the conceptual terrain involved. One has a sense of being 'lost', balked, and frustrated.

A philosophical problem has the form: "I don't know my way about."[88]

The typical character of a philosophic problem is also described as a 'mental cramp', the experience of 'a knot in our thinking'. A philosopher is compared to a fly caught in a fly-bottle. The goal of philosophy as therapy, as Wittgenstein would practice it, is to relieve the mental cramps, untie the knots, show the fly the way out of the fly-bottle, dissolve the philosophic pseudoproblems that afflict people's thinking.[89]

Wittgenstein recognizes that the existence of a philosophic problem is not ordinarily due to some simple or trivial error. The fact that such problems engage the attention of many extremely powerful minds, sometimes over long periods, suggests that the 'illness' is not a superficial one or easily treated. Wittgenstein contends that the problems result from certain underlying linguistic failures. The pervasiveness of our linguistic patterns and either the habitual misuse of these patterns or the desire to break away from the prevalent patterns and create new ones accounts for the persistence of the problems.

The problems arising through a misinterpretation of our forms of language have the character of *depth*. They are deep disquietudes; their roots are as deep in us as the forms of our language and their significance is as great as the importance of our language.[90]

Sometimes philosophic controversies and 'problems' emerge from the unrecognized presence of a proposal to introduce a new conceptual notation, a new language-game. Instead of realizing that what is involved is a dispute over notational matters, we treat the matter as a substantive or factual disagreement. Such, Wittgenstein says, is the character of the dispute between those who say that there are unconscious thoughts as well as conscious ones, and those who deny this; or, to take another example, the dispute between the solipsist and the common-sense realist.

Now when the solipsist says that only his own experiences are real, it is no use answering him: "Why do you tell us this if you don't believe that we really hear it?" Or anyhow, if we give him this answer, we mustn't believe that we have answered his difficulty. There is no common sense answer to a philosophical problem. One can defend common sense against the attacks of philosophers only by solving their puzzles, i.e., by curing them of the temptation to attack common sense; not by restating the views of common sense. A philosopher is not a man out of his senses, a man who doesn't see what everybody sees; nor on the other hand is his disagreement with common sense that of the scientist disagreeing with the coarse views of the man in the street. That is, his disagreement is not founded on a more subtle knowledge of fact. We therefore have to look round for the *source* of his puzzlement. And we find that there is puzzlement and mental discomfort, not only when our curiosity about certain facts is not satisfied or when we can't find a law of nature fitting in with all our experience, but also when a notation dissatisfies us—perhaps because of various associations which it calls up. Our ordinary language, which of all possible notations is the one which pervades all our life, holds our mind rigidly in one position, as it were, and in this position sometimes it feels cramped, having a desire for other positions as well. Thus we sometimes wish for a notation which stresses a difference more strongly, makes it more obvious, than ordinary language does, or one which in a particular case uses more closely similar forms of expression than our ordinary language. Our mental cramp is loosened when we are shown the notations which fulfil these needs. These needs can be of the greatest variety.[91]

If the existence and persistence of various philosophic problems, puzzlements, and disputes is the occasion for helpful and sound philosophical activity, the goal of such activity is the therapeutic one of getting rid of the problems, not by solving them but by dissolving them. By coming to understand the source of our puzzlements and mental cramps, we see through them and are no longer enmeshed or tormented by them.

The real discovery is the one that makes me capable of stopping doing philosophy when I want to.—The one that gives philosophy peace, so that it is no longer tormented by questions which bring *itself* in question.—Instead, we now demonstrate a method, by examples; and the series of examples can be broken off. Problems are solved (difficulties eliminated), not a *single* problem.

There is not *a* philosophical method, though there are indeed methods, like different therapies.[92]

The way in which philosophy when properly practiced achieves its therapeutic results is by making a careful analysis of the uses of language. It does this by examining numerous examples, noting similarities and differences. Its role is wholly descriptive. It focuses on how language is actually used in language-games. By bringing to light—by making explicit and evident—how we use linguistic expressions, the conventions and rules that govern their use—we thereby find that our initial confusions and entanglements, our puzzlements have disappeared!

The role of philosophy, in being purely descriptive, is not to *explain* the use of language, in the sense of producing a scientific theory of the causes and mechanisms (whether physiological, psychological, social, and so on) that lay bare the empirical conditions for the use of language and the factual results or effects of such uses.

We may not advance any kind of theory. There must not be anything hypothetical in our considerations. We must do away with all *explanation,* and description alone must take its place. And this description gets its power of illumination—i.e., its purpose—from the philosophic problems. These are, of course, not empirical problems; they are solved, rather, by looking into the workings of our language, and that in such a way as to make us recognize those workings: *in despite of* an urge to misunderstand them. The problems are solved, not by giving new information, but by arranging what we have always known. Philosophy is a battle against the bewitchment of our intelligence by means of language.

. . . .

Philosophy simply puts everything before us, and neither explains nor deduces anything.—Since everything lies open to view there is nothing to explain. For what is hidden, for example, is of no interest to us.

. . . .

Philosophy may in no way interfere with the actual use of language; it can in the end only describe it.

For it cannot give it any foundation either. It leaves everything as it is.

. . . .

The work of the philosopher consists in assembling reminders for a particular purpose.[93]

Through the assembly of these reminders, this descriptive calling attention to the actual variety of uses and rules of language, the loosening of the grip of the pseudoproblems of philosophy is gradually accomplished.

Wittgenstein's emphasis upon the therapeutic role of philosophy, its laborious and patient activity of untying particular knots, carries with it a disinclination on his part to think of philosophy as engaged in any constructive activity of system-building. He tends to be cautious, if not downright sceptical of the pretensions of many philosophers to have set out once and for all the ground plan of reality.

Disquiet in philosophy might be said to arise from looking at philosophy wrongly, seeing it wrong, namely as if it were divided into (infinite) longitudinal strips instead of into (finite) cross strips. This inversion of our conception produces the *greatest* difficulty. So we try as it were to grasp the unlimited strips and complain that it cannot be done piecemeal. To be sure it cannot, if by a piece one means an infinite longitudinal strip. But it may well be done, if one means a crossstrip.—But in that case we never get to the end of our work!—Of course not, for it has no end.

(We want to replace wild conjectures and explanations by quiet weighing of linguistic facts.)

. . . .

Philosophical investigations: conceptual investigations. The essential thing about metaphysics: it obliterates the distinction between factual and conceptual investigations.[94]

On the view proposed in the *Tractatus,* there is an underlying structure or common form possessed by logic, the depth-grammar of language when brought to light by logic, and the ontological nature of the world. Philosophy, as an activity, elicits this identity of form by using various formal concepts such as 'object', 'proposition', 'form', 'property', 'structure', 'relation', and the like. It cannot say (in propositions) what that

structure is, but it can 'show' it by using these various formal co[
Once having used them, philosophy "throws the ladder away." At least
then, in an indirect way and despite its speaking 'nonsense', philosophy
can and does 'formulate' an ontology, just as in another direction, it formulates a logic.

However, even this much of a concern with adumbrating an ontology is no longer present in Wittgenstein's later writings. Instead of offering an account of what the 'essential structure' of the world is, as this can
be schematically set out and 'shown' by philosophy, Wittgenstein now
restricts philosophy entirely to a therapeutic role. The quest for an ontology is thus surrendered altogether. In its place there is only the attention
given to forms of representation, to various modes of language-uses and
conceptual resources. Whatever can be informatively said about the
world is left entirely to the natural sciences to put into language. Philosophy cannot even provide a schematic framework, whose details are to be
filled in by the sciences. The only fruitful and legitimate role for philosophy is to turn away from a concern with an alleged metaphysical structure
or essence of the world toward the uses of language. The primary goal of
philosophy is to cure us of our conceptual ensnarements, to free us from
futile mental anxieties and philosophic 'problems'. Having thus been
freed, men then may go about their business in genuinely constructive
activities, whether in daily living, in the sciences, or in the arts. Philosophy thus leaves everything 'as it is'. When liberated from pseudoproblems people can turn their attention to the solution of genuine
problems, to the creation of novel and beneficent patterns of thought and
action.

COMMON SENSE AND CERTAINTY: A CRITIQUE OF
G. E. MOORE

During the last year and a half of his life, Wittgenstein worked on a manuscript that was published after his death under the title *On Certainty*. In it
he examines a number of interrelated themes suggested by his reading of
Moore's well-known papers "A Defence of Common Sense" and "Proof
of an External World." In these papers Moore formulates his commitment to a philosophy of Common Sense realism. As a fundamental aspect
of this philosophy he offers a number of truisms—propositions he claims
to know with certainty to be true—e.g., "There exists at present a living
human body, which is *my* body," "Here is one hand, and here is another," "The earth had existed for many years before my body was
born," and so on. Wittgenstein examines these and similar propositions in
order to determine what can be said in favor of their being known with
certainty. What is the logical status of such propositions? How is one to

analyze the use of the phrase 'I know————' when used in connection with one or another of propositions such as the above? This is the central question to which Wittgenstein addresses himself. What he has to say on this topic offers both an important example of the philosophic technique he employs throughout his later philosophy, as well as a means for rounding out in an important direction the content and scope of that later philosophy.

In 1953 G. E. Moore (1873–1958) published under the title *Some Main Problems of Philosophy* a series of lectures he had given some forty years earlier. In the first chapter of that book Moore formulates what he takes to be the essential characteristics of 'the views of Common Sense'. In 1925 Moore contributed the paper "A Defence of Common Sense" to *Contemporary British Philosophy* (Hywel D. Lewis, editor). He there gives a list of propositions as belonging to a Common Sense view of the world, each of which he claims to know with certainty to be true. Let us examine this characterization and this defense of a Common Sense philosophy as Moore presents them.

In *Some Main Problems of Philosophy* Moore begins by making some general introductory remarks about philosophy. He describes one of its purposes as follows:

> To give a general description of the *whole* of the Universe, mentioning all the most important kinds of things which we *know* to be in it, considering how far it is likely that there are in it important kinds of things which we do not absolutely *know* to be in it, and also considering the most important ways in which these various kinds of things are related to one another.[95]

As an example of what it is to have a comprehensive view of the principal kinds of things in the Universe and their relations, Moore describes the main features of Common Sense. He offers this characterization at the very outset, because although according to him such a Common Sense view is held by "almost everybody," and is one to which he himself would subscribe, it is nevertheless challenged and rejected in whole or in part by some philosophers. Of these philosophers Moore says:

> It seems to me that what is most amazing and most interesting about the views of many philosophers, is the way in which they go beyond or positively contradict the views of Common Sense: they profess to know that there are in the Universe most important kinds of things, which Common Sense does not profess to know of, and also they profess to know that there are *not* in the Universe (or, at least, that, if there are, we do not know it), things of the existence of which Common Sense is most sure.[96]

Those who share a Common Sense view of the world would accept a certain number of basic beliefs. One of these is the belief that "there are in the Universe a great number of material objects." As examples of material objects, Moore mentions the bodies of human beings, animals plants, mountains, grains of sand, minerals, soils, rivers, seas, manufactured articles ("houses and chairs and tables and railway engines"), as well as the enormous masses of matter beyond the Earth itself—the Moon, Sun, stars and other heavenly bodies.

A second fundamental component of Common Sense is the belief that in addition to the existence of material objects, there are also in the Universe very many instances of acts of consciousness.

We see and hear and feel and remember and imagine and think and believe and desire and like and dislike and will and love and are angry and afraid, etc. These things that we do are all of them mental acts—acts of mind or acts of *consciousness*. . . . and these acts are something very different from material objects. To hear is not *itself* a material object, however closely it may be related to certain material objects: and so on with all the rest—seeing, remembering, feeling, thinking, etc. . . . There are, therefore, in the Universe at any moment millions of different acts of consciousness being performed by millions of different men, and perhaps also by many kinds of animals. It is, I think, certainly Common Sense to believe all this.[97]

While acts of consciousness are, in the case of human beings and some animals, attached to their bodies, in the case of the vast majority of material objects in the Universe there are *no* acts of consciousness attached at all.

We are sure that chairs and tables and houses and mountains and stones do not really see or hear or feel or think or perform any other mental acts: we are sure they are *not* conscious. We are sure too that the sun and moon and stars and earth are not conscious—that no conscious acts are attached to them, in the sense in which our conscious acts are attached to our bodies: *they* do not feel or hear or see, as *we* do. . . . This, I think, may fairly be said to be the view of Common Sense nowadays.[98]

Moreover, it is part of the Common Sense view to believe that all material objects are in space, i.e., that they are at definite distances and directions from one another. Again, it is part of Common Sense to believe that "all material objects, and all the acts of consciousness of ourselves and other animals upon the earth, are in *time*," i.e., "*either* have been in time *or* are so now, *or* will be so in the future."[99]

Connected with these beliefs about material objects, minds, space, and time, Moore claims it is also part of Common Sense to believe that

material objects are all of such a kind that they may exist, even when we are not conscious of them, and that many do in fact so exist. And . . . there *may* have been a time when acts of consciousness were attached to *no* material bodies anywhere in the Universe, and *may* again be such a time; and that there almost certainly was a time when there were no human bodies, with human consciousness attached to them, upon this earth.[100]

According to Moore, while Common Sense claims there are these two kinds of things in the Universe, namely material objects and acts of consciousness, it nevertheless falls short of making any claims about the *whole* Universe. It does not exclude the possibility that there may indeed be other kinds of entities in the Universe (i.e., in the totality of whatever is real). Thus while many persons may wish to make various *additions* to a Common Sense view as thus far characterized, that view cannot be characterized as including such additions, even though such additions may not be actually incompatible with it. For example, while very many persons believe in the existence of God as a Divine Mind, and as distinct from the existence of material objects or finite acts of consciousness, the viewpoint of Common Sense cannot be said to include this belief, since it is not universally shared.

On the whole, I think it fairest to say, that Common Sense has *no* view on the question whether we do know that there is a God or not: that it neither asserts that we do know this, nor yet that we do not; and that, therefore, Common Sense has *no* view as to the Universe as a *whole*. We may, therefore, say that those philosophers who assert that there certainly *is* a God in the Universe do go *beyond* the views of Common Sense. They make a most important addition to what Common Sense believes about the Universe. For by a God is meant something so different from both material objects and from our minds, that to add that, besides these, there is also a God, is certainly to make an important addition to our view of the Universe.[101]

Moore makes the same type of comment with respect to another widely but not universally shared belief, namely that there is a life after death in the form of the survival of a person's mind independently of the body.

So many people believe that, even if we have a future life, we certainly do not *know* that we have one; that here again it is perhaps fairest to say that Common Sense has no view on the point: that it asserts neither that we *do* know of a future life nor that do *not*.[102]

Moore points out, finally, that it is not impossible there *may* be still other kinds of entities in the Universe of which we have no present knowledge, or that may be altogether unknowable. Surely, however, a Common Sense world view cannot commit itself to the existence of such entities. Any such additions, therefore, would also have to be excluded from a characterization of a Common Sense view of the world.

In his paper "A Defence of Common Sense" Moore is concerned, as the title of the paper indicates, not simply to characterize what the viewpoint of Common Sense is, but to show to what extent and in what specific ways he wishes to come to its defense. He does this principally by listing a number of propositions whose truth he says he knows with certainty. And he gives the following examples of propositions that fall into this class.

There exists at present a living human body, which is *my* body. This body was born at a certain time in the past, and has existed continuously ever since, though not without undergoing changes; it was, for instance, much smaller when it was born, and for some time afterwards, than it is now. Ever since it was born, it has been either in contact with or not far from the surface of the earth; and, at every moment since it was born, there have also existed many other things, having shape and size in three dimensions (in the same familiar sense in which it has), from which it has been *at various distances* (in the familiar sense in which it is now at a distance both from that mantelpiece and from that bookcase, and at a greater distance from the bookcase than it is from the mantelpiece); also there have (very often, at all events) existed some other things of this kind with which it was *in contact* (in the familiar sense in which it is now in contact with the pen I am holding in my right hand and with some of the clothes I am wearing). Among the things which have, in this sense, formed part of its environment (i.e., have been either in contact with it, or at *some* distance from it, however *great*) there have, at every moment since its birth, been large numbers of other living human bodies each of which has, like it, *(a)* at some time been born, *(b)* continued to exist from some time after birth, *(c)* been, at every moment of its life after birth, either in contact with or not far from the surface of the earth; and many of these bodies have already died and ceased to exist. But the earth had existed also for many years before my body was born; and for many of these years, also, large numbers of human bodies had, at every moment, been alive upon it; and many of these bodies had died and ceased to exist before it was born. Finally (to come to a different class of propositions), I am a human being, and I have, at different times since my body was born, had many different experiences, of each of many different kinds: e.g., I have often perceived both my own body and other things which formed part of its environment, including other human bodies; I have not only perceived things of this kind, but have also observed facts about them, such as, for instance, the fact which I am now observing, that that mantelpiece is at present nearer to my body than that bookcase; I have been aware of other facts, which I was not at the time observing, such as, for instance, the fact, of which I am now aware, that my body existed yesterday and was then also for some time nearer to that mantelpiece than to that bookcase; I have had expectations with regard to the future, and many beliefs of other kinds, both true and false; I have thought of imaginary things and persons and incidents, in the reality of which I did not believe; I have had dreams; and I have had feelings of many different kinds. And, just as my body has been the body of a human being, namely myself, who has, during his lifetime, had many experiences of each of these (and other) different kinds; so, in the case of very many of the other human bodies which have lived upon the earth, each has been the body of a different human being, who has during the lifetime of that body, had many different experiences of each of these (and other) different kinds.[103]

In addition to the foregoing list of truisms, Moore proposes a number of others. Thus, he says he knows that other human beings, besides himself, have known a corresponding list of true propositions that he, Moore, knows about himself.

Moore also points out that in claiming he knows with certainty the propositions just listed, or, in addition various others, e.g., the proposition "The earth has existed for many years past," he does not wish to deny that there is a distinction to be made between the *analysis* of any one of these propositions, as distinct from the common *understanding* of the proposition. He admits there may be all sorts of difficulties or controversies arising from the effort to provide a satisfactory analysis. Yet, however this may be, such possible difficulties need not in any way qualify the legitimate claim to know these truistic propositions.

In what I have just said, I have assumed that there is some meaning which is *the* ordinary or popular meaning of such expressions as 'The earth has existed for many years past'. And this, I am afraid, is an assumption which some philosophers are capable of disputing. They seem to think that the question 'Do you believe that the earth has existed for many years past?' is not a plain question, such as should be met either by a plain 'Yes' or 'No', or by a plain 'I can't make up my mind', but is the sort of question which can be properly met by: 'It all depends on what you mean by "the earth" and "exists" and "years": if you mean so and so, and so and so, and so and so, then I do; but if you mean so and so, and so and so, and so and so, and so and so, or so and so, and so and so, and so and so, or so and so, and so and so, and so and so, then I don't, or at least I think it is extremely doubtful.' It seems to me that such a view is as profoundly mistaken as any view can be. Such an expression as 'The earth has existed for many years past' is the very type of an unambiguous expression, the meaning of which we all understand. Anyone who takes a contrary view must, I suppose, be confusing the question whether we understand its meaning (which we all certainly do) with the entirely different question whether we *know what it means,* in the sense that we are able to give *a correct analysis* of its meaning. The question what is the correct analysis of *the* proposition meant *on any occasion* . . . by 'The earth has existed for many years past' is, it seems to me, a profoundly difficult question, and one to which . . . no one knows the answer. But to hold that we do not know what, in certain respects, is the analysis of what we understand by such an expression, is an entirely different thing from holding that we do not understand the expression. It is obvious that we cannot even raise the question how what we do understand by it is to be analyzed, unless we do understand it. So soon, therefore, as we know that a person who uses such an expression is using it in its ordinary sense, we understand his meaning. So that in explaining that I was using the expressions . . . in their ordinary sense (those of them which have an ordinary sense, which is not the case with quite all of them), I have done all that is required to make my meaning clear.[104]

A further point that Moore makes in connection with the set of propositions he says he knows with certainty to be true is that most of them are not known by him (or correspondingly by other human beings) *directly,* but only on the basis of evidence of one sort or another.

I do not know them *directly:* that is to say, I only know them because, in the past, I have known to be true *other* propositions which were evidence for them. If, for instance, I do know that the earth had existed for many years before I was born, I certainly only know this because I have known other things in the past which were evidence for it. And I certainly do not know exactly what the evidence was. Yet all this seems to me to be no good reason for doubting that I do know it. We are all, I think, in this strange position that we do *know* many things, with regard to which we *know* further that we must have had evidence for them, and yet we do not know *how* we know them, i.e., we do not know what the evidence was.[105]

Moore characterizes the type of philosophy that insists on the truth of the various propositions listed above as a "Common Sense view of the world." He argues that not only does he himself uphold such a view, but that *all* other philosophers in fact also uphold such a view, even though many philosophers would deny that they do. Moore maintains that the Common Sense view of the world rests upon the acceptance of a universally shared set of known truths, whatever some philosophers may say to the contrary, and despite the fact that they would wish to reject such a view.

I am one of those philosophers who have held that the 'Common Sense view of the world' is, in certain fundamental features, *wholly* true. But it must be remembered that, according to me, *all* philosophers, without exception, have agreed with me in holding this: and that the real difference, which is commonly expressed in this way, is only a difference between those philosophers, who have *also* held views inconsistent with these features in 'the Common Sense view of the world', and those who have not.

. . . .

The phrases 'Common Sense view of the world' or 'Common Sense beliefs' (as used by philosophers) are, of course, extraordinarily vague; and, for all I know, there may be many propositions which may be properly called features in 'the Common Sense view of the world' or 'Common Sense beliefs', which are not true, and which deserve to be mentioned with the contempt with which some philosophers speak of 'Common Sense beliefs'. But to speak with contempt of those 'Common Sense beliefs' which I have mentioned is quite certainly the height of absurdity. And there are, of course, enormous numbers of other features in 'the Common Sense view of the world' which, if these are true, are quite certainly true too: e.g., that there have lived upon the surface of the earth not only human beings, but also many different species of plants and animals, etc. etc.[106]

With respect to the distinction between physical facts and mental facts, Moore asserts there is no good reason to believe that every physical fact is either logically dependent or causally dependent on some mental fact.

With respect to 'logical dependence', he makes clear in what sense he is using this expression.

I hold, then, that there is no good reason to suppose that *every* physical fact is *logically* dependent upon some mental fact. And I use the phrase, with regard to two facts, F_1 and F_2, 'F_1 is *logically dependent* on F_2', wherever and only where F_1 *entails* F_2, either in the sense in which the proposition 'I am seeing now' *entails* the proposition 'I am conscious now', or the proposition (with regard to any particular thing) 'This is red' entails the proposition (with regard to the same thing) 'This is coloured', or else in the more strictly logical sense in which (for instance) the conjunctive proposition 'All men are mortal, and Mr. Baldwin is a man' entails the proposition 'Mr. Baldwin is mortal'. To say then, of two facts, F_1 and F_2, that F_1 is *not* logically dependent upon F_2, is only to say that F_1 *might* have been a fact, even if there had been no such fact as F_2; or that the conjunctive proposition of 'F_1 is a fact, but there is no such fact as F_2' is a proposition which is not self-contradictory, i.e., does not entail both of two mutually incompatible propositions.

I hold, then, that, in the case of *some* physical facts, there is no good reason to suppose that there is some mental fact, such that the physical fact in question could not have been a fact unless the mental fact in question had also been one.[107]

And with respect to causal independence, Moore also makes clear in what sense he would maintain that there are, in his view, some physical facts that are causally independent of any mental fact.

I also hold that there is no good reason to suppose that *every* physical fact is *causally* dependent upon some mental fact. By saying that F_1 is *causally* dependent on F_2, I mean only that F_1 *wouldn't* have been a fact unless F_2 had been; *not* (which is what 'logically dependent' asserts) that F_1 *couldn't conceivably* have been a fact, unless F_2 had been. And I can illustrate my meaning by reference to the example which I have just given. The fact that that mantelpiece is at present nearer to my body than that bookcase, is (as I have just explained) so far as I can see, not *logically* dependent upon any mental fact; it *might* have been a fact, even if there had been no mental facts. But it certainly is *causally* dependent on many mental facts: my body *would* not have been here unless I had been conscious in various ways in the past; and the mantelpiece and the bookcase certainly *would* not have existed, unless other men had been conscious too.

But with regard to two of the facts, which I gave as instances of physical facts, namely the fact that the earth has existed for many years past, and the fact that the moon has for many years past been nearer to the earth than to the sun, I hold that there is no good reason to suppose that these are *causally* dependent upon any mental fact. So far as I can see, there is no reason to suppose that there is any mental fact of which it could be truly said: unless this fact had been a fact, the earth would not have existed for many years past. And in holding this, again, I think I differ from some philosophers. I differ, for instance, from those who have held that all material things were created by God, and that they had good reasons for supposing this.[108]

We have been examining Moore's *characterization* of a Common Sense view of the world and his *defense* of it. The two need to be distinguished. It is possible for someone to give a fair, clear, and comprehensive characterization of a philosophical viewpoint without at the same time subscribing to it. In Moore's case, however, while he surely can be credited with giving such a characterization of Common Sense, he wishes to do more. He wishes to subscribe to it. This he does, especially in his paper "A Defence of Common Sense," by enumerating a list of propositions belonging to a Common Sense view which he claims on his own behalf *he knows with certainty to be true*. He also claims that not only he but others as well would make corresponding claims about their knowledge of the truth of each of these propositions. Moore's defense is signaled by the use of the phrase '*I know with certainty——to be true*', where the blank, in each case, is filled by some proposition belonging to Common Sense, e.g., 'The earth has existed for many years before I was born'.

In the light of the distinction between characterization and defense, it would be possible for some critic who wishes to examine Moore's account of Common Sense to examine either his characterization or his use of the phrase 'I know with certainty——to be true' as conveying his (Moore's) defense of a Common Sense view, or both. Wittgenstein's critique of Moore is largely preoccupied with the analysis of the role of phrases such as 'I know' and 'I am certain', rather than primarily with Common Sense or Moore's characterization of it. This is not to suggest that Wittgenstein is dissatisfied with or uninterested altogether in Moore's characterization of Common Sense, and that he, Wittgenstein, would wish to dispute the characterization or that he would wish to come to the defense of those whom Moore criticizes, for example the idealist metaphysician or the sceptic. On the contrary, there is every indication that Wittgenstein would align himself with those who would accept the Common Sense outlook Moore describes. The fact remains that Wittgenstein's interests lie elsewhere. His dissatisfaction with Moore's account has to do not with the latter's characterization of Common Sense but with the way in which Moore chooses to come to its defense. In short, Wittgenstein fastens his attention on the typical formula Moore uses in stating his defense, namely 'I know with certainty——to be true'. Wittgenstein will argue that Moore's use of this phrase is altogether faulty and wide of the mark. It will be Wittgenstein's contention that Moore has failed to study sufficiently the use of the phrase 'I know——' and therefore that his defense of a Common Sense view is not sound. In setting out his own analysis of the use of this phrase, Wittgenstein will be giving us what amounts to his own 'theory of knowledge', or more accurately his own analysis of the language-games in which the expressions 'I know' and 'I am certain' play their roles.

The principal thesis Wittgenstein argues for is that it is a *misuse* of the phrase 'I know' to say, as Moore does, and without further clarification, 'I know——to be true', where the blank is filled by any of the propositions in Moore's list. The expression 'I know' cannot properly be used in connection with propositions such as these, in the same way in which the phrase 'I know' is used in connection with other propositions.

The truisms Moore enumerates play such a special role in our language, thought, reasonings, and inquiries that it is an error to say we *know* them in the *ordinary* sense of this term. Their status is so fundamental that they provide the *grounds* and *framework* for determining the certainty or uncertainty, the truth or falsity, for other propositions. They themselves, however, are without grounds and are incapable of being justified or supported by evidence. One might say these 'truisms' are prelogical even 'animal' in character. They determine the framework of a language system, but are not themselves hypotheses or suppositions, stated within the language-game they help to define.

It is Wittgenstein's basic contention that we should not be misled by the ordinary use of expressions such as 'I know', 'I am certain', 'factual truth', 'empirical proposition', and the like, into assuming that their logical role is always the same. He would argue, for example, that the distinctions ordinarily made between empirical (factual) propositions and formal (grammatical) ones do not add up to a single, sharp, absolute division, or constitute a fixed mode of classification such that any given sentence falls definitely into one or the other of these categories. His thesis is a more radical one, offering a new way of regarding, from a logical point of view, the role of any sentence. What he has to say on this topic marks in some ways a significant change from the kinds of things he stressed in *The Blue Book* and *Philosophical Investigations,* let alone the *Tractatus*.

A central theme in his new approach has to do with the important role played in our thought by a *world-picture*—an entire language system or set of beliefs. Such a world-picture serves as a background or encompassing conceptual framework for more restricted and limited language-games, as well as for the 'moves' we make in the latter. In his *Tractatus* Wittgenstein stressed the role of logically independent elementary propositions, each of which depicts some particular possible state of affairs. In his later writings, especially in *The Blue Book* and *Philosophical Investigations,* he stressed the role of language-games as making clear the uses to which various expressions are put. We come to understand the use (and so the 'meaning') of a linguistic expression by making explicit the grammar of the language-game in accordance with which it performs its role. In *On Certainty,* without in the least minimizing or abandoning the importance of the notion of a language-game, Wittgenstein broadens the scope of his analysis by stressing that it is not only particular language-games to which we must attend in order to see how various expressions are used. There is something even more inclusive and basic than a language-game of some restricted variety to be taken into account. He calls this a 'world-picture'. It represents an entire network or framework of propositions, concepts, beliefs, and practices—in short a 'form of life'.

In order to understand certain expressions from a philosophical point of view (to get at their genuine and effective 'logical status'), it is important, he would say, to determine whether it is being used in the context of stating a world-picture, or on the other hand plays a role in some more limited language-game. To take an example, the category of 'empirical propositions' cannot be fruitfully examined without asking ourselves whether the empirical proposition in question belongs to a world-picture, or to one or another of the natural sciences, or is used in some special situation or circumstance of everyday life. The logical status and role of a particular empirical proposition (e.g., 'This is a tree', 'I have two hands') will *differ* as we assign it to one or another of these categories. Similarly, he would say, when we come to analyze such an expression as 'I know', 'I am certain', 'true', 'ground', we must consider its role in the kind of language-game to which it belongs and ask whether it is part of an entire world-picture or involves a language-game different from this. Wittgenstein's critique of Moore has to do with the latter's failure to take note of these differences, and his tendency to assimilate all uses, for example, of 'I know' or 'I am certain', to one another, as if they shared in the same basic characteristics. In this Moore was in error, Wittgenstein would say. The role of 'I know' or 'I am certain', and so on in connection with propositions that belong to the expression of a world-picture is quite different from that which it has when attached to a proposition that is not part of the very framework of a world-picture.

If Moore says he knows the earth existed etc., most of us will grant him that it has existed all that time, and also believe him when he says he is convinced of it. . . .

However, we can ask: May someone have telling grounds for believing that the earth has only existed for a short time, say since his own birth?—Suppose he had always been told that,—would he have any good reason to doubt it? Men have believed that they could make rain; why should not a king be brought up in the belief that the world began with him? And if Moore and this king were to meet and discuss, could Moore really prove his belief to be the right one? I do not say that Moore could not convert the king to his view, but it would be a conversion of a special kind; the king would be brought to look at the world in a different way. . . .

The propositions presenting what Moore '*knows*' are all of such a kind that it is difficult to imagine *why* anyone should believe the contrary. E.g., the proposition that Moore has spent his whole life in close proximity to the earth.—Once more I can speak of myself here instead of speaking of Moore. What could induce me to believe the opposite? Either a memory, or having been told.—

Everything that I have seen or heard gives me the conviction that no man has ever been far from the earth. Nothing in my picture of the world speaks in favour of the opposite.

But I did not get my picture of the world by satisfying myself of its correctness; nor do I have it because I am satisfied of its correctness. No: it is the inherited background against which I distinguish between true and false.

The propositions describing this world-picture might be part of a kind of mythology. And their role is like that of rules of a game; and the game can be learned purely practically, without learning any explicit rules.

It might be imagined that some propositions, of the form of empirical propositions, were hardened and functioned as channels for such empirical propositions as were not hardened but fluid; and that this relation altered with time, in that fluid propositions hardened, and hard ones became fluid.

The mythology may change back into a state of flux, the river-bed of thoughts may shift. But I distinguish between the movement of the waters on the river-bed and the shift of the bed itself; though there is not a sharp division of the one from the other.

But if someone were to say "So logic too is an empirical science" he would be wrong. Yet this is right: the same proposition may get treated at one time as something to test by experience, at another as a rule of testing.

And the bank of that river consists partly of hard rock, subject to no alteration or only to an imperceptible one, partly of sand, which now in one place now in another gets washed away, or deposited.

The truths which Moore says he knows, are such as, roughly speaking, all of us know, if he knows them.

Such a proposition might be e.g., "My body has never disappeared and reappeared again after an interval."

Might I not believe that once, without knowing it, perhaps in a state of unconsciousness, I was taken far away from the earth—that other people even know this, but do not mention it to me? But this would not fit into the rest of my convictions. Not that I could describe the system of these convictions. Yet my convictions do form a system, a structure.

And now if I were to say "It is my unshakeable conviction that etc.", this means in the present case too that I have not consciously arrived at the conviction by following a particular line of thought, but that it is anchored in all my *questions and answers,* so anchored that I cannot touch it.

I am for example also convinced that the sun is not a hole in the vault of heaven.

All testing, all confirmation and disconfirmation of a hypothesis takes place already within a system. And this system is not a more or less arbitrary and doubtful point of departure for all our arguments: no, it belongs to the essence of what we call an argument. The system is not so much the point of departure, as the element in which arguments have their life.[109]

In the foregoing passage, Wittgenstein touches on all the salient points to which he comes back over and over again in *On Certainty,* sometimes by varying his examples and his metaphors, sometimes by developing a point in greater detail, or by showing its connection with other matters from a different perspective. Let us attempt, now, to disentangle the strands in Wittgenstein's argument by considering a number of these fundamental aspects. Since these are interwoven with one another in a multitude of ways, it is not to be assumed that the order in which I shall discuss them in what follows represents a special order of logical priority or of relative importance.

1. The truisms that Moore claims to know belong, each of them, to what Wittgenstein calls a 'world-picture'. A world-picture is described by Wittgenstein by means of various metaphors. In the passage quoted above, he speaks of it as an 'inherited background', as 'the river-bed of thoughts', and as a 'system'. Elsewhere he compares it to an 'axis'.

I do not explicitly learn the propositions that stand fast for me. I can *discover* them subsequently like the axis around which a body rotates. This axis is not fixed in the sense that anything holds it fast, but the movement around it determines its immobility.[110]

Or again, he sometimes compares a world-picture to a 'scaffolding', to a 'whole picture', to 'an unused siding'.

I have a telephone conversation with New York. My friend tells me that his young trees have buds of such and such a kind. I am now convinced that his tree is. . . . Am I also convinced that the earth exists?
The existence of the earth is rather part of the whole *picture* which forms the starting-point of belief for me.
Does my telephone call to New York strengthen my conviction that the earth exists?
Much seems to be fixed, and it is removed from the traffic. It is so to speak shunted onto an unused siding.
Now it gives our way of looking at things, and our researches, their form. Perhaps it was once disputed. But perhaps, for unthinkable ages, it has belonged to the *scaffolding* of our thoughts. (Every human being has parents.)[111]

Again, he compares a world-picture to the 'hinges' of our thoughts and actions.

That is to say, the *questions* that we raise and our *doubts* depend on the fact that some propositions are exempt from doubt, are as it were like hinges on which those turn.
That is to say, it belongs to the logic of our investigations that certain things are *in deed* not doubted.
But it isn't that the situation is like this: We just *can't* investigate everything, and for that reason we are forced to rest content with assumption. If I want the door to turn, the hinges must stay put.[112]

Wittgenstein sometimes uses the metaphor of 'foundations' or 'grounds' in connection with the role of a world-picture. While a world-picture provides a ground or foundation for other propositions or beliefs, he says, it itself has no foundation, it is 'groundless'.

At the foundation of well-founded belief lies belief that is not founded.[113]

The metaphor of 'foundations' ('grounds'), as Wittgenstein appeals to it, should not be thought of in the sense in which other philosophers or scientists have sometimes used it. He does not think of our system of beliefs as made to fall into a deductive arrangement in which certain more general principles, axioms, and premises will serve as the 'foundation' for others derived from them. (This use of the notion of 'foundations', as modeled on Euclid's system, was at the back of such 'foundational' systems as Spinoza's *Ethics*, Descartes' *Principles of Philosophy*, and Newton's *Mathematical Principles of Natural Philosophy*.) The propositions or 'beliefs' of a world-picture, in Wittgenstein's sense, do not constitute a set of axioms, principles, or general hypotheses, with respect to other propositions or beliefs. A world-picture does not 'provide a foundation' in this sense. Rather, in Wittgenstein's metaphor, one might form the image of an entire wall-structure of a house, or of the structure of a nest of twigs.

What I hold fast to is not *one* proposition but a nest of propositions.

. . . .

When we first begin to *believe* anything, what we believe is not a single proposition, it is a whole system of propositions. (Light dawns gradually over the whole.)

It is not single axioms that strike me as obvious, it is a system in which consequences and premises give one another *mutual* support.

. . . .

What would it be like to doubt now whether I have two hands? Why can't I imagine it at all? What would I believe if I didn't believe that? So far I have no system at all within which this doubt might exist.

I have arrived at the rock bottom of my convictions.

And one might almost say that these foundation-walls are carried by the whole house.[114]

Like the individual twigs in a nest, the beliefs of a world-picture, including the truisms Moore mentions, mutually support one another. It is because they form a network of beliefs and propositions, that they not only support one another but also any items that may come to 'rest' 'within' or 'upon' them.

2. How is a world-picture acquired? There are various sources or 'inputs'. Many of these are often unconscious, not explicitly recognized by the individual. We take many things on authority, on trust. It is not always a matter of 'experience teaching us' so-and-so, or of our deliberately setting out to test the truth or falsity of some belief, or of having a question answered or a doubt removed. Rather, as we acquire a host of beliefs, some might later be called 'empirical propositions', others 'mathematical', 'methodological', or 'grammatical' rules, still others 'definitions', and so on.

The child learns to believe a host of things. I.e. it learns to act according to these beliefs. Bit by bit there forms a system of what is believed, and in that system some things stand unshakeably fast and some are more or less liable to shift. What stands fast does so, not because it is intrinsically obvious or convincing; it is rather held fast by what lies around it.

· · · · · · · ·

As children we learn facts; e.g., that every human being has a brain, and we take them on trust. I believe that there is an island, Australia, of such-and-such a shape, and so on and so on; I believe that I had great-grandparents, that the people who gave themselves out as my parents really were my parents, etc. This belief may never have been expressed; even the thought that it was so, never thought.

The child learns by believing the adult. Doubt comes *after* belief.

I learned an enormous amount and accepted it on human authority, and then I found some things confirmed or disconfirmed by my own experience.

In general, I take as true what is found in text-books, of geography for example. Why? I say: All these facts have been confirmed a hundred times over. But how do I know that? What is my evidence for it? I have a world-picture. Is it true or false? Above all it is the substratum of all my enquiring and asserting. The propositions describing it are not all equally subject to testing.[115]

3. In the light of Wittgenstein's emphasis on the role of various beliefs and propositions that constitute the framework of a world-picture, as contrasted with those that do not function in this way, he points out that, for example, simply to label a proposition an 'empirical proposition' does not thereby tell us what its actual logical status and role is. "Our 'empirical propositions' do not form a homogeneous mass."[116] The truths Moore claims to know with certainty may admittedly be labeled 'empirical' (or 'factual') propositions. Wittgenstein's point is that if we do so label them it is important to recognize that they function in a different way from others also so labeled.

When Moore says he *knows* such and such, he is really enumerating a lot of empirical propositions which we affirm without special testing; propositions, that is, which have a peculiar logical role in the system of our empirical propositions.[117]

Thus, superficially, the statements 'The earth existed for many years before I was born' and 'There are live volcanoes on some of Jupiter's moons' may be assigned to the same broad category of 'empirical propositions'. Or the statements 'There are material objects in the world' and 'There are lions in Africa' may also be thought to belong to the same category of 'empirical' propositions. Their logical status and role, however, is completely different in the way they would normally be used. The first of these empirical propositions in each pair would normally not be investigated, tested, or accepted, on the ground that 'it rests on experience' and 'is in agreement with reality'. Not every empirical proposition is examined to see whether it 'agrees with reality' and is tested by an 'appeal to experience'. 'Agreement with reality' and an 'appeal to experience' will themselves be determined by the world-picture we use, and will not apply to the beliefs that make up a world-picture. Insofar as one already uses and accepts a world-picture, one does not ask about it as a composite whole or about its component beliefs, "Is it in agreement with reality? Does experience support it?" Rather it is the world-picture that provides the norms, criteria, and rules for testing other propositions, for determining whether *they* are 'in agreement with reality'. "If the true is what is grounded, then the ground is not *true,* nor yet false."[118] Concerning the beliefs that make up our world-picture, and those that Moore calls 'truisms', "we don't for example, arrive at any of them as a result of investigation. There are e.g. historical investigations and investigations into the shape and also the age of the earth, but not into whether the earth has existed during the last hundred years."[119]

At a given stage of human development, or for a community that shares a world-view, certain factual claims may still be open to test or subject to doubt and inquiry. At another stage of development, or for other communities, some 'empirical propositions' will be part of the framework of the world-picture; they will have become 'fossilized', made part of the 'bedrock'. In other words, a particular empirical proposition may shift its status from being still free-floating to becoming fixed, from being "on the route traveled by inquiry" to being "shifted to an unused siding." We cannot tell of any sentence, *taken in isolation,* where it belongs. One has to examine it in its particular circumstances of use. For some situations, the statement 'I have two hands' (if, for example, uttered by an amputee who is suffering from hallucinations) would be open to the test of experience and therefore falsifiable, whereas the same sentence (as one of Moore's truisms) would not be uttered as a hypothesis to be tested if it is simply one of many beliefs we take for granted in our daily practice and actions. We rely on it, as on innumerable other beliefs, as part of our fixed background, our world-picture.

Does anyone ever test whether this table remains in existence when no one is paying attention to it?

We check the story of Napoleon, but not whether all the reports about him are based on sense-deception, forgery and the like. For whenever we test anything, we are already presupposing something that is not tested. Now am I to say that the experiment which perhaps I make in order to test the truth of a proposition presupposes the truth of the proposition that the apparatus I believe I see is really there (and the like)?

Doesn't testing come to an end?

. . . .

It is clear that our empirical propositions do not all have the same status, since one can lay down such a proposition and turn it from an empirical proposition into a norm of description.

Think of chemical investigations. Lavoisier makes experiments with substances in his laboratory and now he concludes that this and that takes place when
there is burning. He does not say that it might happen otherwise another time. He
has got hold of a definite world-picture—not of course one that he invented: he
learned it as a child. I say world-picture and not hypothesis, because it is the
matter-of-course foundation for his research and as such also goes unmen-
tioned.[120]

The propositions Lavoisier *discovers* as a result of experiments and
accepts henceforth as true are empirical propositions to be distinguished
from those already part of his world-picture. However, *some* of what
Lavoisier discovers may later become shunted into the framework of a
world-picture and no longer be tested. The converse process is possible as
well. At one time it was part of a widely held world-picture that the earth
was at the center of the universe. Following upon the upheaval accomplished by the Copernican revolution, what belonged to the 'bedrock' of
men's beliefs was dislodged (along with many other beliefs) and made
'fluid' once more. In the process a new constellation of beliefs, a largely
new world-picture, came to take its place. Even the king Wittgenstein
alludes to (the one who disagrees with Moore about whether the earth had
existed for many years) might eventually be persuaded to change his
world-picture.

To take a final example, the claim a person might make at one stage
of history that he has been on the moon will be rejected as so greatly in
violent conflict with the whole system of accepted beliefs that he will be
regarded as 'demented'; yet *now* this statement will be acknowledged as
perfectly meaningful, even possibly true. Our standards of 'reasonableness' and 'intelligibility'—what is shared at a given time by an entire community as part of its world-picture—may undergo change. Wittgenstein's
use of the following example, written by him *before* man's historic first
landing on the moon, is a case in point.

Suppose some adult had told a child that he had been on the moon. The
child tells me the story, and I say it was only a joke, the man hadn't been on the
moon; no one has ever been on the moon; the moon is a long way off and it is
impossible to climb up there or fly there.—If now the child insists, saying perhaps
there is a way of getting there which I don't know, etc. what reply could I make to
him? What reply could I make to the adults of a tribe who believe that people
sometimes go to the moon (perhaps that is how they interpret their dreams), and
who indeed grant that there are no ordinary means of climbing up to it or flying
there?—But a child will not ordinarily stick to such a belief and will soon be
convinced by what we tell him seriously.

Isn't this altogether like the way one can instruct a child to believe in God,
or that none exists, and it will accordingly be able to produce apparently telling
grounds for the one or the other?

"But is there then no objective truth? Isn't it true, or false, that someone
has been on the moon?" If we are thinking within our system, then it is certain

338   *Contemporary Analytic Philosophy*

that no one has ever been on the moon. Not merely is nothing of the sort ever seriously reported to us by reasonable people, but our whole system of physics forbids us to believe it. For this demands answers to the questions "How did he overcome the force of gravity?" "How could he live without an atmosphere?" and a thousand others which could not be answered. But suppose that instead of all these answers we met the reply: "We don't know *how* one gets to the moon, but those who get there know at once that they are there; and even you can't explain everything." We should feel ourselves intellectually very distant from someone who said this.[121]

4. The component items of a world-picture are sometimes described by Wittgenstein as being 'judgments'. In using this expression Wittgenstein wishes to stress that a world-picture and its component 'concepts', 'beliefs', 'rules', and 'propositions' form a network that is not simply a detached and purely intellectual construction. It is, rather, interwoven in countless ways and on countless occasions with our daily practices. A world-picture is, like every other restricted language-game, grounded in a form of life, a 'praxis'. We do not regard the items of our world-picture as 'assumptions' or 'hypotheses' to be checked against experience.

If I say "*we assume* that the earth has existed for many years past" (or something similar), then of course it sounds strange that we should *assume* such a thing. But in the entire system of our language-games it belongs to the foundations. The assumption, one might say, forms the basis of action, and therefore, naturally, of thought.[122]

The 'truistic' judgments that make up our world-picture, having been acquired on trust, are acted on unreflectively, uncritically, unquestioningly.

Why do I not satisfy myself that I have two feet when I want to get up from a chair? There is no why. I simply don't. This is how I act.

My judgments themselves characterize the way I judge, characterize the nature of judgment.

How does someone judge which is his right and which his left hand? How do I know that my judgment will agree with someone else's? How do I know that this colour is blue? If I don't trust *myself* here, why should I trust anyone else's judgment? Is there a why? Must I not begin to trust somewhere? That is to say: somewhere I must begin with not-doubting; and that is not, so to speak, hasty but excusable: it is part of judging.[123]

The way we act—what we do, what we avoid, how we manipulate things, interact with objects or persons in our environment—shows the implicit, unexpressed presence of various judgments we rely on in our actions.

My life shows that I know or am certain that there is a chair over there, or a door, and so on.—I tell a friend e.g. "Take that chair over there", "Shut the door", etc. etc.

. . . .

Children do not learn that books exist, that armchairs exist, etc. etc.,—they learn to fetch books, sit in armchairs, etc. etc.

Later, questions about the existence of things do of course arise. "Is there such a thing as a unicorn?" and so on. But such a question is possible only because as a rule no corresponding question presents itself. For how does one know how to set about satisfying oneself of the existence of unicorns? How did one learn the method of determining whether something exists or not?[124]

5. A world-picture is something that is shared and that makes instruction, training, and communication possible. It provides the framework *within* which particular agreements and disagreements, doubts and settlement of doubts, making mistakes and correcting them, can take place. This is not to say that everyone everywhere and throughout history has had the same world-picture. Unlike Moore, who stresses the unique, inescapable, unchanging, and allegedly universally shared world-picture of Common Sense, regardless of what philosophers and others may say to the contrary, Wittgenstein takes the fact of *differences* in world-pictures seriously and considers what is involved when a world-picture is shared, and the possible ways people might come to adopt a different world-picture (at least in part) from the one they already have.

Differences among world-pictures are not simple, like differences between logically contradictory or contrary propositions (e.g., between 'All A are B' and 'Some A are not B', or between 'All A are B' and 'No A are B'), or like the differences that hold between rival scientific hypotheses. These types of differences are identified within a conceptual system (e.g., one that accepts ordinary rules of logic, or ordinary criteria of scientific method). They have to do with oppositions or incompatibilities among particular propositions within a wider framework, where the latter is relatively stable, is accepted and used as a shared basis from which to judge the competing statements as these come to be proposed within the total system, and where the resolution of the conflict (if and when made) leaves the total system for the most part and perhaps wholly unaffected. By contrast, differences, conflicts, and 'oppositions' among world-pictures involve entire frameworks themselves, rather than isolable propositions within a framework. To challenge another framework, or to fail to come to agreement even about this background of beliefs, rules, and standards, is a far more serious type of difference. Where entire systems of beliefs are in conflict, these cannot be reduced to differences of a relatively simple 'logical' or 'factual' sort. For this reason appeal to 'reasons', 'logic', or 'facts' may be of little avail, because the standards of appeal are themselves not shared. To use an example Wittgenstein offers in the quotation below, if Moore says "I know this is wine and not blood" (in connection with the celebration of the Mass) and a Catholic disagrees, this cannot be settled finally in Moore's favor by performing a chemical analysis. The appeal to this type of test is one of the basic matters at issue here.

There are no commonly held adjudicative standards or methods by which the clashes on the level of differences in world-pictures can be resolved. What is called for here is not argument and the giving of reasons, but a type of conversion, the change in one's entire outlook. It calls for what Wittgenstein calls 'persuasion'.

I can imagine a man who had grown up in quite special circumstances and been taught that the earth came into being 50 years ago, and therefore believed this. We might instruct him: the earth has long . . . etc.—We should be trying to give him our picture of the world.
This would happen through a kind of *persuasion.* . . .

. . . .

Is it wrong for me to be guided in my actions by the propositions of physics? Am I to say I have no good ground for doing so? Isn't precisely this what we call a 'good ground'?
Supposing we met people who did not regard that as a telling reason. Now, how do we imagine this? Instead of the physicist, they consult an oracle. (And for that we consider them primitive.) Is it wrong for them to consult an oracle and be guided by it?—If we call this "wrong" aren't we using our language-game as a base from which to *combat* theirs?
And are we right or wrong to combat it? Of course there are all sorts of slogans which will be used to support our proceedings.
Where two principles really do meet which cannot be reconciled with one another, then each man declares the other a fool and heretic.
I said I would 'combat' the other man,—but wouldn't I give him *reasons?* Certainly; but how far do they go? At the end of reasons comes *persuasion.* (Think what happens when missionaries convert natives.)

. . . .

I believe that every human being has two human parents; but Catholics believe that Jesus only had a human mother. And other people might believe that there are human beings with no parents, and give no credence to all the contrary evidence. Catholics believe as well that in certain circumstances a wafer completely changes its nature, and at the same time that all evidence proves the contrary. And so if Moore said "I know that this is wine and not blood", Catholics would contradict him.
What is the belief that all human beings have parents based on? On experience. And how can I base this sure belief on my experience? Well, I base it not only on the fact that I have known the parents of certain people but on everything that I have learnt about the sexual life of human beings and their anatomy and physiology: also on what I have heard and seen of animals. But then is that really a proof?

. . . .

But what men consider reasonable or unreasonable alters. At certain periods men find reasonable what at other periods they found unreasonable. And vice versa.

But is there not objective character here?
Very intelligent and well-educated people believe in the story of creation in the Bible, while others hold it as proven false, and the grounds are well known to the former.[125]

6. Wittgenstein repeatedly calls attention to the basic difference between 'explanation' and 'description'. The former involves giving a *justification* of one's claims by appealing to what, if accepted, will provide the grounds and reasons for one's position with respect to what is in question, under dispute, or subject to doubt. However, the process of giving reasons, grounds, and justifications must itself come to an end at some point.

At some point one has to pass from explanation to mere description.

. . . .

Well, if everything speaks for an hypothesis and nothing against it—is it then certainly true? One may designate it as such.—But does it certainly agree with reality, with the facts?—With this question you are already going round in a circle.
To be sure there is justification, but justification comes to an end.[126]

When justification (explanation, giving of reasons and grounds) does come to an end, all one can do is to give *descriptions,* and say "*this* is how it is done," "*this* is what I accept," "*these* are the standards (rules) to be used."
Where, then, an appeal to a world-picture is involved in the process of giving grounds for some belief, proposition, hypothesis, proposal, within the world-picture, one cannot, in pursuing the chain of grounds and reasons, also give reasons, grounds, and justifications for the world-picture itself. When one reaches a statement or network of statements that belong to (or constitute part of) the very fabric of a world-picture, at that level 'giving grounds' and justifications ceases, and 'description' takes over. Hence if there is a fundamental clash among different world-pictures, one cannot appeal to some 'higher', 'independent', or 'neutral' source of adjudication as a way of determining which, if any, among these competing points of view is true. Unless the conflicting world-pictures share a set of 'higher' adjudicating standards, each will fall back on its own rules and beliefs to provide the grounds for its own choices. At that point one has reached the 'bedrock' of the world-picture; at that point one can only describe it, not justify it. For this reason Wittgenstein would say that the attempt by some philosophers to give reasons and justifications for the soundness of a particular world-picture on the ground that it is "in agreement with reality" or "rests on experience" is ineffective. "Here we see that the idea of 'agreement with reality' does not have any clear application."[127] The use of any such 'criterion' reveals a set of rules, beliefs, and standards internal to, and constitutive of, a particular world-

picture; these are not necessarily binding on a world-picture wholly at variance with it. The most one can hope for at this level is a process of 'conversion' or 'persuasion', not the compelling force of arguments, reasons, grounds, and justifications.

7. For Moore, the expression 'I know', 'I am certain', and 'I cannot be mistaken' are used interchangeably. When Moore says in connection with one of his truisms "I know such and such," it is tantamount to his saying "I am certain that such and such is true," or "I cannot be mistaken that such and such is the case." Wittgenstein criticizes Moore for treating these expressions in this way. He does so on several grounds. The basic one has to do with Wittgenstein's interest in making the distinction we have been examining between what belongs to a world-picture and what does not.

Taken in isolation, apart from a knowledge of the context in which it is used, a sentence—e.g., "This is a tree," "The earth existed for many years before I was born," "My name is M. K. M.," "I have two hands"—cannot be recognized to belong to a world-picture framework or not. Its logical role and status will depend upon the circumstances of its use and whether it belongs to a world-picture or not. Once this has been established, Wittgenstein would say, we can determine the appropriateness of using such expressions as 'I know ———', 'I am certain ———', 'I cannot be mistaken that ——— is true', and so on. In his criticisms of Moore's use of these expressions, Wittgenstein appeals to those language-games in which these expressions are ordinarily used, i.e., in which they are used in connection with propositions that *do not* form part of a world-picture.

One of the principal criticisms Wittgenstein makes of Moore's attempt to defend common sense is that the defense is a misplaced one. The use Moore makes of the phrases 'I know ———' or 'I am certain ——— is true' is a misuse. Each of the propositions in Moore's list of truisms belongs to what Wittgenstein calls a 'world-picture', and in connection with propositions that belong to a world-picture it is inappropriate to use 'I know' or 'I am certain'. These expressions, as normally used, apply to other propositions, those that do not form part of a world-picture.

8. On the topic of 'doubt', Wittgenstein takes a position that has a strong resemblance to Peirce's attack on Descartes' proposed use of the method of universal doubt. "If you tried to doubt everything you would not get as far as doubting anything. The game of doubting itself presupposes certainty."[128] Like Peirce, Wittgenstein asserts that genuine doubt takes place against a background of belief that is undoubted. This background provides the unquestioned rules, beliefs, and standards by which to resolve particular doubts as these arise at particular junctures of experience. In order to genuinely doubt something, there must be *grounds* for

doubt. These grounds cannot, at the same time, be doubted. The grounds for doubt are kept fixed and undoubted in order to state what is in doubt and to proceed with appropriate steps to try to remove the doubt.

If e.g. someone says "I don't know if there's a hand here" he might be told "Look closer."—This possibility of satisfying oneself is part of the language-game. Is one of its essential features.[129]

If we tell him "look closer" it is because in the present context we are not doubting the reliability of using one's eyes, or other suitable methods of testing the truth of the statement. Further, if someone doubted that he had a hand, he must at least be certain about the meaning of the words he uses in expressing his doubt. "If you are not certain of any fact, you cannot be certain of the meaning of your words either."[130] If someone were to say "I don't know if this is a hand," Wittgenstein would reply:

But do you know what the word "hand" means? And don't say "I know what it means now for me". And isn't it an empirical fact—that *this* word is used like *this?*

And here the strange thing is that when I am quite certain of how the words are used, have no doubt about it, I can still give no *grounds* for my way of going on. If I tried I could give a thousand, but none as certain as the very thing they were supposed to be grounds for.[131]

The propositions one accepts as part of one's world-picture are not in doubt.

Admittedly, if you are obeying the order "Bring me a book", you may have to check whether the thing you see over there really is a book, but then you do at least know what people mean by "book"; and if you don't you can look it up,— but then you must know what some other word means. And the fact that a word means such-and-such, is used in such-and-such a way, is in turn an empirical fact, like the fact that what you see over there is a book.

Therefore, in order for you to be able to carry out an order there must be some empirical fact about which you are not in doubt. Doubt itself rests on what is beyond doubt.

. . . .

"I know that I am a human being." In order to see how unclear the sense of this proposition is, consider its negation. At most it might be taken to mean "I know I have the organs of a human". (E.g. a brain which, after all, no one has ever yet seen.) But what about such a proposition as "I know I have a brain"? Can I doubt it? Grounds for *doubt* are lacking! Everything speaks in its favour, nothing against it. Nevertheless it is imaginable that my skull should turn out empty when it was operated on.[132]

The various propositions Moore enumerates belong to a world-picture, and so are not open to doubt. In falling back on them, in taking them for granted, they provide grounds for other propositions that are in doubt, or for which grounds can be given if needed. As part of a world-picture, they are neither in doubt nor have nor need grounds. If they were doubted, this would normally be taken as a sign either of madness or of the challenge faced by a rival world-picture.

I, L. W., believe, am sure, that my friend hasn't sawdust in his body or in his head, even though I have no direct evidence of my senses to the contrary. I am sure, by reason of what has been said to me, of what I have read, and of my experience. To have doubts about it would seem to me madness—of course, this is also in agreement with other people; but *I* agree with them.[133]

9. Under what conditions do we say that someone is *mistaken?* Wittgenstein points out that if the beliefs under consideration belong to a world-picture, we should not say of anyone who rejected them that he was mistaken. These are on a different level from ordinary propositions and beliefs about which one *might* be mistaken. In some cases a challenge to or a rejection of the propositions belonging to the world-picture of Common Sense may be set down to a radical and pervasive mental disturbance, in other cases to a genuine difference in world-picture. Where such oppositions, differences, and incompatibilities of entire systems of belief are involved, we do not say that the person has made a mistake. Something more fundamental is involved. Even to express certain kinds of 'doubts' may reveal a fundamental difference in an entire system of beliefs, a difference whose existence tells us that more than the simple possibility of correcting a mistake is present.

If someone said to me that he doubted whether he had a body I should take him to be a half-wit. But I shouldn't know what it would mean to try to convince him that he had one. And if I had said something, and that had removed his doubt, I should not know how or why.[134]

There are certain propositions that one may take to be true, and yet be mistaken, i.e., discover that they are false. To recognize such mistakes does not mean that one is thereby upsetting or challenging an entire world-picture.

We may be dealing, for example, with the certainty of memory, or again of perception. I may be sure of something, but still know what test might convince me of error. I am e.g. quite sure of the date of a battle, but if I should find a different date in a recognized work of history, I should alter my opinion, and this would not mean I lost all faith in judging.[135]

On the other hand, consider the following situations:

For months I have lived at address A, I have read the name of the street and the number of the house countless times, have received countless letters here and given countless people the address. If I am wrong about it, the mistake is hardly less than if I were (wrongly) to believe I was writing Chinese and not German.

If my friend were to imagine one day that he had been living for a long time past in such and such a place, etc. etc., I should not call this a *mistake,* but rather a mental disturbance, perhaps a transient one.

Not every false belief of this sort is a mistake.[136]

Thus if one makes a mistake, not only does it have a cause (perhaps some temporary and relatively minor psychological disturbance, the effect of taking some drug, physical exhaustion, and so on) but one can appeal to certain procedures and rules in terms of which we should judge that a mistake has been made. One adds a column of figures and discovers after rechecking that a mistake had been made. In order to do this one appeals to the accepted rules of arithmetic and to the reliability of the procedures used in making the recheck.

When someone makes a mistake, this can be fitted into what he knows aright.

. . . .

If someone supposed that *all* our calculations were uncertain and that we could rely on none of them (justifying himself by saying that mistakes are always possible) perhaps we would say he was crazy. But can we say he is in error? Does he not just react differently? We rely on calculations, he doesn't; we are sure, he isn't.[137]

10. What, finally, of the use of the phrase 'I know'? Wittgenstein's argument is that when we examine the typical language-games in which 'I know' is employed, we do not find that Moore's use of this phrase in the examples he gives falls into any of them. Moore's defense therefore fails; he misconceives the status and role of the propositions he adduces. They are not propositions about which it is appropriate to say that he *knows* each of them to be true. Nor, in challenging the appropriateness of Moore's using the phrase, is Wittgenstein saying to Moore, "No, you don't know them," meaning by that that each of these propositions is *false.* In saying to Moore, "You don't *know* it," Wittgenstein is saying rather that it is a *misuse* of the expression 'I know' to apply it in the way Moore does.

What, then, according to Wittgenstein, are the ordinary uses of 'I know'?

The correct use of the expression "I know". Someone with bad sight asks me: do you believe that the thing we can see there is a tree?" I reply "I *know* it is; I can see it clearly and am familiar with it"—A: "Is N. N. at home?"—I: "I believe he is."—A: "Was he at home yesterday?"—I: "Yesterday he was—I know he was; I spoke to him."—A: "Do you know or only believe that this part of the house is built on later than the rest?"—I: "I *know* it is; I asked so and so about it."

. . . .

"I know" often means: I have the proper grounds for my statement. So if the other person is acquainted with the language-game, he would admit that I know. The other, if he is acquainted with the language-game, must be able to imagine *how* one may know something of the kind.

. . . .

If someone believes something, we needn't always be able to answer the question 'why he believes it'; but if he knows something, then the question "how does he know?" must be capable of being answered.

. . . .

Instead of "I know it" one may say in some cases "That's how it is—rely upon it." In some cases, however "I learned it years and years ago"; and sometimes: "I am sure it is so."[138]

Furthermore, when someone says 'I know————', it makes sense to *doubt* what he claims to know; it also makes sense to say that he may be *mistaken* in what he says.

In particular circumstances one says "you can rely on this"; and this assurance may be justified or unjustified in everyday language, and it may also count as justified even when what was foretold does not occur. A *language-game exists* in which this assurance is employed.[139]

And if one uses the expression 'I know————', it must be appropriate in the circumstances.

My difficulty can also be shown like this: I am sitting talking to a friend. Suddenly I say: "I knew all along that you were so-and-so." Is that really just a superfluous, though true, remark?

I feel as if these words were like "Good morning" said to someone in the middle of a conversation.[140]

The nub of Wittgenstein's argument and criticism of Moore can be stated as follows. The language-games in which 'I know' receives its ordinary meaning can be specified as being of two sorts. In one, for someone to say 'I know' is a way of giving assurance to others that the speaker (or writer) can be relied upon. He has *special qualifications* that entitle him to give assurance to others of the truth of the proposition he claims to know. He has 'looked into the matter' and what he reports is to be accepted as a true account of the matter. "If someone says he *knows* something, it must be something that, by general consent, he is in a position to know."[141] Of course, despite these assurances, it is open to someone to legitimately *doubt* the proposition in question.

In the second use of 'I know', the emphasis falls not so much on the competence or special qualifications of the one putting forth the proposition as on the truth of the proposition itself. It is to be accepted as true because *compelling grounds* can be given to show that the proposition *is* true.

One says "I know" when one is ready to give compelling grounds. "I know" relates to a possibility of demonstrating the truth. . . . But if what he believes is of such kind that the grounds that he can give are no surer than his assertion, then he cannot say that he knows what he believes.

· · · · · · · ·

Whether *I know* something depends on whether the evidence backs me up or contradicts me.[142]

Wittgenstein's criticism of Moore is that neither of the foregoing ordinary uses of 'I know', whether taken singly or in conjunction, applies to the propositions Moore offers in his defense of Common Sense. It is *inappropriate* to use 'I know' in connection with any of the propositions Moore considers, e.g., 'I know the earth existed for many years before I was born', 'I know I have two hands'.

In the first place, there is *no special qualification* on the part of the speaker that he can offer as the basis for our relying on him.

Moore says he *knows* that the earth existed long before his birth. And put like that it seems to be a personal statement about him, even if it is in addition a statement about the physical world. Now it is philosophically uninteresting whether Moore knows this or that, but it is interesting that, and how, it can be known. If Moore had informed us that he knew the distance separating certain stars, we might conclude from that that he had made some special investigations, and we shall want to know what these were. But Moore chooses precisely a case in which we all seem to know the same as he, and without being able to say how. I believe e.g. that I know as much about this matter (the existence of the earth) as Moore does, and if he knows that it is as he says, then *I* know it too. For it isn't, either, as if he had arrived at his proposition by pursuing some line of thought which, while it is open to me, I have not in fact pursued.

· · · · · · · ·

Why doesn't Moore produce as one of the things that he knows, for example, that in such-and-such a part of England there is a village called so-and-so? In other words: why doesn't he mention a fact that is known to him and not to *every one* of us?[143]

In the second place, the propositions Moore offers as true in his defense of Common Sense cannot be said to be *known,* because they are in fact without grounds; they are groundless. "I cannot say that I have good grounds for the opinion that cats do not grow on trees or that I had a father and a mother."[144] One cannot give compelling grounds, reasons, or evidence to support any one of Moore's propositions, since they belong to a world-picture (a 'bedrock' or 'foundation').

I should like to say: Moore does not *know* what he asserts he knows, but it stands fast for him, as also for me; regarding it as absolutely solid is part of our *method* of doubt and enquiry.[145]

As parts of an entire system of propositions making up a world-picture, the propositions in question are accepted as true. However, no reasons or grounds are given or required, for nothing can be more fundamental than they already are. The entire framework itself is not grounded, not justified.

Hence, for both of these kinds of reasons, it is a misuse of the phrase 'I know' on Moore's part to use it in connection with any of the propositions he lists. At the same time, Wittgenstein does not overlook or deny the possibility that *there may be special circumstances* in which someone may *appropriately* use the phrase 'I know' in connection with one or another of the propositions Moore considers. Thus, a child learning arithmetic may say "I know 12 × 12 = 144," or in learning the names of colors may say "I know this is blue"; or someone who has been recovering from amnesia may say "I know my name is N. N."; or in a field full of mixed vegetation, where bushes, trees, and plants of all sorts are intertwined, a botanist may say, pointing to a particular specimen, "I know this is a tree."

> Suppose you were guiding a blind man's hand, and as you were guiding it along yours you said "this is my hand"; if he then said "are you sure?" or "do you know it is?", it would take very special circumstances for that to make sense.[146]

None of these cases, however, is in conflict with the basic point Wittgenstein is making. Moore's examples are not taken from any of these special situations in which the phrase 'I know' may be appropriately used.

CHAPTER VIII

Ontological Commitments

WILLARD V. O. QUINE

Willard Van Orman Quine (1908–), Professor of Philosophy at Harvard University, is a major representative of the tradition of analytic philosophy that derives from Frege and Russell. As with the two earlier thinkers, Quine's initial entry into philosophy was via the discipline of mathematics. As in the case of his predecessors, he has devoted a major share of his attention to the study of logic. Typically, too, his extensive writings in logic are not self-contained projects; his interest in their themes has been pursued with an eye to their manifold applications within the broader areas of philosophic concern. These include studies in the philosophy of mathematics, as one would expect, and much else besides. We might sum up his major preoccupations as a philosopher under two general headings—those having to do with the philosophy of language (or theory of meaning) and those having to do with ontology—both topics having, in his treatment, close interconnections. What he has to say in both these areas has marked affinities with the general orientation of empiricist and pragmatist philosophies. At the same time Quine has not hesitated to deviate, in certain respects, from these viewpoints. His work has had a large audience and wide impact, while also provoking much dissent and controversy. A study of the major lineaments of his thought offers, therefore, a good opportunity to examine some recent phases in the development of analytic philosophy. Two of Quine's papers, "On What There Is" and "Two Dogmas of Empiricism," have already achieved the status of classics.[1] In them Quine sets out in brief compass some of his characteristic and innovative claims. It will be helpful, in obtaining a preliminary

349

overview of his philosophy, to begin by examining the arguments presented in these papers.

"ON WHAT THERE IS"

The paper "On What There Is" deals with ontology, for this indeed is
how Quine would characterize that branch of philosophy; it seeks to determine the basic types or kinds of 'things there are'. In order to clarify
what this comes to, he begins by mentioning a few examples of answers to
this question that have been offered by various philosophers in setting out
their own ontologies—answers that, far from being universally accepted,
have generated much controversy. There are some philosophers who
claim we must acknowledge the *being* of nonexistent entities. Some
would give such ontologic status to individuals named in fiction or myth
(e.g., Pegasus); others would draw a distinction between actual entities
and possible ones, giving the latter a special status among things there
are; finally, there is a long and influential tradition of philosophers who
draw a fundamental contrast between the realm of particulars and that of
universals, the latter, it is said, enjoying objective and timeless reality.
Quine makes clear his distinct lack of sympathy for any of these types of
ontology. He points to the faulty grounds and misleading considerations
on which they have been based, and shows how one may avoid accepting
their conclusions. In addition to the foregoing he offers what he thinks is
at least a clear and neutral criterion for determining what are a philosopher's ontological commitments. This criterion would give us an important means for sorting out the point at which differences and rivalries
among ontologies emerge.

Let us consider, first, the philosophic view that claims that corresponding to the use of every singular term (e.g., a proper name) and as
giving that term its meaning, there is an entity having some type of being,
though not necessarily one of actual space-time existence. Quine invents
the names 'Mc X' and 'Wyman' to represent the class of those philosophers who would uphold such a position. Take the case of Pegasus.

If Pegasus *were* not, McX argues, we should not be talking about anything
when we use the word; therefore it would be nonsense to say even that Pegasus is
not. Thinking to show thus that the denial of Pegasus cannot be coherently maintained, he concludes that Pegasus is.

. . . .

Pegasus, Wyman maintains, has his being as an unactualized possible.
When we say of Pegasus that there is no such thing, we are saying, more pre-
cisely, that Pegasus does not have the special attribute of actuality. Saying that
Pegasus is not actual is on a par, logically, with saying that the Parthenon is not

red; in either case we are saying something about an entity whose being is unquestioned.[2]

There are several grounds on which Quine voices his dissatisfaction with the kind of ontology that claims, as in the above, that *there are* individual entities—whether possible, fictional (and so nonexistent), or otherwise—that are being named and so have being wherever any singular term is used. Two of his principal objections are the following.

One objection has to do with the lack of any clear criterion of identity by which one may identify and distinguish within the domain of individual possible entities one such possible individual from the others. "No entity without identity" is a much-quoted slogan coined by Quine to sum up his position here.

Take, for instance, the possible fat man in that doorway; and, again, the possible bald man in that doorway. Are they the same possible man, or two possible men? How do we decide? How many possible men are there in that doorway? Are there more possible thin ones that fat ones? How many of them are alike? Or would their being alike make them one? Are no *two* possible things alike? Is this the same as saying that it is impossible for two things to be alike? Or, finally, is the concept of identity simply inapplicable to unactualized possibles? But what sense can be found in talking of entities which cannot meaningfully be said to be identical with themselves and distinct from one another? These elements are well-nigh incorrigible. By a Fregean therapy of individual concepts, some effort might be made at rehabilitation; but I feel we'd do better simply to clear Wyman's slum and be done with it.[3]

For Quine, a second objection to the ontology of 'Wyman' and 'Mc X' is that it rests on the fallacy of equating meaning and naming. Such a philosophy presumes that if a singular term is meaningfully used it must name something, that there must *be* something for the name to designate or refer to. This view, Quine points out, is an error that was classically exposed in Russell's Theory of Definite Descriptions. The technique of analysis employed in that theory showed how one can transform a sentence containing a singular term into a sentence in which, without loss of meaning, that singular term is no longer present; what remain are only quantified variables, predicate (descriptive) expressions, and relevant logical constants. There is no need to posit an *entity* to correspond to or be named by the singular term (e.g., name or definite descriptive phrase), since the singular term has been eliminated in reparsing the sentence in accordance with the devices and rules of the predicate calculus.

When a statement of being or nonbeing is analyzed by Russell's theory of descriptions, it ceases to contain any expression which even purports to name the alleged entity whose being is in question, so that the meaningfulness of the statement no longer can be thought to presuppose that there be such an entity.[4]

Quine further points out how, for example, this Russellian approach, which he accepts, can be effectively used to avoid having to say there is an entity named by 'Pegasus'.

Now what of 'Pegasus'? This being a word rather than a descriptive phrase, Russell's argument does not immediately apply to it. However, it can easily be made to apply. We have only to rephrase 'Pegasus' as a description, in any way that seems adequately to single out our idea: say, 'the winged horse that was captured by Bellerophon'. Substituting such a phrase for 'Pegasus', we can then proceed to analyze the statement 'Pegasus is', or 'Pegasus is not', precisely on the analogy of Russell's analysis of 'The author of *Waverley* is' and 'The author of *Waverley* is not'.

In order thus to subsume a one-word name or alleged name such as 'Pegasus' under Russell's theory of description, we must, of course, be able first to translate the word into a description. But this is no real restriction. If the notion of Pegasus had been so obscure or so basic a one that no pat translation into a descriptive phrase had offered itself along familiar lines, we could still have availed ourselves of the following artificial and trivial-seeming device: we could have appealed to the *ex-hypothesi* unanalyzable, irreducible attribute of *being Pegasus*, adopting, for its expression, the verb 'is-Pegasus', or 'pegasizes'. The noun 'Pegasus' itself could then be treated as derivative, and identified after all with a description: 'the thing that is-Pegasus', 'the thing that pegasizes'.[5]

In criticizing those who confuse meaning and naming, Quine makes it clear that in his own use of 'meaning' in this context he would fall back on Frege's distinction between sense and reference. A term may have sense (i.e., 'meaning' as Quine uses this latter term) without necessarily having a reference, i.e., without there being some entity which it names or to which it refers.

What about those ontologies that claim that among the kinds of things there are one should include universals? Are there "such entities as attributes, relations, classes, numbers, functions"?[6] In examining this traditional controversial question, Quine singles out the case of attributes (qualities, properties) and shows why in his opinion there is no need to posit such entities. (He does not, in "On What There Is," give a full-fledged discussion of all the other varieties of claims in behalf of universals; nevertheless one readily detects, from the example he does discuss, his general reluctance to 'countenance' universals of any kind in his own ontological commitments.) There are those who, like McX, say that since there are red houses, red roses, red sunsets that have something in common, namely their redness, it is unquestionably true that *there is* such an attribute—redness. To this claim Quine offers the objection that the use of the abstract noun 'redness' does not commit us to saying there is a special entity (a universal), redness, being named by this noun; nor, of course, would he allow that the use of the general term 'red' as a predicate obliges us to posit some special entity, a universal, which *it* names or to which it refers.

On the first point, Quine denies that we must treat an abstract noun as a name for an entity, since we can always regard it as replaceable by a *predicate* expression that is either *true of* or *false of* the individual object it would describe, without itself designating some special type of individual entity.

One may admit that there are red houses, roses, and sunsets, but deny, except as a popular and misleading manner of speaking, that they have anything in common. The words 'houses', 'roses', and 'sunsets' are true of sundry individual entities which are houses and roses and sunsets, and the word 'red' or 'red object' is true of each of sundry individual entities which are red houses, red roses, red sunsets; but there is not, in addition, any entity whatever, individual or otherwise, which is named by the word 'redness', nor, for that matter, by the word 'househood', 'rosehood', 'sunsethood'. That the houses and roses and sunsets are all of them red may be taken as ultimate and irreducible, and it may be held that McX is no better off, in point of real explanatory power, for all the occult entities which he posits under such names as 'redness'.[7]

As for the claim that the predicative use of a general term such as 'red' also commits us to saying that it *names* an entity (the universal, redness), Quine points out the confusion involved. Once again, to say this is to overlook the important difference between naming and meaning. It does not follow that because a general term used predicatively is meaningful, its *meaningfulness* consists in its serving as a *name* for an entity.

McX cannot argue that predicates such as 'red' or 'is-red', which we all concur in using, must be regarded as names each of a single universal entity in order that they be meaningful at all. For we have seen that being a name of something is a much more special feature than being meaningful. He cannot even charge us—at least not by *that* argument—with having posited an attribute of pegasizing by our adoption of the predicate 'pegasizes'.[8]

Finally, Quine rejects any attempt to introduce universals under the heading of 'meanings' as that which general terms allegedly designate. He denies that we need such a category of entity as 'meanings' altogether. We can get along perfectly well by making the necessary distinction between what is *meaningful* and *meaningless* (difficult as the clarification of these terms may be) without having to admit as required for such clarification that there are some "special and irreducible intermediary entities called meanings."[9]

It is one of Quine's central purposes in his paper "On What There Is," as we have just seen, to point out certain typical differences among philosophers in their views of what kinds of entity there are, and not only to indicate his disagreement with some of these views but also to hint at the direction toward which he would gravitate in stating his own preferences for a sound ontological theory. Quine has another purpose in view as well. It is to formulate a clear criterion or standard, based on the use of logic, by which one could determine in an explicit and perspicuous way at what point differences in ontologies emerge. This is Quine's celebrated *criterion of ontological commitment*. It is a criterion that takes advantage of some of the familiar notational devices and distinctions of the predicate calculus.

The articulation and use of the criterion of ontological commitment has served as a focal point in Quine's approach to philosophy. In giving this entire topic the prominence he does, Quine has made a major contribution, as an analytical philosopher and logician, toward overcoming the prevailing hostility to 'metaphysics' that pervaded analytical philosophy during the period when it was dominated by logical positivism. This is not to say that Quine would encourage a return to cultivating metaphysics of the sort the positivists condemned. Quine is just as hostile to the excesses of 'speculative' and 'transcendent' metaphysics as were the positivists, yet his views may be taken as subscribing to the cautionary advice that one should not throw out the baby with the bath water. Rather than stress, as the positivists did, a wholly negative and polemical approach, Quine takes a positive stance with respect to the importance and need to cultivate sound ontological views. It does not follow that because some species of metaphysical writing is to be condemned, therefore the entire discipline is also to be shunned. Quine would revitalize and rehabilitate metaphysics as ontology. This can be done by reconstructing the formulation of the questions with which ontology deals in accordance with the guiding principles of modern logic. We could then be clear about what can be profitably inquired into, where legitimate differences arise among competing ontologies, and how one might proceed to try to resolve these differences. Of course, Quine's proposals have by no means been greeted with universal acceptance. On the contrary, much controversy continues to swirl about what he may be thought to have accomplished. Nevertheless, it must be recognized that he did succeed in restoring to respectability and central importance an area of traditional philosophic concern that other analytic philosophers had been prepared to abandon altogether. For this Quine deserves full credit, regardless of whether one comes finally to agree with him either about the formulation he gives to his criterion of ontological commitment or with his choices of such commitments to mark his own ontological viewpoint.

What, then, is the criterion of ontological commitment? To state this, we must remember above all that Quine is steeped in the Frege-Russell tradition of the new logic. For all his modifications, here and there, of that heritage, Quine remains convinced of the great power and intellectual value of calling upon the resources of modern logic in order to state the 'depth-grammar' of language wherever that language is used to convey our attempts to give a cognitively true account of the world in which we live. Quine, following Frege and Russell, sees the power of logic to introduce clarity and precision into our language when that language is stripped of irrelevancies and obfuscations. In particular, he shows the great power of the use of the predicate calculus, at the heart of which, as we had seen earlier in connection with Frege, is the use of the methods of quantification, i.e., the use of bound variables to express forms of generality.

If, then, given some stretch of discourse (whether in everyday language, science, or in the writings of philosophers), we seek to determine the ontological commitments embedded in such discourse, the first thing we must be prepared to do is re-write the relevant statements to disclose their underlying logical patterns. This would involve employing the universal and particular ('existential') quantifiers, various logical constants (negation, identity, conjunction, and so on), and constants or variables to represent various singular terms or predicate expressions. The quantifiers (which translate the use of such ordinary expressions as 'everything', 'something', 'nothing') are used to bind variables.* The variables 'range over' a domain of possible values. Quine would say this is made evident by translating every statement of ordinary language, science, or philosophy (not already in this form) with the aid of the 'canonic notation' of the formulae of first-order statements. The best way to understand what this comes to is to go back to Frege's basic distinction between *objects* on the one side and *concepts* (along with relations and functions) on the other. A first-order quantified proposition is one in which the bound variables range over *individual objects*. These objects, as making up the domain of possible values over which the quantified individual variables range, may be of any type one chooses to distinguish in one's ontology, including the making of a broad distinction between concrete and abstract objects. For Quine, the differences among ontologies have to do primarily with what kinds of *objects* are said to make up 'what there is', and so are represented by different types of individual variables. Thus, for Quine, it is enough for purposes of clarifying one's ontological commitments to make use of first-order quantifications where the quantified variables range over one or more types of individual objects. In such first-order generalizations, predicate expressions (concepts), since they do not name or represent objects, are not quantified. Also, of course, various logical constants do not designate or name special kinds of objects, and so do not appear as quantified variables. Thus all expressions (quantifiers, bound variables, predicate expressions, and logical constants) assume their

---

*In sentence '$(x)\,Fx$', the brackets (　　　) serve as an expression in which the gap is filled by a variable for the universal quantifier, and the entire sentence is read 'for all x, Fx'. Similarly, in the sentence '$(\exists x)\,Fx$', the expression '$(\exists x)$' stands for the particular quantifier, and the entire sentence would be read 'for at least one (for some) x, Fx'. The variable x, m both these examples, which is inside the scope of the quantifiers, is said to be *bound* by the quantifier. Where a variable occurs in a sentence that is not so bound, as e.g., y is in '$(\exists x)\,Fx.Gy$', it is said to be *free*. A sentence containing one or more free variables is known as an *open* sentence. A *closed* sentence is one in which there are no free variables.

proper place in logically 're-parsed' sentences. Given such sentences, we are then in a position to see where ontological commitments are present. They are to be found in the range of values allowed for and governed by its bound variables. Quine's famous statement, "To be is to be the value of a variable," may accordingly serve as a slogan to sum up the criterion of ontological commitment.

We may say, for example, that some dogs are white and not thereby commit ourselves to recognizing either doghood or whiteness as entities. 'Some dogs are white' says that some things that are dogs are white; and, in order that this statement be true, the things over which the bound variable 'something' ranges must include some white dogs, but need not include doghood or whiteness. On the other hand, when we say that some zoological species are cross-fertile we are committing ourselves to recognizing as entities the several species themselves, abstract though they are. We remain so committed at least until we devise some way of so paraphrasing the statement as to show that the seeming reference to species on the part of our bound variable was an avoidable manner of speaking.

. . . .

We now have a more explicit standard whereby to decide what ontology a given theory or form of discourse is committed to: a theory is committed to those and only those entities to which the bound variables of the theory must be capable of referring in order that the affirmations made in the theory be true.[10]*

Quine makes clear that in stating his criterion of ontological commitment he is not thereby providing a means for adjudicating among rival ontologies. The criterion only helps to bring out into the open the differences among philosophers on *what they say* there is. It does not settle the question what there is or isn't (whether what they say is *true*); yet making clear how the differences can be formulated is an important step. He calls it the method of 'semantic ascent', because it first transposes differences of a substantive sort into linguistic differences, i.e., differences with respect to the ranges of variables being quantified. Having located differences on that level, one may then proceed to consider the substantive differences in their own right. One asks whether this or that quantified range or domain should be 'countenanced', i.e., included in our ontology in order to give a true account of what there is. Questions of the eliminability of certain domains (types of object), of simplicity, of reduction, and so on, will then come to the fore. However difficult it may be to settle those questions, at least progress will have been made in isolating where

* Quine has given various formulations to the criterion. Another one reads:

"As applied to discourse in an explicitly quantificational form of language, the notion of ontological commitment belongs to the theory of reference. For to say that a given existential quantification presupposes objects of a given kind is to say simply that the open sentence which follows the quantifier is true of some objects of that kind and none not of that kind."[11]

the differences lie and in pointing to the kinds of issues that need to be resolved.

Now how are we to adjudicate among rival ontologies? Certainly the answer is not provided by the semantical formula "To be is to be the value of a variable"; this formula serves rather, conversely, in testing the conformity of a given remark or doctrine to a prior ontological standard. We look to bound variables in connection with ontology not in order to know what there is, but in order to know what a given remark or doctrine, ours or someone else's, *says* there is; and this much is quite properly a problem involving language. But what there is is another question.[12]

In facing issues of the sort that remain, even after one has made the "semantic ascent," Quine recommends a pragmatic approach.

I advanced an explicit standard whereby to decide what the ontological commitments of a theory are. But the question what ontology actually to adopt still stands open, and the obvious counsel is tolerance and an experimental spirit.[13]

THE CRITIQUE OF EMPIRICISM

In clarifying the title of his paper "Two Dogmas of Empiricism," Quine identifies the two dogmas he proposes to subject to criticism. The first insists on "the fundamental cleavage between truths which are *analytic,* or grounded in meanings independently of matters of fact, and truths which are *synthetic,* or grounded in fact. The other dogma is *reductionism:* the belief that each meaningful statement is equivalent to some logical construct upon terms which refer to immediate experience."[14] Toward the end of the paper, having shown his reasons for rejecting both these dogmas, Quine gives a brief but important discussion of the need—in considering questions of truth and of what needs to be taken into account in modifying one's beliefs—not to confine one's attention to individual statements, taken singly, but rather to attend to *entire systems of thought.* It is only when we take into account such holistic networks of statements—the interconnected web of laws, logical principles, observational reports, and so on—that we are in a position to determine the grounds of our acceptance, rejection, or modification of any single belief. This thesis of Quine's is a restatement and extension of a similar one enunciated in an earlier period by the great French historian and philosopher of science, Pierre Duhem. (Hence this general argument is nowadays referred to as the "Duhem-Quine thesis.")[15] This thesis is of central importance in understanding Quine's philosophy. From the point of view of our present discussion, it sums up in a positive vein the reasons why Quine finds it necessary to reject the two dogmas mentioned above. His defense of a reformulated empiricist-pragmatist philosophy incorporates 'holism' as a central feature. It is because of this emphasis on the importance of always seeing the role of an entire web or network of beliefs that Quine rejects the traditional analytic-synthetic dualism (on which the logical positivists, among others, had placed such great store), as well as another dogma of logical positivism, the verificationist theory of the meaningfulness of any single 'synthetic' statement.

A traditional method for supporting the claim that it is both possible and important to distinguish analytic and synthetic statements is this: A statement is analytic if it can be shown to be ultimately reducible to a form governed by the logical law of identity, 'A is A'. A statement is non-analytic (i.e., synthetic) if it cannot be shown to be reducible to a statement that is basically of the form of an identity statement.

Thus it would be said that the statement 'All married men are married' would clearly qualify as being analytic on the above criterion, for it falls within the pattern 'All A is A'. Similarly, the statement 'No unmarried men are married' would also be analytic since it too reduces to an identity. What now of the statement 'All bachelors are unmarried'? Here, too, many philosophers would claim that this statement is analytic, for, they would say, since 'bachelor' means the same as 'being unmarried', if we replace the term 'bachelor' by its synonymous expression, we obtain once again a statement ('No unmarried men are married') which conforms to the logical law of identity, and so is analytic. The route by which this classification of a statement as analytic is accomplished is through an appeal to the notion of synonymy (sameness of meaning). Hence any statement that involves or states a relation of synonymy, or sameness of meaning, is at bottom one of identity, and so analytic. All analytic statements are identity statements, whereas nonanalytic (synthetic) statements cannot be shown to rest on the relation of identity of meanings to sanction their truth. Quine argues that this traditional method for identifying analytic statements is unsuccessful, since in appealing to the notion of synonymy or sameness of meaning it makes use of a concept that is just as unclear and in need of further analysis as is the original concept of 'analyticity'. Moreover, those who have attempted to render it clear have used arguments or doctrines that are highly questionable. If, for example, one were to attempt to clarify what 'synonymy' means by saying it is a matter of how, *in fact*, people use two expressions interchangeably, this makes synonymy depend on the empirical (sociological, historical) facts of *linguistic usage*. Since the initial aim was to clarify wherein an analytic statement consists, that would differentiate it from a synthetic one, with the latter's dependence on a recourse to experience, this approach will obviously not succeed. Nor will the device of appealing to 'meanings', those alleged entities *designated* by terms; for Quine, as we have seen, would claim that any appeal to such shadowy 'entities' rests on a confusion of naming (an object) and sense (being meaningful). In short, the foregoing and every other known, standard proposal for characterizing 'synonymy' fails to provide the needed clarification; they rest upon arguments, distinctions, or doctrines in which one cannot have any confidence.

The problem of analyticity then confronts us anew. Statements which are analytic by general philosophical acclaim are not, indeed, far to seek. They fall into two classes. Those of the first class, which may be called *logically true,* are typified by:

(1) No unmarried man is married.

The relevant feature of this example is that it not merely is true as it stands, but remains true under any and all reinterpretations of 'man' and 'married'. If we suppose a prior inventory of *logical* particles, comprising 'no', 'un-', 'not', 'if', 'then', 'and', etc., then in general a logical truth is a statement which is true and remains true under all reinterpretations of its components other than the logical particles.

But there is also a second class of analytic statements, typified by:

(2) No bachelor is married.

The characteristic of such a statement is that it can be turned into a logical truth by putting synonyms for synonyms; thus (2) can be turned into (1) by putting 'unmarried man' for its synonym 'bachelor'. We still lack a proper characterization of this second class of analytic statements, and therewith of analyticity generally, inasmuch as we have had in the above description to lean on a notion of "synonymy" which is no less in need of clarification than analyticity itself.[16]

Quine proceeds to examine various maneuvers by which philosophers have sought to make the notion of analyticity clear, by focusing on the concept of synonymy and its near relatives; however, he does not find any of these efforts successful. Of course, one could always leave 'analytic' undefined, or one could indulge unawares in a circular argument in which in attempting to clarify the concept of analyticity one appeals to this very concept. This would be obviously unsatisfactory. Quine searches in vain for a way of specifying what analytic statements are that is clear, rigorous, and an unmistakable means for discriminating them from synthetic ones. He claims he has found no such effective criterion of accomplishing this distinction. He concludes:

For all its a priori reasonableness, a boundary between analytic and synthetic statements simply has not been drawn. That there is such a distinction to be drawn at all is an unempirical dogma of empiricists, a metaphysical article of faith.[17]

Quine examines one further type of approach by which positivists and others have sought to provide a clear criterion for making the distinction between analytic and synthetic statements. By adopting, with the positivists, the verifiability theory of meaning, which appeals to sense experience to confirm or disconfirm any purported fact-stating sentence, one might say that the distinction between an analytic and synthetic statement is this: A synthetic statement is open to disconfirmation by what is found in observation. If a statement is analytic, it could never be disconfirmed; it would always be confirmed, no matter what the world is like, and no matter what our ongoing experience discloses.

The verification theory of meaning, which has been conspicuous in the literature from Peirce onward, is that the meaning of a statement is the method of empirically confirming or infirming it. An analytic statement is that limiting case which is confirmed no matter what.[18]

It should be noticed that the approach to characterizing the nature of an 'analytic' statement by saying that its *truth* is confirmed "no matter what" is different from the method previously mentioned by which the criterion employed for identifying an analytic statement makes use of the notion of synonymy, or sameness of meaning. In the latter case, 'analytic' is a matter of (sameness of) *meaning;* in the present case, even though one is appealing to the verifiability theory of meaning, what is actually important is the matter of *truth*, not primarily that of *meaning*. Now the proposed criterion places the emphasis on the fact that in order to establish the *truth* of a synthetic statement one has recourse to sense experience; and this is attended by all the uncertainties and hazards that this kind of appeal has. On the other hand, the *truth* of an analytic statement does not depend on the vagaries or uncertainties of experience. *Its truth* can be established without recourse to experience, because experience can never upset it. Another way of putting the same point is to say that even if one does appeal to experience, experience will *always* confirm it. What this comes down to, then, is that by this second route analyticity amounts to *a prioricity*—independence of experience—as contrasted with the *a posteriori* character of synthetic statements. The first method of discriminating analytic and synthetic statements that we examined earlier had to do with the question of whether or not there is a *synonymy of meanings* present. If there is it is an analytic statement, otherwise it is synthetic (nonanalytic). These are two quite different criteria for accomplishing the distinction between analytic and synthetic statements.

In any case, it is important to realize, in understanding Quine's philosophy, that neither route, according to him, proves to be satisfactory for effecting the distinction between analytic and synthetic statements. The earlier 'meaning' approach in terms of synonymy fails because we have no satisfactory way of making that notion clear or the arguments behind it convincing. The present 'truth' approach (in terms of the distinction between what is *a priori* and *a posteriori,* where the mark of an analytic statement is that its truth is assured under all and any conditions of sense experience, and so is in that sense not 'contingent' upon it, i.e., it is independent of such an appeal) is also, for Quine, just as unsatisfactory. This time, in order to show why it is unsatisfactory, he does not dwell on the shortcomings of finding a sound method of characterizing synonymy. Instead, since matters of truth and knowing the truth are at stake, he turns to other considerations. He shows that when we take into account the grounds upon which we accept the truth of a statement, as well as the grounds upon which we may find it necessary to reject or modify our claims to know the truth, we can no longer draw the kind of distinction previously appealed to between *a priori* statements (those whose truth is assured, no matter what) and the synthetic *a posteriori* ones (those subject to confirmation or disconfirmation by sense experience). The alleged distinction is a faulty one, because *any* statement is open to modification or rejection. There are no analytic statements as such, forever immune to all revision or rejection. The basic reason is that we must always take into account the entire network of statements related to any given statement. In determining the truth and our knowledge of the truth we should not consider an individual sentence, taken singly and apart from its interrelations with other statements in a total network or web of beliefs. Always, in the face of challenge by observational data, it is not a single statement that is being tested but a whole network of beliefs. Therefore even those beliefs, otherwise thought to be immune from disconfirmation by experience, are vulnerable and also subject to modification or replacement under radical scrutiny and overhaul. This is tantamount to saying there is no fixed, sharp distinction between analytic *a priori* statements and synthetic *a posteriori* ones. To drive home this point, and so to register his objection to the alleged distinction between analytic and synthetic judgments, is the main purpose of Quine's restatement of the 'holistic' thesis first enunciated by Pierre Duhem; it is a thesis he now emphatically calls to his support.

The totality of our so-called knowledge or beliefs, from the most casual matters of geography and history to the profoundest laws of atomic physics or even of pure mathematics and logic, is a man-made fabric which impinges on experience only along the edges. Or, to change the figure, total science is like a field of force whose boundary conditions are experience. A conflict with experience at the periphery occasions readjustments in the interior of the field. Truth values have to be redistributed over some of our statements. Reëvaluation of some statements entails reëvaluation of others, because of their logical interconnections—the logical laws being in turn simply certain further statements of the system, certain further elements of the field. Having reëvaluated one statement we must reëvaluate some others, which may be statements logically connected with the first or may be the statements of logical connections themselves. But the total field is so underdetermined by its boundary conditions, experience, that there is much latitude of choice as to what statements to reëvaluate in the light of any single contrary experience. No particular experiences are linked with any particular statements in the interior of the field, except indirectly through considerations of equilibrium affecting the field as a whole.

If this view is right, it is misleading to speak of the empirical content of an individual statement—especially if it is a statement at all remote from the experiential periphery of the field. Furthermore it becomes folly to seek a boundary between synthetic statements, which hold contingently on experience, and analytic statements, which hold come what may. Any statement can be held true come what may, if we make drastic enough adjustments elsewhere in the system. Even a statement very close to the periphery can be held true in the face of recalcitrant experience by pleading hallucination or by amending certain statements of the kind called logical laws. Conversely, by the same token, no statement is immune to revision. Revision even of the logical law of the excluded middle has been proposed as a means of simplifying quantum mechanics; and what difference is there in principle between such a shift and the shift whereby Kepler superseded Ptolemy, or Einstein Newton, or Darwin Aristotle?

For vividness I have been speaking in terms of varying distances from a sensory periphery. Let me try now to clarify this notion without metaphor. Certain statements, though *about* physical objects and not sense experience, seem peculiarly germane to sense experience—and in a selective way: some statements to some experiences, others to others. Such statements, especially germane to particular experiences, I picture as near the periphery. But in this relation of "germaneness" I envisage nothing more than a loose association reflecting the relative likelihood, in practice, of our choosing one statement rather than another for revision in the event of recalcitrant experience. For example, we can imagine recalcitrant experiences to which we would surely be inclined to accommodate our system by reëvaluating just the statement that there are brick houses on Elm Street, together with related statements on the same topic. We can imagine other recalcitrant experiences to which we could be inclined to accommodate our system by reëvaluating just the statement that there are no centaurs, along with kindred statements. A recalcitrant experience can, I have urged, be accommodated by any of various alternative reëvaluations in various alternative quarters of the total system; but, in the cases which we are now imagining, our natural tendency to disturb the total system as little as possible would lead us to focus our revisions upon these specific statements concerning brick houses or centaurs. These statements are felt, therefore, to have a sharper empirical reference than highly theoretical statements of physics or logic or ontology. The latter statements may be thought of as relatively centrally located within the total network, meaning merely that little preferential connection with any particular sense data obtrudes itself.

As an empiricist I continue to think of the conceptual scheme of science as a tool, ultimately, for predicting future experience in the light of past experience. Physical objects are conceptually imported into the situation as convenient intermediaries—not by definition in terms of experience, but simply as irreducible posits comparable, epistemologically, to the gods of Homer. For my part I do, qua lay physicist, believe in physical objects and not in Homer's gods; and I consider it a scientific error to believe otherwise. But in point of epistemological footing the physical objects and the gods differ only in degree and not in kind. Both sorts of entities enter our conception only as cultural posits. The myth of physical objects is epistemologically superior to most in that it has proved more efficacious than other myths as a device for working a manageable structure into the flux of experience.

. . . .

Ontological questions, under this view, are on a par with questions of natural science. Consider the question whether to countenance classes as entities. This, as I have argued elsewhere, is the question whether to quantify with respect to variables which take classes as values. Now Carnap has maintained that this is a question not of matters of fact but of choosing a convenient language form, a convenient conceptual scheme or framework for science. With this I agree, but only on the proviso that the same be conceded regarding scientific hypotheses generally. Carnap has recognized that he is able to preserve a double standard for ontological questions and scientific hypotheses only by assuming an absolute distinction between the analytic and the synthetic; and I need not say again that this is a distinction which I reject.

The issue over there being classes seems more a question of convenient conceptual scheme; the issue over there being centaurs, or brick houses on Elm Street, seems more a question of fact. But I have been urging that this difference is only one of degree, and that it turns upon our vaguely pragmatic inclination to adjust one strand of the fabric of science rather than another in accommodating some particular recalcitrant experience. Conservatism figures in such choices, and so does the quest for simplicity.

Carnap, Lewis, and others take a pragmatic stand on the question of choosing between language forms, scientific frameworks; but their pragmatism leaves off at the imagined boundary between the analytic and the synthetic. In repudiating such a boundary I espouse a more thorough pragmatism. Each man is given a scientific heritage plus a continuing barrage of sensory stimulation; and the considerations which guide him in warping his scientific heritage to fit his continuing sensory promptings are, where rational, pragmatic.[19]

OBJECTS, QUANTIFICATION, AND ONTOLOGY

We have seen that for Quine ontology—as a saying of what there is—is to be understood basically as a matter of speaking of objects. Accordingly, ontologies may be identified, and the differences among them recognized, by what kinds of objects they posit or countenance. The sophisticated language of quantification, as used in logic, helps to make clear what ontological commitments are involved in some stretch of discourse. Since on this approach much hinges on the interconnections among 'object', 'reference to objects', 'quantification', and 'ontology', Quine has devoted a great deal of attention to these topics. He has done so by way of giving a deeper analysis to these themes than he had sketched in "On What There Is," under the pressure of having to respond to various critics. Our task now, in coming to closer grips with Quine's philosophy, is to follow him in some of these further details.

Despite the great stress that Quine places on the role of logic in refining and regimenting our language for purposes of giving the latter greater power as a cognitive instrument, he is not so preoccupied with the importance of logic that he fails to take into account the wider setting in which it comes to play its role. On the contrary, he gives much attention in various directions to this wider setting, thereby making the understanding and appreciation of the positive powers of logic deeper. He also drives home our sense of the human origins of logic and of the inescapable relativity inherent in any of our conceptual tools. Thus Quine's study of the relations of logic to language engages him, among other matters, in an examination of the psychological and social factors involved in the learning process by the individual, and of the multiple uses of language. It encourages him to take note of the social factors at work in developing many different languages, as well as the interpersonal role that language plays in communication. These questions have to do, among other things, with what he calls the 'ontogenesis of reference'—the discrimination of the various stages in the growth of an individual, from the earliest steps taken in early childhood in learning to use language to the later mastery of the most sophisticated language-use by the mature adult. In short, Quine is aware of the numerous forces at work in human nature and the surrounding natural and social environment that affect the use of language. He is on guard not to fall into the trap himself of taking formal logic as a heaven-sent, self-contained tool that does not have its earthly roots in human nature.

Quine is sensitive, in another direction, to what logic can and cannot do. He is deeply aware of the matter of the diversity of conceptual systems, and of the fact that we cannot get 'outside' the use of *some* conceptual system, however pervasive and taken-for granted it may be. We cannot divest ourselves of the grid or filter of a conceptual system in order to determine what the world is like independently and absolutely—that is, apart from the use of such a conceptual system and what is *says* the world is like. Quine thus takes seriously the matter of conceptual *relativity*. He drives home this point by examining the intimate connection of thought and language. He upholds what we may think of as a severely modified form of 'Kantianism'—a type of linguistic relativism. Logic, for all its importance in regimenting language, and in improving the rigor and clarity of linguistic expressions, does not give us the means for achieving some set of unique, absolute, and eternally valid insights. Logic itself is hedged in by all our human limitations; it is relative to the encompassing contextual uses of multiple human languages.

Let us turn to see, in specific examples, how Quine works out his support for these general points. Let us consider, first, the whole question of how we come to develop and use the term 'object' itself. This is a term that is important (as we have seen) in understanding the very enterprise of ontology, in the use of first-order quantification, and in examining what lies at the bottom of many philosophic controversies—especially those about whether, in addition to physical objects, we must acknowledge other types of object as well, for example abstract, intensional, or possible ones.

Let us consider first, as Quine recounts it, the way in which a child, at a very early stage, long before it comes to be in a position to discriminate *objects* as such, acquires its first items of vocabulary. Consider, in other words, the character of early, unsophisticated language-use. It occurs when a child learns to respond to or use its first few words. Out of this matrix it will come at a later stage, and with the help of adults and their tools already-acquired, to discriminate and identify *objects*.

Consider the acquisition of such terms as 'mama', 'water', and 'red', at an early stage of the child's development.

We in our maturity have come to look upon the child's mother as an integral body who, in an irregular closed orbit, revisits the child from time to time; and to look upon red in a radically different way, viz., as scattered about. Water, for us, is rather like red, but not quite; things are red, stuff alone is water. But the mother, red, and water are for the infant all of a type; each is just a history of sporadic encounter, a scattered portion of what goes on. His first learning of the three words is uniformly a matter of learning how much of what goes on about him counts as the mother, or as red, or as water. It is not for the child to say in the first case 'Hello! mama again', in the second case 'Hello! another red thing', and in the third case 'Hello! more water'. They are all on a par: Hello! more mama, more red, more water.[20]

In order for the child to be able to use words in such a way that it can be said to have begun to master the conceptual scheme employed by adults, it must learn to be able to refer to or talk about *individual objects, recognized as such.* For this purpose it needs to learn how to use *individuative terms.*

It is only when the child has got on to the full and proper use of *individuative* terms like "apple" that he can properly be said to have taken to using terms as terms, and speaking of objects. Words like "apple," and not words like "mama" or "water" or "red," are the terms whose ontological involvement runs deep. To learn "apple" it is not sufficient to learn how much of what goes on counts as apple; we must learn how much counts as *an* apple, and how much as another. Such terms possess built-in modes of individuation.[21]

A physical object such as *an* apple has an individual identity, marking it out from other objects, closely similar or not. Its individual identity enables one to identify it as the *same* object from one moment to the next, or as enduring over a stretch of time; and, if it is a movable or moving physical object, as the same object that moves from one place to another. Individual physical objects are the first and paradigmatic examples of 'object'. The terms we use to refer to individual physical objects, one at a time—individuative (singular) terms—accomplish this by what Quine calls 'divided reference'.

Individuative terms, however, need to be carefully distinguished from 'mass (or bulk) terms' that might sometimes be confused with the individuative ones. Thus there is a difference between the use of the term 'apple' to represent a kind of stuff, 'apple-stuff', as distinguished from *an* apple' or *'these* apple*s*' or *'this* apple', where the latter expressions show the use of *individuating* (divided reference) devices of language, used to refer to individual objects.

Individuative terms are commonly made to double as bulk terms. Thus we may say "There is some apple in the salad," not meaning "some apple or other"; just as we may say "Mary had a little lamb" in either of two senses. Now we have appreciated that the child can learn the terms "mama," "red," and "water" quite well before he ever has mastered the ins and outs of our adult conceptual scheme of mobile enduring physical objects, identical from time to time and place to place; and in principle he might do the same for "apple," as a bulk term for uncut apple stuff. But he can never fully master "apple" in its individuative use, except as he gets on with the scheme of enduring and recurrent physical objects.

. . . .

How can we ever tell, then, whether the child has really got the trick of individuation? Only by engaging him in sophisticated discourse of "that apple," "not that apple," "an apple," "same apple," "another apple," "these apples."

. . . .

Until individuation emerges, the child can scarcely be said to have general *or* singular terms, there being no express talk of objects. The pre-individuative term "mama," and likewise "water" and "red" (for children who happen to learn "water" and "red" before mastering individuation), hark back to a primitive phase to which the distinction between singular and general is irrelevant. Once the child has pulled through the individuative crisis, though, he is prepared to reassess prior terms. "Mama," in particular, gets set up retroactively as the name of a broad and recurrent but withal individual object, and thus as a singular term *par excellence*. Occasions eliciting "mama" being just as discontinuous as those eliciting "water," the two terms had been on a par; but with the advent of individuation the mother becomes integrated into a cohesive spatiotemporal convexity, while water remains scattered even in space-time. The two terms thus part company.

The mastery of individuation seems scarcely to affect people's attitude toward "water." For "water," "sugar," and the like the category of bulk terms remains, a survival of the pre-individuative phase, ill fitting the dichotomy into general and singular. But the philosophical mind sees its way to pressing this archaic category into the dichotomy. The bulk term "water" after the copula can usually be smoothly reconstrued as a general term true of each portion of water, while in other positions it is more simply construed as a singular term naming that spatiotemporally diffuse object which is the totality of the world's water.[22]

As we have just seen, in his exploration of the powers and uses of language, Quine studies some of the features of the acquisition of competency in the use of language in its first, tentative, and relatively crude stages in early childhood. At the same time, 'language', as Quine and every one else realizes, covers an enormously rich, complex, and diversified aspect of human culture and behavior. In the study of that complexity Quine is much concerned to stress the importance of using the refined tools of language that come to the fore in the development of the technical vocabularies of science, mathematics, and logic. In particular, as a logician working within the broad tradition of the new logic inspired by the pioneering studies of Frege, Quine has devoted himself to showing the contribution logic can make toward achieving economy, exactness, and rigor in our use of language for cognitive purposes. It does so by what Quine calls a process of 'regimenting discourse' and by offering a 'canonic notation' for codifying the underlying structure of language.

Among these logician's tools there is the powerful and important use *of* the predicate calculus, along with the use *in* the calculus, of the techniques of quantifying variables. The understanding of what is involved in the use of this calculus leads directly to raising various questions about the nature and extent of the domains to be ranged over in quantification, the meaning of such terms as 'existence' and 'identity', the matter of the decidability or undecidability of the truth-value of quantified sentences, and many other related topics. These questions have obvious connections with certain traditional concerns of philosophy, particularly in metaphysics (ontology). In our summary of Quine's papers, "On What There Is" and "Two Dogmas of Empiricism," we have had a glimpse of his approach to these kinds of questions. Let us now fill in some of the details by taking advantage of his later writings, among them his major work *Word and Object*.

According to Quine, the advantages of using the formal devices of the predicate calculus become wholly clear if we restrict our attention to the use of first-order quantifications. In such quantifications we make use of the universal quantifier, '(x)', which is read 'everything x is such that _____', and the particular (sometimes called the 'existential') quantifier, '$(\exists x)$', read as 'something x is such that_____'. In first-order quantifications these quantifiers are attached to individual variables, i.e., to variables that range over individual objects. Although there are just these two quantifiers, the universal and the particular, each can be defined in terms of the other, so that for purposes of economy we can get along with one quantifier only. Thus '$(\exists x)(\_\_\_\_\_x)$' can be rewritten as 'not (x) not

(———*x*)', and in turn '(*x*)(———*x*)' can be rewritten as 'not (Ⅎ*x*) not (———*x*).'[23]

For purposes of determining the ontological commitments of language that makes use of quantifiers, such commitments are clearly revealed by the use of *either* type of quantifier, universal or particular. Each type of quantifier, as attached to a variable, ranges over a domain of objects (values of the variable) as bound by the quantifier in question. Thus the so-called 'existential' quantifier (the particular quantifier) has no greater role in revealing ontological commitments than does the universal quantifier. However, in his earlier writings, and in his later writings as well, Quine sometimes features the use of the 'existential' quantifier in discussing the criterion of ontological commitment, as well as in connection with the meaning of the term 'existence'. While his stress on the use of the existential quantifier could lead to some misunderstanding, it should be emphasized that the use of the universal quantifier is just as involved in expressing ontological commitments as is the particular one, for it is the *kind of objects* represented by the domain over which the quantified variables range that determines the ontological commitments of a given theory. The question of general ontological commitments has to do with the *semantics* of the language. For this purpose, the use of quantifiers, whether universal or particular, will serve equally well to indicate the domain of objects over which the quantifiers range. On the other hand, the use of some one of the quantifiers or some array of them to translate the logical structure of a specific sentence has to do with the *truth-conditions for that specific sentence*. It is more pointed in its concerns than the broader 'semantic' question of the ontological commitments presupposed in using the quantifiers as ranging over some posited type or kind of objects.

We come now to a further point. For Quine there is an important distinction to be made between *variables* and *schematic letters*. Thus quantifiers are only to be used in connection with variables, not with schematic letters. Variables are those expressions which, in first-order quantifications, range over the domain of values that are the individual objects making up that domain. In first-order quantification the quantified variables are always individual variables. None of the other expressions used, e.g. predicate expressions, can be quantified, since predicates do not stand for objects.

When we schematize a sentence in the predicative way "*Fa*," or "*a* is an *F*," our recognition of an "*a*" part and an "*F*" part turns strictly on our use of variables of quantification; the "*a*" represents a part of the sentence that stands where a quantified variable could stand, and the "*F*" represents the rest.[24]

Thus, where predicates or other nonquantifiable expressions are used, these are represented by schematic letters, *not* by variables. Accordingly, while certain appropriate linguistic expressions may be substituted both for individual variables and for schematic letters, those expressions that can be substituted for individual variables would typically be names or other singular terms and would represent individual objects in the domain of *values* of the variable. However, linguistic expressions that could be used as *substitutions* for schematic letters do not oblige us to consider them as designating some object or as representing some kind of nonlinguistic entity. Whereas variables range over values (a domain of objects), schematic letters are linguistic expressions for which other linguistic expressions may be substituted. It is therefore the *variables,* as quantified, that carry ontological commitments, not schematic letters.

The importance of making the foregoing distinction comes out in connection with Quine's discussion of the topic of 'existence'. It is here, according to him, that the role of quantifying *variables* makes clear what claims to existence amount to.

What we have to get clear on is when to consider that a sentence mentions certain things and thereby assumes their existence. Looking for names is no help, since anyone can disclaim assumption of the object by declaring that the alleged name is not a name. What counts, rather, are the variables. The objects assumed in a given discourse are the values of the variables. They are the things in the universe over which the variables are interpreted as ranging. If a man's assertions are such that protons, unicorns, or universals have to be among the values of the variables in order for the assertions to be true, then he has no business denying the assumption of protons or unicorns or universals.

We have the modern logic of quantification to thank for making evident the existential force of the variable. The existential quantifier "$(\exists x)$" is the distilled essence of existential talk. All imputations of existence can be put as existential quantifications. Moreover, all the other uses of variables—in universal quantification, in singular description, in class abstraction, in algebra—can be paraphrased in familiar ways so that the variables end up as variables of existential quantification.

This existential role belongs to variables only in the strict sense of the word; not to schematic letters. Schematic letters, such as the sentence letters of truth-function logic and the predicate letters of quantification theory, occur only in schemata and not in sentences, and they take only substitutions and not values. By variables I mean bound or bindable variables. These, if we construct our discourse along the lines of neoclassical logic, are the primary instrument of reference to objects. The objects are the values of the variables.[25]

We have been examining Quine's views of the scope and character of ontology. In the judgment of some philosophers, Quine's efforts to restore the legitimacy, meaningfulness, and importance of this branch of philosophical injury are of no avail. According to these critics, those who engage in ontological discussions and disputes are not able to bring their discussions to a successful resolution; the questions they raise and *a fortiori* the proposed answers they would give are pseudoquestions and pseudoanswers. One of these critics is Rudolf Carnap. This type of charge was made by him in a well-known paper entitled "Empiricism, Semantics, and Ontology."[26] To this Quine responded, for instance in his paper "On Carnap's Views on Ontology."[27] In the course of this response he seeks to show his grounds for divergence from Carnap, and thereby to uphold what he takes to be the genuine, legitimate cognitive status of ontology. It will be of interest for us to explore this dispute as a way of obtaining a further clarification of Quine's views on the nature of ontology. As we explore Quine's answer, we shall find that in some respects he shows himself to *share* with Carnap certain views about the nature of cognitive inquiry. It is a position we might characterize (roughly) as a type of 'conventionalism', 'pragmatism', 'linguistic relativism', or (severely modified) 'Kantianism'. In any case, as we explore these points we shall at the same time be laying the groundwork for our examination, later in this chapter, of certain other aspects of Quine's philosophy, in particular his stance on modality and the indeterminacy of translation.

Let us turn first to Carnap's strictures on 'ontology' and the way he would characterize its status. Carnap begins his discussion by pointing out that when philosophers engage in a dispute about, for example, whether there are certain abstract entities such as properties, classes, numbers, and propositions—with philosophers called 'realists' (in the Platonic sense) giving an affirmative answer and those called 'nominalists' giving a negative answer—this dispute cannot be resolved as long as it is conducted in the traditional manner. For, Carnap maintains, the dispute so conducted fails to take into account an important distinction—that between 'internal' and 'external' questions. The failure to draw and acknowledge this distinction is common to all sides in the dispute. It is only by making this distinction that one is in a position to settle the dispute. One will then realize that insofar as the dispute concerns an 'external' question it is a pseudoquestion and there is no possible meaningful or correct (true) answer that could be given. The question has no genuine cognitive validity, and hence cannot be answered by a 'yes' or 'no' on the basis of some kind of relevant objective evidence. This type of 'external' question underlies the dispute between the realists and nominalists regarding whether there are or are not abstract entities of one kind or another. It is also characteristic of other types of disputes in ontology. They are all equally 'metaphysical', i.e. 'meaningless', hence cognitively irresolvable. On the other hand, if the question were seen as simply an 'internal' question, then it is not only meaningful but in many cases relatively trivial because easily solvable, or at any rate, if not already solved, one for which the procedure for obtaining a solution is readily available. In order to understand this fundamental distinction between 'external' and 'internal' questions, we first have to follow Carnap as he introduces the notion of a *framework*.

Are there properties, classes, numbers, propositions? In order to understand more clearly the nature of these and related problems, it is above all necessary to recognize a fundamental distinction between two kinds of questions concerning the existence or reality of entities. If someone wishes to speak in his language about a new kind of entities, he has to introduce a system of new ways of speaking, subject to new rules; we shall call this procedure the construction of a *framework* for the new entities in question. And now we must distinguish two kinds of questions of existence: first, questions of the existence of certain entities of the new kind *within the framework;* we call them *internal questions;* and second, questions concerning the existence or reality *of the framework itself,* called *external questions.* Internal questions and possible answers to them are formulated with the help of the new forms of expressions. The answers may be found either by purely logical methods or by empirical methods, depending upon whether the framework is a logical or a factual one. An external question is of a problematic character which is in need of closer examination.[28]

To bring out the force of these distinctions Carnap considers a number of examples. Consider first the use of the linguistic framework in daily use in which we talk about and describe ordinary observable physical objects and events—tables, chairs, walking, raining, and so on. Carnap calls the use of this framework the use of the 'thing-language'.

Once we have accepted this thing-language and thereby the framework of things, we can raise and answer internal questions, e.g., "Is there a white piece of paper on my desk?", "Did King Arthur actually live?", "Are unicorns and centaurs real or merely imaginary?", and the like. These questions are to be answered by empirical investigations. Results of observations are evaluated according to certain rules as confirming or disconfirming evidence for possible answers.[29]

Suppose that instead of asking specific questions about things of the kind just illustrated (internal questions that can be answered by empirical investigation), one were to ask "Are there really things in the world?" Carnap says that this *kind* of question is no longer answerable by appropriate empirical methods. It is an 'external' question.

In contrast to the former questions, this question is raised neither by the man in the street nor by scientists, but only by philosophers. Realists give an affirmative answer, subjective idealists a negative one, and the controversy goes on for centuries without being solved. And it cannot be solved because it is framed in a wrong way. To be real in the scientific sense means to be an element of the framework; hence this concept cannot be meaningfully applied to the framework itself.

. . . .

To accept the thing world means nothing more than to accept a certain form of language, in other words, to accept rules for forming statements and for testing, accepting, or rejecting them. Thus the acceptance of the thing language leads, on the basis of observations made, also to the acceptance, belief, and assertion of certain statements. But the thesis of the reality of the thing world cannot be among these statements, because it cannot be formulated in the thing language or, it seems, in any other theoretical language.[30]

Consider, as another example, the language concerning the natural numbers, in which use is made of such expressions as 'five', 'one million', 'odd', 'prime', 'plus', and so on.

Here again there are internal questions, e.g., "Is there a prime number greater than hundred?" Here, however, the answers are found, not by empirical investigation based on observations, but by logical analysis based on the rules for the new expressions. Therefore the answers are here analytic, i.e. logically true.[31]

Suppose, once more, that the external, 'ontological' question were raised concerning the existence or reality of numbers as such. To this Carnap replies:

Those philosophers who treat the question of the existence of numbers as a serious philosophical problem and offer lengthy arguments on either side, do not have in mind the internal question. And, indeed, if we were to ask them: "Do you mean the question as to whether the system of numbers, *if* we were to accept it, would be found to be empty or not?", they would probably reply: "Not at all; we mean a question prior to the acceptance of the new framework". They might try to explain what they mean by saying that it is a question of the ontological status of numbers; the question whether or not numbers have a certain metaphysical characteristic called reality (but a kind of ideal reality, different from the material reality of the thing world) or subsistence or status of "independent entities". Unfortunately, these philosophers have so far not given a formulation of their question in terms of the common scientific language. Therefore our judgment must be that they have not succeeded in giving to the external question and to the possible answers any cognitive content. Unless and until they supply a clear cognitive interpretation, we are justified in our suspicion that their question is a pseudo-question, that is, one disguised in the form of a theoretical question while in fact it is non-theoretical; in the present case it is the practical problem whether or not to incorporate into the language the new linguistic forms which represent the framework of numbers.[32]

To summarize the main point that Carnap makes: We need to distinguish genuine questions that have a possible answer by the use of suitable scientific, logical, or mathematical procedures. These are 'internal' to a framework, to the use of an adopted language. On the other hand, questions raised in ontology about the 'reality' or 'existence' of certain entities (things, numbers, abstract entities such as classes, propositions, properties, and so on) are 'external' questions. They have no genuine merit as theoretical, cognitive questions, because there is no acceptable way of answering them. There is, in short, an important division between science and ontology; the former raises 'internal' questions, the later 'external' questions.

In his response to Carnap, Quine disagrees with the distinction

Carnap draws between science and ontology, insofar as Carnap would limit the first to the raising of internal questions and criticize the latter for raising external ones. Quine *agrees* with Carnap about the relevance and importance of considering what is involved in the adoption of a 'framework' (a language or conceptual scheme). And he agrees with Carnap that we cannot 'step outside' the use of some language to ask about what there is in reality, apart from our using some language or other to *say* what there is. He agrees, furthermore, with Carnap that the choice among different available languages, old or newly proposed, is a matter that ultimately calls for decision on grounds of 'practical', i.e. pragmatic, considerations—that is, how well, in comparisons with others, a language or conceptual scheme works, as judged in terms of considerations of simplicity, economy, and the like. Quine's main point of divergence from Carnap has to do with Carnap's insisting on making a sharp distinction between science and ontology. For Quine, *both* science *and* ontology require the use of some language or other, and what holds true for the one holds for the other. When properly construed, ontology is not mired down in raising pseudoquestions; it has as sound a status in cognitive inquiry as does any branch of science, and is bound by the same typical conditions or constraints that apply to any legitimate inquiry. *Any* inquiry must make use of some language. All 'saying' is relative to the resources of the language used for doing the saying. Since we can never dispense with the use of some language, this holds as much for science and mathematics as it does for ontology. The only relevant considerations have to do with judgments of a comparative sort, in which one language or conceptual system is compared with another, but never with something 'outside', i.e., with 'reality' as it exists independently and apart from the use of a language system.

In supporting these general points of disagreement (and also agreement) with Carnap, Quine chooses to call attention to what he considers a more fruitful distinction than the one Carnap makes between 'internal' and 'external' questions. Instead of saying that ontology raises the latter kind of questions, and science the former kind, Quine says that if we properly understand what ontology is about we will say that ontology is interested in working with certain broad *category* expressions, whereas science is preoccupied with what may be called expressions for *subclasses*. This is a question of a breadth or range of interest; it is a question of degree, not of kind. It is not that category-expressions as used by ontology are on 'the other side' of the framework, and subclasses on 'this side'. *Both* are on 'this side'. Both ontology and science must employ language, and cannot raise 'external' questions. But instead of condemning ontology for working with 'category' expressions, as distinguished from the more limited domains of one or another science, one should recognize that it is every bit as legitimate an inquiry as that of science.

Carnap's dichotomy of questions of existence is a dichotomy between questions of the form "Are there so-and-so's?" where the so-and-so's purport to exhaust the range of a particular style of bound variables, and questions of the form "Are there so-and-so's?" where the so-and-so's do not purport to exhaust the range of a particular style of bound variables. Let me call the former questions *category* questions, and the latter ones *subclass* questions. I need this new terminology because Carnap's terms 'external' and 'internal' draw a somewhat different distinction which is derivative from the distinction between category questions and subclass questions. The external questions are the category questions conceived as propounded before the adoption of a given language; and they are, Carnap holds, properly to be construed as questions of the desirability of a given language form. The internal questions comprise the subclass questions and, in addition, the category questions when these are construed as treated within an adopted language as questions having trivially analytic or contradictory answers.

But now I want to examine the dichotomy which, as we see, underlies Carnap's distinction of external and internal, and which I am phrasing as the distinction between category questions and subclass questions. It is evident that the question whether there are numbers will be a category question only with respect to languages which appropriate a separate style of variables for the exclusive purpose of referring to numbers. If our language refers to numbers through variables which also take classes other than numbers as values, then the question whether there are numbers becomes a subclass question, on a par with the question whether there are primes over a hundred.[33]

According to Quine, then, the basic distinction between ontology and science is not where Carnap draws it, but has to do with the kinds of bound variables that a discipline chooses to deal with. If the bound variables are of the type and scope that belong to category words one may say this marks an ontological statement, whereas if it is of the subclass variety it may be part of a statement belonging to one or another of the sciences. This distinction is not an absolute one, and will vary with the kind of language in use. Since both ontology and science have to adopt some language or other, and quantify over some range of variables, there is no essential difference in cognitive status, or with respect to 'meaningfulness', that divides ontology from science. At best, the difference between ontology and science is a question of degree of scope, of range of subject matter, of role within a *total system* of beliefs.

Within natural science there is a continuum of gradations, from the statements which report observations to those which reflect basic features say of quantum theory or the theory of relativity. The view which I end up with . . . . is that statements of ontology or even of mathematics and logic form a continuation of this continuum, a continuation which is perhaps yet more remote from observation than are the central principles of quantum theory or relativity. The differences here are in my view differences only in degree and not in kind. Science is a unified structure, and in principle it is the structure as a whole, and not its component statements, one by one, that experience confirms or shows to be imperfect.

Carnap maintains that ontological questions, and likewise questions of logical or mathematical principle, are questions not of fact but of choosing a convenient scheme or framework for science; and with this I agree only if the same be conceded for every scientific hypothesis.[34]

THE INDETERMINACY THESIS AND ONTOLOGICAL RELATIVITY

We now move on to examine other aspects of Quine's views about ontology—particularly the matter of conceptual relativity. There is a close interconnection, in Quine's philosophy, between his views on the nature of language and his conception of the enterprises of ontology and science. One cannot give an account, he would say, of *what there is* without at the same time paying special attention to the terms used in giving the *account* of what there is, that is, to the conditions, mechanisms, and possible limitations involved in the use of language itself.

   Quine's approach to language is that of an empiricist and behaviorist. He stresses the need for a thorough empirical study of the behavioral and publicly observable responses of individuals under particular nonverbal and verbal stimulations in the course of learning a language. The pattern of these stimulations and responses gets channeled into specific speech dispositions, and constitutes the basis for claiming that someone has acquired mastery of a particular language. At the same time, for all the emphasis Quine gives to the requirement of an empirical orientation for a study of language, he recognizes, precisely as the result of this orientation that we have no direct access to 'things themselves'. Our access is always filtered through, and inevitably colored by, the distinctive characteristics of one or another set of linguistic tools. The empiricism and behaviorism that characterize his approach to understanding the phenomenon of language become the very ground for his adoption of relativism, pragmatism, and holism, as qualifying all claims to knowledge in the domains of ontology and science. (This latter feature of Quine's philosophy is what I have been calling 'Quine's version of a severely modified Kantianism'.) Because Quine, through his empirical studies of language, is aware of the plurality of languages, the social dimensions of language sharing, and the psychogenetic factors involved in acquisition of language-mastery, he has given emphasis to certain distinctive theses identified as 'the indeterminacy thesis' and the doctrine of 'ontological relativity'. We turn next to a brief examination of these ideas.

   Quine uses the metaphor of 'the myth of the museum' to describe a common misconception of the role of language. According to it, language provides the labels for 'meanings' as mental entities, but since the labels can be switched, the referents—like the exhibits on display in a museum case—are unaffected by and indifferent to any change of labels. Quine protests this 'museum myth' conception of language.

Uncritical semantics is the myth of a museum in which the exhibits are meanings and the words are labels. To switch languages is to change the labels. Now the naturalist's primary objection to this view is not an objection to meanings on account of their being mental entities, though that could be objection enough. The primary objection persists even if we take the labeled exhibits not as mental ideas but as Platonic ideas or even as the denoted concrete objects. Semantics is vitiated by a pernicious mentalism as long as we regard a man's semantics as somehow determinate in his mind beyond what might be implicit in his dispositions to overt behavior. It is the very facts about meaning, not the entities meant, that must be construed in terms of behavior.

. . . .

When . . . we turn toward a naturalistic view of language and a behavioral view of meaning, what we give up is not just the museum of figure of speech. We give up an assurance of determinacy. Seen according to the museum myth, the words and sentences of a language have their determinate meanings. To discover the meanings of the native's words we may have to observe his behavior, but still the meanings of the words are supposed to be determinate in the native's *mind*, his mental museum, even in cases where behavioral criteria are powerless to discover them for us. When on the other hand we recognize with Dewey that "meaning . . . is primarily a property of behavior," we recognize that there are no meanings, nor likenesses nor distinctions of meaning, beyond what are implicit in people's dispositions to overt behavior. For naturalism the question whether two expressions are alike or unlike in meaning has no determinate answer, known or unknown, except insofar as the answer is settled in principle by people's speech dispositions, known or unknown. If by these standards there are indeterminate cases, so much the worse for the terminology of meaning and likeness of meaning.[35]

If, following Quine, we replace the museum myth of how language is learned and functions with a more responsible, empirically based account, we should be led to acknowledge the presence of elements of *indeterminacy* and *relativity*, in some form or degree, in every use of language from the most commonplace and ordinary to the most sophisticated, technical, or recondite.

By 'indeterminacy' in general we shall understand that even under the most carefully controlled conditions of providing certain particular, publicly given stimuli, it will not be the case that different linguistic responses in the face of those stimulations can be discovered to match each other completely in meaning or reference. There will always remain the possibility of an element of indeterminateness, of 'surplus' interpretation, which would be impossible to detect and capture in the attempt to go from one linguistic response to another in the face of the same stimuli. Another way of putting this is to say that there is an 'empirical slack' in our adoption and use of language and belief, that these are *underdetermined* by sheer observational or sensory experience. Quine's favorite way of illustrating what he means by 'indeterminacy' is to point to the indeterminacy of translation in going from one language to another. To make this clear he takes not the ordinary case of translating from one familiar language to another (say from French to English), but the extreme case of what he calls *radical translation*. This is the kind of challenge experienced by a field linguist who must translate the language of a "hitherto untouched people."

To see what such indeterminacy would be like, suppose there were an expression in a remote language that could be translated into English equally defensibly in either of two ways, unlike in meaning in English. I am not speaking of ambiguity within the native language. I am supposing that one and the same native use of the expression can be given either of the English translations, each being accommodated by compensating adjustments in the translation of other words. Suppose both translations, along with these accommodations in each case, accord equally well with all observable behavior on the part of speakers of the remote language and speakers of English. Suppose they accord perfectly not only with behavior actually observed, but with all dispositions to behavior on the part of all the speakers concerned. On these assumptions it would be forever impossible to know of one of these translations that it was the right one, and the other wrong. Still, if the museum myth were true, there would be a right and wrong of the matter; it is just that we would never know, not having access to the museum. See language naturalistically, on the other hand, and you have to see the notion of likeness of meaning in such a case simply as nonsense.[36]

What this comes to can be put into terms of the notion of constructing a *manual of translation* from some foreign language, *N,* into one's own language, *E.* The principle of the indeterminacy of translation asserts that one may construct two different manuals of translation, each of which is acceptable, and in accordance with which a sentence of *N* will be translated into a sentence of *E,* and yet such that the sentence in *N* as translated into distinct sentences of *E* will have *different* truth-values, according to whether one uses one manual rather than the other. However, it would be impossible to establish that one of these manuals of translation is right and the other wrong!

To illustrate this situation, Quine considers the case of a field linguist and a native both of whom are confronted by the same stimuli.

A rabbit scurries by, the native says 'Gavagai', and the linguist notes down the sentence 'Rabbit' (or 'Lo, a rabbit') as tentative translation, subject to testing in further cases.

So we have the linguist asking 'Gavagai?' in each of various stimulatory situations, and noting each time whether the native assents, dissents, or neither.[37]

The indeterminacy of translation arises, and qualifies any manual of translation the linguist may wish to construct, due to the following circumstance:

A whole rabbit is present when and only when an undetached part of a rabbit is present; also when and only when a temporal stage of a rabbit is present. If we are wondering whether to translate a native expression "gavagai" as "rabbit" or as "undetached rabbit part" or as "rabbit stage," we can never settle the matter simply by ostension—that is, simply by repeatedly querying the expressions "gavagai" for the native's assent or dissent in the presence of assorted stimulations.

. . . .

Thus consider specifically the problem of deciding between "rabbit" and "undetached rabbit part" as translation of "gavagai." No word of the native language is known, except that we have settled on some working hypothesis as to what native words or gestures to construe as assent and dissent in response to our pointings and queryings. Now the trouble is that whenever we point to different parts of the rabbit, even sometimes screening the rest of the rabbit, we are pointing also each time to the rabbit. When, conversely, we indicate the whole rabbit with a sweeping gesture, we are still pointing to a multitude of rabbit parts. And note that we do not have even a native analogue of our plural ending to exploit, in asking "gavagai?" It seems clear that no even tentative decision between "rabbit" and "undetached rabbit part" is to be sought at this level.[38]

Quine makes clear that even if one were to marshall various techniques and resources for reducing the zone of indeterminacy, that indeterminacy, in some degree or form, could not be eliminated altogether. It will always be possible that in going from one language (or conceptual scheme) to another there will not be a unique and complete match of translatability that could be brought about by a single manual of translation. This unavoidable residual indeterminacy of translation has, for Quine, a general philosophical significance. That significance consists in his stress upon what we may call the thesis (or principle) of *conceptual relativity*. It underlies the account he gives of the notion of *ontological relativity*.

One way in which Quine makes clear the idea of conceptual (or ontological) relativity is by comparing what is involved in using some particular language (or conceptual scheme) as a 'frame of reference' in terms of which meanings and referents are specified, to what is involved in determining the position and motion of a body by using a frame of reference (a coordinate system) to specify locations of position or displacements. Thus we cannot, in the case of location of bodies, assign some *absolute* position or series of displacement positions if it is thought (erroneously) that such 'absolute' specifications can be accomplished without making use of any frame of reference or coordinate scheme, conventionally chosen. Instead we must adopt *some* frame of reference, with its arbitrarily chosen 'origin of coordinates' and grid of coordinates. Relative to the Sun, for example, the Earth is in such and such a position, or moving along such and such an orbit; relative to the fixed walls of my room, I walk about in it, and so on. In the same way, the first step in understanding the notions of meaning and reference is to realize that the means we use to convey these is *relative* to some specific, arbitrarily or conventionally chosen linguistic frame of reference, and cannot be accomplished in an absolute way, that is, by hoping to escape from and dispense with their use altogether.

It is meaningless to ask whether, in general, our terms "rabbit," "rabbit part," "number," etc., really refer respectively to rabbits, rabbit parts, numbers, etc., rather than to some ingeniously permuted denotations. It is meaningless to ask this absolutely; we can meaningfully ask it only relative to some background language. When we ask, "Does 'rabbit' really refer to rabbits?" someone can counter with the question: "Refer to rabbits in what sense of 'rabbits'?" thus launching a regress; and we need the background language to regress into. The background language gives the query sense, if only relative sense; sense relative in turn to it, this background language. Querying reference in any more absolute way would be like asking absolute position, or absolute velocity, rather than position or velocity relative to a given frame of reference. Also it is very much like asking whether our neighbor may not systematically see everything upside down, or in complementary color, forever undetectably.[39]

Of course, the question can immediately arise whether, if we arbitrarily adopt some frame of reference—spatial, linguistic, or whatever—we are not able to subsume (translate, place, re-express) the given frame within some *other* one, and whether in realizing that we can we are not thereby launched into an infinite regress. Quine's reply is that we avoid such an infinite regress only by realizing that if it is spurred on by the hope to find some final, absolute, and uniquely correct resting place, this is an illusory hope or search. There is no such ultimate, absolute frame.

We need a background language, I said, to regress into. Are we involved now in an infinite regress? If questions of reference of the sort we are considering make sense only relative to a background language, then evidently questions of reference for the background language make sense in turn only relative to a further background language. In these terms the situation sounds desperate, but in fact it is little different from questions of position and velocity. When we are given position and velocity relative to a given coordinate system, we can always ask in turn about the placing of origin and orientation of axes of that system of coordinates; and there is no end to the succession of further coordinate systems that could be adduced in answering the successive questions thus generated.

In practice of course we end the regress of coordinate systems by something like pointing. And in practice we end the regress of background languages, in discussions of reference, by acquiescing in our mother tongue and taking its words at face value.

Very well; in the case of position and velocity, in practice, pointing breaks the regress. But what of position and velocity apart from practice? what of regress then? The answer, of course, is the relational doctrine of space; there is no absolute position or velocity; there are just the relations of coordinate systems to one another, and ultimately of things to one another. And I think that the parallel question regarding denotation calls for a parallel answer, a relational theory of what the objects of theories are. What makes sense is to say not what the objects of a theory are, absolutely speaking, but how one theory of objects is interpretable or reinterpretable in another.

. . . .

What our present reflections are leading us to appreciate is that the riddle about seeing things upside down, or in complementary colors, should be taken seriously and its moral applied widely. The relativistic thesis to which we have come is this, to repeat: it makes no sense to say what the objects of a theory are, beyond saying how to interpret or reinterpret that theory in another. Suppose we are working within a theory and thus treating of its objects. We do so by using the variables of the theory, whose values those objects are, though there be no ultimate sense in which that universe can have been specified. In the language of the theory there are predicates by which to distinguish portions of this universe from other portions, and these predicates differ from one another purely in the roles they play in the laws of the theory. Within this background theory we can show how some subordinate theory, whose universe is some portion of the background universe, can by a reinterpretation be reduced to another subordinate theory whose universe is some lesser portion. Such talk of subordinate theories and their ontologies *is* meaningful, but only relative to the background theory with its own primitively adopted and ultimately inscrutable ontology.[40]

There is no "absolute fact of the matter." In the case of accomplishing reference, Quine expresses this as the doctrine of the "inscrutability of reference"; there is nothing to "scrute" independently and apart from the use of some conceptual (linguistic) scheme of referring devices. At best we may attempt to 'translate' one background 'theory' or arbitrarily chosen and adopted conceptual scheme into another, but there is no guarantee that these are strictly equivalent to one another, i.e., that the symbols chosen by one scheme have a unique match or corresponding symbol in another language, in the way in which the mathematician or physicist can translate the symbols of one coordinate frame into those of another, within some commonly accepted background language or theory, by means of a system of transformation equations.

REFERENTIAL OPACITY, MODALITY, AND ESSENTIALISM: SAUL KRIPKE

In our earlier summary of Quine's paper, "On What There Is," we saw that in hinting at his own ontological views he raised various difficulties with—and therefore expressed strong reservations about—the need to include *possible objects* among 'those that there are'. In the present section we shall examine some further refinements of Quine's views on the general topic of modality—that area of philosophy and logic that undertakes to clarify the concepts of necessity and possibility, or the use of the expressions 'necessarily' and 'possibly'.

The basic groundwork for a classical sentential and predicate logic was established by Frege. This logic involved two sets of central ideas: those having to do with a two-valued truth-functional system for dealing with propositions, and that of generality, as reflected in the use of quantifiers. The publication of Whitehead and Russell's *Principia Mathematica* marks a major milestone in the history of logic that built on these ideas. Quine's work, for all its innovative contributions, is essentially a working out of some further details within this tradition initiated by Frege and Russell. In recent decades, various departures from and rivals to the classical system of *Principia* have characterized the lively and richly flowering field of logic. Various types of formal calculi have been developed—many-valued logics, tense-logics, deontic logics, epistemic logics, erotetic (interrogative) logics, and so on.* Among these developments is the construction of systems of *modal logic*. Various logicians, including Clarence I. Lewis, Jaakko Hintikka, Ruth Barcan Marcus, Saul Kripke, and others have contributed to the development of such modal calculi, including the use of devices of quantification, in order to give precise expression to the notions of necessity and possibility. In addition, they have sought to work out a 'semantics' (schemes for determining the application and interpretation) of these formal calculi. Furthermore, an extensive philosophical literature surrounding these formal developments has grown up in which diverse views are presented for evaluating the significance or merit of what has thereby been achieved. It is in the context of these recent developments that Quine's comments on modality are to be understood. He has expressed his strong misgivings about the logical and philosophical soundness of the claims made in behalf of quantified modal logic. Although the topic is a complex and technical one, with details beyond the scope of the present book, it will nevertheless be of some importance to an understanding both of Quine's views and of some recent lines of thought in analytic philosophy (e.g., in the work of Saul Kripke) to briefly explore some general features of the controversy thus engendered.

Let us begin by considering the following sentences, the combination of which illustrates some of the difficulties that arise, Quine would

---

* Many-valued systems are not restricted, as classical Fregean logic is, to the two truth-values 'true' and 'false'; tense logics deal with such expressions as 'earlier than', 'it will be the case', 'it used to be the case that'; deontic logics with expressions as 'may' ('it is permitted'), 'ought' and the like; epistemic logics with terms such as 'believes' and 'knows'; erotetic logics with 'questions' and 'answers'.

say, when we try to combine modal concepts and those of the standard classical predicate logic.*

1.   9 = the number of the planets,
2.   □ (9 > 7),
3.   □ (the number of the planets > 7).

The first sentence can be read '9 is (the same as) the number of the planets'; it is true. The second can be read as 'Necessarily 9 is greater than 7', and is also true. However, the third sentence, which can be read 'Necessarily, the number of planets is greater than 7', is false, for it is logically possible (non-necessary) that the number of planets is not greater than 7. It would seem to be required, however, that sentence *3* follows from sentences *1* and *2*, once we perform the relevant substitutions. Yet clearly something is wrong if we can obtain as a conclusion a false sentence from two true premisses.

In carrying out his critical analysis of this situation, Quine shows the role played by the principle of identity, taken as a *principle of substitutivity*. If we have a statement of identity, with the identity sign flanked on either side by a singular term, then the principle of substitutivity asserts that "*given a true statement of identity, one of its two terms may be substituted for the other in any true statement and the result will be true.*"[41] This principle is sometimes also expressed by saying that terms shown to be identical are intersubstitutive *salva veritate*. (The expression '*salva veritate*' means, effectively, 'without change of truth-value': that is, if a statement is true, and we replace a singular referring expression in it by one of its equivalents, the truth of the statement as a whole is unaffected—its truth is 'saved' or preserved—despite this replacement.)

Two expressions will designate the same individual if each expression is used *directly* or in a *purely referential* way to refer to its object (its referent). On the other hand, if a term is not used in a direct or purely referential way it will have what Quine calls *referential opacity*. Thus in order for the principle of substitutivity to hold, the singular expressions (e.g., names) must be used in a purely referential way and not be referentially opaque. "For it is clear that whatever can be affirmed about the object remains true when we refer to the object by any other name."[42]

Thus, if 'Socrates = the teacher of Plato = the husband of Xanthippe', and if the sentence 'Socrates was made to drink the hemlock' is true, in accordance with the statement of identity one could replace the expression 'Socrates' by either of the expressions 'the teacher of Plato' or 'the husband of Xanthippe', and the sentence as a whole will retain its

---

* In modal logic, the two key ideas are 'necessarily' and 'possibly'. The former is symbolized as '□' and the latter as ◇. Alternative symbolizations in common use are 'L' for 'necessarily', and 'M' for 'possibly'.

truth. The predicate 'was made to drink the hemlock' would continue to be true of the individual referred to by any one of these equivalent, intersubstitutive, purely referential expressions.

However, there are some sentences in which names (or other singular expressions) are not used in a purely referential way. In these cases, the principle of substitutivity will not hold, i.e., it will *not* generally or necessarily be the case that by replacing some singular term by its equivalent the truth of the entire sentence will be preserved. Thus, take Quine's example of the true identity

Tegucigalpa=the capital of Honduras

and consider the true sentence concerning the *belief* of a certain person, namely Philip.

Philip believes that Tegucigalpa is in Nicaragua.

On the assumption that Philip realizes that Honduras and Nicaragua are different countries, it would be false that

Philip believes that the capital of Honduras is in Nicaragua.

The replacement of the intersubstitutive terms 'Tegucigalpa' by 'the capital of Honduras' does *not* preserve the truth of the sentence that describes a person's belief. In such a sentence ('Philip believes that Tegucigalpa is in Nicaragua') the use of the expressions 'Tegucigalpa' and 'Nicaragua' is *not* purely referential. They occur in this kind of sentence in a referentially opaque way. (Frege called such occurrences 'indirect', *ungerade*, as contrasted with 'direct', *gerade*, uses). In sentences containing terms marked by referential opacity, the principle of substitutivity is not applicable; it does not guarantee truth preservation.

There are many other examples of sentences in which the singular terms present in them have referential opacity in *those* sentences. This is the case, for example, with the whole group of sentences that convey various types of 'propositional attitude', for example, '*x* fears that———', '*x* believes that———', '*x* knows that———', '*x* expects that———', '*x* says that———, '*x* doubts that———', '*x* is surprised that———', and so on. In all of these, if singular terms are embedded in the clauses that follow the 'that ———', they suffer from referential opacity.

Other examples where referential opacity is present occur wherever the distinction needs to be made between the *use* and *mention* of a term, and where the latter is marked by the presence of quotation marks around the term in question. Thus in the sentence

Cicero was an orator

one is *using* the proper name to refer to a particular individual. On the basis of the identity sentence

$$Tully = Cicero$$

we can replace a sentence in which one of these proper names is *used* by another sentence in which the other name is used without affecting the truth-value. Now, however, consider the sentence

'Tully' has five letters.

While this sentence is true, we cannot replace 'Tully' by 'Cicero' since we should then get a *false* sentence. By employing quotation marks, as in 'Tully', one is no longer *using* the proper name in a purely referential way. Instead, one is *mentioning* Tully by means of the quoted expression. The quoted expression is referentially opaque; it does not refer to the person named.

Quine's principal argument is that one of the major weaknesses of modal sentences involving the expressions 'necessarily' or 'possibly', as codified and symbolized in quantified modal logic, is that they too suffer from or induce referential opacity, and thereby defeat the legitimate use of quantified variables.

As a preparation and background for understanding Quine's criticisms, let us pause to take note, first, of a distinction commonly made by many philosophers with respect to the use of the terms 'necessary' and 'possible'. Each of these terms, it will be said, can be used in either of two ways, *de dicto* and *de re*. (These latter expressions can be translated, respectively, as 'having to do with the dictum or proposition' and 'having to do with the thing'). Thus consider the following sentences:

Necessarily, a = a

and

Necessarily, if 'All men are mortal, and Socrates is a man, then Socrates is mortal'.

In each case one can say that the term 'necessarily' is used in such a way that it applies to the *proposition* as a whole that follows immediately after the term 'necessarily'. If one says of the proposition 'a = a' that it is necessary, this is to say that, in conveying the principle of identity, it is true universally, without exception. Similarly, the entire statement 'If all men are mortal, and Socrates is a man, then Socrates is mortal', is necessarily true as a whole because it conforms to the schema '(p → q). (p) → q', i.e., 'If (if p then q) and (p), then q'. This pattern states a logically true principle that holds without exception.

On the other hand, if one says 'A man is necessarily a rational animal', the term 'necessarily' describes a property belonging to an individual essentially. Thus on the traditional view, God is a being whose existence is necessary (it is not possible for God not to exist), whereas the existence of his creatures (of any finite entity, or of the world itself) is non-necessary or contingent. Or again, the property of being a rational animal is necessary (essential) to what it is to be a man; however, it is not essential to being a man that he speak Spanish; that property belongs to some individuals, not to others. A man possibly speaks Spanish, but necessarily is a rational animal.

Our first group of examples, those having to do with the use of 'necessarily' in connection with propositions as a whole, belong to the *de dicto* use of 'necessarily'; the second group of examples, those having to do with the essential properties of an individual object (or person) have to do with the use of 'necessarily' *de re*.

Analogously, one could make a distinction between two uses of the term 'possibly'. Consider the two sentences

Possibly Socrates was a vegetarian

Socrates was possibly a vegetarian.

In the first case, the use of the term 'possibly' governs the entire proposition 'Socrates was a vegetarian' and its truth-value. It may be true or it may be false. On the other hand, in the sentence 'Socrates was possibly a vegetarian', the use of the term 'possibly' tells us something about the applicability of the predicate 'was a vegetarian' (the property of being a vegetarian) in connection with Socrates. As a person who has the capacity to adopt a particular kind of diet or change it, he may or may not have had that property at a particular time. The first use of 'possibly' is *de dicto*, the second use *de re*.

A *de dicto* use of 'necessarily' or 'possibly' has to do with the truth or falsity of some proposition as a whole; the *de re* use of modal terms has to do with the thing (*res*) or state of affairs, with whether the property in question belongs to the object essentially or not.

There is one further point we need to introduce in connection with the use of quantified variables, before we put our various preliminary reminders together and return to Quine's indictment of quantified modal logic. This point concerns the use of the *principle of existential generalization*. According to this standard rule of classical predicate logic, if we are given a sentence in which a predicate expression is attached to a name and predicated of the object referred to by the name, we may apply the rule of existential generalization by dropping the use of the name and replacing it by a variable that is then quantified (bound) by the existential quantifier. Thus, given the sentence

Socrates is a man

we may use the rule of existential generalization to obtain the sentence

$(\exists x)\, x$ is a man.

Or, again, if we are given the sentence

$$9 > 7,$$

we may apply the rule of existential generalization to obtain

$$(\exists x)\, x > 7.$$

In each of the above cases, the expression following the quantified variable is said to lie within the scope of the quantified variable. Thus 'x is a man' or '$x > 7$' lies within the scope of the quantified variable $(\exists x)$.

We have seen previously that, as used in ordinary language, the expressions 'necessarily' and 'possibly' suffer from certain ambiguities of scope. A modal term may in some cases be used as a *sentential operator* and apply to the entire sentence, which may be said to lie within its scope. On the other hand, the modal expression may be used to apply to only a fragment of the sentence, and thereby have only that fragment within its scope. The introduction of quantifiers in predicate logic is a device one of whose principal uses is the elimination of such troublesome ambiguities of scope.

Let us next consider the complication presented by the attempt to combine the use of quantifiers and modal expressions. Take the case, previously mentioned, in which the following expression is obtained as a result of applying the rule of existential generalization:

$$(\exists x)\, Fx$$

where 'F' is a predicate expression, and x is an individual variable. If, now, we introduce the use of modal expressions, such as 'necessarily' alongside the standard use of quantifiers, individual variables, predicate expressions and other logical constants, it is clearly important, in the light of what we said earlier, to be able to distinguish

$$\Box\,(\exists x)\, Fx$$

and

$$(\exists x)\,\Box\, Fx.$$

In the first case, the modal expression lies outside the range of the quantifier and serves as a sentential operator. In the second case, the modal expression lies *within* the scope of the quantified variable. The first sentence may be read

Necessarily, for some x, Fx.

And the second sentence may be read

For some x, necessarily Fx.

Quine's questions and criticisms of quantified modal logic have to do primarily with the use of modal expressions *within* the scope of quantified variables, although he also has some qualms about the other uses as well. In order to see what Quine's objections are, I shall summarize these as falling within a two-pronged dilemma, each of whose horns, as we may interpret Quine, presents serious difficulties. Hence (to anticipate) instead of searching for a way of 'escaping between the horns' (as some have sought to do), he would maintain that the whole enterprise and program of quantified modal logic was "conceived in sin." It is philosophically misbegotten and should be abandoned.

In examining a typical example of quantified modal logic, let us go back to the case with thich we started our discussion: that involving 9, the number of the planets, and the property of being greater than 7. Let us now introduce the use both of quantifiers (through the use of existential generalization) *and* the use of the modal expression 'necessarily' within the scope of the quantified variable. Thus from

$$9 > 7$$

we obtain (by existential generalization)

$$(\exists x)\, x > 7.$$

And from

9 is necessarily greater than 7

where 'necessarily' is taken as applying to a part of the entire sentence, i.e., as lying within the scope of the quantifier, we obtain

$$(\exists x)\, \Box\, x > 7.$$

The problem, for Quine, may now be put in the form of a dilemma, each of whose horns has unpalatable consequences in his eyes.

1. Let us go back to the standard interpretation of the use of quantifiers as we find it in the classical predicate calculus. Let us take the case of where, for a quantified variable, we insert as an argument for the variable a singular referring expression; and let us assume that as a result we obtain a true statement. (For '$(\exists x)\, x$ is a man' we replace 'x' by 'Socrates', and obtain the true statement 'Socrates is a man'.) According to the principle of substitutivity, we should also obtain the same truth-value (*salva veritate*) by substituting for 'Socrates' any singular referring expression that refers—as a purely referential term—to the same individual, in other words is intersubstitutive with 'Socrates' (e.g., 'the teacher of Plato'). According to the rules of classical predicate logic, one could always use the principle of substitutivity in this way for terms within the range of values (or arguments) of a bound variable.

However, we find that by adding the use of modal expressions within the scope of bound variables the situation changes drastically. Recall the argument in which we obtained the false conclusion 'The number of the planets is necessarily greater than 7' from the two true premises

'9 is necessarily greater than 7' and '9 is the number of the planets'. We assumed, in obtaining this result, that we could rely with confidence on the principle of substitutivity, which sanctioned the substitution of 'the number of the planets' for '9'. In making this substitution, we assumed that each of these expressions is here being used in a purely referential way. If now, however, as a result of this we obtain the unwelcome outcome of obtaining a false conclusion from two true premisses, we must go back and question what we have accepted and assumed along the way. The suspicion falls on the assumption that the singular terms were used in a purely referential way, and therefore subject to the principle of substitutivity. If we surrender this assumption, it means that far from the singular terms being used in a purely referential way, they are in fact referentially opaque! What has brought about this change is the use of the modal expression joined to the singular term within the scope of the quantifier. Unlike the situation in classical quantificational logic that is unencumbered by modal expressions, the introduction of these expressions (like the use of verbs of propositional attitudes, or quotation marks) transforms the role and status of a singular term used in a purely referential way to one where it is now referentially opaque. Of course, under these conditions one can no longer use the principle of substitutivity to sanction replacement of singular terms by their equivalents. Clearly, we cannot complacently accommodate ourselves to this situation. Either we must discard or change our standard rules for the use of the quantifiers, or else we must surrender the use of modal terms in the way they appear here. The choice, for Quine, is obvious. He thinks the enormous strength, clarity, consistency, and successes of classical first-order predicate logic (including the use of the principle of substitutivity) are so well established that it is preferable by all odds to give up the attempt to combine the use of quantifiers and modal terms.

2. Now let us turn to the other possible route, the other horn of the dilemma. It might be suggested that it is really not required that we give up the combined use of quantifiers and modal terms, since in the case of the term 'necessarily', as it appears in 'an x which is necessarily F', we are appealing to the notion of *essential properties,* and this is a wholly respectable philosophic concept. We could call upon the philosophical doctrine of *essentialism,* of the sort that Aristotle or others influenced by him espouse. Such a doctrine commits one to speaking of objects as having essential or nonessential (contingent) properties; in short, to a conception of *de re* modalities. However, this 'way out' is equally unappealing to Quine.

The only course open to the champion of quantified modal logic is to meet my strictures head on: to argue in the case of 9 and the number of the planets that this number is, of itself and independently of mode of specification, something that necessarily, not contingently, exceeds 7. This means adopting a frankly inequalitarian attitude toward the various ways of specifying the number. One of the determining traits, the succeeding of 8, is counted as a necessary trait of the number. So are any traits that follow from that one, notably the exceeding of 7. Other uniquely determining traits of the number, notably its numbering of the planets, are discounted as contingent traits of the number and held not to belie the fact that the number does still necessarily exceed 7.

This is how essentialism comes in: the invidious distinction between some traits of an object as essential to *it* (by whatever name) and other traits of it as accidental. I do not say that such essentialism, however uncongenial to me, should be uncongenial to the champion of quantified modal logic. On the contrary, it should be every bit as congenial as quantified modal logic itself.[43]

Quine confesses that he finds it bewildering to talk about the difference between necessary and contingent (accidental, non-necessary) properties:

Perhaps I can evoke the appropriate sense of bewilderment as follows. Mathematicians may conceivably be said to be necessarily rational and not necessarily two-legged; and cyclists necessarily two-legged and not necessarily rational. But what of an individual who counts among his eccentricities both mathematics and cycling? Is this concrete individual necessarily rational and contingently two-legged or vice versa? Just insofar as we are talking referentially of the object, with no special bias toward a background grouping of mathematicians as against cyclists or vice versa, there is no semblance of sense in rating some of his attributes as necessary and others as contingent. Some of his attributes count as important and others as unimportant, yes: some as enduring and others as fleeting; but none as necessary or contingent.

Curiously, a philosophical tradition does exist for just such a distinction between necessary and contingent attributes. It lives on in the terms 'essence' and 'accident', 'internal relation' and 'external relation'. It is a distinction that one attributes to Aristotle (subject to contradiction by scholars, such being the penalty for attributions to Aristotle). But, however venerable the distinction, it is surely indefensible.[44]

Quine's strictures concerning modal logic have provoked much discussion. Various lines of defense and support have been proposed in order to show the philosophic soundness of the basic ideas of modal logic. Some have insisted on retaining the traditional doctrine of essentialism and *de re* modalities. Others have adopted a special interpretation of the quantifiers as used in modal quantification—calling it 'substitutional quantification'—as a way of reconciling the use of quantifiers and modal concepts. A major development in recent decades has been the working out of a semantics (a way of specifying the possible applications and interpretations of the formal, syntactic formulae of modal logic) that appeals to the notion of 'models' or 'possible worlds'.[45] Such accounts of 'possible worlds semantics' have been very much in the forefront of recent discussions of quantified modal logic, and serve as the framework within which most of the responses to Quine have been expressed. This type of semantics has been elaborated largely since the time when Quine first expressed his doubts about modal logic. Many philosophers and logicians think they see in these recent developments a way of answering Quine. However, it should be noted that those who rely on these recent developments do not always agree among themselves how it would be best to interpret what we are to understand by a 'possible world', and thus differ among themselves about what such an appeal amounts to. Quine, let it be remarked, is not convinced that *any* one or a combination of these defenses, whether in terms of essentialism, substitutional quantification, or some form of possible-worlds semantics, is really adequate to or successful in meeting his criticisms.

Let us examine one example of these recent moves by modal logicians to defend themselves against Quine, the views of Saul Kripke. He is one of the chief contributors to and pioneers in formulating a possible-worlds semantics (on the formal side); also, in subsequent philosophical articles—especially "Identity and Necessity" and "Naming and Necessity"—he shows how one may support essentialism.[46] One of the main ideas Kripke works out for these philosophic purposes is that of 'rigid designators'. His proposals have in turn sparked a good deal of recent discussion. It will be of interest to explore these suggestions.

In order to understand the main lines of Kripke's views and wherein they differ from those of Quine, we need first to follow Kripke as he draws a number of distinctions. It is Quine's failure (as well as that of many other philosophers) to draw the following distinctions, Kripke would maintain, that accounts for the considerable confusion and disagreements that persist in the discussion of modal concepts.

Why can one say that 9 is necessarily greater than 7, whereas we cannot say that the number of the planets is necessarily greater than 7? The intuitive response is that while the number of the planets might have been different from what in fact it is, 9 could not be different from what it is. This difference, intuitively sensed, is, for Kripke, captured and made explicit by the distinction between *rigid* and *nonrigid designators*. What, then, is this distinction? What do these terms mean?

As an example of a nonrigid designator, I can give an expression such as 'the inventor of bifocals'. Let us suppose it was Benjamin Franklin who invented bifocals, and so the expression, 'the inventor of bifocals', designates or refers to a certain man, namely, Benjamin Franklin. However, we can easily imagine that the world could have been different, that under different circumstances someone else would have come upon this invention before Benjamin Franklin did, and in that case, *he* would have been the inventor of bifocals. So, in this sense, the expression 'the inventor of bifocals' is nonrigid: Under certain circumstances one man would have been the inventor of bifocals; under other circumstances, another man would have. In contrast, consider the expression 'the square root of 25'. Independently of the empirical facts, we can give an arithmetical proof that the square root of 25 is in fact the number 5, and because we have proved this mathematically, what we have proved is necessary. If we think of numbers as entities at all, and let us suppose, at least for the purpose of this lecture, that we do, then the expression 'the square root of 25' necessarily designates a certain number, namely 5. Such an expression I call 'a *rigid* designator' . . . . What do I mean by a 'rigid designator'? I mean a term that designates the same object in all possible worlds.[47]

If we accept the foregoing distinction between rigid and nonrigid designators, we should say that the sentence '9 = the number of the planets', although presented as an identity, is one that contains two different types of referring expressions: '9', as a numeral referring to the number 9, is a *rigid designator*; on the other hand, the phrase 'the number of the planets' is a *nonrigid designator*. One of the reasons Quine is able to point out the difficulties arising from combining this sentence with modal expressions has nothing to do with the use of modal expressions as such. The difficulties result from a failure to realize that if a true identity statement is to be employed in an argument and as expressing a *necessary* intersubstitutivity of the expressions on either side of the identity sign, it must be one in which these expressions are *both rigid designators*. Thus 'the square root of 25 is 4 + 1' is a necessarily true identity statement in which both referring expressions are rigid designators. So is the sentence 'Tully is Cicero'.

Kripke offers further clarifications of what he means by a rigid designator as distinguished from a nonrigid designator. The difference is *not* to be assigned to some difference in the conventional (arbitrary) way in which certain expressions are used in one linguistic community as compared to another.

To get rid of one confusion which certainly is not mine, I do not use "might have designated a different object" to refer to the fact that language might have been used differently. For example, the expression 'the inventor of bifocals' might have been used by inhabitants of this planet always to refer to the man who corrupted Hadleyburg. This would have been the case, if, first, the people on this planet had not spoken English, but some other language, which phonetically overlapped with English; and if, second, in that language the expression 'the inventor of bifocals' meant the 'man who corrupted Hadleyburg'. Then it would refer, of course, in their language, to whoever in fact corrupted Hadleyburg in this counterfactual situation. That is not what I mean. What I mean by saying that a description might have referred to something different, I mean that in *our* language as *we* use it in describing a counterfactual situation, there might have been a different object satisfying the descriptive conditions *we* give for reference. So, for example, we use the phrase 'the inventor of bifocals', when we are talking about another possible world or a counterfactual situation, to refer to whoever in that counterfactual situation would have invented bifocals, not to the person whom people *in* that counterfactual situation would have called 'the inventor of bifocals'. *They* might have spoken a different language which phonetically overlapped with

English in which 'the inventor of bifocals' is used in some other way. I am *not* concerned with that question here. For that matter, they might have been deaf and dumb, or there might have been no people at all. (There still could have been an inventor of bifocals even if there were no people—God, or Satan, will do).[48]

One way in which Kripke characterizes a rigid designator is by saying that it is an expression that designates the same object in all possible worlds. How, then, are we to understand the notion of a *possible world?* Very roughly, a possible world is a counterfactual situation. On Kripke's approach, the key idea in all talk about 'possible worlds' is that we start with the notion of this actual world, with the objects existent in it, and build our conception of a possible world by describing or stipulating a counterfactual situation. In our description of that possible world we retain some entities or features from the actual world—but not all. A possible world is not something having its own independent mode of being that we can *discover* apart from all reference to the actual world.

So, we do not begin with worlds (which are supposed somehow to be real, and whose qualities, but not whose objects, are perceptible to us), and then ask about criteria of transworld identification; on the contrary, we begin with the objects which we *have,* and can identify, in the actual world. We can then ask whether certain things might have been true of the objects.[49]

If one accepts this approach to the concept of a possible world—and possible objects—then one of Quine's objections to the notion of possible objects can be removed. For, it will be recalled, Quine asks how one can provide a criterion of identity for distinguishing, say, the number of possible fat and/or bald men in that doorway! The reply would be that one cannot meaningfully discuss the abstract notion of *a* fat or *a* bald man in the doorway, or for that matter several fat and/or bald men in the doorway, as abstract entities described wholly in terms of certain qualities, and still apply a criterion of identity for *individual* objects to these. Quine is justified in raising doubts about *that* conception of a possible object. However, if one starts by referring to a given (existent) fat person (or a given person who could become fat or bald) or several such actual persons, who are not at a given time standing simultaneously in *that* particular doorway, and asks counterfactually; "How many of *these* persons could fit into *that* doorway?" then the matter of providing a criterion of identity for these 'possible' individuals is no longer unanswerable.

In the actual world, things are as they are and have the properties and relations they do. A possible world is different from the actual world either because in part the constituents of the world would be different, or, if having the same constituents, would differ in terms of some of their properties or relations. Let us consider the case where we identify an individual as existing in the actual world. There may be some possible worlds to which *that* individual does not belong as a constituent. For example, we can conceive (i.e., stipulate, describe) a possible world containing the two *persons* whom you in this actual world call your parents, but who in that possible world never do meet, never get married, and never produce you as their child. In that possible world *you* would not 'exist', although the individual persons whom you *now* call your parents *would* 'exist'. Or again, we may think of a possible world as one to which certain individual objects or persons belong, but do not have certain properties or relations that they do in the actual world. We may conceive of a possible world in which Shakespeare did not write *Hamlet,* or a possible world in which, as a child, I would have been given lessons in how to play the clarinet rather than the violin.

If there is some object that exists in *all* possible worlds, Kripke would say it is a necessary existent, or has necessary existence. On the other hand, there are some individual entities that exist in some worlds but not necessarily in all possible worlds; in that case such individual entities will be said to have contingent existence.

If we identify an individual object as existing in this world, and also conceive of one or more possible worlds to which that same individual also belongs, then the expression that serves to designate *that* individual both in the actual and in those possible worlds will be said to be a *rigid designator.*

In talking about the notion of a rigid designator, I do not mean to imply that the object referred to has to exist in all possible worlds, that is, that it has to necessarily exist. Some things, perhaps mathematical entities such as the positive integers, if they exist at all, necessarily exist. Some people have held that God both exists and necessarily exists; others, that He contingently exists; others, that He contingently fails to exist; and others, that He necessarily fails to exist: all four options have been tried. But at any rate, when I use the notion of rigid designator, I do not imply that the object referred to necessarily exists. All I mean is that in any possible world where the object in question *does* exist, in any situation where the object *would* exist, we use the designator in question to designate that object. In a situation where the object does not exist, then we should say that the designator has no referent and the object in question so designated does not exist.[50]

For Kripke, a proper name is always a rigid designator, whereas other ways of referring to the individual need not be rigid designators. He claims there is a simple intuitive test for distinguishing rigid and nonrigid designators.

We can say, for example, that the number of planets might have been a different number from the number it in fact is. For example, there might have been only seven planets. We can say the the inventor of bifocals might have been someone other than the man who *in fact* invented bifocals. We cannot say, though, that the square root of 81 might have been a different number from the number it in fact is, for that number just has to be 9. If we apply this intuitive test to proper names, such as for example 'Richard Nixon', they would seem intuitively to come out to be rigid designators. First, when we talk even about the counterfactual situation in which we suppose Nixon to have done different things, we assume we are still talking about Nixon himself. We say, "If Nixon had bribed a certain Senator, he would have gotten Carswell through," and we assume that by 'Nixon' and 'Carswell' we are still referring to the very same people as in the actual world. And it seems that we cannot say "Nixon might have been a different man from the man he in fact was," unless, of couse, we mean it metaphorically: He might have been a different *sort* of person (if you believe in free will and that people are not inherently corrupt). You might think the statement true in that sense, but Nixon could not have been in the other literal sense a different person from the person he, in fact, is, even though the thirty-seventh President of the United States might have been Humphrey. So the phrase "the thirty-seventh President" is nonrigid, but 'Nixon', it would seem, is rigid.[51]

Another set of distinctions overlooked by most philosophers, according to Kripke, but important in all discussions of modal logic, has to do with the contrasting pairs of terms, '*a priori* / *a posteriori*' and 'necessary / contingent'. He points out that for many philosophers the terms '*a priori*', 'necessary', 'analytic', and 'certain' are used interchangeably to characterize one whole group of statements, whereas, it is claimed, those which are *a posteriori* are contingent, synthetic, and uncertain (probable). Orthodox logical positivists (empiricists) would fall into this group. On the other hand, philosophers such as Quine would deny the meaningfulness of this sharp distinction. Kripke believes *both* groups of philosophers (the empiricists and their opponents) to be equally at fault in not drawing certain distinctions. If accepted, the *separation* of *a priori* statements from necessary ones will provide one crucial way of dealing with the concepts of modal logic, and will also be of value in judging the elements of soundness in essentialist doctrines.

What do we mean by calling a statement *necessary?* We simply mean that the statement in question, first, is true, and second, that it could not have been otherwise. When we say that something is *contingently* true, we mean that, though it is in fact the case, it could have been the case that things would have been otherwise. If we wish to assign this distinction to a branch of philosophy, we should assign it to metaphysics. To the contrary, there is the notion of an *a priori* truth. An *a priori* truth is supposed to be one which can be *known* to be true independently of all experience. Notice that this does not in and of itself say anything about all possible worlds, unless this is put into the definition. All that it says is that it can be known to be true of the actual world, independently of all experience. It may, by some philosophical argument, follow from our knowing, independently of experience, that something is true of the actual world, that it has to be known to be true also of all possible worlds. But if this is to be established, it requires some philosophical argument to establish it. Now, *this* notion, if we were to assign it to a branch of philosophy, belongs, not to metaphysics, but to epistemology. It has to do with the way we can know certain things to be in fact true. Now, it may be the case, of course, that anything which is necessary is something which *can* be known *a priori* . . . these two notions are by no means trivially the same. If they are coextensive, it takes some philosophical argument to establish it. As stated, they belong to different domains of philosophy. One of them has something to do with *knowledge,* of what can be known in certain ways about the actual world. The other one has to do with *metaphysics,* how the world *could* have been; given that it is the way it is, could it have been otherwise, in certain ways? Now I hold, as a matter of fact, that neither class of statements is contained in the other.[52]

Having drawn the foregoing distinctions—between rigid and non-rigid designators, between the actual world and possible worlds, and between *a prioricity* and necessity—Kripke puts these distinctions to work in dealing with a number of controversial themes arising from developments in modal logic. As examples of these applications, and to show specifically how Kripke's approach differs from that of Quine, we turn now to examine his views on essentialism (the doctrine of *de re* necessities) and the analysis he gives of identity statements.

With respect to the question of essentialism, Kripke makes it clear that since the question of necessity is a metaphysical question, and therefore to be kept separate from epistemological questions concerning our knowledge about something (whether our *account* is *a priori, a posteriori,* certain or uncertain, and so on), there is no reason why one should not say that, for example, a particular object has, *necessarily and as belonging to it essentially (de re),* certain properties.

Here is a lectern. A question which has often been raised in philosophy is: What are its essential properties? What properties, aside from trivial ones like self-identity, are such that this object has to have them if it exists at all, are such that if an object did not have it, it would not be this object? For example, being made of wood, and not of ice, might be an essential property of this lectern. Let us just take the weaker statement that it is not made of ice. That will establish it as strongly as we need it, perhaps as dramatically. Supposing this lectern is in fact made of wood, could this very lectern have been made from the very beginning of its existence from ice, say frozen from water in the Thames? One has a considerable feeling that it could *not*, though in fact one certainly could have made a lectern from water from the Thames, frozen it into ice by some process, and put it right there in place of this thing. If one had done so, one would have made, of course, a *different* object. It would not have been *this very lectern,* and so one would not have a case in which this very lectern here was made of ice, or was made from water from the Thames. The question of whether it could afterward, say in a minute from now, turn into ice is something else. So, it would seem, if an example like this is correct—and this is what advocates of essentialism have held—that this lectern could not have been made of ice, that is in any counterfactual situation of which we would say that this lectern existed at all, we would have to say also that it was not made from water from the Thames frozen into ice . . . . We can talk about *this very object,* and whether it could have had certain properties which it does not in fact have. For example, it could have been in another room from the room it in fact is in, even at this very time, but it could not have been made from the very beginning from water frozen into ice.

If the essentialist view is correct, it can only be correct if we sharply distinguish between the notions of a posteriori and a priori truth on the one hand, and contingent and necessary truth on the other hand, for although the statement that this table, if it exists at all, was not made of ice, is necessary, it certainly is not something that we know a priori. What we know is that first, lecterns usually are not made of ice, they are usually made of wood. This looks like wood. It does not feel cold and it probably would if it were made of ice. Therefore, I conclude, probably this is not made of ice. Here my entire judgment is a posteriori. I could find out that an ingenious trick has been played upon me and that, in fact, this lectern is made of ice; but what I am saying is, given that it is in fact not made of ice, in fact is made of wood, one cannot imagine that under certain circumstances it could have been made of ice. So we have to say that though we cannot know a priori whether this table was made of ice or not, given that it is not made of ice, it is *necessarily* not made of ice. In other words, if P is the statement that the lectern is not made of ice, one knows by a priori philosophical analysis, some conditional of the form "if P, then necessarily P." If the table is not made of ice, it is necessarily not made of ice. On the other hand, then, we know by empirical investigation that P, the antecedent of the conditional, is true—that this table is not made of ice. We can conclude by *modus ponens*:

$$P \supset \square\, P$$
$$P$$
$$\overline{\qquad\qquad}$$
$$\square\, P$$

The conclusion—'$\square\, P$'—is that it is necessary that the table not be made of ice, and this conclusion is known a posteriori. So, the notion of essential properties can be maintained only by distinguishing between the notions of a priori and necessary truth, and I do maintain it.[53]

One way in which Kripke seeks to show the value of making the distinctions he does has to do with the understanding of identity statements, particularly those that are called 'contingent identity statements' and that have been a matter of great puzzlement to many philosophers. Consider the following standard argument by which some philosophers claim we are obliged to recognize *contingent identity statements*, whereas other philosophers consider such a result highly paradoxical and therefore argue there cannot be such contingent identity statements.

First, the law of the substitutivity of identity says that, for any objects x and y, if x is identical to y, then if x has a certain property F, so does y:

$$(1)\ (x)\,(y)\ [(x = y) \supset (Fx \supset Fy)]$$

On the other hand, every object surely is necessarily self-identical:

$$(2)\ (x)\ \square\ (x = x)$$

But

$$(3) \ (x) \ (y) \ (x=y) \supset [\Box \ (x=x) \supset \Box \ (x=y)]$$

is a substitution instance of (1), the substitutivity law. From (2) and (3), we can conclude that, for every x and y, if x equals y, then, it is necessary that x equals y:

$$(4) \ (x) \ (y) \ ((x = y) \supset \Box \ (x = y))$$

This is because the clause $\Box \ (x = x)$ of the conditional drops out because it is known to be true.[54]

According to Kripke, if we are going to make a proper assessment of the kind of identity statement some particular combination of expressions compose, we must first determine how the expressions flanking the identity sign are being used, and if we say the entire statement is true, what warrant there is for this. Are the expressions used to fix the reference of the referent? Are the terms rigid designators or nonrigid designators? Are the expressions names or descriptive phrases? Is the warrant for accepting the truth of the statement as a whole *a priori* or *a posteriori*? Finally (bearing in mind that necessity is not the same as *a prioricity*, or contingency the same as empirical warrantedness), is the identity necessary or contingent? Kripke's view is that some identity statements are necessary, and cannot be contingent if they consist of the use of names as rigid designators, or indeed if they consist of any type of rigid designator. Such identity statements are necessary insofar as they have to do with an objective, metaphysical *de re* situation, e.g., the identity of an object with itself. If, on the other hand, an identity statement is contingent, this could only be the case if the expressions used to fix the reference are nonrigid designators and do not refer to an essential property. The epistemic character of a statement—the way in which the truth of an identity statement comes to be known and warranted—does not as such tell us whether the particular identity statement is of a necessary or contingent variety since the latter difference is a metaphysical one, not an epistemic one. Some necessary identity statements are known *a priori*, some *a posteriori*; some contingent identity statements may be known *a priori*, some *a posteriori*.

Concerning the statement 'Hesperus is Phosphorus' or the statement 'Cicero is Tully', one can find all of these out by empirical investigation, and we might turn out to be wrong in our empirical beliefs. So, it is usually argued, such statements must therefore be contingent. Some have embraced the other side of the coin and have held "Because of this argument about necessity, identity statements between names have to be knowable a priori, so, only a very special category of names, possibly, really works as names; the other things are bogus names, disguised descriptions, or something of the sort. However, a certain very narrow class of statements of identity are known a priori, and these are the ones which contain the genuine names." If one accepts the distinctions that I have made, one need not jump to either conclusion. One can hold that certain statements of identity between names, though often known a posteriori, and maybe not knowable a priori, are in fact necessary, if true. So, we have some room to hold this. But, of course, to have some room to hold it does not mean that we should hold it. So let us see what the evidence is. First, recall the remark that I made that proper names seem to be rigid designators, as when we use the name 'Nixon' to talk about a certain man, even in counterfactual situations. If we say, "If Nixon had not written the letter to Saxbe, maybe he would have gotten Carswell through," we are in this statement talking about Nixon, Saxbe, and Carswell, the very same men as in the actual world, and what would have happened to them under certain counterfactual circumstances. If names are rigid designators, then there can be no question about identities being necessary, because '*a*' and '*b*' will be rigid designators of a certain man or thing *x*. Then even in every possible world, *a* and *b* will both refer to this same object *x*, and to no other, and so there will be no situation in which *a* might not have been *b*. That would have to be a situation in which the object which we are also now calling '*x*' would not have been identical with itself. Then one could not possibly have a situation in which Cicero would not have been Tully or Hesperus would not have been Phosphorus.[55]

To further clarify the difference between a necessary identity statement and a contingent one, consider the difference between 'Cicero is Tully' and 'The man who denounced Cataline is the author of certain books read in third year Latin courses'. The first is a necessary identity statement, the second a contingent one.

Suppose someone uses 'Tully' to refer to the Roman orator who denounced Cataline and uses the name 'Cicero' to refer to the man whose works he had to study in third-year Latin in high school. Of course, he may not know in advance that the very same man who denounced Cataline wrote these works, and that is a contingent statement. But the fact that this statement is contingent should not make us think that the statement that Cicero is Tully, if it is true, and it is in fact true, is contingent. Suppose, for example, that Cicero actually did denounce Cataline, but thought that this political achievement was so great that he should not bother writing any literary works. Would we say that these would be circumstances under which he would not have been Cicero? It seems to me that the answer is no, that instead we would say that, under such circumstances, Cicero would not have written any literary works. It is not a necessary property of Cicero—the way the shadow follows the man—that he should have written certain works; we can easily imagine a situation in which Shakespeare would not have written the works of Shakespeare, or one in which Cicero would not have written the works of Cicero. What may be the case is that we *fix the reference* of the term 'Cicero' by use of some descriptive phrase, such as 'the author of these works'. But once we have this reference fixed, we then use the name 'Cicero' *rigidly* to designate the man who in fact we have identified by his authorship of these works. We do not use it to designate whoever would have written these works in place of Cicero, if someone wrote them. It might have been the case that the man who wrote these works was not the man who denounced Cataline. Cassius might have written these works. But we would not then say that Cicero would have been Cassius, unless we were speaking in a very loose and metaphorical way. We would say that Cicero, whom we may have identified and come to know by his works, would not have written them, and that someone else, say Cassius, would have written them in his place.

Such examples are not grounds for thinking that identity statements are contingent. To take them as such grounds is to misconstrue the relation between a *name* and a *description used to fix its reference,* to take them to be *synonyms.* Even if we fix the reference of such a name as 'Cicero' as the man who wrote such and such works, in speaking of counterfactual situations, when we speak of Cicero, we do not then speak of whoever in such counterfactual situations *would* have written such and such works, but rather of Cicero, whom we have identified by the contingent property that he is the man who in fact, that is, in the actual world, wrote certain works.[56]

In the foregoing we have followed Kripke's efforts to provide the kind of philosophic distinctions and analyses that would lend support to the use of such terms as 'necessarily' and 'possibly' as these occur characteristically in the formulae of modal logic, and their applications to ordinary discourse. Needless to say, these efforts have not themselves met with universal acceptance, and the debate goes on. In particular, Quine himself remains unconvinced; he has written:

The notion of possible world did indeed contribute to the semantics of modal logic, and it behooves us to recognize the nature of its contribution: it led to Kripke's precocious and significant theory of modal logic. Models afford consistency proofs; also they have heuristic value; but they do not constitute explication. Models, however clear they be in themselves, may leave us still at a loss for the primary, intended interpretation. When modal logic has been paraphrased in terms of such notions as possible world or rigid designator, where the displaced fog settles is on the question when to identify objects between worlds, or when to treat a designator as rigid, or where to attribute metaphysical necessity.[57]

Our survey of analytic philosophy from Frege to Quine has concluded with a brief account of recent controversies concerning modal logic. These controversies are not to be taken, of course, as either exhausting or dominating the entire range of discussions and philosophical preoccupations of contemporary analytical philosophers. They are, indeed, only one strand in a complex web whose fabric is still very much in the process of being woven.

REFERENCE NOTES

CHAPTER II: BELIEF, INQUIRY AND MEANING

1. In this connection it is interesting to read Dewey's essays, "The Pragmatism of Peirce," in Peirce Commemorative Issue, *Journal of Philosophy, Psychology, and Scientific Methods*, 1916, pp. 709–715, reprinted in Cohen, ed., *Chance, Love, and Logic*, pp. 301–308; and "The Development of American Pragmatism," in *Studies in the History of Ideas*, 2:353–377, reprinted in Dewey, *Philosophy and Civilization*, pp. 13–35.

2. Peirce, *Collected Papers of Charles S. Peirce*, 5.223n. (Hereafter referred to as *CP*). (References will generally be made to volume number and section. Thus 5.223 refers to volume 5, section 223.)

3. *CP*, 5.415.

4. Peirce, *The New Elements of Mathematics of Charles S. Peirce*, 3(1):159. (Hereafter referred to as *NEM*.)

5. *NEM*, 4:v (notebook fragment from MS 905).

6. *NEM*, 3(1):129n (from MS 823).

7. M. A. De Wolfe Howe, ed., *John Jay Chapman and His Letters* (Boston: Houghton Mifflin, 1937), pp. 94–96.

8. *CP*, 5.12–13 (from MS ca. 1906). The paper to which Peirce refers at the conclusion of this quotation, in which he formulates the basic ideas of pragmatism, was expanded by him into two papers, viz., "The Fixation of Belief," published in *Popular Science Monthly* 12 (1877): 1–15; and "How to Make Our Ideas Clear," in *Popular Science Monthly* 13 (1878): 286–302. The pragmatic maxim was stated by Peirce in the second of these papers, although the *term* 'pragmatism' is not used by Peirce in that statement. He did not, in fact, use the term 'pragmatism' in print until 1902, when it appears in his article, "Pragmatism," in the *Baldwin Dictionary*.

   On 'The Metaphysical Club' and related matters, see Wiener, *Evolution and the Founders of Pragmatism;* and Max H. Fisch, "Was There a Metaphysical Club in Cambridge?" in Moore and Robin, eds., *Studies in the Philosophy of Charles Sanders Peirce*, pp. 3–32.

9. James, *Pragmatism*, p. 5.

10. Ralph B. Perry, *The Thought and Character of William James*, 2 vols. (Boston: Little, Brown and Co., 1935; reprinted, Westport Ct.: Greenwood Press, Vol. II, p. 117.)

11. *NEM*, 3(1):129–130.

12. *NEM*, 4:152 (from "Lectures on Pragmatism," Lecture 2, pp. 302, 303).

13. Victor F. Lenzen, "Reminiscences of a Mission to Milford, Pennsylvania," *Transactions of the Charles S. Peirce Society* 1, no. 1 (Spring 1965):11.

14. *CP*, 1.3–14 (from MS ca. 1897).

15. *CP*, 5.542; cf. 3.456–467.

16. *NEM*, 4:39, (L.75); cf. NEM, 4:248.

17. *CP*, 5.30–31.

18. *CP*, 5.543.

19. *CP*, 7.356; cf. 5.538.

20 *CP*, 5.538.
21 *CP*, 5.487, note.
22 *CP*, 5.398–399.
23 *CP*, 7.313.
24 *NEM*, 4:41.
25 *CP*, 5.376.
26 *CP*, 5.264.
27 Cf. *CP*, 5.451, 5.514.
28 *CP*, 7.314, note 4 (from a fragment).
29 *CP*, 5.371.
30 *CP*, 5.372.
31 *CP*, 5.375.
32 *CP*, 5.317.
33 *CP*, 7.315, note 5; 7.317.
34 *CP*, 5.377.
35 *CP*, 5.378.
36 *CP*, 5.379.
37 *CP*, 5.380.
38 *CP*, 5.381–382.
39 *CP*, 5.382–383.
40 *CP*, 7.315–316.
41 *CP*, 7.317–319.
42 *CP*, 7.321.
43 *CP*, 5.430.
44 *CP*, 7.336.
45 *CP*, 7.336, note. (From "*Logic,* Chap. 6th" March 10, 1873).
46 *CP*, 5.409.
47 *CP*, 5.257.
48 *CP*, 7.340, 7.344–345.
49 *CP*, 5.384, note (1893).
50 *CP*, 5.416.
51 *CP*, 5.407–408.
52 *CP*, 5.393.
53 *CP*, 5.402, note.
54 *CP*, 5.410.
55 *CP*, 5.402.
56 *CP*, 5.400.
57 *CP*, 5.403–404.
58 *CP*, 2.330.
59 *CP*, 5.467.
60 *CP*, 5.429.
61 Cf. *CP*, 5.256.
62 *CP*, 5.483.
63 *CP*, 1.615.
64 *CP*, 5.411.
65 *CP*, 7.187.
66 *CP*, 5.423.
67 *CP*, 1.23–26, 1.340.

68 Cf. *NEM*, 3 (1): 343.
69 *CP*, 1.53.
70 *NEM*, 3 (1): 40–41.
71 *CP*, 5.429.
72 *CP*, 5.403, note 3.
73 James, *Pragmatism*. pp. 45–46.
74 Ibid., pp. 49–50.
75 Ibid., p. 200.
76 Ibid., p. 201.
77 Ibid., p. 222.

CHAPTER III: THE NEW LOGIC

1 Russell, *A History of Western Philosophy*, p. 830.
2 Idem, *Introduction to Mathematical Philosophy*, p.25n. Cf. Frege, *Conceptual Notation and Related Articles*, pp. 48ff.
3 Russell and Whitehead, *Principia Mathematica*, 1:viii.
4 Wittgenstein, *Tractatus Logico-Philosophicus*, p. 3.
5 Anscombe, *An Introduction to Wittgenstein's Tractatus*, p. 12.
6 Schilpp, ed., *The Philosophy of Rudolf Carnap*, p. 6.
7 This conversation is reported by Geach in Anscombe and Geach, *Three Philosophers*, p. 130.
8 Dummett, *Frege: Philosophy of Language*, p. xii.
9 Cf. Dummett, *Frege: Philosophy of Language*, chap. 18, "The Evolution of Frege's Thought"; and Bynum, "On the Life and Work of Gottlob Frege," in Frege, *Conceptual Notation*, pp. 1–54.
10 Cf. Frege, *Conceptual Notation*, pp. 74–75, 167–202.
11 Idem, *The Foundations of Arithmetic*, p.x.
12 Idem, *The Basic Laws of Arithmetic*, [Vol. 2 (app.)]:127–128.
13 Idem, *Foundations of Arithmetic*, §3, pp. 3–4.
14 For a recent attempt to defend a form of the Fregean logicist thesis, see David Bostock, *Logic and Arithmetic*, vols. I, II (Oxford: Oxford University Press, 1974, 1979).
15 Frege, *Conceptual Notation*, p. 123.
16 Idem, *Logical Investigations*, chap. 1, "Thought," p. 7.
17 Ibid., pp. 8–9.
18 Frege, *Translations from the Philosophical Writings of Gottlob Frege*, "Function and Concept," p. 24.
19 Ibid., p. 25.
20 Ibid., p. 30.
21 Frege, *Foundations of Arithmetic*, pp. 82–83.
22 Idem, *Translations from the Philosophical Writings*, "Concept and Object," pp. 51–52.
23 Idem, *Basic Laws of Arithmetic*, p. 11.
24 Cf. Anscombe and Geach, *Three Philosophers*, pp. 148f.; Dummett, *Frege: Philosophy of Language*, chap. 3; Frege, *Translations*, "Function and Concept."

25 Frege, *Foundations of Arithmetic*, p. 87.
26 Ibid., pp. 87–88n.
27 Frege, *Foundations of Arithmetic*, §46, p. 59.
28 Cf. Dummett, *Frege: Philosophy of Language*, p. 262.
29 Frege, *Foundations of Arithmetic*, §53, p. 65.
30 See Munitz, *Existence and Logic*, chap. 4; Dummett, *Frege: Philosophy of Language*, chap. 14.
31 From a letter from Frege to Heinrich Liebmann (8.25.1900) in Frege, *On the Foundations of Geometry and Formal Theories of Arithmetic*, pp. 3–5.
32 Frege, *Foundations of Arithmetic*, §§47, 51, pp. 60–61, 63–64.
33 Idem, *Translations from the Philosophical Writings*, pp. 56–58.
34 Idem.
35 Ibid, pp. 59–60.
36 Ibid., p. 63.
37 Ibid., pp. 58–59.

CHAPTER IV: LOGICAL ATOMISM

1 Russell, *Portraits from Memory*, p. 9.
2 Idem, *My Philosophical Development*, p. 11.
3 Idem, *Portraits from Memory*, pp. 21–22.
4 Idem, *My Philosophical Development*, pp. 39–40.
5 Idem, "My Mental Development," in Schilpp, ed., *The Philosophy of Bertrand Russell*, pp. 11–12.
6 Idem, *My Philosophical Development*, p. 62.
7 Idem, "The Nature of Truth," *Proceedings of the Aristotelian Society*, 1906–1907; reprinted in Russell, *Philosophical Essays* as "The Monistic Theory of Truth."
8 Idem, *My Philosophical Development*, pp. 54–55.
9 Ibid., pp. 63–64.
10 Ibid., p. 11.
11 Russell, "My Mental Development," op. cit., pp. 12–13.
12 Idem, *Portraits from Memory*, pp. 25–26.
13 Idem, *My Philosophical Development*, pp. 112–113.
14 Russell, "My Mental Development," op. cit., pp. 19–20.
15 Idem, *Logic and Knowledge*, "Logical Atomism," p. 178.
16 Ibid. pp. 197–198.
17 Ibid. p. 326.
18 Idem, "My Mental Development," op. cit, p. 14; cf. Russell, *Human Knowledge: Its Scope and Limits*, pp. 242–249.
19 Idem, *Mysticism and Logic*, chap. 8, "The Relation of Sense-Data to Physics," sec. 6., pp. 155–156.
20 Idem, *Our Knowledge of the External World*, pp. 52–53.
21 Cf. Idem, *Portraits from Memory*, p. 90. Cf. George Santayana *Winds of Doctrine* (New York: Charles Scribners Sons, 1913), Chapter IV, "The Philosophy of Mr. Bertrand Russell," Sec. 4.
22 Idem, *The Problems of Philosophy*, pp. 73–74.

23 Ibid., pp. 76–77.
24 Russell: *Problems of Philosophy*, p. 81; *Mysticism and Logic*, "Knowledge by Acquaintance and Knowledge by Description," pp. 212–213.
25 Idem, *Problems of Philosophy*, p. 82.
26 Ibid., pp. 82–83.
27 Ibid., p. 90.
28 Russell, "Knowledge by Acquaintance and Knowledge by Description," op. cit., p. 219.
29 Ibid., pp. 216–218.
30 Frank P. Ramsey, *The Foundations of Mathematics*. New York: Humanities Press, 1950, p. 263, note.
31 Russell, *Logic and Knowledge*, "On Denoting," p. 48.
32 Idem, *Principles of Mathematics*, p. 449, par. 427.
33 Moore, *Some Main Problems of Philosophy*, pp. 212–213; cf. ibid., p. 89.
34 Meinong's theory of objects is presented in "Über Gegenstandstheorie" (1904), an article translated as "The Theory of Objects" in Roderick M. Chisholm, ed., *Realism and the Background of Phenomenology* (New York: Free Press, 1960). Cf. John N. Findlay, *Meinong's Theory of Objects and Values* (2nd ed., Oxford, 1963); also, Bertrand Russell, "Meinong's Theory of Complexes and Assumptions," three articles in *Mind*, 13 (1904), 204–219, 336–354, 509–524.
35 Russell, *Introduction to Mathematical Philosophy*, 2nd ed., pp. 169–170.
36 Idem, "On Denoting," op. cit., p. 48.
37 Cf. Peter T. Geach, *Reference and Generality* (Cornell University Press, 1962), sec. 106, *Logic Matters* (Basil Blackwell, Oxford, 1972); Peter F. Strawson, *Logico-Linguistic Papers* (London; Methuen & Co., 1971), "On Referring" and "Identifying Reference and Truth-Values."
38 Russell, "On Denoting", op. cit., pp. 47–48.
39 Idem, *Logic and Knowledge*, "The Philosophy of Logical Atomism," pp. 200–202.
40 Idem, *Introduction to Mathematical Philosophy*, p. 174.
41 Idem, "The Philosophy of Logical Atomism," p. 251.
42 Idem, *My Philosophical Development*, p.84.
43 Idem, "The Philosophy of Logical Atomism," op. cit., pp. 249–250.
44 Ibid., pp. 252–253.
45 Russell, "On Denoting," op. cit., p. 51.
46 Ibid., pp. 51–52.
47 Russell, "The Philosophy of Logical Atomism," op. cit., pp. 244, 245–256.
48 Ibid., pp. 200–201.
49 Ibid., p. 243.
50 Ibid., p. 201.
51 Russell, *Introduction to Mathematical Philosophy*, pp. 11, 14–18.
52 Idem, "The Philosophy of Logical Atomism," op. cit., pp. 259–260.
53 Ibid., pp. 260–261.
54 Ibid., p. 262.
55 Ibid., pp. 262–264.
56 Russell and Whitehead, *Principia Mathematica*, chap. 2, sec. 1.
57 Idem, *My Philosophical Development*, pp. 81–83.

58 Idem, *Logic and Knowledge,* "Mathematical Logic as based on the Theory of Types" (1908), p. 75.
59 Idem, *Principia Mathematica,* 1; 62–63.
60 Idem, "Philosophy of Logical Atomism," op. cit., pp. 264–265.
61 Idem, *The Problems of Philosophy,* pp. 156–157.
62 Idem, *My Philosophical Development,* p. 219.

CHAPTER V: THE LIMITS OF LANGUAGE

1 Wittgenstein, *Letters to Russell, Keynes and Moore* (letter R. 37, Cassino, 19.8.19), p. 71.
2 Leitner, *The Architecture of Ludwig Wittgenstein: A Documentation with Excerpts from the Family Recollections by Hermine Wittgenstein,* p. 20.
3 For a study of these influences see Janik and Toulmin,*Wittgenstein's Vienna.*
4 Cf. Fania Pascal, "Wittgenstein: A Personal Memoir," in Luckhardt, ed., *Wittgenstein: Sources and Perspectives,* pp. 46–47; and Janik and Toulmin, *Wittgenstein's Vienna,* pp. 172–173.
5 Wolfe Mays, "Recollections of Wittgenstein," in Fann, ed. *Ludwig Wittgenstein; The Man and His Philosophy,* p. 87.
6 Russell, *Autobiography,* 2:98–99.
7 Cf. Wittgenstein: *Notebooks 1914–1916;* and *Prototractatus: An Early Version of the Tractatus Logico-Philosophicus.*
8 The details of the events that led up to the publication of the *Tractatus* are given in von Wright, "The Origin of Wittgenstein's *Tractatus,*" in Luckhardt, ed., *Wittgenstein,* pp. 99–137. Cf. von Wright's introduction in *Prototractatus,* pp. 1–34.
9 Wittgenstein, *Letters to Russell, Keynes and Moore* (R. 35), p. 68.
10 Ibid. (R. 48), p. 89.
11 Cf. Malcolm, *Ludwig Wittgenstein, a Memoir;* Fann, ed., *Ludwig Wittgenstein;* Bartley, *Wittgenstein.*
12 Carnap, "Intellectual Autobiography," in Schilpp, ed., *The Philosophy of Rudolf Carnap,* pp. 25–26.
13 Karl Britton, "Portrait of a Philosopher," in Fann, ed., *Ludwig Wittgenstein,* pp. 56–57.
14 Engelmann, *Letters from Ludwig Wittgenstein, with a Memoir,* p. 142.
15 M. O'C. Drury, "A Symposium," in Fann, ed., *Ludwig Wittgenstein,* p. 67.
16 Cf. Allan Janik, "Wittgenstein, Ficker, and *Der Brenner,*" in Luckhardt, ed., *Wittgenstein,* pp. 161–189; "Letters to Ludwig von Ficker," ibid., pp. 82–98.
17 I have used the translation of the letter to von Ficker that appears in Engelmann, *Letters from Ludwig Wittgenstein,* pp. 143–144.
18 Wittgenstein, *Tractatus,* p. 3.
19 Ibid., pp. 149, 151.
20 Reproduced in Wittgenstein, *Letters to Russell, Keynes, and Moore,* p. 82.
21 Engelmann, *Letters from Ludwig Wittgenstein,* pp. 96–97.
22 See P. M. S. Hacker, "Semantic Holism: Frege and Wittgenstein," in Luckhardt, *Wittgenstein,* pp. 213–242.
23 Cf. Wittgenstein, *Tractatus,* 3.323: "In the proposition, 'Green is green'—

where the first word is the proper name of a person and the last an adjective—these words do not merely have different meanings: they are *different symbols.*"

24 I borrow this analogy from Stenius, *Wittgenstein's Tractatus,* chap. 4, where it is worked out in great detail.

25 Cf. Griffin, *Wittgenstein's Logical Atomism,* pp. 36–38; Stenius, 38–60.

26 Von Wright, "Biographical Sketch," in Malcolm, *Ludwig Wittgenstein; A Memoir,* pp. 7–8; Cf. Wittgenstein, *Notebooks 1914–1916,* p.7.

27 Wittgenstein, *Letters to Russell, Keynes and Moore* (R. 37, 19.8.19), p. 72.

28 Ibid, p. 72.

29 Ibid (Cassino, 19.8.19), p. 72.

30 These materials are published in *Philosophical Review* 74 (Jan. 1965): 3–26.

31 Wittgenstein, "Lecture on Ethics," *Philosophical Review* 74 (Jan. 1965): 5.

32 "Notes on Talks with Wittgenstein," *Philosophical Review* 74 (Jan. 1965) : 13.

33 Wittgenstein, *Notebooks,* pp. 77, 79.

34 Ibid., p. 82.

35 Ibid., p. 79.

36 Ibid., p. 78.

37 Ibid., p. 82.

38 Wittgenstein, "Lecture on Ethics," op. cit., pp. 11–12.

39 Idem, *Notebooks,* 83.

40 Ibid., pp. 74–75.

41 Wittgenstein, "Lecture on Ethics," op. cit., pp. 8–9.

CHAPTER VI: VERIFICATIONISM

1 Wittgenstein, *Letters to C. K. Ogden* (with comments on the English translation of the *Tractatus Logico-Philosophicus* and an appendix of letters by F. P. Ramsey), pp. 77–78.

2 Wittgenstein, *Philosophical Investigations,* preface, p.x.

3 For a detailed account of this period see Bartley, *Wittgenstein,* pp. 53–96.

4 See Leitner, *Architecture of Ludwig Wittgenstein.*

5 In appendix by McGuinness in Engelmann, *Letters from Wittgenstein,* p. 146.

6 Waismann, *Wittgenstein and the Vienna Circle* (shorthand notes recorded by Waismann, edited by McGuinness).

7 Carnap, "Intellectual Autobiography," in Schilpp, ed., *The Philosophy of Rudolf Carnap,* pp. 12–13.

8 Ibid., pp. 24–25.

9 Clark, *The Life of Bertrand Russell,* p. 438.

10 Russell, *Autobiography,* vol. 2 (1914–1944), pp. 196–197.

11 Ibid., p. 200.

12 Quoted by D. A. T. Gasking and A. C. Jackson, "Wittgenstein as a Teacher," in Fann, ed., *Ludwig Wittgenstein,* p. 54.

13 Wittgenstein, *Philosophical Remarks,* p. 200.

14 Ibid., pp. 66–67.

15 Ibid., p. 77.

16 Ibid., p. 174.
17 Ibid., p. 200.
18 Waismann, *Ludwig Wittgenstein and the Vienna Circle*, p. 79.
19 Ibid., p. 47.
20 Wittgenstein, *Philosophical Remarks*, p. 282.
21 Ibid., pp. 282–283.
22 Wittgenstein, *Philosophical Grammar*, p. 219.
23 Idem, *Philosophical Remarks*, pp. 283–284.
24 Idem, *Philosophical Grammar*, pp. 221–222.
25 Ibid., p. 219.
26 Ibid., p. 222.
27 Ibid., p. 222.
28 Wittgenstein, *Philosophical Remarks*, p. 283.
29 Idem, *Philosophical Grammar*, p.224.
30 Idem, *Philosophical Remarks*, p. 285.
31 Schlick, *General Theory of Knowledge*, p. 3.
32 Published in English translation as "The Scientific Conception of the World" in Otto Neurath, *Empiricism and Sociology*.
33 David Hume, *Enquiry Concerning Human Understanding*, Sec. 12, Part III.
34 Carnap, "The Elimination of Metaphysics Through Logical Analysis of Language" (*Erkenntnis*, vol. 2 (1932), translated from the German by Arthur Pap, in Ayer, ed., *Logical Positivism*, p. 76.
35 Carnap, "The Elimination of Metaphysics," op. cit., pp. 72–73.
36 Schlick,"Positivism and Realism," in Ayer, ed., *Logical Positivism*, pp. 86–87.
37 Ibid., pp. 88–89.
38 Carnap, *Philosophy and Logical Syntax* (London: Psyche Miniatures, 1935), sec. 1, reprinted with terminological changes suggested by Carnap, in W. P. Alston and G. Nakhnikian, *Readings in Twentieth Century Philosophy* (New York: Macmillan, Free Press, 1963), pp. 425–427.
39 Schlick, "Positivism and Realism," op. cit., sec. 3 (pp. 100–101).
40 Ibid., p. 101.
41 Ibid., p. 102.
42 Ibid., pp. 106, 107.
43 Quoted in Carnap, "The Elimination of Metaphysics," op. cit., p. 69. Heidegger's essay, "What is Metaphysics," appears in a translation by R. F. C. Hull and A. Crick in Heidegger, *Existence and Being*, ed. W. Brock (London: Vision Press, 1949), pp. 353ff.
44 Carnap, op. cit., pp. 69–72.
45 Schlick, *Problems of Ethics*, tr. D. Rynin, chap. 1, secs. 8, 10, 11; reprinted in Ayer, ed., *Logical Positivism*, pp. 256, 261, 263.
46 Carnap, *Philosophy and Logical Syntax*, sec. 4.
47 Schlick, "Positivism and Realism," op cit., pp. 91–92.
48 Schlick, "The Foundation of Knowledge," in Ayer, ed., *Logical Positivism*, pp. 221–227; this article originally appeared in *Erkenntnis*, vol. 4 (1934), under the title "Über das Fundament der Erkenntnis."
49 Otto Neurath, "Protocol Sentences," in Ayer, ed., *Logical Positivism*, pp. 201, 202–203, 204, 205, 207; this article first appeared in *Erkenntnis*, vol. 3 (1932–1933).

50 Carnap, "Intellectual Autobiography," op. cit., p. 57.
51 Carnap, "On the Character of Philosophic Problems," *Philosophy of Science* 1 (1934):5–19; reprinted in Richard Rorty, ed., *The Linguistic Turn*, p. 55.
52 Carnap, ibid., in Rorty, ed., pp. 54–55.
53 Carnap, ibid., in Rorty, ed., pp. 61–62.
54 Ayer, Introduction to *Logical Positivism* (op. cit.), pp. 15–16.
55 Ayer, *Language, Truth and Logic*, p. 16.

CHAPTER VII: LANGUAGE-GAMES

1 Wittgenstein, *Notebooks 1914–1916*, p. 39.
2 Idem, *The Blue and Brown Books*, p. 28 (hereafter called *The Blue Book*).
3 Idem, *Philosophical Investigations*, sec. 132.
4 L. E. J. Brouwer, "Mathematik, Wissenschaft und Sprache," *Monatshefte für Mathematik und Physik*, 36 (1929): 153–164; cf. Hacker, *Insight and Illusion*, pp. 98–104.
5 Quoted in Pitcher, *The Philosophy of Wittgenstein*, p. 8n.
6 Wittgenstein, *The Blue Book*, pp. 17–20.
7 Idem, *Philosophical Investigations*, sec. 67.
8 Ibid., sec. 66.
9 Ibid., sec. 67.
10 Wittgenstein, *The Blue Book*, pp. 27–28
11 Idem, *Philosophical Investigations*, sec. 1.
12 Idem, *Philosophical Grammar*, p. 190.
13 Idem, *Philosophical Investigations*, sec. 65.
14 Ibid., secs. 13,14.
15 Ibid., sec. 11.
16 Ibid., sec. 12.
17 Wittgenstein, *Philosophical Grammar*, pp. 58, 59.
18 Ibid., 59.
19 Wittgenstein, *Philosophical Investigations*, sec. 120.
20 Idem, *Philosophical Grammar*, p. 63.
21 Idem, *Philosophical Investigations*, sec. 27.
22 Idem, *The Blue Book*, p. 1.
23 Idem, *Philosophical Investigations*, sec. 2, 3.
24 Ibid., sec. 1.
25 Ibid., sec. 23.
26 Wittgenstein, *The Blue Book*, p. 17.
27 Idem, *Philosophical Investigations*, sec. 19.
28 Idem, *Philosophical Grammar*, pp. 59–60.
29 Idem, *Philosophical Investigations*, sec. 40.
30 Ibid., sec. 39.
31 Wittgenstein, *The Blue Book*, p. 56; *Philosophical Investigations*, secs. 251–252.
32 Idem, *The Blue Book*, p. 26.
33 Cf. Idem, *Philosophical Investigations*, sec. 251.
34 Waismann, *Ludwig Wittgenstein and the Vienna Circle*, pp. 61–63.

35 Wittgenstein, *Philosophical Grammar*, p. 67.
36 Idem, *Philosophical Investigations*, secs. 96, 97.
37 Idem, *The Blue Book*, pp. 25–26.
38 Idem, *Philosophical Grammar*, p. 88.
39 Cf. Idem, *Philosophical Investigations*, sec. 50.
40 Ibid., sec. 50.
41 Ibid., sec. 50.
42 Wittgenstein, *Philosophical Grammar*, pp. 60–61.
43 Idem, *Philosophical Investigations*, sec. 30, 31.
44 Idem, *Philosophical Grammar*, p. 184.
45 Ibid., p. 185.
46 Ibid., p. 97.
47 Wittgenstein, *Philosophical Remarks*, p. 54.
48 Ibid., p. 55.
49 Wittgenstein, *Philosophical Grammar*, p. 184.
50 Ibid., pp. 186–187.
51 Moore, "Wittgenstein's Lectures in 1930–33," in Moore, *Philosophical Papers*, p. 280.
52 Wittgenstein, *Philosophical Grammar*, p. 97.
53 Cf. W. Gregory Lycan, "Noninductive Evidence: Recent Work on Wittgenstein's Criteria," *American Philosophical Quarterly*, 8, no. 2 (1971): 109–125; Gordon Baker, "Criteria: A New Foundation for Semantics," *Ratio*, 16 (1974): 156–189.
54 Wittgenstein, *Philosophical Investigations*, sec. 79.
55 Idem, *The Blue Book*, p. 61.
56 Idem, *Zettel*, sec. 440.
57 Idem, *The Blue Book*, p. 51.
58 Cf. Idem, *Philosophical Investigations*, sec. 354.
59 Idem, *The Blue Book*, pp. 24–25.
60 Ibid., p. 25.
61 Wittgenstein, *Zettel*, sec. 438.
62 Idem, *Philosophical Investigations*, sec. 665.
63 Ibid., p. 218.
64 Wittgenstein, *Philosophical Grammar*, pp. 64–65.
65 Ibid., p. 50.
66 Ibid., 148.
67 Wittgenstein, *Philosophical Investigations*, secs. 580, 503–504.
68 Cf. Gilbert Ryle, *The Concept of Mind* (London: Hutchinson, 1949), chap. 1.
69 John Locke, *An Essay Concerning Human Understanding*, book 3, chap. 2, sec. 2.
70 Wittgenstein, *Philosophical Investigations*, sec. 243.
71 Peter Geach, *Mental Acts* (London: Routledge & Kegan Paul, 1957), p. 3.
72 Wittgenstein, *Philosophical Investigations*, sec. 243.
73 Ibid., sec. 274.
74 Wittgenstein, "Notes for Lectures on 'Private Experience' and 'Sense Data'," *Philosophical Review*, LXXVII (1968): 289–290.
75 Idem, *Philosophical Investigations*, sec. 303.
76 Ibid., sec. 246.

77 Ibid., sec. 253.
78 Ibid., secs. 258, 265.
79 Wittgenstein, "Notes for Lectures," op.cit., 289.
80 Idem, *Philosophical Investigations,* sec. 293.
81 Ibid., sec. 272.
82 Ibid., sec. 246.
83 Wittgenstein, *The Blue Book,* p. 28.
84 Moore, "Wittgenstein's Lectures in 1930–33," op.cit., p. 322.
85 Wittgenstein, *Philosophical Investigations,* sec. 122.
86 Idem, *Remarks on the Foundations of Mathematics,* p. 157.
87 Idem, *Philosophical Investigations,* sec. 255.
88 Ibid., sec. 123.
89 Cf. Ibid., sec. 309.
90 Ibid., sec. 111.
91 Wittgenstein, *The Blue Book,* pp. 58–59.
92 Idem, *Philosophical Investigation,* sec. 133.
93 Ibid., secs. 109, 126, 124, 127.
94 Wittgenstein, *Zettel,* secs. 447, 458.
95 Moore, *Some Main Problems of Philosophy,* p. 1.
96 Ibid., p. 2.
97 Ibid., p. 4.
98 Ibid., p. 8.
99 Ibid., p. 11.
100 Ibid., p. 11.
101 Ibid., p. 17.
102 Ibid., p. 18.
103 Moore, *Philosophical Papers,* pp. 33–34.
104 Ibid., pp. 36–37.
105 Ibid., p. 44.
106 Ibid., pp. 44–45.
107 Ibid., pp. 50–51.
108 Ibid., pp. 52.
109 Wittgenstein, *On Certainty,* 91–105. (All references are to numbered passages of this work.)
110 Ibid., 152.
111 Ibid., 208–211.
112 Ibid., 341–343.
113 Ibid., 253.
114 Ibid., 225, 141–142, 247–248.
115 Ibid., 144, 159–162.
116 Ibid., 213.
117 Ibid., 136.
118 Ibid., 205.
119 Ibid., 138.
120 Ibid., 163, 164, 167.
121 Ibid., 106–108.
122 Ibid., 411.
123 Ibid., 148–150.

124　Ibid., 7, 476.
125　Ibid., 262, 608–612, 239–242, 336.
126　Ibid., 189, 191, 192.
127　Ibid., 215.
128　Ibid., 115.
129　Ibid., 3.
130　Ibid., 114.
131　Ibid., 306–307.
132　Ibid., 519,4.
133　Ibid., 281.
134　Ibid., 257.
135　Ibid., 66.
136　Ibid., 70–72.
137　Ibid., 74, 217.
138　Ibid., 483, 18, 550, 176.
139　Ibid., 620.
140　Ibid., 464.
141　Ibid., 555.
142　Ibid., 243, 504.
143　Ibid., 84, 462.
144　Ibid., 282.
145　Ibid., 151.
146　Ibid., 413.

CHAPTER VIII: ONTOLOGICAL COMMITMENTS

1　Both papers are contained in Quine, *From a Logical Point of View;* references to them will be to this source.
2　Quine, *From a Logical Point of View,* pp. 2, 3.
3　Ibid., p. 4.
4　Ibid., p. 7.
5　Ibid., pp. 7–8.
6　Ibid., p. 9.
7　Ibid., p. 10.
8　Ibid., p. 11.
9　Ibid., p. 12.
10　Ibid., pp. 13–14.
11　Ibid., pp. 130–131.
12　Ibid., pp. 15–16.
13　Ibid., p. 19.
14　Ibid., p. 20.
15　Cf. Sandra G. Harding, ed., *Can Theories Be Refuted?: Essays on the Duhem-Quine Thesis* (Hingham, Mass.: Reidel, 1976).
16　Quine, *From a Logical Point of View,* pp. 22–23.
17　Ibid., p. 37.

18 Ibid., p. 37.
19 Ibid., pp. 42–46.
20 Quine, *Word and Object*, p. 92.
21 Quine, *Ontological Relativity and Other Essays*, p. 8.
22 Ibid., pp. 8–11.
23 Cf. Quine, *Methods of Logic*, 3d. ed. (1972), p. 115.
24 Quine, *Ontological Relativity and Other Essays*, p. 95
25 Quine, "Existence," in W. Yourgrau and A. D. Breck, eds., *Physics, Logic, and History* (New York: Plenum Press, 1970), p. 90.
26 Carnap, "Empiricism, Semantics, and Ontology," *Revue Internationale de Philosophie*, 11 (1950): 20–40.
27 Quine, *The Ways of Paradox and Other Essays*, pp. 126–134.
28 Carnap, op. cit., pp. 21–22.
29 Ibid., p. 22.
30 Ibid., pp. 22–23.
31 Ibid., p. 24.
32 Ibid., p. 25.
33 Quine, *Ways of Paradox*, pp. 130–131.
34 Ibid., p. 134.
35 Quine, *Ontological Relativity and Other Essays*, pp. 27–29.
36 Ibid., pp. 29–30.
37 Quine, *Word and Object*, p. 29.
38 Idem, *Ontological Relativity*, pp. 30–31, 32.
39 Ibid., pp. 48–49.
40 Ibid., pp. 49–51.
41 Quine, *From a Logical Point of View*, p. 139.
42 Ibid., p. 140.
43 Quine, *Ways of Paradox*, p. 182.
44 Idem, *Word and Object*, pp. 199–200.
45 Cf. Leonard Linsky, ed., *Reference and Modality* (New York: Oxford University Press, 1971).
46 Kripke: "Identity and Necessity," in Munitz, ed., *Identity and Individuation;* "Naming and Necessity," in D. Davidson and G. Harman, eds., *Semantics of Natural Language* (Hingham, Mass.: Reidel, 1973).
47 Idem, "Identity and Necessity," op.cit., pp. 144–145.
48 Ibid., p. 145.
49 Kripke, "Naming and Necessity", op.cit., p. 273.
50 Kripke, "Identity and Necessity," op.cit., pp. 145–146.
51 Ibid., pp. 148–149.
52 Ibid., p. 150.
53 Ibid., pp. 151–153.
54 Ibid., p. 136.
55 Ibid., pp. 153–154.
56 Ibid., 156–157.
57 Quine, review of Munitz, ed., *Identity and Individuation*, in *Journal of Philosophy*, 69 (1972): pp. 492–493.

SELECTED BIBLIOGRAPHY

GENERAL WORKS

Ammerman, Robert R., ed. *Classics of Analytic Philosophy.* New York: McGraw-Hill Book Company, 1964.

Ayer, Alfred J., et al. *The Revolution in Philosophy.* London: Macmillan & Company Ltd., 1956.

Barrett, William. *The Illusion of Technique: A Search for Meaning in Technological Civilization.* New York: Doubleday & Company, Inc., 1979.

Black, Max, ed. *Philosophy in America,* Ithaca: Cornell University Press, 1965.

Brown, Robert, and Rollins, C. D., eds. *Contemporary Philosophy in Australia.* London: George Allen & Unwin Ltd.; Atlantic Highlands, N.J., Humanities Press, Inc., 1969.

Butler, Ronald J., ed. *Analytical Philosophy.* First series. Oxford: Basil Blackwell, Publisher, 1963.

———. *Analytical Philosophy.* Second series, Oxford: Basil Blackwell, Publisher, 1965.

Copi, Irving M., and Gould, James A., eds. *Contemporary Philosophical Logic.* New York: St. Martin's Press, Inc., 1978.

Copleston, Frederick. *Contemporary Philosophy: Studies of Logical Positivism and Existentialism.* London: Burns, Oates & Washburn Ltd., 1956; Search Press Ltd., 1972. (Rev. ed., New York: Barnes & Noble Books, 1979.)

Edwards, Paul, ed. *The Encyclopedia of Philosophy.* 8 vols. New York: Macmillan Publishing Co., Inc., The Free Press, 1967. (4 vols. The Free Press, 1973.)

Feigl, Herbert; Sellars, Wilfred; and Lehrer, Keith., eds. *New Readings in Philosophical Analysis.* New York: Appleton-Century-Crofts, 1972.

Flew, Antony G. *Essays in Conceptual Analysis.* London: Macmillan & Company Ltd., 1956.

———. *Logic and Language.* First series. Oxford: Basil Blackwell, Publisher, 1951.

———. *Logic and Language.* Second series. Oxford: Basil Blackwell, Publisher, 1953, 1976.

Foster, Lawrence, and Swanson, J. W., eds. *Experience and Theory.* London: Gerald Duckworth & Co. Ltd., 1971; Amherst: University of Massachusetts Press, 1970.

French, Peter A.; Uehling, T. E.; and Wettstein, H. K., eds. *Studies in Metaphysics.* Midwest Studies in Philosophy, vol. 4. Minneapolis: University of Minnesota Press, 1979.

———. *Studies in the Philosophy of Language.* Midwest Studies in Philosophy, vol. 2. Minneapolis: University of Minnesota Press, 1977.

Körner, Stephen, ed. *Philosophy of Logic.* Oxford: Basil Blackwell, Publisher; Berkeley, University of California Press, 1976.

Lewis, Hywel D., ed. *Clarity is not Enough: Essays in Criticism of Linguistic Philosophy.* London: George Allen & Unwin Ltd., 1963.

———. *Contemporary British Philosophy.* Third series. London: George Allen & Unwin Ltd., 1956.

_____. *Contemporary British Philosophy*. Fourth series. London: George Allen & Unwin Ltd., 1976.

Macdonald, Margaret, ed. *Philosophy and Analysis*. Oxford: Basil Blackwell, Publisher, 1954.

Mace, C. A., ed. *British Philosophy in the Mid-Century*. London: George Allen & Unwin, 1957.

Magee, Bryan. *Men of Ideas: Some Creators of Contemporary Philosophy*. London: BBC Publications, 1978; New York: The Viking Press, Inc., 1979.

_____. *Modern British Philosophy*. London: Secker & Warburg Ltd.; New York: St. Martin's Press, Inc., 1971.

Munitz, Milton K. *Existence and Logic*. New York: New York University Press, 1974.

Munitz, Milton K., ed. *Identity and Individuation*. Studies in Contemporary Philosophy. New York: New York University Press, 1971.

_____. *Logic and Ontology*. Studies in Contemporary Philosophy. New York: New York University Press, 1973.

Munitz, Milton K., and Kiefer, Howard, eds. *Contemporary Philosophic Thought: The International Philosophy Year Conferences at Brockport*. 4 vols. Vol. 1, *Language, Belief and Metaphysics;* vol. 2, *Mind, Science, and History;* vol. 3, *Perspectives in Education, Religion, and the Arts;* vol. 4, *Ethics and Social Justice*. Albany: State University of New York Press, 1968, 1970.

Munitz, Milton K., and Unger, P., eds. *Semantics and Philosophy*. Studies in Contemporary Philosophy. New York: New York University Press, 1974.

Naess, Arne. *Four Modern Philosophers: Carnap, Wittgenstein, Heidegger, and Sartre*. Translated by A. Hannay. Chicago: University of Chicago Press, 1968.

Olson, Raymond E., and Paul, Anthony M., eds. *Contemporary Philosophy in Scandinavia*. Baltimore: The Johns Hopkins University Press, 1972.

Passmore, John. *A Hundred Years of Philosophy*. New York: Basic Books, Inc., Publishers, 1957, 1966.

Rorty, Richard, ed. *The Linguistic Turn: Recent Essays in Philosophical Method*. Chicago: University of Chicago Press, 1967.

Ryle, Gilbert, ed. *Contemporary Aspects of Philosophy*. London: Oriel Press Ltd., 1977.

Skolimowski, Henryk. *Polish Analytical Philosophy: A Survey and a Comparison with British Analytical Philosophy*. London: Kegan Paul, Trench, Trubner & Co.; Atlantic Highlands, N.J., Humanities Press, Inc., 1967.

Stegmueller, Wolfgang. *Main Currents in Contemporary German, British and American Philosophy*. Translated by A. E. Blumberg. Bloomington: Indiana University Press, 1970.

Urmson, J. O. *Philosophical Analysis: Its Development Between the Two World Wars*. Oxford and New York: Oxford University Press, 1956.

Warnock, Geoffrey J. *English Philosophy Since 1900*. Oxford: Oxford University Press, 1958. (Sec. ed., Oxford and New York: Oxford University Press 1969.)

Williams, Bernard, and Montefiore, Alan, eds. *British Analytical Philosophy*. Atlantic Highlands, N.J., Humanities Press, Inc., 1966.

PEIRCE: PRAGMATISM

Ayer, Alfred J. *The Origins of Pragmatism: Studies in the Philosophy of Charles Sanders Peirce and William James*. San Francisco: W. H. Freeman and Company, Publishers, 1968.

Bernstein, Richard J., ed. *Perspectives on Peirce*. New Haven: Yale University Press, 1965.

Buchler, Justus. *Charles Peirce's Empiricism*. New York: Harcourt Brace Jovanovich, Inc., 1939. (New York: Octagon Books, 1966.)

Buchler, Justus, ed. *The Philosophy of Peirce: Selected Writings*. London: Kegan Paul, Trench, Trubner & Co., 1940.

Cohen, Morris R., ed. *Chance, Love, and Logic*. New York: Harcourt Brace Jovanovich, Inc., 1923.

Dewey, John. *Essays in Experimental Logic*. Chicago: University of Chicago Press, 1916.

————. *Logic: The Theory of Inquiry*. New York: Holt, Rinehart and Winston, 1938. (New York: Irvington Publishers, Inc., n.d.)

————. "The Development of American Pragmatism." In *Studies in the History of Ideas*, 2:353–377. New York: Columbia University Press, 1925. Reprinted in John Dewey, *Philosophy and Civilization*. New York: G. P. Putnam's Sons, 1931. (Magnolia, Mass.: Peter Smith Publisher, Inc., n.d.)

————. "The Pragmatism of Peirce." Reprinted in Cohen, *Chance, Love, and Logic*, pp. 301–308.

Gallie, W. B. *Peirce and Pragmatism*. London: Penguin Books, 1952. (London, Greenwood Press, Inc., 1976; Westport, Ct.: Greenwood Press, Inc., 1975.)

Goudge, T. A. *The Thought of C. S. Peirce*. Toronto: University of Toronto Press, 1950. (New York: Dover Publications, Inc., 1969.)

James, William. *The Meaning of Truth: A Sequel to "Pragmatism."* New York: Longman, Inc., 1909. (Ann Arbor, University of Michigan Press, 1970.)

————. *Pragmatism: A New Name for Some Old Ways of Thinking*. New York: Longman, Inc., 1907, 1943. (Cambridge: Harvard University Press, 1976, edited by Frederick Burkhardt et al.)

————. *The Will to Believe and Other Essays in Popular Philosophy*. New York: Longman, Inc., 1897. (Magnolia, Mass.: Peter Smith Publisher, Inc., n.d.)

————. "What Pragmatism Means." In Ralph B. Perry, ed., *Collected Essays and Reviews*. New York: Longman, Inc., 1920. (Reprinted, New York: Atheneum Publishers, Russell & Russell, 1969.)

Lewis, Clarence I. *An Analysis of Knowledge and Valuation*. La Salle, Ill.: Open Court Publishing Company, 1946, 1971.

Madden, Edward H. *Chauncey Wright and the Foundations of Pragmatism*. Seattle: University of Washington Press, 1963.

Mead, G. H. *Mind, Self, and Society*. Chicago: University of Chicago Press, 1934, 1967.

————. *The Philosophy of the Present*. La Salle, Ill.: Open Court Publishing Company, 1932, 1959.

Moore, E. C., and Robin, Richard S., eds. *Studies in the Philosophy of Charles Sanders Peirce*. Second series. Amherst: University of Massachusetts Press, 1964.

Morris, Charles W. *Logical Positivism, Pragmatism, and Scientific Empiricism*. Paris: Hermann, 1937. (New York: AMS Press, Inc., 1976.)

Murphey, Murray G. *The Development of Peirce's Philosophy*. Cambridge: Harvard University Press, 1961.

Peirce, Charles S. *Charles S. Peirce's Letters to Lady Welby*. Edited by I. Lieb. New Haven: Whitlock's, 1953.

————. *The Collected Papers of Charles Sanders Peirce*. 8 vols. Vols. 1–6 edited by C. Hartshorne and P. Weiss; vols. 7–8 edited by A. W. Burks. Cambridge: Harvard University Press, 1931–1958.

————. *The New Elements of Mathematics of Charles S. Peirce*. 4 vols. Edited by C. Eisele. Atlantic Highlands, N. J.: Humanities Press, Inc., 1976.

Peirce Commemorative Issue, *Journal of Philosophy, Psychology and Scientific Methods*, Dec. 1916.

Perry, Ralph B. *The Thought and Character of William James*. 2 vols., Boston: Little, Brown, and Company, 1935.

Rorty, Amelie O., ed. *Pragmatic Philosophy*. New York: Doubleday & Company, Inc., Anchor Books, 1966.

Scheffler, Israel. *Four Pragmatists: A Critical Introduction to Peirce, James, Mead and Dewey*. London: Kegan Paul, Trench, Trubner & Co.; Atlantic Highlands, N. J.: Humanities Press, Inc., 1974.

Smith, John E. *Purpose and Thought: The Meaning of Pragmatism*. New Haven: Yale University Press, 1978.

Thayer, H. S. *Meaning and Action: A Critical History of Pragmatism*. Indianapolis: The Bobbs-Merrill Co., Inc., 1968.

Thompson, Manley. *The Pragmatic Philosophy of C. S. Peirce*. Chicago: University of Chicago Press, 1953.

Wiener, Philip P. *Evolution and the Founders of Pragmatism*. Cambridge: Harvard University Press, 1949. (Philadelphia, University of Pennsylvania Press, 1972.)

Wiener, Philip P., and Young, F.. H., eds. *Studies in the Philosophy of Charles Sanders Peirce*. Cambridge: Harvard University Press, 1952.

FREGE

Angelelli, Ignacio. *Studies on Gottlob Frege and Traditional Philosophy*. Atlantic Highlands, N.J.: Humanities Press, Inc., 1967.

Anscombe, Gertrude E. M., and Geach, Peter. *Three Philosophers*. (Aristotle, Aquinas, and Frege.) Oxford: Basil Blackwell, Publisher; Ithaca, N.Y.: Cornell University Press, 1961.

Bell, David. *Frege's Theory of Judgement*. Oxford: Clarendon Press, 1979.

Birjukov, B. V. *Two Soviet Studies on Frege*. Translated by I. Angelelli. Oxford: Basil Blackwell, Publisher; Hingham, Mass.: Kluwer, 1964.

Dummett, Michael. *Frege: Philosophy of Language*. London: Gerald Duckworth & Co. Ltd., 1973.

————. *Truth and Other Enigmas*. London: Gerald Duckworth & Co. Ltd.; Cambridge: Harvard University Press, 1978.

Frege, Gottlob. *The Basic Laws of Arithmetic: Exposition of the System*. Translated and edited by Montgomery Furth. Berkeley: University of California Press, 1965.

———. *Conceptual Notation and Related Articles*. Translated by T. W. Bynum. Oxford: Clarendon Press; New York: Oxford University Press, 1972.

———. *The Foundations of Arithmetic: A Logico-Mathematical Enquiry into the Concept of Number*. Translated by J. L. Austin. Oxford: Basil Blackwell, Publisher, 1950, 1953, 1956. (Evanston, Ill.: Northwestern University Press, 1968.)

———. *Logical Investigations*. Edited by Peter Geach and R. H. Stoothoff. Oxford: Basil Blackwell, Publisher; New Haven: Yale University Press, 1977.

———. *On the Foundations of Geometry and Formal Theories of Arithmetic*. Translated by Eike-Henner W. Kluge. New Haven: Yale University Press, 1971.

———. *Philosophical and Mathematical Correspondence*. Translated by H. Kaal. Oxford: Basil Blackwell, Publisher, 1979.

———. *Posthumous Writings*. Edited by H. Hermes, F. Kambartel, and F. Kaulbach. Translated by P. Long and R. White. Oxford: Basil Blackwell, Publisher; Chicago: University of Chicago Press, 1979.

———. *Translations from the Philosophical Writings of Gottlob Frege*. Edited by P. Geach and M. Black. Oxford: Basil Blackwell, Publisher, 1952, 1960, 1980.

Grossman, Reinhardt. *Reflections on Frege's Philosophy*. Evanston, Ill.: Northwestern University Press, 1969.

Klemke, E. D., ed. *Essays on Frege*. Urbana: University of Illinois Press, 1968.

Sternfeld, Robert. *Frege's Logical Theory*. Carbondale: Southern Illinois University Press, 1966.

Thiel, Christian. *Sense and Reference in Frege's Logic*. Translated by T. J. Blakeley. Dordrecht, Holland, and Hingham, Mass.: D. Reidel Publishing Co., 1968.

Van Heijenoort, Jean, ed. *From Frege to Gödel: A Source Book in Mathematical Logic 1879–1931*. Cambridge: Harvard University Press, 1967.

Walker, Jeremy D. B. *A Study of Frege*. Ithaca, N.Y.: Cornell University Press, 1965.

RUSSELL

Ayer, Alfred J. *Russell and Moore: The Analytical Heritage*. London: Macmillan and Company Ltd.; Cambridge: Harvard University Press, 1971.

Clark, Ronald W. *The Life of Bertrand Russell*. London: Weidenfeld and Nicolson, 1975; New York: Alfred A. Knopf, Inc., 1976.

Crawshay-Williams, Rupert. *Russell Remembered*. Oxford: Oxford University Press, 1970.

Dewey, John, and Kallen, H. M., eds. *The Bertrand Russell Case*. New York: The Viking Press, Inc., 1941. (Reprint, New York: Da Capo Press, Inc., 1972.)

Feinberg, Barry, and Kasrils, Ronald. *Bertrand Russell's America*. London: George Allen & Unwin Ltd., 1973.

Fritz, Charles A., Jr. *Bertrand Russell's Construction of the External World*. Atlantic Highlands, N.J.: Humanities Press, Inc., 1952. (Reprinted, Westport, Ct., Greenwood Press, Inc., 1974.)

Grattan-Guiness, I. *Dear Russell–Dear Jourdain*. New York: Columbia University Press, 1977.

Jager, Ronald. *The Development of Bertrand Russell's Philosophy*. London: George Allen & Unwin Ltd.; Atlantic Highlands, N. J.; Humanities Press, Inc., 1972.

Klemke, E. D., ed. *Essays on Bertrand Russell*. Urbana: University of Illinois Press, 1970.

Nakhnikian, George, ed. *Bertrand Russell's Philosophy*. New York: Harper & Row, Publishers, 1974.

Pears, David F., ed. *Bertrand Russell: A Collection of Critical Essays*. New York: Doubleday & Company, Inc., Anchor Books, 1972.

———. *Bertrand Russell and the British Tradition in Philosophy*. New York: Random House, Inc., 1967.

Roberts, George W. *Bertrand Russell: The Memorial Volume*. Atlantic Highlands, N.J.: Humanities Press, Inc., 1979.

Russell, Bertrand. *The Analysis of Matter*. London: Kegan Paul, Trench, Trubner & Co., 1927.

———. *Analysis of Mind*. London: George Allen & Unwin Ltd., 1921. (Atlantic Highlands, N.J.: Humanities Press, Inc., 1978.)

———. *Authority and the Individual*. London: George Allen & Unwin Ltd., 1949, 1977. (New York: AMS Press, Inc., n.d.)

———. *Autobiography*. 3 vols. London: George Alien & Unwin Ltd., 1967–1969.

———. *The Conquest of Happiness*. London: George Allen & Unwin Ltd., 1930, 1975.

———. *A Critical Exposition of the Philosophy of Leibniz*. London: George Allen & Unwin Ltd., 1900, 1937. (Atlantic Highlands, N.J., Humanities Press, Inc., 1961.)

———. *An Essay on the Foundations of Geometry*. Cambridge: Cambridge University Press, 1897.

———. *Essays in Analysis*. Edited by D. Lackey. New York: George Braziller, Inc., 1973.

———. *Freedom and Organization: 1814–1914*. London: George Allen & Unwin; New York: W. W. Norton & Company, Inc., 1934.

———. *German Social Democracy*. London: Longman Group Limited, 1896. (New York: Simon & Schuster, Inc., 1965.)

———. *A History of Western Philosophy*. New York: Simon & Schuster, Inc., 1945.

———. *Human Knowledge: Its Scope and Limits*. London: George Allen & Unwin Ltd.; New York: Simon & Schuster, Inc., 1948.

———. *Human Society in Ethics and Politics*. London: George Allen & Unwin Ltd., 1954.

———. *The Impact of Science on Society*. London: George Allen & Unwin Ltd., 1952, 1968

———. *An Inquiry into Meaning and Truth*. London: George Allen & Unwin Ltd.; Atlantic Highlands, N.J.: Humanities Press, Inc., 1940.

———. *Introduction to Mathematical Philosophy*. London: George Allen & Unwin Ltd., 1919. (New York: Simon & Schuster, Inc., 1971.)

———. *Logic and Knowledge*. Edited by R. C. Marsh. London: George Allen & Unwin Ltd., 1956.

———. *Marriage and Morals*. London: George Allen & Unwin Ltd., 1929, 1976.

———. *My Philosophical Development*. London: George Allen & Unwin Ltd., 1959.

———. *Mysticism and Logic and Other Essays*. London: George Allen & Unwin Ltd., 1917.

———. *New Hopes for a Changing World*. London: George Allen & Unwin Ltd., 1951.

———. *Our Knowledge of the External World as a Field for Scientific Method in Philosophy*. La Salle, Ill.: Open Court Publishing Company, 1914. (2d ed., Atlantic Highlands, N.J.: Humanities Press, Inc., 1972.)

———. *Philosophical Essays*. 2d ed. London: George Allen & Unwin Ltd., 1966; New York, Simon & Schuster, Inc., 1968.

———. *Portraits from Memory and Other Essays*. London: George Allen & Unwin Ltd., 1956.

———. *Power: A New Social Analysis*. New York: W. W. Norton & Company, Inc., 1938, 1969.

———. *The Practice and Theory of Bolshevism*. London: George Allen & Unwin Ltd., 1920, 1963.

———. *The Principles of Mathematics*. 1st ed. 1903, 2d ed. 1937. New York: W. W. Norton & Company, Inc., 1937, 1964.

———. "The Philosophy of Logical Atomism" (in *Logic and Knowledge*).

———. *Principles of Social Reconstruction*. London: George Allen & Unwin Ltd., 1916, 1972.

———. *The Problems of Philosophy*. London: Williams & Norgate, 1912, 1967. New York, Oxford University Press, 1967.

———. *Religion and Science*. London: Thornton Butterworth Ltd., 1935. (New York: Oxford University Press, 1961.)

———. *Roads to Freedom: Socialism, Anarchism and Syndicalism*. London: George Allen & Unwin Ltd., 1918, 1966, 1967.

———. *Sceptical Essays*. London: George Allen & Unwin Ltd., 1928, 1935, 1977.

———. *The Scientific Outlook*. London: George Allen & Unwin Ltd., 1931. (New York: W. W. Norton & Company, Inc., 1962.)

———. *Why I Am Not a Christian*. Edited by P. Edwards. London: George Allen & Unwin Ltd., 1957, 1975; New York: Simon & Schuster, 1957.

Russell, Bertrand, and Whitehead, Alfred North. *Principia Mathematica*. 3 vols. Vol. 1, 1910, 2d ed. 1925; vol. 2, 1912; vol. 3, 1913. Cambridge: Cambridge University Press, 1962.

Sainsbury, R. M. *Russell*. London: Kegan Paul, Trench, Trubner & Co., 1979.

Schilpp, Paul A., ed. *The Philosophy of Bertrand Russell*. The Library of Living Philosophers. Evanston, Ill.: Northwestern University Press, 1944. (La Salle, Ill.: Open Court Publishing Company, 1979.)

Schoenman, Ralph, ed. *Bertrand Russell, Philosopher of the Century*. London: George Allen & Unwin Ltd., 1967.

Wood, Alan. *Bertrand Russell: The Passionate Sceptic.* London: George Allen & Unwin Ltd., 1957.

MOORE

Ambrose, Alice, and Lazerowitz, Morris, eds. *G. E. Moore: Essays in Retrospect.* London: George Allen & Unwin; Atlantic Highlands, N.J.: Humanities Press, Inc., 1970.

Ayer, Alfred J. *Russell and Moore: The Analytical Heritage.* London: Macmillan & Company Ltd.; Cambridge, Harvard University Press, 1971.

Klemke, E. D., ed. *Studies in the Philosophy of G. E. Moore.* Chicago: University of Chicago Press, 1969.

Moore, George E. *Commonplace Book, 1919–1953.* Edited by C. Lewy. London: George Allen & Unwin Ltd., 1962. (Atlantic Highlands, N.J.: Humanities Press, Inc., 1962, 1978.)

———. *Ethics.* London: Williams & Norgate, 1912. (Oxford: Oxford University Press, 1966; New York: Oxford University Press, 1967.)

———. *Lectures on Philosophy.* Edited by C. Lewy. London: George Allen & Unwin Ltd., 1967.

———. *Philosophical Papers.* London: George Allen & Unwin Ltd., 1959. (Reprint, Atlantic Highlands, N.J.: Humanities Press, Inc., 1977.)

———. *Philosophical Studies.* London: Kegan Paul, Trench, Trubner & Co.; Atlantic Highlands, N.J.: Humanities Press, Inc., 1922.

———. *Principia Ethica.* Cambridge: Cambridge University Press, 1903. (New York: Cambridge University Press, 1959.)

———. *Some Main Problems of Philosophy.* London: George Allen & Unwin Ltd., 1953. (Atlantic Highlands, N.J.: Humanities Press, Inc., 1978.)

Schilpp, Paul A., ed. *The Philosophy of G. E. Moore.* The Library of Living Philosophers, vol. 4. Evanston, Ill.: Northwestern University Press, 1942.

White, Alan R. *G. E. Moore: A Critical Exposition.* Oxford: Basil Blackwell, Publisher, 1958. (Westport, Ct.; Greenwood Press, Inc., 1979.)

WITTGENSTEIN

Ambrose, Alice, and Lazerowitz, Morris, eds. *Ludwig Wittgenstein: Philosophy and Language.* London: George Allen & Unwin Ltd.; Atlantic Highlands, N.J.: Humanities Press, Inc., 1972.

Anscombe, Gertrude E. M. *An Introduction to Wittgenstein's Tractatus.* London: Hutchinson Publishing Group, 1959, 1963. (Philadelphia, University of Pennsylvania Press, 1971.)

Baker, G. P., and Hacker, P. M. S. *Wittgenstein—Understanding and Meaning: An Analytical Commentary on the Philosophical Investigations,* vol. 1. Oxford: Basil Blackwell, Publisher; Chicago: University of Chicago Press, 1980.

Bartley, William Warren, III. *Wittgenstein.* London: Quartet Books Ltd., 1974, 1976; New York: J. B. Lippincott Company, 1973.

Black, Max. *A Companion to Wittgenstein's Tractatus*. Ithaca, N. Y.: Cornell University Press, 1964.

Bogen, James. *Wittgenstein's Philosophy of Language: Some Aspects of Its Development*. London: Kegan Paul, Trench, Trubner & Co.; Atlantic Highlands, N. J.: Humanities Press, 1972.

Brand, Gerd. *The Basic Texts of Wittgenstein*. Oxford: Basil Blackwell, Publisher, 1979.

Coope, Christopher; Geach, Peter; et al. *A Wittgenstein Workbook*. Oxford: Basil Blackwell, Publisher; Berkeley: University of California Press, 1970.

Copi, Irving M., and Beard, Robert W., eds. *Essays on Wittgenstein's Tractatus*. New York: Macmillan Publishing Co., Inc., 1966.

De Mauro, Tullio. *Ludwig Wittgenstein: His Place in the Development of Semantics*. Dordrecht, Holland: Reidel; Atlantic Highlands, N.J.: Humanities Press, Inc., 1967.

Dilman, Ilham. *Induction and Deduction: A Study in Wittgenstein*. Oxford: Basil Blackwell, Publisher; New York: Barnes & Noble Books, 1973.

Engel, S. M. *Wittgenstein's Doctrine of the Tyranny of Language*. The Hague: Martinus Nijhoff, Publishers, 1975.

Engelmann, Paul. *Letters from Ludwig Wittgenstein, with a Memoir*. Translated by L. Furtmuller. Edited by B. McGuiness. Oxford: Basil Blackwell, Publisher, 1968. (New York: Horizon Press, 1974.)

Fann, K. T. *Wittgenstein's Conception of Philosophy*. Oxford: Basil Blackwell, Publisher; Berkeley: University of California Press, 1969.

Fann, K. T., ed. *Ludwig Wittgenstein, the Man and His Philosophy*. New York: Dell Publishing Co., Inc., 1967. (Atlantic Highlands, N.J.: Humanities Press, Inc., 1978.)

Favrholdt, David. *An Interpretation and Critique of Wittgenstein's Tractatus*. Copenhagen: Munksgaard, 1965.

Finch, Henry Le Roy. *Wittgenstein, The Early Philosophy: An Exposition of the Tractatus*. Atlantic Highlands, N.J.: Humanities Press, Inc., 1971.

———. *Wittgenstein, The Later Philosophy: An Exposition of the Philosophical Investigations*. Atlantic Highlands, N.J.: Humanities Press, Inc., 1977.

Fogelin, Robert J. *Wittgenstein*. London: Kegan Paul, Trench, Trubner & Co., 1976.

Griffin, James. *Wittenstein's Logical Atomism*. Oxford: Oxford University Press, 1964.

Gudmunsen, Chris. *Wittgenstein and Buddhism*. London: Macmillan & Company Ltd.; New York: Barnes & Noble Books, 1977.

Hacker, P. M. S. *Insight and Illusion: Wittgenstein on Philosophy and the Metaphysics of Experience*. Oxford and New York: Oxford University Press, 1972.

Hallett, Garth. *A Companion to Wittgenstein's "Philosophical Investigations."* Ithaca, N.Y.: Cornell University Press, 1977.

———. *Wittgenstein's Definition of Meaning as Use*. New York: Fordham University Press, 1967.

Hartnack, Justus. *Wittgenstein and Modern Philosophy*. New York: Doubleday & Company, Inc., Anchor Books, 1965.

High, D. M. *Language, Persons and Belief*. Studies in Wittgenstein's *Philosophi-*

cal Investigations and Religious Use of Language. New York: Oxford University Press, Inc., 1967.

Janik, Allan, and Toulmin, Stephen. *Wittgenstein's Vienna.* New York: Simon & Schuster, Inc., 1974.

Jones, Owen R., ed. *The Private Language Argument.* London: Macmillan & Company Ltd.; New York: St. Martin's Press, Inc., 1971.

Kenny, Anthony. *Wittgenstein.* London: Allen Lane, Penguin Press Ltd., 1975; Cambridge: Harvard University Press, 1974.

Leinfellner, Elizabeth, et al, eds. *Wittgenstein and His Impact on Contemporary Thought.* Proceedings of the Second International Wittgenstein Symposium, September 1977. Vienna: Holder, Pichler, Tempsky, 1978.

Leitner, Bernhard. *The Architecture of Ludwig Wittgenstein: A Documentation with Excerpts from the Family Recollections by Hermine Wittgenstein.* Halifax, Canada: The Press of Nova Scotia College of Art and Design, 1973. (New York: New York University Press, 1976.)

Luckhardt, C. Grant, ed. *Wittgenstein: Sources and Perspectives.* Ithaca, N.Y.: Cornell University Press, 1979.

Malcolm, Norman, and von Wright, Georg H. *Ludwig Wittgenstein: a Memoir.* Oxford: Oxford University Press, 1958. (New York: Oxford University Press, 1967.)

Morawetz, Thomas. *Wittgenstein and Knowledge: The Importance of "On Certainty."* Amherst: University of Massachusetts Press, 1978.

Morick, Harold, ed. *Wittgenstein and the Problem of Other Minds.* New York: McGraw-Hill Book Company, 1967.

Pears, David. *Ludwig Wittgenstein.* New York: The Viking Press, Inc., 1970.

Pitcher, George. *The Philosophy of Wittgenstein.* Englewood Cliffs, N.J.: Prentice-Hall, Inc., 1964.

Pitcher, George, ed. *Wittgenstein: The Philosophical Investigations.* New York: Doubleday & Company, Inc., 1966. (Notre Dame, Ind.: University of Notre Dame Press, 1968, 1974.)

Pitkin, Hanna F. *Wittgenstein and Justice.* Berkeley: University of California Press, 1972.

Plochmann, George K., and Lawson, J. B. *Terms in Their Propositional Contexts in Wittgenstein's Tractatus: An Index.* Carbondale: Southern Illinois University Press, 1962.

Pole, David. *The Later Philosophy of Wittgenstein.* London: The Athlone Press, University of London, 1958

Rhees, Rush. *Discussions of Wittgenstein.* London: Kegan Paul, Trench, Trubner & Co., 1970.

Specht, Ernest Konrad. *The Foundations of Wittgenstein's Late Philosophy.* Translated by D. E. Walford, Manchester: Manchester University Press, 1969.

Stenius, Erik. *Wittgenstein's Tractatus.* Oxford: Basil Blackwell, Publisher, 1960.

Vesey, Godfrey, ed. *Understanding Wittgenstein.* (Vol. 7, Royal Institute of Philosophy Lectures). Ithaca, N. Y.: Cornell University Press, 1974, 1976.

Waismann, Friedrich. *The Principles of Linguistic Philosophy.* London: Macmillan & Company Ltd., 1965, 1969. (New York: St. Martin's Press, Inc., 1976, edited by R. Harré.)

————. *Wittgenstein and the Vienna Circle: Conversations Recorded by Friedrich Waismann*. Edited by B. McGuiness. Translated by J. Schulte. Oxford: Basil Blackwell, Publisher, 1979.

Winch, Peter, ed. *Studies in the Philosophy of Wittgenstein*. London: Kegan Paul, Trench, Trubner & Co.; Atlantic Highlands, N.J.: Humanities Press, Inc., 1969.

Wittgenstein, Ludwig. *The Blue and Brown Books*. 2d ed. Oxford: Basil Blackwell, Publisher, 1969. (New York: Harper & Row, Publishers, n.d.)

————. "A Lecture on Ethics", *Philosophical Review* 74 (1965), 3–12.

————. *Lectures and Conversations on Aesthetics, Psychology and Religious Belief*. Edited by Cyril Barrett. Oxford: Basil Blackwell, Publisher, 1966. Berkeley: University of California Press, 1967.

————. *Letters to C. K. Ogden*. Edited by G. H. von Wright. Oxford: Basil Blackwell, Publishers; Routledge & Kegan Paul, London and Boston, 1973.

————. *Letters to Russell, Keynes and Moore*. Edited by G. H. von Wright. Oxford: Basil Blackwell, 1974.

————. *Notebooks 1914–1916*. 2d ed. Edited by G. H. von Wright and G. E. M. Anscombe. Translated by G. E. M. Anscombe. Oxford: Basil Blackwell, Publisher, 1961.

————. "Notes for Lectures on 'Private Experience' and 'Sense Data'", edited by R. Rhees, *Philosophical Review*, 77 (1968), 275–320.

————. *On Certainty*. Edited by G. E. M. Anscombe and G. H. von Wright. Oxford: Basil Blackwell, Publisher, 1969, 1975. (New York: Harper & Row, Publishers, 1972.)

————. *Philosophical Grammar*. Edited by Rush Rhees. Translated by Anthony Kenny. Oxford: Basil Blackwell, Publisher; Berkeley: University of California Press, 1974.

————. *Philosophical Investigations*. 3d ed. Translated by G. E. M. Anscombe. Oxford: Basil Blackwell, Publisher, 1967. (New York: Macmillan Publishing Co., Inc., 1973.)

————. *Philosophical Remarks*. Edited by Rush Rhees. Oxford: Basil Blackwell, Publisher; New York: Barnes & Noble Books, 1975.

————. *Prototractatus: An Early Version of Tractatus Logico-Philosophicus*. Edited by B. F. McGuiness, T. Nyberg, and G. H. von Wright. Translated by B. F. McGuiness and D. F. Pears. Ithaca, N. Y.: Cornell University Press, 1971.

————. *Remarks on Colour*. Edited by G. E. M. Anscombe. Translated by Linda L. McAlister and Margarete Schättle. Oxford: Basil Blackwell, Publisher; Berkeley: University of California Press, 1978.

————. *Remarks on the Foundations of Mathematics*. 3d ed. Edited by G. H. von Wright, R. Rhees, and G. E. M. Anscombe. Translated by G. E. M. Anscombe. Oxford: Basil Blackwell, Publisher; Cambridge: M.I.T. Press, 1978.

————. "Remarks on Frazer's *Golden Bough*." Translated by John Beversluis. In C. G. Luckhardt, ed., *Wittgenstein: Sources and Perspectives*, 61–81.

————. *Remarks on the Philosophy of Psychology*. Edited by G. H. Von Wright and Heikki Nyman, three volumes: Oxford, Basil Blackwell, Publisher, 1980.

————. "Some Remarks on Logical Form." *Proceedings of the Aristotelian Society*, supplementary volume IX (1929), 162–71.

————. *Tractatus Logico-Philosophicus*. Translated by D. F. Pears and B. F. McGuiness. Introduction by Bertrand Russell. 2d ed. London: Kegan Paul, Trench, Trubner & Co., 1961.

————. *Wittgenstein's Lectures on the Foundations of Mathematics*, Cambridge 1939. Edited by Cora Diamond. Ithaca, N. Y.: Cornell University Press, 1976.

————. *Wittgenstein's Lectures: Cambridge 1930–1932*. Edited by Desmond Lee. Oxford: Basil Blackwell, Publisher, 1979.

————. *Wittgenstein's Lectures: Cambridge 1932–1935*. Edited by Alice Ambrose. Oxford: Basil Blackwell, Publisher, 1979.

————. *Zettel*. Edited by G. E. M. Anscombe and G. H. von Wright. Translated by G. E. M. Anscombe. Oxford: Basil Blackwell, Publisher; Berkeley: University of California Press, 1967.

Wright, Crispin. *Wittgenstein on the Foundations of Mathematics*. London: Duckworth; Cambridge: Harvard University Press, 1980.

LOGICAL POSITIVISM

Achinstein, Peter, and Barker, Stephen, eds. *The Legacy of Logical Positivism for the Philosophy of Science*. Baltimore: The Johns Hopkins University Press, 1969.

Ayer, Alfred J. *Language, Truth, and Logic*. 2d ed. London: Victor Gollancz Ltd..; New York: Dover Publications, Inc., 1936.

Ayer, Alfred J., ed. *Logical Positivism*. New York: Macmillan Publishing Co., Inc., The Free Press, 1959. (London and Westport, Ct.: Greenwood Press, 1978.)

Bergmann, Gustav. *The Metaphysics of Logical Positivism*. London: Longman Group Ltd., 1954. (London and Westport, Ct.: Greenwood Press, 1978.)

Buck, R. C., and Cohen, R. S., eds. *PSA 1970: In Memory of Rudolf Carnap*. Proceedings of the 1970 Meeting of the Philosophy of Science Association. Atlantic Highlands, N.J.: Humanities Press, Inc., 1971.

Carnap, Rudolf. *The Continuum of Inductive Methods*. Chicago: University of Chicago Press, 1952

————. *Foundations of Logic and Mathematics*. Foundations of the Unity of Science Series, vol. 1, no. 3. Chicago: University Press, 1937.

————. *Introduction to Semantics and Formalization of Logic*. Cambridge: Harvard University Press, 1959.

————. *Logical Foundations of Probability*. Chicago: University of Chicago Press, 1950.

————. *The Logical Structure of the World* and *Pseudoproblems in Philosophy*. Berkeley: University of California Press, 1967.

————. *The Logical Syntax of Language*. New York: Harcourt Brace Jovanovich, Inc., 1937. (Atlantic Highlands, N.J.: Humanities Press, Inc., 1964.)

————. *Meaning and Necessity: A Study in Semantics and Modal Logic.* Enlarged ed. Chicago: University of Chicago Press, 1956.

————. *Philosophy and Logical Syntax.* London: Kegan Paul, Trench, Trubner & Co., 1935. (New York: AMS Press, Inc., 1976.)

Edwards, Paul. *The Logic of Moral Discourse.* New York: Macmillan Publishing Co., Inc., The Free Press, 1955.

Frank, Philipp. *Between Physics and Philosophy.* Cambridge: Harvard University Press, 1941.

————. *Modern Science and Its Philosophy.* Cambridge: Harvard University Press, 1949. (New York: Arno Press, Inc., 1975.)

Hempel, Carl G. *Aspects of Scientific Explanation and Other Essays in the Philosophy of Science.* New York: Macmillan Publishing Co., Inc., The Free Press, 1965, 1970.

————. *Fundamentals of Concept Formation in Empirical Science.* Foundations of the Unity of Science Series. Chicago: University of Chicago Press, 1952.

Hintikka, Jaakko, ed. *Rudolf Carnap, Logical Empiricist: Materials and Perspectives.* Dordrecht, Holland: D. Reidel Publishing Co., 1976.

Jordan, A. *On the Development of Mathematical Logic and of Logical Positivism in Poland.* Oxford: Oxford University Press, 1946.

Jörgenson, Jörgen. *The Development of Logical Empiricism.*. International Encyclopedia of Unified Science. Chicago: University of Chicago Press, 1951.

Juhos, Béla. *Selected Papers on Epistemology and Physics.* Edited by G. Frey. Dordrecht, Holland: D. Reidel Publishing Co., 1976.

Kazemier, B. H., and Vusje, D., eds. *Logic and Language: Studies Dedicated to Professor Carnap.* Hingham, Mass.: D. Reidel Publishing Co., Inc., 1962.

Kraft, Viktor. *The Vienna Circle, the Origins of Neo-Positivism.* New York: Philosophical Library, Inc., 1953.

Morris, Charles W. *Logical Positivism, Pragmatism, and Scientific Empiricism.* Paris: Hermann, 1937. (New York: AMS Press, Inc.)

————. *Signs, Language, and Behavior.* Englewood Cliffs, N.J.: Prentice-Hall, Inc., 1946. (New York: George Braziller, Inc., 1955.)

Nagel, Ernest. *Logic Without Metaphysics.* New York: Macmillan Publishing Co., Inc., The Free Press, 1956.

————. *Principles of the Theory of Probability.*. Foundations of the Unity of Science Series. Chicago: University of Chicago Press, Phoenix Books, 1939.

————. *Sovereign Reason.* New York: Macmillan Publishing Co., Inc., The Free Press, 1954.

————. *The Structure of Science.* New York: Harcourt Brace Jovanovich, Inc., 1961.

————. *Teleology Revisited and Other Essays in the Philosophy and History of Science.* New York: Columbia University Press, 1979.

Neurath, Otto. *Empiricism and Sociology: The Life and Works of Otto Neurath.* Edited by Marie Neurath and R. S. Cohen. Translated by Paul Foulkes. Dordrecht, Holland, and Hingham, Mass.: D. Reidel Publishing Co., 1973.

————. *Foundations of the Social Sciences.* Foundations of the Unity of Science Series. Chicago: University of Chicago Press, 1944.

Neurath, Otto, et al. *Encyclopedia and Unified Science.* Foundations of the Unity of Science Series. Chicago: University of Chicago Press, 1938.

Norton, Bryan G. *Linguistic Frameworks and Ontology: A Re-examination of Carnap's Metaphilosophy*. The Hague: Mouton Publishers, 1977.
Popper, Karl. *Conjectures and Refutations: The Growth of Scientific Knowledge*. New York: Basic Books, Inc., Publishers, 1962.
———. *The Logic of Scientific Discovery*. London: Hutchinson, 1959. (Rev. ed., 1972, 1974; New York: Harper & Row, Publishers, Torchbooks, 1959.)
Reichenbach, Hans. *Experience and Prediction: An Analysis of the Foundations and the Structure of Knowledge*. Chicago: University of Chicago Press, 1938, 1976.
———. *The Rise of Scientific Philosophy*. Berkeley: University of California Press, 1951.
Reichenbach, Maria, and Cohen, R. S., eds. *Hans Reichenbach: Selected Writings (1909–1953)*, vols. 1 and 2. Dordrecht, Holland: D. Reidel Publishing Co., 1978.
Schilpp, Paul A., ed. *The Philosophy of Rudolf Carnap*. Library of Living Philosophers, vol. 11. La Salle, Ill.: Open Court Publishing Company, 1963.
Schlick, Moritz. *General Theory of Knowledge*. Translated by A. E. Blumberg. New York: Springer-Verlag, Inc., 1974.
———. *Philosophical Papers*. Vol. 1, 1909–1922. Translated by P. Heath. Dordrecht, Holland: D. Reidel Publishing Co., 1978.
Stevenson, Charles. *Ethics and Language*. New Haven: Yale University Press, 1945. (New York: AMS Press, Inc., 1976.)
Von Mises, Richard. *Positivism: A Study in Human Understanding*. Cambridge: Harvard University Press, 1951.
Waismann, Friedrich. *Philosophical Papers*. Edited by B. McGuiness. Dordrecht, Holland: D. Reidel Publishing Co., 1977.
Weinberg, Julius R. *An Examination of Logical Positivism*. London: Kegan Paul, Trench, Trubner & Co., 1936.

QUINE

Davidson, Donald, and Hintikka, Jaakko, eds. *Words and Objections: Essays on the Work of W. V. Quine*. Dordrecht, Holland, and Hingham, Mass.: D. Reidel Publishing Co., 1975.
Orenstein, Alex. *Willard Van Orman Quine*. Boston: Twayne Publishers, 1977.
Quine, Willard Van Orman. *Elementary Logic*. Lexington, Mass.: Ginn and Company, 1941, 1966.
———. *From a Logical Point of View*. Cambridge: Harvard University Press, 1953, 1961.
———. *Mathematical Logic*. Cambridge: Harvard University Press, 1940, 1951.
———. *Methods of Logic*. Holt, Rinehart and Winston, 1950, 1972.
———. *Ontological Relativity and Other Essays*. New York: Columbia University Press, 1969.
———. *The Philosophy of Logic*. Englewood Cliffs, N.J.: Prentice-Hall, Inc., 1970.
———. *The Roots of Reference*. La Salle, Ill.: Open Court Publishing Company, 1974.

————. *Selected Logical Papers.* New York: Random House, Inc., 1966.

————. *Set Theory and Its Logic.* Cambridge, Mass.: Harvard University Press, 1969.

————. *A System of Logistic.* Cambridge, Mass.: Cambridge: Harvard University Press, 1934.

————. *The Ways of Paradox and Other Essays.* New York: Random House, Inc., 1966.

Quine, W. V. O., and Ullian, J. S. *The Web of Belief.* New York: Random House, Inc., 1970, 1978.

————. *Word and Object.* Cambridge: MIT Press, and New York: John Wiley, Inc., 1960.

Severens, R. H., ed. *Ontological Commitment.* Athens, Ga.: University of Georgia Press, 1974.

Shahan, Robert W., and Swayer, Chris., eds. *Essays on the Philosophy of W. V. Quine.* Norman, Okla.: University of Oklahoma Press, 1979.

KRIPKE

Kripke, Saul A. "Semantical Considerations on Modal Logic," *Acta Philosophica Fennica,* xvi (1963), 83–94.

————. "Identity and Necessity," In M. K. Munitz, editor, *Identity and Individuation.* New York: New York University Press, 1971, 1980, 135–164.

————. "Is There a Problem about Substitutional Quantification?" In Gareth Evans and John McDowell, editors, *Truth and Meaning.* Oxford: Clarendon Press, 1976, 324–419.

————. *Naming and Necessity.* Cambridge: Harvard University Press, 1980.

————. "Outline of a Theory of Truth." *Journal of Philosophy,* lxxii (1975), 690–716.

————. "Speaker's Reference and Semantic Reference." In P. A. French, T. E. Uehling, H. K. Wettstein, editors, *Studies in the Philosophy of Language,* Volume II, *Midwest Studies In Philosophy.* Morris, Minnesota: The University of Minnesota, Morris, 1977.

INDEX

A

'*A posteriori*', 79, 360, 394, 397
'*A priori*', 79, 113, 200, 209, 240, 274, 360f., 394, 397
A priori, method, 40ff.
Agnosticism, 242
Analysis, 3, 9ff., 132ff., 141, 187ff., 273
Analytic, 79, 357ff., 394f.
  analyticity, 359f.
Analytic *a priori*, 77, 79f., 240f.
Analytic philosophy, 3–13, 65f., 67–69, 141, 164f., 399
Anaximander, 1
Anscombe, Gertrude, E. M., 69
Anselm, St., 1
Antimetaphysics, 247–252
Aquinas, Thomas, St., 1
Argument, 73, 83, 86ff., 88ff., 97ff., 148f.
Aristotle, 1, 11, 12, 388
Arithmetic, 72ff., 79
Assertible content, 83f.
Assertion, 28f., 83ff.
  direct, 117
Assertoric force, 83
Atomic facts, 191, 200
Atomic simples, 132ff., 134
Augustine, St., 279ff., 283, 288
Austin, John, 4
Authority, method, 36–40
Avicenna, 1
Ayer, Alfred J., 4, 239, 266ff.

B

Bacon, Francis, 1
Being, 142, 350
Belief, 26, 27–33, 334f.
  and doubt, 31ff.
  and habit, 29f.
  settlement of, 34–48
Berkeley, George, 1, 4, 6, 50, 123
Boltzmann, Ludwig, 171
Boole, George, 12

Bradley, F. H., 46, 121
Britton, Karl, 176
Brouwer, L. E. J., 272f.
Buddhism, 171, 209

C

Cantor, Georg, 75, 158
Carnap, Rudolf, 3, 4, 11, 65, 68, 69, 175, 224f., 237, 238, 239, 250ff., 254, 256f., 260, 263ff., 370–375
Causal connections, 6
Certainty, 231, 233, 261ff., 321–347
Change, 188
Chapman, J. C., 20
Chomsky, Noam, 11
Church, Alonzo, 65
Class, 74, 156–165
Common sense, 44, 321–332, 339, 344, 347
Concepts, 53ff., 73, 76ff., 82–104, 295, 355ff.
  descriptive, 54f.
  and 'falling under', 94ff.
  and 'falling within', 97ff.
  formal, 54f., 204
  and functions, 85ff.
  as incomplete, 93
  levels, 96ff., 98ff.
  marks of, 95ff.
  and predicates, 90ff., 93
Concept-words, 76, 83, 85ff., 89, 107, 186
Conceptual analysis, 10
Conceptual notation, 73ff.
Conceptual relativity, 364ff., 378
Contradiction, 198, 207
Criteria, 236, 299–303
Criterion of identification, 114

D

Davidson, Donald, 4, 11, 69
Death, 215

429

Democritus, 1
Denotation, 146f., 153
Descartes, René, 1, 4, 5, 32, 50, 307ff.,
    334
Description, 138ff.
    and existence, 140–155
Designators, rigid, nonrigid, 390–395
Dewey, John, 15, 16, 17, 21, 64f.
Dostoyevsky, Fyodor, 171
Doubt, 31–33, 342–344
Drury, M. O. C., 176
Duhem, Pierre, 357
Dummett, Michael, 2, 4, 11, 65, 69, 71

E

Egolessness, 213–215
Empirical propositions, 335
Empiricism, 4, 5ff., 50, 160, 236, 259,
    264, 357–363, 394
Engelmann, Paul, 170, 176, 180, 223
Epistemology, 4ff., 46, 394f.
Essences, 274–279, 388
Essentialism, 388ff.
Ethics, 134, 209–216, 252–257
Euclid, 334
Evidence, 300–303
Existence, 98ff., 151ff., 191, 217ff.,
    369f., 392f.
Experience, 50, 53, 58, 216
    private, 308–315
    sense, 5, 230, 236ff.
Expressions,
    formal, 54, 133, 204
    linguistic, 76, 89, 107ff., 133, 205,
        270ff., 273, 279, 280ff., 293ff.,
        319f.
    syncategorematic, 54
External world, 4ff., 248–250

F

Facts, 116, 191
Fallibilism, 26
Family resemblances, 274–279

Feigl, Herbert, 238, 271f.
Ficker, Ludwig von, 177, 209
Form, 189ff.
Formal concepts, 204, 207ff.
Frege, Gottlob, 3, 12, 65, 66, 67–118,
    119, 125, 126, 130, 135, 144ff.,
    147, 151, 156f., 163, 169f., 172,
    183, 184, 185, 224, 233, 234, 237,
    259, 272, 274, 292, 349, 352, 354,
    381, 399
Function, 73, 85, 86
    and concept, 87f.
    descriptive, 88
    orders of, 96ff.
    unsaturated, 86

G

Geach, Peter, 65, 69, 309
Generality, 53, 73, 83, 100ff., 274–279
    multiple, 102
Generalizations, 101
Geometry, 79, 122
Gödel, Kurt, 12, 238
Grammar, 31, 82, 83, 273, 287–293
    autonomy, 295–299
Grammatical rules, 236, 287–293,
    296–299, 306
Grelling, Kurt, 239

H

Hahn, Hans, 223, 238
Hegel, G., 1, 122, 123
Heidegger, Martin, 250–252
Hempel, Carl, 239
Heraclitus, 1
Hertz, Heinrich, 171, 272
Hintikka, Jaakko, 4, 381
Hobbes, Thomas, 1
Holism, 357f.
Holmes, O. W. Jr., 20
Hume, David, 1, 4, 6, 7, 135, 238,
    240
Husserl, Edmund, 75

Hypothesis, 229–233, 235ff., 260–265

I

'I', 212ff.
Idealist metaphysics, 121ff.
Ideas, 50, 53
Identity, 93, 105–113, 144ff., 152, 358ff., 382ff., 396ff.
Illegitimate totalities, 158, 160f.
Incomplete symbols, 147f., 152
Indeterminacy thesis, 375–380
Indirect speech, 116–118
Individuation, 365ff.
Indubitability, 32f.
Induction, 19
Inquiry, 48, 64
Instantiation, 98ff.
Intelligence, 64
Intending, 303–307
Interrogatory force, 83
'Is', 93ff.

J

James, William, 15, 16, 17, 20, 21, 22, 62f., 171
Joergensen, Joergen, 239
Juhos, Bela von, 238
Justification, 34f., 79, 341f.

K

Kaila, Eino, 239
Kant, I., 1, 4, 5, 6, 7, 12, 77, 79, 171, 240
Keynes, John Maynard, 222
Kierkegaard, Sören, 171
Knowledge, 45, 115, 136, 329–332, 342–348
  by acquaintance, 135ff.
  by description, 135f., 138ff.
Kraft, Victor, 238

Kraus, Karl, 170
Kripke, Saul, 2, 4, 69, 381, 390–399

L

Ladd-Franklin, Christine, 21
Language, 9ff., 76, 80ff., 104f., 169–205, 270, 279ff., 298f., 354ff., 364ff.
  critique of, 315
  emotive uses, 253ff., 256
  ideal, 80ff., 130, 182ff., 234, 275f., 301f.
  natural, 80ff., 100f., 130, 234ff., 268, 279ff.
  ordinary, 271f., 301f., 319ff.
  private, 307–315
Language-games, 283–287
Law, 230
Law of contradiction, 158
Law of excluded middle, 144
Laws of logic, 198ff.
Leibniz, G., 1, 4
Leśniewski, Stanislaw, 12, 79
Lewis, Clarence, I., 16, 381
Limit, 180ff., 182
Locke, John, 1, 4, 6, 308
Logic, 8ff., 18, 21ff., 43, 61, 72ff., 80ff., 130, 181, 182ff., 198ff., 292, 349, 364ff.
  formal, 12, 19, 133, 367ff.
  of inquiry, 7ff.
  modal, 381ff.
  philosophical, 75ff.
  of relations, 19
Logical atomism, 119–168, 187, 286
Logical constants, 200, 355
Logical constructions, 131ff.
Logical form, 195, 197, 202–205
Logical positivism, 10, 165, 178, 224, 227f., 235, 237–268, 358, 394
Logical space, 192, 196f., 201, 207, 216
Logical syntax, 203, 208, 265ff.
Logically proper names, 155, 186
Logicism, 70, 77ff., 156f.
Loos, Adolf, 170

M

Mach, Ernst, 238, 259
Maimonides, 1
Marcus, Ruth Barcan, 381
Mathematics, 58ff., 70, 121, 272, 287
Mauthner, Fritz, 170
Mc Taggart, John, M. E., 121
Mead, George H., 16, 17
Meaning, 9ff., 15, 43, 48–56, 76, 77,
    104–118, 130, 133ff., 135, 146,
    186ff., 214, 234ff., 243ff., 279–
    283, 286, 302, 303ff., 353ff.,
    360ff.
Meaning of life, 211–216
Meaningfulness, 241–247, 253f., 258f.,
    353
Meinong, Alexius, 142
Menger, Karl, 238
Mentioning, 117, 383f.
Metaphysics, 10, 19, 58ff., 165, 247–
    252, 354, 394f.
Methodology, 7, 19
Mill, John Stuart, 18, 121
Mind, 4ff., 304ff., 307ff.
Minimum vocabulary, 131
Modal logic, 381ff.
    quantified, 386ff.
Monistic metaphysics, 123
Moore, G. E., 4, 9, 46, 121ff., 134, 211,
    225f., 269, 316, 321–347
Moral concepts, 134
Morris, Charles W., 239
Musil, Robert, 170
Mysticism, 178f., 201ff., 217

N

Nagel, Ernest, 11, 239
Names, 54, 85ff., 88ff., 93, 184ff.,
    279–283, 352ff., 393
Necessity, 182, 193, 200, 207, 384–399
Negative existential statements, 141ff.,
    153
Neurath, Otto, 238, 260, 263
Newton, Isaac, 334
Nietzsche, Friedrich, 1

Non-existence, 141ff., 191, 219f., 350f.
Nonsense, 164, 206ff., 209, 214
Norms, 253–257
Nothing, 250–252
Number, 72, 77, 98f., 156ff.
Numerals, 77

O

Objects, 76, 82ff., 108ff., 186ff., 355ff.,
    363–375
    abstract, 77, 99
Ockham, William of, 1
Ockham's Razor (Ockham's Principle),
    131ff., 140, 157, 166
Ogden, C. K., 221
Ontological commitments, 142, 157,
    350–357
Ontological relativity, 375–380
Ontology, 129ff., 140, 165, 182, 349–
    380
Ostensive definitions, 293–295, 311
Oxford school, 4, 10, 239

P

Papini, G., 16
Paradigms, 293–295
Parmenides, 1
Peano, Guiseppe, 124ff., 130
Peirce, Benjamin, 17f., 60
Peirce, Charles S., 10, 11, 12, 15–66,
    130, 237, 342
Philosophy, 3, 205–209, 253f., 265,
    273f., 315–321
Pictorial form, 194ff., 234
Picture theory of language, 193ff., 227
Planck, Max, 237
Plato, 1, 122, 141, 166, 274, 279
Platonism, 77, 135, 166
Pluralistic metaphysics, 123ff.
Possible worlds, 188, 389–393
Possibles, 59, 191, 196, 217
'Possibly', 385f.
Pragmaticism, 15
Pragmatism, 14–66, 239

Predicates, 73, 83, 90ff., 100f., 145f., 150, 163, 353
Principle of substitutivity, 382–389, 396f.
Principle of verification, 227ff., 239, 243–247, 257–268
Private language argument, 307–315
Probability, 232f., 261ff.
  theory of, 19
Proof, 72
Proper names, 54, 76, 83, 94, 107, 115, 145f., 152–155, 186
Property, 95ff., 189ff.
  contingent, 388ff.
  essential, 388ff.
Proposition, 27–29, 83, 115, 163f., 190ff., 193, 196ff., 206ff., 228–237, 270, 274f., 296f., 331
Propositional attitudes, 28, 83
Propositional functions, 148f., 163f.
Pseudo-propositions, 207ff., 240ff., 244, 250ff.
Psychologism, 72, 76

Q

Quantification, 19, 83, 100ff., 355, 363–375, 381–389
Questions, 31f.
Quine, W. V. O., 3, 4, 12, 69, 239, 349–399

R

Ramsey, Frank P., 140, 221f.
Rationalism, 4, 5ff.
Realism, 76, 123, 236
Reality, 42–48, 123, 193, 229ff., 273
Reductionism, 357
Reference, 104–118, 184, 204, 352
  and referents, 112ff., 143, 146
Referential opacity, 382–389
Reichenbach, Hans, 4, 11, 237, 238, 239
Relations, 123ff., 190
Relation-expressions, 76, 186
Representational dualism, 5

Royce, Josiah, 21, 46
Russell, Bertrand, 3, 4, 11, 12, 46, 65, 68, 69, 78, 119–168, 169f., 172, 174, 183, 186, 208, 224, 225f., 237, 272, 274, 349, 351, 381
Russell, Lord John
Russell paradox, 78ff., 125, 157ff.
Ryle, Gilbert, 308

S

Santayana, George, 64, 134
Scepticism, 6ff.
Schiller, F. C. S., 16
Schlick, Moritz, 4, 209, 211, 223, 224, 226f., 228, 235, 237ff., 243f., 247–250, 254, 260ff.
Schönberg, Arnold, 171
Schopenhauer, Arthur, 1, 171, 209, 272
Schröder, Ernst, 19
Science, 42–48, 57–61, 240ff.
Scotus, Duns, 1
Self, 212ff.
Semantics, 76, 140, 186, 236, 368, 381
Semiotics, 19, 42
Sense, 104–118, 146, 164, 184, 188, 196ff., 206f., 352
Sense-data, 137, 155, 186
Sentence, 76, 82ff., 88f., 107f., 115, 145, 184ff., 229f.
Sidgwick, Henry, 121
Singular terms, 146ff., 186
Socrates, 1, 9
Solipsism, 213ff., 318f.
Spinoza, B., 1, 175, 334
States of affairs, 189ff., 207
Stebbing, Susan, 239
Stout, George F., 121
Strawson, Peter F., 2, 4, 69
Structure, 190
Subjects, 27ff., 73, 91ff.
Subsistence, 141
Synonymy, 358ff.
Syntax, 133
Synthetic, 79, 357
  a priori, 77, 79f., 240ff.

T

Tautology, 198ff., 207, 218ff.
Tenacity, method of, 34ff.
'The', 138
Theory of definite descriptions, 125,
  130, 140– 155, 351
Theory of knowledge, 129ff., 167
Theory of meaning, 130, 349
Theory of Types, 125, 156– 165, 208
Thought, 44f., 82, 83, 104, 115, 193, 195,
  316f.
Tolstoy, Leo, 171, 209
Tone, 81, 83f.
Transcendent, 178, 214, 249
Truth, 15, 42– 48, 56, 57ff., 63, 89, 104f.,
  115, 234ff., 360ff.
  formal, 60
Truth-conditions, 76, 105, 184, 234, 368
Truth-functions, 200f., 203, 234, 381ff.
Truth-values, 73, 76, 81, 83, 84, 87, 92f.,
  116, 199ff

U

Understanding, 115, 135, 184, 196,
  303– 307, 311, 317
Universals, 99, 137, 352ff.
Use-conditions, 236, 273, 279– 283,
  284ff.

V

Variables, 368f.
Veblen, Thorstein, 21

Verificationism, 221– 268
Verifications, strong and weak, 259–
  265
Vicious-circle principle, 158, 160f.
Vienna Circle, 223ff., 226f., 237– 268

W

Waismann, Friedrich, 209, 211, 224,
  226f., 228, 235, 238, 260ff.,
  271
Ward, James, 121
Weininger, Otto, 171
Whitehead, Alfred N., 12, 68, 121,
  130
Will, 212f.
Wittgenstein, Hermine, 170
Wittgenstein, Ludwig, 3, 4, 10, 12, 65,
  68, 69, 116, 125ff., 134, 135, 165,
  168, 169– 220, 221– 237, 239,
  259ff., 265, 269– 347
Wonder, 218– 220
World, The, 182ff., 187, 192ff., 211ff.,
  216– 230, 248– 250
World-picture, 330f., 333– 344
Wright, Chauncey, 20
Wright, G. H. von, 194

Z

Zen, 209
Zilsel, Edgar, 238